Novello's Collection of Words of Anthems

To My Rector
The Ven: Archdeacon Cody. D.D. L.L.D.

With Xmas Greetings and
affectionate Regards
From his Organist
T. J. Palmer

Xmas. 1910

WORDS OF ANTHEMS.

NEW AND ENLARGED EDITION.

WITH APPENDIX, 1898.

NOVELLO'S COLLECTION

OF

WORDS

OF

ANTHEMS

London: NOVELLO AND COMPANY, Limited

AND

NOVELLO, EWER AND CO., NEW YORK.

LONDON :
NOVELLO AND COMPANY, LIMITED,
PRINTERS.

PREFACE.

THE following Collection of "WORDS OF ANTHEMS" is mainly founded on that issued some years ago under the joint Editorship of the Rev. W. RAYSON, M.A., Sir JOHN STAINER, M.A., Mus. Doc., and the Rev. J. TROUTBECK, D.D.

Not only, however, has it been made more comprehensive, but it has been almost entirely re-arranged on a plan commending itself to many distinguished and experienced Church Musicians, from whom also many valuable hints and much kind help have been received.

In grateful recognition of such help, the Compiler desires especially to mention the names of W. A. Barrett, Mus. Bac., Vicar Choral of St. Paul's Cathedral; C. S. Jekyll, Organist and Composer to Her Majesty's Chapels Royal; the Rev. S. Flood Jones, M.A., Precentor of Westminster Abbey; C. Harford Lloyd, M.A., Mus. Bac., Organist of Christ Church Cathedral, Oxford; A. H. Mann, Mus. Doc., Organist of King's College, Cambridge; the Rev. Sir F. A. Gore Ouseley, Bart., M.A., Mus. Doc., Professor of Music in the University of Oxford; J. V. Roberts, Mus. Doc., Organist of Magdalen College, Oxford; the Rev. W. Russell, M.A., Mus. Bac., Succentor of St. Paul's Cathedral; Sir John Stainer, M.A., Mus. Doc.; Sir Robert P. Stewart, Mus. Doc., Professor of Music in Trinity College, Dublin; and the Rev. J. Troutbeck, D.D., Chaplain to the Queen and Minor Canon of Westminster Abbey.

Thanks are due also to C. Villiers Stanford, M.A., Mus. Doc., Professor of Music in the University of Cambridge, for

PREFACE.

his kind permission to print the words of Nos. 1546—1548 ; to Sir Herbert S. Oakeley, M.A., Mus. Doc., Professor of Music in the University of Edinburgh, for his kind permission to print the words of No. 1222, his copyright ; to the late Mr. Henry Littleton, who took a great interest in the work during the early stages of its compilation ; and to many others for advice and assistance.

HENRY KING,

Assistant Vicar Choral, St. Paul's Cathedral.

November 2, 1888.

In issuing this new edition with an Appendix consisting of upwards of four hundred Anthems which have recently appeared, the special attention of Precentors, Organists, and Choirmasters is directed to the index of "*Anthems suitable for certain days or seasons,*" which has been considerably enlarged, in the hope that it will be found more valuable to those whose duty it is to select the music for "quires and places where they sing," and to assist them in making their selections with due regard to the sentiment of the words and their suitability for "*certain days or seasons.*"

Thanks are hereby tendered to the proprietors of "Hymns Ancient and Modern," for their kind permission to print the words of several hymns ; also to the Rev. F. G. Ellerton for No. 1766, to Messrs. Macmillan & Co., for Nos. 1666 and 1741, by the late Lord Tennyson ; to Messrs. James Nisbet & Co., for Nos. 1686 and 1901, by the late Dr. Bonar ; to Messrs. Smith, Elder & Co., for No. 1738, by the late Mrs. Browning ; and to the Committee of the Providence (Row) Night Refuge, for whose benefit 1769 was written by the late Miss Proctor.

H. K.

ASCENSION DAY,
May 17, 1898.

CONTENTS.

The Anthems are arranged in the chronological order of their Composers. Where the same words have been set by more than one Composer, their names are added in alphabetical order. The names of Composers who have set part of the words only are subjoined under consecutive numbers.

The words within square brackets do not belong to the first setting, but to one or more of those following.

NAMES OF COMPOSERS,

WITH

LIST OF THEIR ANTHEMS.

ABT, FRANZ WILHELM. Born 1819. Died 1885.

O LORD, most holy 970

ADAMS, THOMAS. Organist of St. Alban's, Holborn.

Alleluia! Now is CHRIST risen. 1895	Like as the hart 92
Come unto Me 364	Nearer, my GOD, to Thee ... 1861
He shall be great 1915	Oh, how great is Thy goodness 1863
If any man sin 1859	The earth brought forth grass ... 1862
If I go not away 1860	The eyes of all 406

ADLAM, FRANK.

Open to me the gates ... ... 1854 | Unto us a Child is born ... 1855

AGUTTER, B. Mus. Bac., Oxon., 1870. Mus. Doc., Cantuar, 1891.
Organist of St. Peter's, Streatham, 1867.

Arise, O LORD 1458

AITKEN, G. B. J. Organist of Hampstead Parish Church.

CHRIST is risen from the dead 1747

ALBERT, PRINCE CONSORT. Born at Rosenau, Coburg, 1819. Died
1861.

Out of the deep 1333

ALCOCK, JOHN. Mus. Doc., Oxon., 1761 (? 1765). Born 1715. Chorister
of St. Paul's. Organist of Lichfield Cathedral, 1749. Died 1806.

Out of the deep ... ... 1334 | Wherewithal shall a young man? 333

ALDRICH, VERY REV. HENRY, D.D. Born 1647. Dean of Christ
Church, Oxford, 1689. Died 1710.

Behold now, praise the LORD ... 206	Not unto us 256
By the waters of Babylon ... 570	O give thanks unto the LORD ... 904
GOD is our Hope and Strength 251	O praise the LORD, all ye heathen 278
Hide not Thou Thy face .. 11	Out of the deep 1334
I am well pleased 257	We have heard with our ears ... 258

BATES, FRANK. Mus. Doc., Dublin, 1884. Organist of Norwich Cathedral, December, 1885.

GOD is our hope...	1843	I will sing unto the LORD ...	1845
Hear my prayer, O LORD ...	1844	O LORD, correct me	869
I will lay me down	1292		

BATSON, A. WELLESLEY. Mus. Bac., Oxon., 1878.

Blessed are they that mourn ...	1941	The LORD is loving	1623
Make me a clean heart... ...	1731	They that sow in tears... ...	1942
O GOD, Who hast prepared ...	697		

BATTEN, ADRIAN. Lay Vicar of Westminster Abbey, 1614. Organist and Vicar Choral of St. Paul's Cathedral, 1624. Died about 1640.

Deliver us, O LORD	905	My soul truly waiteth	1323
Haste Thee, O GOD	96	O praise the LORD, all ye ...	279
Hear my prayer, O GOD ...	537	Sing we merrily	51
Let my complaint	419	When the LORD turned again ...	1517

BATTISHILL, JONATHAN. Born 1738. Organist of Christ Church, Newgate Street, London. Died 1801.

Behold, how good and joyful ...	631	I will magnify Thee	661
Call to remembrance	341	O LORD, look down	443
Deliver us, O LORD our GOD ...	662	Unto Thee, lift I up mine eyes	663
How long wilt Thou forget me?	64		

BAYLEY, CLOWES.

Be Thou exalted	1677	Bless thou the LORD	1678

BEALE, WILLIAM. Born January 1, 1784. Gentleman of the Chapels Royal. Died May 3, 1854.

Bow down Thine ear to me, O LORD	1600

BECKWITH, JOHN CHRISTMAS. Mus. Doc., Oxon., 1803. Born 1750. Organist of Norwich Cathedral, 1808. Died 1809.

I bow my knee	803	My soul is weary	682
I will alway give thanks ...	1193	The LORD is very great... ...	683

BEETHOVEN, LUDWIG VAN. Born at Bonn, 1770. Died at Vienna, 1827.

Great GOD of all	702	He is blessed	1588
Hallelujah to the Father ...	703	O Lamb of GOD...	1589
Hallelujah unto GOD's Almighty		We worship, we confess Thee	
Son (*2nd version*)	703	LORD	705
Hear my crying	704	When I call upon Thee ...	706

BELL, WALTER BEDFORD. Organist of St. Stephen's, Bury.

Let Thy merciful ears, O LORD	1880

ELLIOTT, J. W. Organist of St. Mark's, Hamilton Terrace, 1874.

O most merciful 1479	The LORD is in His Holy Temple 1289
O ye that love the LORD ... 1674	Thou visitest the earth 1208
Praise the LORD, O my soul ... 1785	

ELVEY, GEORGE J. Born 1816. Mus. Doc., Oxon., 1840. Organist of St. George's Chapel, Windsor, 1835—1882. Knighted 1871. Died 1893.

And it was the third hour ... 1024	O do well unto Thy servant ... 1033
Arise, shine 1358	O give thanks unto the LORD ... 114
Behold, O GOD 1023	O praise the LORD of Heaven... 948
Blessed are the dead 1138	O ye that love the LORD ... 742
Blessed are they that fear ... 58	Praise the LORD, and call ... 1034
Bow down Thine ear 1027	Rejoice in the LORD, O ye ... 1088
Christ being raised 1346	Teach me, O LORD 1610
Christ is risen from the dead ... 1028	The eyes of all 1611
Come, Holy Ghost 13	The souls of the righteous ... 847
Come unto Me 864	They that go down to the sea... 198
Daughters of Jerusalem ... 1047	This is the day 1035
Enable with perpetual light ... *13	Unto Thee have I cried ... 1036
I beheld, and lo! 1025	Wherewithal shall a young man 333
In that day 1029	While shepherds watched ... 1636
I was glad 108	Whom have I in heaven ... 1612
O be joyful in GOD 1032	

ELVEY, MARY.

Grant, we beseech Thee 731

ELY, GEORGE H., B.A. Organist of St. Leonard's Church, Ayr.

All Thy works shall praise Thee 1943

EVANS, CHARLES SMART. Born 1778. Gentleman of the Chapels Royal, 1808. Died 1849.

Almighty Father, Who hast ... 799 | O GOD, the strength of all ... 800

FANING, EATON. Mendelssohn Scholar, 1873. Director of the Music at Harrow School, 1885. Mus. Bac., Cantab., 1894. Mus. Doc., 1900.

Christ is not entered into the holy places 1777

FAREBROTHER, B.

Lo, the winter is past 1605

FARRANT, RICHARD. Born 1530. Gentleman of the Chapels Royal till 1564, when he was appointed Master of the Boys and Organist of St. George's Chapel, Windsor. In 1569 he was reinstated Gentleman of the Chapels Royal. Died 1580 or 1581.

Call to remembrance 341	LORD, for Thy tender mercies'
Hide not Thou Thy face ... 11	sake 12

FIELD, J. T.   Organist of Christ Church, Lee Park, Kent, 1874.

God shall wipe away all tears .. 1773	Lord of our life 1774
Hail, gladdening Light... .. 1045	Send out Thy light 587
Let us now go 1531	Whosoever drinketh 1775

FISHER, ARTHUR COLBORNE.   Born 1864.   F.R.C.O.   Organist of St. George's Church, Cannes.   Died December, 1896.

Blessed city, heavenly Salem .. 1639	God, that madest earth and heaven 1565

FOOTE, ARTHUR.

God is our refuge and strength... 1818

FORD, ERNEST.

Domine Deus salutis meæ ... 1576 | O Lord God of my salvation... 1576

FORD, H. E.   Organist of Carlisle Cathedral since 1842.   Mus. Doc., Cantuar, 1891.

Love not the world ... .. 1424 | The Lord hear thee 1401

FORDE, T.   Born c. 1580.   Died 1648.

Almighty God, Who hast me brought 1591

FOSTER, JOHN.   Gentleman of the Chapels Royal, and Lay Vicar of Westminster Abbey, 1856.   Retired Christmas, 1898.

Forsake me not, O Lord my God 451

FOSTER, MYLES B.   Organist of the Foundling Hospital, 1880.   Resigned, 1892.

As it began to dawn 1778	O God, who is like unto Thee ... 1787
Eye hath not seen 1779	The eyes of all wait upon Thee 1788
Hearken unto Me 1780	The night is far spent 1789
If ye then be risen with Christ 1781	There were Shepherds (4 voices) 1790
Is it nothing to you ? 1782	There were Shepherds (2-part).. 1791
Let not your heart be troubled... 1783	The souls of the righteous .. 848
My heart is inditing 1784	The Story of the Cross 1715
O come, let us sing 1786	When the Sabbath was past .. 1793
O for a closer walk with God ... 1537	Why seek ye the living ? ... 1794

FRANZ, ROBERT.

Praise ye the Lord, all ye nations 1657

FROST, C. J.   Mus. Doc., Cantab., 1882.   Organist of St. Peter's Church, Brockley, 1884.

Hear my prayer, O Lord ... 796	Thou shalt shew us 1515
Save me, O God... 190	When the Lord turned again .. 1510

FROST, W. A.   Vicar-Choral of St. Paul's Cathedral, 1891.

I will go unto the Altar of God . 1536 | O blest memorial ... *1530

NARES, JAMES. Mus. Doc., Cantab., 1757. Born 1715. Organist of York Minster, 1734. Succeeded John Travers as Organist and Composer to the Chapels Royal, 1758. Died 1783.

Arise, Thou Judge of the world.	636	O LORD, grant the king	...	455
Awake up, my glory ...	157	O LORD, my GOD ...	...	82
Behold, how good and joyful	.. 629	Save me, O GOD...	...	253
Blessed be the LORD GOD	... 276	The eyes of the LORD ...	...	627
Blessed is he that considereth...	815	The LORD hear thee ...	...	1407
By the waters of Babylon	... 572	The souls of the righteous	...	637
Call to remembrance ..	... 341	Try me, O GOD	...	292
Hide not Thou Thy face	... 635	When the LORD turned again ...		1517
O come, let us sing ...	... 515			

NAUMANN, G. A. Born 1741. Died 1801.

JESU, LORD of life and glory ...	661	Lauda Sion	.. ...	768

NAYLOR, CHAS. LEGH, M.A. Mus. Bac., Cantab., 1892. Organist of St. Peter's, Harrogate.

GOD that madest earth and heaven 1565	Lead, kindly Light	...	... 1377

NAYLOR, EDWARD WOODALL, M.A. Mus. Bac., Cantab., 1891.

CHRIST both died and rose	... 1927	O Jerusalem, look about thee	... 1928

NAYLOR, JOHN. Mus. Doc., Oxon., 1872. Organist of York Minster, 1883. Resigned, 1897. Born 1838. Died at sea, May 15, 1897.

If ye then be risen	... 1544	Out of the deep	...	1332
My soul truly waiteth ...	... 1328	O ye that love the LORD	...	742
O praise the LORD with me	... 1201	Sing, O daughter of Zion	..	1341

NEUKOMM, SIGISMUND. Born at Salzburg, 1778. Died 1858.

Holy is the LORD our GOD	...	...	...	...	...	...	831

NORRIS, T. Mus. Bac., Oxon., 1765. Born 1741. Organist of Christ Church Cathedral and St. John's College, Oxford, 1765. Lay Clerk of Magdalen College, Oxford, 1771. Died September 3, 1790.

Hear my prayer, O GOD	... 538	Hear my prayer, O LORD	.. 796

NOVELLO, VINCENT. Born 1781. Organist to the Portuguese Embassy, London. Died 1861.

In manus Tuas ...	...	... 853	Sing unto the LORD a new song	855
Like as the hart ...	...	... 853	The LORD is great in Zion	... 852
Miserere mei, Deus	...	... 18	The LORD is my strength	... 223
Praise the LORD, ye servants	... 854	Therefore with Angels ...	... 79

OAKELEY, SIR HERBERT, M.A., LL.D. Mus. Doc., Oxon., 1879. Mus. Doc., Cantuar, 1871. Professor of Music in the University of Edinburgh, 1865. Retired 1891. Born July 22, 1830. Died October 26, 1903.

Adown the river year by year	... 1665	O GOD, Who hast prepared	...	697
Behold now, praise the LORD	... 206	O praise the LORD, all ye nations	1225
Comes, at times, a stillness	... 1222	Strong Son of GOD	...	... 1666
Come unto Me ...	.. 364	The day beam dies		... 1667
Now unto the King eternal	1221	This is the day		... 224
O everlasting GOD	.. 1226	Whatsoever is born		... 1226
O GOD, our Refuge ...	... 1221	Who is this? ...	..	... 594

OBERTHUR, CARL.   Born 1819.   Died 1895.

OSBORNE, G. A.   Born 1806.   Died 1893.

OUSELEY, REV. SIR F. A. GORE, Bart., M.A.   Mus. Doc., Oxon., 1854, et Cantab., 1862.   Professor of Music in the University of Oxford, 1855.   Canon and Precentor of Hereford Cathedral, 1855.   Born 1825   Died April 6, 1889.

PAGE, A. J.   Organist of St. Mary's, Nottingham, 1867.

REAY, SAMUEL. Mus. Bac., Oxon., 1871. Organist of the Parish Church, Newark, 1864.

I will go to the Altar of God	... 1212	The Gentiles shall come	... 1215
O Lord, why sleepest Thou ?	... 1213	The love of God... ...	... 1216
Rejoice in the Lord alway	... 1214	This is the day	.. 225

REDFORD, JOHN. Organist of St. Paul's Cathedral and Master of the Boys, about 1543.

Rejoice in the Lord alway 2

REISSIGER, CARL GOTTLIEB. Born 1798. Died 1859.

Beati omnes	... 845	Hear my prayer, O Lord	... 846
Blessed are those ...	... 845	Justorum animæ... ...	... 847
Domine exaudi	... 846		

REYNOLDS, JOHN. Gentleman of the Chapels Royal. Died 1770.

My God, my God, look upon me 488

RHEINBERGER, JOSEPH. Born 1839. Died November 25, 1901.

I am well pleased ...	... 1352	The Lord give ear ...	... 1354
Rejoice, O ye righteous...	... 1353	Why assemble the heathen	... 1356
The fool within his heart	.. 1355		

RICHARDS, HY. W. Mus. Bac., Dunelm, 1895. Organist of Christ Church, Lancaster Gate.

Ye holy Angels bright 1908

RICHARDSON, JOHN E. Organist of Salisbury Cathedral, 1863—1881.

Lay not up (No. 2) 1583

RICHARDSON, VAUGHAN. Pupil of Dr. Blow. Organist of Winchester Cathedral, 1695. Died 1729.

O how amiable 911

RIGHINI, VINCENZO. Chapelmaster at Berlin. Born 1756. Died 1812.

O praise the Lord, all ye heathen 277 | Great is the Lord and marvellous 684

ROBERTS, J. H. Mus. Bac., Cantab., 1882.

Through peace to light (I do not ask, O Lord) 1769

ROBERTS, J. V. Mus. Doc., Oxon., 1876. Organist of Magdalen College, Oxford, 1882.

Behold, I send the promise	.. 1719	O Saviour of the world ...	... 255
Blessed are the merciful	.*1415	Peace I leave with you .	... 1723
Christ is risen	.. 1642	Seek ye the Lord ...	... 1485
God so loved the world...	... 1912	Shew me Thy ways, O Lord	... 1724
Grant, we beseech Thee	... 731	The Lord is full of compassion	1415
I am Alpha and Omega	... 1720	The Lord is righteous ...	... 1416
In the fear of the Lord...	... 1721	The Lord shall be thy confidence	1725
I will magnify Thee, O God	... 411	The path of the just ...	... 1726
I will sing unto the Lord	... 1417	The Story of the Cross ...	... 1715
Jesu, priceless treasure...	1722	The whole earth is at rest	... 1727
Lord, we pray Thee	675	Try me, O G D	... 1728
Lord, who shall dwell?...	582	When Christ, Who is our Life	1748
O God, Who hast prepared	... 697 .		

SAUNDERS, GORDON. Mus. Doc., Oxon., 1878.

The LORD is in His holy Temple 1288

SAWYER, F. J. Mus. Doc., Oxon., 1883.

Ponder my words, O LORD 602

SCHARTAU, H. W. Lay Vicar of Westminster Abbey.

Rend your heart 100

SCHUBERT, FRANZ P. Born 1797. Died in Vienna, 1828.

Great is Jehovah	 707	The LORD is my Shepherd	... 709
Song of Miriam, The	 708	Where Thou reignest ...	... 1599
Strike your timbrels	 708		

SCHUMANN, ROBERT. Born at Zwickau, in Saxony, 1810. Died 1856.

Advent Hymn ...	 812	Te decet hymnus	 813
In lowly guise ...	 812		

SCOTT, J. Born 1776. Organist at Spanish Town, Jamaica. Died 1815.

Praise the LORD, O Jerusalem 687

SELBY, B. LUARD. Organist of Salisbury Cathedral, 1881—1883; Rochester Cathedral, 1900.

All nations, whom Thou hast .	1558	O GOD, Thou art my GOD	... 1816
Blessed is he whose .	... 1815	Thou, O GOD, art praised	... 1817
I will magnify Thee ...	... 403		

SEWELL, JOHN. Organist, Bridgenorth.

Blessed are the undefiled	... 1522	They that wait	... 1384
Break forth into joy ...	... 1524	This is the day	... 1523

SHAW, JAMES. Organist of the Parish Church, Hampstead.

Have mercy upon me	. 1729	The LORD is my Shepherd	... 544
I will magnify Thee, O GOD	... 399		

SHEPHERD, J. Mus. Bac., Oxon., 1554. Chorister of St. Paul's Cathedral. Organist of Magdalen College, Oxford, 1542.

Haste Thee, O GOD 98

SILAS, E. Professor at the Guildhall School of Music.

The light hath shined 1211

SMART, SIR GEORGE T. Born 1776. Organist to the Chapels Royal, 1822. Composer to the same on the death of Attwood, 1838. Died 1867.

I will lift up mine eyes ... .. 281 | O GOD, Who art the Author ... 863

STAINER, JOHN, Knt., M.A., D.C.L.   Mus. Doc., Oxon., 1865. Organist of Magdalen College, Oxford, 1860—1872. Organist of St. Paul's Cathedral, 1872—1888. Inspector of Music to the Education Department, 1882. Professor of Music in the University of Oxford, 1889—1899. Born June 6, 1814. Died at Verona on Palm Sunday, March 31, 1901. Buried at Oxford on Easter Eve

STANFORD, CHARLES VILLIERS, M.A. Mus. Doc., Oxon., 1883, et Cantab., 1888. Organist of Trinity College, Cambridge, 1873—1892. Succeeded Sir G. A. Macfarren as Professor of Music in the University of Cambridge, 1887.

STATHAM, F. REGINALD.

Rejoice in the LORD alway   2

STEANE, BRUCE, H. D.   Organist of St. Mary's, Cuddington, Surrey.

Almighty Father, GOD of love...	1919	Joy in harvest (*Title*) ...	... 1919
Be glad and rejoice (*Title*) ...	1925	My soul truly waiteth ...	... 1920
Break forth into joy ...	1917	O give thanks	... 1921
Great is the LORD ...	1918	The first day of the week	... 1922
Hallelujah! CHRIST is risen ...	1923	The night is far spent ...	... 1924
If ye love Me	16	The strife is o'er (*Title*)...	... 1926
I will not leave you comfortless	1849	While the earth remaineth ...	... 1925
JESUS, Saviour, I am Thine ...	374	Why seek ye the living?	... 1926

STEGGALL, CHARLES.   Mus. Doc., Cantab., 1851.   Organist of Lincoln's Inn, 1864.

GOD came from Teman...	... 1177	O clap your hands ...	... 1238
Have mercy upon me, O GOD ...	30	Praised be the LORD ...	... 1183
Hear ye, and give ear ...	... 1178	Remember now Thy Creator	... 1179
He was as the morning star ...	1181	Turn Thy face from my sins ...	31
I will cry unto GOD ...	... 1182	We have heard	259
LORD, what love have I ...	288		

STEVENSON, JOHN A.   Born 1762.   Mus. Doc., Dublin, 1791.   Vicar Choral of Christ Church and St. Patrick's Cathedrals, Dublin, 1800. Knighted 1803.   Died 1833.

Behold, how good and joyful ...	634	O LORD our Governour ...	173
By the waters of Babylon ...	571	The LORD is King	743
Grant to us, LORD ...	... 1104	The LORD is my Shepherd ...	545
LORD, how are they increased?	244		

STEWART, ROBERT P.   Born 1825.   Mus. Doc., Dublin, 1851.   Organist of Christ Church and St. Patrick's Cathedrals, 1844.   Professor of Music at Trinity College, Dublin, 1861.   Knighted 1872.   Died 1894.

If ye love Me	... 1160	O LORD, my GOD ...	... 1162
In the LORD put I my trust ...	1161	The King shall rejoice ...	... 1164
LORD, who shall dwell	584	Thou, O GOD, art praised ...	1165

STROUD, CHARLES.   One of the Children of the Chapels Royal.   Born 1705.   Died, April 26, 1726.   ("Having been educated under Dr. Croft, he was his Deputy and Organist at Whitehall Chapel.")

Hear my prayer, O GOD   537

STURGES, E.   Organist of the Foundling Hospital.   Born 1808.   Died 1848.

I know their sorrow, ...   801

SULLIVAN, ARTHUR S.   First Mendelssohn Scholar, 1856. Mus. Doc., Cantab., 1876, et Oxon., 1879. Knighted 1883. Born May 13, 1842. Died November 22, 1900. Buried in St. Paul's Cathedral.

SWEELINCK, JAN PETER.   A famous Dutch Organist. Born 1562. Died at Amsterdam, 1621.

SWIFT, GEORGE H.

SYDENHAM, EDWIN AUGUSTUS.   Born 1847. Organist of All Saints', Scarborough, 1882. Died 1891.

TALLIS, THOMAS.   Born about 1520. Gentleman of the Chapels Royal during the reigns of Henry VIII., Edward VI., and Mary. Organist of the same in the reign of Elizabeth. Died 1585.

ANTHEMS SUITABLE FOR CERTAIN DAYS OR SEASONS.

NOTE.—Many of the following Anthems, although assigned to other special seasons, may be sung also between Trinity Sunday and Advent.

MORNING.

EVENING.

ADVENT.

ADVENT—*continued.*

ADVENT—*continued.*

CHRISTMAS.

CHRISTMAS—*continued.*

CHRISTMAS—*continued*

NEW YEAR—CIRCUMCISION.

EPIPHANY—*continued.*

QUINQUAGESIMA.

		No
Awake, my heart	...*Stanford*	1550
Behold, how good and joyful	*Baildon*	630
Behold, how good and joyful	*Battishill*	631
Behold, how good and joyful	*Ebdon*	633
Behold, how good and joyful	*Blow, Child, J. H. Clarke, W. H. Gladstone, Jekyll, Ouseley, B. Rogers, Whitfeld*	632
Behold, how good and joyful	*Nares*	629
Beloved, let us love one another	*Cobb*	1700
Be ye all of one mind	... *Godfrey*	1932
Be ye kind one to another	*M. Smith*	1116
Blessed are the merciful	... *Hiles*	1168
Blessed are they that mourn	.. *Batson*	1941
Blessed are they that mourn	... *Brahms*	1229
Blessed be the God and Father .. .	*S. S. Wesley*	889
Bow Thine ear, O Lord	... *Bird*	47
Hear my prayer, O God	.. *Mendelssohn*	764
Henceforth, when ye hear (No. 5)	... *Mendelssohn*	.779
Let your light so shine (No. 1)	..*Barnby, Calkin*	1583
Lord, do Thou well (No. 3)	. *Hiller*	978
Love, that caused us first to be	... *Gregory*	1578
O Lord, Who hast taught us	...*Iggulden*	710
O Lord, Who hast taught us	.. *Marsh*	710
See what love hath the Father	*Mendelssohn*	*793
Where Thou reignest	...*Schubert*	1599

ASH WEDNESDAY.

Blessed is he whose unrighteousness	*Selby*	1815
Come, and let us return	*Goss*	939
Hear, O heavens	*Humphreys*	90
Hear, O Lord	*Goss*	940
Hear us, O Saviour	*Hauptmann*	849
It is of the Lord's mercies we are not consumed	*Thorne*	1679
Lord, for Thy tender mercies' sake	...*Farrant Vicars*	12
Make me a clean heart, O God...	.. *Barnby*	22
Now, saith the Lord	.. *Macfarren*	1001
Remember, O Lord	*T. A. Walmisley*	829
Thus saith the Lord, Turn ye even to Me	... *Garrett*	1258
Thus saith the Lord, Turn ye to Me	. *Cobb*	1857
Turn Thou us, O good Lord . . .	... *Purcell*	202
Turn ye unto Me	... *Barrett*	1278
Turn Thy face from my sins	. *Attwood*	20

LENT.

Adoramus Te, Christe	*Palestrina*	17
All ye who weep	.. *Gounod*	1041
And He shall redeem thee (§ 4)	. *Gounod*	1055
And Jacob was left alone	. *Stainer*	1705
Arise, O Lord God .	*Jekyll*	1439
Art thou weary .	*C. H. Lloyd*	1526
As the hart pants (Nos. 1, 2, 4) F..th Sunday.. ..	*Mendelssohn*	748
As pants the hart *First Sunday*	*King, Spohr*	838

LENT—*continued.*

. LENT—*continued.*

LENT—*continued.*

LENT—*continued.*

LENT—*continued.*

LENT—*continued.*

LENT—*continued.*

PASSIONTIDE—*continued.*

PALM SUNDAY.

GOOD FRIDAY—*continued*.

		No
Is it nothing to you ? ... ... *Stainer*	1708
Jesu, Blessed Word of God Incarnate ... . *Gounod*	641
Jesus, Saviour, I am Thine . .. . *J. S. Bach*	874
Jesu. Word of God Incarnate .. .. *Docker, Mozart*	640
Jesu, Word of God Incarnate ... ...*Gounod, Hoyte, White*	642
Lord, on our offences ... ... *Mendelssohn*	775
My God, my God ... ... *Greene*	437
My God, my God ... ... *Mendelssohn*	777
O come near to the Cross ... ... *Gounod*	1050
O day of penitence ... ... *Gounod*	1051
O death, where is thy sting (No. 53) ... . *Handel*	502
O Fount of love unbounded . . .. *J. S. Bach*	*374
O Lamb of God ... . . *Barnby, Gounod, Luke, Miller*	1589
O Lord. my God. why hast Thou forsaken me .. *Humphreys*	94
O My vineyard .. .. *Gounod*	1060
O Saving Victim ... . *Gounod (Men's voices), Stainer*	1053
O Saving Victim ... . *Cruickshank*	1823
O Saving Victim ... ... *Kœnig*	1947
O Saving Victim ... . *Rossini*	865
O Saving Victim ... ... ' .. *Gounod, Tours*	1054
O Saving Victim ... ... *Miller, Powell*	1451
O Saviour of the world .. {*Goss, Greatheed, Havergal, Macfarren.* / *Ouseley, Palestrina, J. V. Roberts* }	255
O Thou, Whose Head was wounded ... ... *J. S. Bach*	379
Salvator mundi .. . . *Blow*	255
Surely He hath borne our griefs (No. 24) ... ... *Handel*	495
There is a green hill far away ... ... · *Gounod, Somerset*	1530
The Story of the Cross *Stainer, M. B Foster, J V. Roberts, Somervell*	1715
Thy rebuke (No 29) ... ... *Handel*	497
Who hath believed our report ... . *Purcell*	201
Word of God Incarnate ... ' ... ... *Gounod*	648

EASTER EVE.

Achieved is the glorious work ... . ' ... *F. J. Haydn*	*668
As Christ was raised ... ... *Macfarren*	995
Behold the Lamb that was slain---All glory to the Lamb ... *Spohr*	844
But Thou didst not leave—Hallelujah... ... ... *Handel* 497 & 500
Jesus, Saviour, I am Thine . .. *Bach*	874
My hope is in the Everlasting ... ... *Stainer*	1395
Yea, though I walk (§ 16) .. ..*Sullivan*	1419

EASTER-TIDE.

Above all praise and all majesty . . *Mendelssohn*	746
Alleluia! Christus surrexit . . .. *Anerio*	44
Alleluia! Christ is risen . . . ... · ... *Anerio*	44
Alleluia! now is Christ risen .. .. *T. Adams*	1895
All glory to the Lamb (No. 8) ... ... *Spohr*	844
All men, all things .. *Mendelssohn*	747
Almighty Father, Who hast ... e. *F. in*	799
And when the Sabbath was pa t ... .*Walting*	1846

EASTER-TIDE—*continued.*

						No
As CHRIST was raised from the dead	...		...	..	*Macfarren*	995
As it began to dawn	...	...	...	...	*M. B. Foster*	1778
As it began to dawn	...	...	...	...	.. *Martin*	1732
As it began to dawn	...	...	...	..	... *Vincent*	1806
As Moses lifted up the serpent	...	...	...	...	...*Gostelow*	1911
As we have borne the image	...	..	...	...	... *Barnby*	1294
At the Lamb's high feast we sing		...	...	...	... *Hall*	1687
At the Sepulchre (*Title*)...	...	...	...	...	.. *Wareing*	1846
Awake, my heart ...	...	...	..	...	...	...*Stanford*	1550
Awake, thou that sleepest	...	...	...	...	... *Ouseley*	1122
Awake, thou that sleepest	.	...	...	..	... *Stainer*	*1395
Awake up, my glory	...	...	...	...	*Nares, Wise*	157
Awake up, my glory	...	...	...	...	... *Barnby*	1624
Awake up, my glory	...	...	...	...	. *Haynes*	1876
Be glad, O ye righteous ...	...	...	..	..	... *Smart*	928
Behold, I shew you a mystery	...	...	...	...	... *Handel*	-502
Behold the Angel of the LORD	..	...	..	...	. *Tours*	1641
Behold the Lamb that was slain (No. 5)			...	...	... *Spohr*	844
Blessed be the GOD and FATHER		..	..	...	*S. S. Wesley*	889
Blessed be Thou, LORD GOD	...	..	..	...	*Bunnett, Kent*	1125
Blessing and glory	...	...	...	..	...	... *Boyce*	235
Blessing, glory, wisdom, and thanks	...		..	...	. *Tours*	1342
Break forth into joy	...	...	...	...	... ... *Barnby*	1298
Break forth into joy	...	.	...	...	...	*Palestrina*	1525
But thanks be to GOD (No. 54)	...	...	...	...	... *Handel*	502
But Thou didst not leave (No. 32)	...	...	...	...	... *Handel*	497
CHRIST being raised from the dead	.	...	.	.	*Elvey*	1346
CHRIST both died and rose	...	..	...	...	*C. L. Naylor*	1927
CHRIST is risen; CHRIST is risen	...	...	...	...*Maunder*	1867
CHRIST is risen from the dead	..	.	...	...	... *Aitken*	1747
CHRIST is risen from the dead	...	.	*J. H. Clarke, Sydenham*	1345
CHRIST is risen from the dead	...	...	..	...	. *Crament*	1746
CHRIST is risen from the dead	..	.	..	...	. *Elvey*	1028
CHRIST is risen from the dead	...	.	...	...	.. *Ouseley*	1127
CHRIST is risen from the dead	..	..	...	.	*J. V. Roberts*	1642
CHRIST is risen! He is the LORD	.	.	..	... *Thorne*	1234
CHRIST our Passover is sacrificed for us	.	...	*Goss, Hall*	1347
CHRIST our Passover is sacrificed for us	...	...	...	... *Tours*	1344
CHRIST the LORD is risen to-day	...	...	...	*E. V. Hall*	1688
Come, ye faithful...	...	...	...	...	...	*E. V. Hall*	1689
Easter hymn	...	...	...	...	...	*G. J. Bennett*	1900
For it became Him	..	...	...	...	...	... *O. King*	1833
For our offences	..	..	...	...	...	*Mendelssohn*	765
For us the CHRIST	...	...	...	...	...	... *Gounod*	1062
From Thy love	...	...	..	...	...	..	... *Gounod*	1063
Give thanks unto GOD	...	...	...	..	...	... *Spohr*	*837
GOD hath appointed a day	...	...	...	...	... *Tours*	1348
GOD hath not appointed us	..	...	...	...	*J. F. Bridge*	1473
GOD so loved the world	...	...	...	...	*J. H. Clarke*	1408
GOD so loved the world	...	...	{ *Goss, Kingston, E. G. Monk,* } { *Stainer, Thorne, Tuckerman* }	1409
GOD so loved the world	...	...	...	...	*J. V. Roberts*	1912
GOD, Who is rich in mercy	...	...	...	...	... *Garrett*	1648
Great is the LORD	.	...	...	...	...	*W. Hayes*	404

EASTER-TIDE—*continued.*

	No.
The LORD is King ... ... *Trimnell*	1189
The LORD is my strength ... . *Coleridge-Taylor*	1939
The LORD is my strength . .. . *Goss*	220
The LORD is my strength ... ... *Smart*	226
The LORD is our good Shepherd. (*Second Sunday*)... *Mendelssohn*	784
The LORD is risen ... ... *Garrett*	1649
The LORD is risen again ... ... *J. S. Bach*	382
The LORD shall comfort Zion ... ... *J. L. Hopkins*	826
The LORD shall comfort Zion ... . *T. A. Walmisley*	825
The LORD shall reign ... . *Handel*	477
The LORD will comfort Zion ... ... *Hiles*	1175
The merciful and gracious LORD .. .. .. *Jekyll*	*1440
The strife is o'er (*Title*) ... ... *Steane*	1926
They have taken away my LORD .. .. *Stainer*	1390
This is the day which the LORD hath made ... . *S. C. Cooke*	1523
This is the day which the LORD hath made ... . *Elvey*	1035
This is the day which the LORD hath made .. .. *E. V. Hall*	1696
This is the day which the LORD hath made ... ... *Marchant*	1776
This is the day which the LORD hath made ... . *Oakeley*	224
This is the day which the LORD hath made .. .. *Sewell*	1523
This is the day which the LORD hath made ... ... *Turle*	959
Thou art the King of Glory (*verse* 14) .. .. *Handel*	674
Thou hast turned my heaviness ... . *Gray*	1563
Thou shalt bring them in .. . . *Handel*	477
Thou wilt keep him in perfect peace . .. ... *Jekyll*	1445
Unto which of the angels . . .. *Handel*	498
We declare unto you . .. . *J. F Bridge*	1487
We declare unto you ... . *Maunder*	1874
We praise Thee, O Father ... . *Gibbons*	78
When CHRIST, Who is our life ... . *J. V. Roberts*	1748
When Israel came out of Egypt .. .. . . *S. Wesley*	721
When Israel out of Egypt came . . .. *Mendelssohn*	797
When my soul fainted within me .... *J. F. Bridge*	1744
When the Sabbath was past ... ... *M. B Foster*	1793
When Thou hadst overcome (*verse* 17) . ... *Handel*	674
Who is like unto Thee ? . . .. *Crotch*	745
Who is like unto Thee ? . . .. *Sullivan*	1434
Why do the heathen ? . . . *Kent*	659
Why rage fiercely the heathen ? . . *Mendelssohn*	798
Why seek ye the living ? ... . *Alexander*	1102
Why seek ye the living ? ... . *M. B Foster*	1794
Why seek ye the living ? . .. . *E. J. Hopkins*	1101
Why seek ye the living ? ... ... *Peel*	1702
Why seek ye the living ? ... ... *Steane*	1926
Worthy is the Lamb .. .. *Barnett*	1699
Worthy is the Lamb (No 56) . ... *Handel*	503
Worthy the Lamb, Omnipotent to save (§ 4)... .. ... *Crotch*	735
Ye sons of Israel . . .. *Mendelssohn*	772

ROGATION DAYS

All-gracious Father (No. 4) ... . *Spohr*	843
By His care are we protected . *Mendelssohn*	770
Give unto the LORD the glory due † *F Bridge*	1474
GOD be merciful unto us . . . .. *Mann*	896

ANTHEMS SUITABLE FOR

ROGATION DAYS—*continued.*

ASCENSION-TIDE.

ASCENSION-TIDE—*continued.*

ASCENSION-TIDE—continued.

		No
Thou art gone up on high	Hatton	249
Thou sittest at the right hand of God (verse 18), ...	Handel	674
Unfold, ye portals	Gounod	1064
Where Thou reignest	Schubert	1599
Who is this, so weak and helpless	Rayner	1797
Who shall ascend into the hill of the Lord ?	J. F. Bridge, Ouseley	309
Who shall ascend into the hill of the Lord ?	Gray	1564
Ye boundless realms of joy (No. 7)	Handel	517
Ye sons of Israel	Mendelssohn	772

WHITSUN-TIDE.

		No
All creatures serve Thee . . ..! ..	Smart	*930
And all the people	Stainer	1864
And when the Day of Pentecost	C. W. Smith	1601
As pants the hart	King, Spohr	338
As the hart pants	Mendelssohn	748
Behold, God the Lord passed by. (Saturday after) ..	Mendelssohn	760
Behold, I send the promise of My Father .	J. V Roberts	1719
Bring unto the Lord, O ye mighty ..	F E. Gladstone	1490
Come, Holy Ghost . Attwood, Elvey, Hatton, Palestrina, Tallis		18
Eye hath not seen	M. B Foster	1779
Fear not, O land . .. . . '. .	Goss	941
Give thanks unto God	Spohr	*837
God came from Teman	Steggall	1177
God is a Spirit (§ 5) .. .	W. S. Bennett	881
Great is the Lord	W. Hayes	404
Grieve not the Holy Spirit.	Stainer	1871
Happy is the man that findeth wisdom	J. F. Bridge	1263
Happy is the man that findeth wisdom	Prout	1262
Holy Spirit, come, O come	Martin	1458
I am Alpha and Omega	Stainer	1373
I am Alpha and Omega	J. V. Roberts	1720
If I go not away	T. Adams	1860
If ye love Me	Bunnett, Huntley	1848
If ye love Me .. Heap, W. H. Monk, Steane, Tallis		16
If ye love Me	Stewart	1160
If ye love Me	Wareing	1847
In my Father's house	Crament	1489
It shall come to pass	Garrett	1251
It shall come to pass	Tours	1643
I will magnify thee O God...	Greene	894
I will magnify Thee, O God	Ouseley	409
I will not leave you comfortless	Steane	1849
I will pour My Spirit (§ 7)	Sullivan	1419
Let God arise	Greene	426
Let God arise	Trimnell	1651
Let not your heart be troubled ..	Trembath	1488
Like as the hart desireth the water brooks . '.	Greene	427
Lord, before Th' footstool . ..	Spohr	835
Lord, Thy truth and loving kindness (. 3. .	Mendelssohn	774
O be joyful in God . .	Smart	981

WHITSUN-TIDE—*continued.*

TRINITY SUNDAY AND TRINITY SEASON. (*General.*)

TRINITY SUNDAY AND TRINITY SEASON—*continued.*

TRINITY SUNDAY AND TRINITY SEASON—*continued*

						No
Quis Te comprehendat	...	...	...	...	.	*Mozart*	651
Rejoice in the LORD	...	...	...	...	..	*Martin*	1462
See what love hath the Father	(*First Sunday after*)	*Mendelssohn*	*793
Sing to the LORD	...	...	...	...	...	*Mendelssohn*	783
Stand up and bless the LORD	...	...	...	.	*Goss*	953
Teach me Thy way	...	...	...	...	..	*W. H. Gladstone*	132
The LORD hath been mindful. .	...	...	...	*G. A. Macfarren*	992
The LORD hath been mindful...	...	...	...	*S. S Wesley*	*888
The LORD is very great and terrible	.	...	*J. C. Beckwith*	683
The LORD will comfort Zion ...	...	...	...	...	*Hiles*	1175
Then said He, on the Throne	...	...	...	...	*Gounod*	1081
Thou art worthy, O LORD	..	...	...	*F. E. Gladstone*	323
Thus saith the LORD, Behold, I create	..	...	*Gaul*	1285
To Thee, Cherubin and Seraphin (*verse* 4)	...	.	*Handel*	674
Thou shalt shew me the path of life	...	...	...	*Gray*	1827
We have heard with our ears	...	...	...	...	*Aldrich*	258
Whatsoever is born of GOD ...	...	...	...	...	*Oakeley*	1226
Who can comprehend Thee ...	...	...	..	...	*Mozart*	651
With cheerful notes (§ 5)	...	...	...	...	...	*Handel*	517

APOSTLES, MARTYRS, AND EVANGELISTS. (*General.*)

And lo ! a mighty host (No. 11)	...	...	...	...	*Spohr*	844
And the wall of the city	...	...	...	...	...	*O King*	1828
And though he be offered	...	...	...	...	*Mendelssohn*	794
Awake, awake, put on thy strength...	...	...	...	*Wise*	121
Awake, awake, put on thy strength...	...	...	...	*Stainer*	1365
Beati mortui in Domino	...	...	...	...	*Mendelssohn*	749
Be thou faithful unto death ...	...	...	...	*Mendelssohn*	*793
Blessed are the dead ...	..	..	...	...	*Spohr, Stanford*	1551
Blessed are the men who fear Him ...	..	...	*Mendelssohn*	*762
Blessed is the man	...	...	...	...	...	*Stainer*	996
Blessed is the man that endureth	...	. .	...	*O. King*	1830
Blest are the departed (No. 19)	...	...	...	...	*Spohr*	844
Come, ye blessed of my Father	...	...	...	...	*Barnby*	1301
For ever blessed are they	...	...	...	...	*Mendelssohn*	749
From Thy love as a Father ...	...	...	...	...	*Gounod*	1063
Give ear, O ye heavens	...	...	..	...	...	*Armes*	1267
Great and wonderful (No. 22)	...	...	...	...	*Spohr*	844
Hallelujah ! what are these ? ..	...	...	..	...	*Stainer*	1369
How beautiful are the feet. (*Solo*) (No. 38)	..	...	*Handel*	499
How beautiful are the feet. (*Duet*)	...	...	...	*Handel*	480
How beautiful upon the mountains ...	...	...	...	*Stainer*	*1365
How lovely are the messengers	...	...	.	*Mendelssohn*	*791
In memoriâ æternâ erit justus	...	...	...	...	*Stanford*	1545
In the sight of the unwise	...	...	...	...	...	*Ouseley*	1556
I saw a new Heaven (No. 20)	...	...	...	...	*Spohr*	811
I saw under the Altar ...	...	...	...	..	..	*Mee*	1541
Jerusalem, Jerusalem ..		'	*M . . J . .' '*	786
Lovely appear over the mountain	.		*G . . .'*	1065
O clap your hands	...			*Stain.*	1383
O give thanks unto the LORD	...	...	. *T. .1. Walmsle*	824

APOSTLES, MARTYRS, AND EVANGELISTS—*continued.*

		No
O where shall wisdom be found ?	*Boyce*	608
Periti autem fulgebunt	*Mendelssohn*	781
Precious in the sight of the LORD	*Chawner*	*864
Sing praises unto the LORD (*Vigil*)	*Gounod*	1057
Their doctrine shall drop as the rain	*Armes*	*1267
Their sound is gone out (No. 39)	*Handel*	499
The LORD gave the word (No. 37)	*Handel*	499
The LORD redeemeth	*Calkin, Macfarren*	1207
Then shall the righteous	*Mendelssohn*	762
The path of the just	*J. V. Roberts*	1726
The pillars of the earth	*Tours*	1646
The righteous live	*Stainer*	1389
The righteous living for ever	*Mendelssohn*	781
The righteous shall flourish	*Calkin*	1804
The salvation of the righteous	*Vincent*	1119
These are they which came	*Dykes*	1870
The souls of the righteous	*Croft*	638
The souls of the righteous	*Elvey, E. V. Hall*	847
The souls of the righteous	*Macfarren*	639
The souls of the righteous	*Nares*	637
The souls of the righteous	*Williams*	1555
The souls of the righteous	*H. H. Woodward*	1557
The sun shall be no more thy light	*H. H. Woodward*	1512
They that in much tribulation (§ 5)	*Mendelssohn*	770
To Thee, O LORD	*Mendelssohn*	*786
What are these ?	*Pierson*	875
What are these ?	*Stainer*	1869

ST ANDREW.

If thou shalt confess	*Stanford*	1809
The salvation of the righteous	*Vincent*	1119

ST. THOMAS.

Blessed are the men who fear Him	*Mendelssohn*	*762
Blessed is the man that endureth temptation	*O King*	1830
How shall I fitly meet Thee? (*Introit*)	*J. S. Bach*	850
If with all your hearts	*Mendelssohn*	753
If with your whole hearts (No. 16)	*Spohr*	844
O that I knew where I might find Him	*W. S. Bennett*	878
Rejoice in the LORD alway	*Miller, Purcell, Redford, Statham,*	2

ST. STEPHEN.

And the witnesses had laid down their clothes	*Mendelssohn*	*786
And they stoned him	*Mendelssohn*	786
As bright the star of morning gleams (*Introit*)	*Mendelssohn*	751
Be thou faithful unto death	*Mendelssohn*	*793
Blessed are the undefiled	*Sewell*	1522

ST. STEPHEN—*continued.*

						No.
Devout men carried Stephen	...	...	...	...	*Chawner*	864
Happy and blest are they	...	...	...	...	*Mendelssohn*	*786
Jerusalem, Jerusalem	...	...	...	...	*Mendelssohn*	786
Lord, Thou alone art God	...	...	...	...	*Mendelssohn*	785
O rest in the Lord	...	...	...	...	*Mendelssohn*	759
Precious in the sight of the Lord	...	...	...	...	*Chawner*	*864
To Thee, O Lord	...	...	...	...	*Mendelssohn*	*786

ST. JOHN THE EVANGELIST.

Children, pray this love (§ 4)	...	...	...	...	*Spohr*	841
Give ear, O ye heavens	...	...	...	...	*Armes*	1267
How beautiful are the feet (No. 38)	...	...	...	*Handel*	499
How lovely are the messengers	...	...	...	*Mendelssohn*	*791
In the beginning. (*Introit*)	...	...	...	...	*Thorne*	1236
O clap your hands	...	...	...	...	*Stainer*	1383
Rejoice in the Lord, O ye righteous	...	...	...	*Martin*	1462
Their doctrine shall drop as the rain	...	...	...	*Armes*	*1267
Then shall the righteous	...	...	...	...	*Mendelssohn*	762

INNOCENTS' DAY.

Come, we pray ye	...	...	...	...	*Leslie*	1110
In Rama was there a voice heard (§ 5)	...	...	...	*Sullivan*	1419
My hope is in the Everlasting (*vv.* 22, 23; and 1396, *v.* 5.)				*Stainer*	1395
O Lord our Governour	...	...	...	...	*Marcello*	326
Refrain thy voice from weeping (§ 6)	...	...	...	*Sullivan*	1419
These are they which follow	...	...	...	...	*Goss*	956

CONVERSION OF ST. PAUL.

And as Saul journeyed	...	...	...	...	*Mendelssohn*	787
And Paul came to the congregation	...	...	...	*Mendelssohn*	791
Hail! Festal day	...	...	...	...	*Powell*	1447
How lovely are the messengers	...	...	...	*Mendelssohn*	*791
Lovely appear over the mountains	...	...	...	*Gounod*	1065

PURIFICATION.

Beloved, now are we the sons of God	...	...	...	*Keeton*	1760
Beloved, now are we the sons of God	...	...	...	*Thorne*	1761
Blessed are the merciful	...	...	...	...	*Hiles*	1168
Blessed are the pure in heart	...	...	...	*Macfarren*	1169
Blessed are the undefiled	...	...	...	...	*Sewell*	1522
His salvation is nigh them that fear Him	...	...	*W. S. Bennett*	881
I will wash my hands	...			*E. J. Hopkins*	696
Lord, who shall dwell?	...		...	*Boyce*	581

PURIFICATION—*continued*

ST. MATTHIAS.

ANNUNCIATION.

ST. MARK.

ST. PHILIP AND ST. JAMES.

ST. BARNABAS.

		No.
Blessed is the man that feareth the LORD ... . *Boyce*		152
O GOD of Saints, to Thee we cry. (*Introit*) ... *H. H. Woodward*		*1512
The LORD gave the word ... . *Handel*		499
They that in much tribulation (§ 5) ... ... *Mendelssohn*		770

ST. JOHN THE BAPTIST.

		No.
Behold, GOD hath sent Elijah . ... *Mendelssohn*		763
Blessed be the LORD GOD of Israel ... ... *W. S. Bennett*		881
Blessed be the LORD GOD of Israel ... ... *Gaul*		1754
Blessed be the LORD GOD of Israel ... . *Heap*		1753
Blessed be the LORD GOD of Israel .. .. *Williams*		1800
Comfort ye, My people—Every valley—And the glory *Handel*		488
How beautiful are the feet (*Solo*) (No 38) . ... *Handel*		499
How beautiful are the feet (*Duet*) . ... *Handel*		480
How beautiful upon the mountains ... . *Stainer*		*1365
How lovely are the messengers ... ... *Mendelssohn*		*791
Listen, O isles ... ... *Allen*		1114
Lovely appear over the mountains ... ... *Gounod*		1065
O thou that tellest ... ... *Handel*		490
Prepare ye the way of the LORD ... ... *Wise*		122
Sleepers, wake ... ... *Mendelssohn*		*787
The voice of one crying ... . *Garrett*		1256
This is the record of John . . ..' .. ... *Gibbons*		77

ST. PETER.

		No.
Be strong and of a good courage .. . ... *Macfarren*		990
Blessed be the GOD and Father . ... *S. S. Wesley*		880
He was as the morning star . . . . *Steggall*		1181
How lovely are the messengers . . . ... *Mendelssohn*		*791
The LORD gave the word (Nos. 37-39) ... ... *Handel*		499
Thou art Peter ... ...' .. '... *Palestrina*		88
Tu es Petrus ... ... *Mendelssohn, Palestrina*		88

ST. JAMES.

		No.
Blessed is the man ... ... *Stainer*		996
Happy and blest are they ... ... *Mendelssohn*		*786
Jerusalem, Jerusalem ... . *Mendelssohn*		786

ST. BARTHOLOMEW.

		No.
Then shall the righteous—Blessed are the men who fear Him *Mendelssohn*		762
The sun shall be no more thy light ... ... *Woodward*		1512

ST. MATTHEW.

		No.
Awake, put on thy strength ... ... *Stainer*		1365
Lovely appear over the mountains ... ... *Gounod*		1065

HOLY COMMUNION.

HOLY MATRIMONY.

BURIALS.

BURIALS—*continued*·

EMBER DAYS.

EMBER DAYS—*continued.*

ORDINATION.

CONSECRATION.

MISSIONS.

IN TIMES OF TROUBLE—*continued.*

THANKSGIVING AFTER WAR—*continued.*

					No.
The LORD is King, be the people	...	...	...	*Boyce*	624
The LORD is my light	...	...	...	*Handel*	518
The LORD is my strength	...	...	...	*Greene*	459
They that go down to the sea	...	...	...	*Elvey*	198
This is the day which the LORD hath made	...	...	...	*Elvey*	1035
Thou shalt bring them in	...	...	...	*Handel*	477
Thy way, O GOD, is holy	...	...	...	*Purcell*	194
Thy way, O GOD, is holy	...	...	...	*Kelway*	195
We praise Thee, O GOD ...	...	...	*Handel, Sullivan*	674
We will rejoice in Thy salvation	...	...	...	*Blow*	1403
We will rejoice in Thy salvation	...	...	...	*Croft*	1404
We worship, we confess Thee LORD	...	...	*Beethoven*	705
Who is like unto Thee, O LORD	...	...	...	*Sullivan*	1434

GENERAL THANKSGIVING.

					No.
A Hymn of Praise	...	...	...	*Mendelssohn*	747
All people that on earth do dwell	...	...	...	*Pole*	1017
All Thy works praise Thee	...	...	...	*Barnby*	1622
Behold, O GOD, our Defender	...	...	*T. A. Walmisley*	823
Blessing, glory, wisdom, and thanks	...	...	...	*Tours*	1342
Bless the LORD, O my soul	...	...	...	*Kingston*	1945
Bless thou the LORD, O my soul	...	...	...	*Bayley*	1678
Bless thou the LORD, O my soul	...	...	...	*O. King*	1831
Exultate Deo, adjutori nostro	...	...	...	*S. Wesley*	719
Fear not, O land	...	...	...	*Goss*	941
Fear not, O land	...	...	...	*C. H. Lloyd*	942
Give the LORD the honour due	...	...	*Kent, C. H. Lloyd*	1493
Give unto the LORD, O ye kindreds	...	...	...	*Parker*	1906
Great is the LORD	...	...	...	*Ouseley*	1131
Great is the LORD	...	...	...	*Steane*	1918
Hear my cry, O GOD	...	...	...	*Verrinder*	1260
Hear my words, ye people	...	...	...	*Parry*	1767
I am well pleased..	...	...	...	*Aldrich*	257
I cried unto the LORD	...	...	...	*Heap*	1755
I did call upon the LORD	...	...	...	*Moir*	1799
If the LORD Himself	...	...	...	*Child*	820
If the LORD Himself	...	...	...	*Dupuis*	821
If the LORD Himself	...	...	...	*Travers*	822
If the LORD Himself	...	...	*T. A. Walmisley*	819
In constant order works the LORD	...	...	...	*Weber*	1598
In my distress	...	...	...	*E. J. Hopkins*	1100
It came even to pass	...	...	...	*Ouseley*	1141
I waited patiently for the LORD	...	...	...	*Croft*	1144
I will alway give thanks	...	...	...	*Greene*	416
I will exalt Thee, O LORD	...	...	...	*Tye*	7
I will extol Thee	...	...	...	*Hudson*	1640
I will give thanks unto Thee	...	...	*E. J. Hopkins*	1095
I will give thanks unto Thee	...	...	...	*Mozart*	1597
I will love Thee, O LORD, my strength	...	...	*J. Clark*	215
I will love Thee, O LORD, my strength	...	...	*Kingston*	1946
I will love Thee, O LORD, my strength	...	...	*Ouseley*	217
I will magnify Thee	...	...	...	*O. King*	1837

GENERAL THANKSGIVING—*continued.*

HARVEST.

HARVEST—*continued.*

		No.
Great and marvellous are Thy works	*J. F Bridge*	1737
Great is the LORD and marvellous	*Sydenham*	412
Great is the LORD	*Steane*	1918
His salvation is nigh them that fear Him (§ 8)	*W. S. Bennett*	881
Honour the LORD with thy substance	*Stainer*	1707
How excellent is Thy loving kindness	*Cowen*	1796
In constant order works the LORD	*Weber*	1598
I will alway give thanks	*Calkin*	1192
I will extol Thee	*Hudson*	1640
I will feed My flock	*J. F. Bridge*	1739
I will give thanks unto Thee, O LORD	*Barnby*	1308
I will greatly rejoice in the LORD	*Cruickshank*	1762
I will magnify Thee, O GOD	*Boyce*	397
I will magnify Thee, O GOD	*Goss, Travers, Tucker*	401
I will magnify Thee, O GOD	*O King*	1837
I will magnify Thee, O GOD	*J. V Roberts*	411
I will open rivers in high places	*Pettman*	1913
I will sing a new song	*Armes*	118
I will sing a new song	*Wise*	117
Joy in harvest (*Title*)	*Steane*	1919
Let us now fear the LORD our GOD	*West*	1891
LORD of the harvest	*Barnby*	1629
LORD of the rich and golden grain	*Tozer*	1857
Lo! summer comes again	*Stainer*	1710
Man goeth forth to his work	*Carnall*	1813
My mouth shall speak the praise	*West*	1892
O be joyful in GOD, all ye lands	*Elvey*	1032
O be joyful in GOD, all ye lands	*West*	1890
O clap your hands together	*Bunnett*	1680
O come, let us sing to the LORD	*Tours*	1343
O give thanks unto the LORD	*Steane*	1921
O give thanks unto the LORD	*Sydenham*	1508
O GOD, who is like unto Thee?	*M. B. Foster*	1787
Oh, how great is Thy goodness	*T Adams*	1863
O how plentiful	*Pattison*	1152
O LORD, how manifold are Thy works	*Barnby*	1314
O LORD, how manifold are Thy works	*Macfarren*	314
O lovely Peace	*Handel*	511
On Thee each living soul awaits	*F. J. Haydn*	671
Open to me the gates	*Adlam*	1854
O praise GOD in His holiness	*Blair, B. Cooke, Distin, Gaul, Purcell*	162
O praise GOD in His holiness	*Goldwin, Trimnell, Whitfeld, Wise*	163
O praise GOD in His holiness	*Weldon*	164
O praise the LORD, all ye nations	*Oakeley*	1225
O praise the LORD of Heaven	*Goss*	947
O praise the LORD of Heaven	*Greene*	949
O sing unto the LORD	*Cruickshank*	1824
O that men would praise the LORD	*J. C. Bridge*	1560
Our GOD is LORD of the harvest	*Mundella*	1638
O worship the King	*E. V. Hall*	1691
Praised be the LORD	*Steggall*	1183
Praise, my soul, the King of heaven	*E. V. Hall*	1692
Praise, O praise, our GOD and King	*E. V. Hall*	1693
Praise the LORD, O Jerusalem	*Bliss*	1284

HARVEST—*continued*

HARVEST—*continued.*

						No
While the earth remaineth	...	...	...	...	.. *Tours*	1351
While the earth remaineth	...	...	...	...	... *Heap*	1498
While the earth remaineth	...	...	...	..	*Maunder*	1875
While the earth remaineth	...	...	..	...	*Williams*	1802
Ye shall dwell in the land	...	...	..	...	... *Stainer*	1391
Ye shall go out with joy...	...	...	..	...	... *Barnby*	1637

DEDICATION OF A CHURCH.

A day in Thy courts	...	...	...	... .	*Macfarren* 994
Arise, O LORD, into Thy resting-place		..	..	*Agutter, Cobb*	1453
Ascribe unto the LORD ...	...	...	...	...	... *Travers* 304
Behold, brethren, how good and joyful		..	..	*.Caldicott*	1658
Behold, how good and joyful	..	.	..	..	*Battishill* 631
Behold, how good and joyful	...	...	..		*Stevenson* 634
Behold now, praise the LORD	...	{*Aldrich, Blow, Creyghton,*} {*Oakeley, B. Rogers, Whitfeld*}			206
Behold now, praise the LORD	..	...	...	... *G. J. Bennett*	207
Behold now, praise the LORD	...	..	..	.. . *Ouseley*	1123
Behold now, praise the LORD	...	..	..	. . *Purcell*	208
Behold now, praise ye the LORD	...	..	..	*Calkin*	1190
Blessed are they that dwell	..	..	..	. *Tours*	918
Blessed art Thou, LORD...	...	...	...	.. . *Torrance*	1266
Blessed be Thou, LORD GOD of Israel...	.	... *Bunnett, Kent*			1125
Blessed City, heavenly Salem .	...	...	.. .	.. *Fisher*	1639
Come, and let us go up .	.	.	..	. . *Barrett*	1277
Give thanks, O Israel .	..	...	..	.. ... *Ouseley*	1129
Give unto the LORD, O ye kindreds	...	...	...	... *Parker*	1906
Glorious and powerful GOD	...	..	...	... .. *Gibbons*	61
Great is the LORD, and highly to be praised	.	..	. . *Ouseley*		1131
Hail ! Festal day '	.	.	.	. *Powell*	1447
Happy, who in Thy house reside (§ 2)...	..	...	. *Spohr*		842
Hear the voice and prayer	.	.	.. *J. L. Hopkins, Tallis*		14
How goodly are thy tents	.	...	...	.. *Ouseley*	1126
How lovely are Thy dwellings fair	...	..	...	... *Spohr*	842
How lovely are Thy habitations	..	..	..	..*Saluman*	1021
How lovely is Thy dwelling-place (§ 4)	.	..	. *Brahms*		1229
I have surely built Thee an house	.	..	. . ... *Boyce*		578
I have surely built Thee an house	..	. .	...	...*Trimnell*	579
It came even to pass	..	...	.	...	.. ... *Ouseley*	1141
I was glad when they said `	...	..	. .	. *Attwood*	106
I was glad when they said		...	. .	... *Gaul*	1682
I was glad when they said	..	.	..	... *Hiles*	1172
I was glad when they said	..		..	. *J. L Hopkins*	110
I was glad when they said	.	..	..	... *Horsley*	111
I was glad when they said	...	..	.	... ...*Pergolesi*	112
I was glad when they said			..	*Purcell*	113
I was glad when they said	. *Bunnett, Thorne, Trimnell, Tucker*				105
Now, my GOD, let, I beseech Thee	.	..	.. *W. S. Bennett*		882
O come, let us sing unto the LORD	.	..	... *Handel*		512
O come, let s worship			*Mendelssohn*		779
O how amiable are Thy dwellings	*Bunnett, B a , R, hardson*				911
O how amiable are Thy dwelling		. *Greene*			914
O how amiable are Thy house			*Pattison*		916

SOVEREIGN'S ACCESSION—*continued.*

		No.
My heart is inditing of a good matter	*Handel*	509
O give thanks unto the LORD	*Turle*	1604
O LORD, grant the King a long life	*Attwood, Child, Croft, Nares*	455
O LORD, grant the King a long life	*Greene*	456
O LORD, grant the King a long life	*Purcell*	458
O LORD, shew Thy mercy upon us	*C. H. Lloyd*	1771
Praise the LORD, O Jerusalem	*...J. Clark*	227
Praise the LORD, O Jerusalem	*...Purcell*	227
The king shall rejoice	*.J Corfe*	1084
The king shall rejoice	*...Greene*	454
The king shall rejoice	*...Handel*	457
The king shall rejoice	*E. J. Hopkins*	1083
Vouchsafe, O LORD (*verse* 26)	*...Sullivan*	674
Zadok the priest	*...Handel*	525

—   —   •

ANTHEMS SUITABLE TO BE SUNG *WITHOUT* ACCOMPANIMENT.

(Those marked † are suitable for Fridays.)

		No.
All people that on earth do dwell	*Pole*	1017
All people that on earth do dwell	*Tallis*	3
† All ye who weep	*Gounod*	1041
Almighty and everlasting GOD	*. Gibbons*	53
† Almighty and merciful GOD	*Goss*	937
† Art thou weary . ..	*C H Lloyd*	1526
† Ave verum	*. Gounod*	642
† Ave verum	*Gounod*	643
Blessed are the dead	*...Stanford*	1551
Blessed are they that mourn	*...Batson*	1941
Blessed is the man	*Goss*	657
Blessing, glory, and wisdom, and thanks	*J. S Bach*	348
† Bow Thine ear, O LORD	*Bird*	47
† Bow Thine ear to me, O LORD	*Dowland*	83
By the waters of Babylon	*Boyce*	571
Call to remembrance, O LORD ..	*Battishill, Farrant, Nares*	341
Come, JESU, come	*J. S. Bach*	363
Come, let us worship	*Palestrina*	516
† Come unto CHRIST, ye mourners	*.Somerset*	1529
† Come unto Him, all ye who labour	*Gounod*	1043
Comfort the soul	*Crotch*	*134
† Daughters of Jerusalem	*Gounod*	1046
† Enter not into judgment	*Attwood, Whitfeld*	464
† Filiæ Jerusalem	*Gounod*	1046
† From sin's dread power	*Graun*	530
† From the deep	*Spohr*	832
† From the morning watch	*Gounod*	1068
Give peace in our time, O LORD	*.W. H. Callcott*	961
GOD hath not appointed us	*J. F. Bridge*	1473
† GOD is a Spirit (§ 5), (also for A.T. L B.) ...	*...W. S. Bennett*	881

ANTHEMS FOR MEN'S VOICES.

Some of these Anthems include short movements in which treble voices are introduced. These can, however, be omitted, the remaining portion of the Anthem being complete in itself, and for men's voices only.

ANTHEMS WITH LATIN WORDS.

WORDS OF ANTHEMS.

1

A PRAYER.

O LORD, the Maker of all thing,
We pray Thee now in this evening
Us to defend through Thy mercy
From all deceit of our enemy:
Let neither us deluded be,
Good LORD, with dream or fantasy;
Our hearts waking in Thee Thou keep,
That we in sin fall not on sleep.
O Father, through Thy blessed Son,
Grant us this our petition;
To Whom, with the Holy Ghost always,
In heaven and earth be laud and praise.

Attributed to HENRY VIII.
Also to WILLIAM MUNDY.

2

PHILIPPIANS iv. 4. Rejoice in the LORD alway; and again I say, Rejoice.

5. Let your moderation be known unto all men. The LORD is at hand.

6. Be careful for nothing; but in every thing by prayer and supplication with thanksgiving let your requests be made known unto GOD.

7. And the peace of GOD, which passeth all understanding, shall keep your hearts and minds through JESUS CHRIST OUR LORD. Amen.

MILLER, PURCELL, REDFORD, STATHAM.

3

PSALM c. (*Old Version*).

All people that on earth do dwell,
    Sing to the LORD with cheerful voice,
Him serve with fear, His praise forth tell,
    Come ye before Him and rejoice.

The LORD, ye know, is GOD indeed,
    Without our aid He did us make;
We are His flock, He doth us feed,
    And for His sheep He doth us take.

O enter then His gates with praise,
    Approach with joy His courts unto;
Praise, laud, and bless His Name always,
    For it is seemly so to do.

For why? the LORD our GOD is good,
    His mercy is for ever sure;
His truth hath always firmly stood,
    And shall from age to age endure.   Amen.
          W. HAYES, LUTHER, TALLIS.

4

Great GOD! what do I see and hear!
    The end of things created;
The Judge of mankind doth appear,
    On clouds of glory seated.
The trumpet sounds! the graves restore
The dead which they contained before:
    Prepare, my soul, to meet Him!
          LUTHER.

5

PSALM lv.   1. Give ear unto my prayer, O LORD my
GOD, and hide not Thyself from my supplication.

     2. Attend to me and hear me: I mourn in my complaint
and make a noise.

4. My heart is sore pained within me. O hear my prayer. Hide not Thyself. I mourn, I mourn, O hear me. LORD GOD, hear my prayer. Amen.

ARCADELT.

6

ST. LUKE i. 28. Hail, thou that art highly favoured, the LORD is with thee. Blessed art thou among women.

30. And the Angel said unto her, Fear not, Mary: for thou hast found favour with GOD.

46, 47. My soul doth magnify the LORD, and, my spirit hath rejoiced in GOD my SAVIOUR.

48. For He hath regarded the low estate of His hand-maiden: for, behold, from henceforth all generations shall call me blessed.

49. For He that is mighty hath done to me great things; and holy is His Name.

50. And His mercy is on them that fear Him, from generation to generation. Amen.

ARCADELT, OSBORNE.

7

*PSALM xxx. 1. I will exalt Thee, O LORD, for Thou hast defended me, and not suffered mine enemies to have their pleasure upon me.

2. O LORD my GOD, I have cried unto Thee, and Thou hast healed me.

3. LORD, Thou hast brought my soul out of hell: Thou hast preserved me from them that descend into the pit.*

*4. Sing unto the LORD, ye that are His Saints: and give thanks with a remembrance of His holiness.

11. The LORD hath heard me, and hath taken mercy upon me: the Lord is made my helper.

12. Thou hast turned my sorrow into joy; Thou hast put off my sackcloth, and hast compassed me with gladness, that my glory may sing to Thee without grief.

13. O LORD my GOD, I shall evermore give thanks to Thee.*

TYE.

* Sometimes sung as a separate Anthem.

· 8

PSALM CXXXIV.

Laudate Nomen Domini, vos servi Domini, ab ortu
solis usque ad occasum ejus.
Decreta Dei justa sunt, et cor exhilarant.
Laudate Deum, principes et omnes populi.

English Version.

O come, ye servants of the LORD,
  And praise His holy Name :
From early morn to setting sun,
  His might on earth proclaim.

His laws are just, and glad the heart;
  He makes His mercies known:
Ye princes come, ye people too,
  And bow before His Throne.

Another Version.

Sing to the LORD in joyful strains,
  Let earth His praise resound,
Ye who amidst the ocean dwell,
  And fill the isles around.

Thou city of the LORD, begin
  The universal song ;
Let all combined with one accord
  The cheerful notes prolong.

Another Version.

PSALM cxix. 85. The proud have digged pits for me,
which are not after Thy law.
  86. They persecute me falsely : O be Thou my help.
  79. Let such as fear Thee and have known Thy
testimonies be turned into me.

TYE.

9

PSALM cxix. 41. Let Thy loving mercy come also unto me, O LORD: even Thy salvation, according unto Thy word.

44. So shall I alway keep Thy law, yea, for ever and ever.

45. And I will walk at liberty, for I seek Thy commandments.

49. O think upon Thy servant, as concerning Thy word, wherein Thou hast caused me to put my trust.

50. The same is my comfort in my trouble : for Thy word hath quickened me.

64. The earth, O LORD, is full of Thy mercy : O teach me Thy statutes.

TYE.

10

PSALM cxix. 89. O LORD, Thy word endureth for ever in heaven.

90. Thy truth also remaineth from one generation to another. Thou hast laid the foundation of the earth, and it abideth.

91. They continue this day according to Thine ordinance, for all things serve Thee.

TYE.

11

Hide not Thou Thy face from us, O LORD, and cast not off Thy servants in Thy displeasure : for we confess our sins unto Thee, and hide not our unrighteousness. For Thy mercies' sake, deliver us from all our sins.

ALDRICH, FARRANT.

12

LORD, for Thy tender mercies' sake, lay not our sins to our charge, but forgive that is past, and give us grace to amend our sinful lives ; to decline from sin, and incline to virtue, that we may walk with a perfect heart before Thee now and evermore. Amen.

FARRANT, VICARS.

13

1. Come, Holy Ghost, our souls inspire,
   And lighten with celestial fire;
   Thou the anointing Spirit art,
   Who dost Thy sevenfold gifts impart.
   Thy blessed Unction from above
   Is comfort, life, and fire of love !—

*2. Enable with perpetual light
   The dulness of our blindèd sight :
   Anoint and cheer our soiled face
   With the abundance of Thy grace ;
   Keep far our foes ; give peace at home ;
   Where Thou art Guide, no ill can come !*

3. Teach us to know the Father, Son,
   And Thee, of Both, to be but One ;
   That, through the ages all along,
   This may be our endless song ;
   Praise to Thy eternal merit,
   Father, Son, and Holy Spirit.   Amen.

ATTWOOD, *ELVEY, HATTON, PALESTRINA, TALLIS.

* —— * Sometimes sung as a separate Anthem.

14

1 KINGS viii. 28. Hear the voice and prayer of Thy servants which they make before Thee this day.

29. That Thine eyes may be open toward this house day and night, even toward this place of which Thou hast said, My Name shall be there.

30. And when Thou hearest, have mercy upon them.

J. L. HOPKINS, TALLIS.

15

I call and cry to Thee, O LORD,
   Give ear unto my plaint :
Bow down Thine eyes, and mark my heavy plight,
   And how my soul doth faint :
   For I have many ways offended Thee.
   Forget my wickedness, O LORD, I beseech Thee.

TALLIS.

16

St. John xiv. 15. If ye love Me, keep My commandments.

16, 17. And I will pray the Father, and He shall give you another Comforter, that He may abide with you for ever, even the Spirit of truth. [Amen.]

HEAP, W. H. MONK, STEANE, TALLIS.

17

Adoramus Te, Christe; et benedicimus Tibi, quia per sanctam crucem Tuam redemisti mundum. Qui passus es pro nobis, Domine, miserere nobis.

PALESTRINA.

18

Psalm li. 1. Miserere mei, Deus, secundum misericordiam Tuam.

2. Et secundum multitudinem miserationum Tuarum, dele iniquitatem meam.

3. Amplius lava me ab iniquitate meâ, et a peccato meo munda me.

4. Quoniam iniquitatem meam ego cognosco, et peccatum meum contra me est semper.

5. Tibi soli peccavi, et malum coram Te feci: ut justificeris in sermonibus Tuis, et vincas cum judicaris.

6. Ecce enim in iniquitatibus conceptus sum, et in peccatis concepit me mater mea.

7. Ecce enim veritatem dilexisti: incerta et occulta sapientiæ Tuæ manifestasti mihi.

8. Asperges me hyssopo, et mundabor: lavabis me, et super nivem dealbabor.

9. Auditui meo dabis gaudium et lætitiam, et exultabunt ossa humiliata.

10. Averte faciem Tuam a peccatis meis, et omnes iniquitates meas dele.

11. Cor mundum crea in me, Deus, et spiritum rectum tum innova in visceribus meis.

12. Ne projicias me a facie Tuâ, et Spiritum Sanctum Tuum ne auferas a me.

13. Redde mihi lætitiam salutis Tuæ, et Spiritu principali confirma me.

14. Docebo iniquos vias Tuas, et impii ad Te convertentur.

15. Libera me de sanguinibus, Deus, Deus salutis meæ, et exultabit lingua mea justitiam Tuam.

16. Domine, labia mea aperies, et os meum annunciabit laudem Tuam.

17. Quoniam si voluisses sacrificium, dedissem utique: holocaustis non delectaberis.

18. Sacrificium Deo spiritus contribulatus: cor contritum et humiliatum, Deus, non despicies.

19. Benigne fac, Domine, in bonâ voluntate Tuâ Sion: ut ædificentur muri Hierusalem.

20. Tunc acceptabis sacrificium justitiæ, oblationes, et holocausta: tunc imponent super altare Tuum vitulos.

Gloria Patri, et Filio, et Spiritui Sancto: sicut erat in principio, et nunc, et semper, et in sæcula sæculorum. Amen.

ALLEGRI, GLUCK, HASSE, M. HAYDN, JOMELLI, LEO,
NOVELLO, PALESTRINA.

English Version.

PSALM li. 1. Have mercy upon me, O GOD, after Thy great goodness: according to the multitude of Thy mercies do away mine offences.

2. Wash me throughly from my wickedness, and cleanse me from my sin.

3. For I acknowledge my faults, and my sin is ever before me.

4. Against Thee only have I sinned, and done this evil in Thy sight: that Thou mightest be justified in Thy saying, and clear when Thou art judged.

5. Behold, I was shapen in wickedness, and in sin hath my mother conceived me.

6. But lo, Thou requirest truth in the inward parts, and shalt make me to understand wisdom secretly.

7. Thou shalt purge me with hyssop, and I shall be clean: Thou shalt wash me, and I shall be whiter than snow.

8. Thou shalt make me hear of joy and gladness, that the bones which Thou hast broken may rejoice.

9. Turn Thy face from my sins, and put out all my misdeeds.

10. Make me a clean heart, O GOD, and renew a right spirit within me.

11. Cast me not away from Thy presence, and take not Thy Holy Spirit from me.

12. O give me the comfort of Thy help again, and stablish me with Thy free Spirit.

13. Then shall I teach Thy ways unto the wicked, and sinners shall be converted unto Thee.

14. Deliver me from blood-guiltiness, O GOD, Thou that art the GOD of my health, and my tongue shall sing of Thy righteousness.

15. Thou shalt open my lips, O LORD, and my mouth shall shew Thy praise.

16. For Thou desirest no sacrifice, else would I give it Thee; but Thou delightest not in burnt-offerings.

17. The sacrifice of GOD is a troubled spirit: a broken and contrite heart, O GOD, shalt Thou not despise.

18. O be favourable and gracious unto Sion: build Thou the walls of Jerusalem.

19. Then shalt Thou be pleased with the sacrifice of righteousness, with the burnt-offerings and oblations: then shall they offer young bullocks upon Thine altar.

BARNBY, PALESTRINA, STAINER.

19 S. ARNOLD, vv. 1, 2, 7, 8.

20 ATTWOOD, SULLIVAN, TUCKERMAN, vv. 9-11.

21 BARNBY, v. 1. Amen.

22 BARNBY, vv. 10-13.

23 BUCK, vv. 1, 9, 12.

24 GOSS, vv. 1-3, 12-14. Hallelujah, Amen. v. 8. Amen.

25 GREENE, vv. 1, 12, 11, 15, 13, 19, 14, 17.

26 HANDEL, vv. 1-4, 8, 10-13.

27 HUMPHREYS, vv. 1-9.

28 KING, vv. 9-12.

29 LONGHURST, MACFARREN, vv. 1. 2.

30 STEGGALL, vv. 1 3.

31 STEGGALL, vv. 9-11, 17. 12, 13.

32

Hodie Christus natus est.　Noé! Noé!
Hodie Salvator apparuit.　Noé! Noé!
Hodie in terrâ canunt Angeli, et lætantur Archangeli.
　Noé! Noé!
Hodie exultant justi, dicentes, Gloria in excelsis Deo.
　Noé! Noé!

English Version.

This day CHRIST was born.　Alleluia!
This day our Saviour hath appeared.　Alleluia!
This day on earth Angels sing, and Archangels share
　our joys.　Alleluia!
This day the righteous rejoice, proclaiming, " Glory to
　GOD in the highest."　Alleluia!

PALESTRINA, SWEELINCK.

33

PSALM ix.　1. I will give thanks to Thee, O LORD, and
magnify Thy holy Name.　How great and wonderful
art Thou in all the world!　Holy, Holy, LORD GOD
of Hosts.

PALESTRINA.

34

PSALM c.　1. O be joyful, all ye lands; serve the LORD
with gladness: come before Him with a song.　Let all
the people worship Him; sing of Him, and praise His
Name.　For the LORD our GOD is great: He is just and
merciful: O that men would praise Him.

PALESTRINA.

35

PSALM vii.　1. O LORD my GOD, in Thee have I put
my trust: save me from all them that persecute me, and
deliver me.

PALESTRINA.

36

1. Stabat mater dolorosa
   Juxta crucem lacrymosa,
   Dum pendebat Filius.

2. Cujus animam gementem
   Contristantem et dolentem
   Pertransivit gladius.

3. O quam tristis et afflicta
   Fuit illa benedicta
   Mater Unigeniti ;

4. Quæ mœrebat et dolebat
   Et tremebat, cum videbat
   Nati pœnas inclyti.

5. Quis est homo qui non fleret,
   Christi matrem si videret
   In tanto supplicio ?

6. Quis non posset contristari
   Piam matrem contemplari
   Dolentem cum Filio ?

7. Pro peccatis suæ gentis
   Vidit Jesum in tormentis,
   Et flagellis subditum.

8. Vidit suum dulcem natum
   Morientem, desolatum,
   Dum emisit spiritum.

ASTORGA, CLARI, DVOŘÁK, PALESTRINA,
PERGOLESI, ROSSINI.

37

PSALM cxxxvii. 1. Super flumina Babylonis, illic sedimus et flevimus, cum recordaremur tui, Sion.

2. In salicibus in medio ejus suspendimus organa nostra.

PUI SIKINA.

38

St. Matthew xvi. 18, 19. Tu es Petrus, et super hanc petram ædificabo Ecclesiam Meam, et portæ inferi non prævalebunt adversus eàm : et tibi dabo claves regni cœlorum. Quodcunque ligàveris super terram erit ligatum et in cœlis, et quodcunque solveris super terram erit solutum et in cœlis.

English Version.

Thou art Peter, and upon this rock I will build My Church ; and the gates of hell shall not prevail against it ; and I will give unto thee the keys of the Kingdom of Heaven ; and whatsoever thou shalt bind on earth shall be bound in Heaven ; and whatsoever thou shalt loose on earth shall be loosed in Heaven.

Mendelssohn, Palestrina.

39

Psalm ii. 1. Why do the heathen rage so furiously against the Lord ?

11. Serve ye, O serve the Lord in fear, and magnify His Name. Glorify Him for evermore.

Palestrina.

40

Save, Lord, hear us ; O hear us, when we call. Forsake us not for ever ; revive us for Thy mercy's sake. We pray Thee, return unto us ; O Lord, forsake us not.

Marenzio.

41

Jesu, dulcis memoria,
Dans vera cordi gaudia ;
Sed super mel et omnia
Ejus dulcis præsentia.
Duræ premunt angustiæ,
Exaudi preces supplicum ;
Fluunt amaræ lacrymæ ;
Exaudi vota pauperum.

†Boiiier, Vittoria.

† For English Version see No. 590.

42

‚O quam gloriosum est regnum in quo cum Christo gaudent omnes sancti ! 'Amicti, stolis albis ‚Agnum sequuntur ‚quocunque ierit.

BIRD, VITTORIA.

43

When to the Temple Mary went, and brought the Holy
    Child,
Him did the aged Simeon see, as it had been revealed.
He took up JESUS in 'his arms, and blessing GOD, he said:
In peace I now depart, my Saviour having seen,
The Hope of Israel, the Light of men.
Help now Thy servants, gracious LORD, that we may
    ever be
As once the faithful Simeon was, rejoicing but in Thee;
And when we must from earth departure take,
May gently fall asleep, and with Thee wake.

ECCARD.

44

1 CORINTHIANS xv. 20. Alleluia. Christus surrexit a mortuis primitiæ dormientium.

21. Alleluia. Quoniam per hominem mors, et per hominem resurrectio mortuorum.

22. Alleluia. ‚Et sicut in Adam omnes moriuntur, ita et in Christo omnes vivificabuntur.

ROMANS iv. 25 ;¹ 1 COR. v. 8. Mortuus est propter delicta nostra, et resurrexit propter justificationem nostram; itaque epulemur in azymis sinceritatis et veritatis. Alleluia.

English Version.

1 CORINTHIANS xv. 20. Alleluia. CHRIST is risen from the dead, the first fruits of them that are asleep.

21. Alleluia. Since by man came death, also came by man the resurrection of the dead.

22. Alleluia. For as in Adam all die, so also in CHRIST shall all be made alive.

ROMANS iv. 25 ; 1 COR. v. 8. CHRIST was delivered up for our offences, and He was raised again for our justification; let us then keep the feast with purity and with truth. Alleluia.

ANERIO.

45

'Arise, O ye servants of GOD, ye who watch in His courts, to serve our GOD and laud His Name, singing praise to Him night and day. O praise ye His Name evermore.

SWEELINCK.

46

O LORD GOD, to Thee be praise evermore. And Thy glory shall be told to the ends of all the earth, while we sing unceasingly the great deeds which Thou hast wrought.

SWEELINCK.

47

PSALM lxxxvi. 1. Bow Thine ear, O LORD, and hear : let Thine anger cease from us.

ISAIAH lxiv. 10. Sion, Thy Sion, is wasted and brought low : Jerusalem is wasted quite : desolate and void.

Another Version.

PSALM lxxxvi. 1. Bow Thine ear, O LORD, and hear me : for I am poor and in misery.

3, 6. O LORD, be merciful unto me : give ear unto my prayer, and ponder the voice of my humble desires.

8, 9. Among the Gods there is none like Thee. All nations shall come and worship Thee, O LORD, and glorify Thy Name.

10. For Thou art great, and dost wondrous things : Thou art GOD alone.

Another Version.

ISAIAH lxiv. 9. Be not wroth very sore, O LORD, neither remember iniquity for ever : see, we beseech Thee, we are Thy people.

10. Zion is a wilderness, Jerusalem a desolation.

11. Our holy and our beautiful house is burnt up with fire.

12. Wilt Thou refrain Thyself, O LORD, for these things ? wilt Thou hold Thy peace. and afflict us very sore ?

BIRD.

48

St. John xiv. 18. I will not leave you comfortless, I
will come again to you, (xvi. 22) and your heart shall
rejoice. Hallelujah.

Bird.

49

O Lord, turn Thy wrath away from us, for Thy mercy's
sake; call to mind no more, O our God, our former sins
and wickedness; look down with Thy merciful eyes, and
see we be Thy people and Thy pasture-sheep.

Bird.

50

Psalm lxxxi. 1. Sing joyfully unto God our strength;
sing loud unto the God of Jacob.

2. Take the song, and bring forth the timbrel, the
pleasant harp, and the viol.

3. Blow the trumpet in the new moon, even in the time
appointed, and at our feast-day.

4. For this is a statute for Israel, and a law of the God
of Jacob.

Bird.

51

Psalm lxxxi. 1. Sing we merrily unto God our
strength: make a cheerful noise unto the God of Jacob.

2. Take the psalm, bring hither the tabret :: the merry
harp with the lute:

3. Blow up the trumpet in the new moon : even in the
time appointed, and upon our solemn feast-day.

4. For this was made a statute for Israel : and a law of
the God of Jacob. [Hallelujah. Amen.]

Batten, Blow, Child, Kefway.

52 Crotch, Tinney, vv. 1-3. [Hallelujah. Amen.]

·53

COLLECT
· For the Third Sunday after the Epiphany..

Almighty and everlasting GOD, mercifully look upon our infirmities: and in all our dangers and necessities stretch forth Thy right hand to help and defend us, through JESUS CHRIST our LORD. Amen.

GIBBONS.

54

ST. LUKE ii. 10. Behold, I bring you glad tidings of great joy, which shall be to all people.

11. That unto us a Child is born, unto us a Son is given, a Saviour, Which is CHRIST the LORD.

14. Glory be to GOD on high, and on earth peace, goodwill toward men.

GIBBONS.

55

PSALM xxxix. 6. Behold, Thou hast made my days as it were a span long; and mine age is even as nothing in respect of Thee; and verily every man living is altogether vanity.

7. For man walketh in a vain shadow, and disquieteth himself in vain: he heapeth up riches, and cannot tell who shall gather them.

8. And now, LORD, what is my hope? truly my hope is even in Thee.

13. Hear my prayer, O LORD, and with Thine ears consider my calling; hold not Thy peace at my tears.

14. For I am a stranger with Thee, and a sojourner, as all my fathers were.

15. O spare me a little, that I may recover my strength, before I go hence, and be no more seen.

GIBBONS.

56

PSALM cxxviii. 1. Blessed are all they that fear the LORD, and walk in His ways.

2. For thou shalt eat the labours of thine hands; O well is thee, and happy shalt thou be.

3. Thy wife shall be as the fruitful vine upon the walls of thine house.

4. Thy children like the olive-branches, round about thy table.

5. Lo, thus shall the man be blessed that feareth the LORD.

6. The LORD [thy GOD] from out of Sion shall so bless thee, that thou shalt see Jerusalem in prosperity all thy life long.

7. Yea, thou shalt see thy children's children, and peace shall be upon Israel.

Glory be to the Father, &c.

GIBBONS.

57 CROFT, W. HAYES, vv. 1-7. [Amen.]
58 ELVEY, vv. 1 (*Blessed are they*), 2 (*2nd part*).
59 E. G. MONK, vv. 1-5.
60 PURCELL, vv. 1-4, 6, 7, 2, 5. Hallelujah.

61

Glorious and Powerful GOD, we understand
  Thy dwelling is on High
  Above the starry sky.
Thou dwell'st not in stone temples made with hand;
But in the flesh hearts of the sons of men
  To dwell is Thy delight,
  Near hand, though out of sight.

We give of Thine own hand, Thy acceptation
  Is very life and blood,
  To all actions good.
Whenever here or hence our supplication,
From pure and with unfeigned hearts, to Thee ascends,
  Be present with Thy grace,
  Shew us Thy loving face.

Oh! down on us full show'rs of mercy send,
  Let Thy love's burning beams
  Dry up all our sin's streams.
Arise, O LORD, and come into Thy rest.
Both now and evermore Thy Name be blest,
  Founder and Foundation
  Of endless habitation. Amen.

GIBBONS.

62

Great LORD of Lords, supreme immortal King,
O give us grace to sing
Thy praise, which makes earth, air, and heaven to ring.

O Word of GOD, from ages unbegun,
The FATHER's only Son,
With Him in power, in substance, Thou art one.

O Holy Ghost, Whose care doth all embrace,
Thy watch is o'er our race,
Thou Source of life, Thou Spring of peace and grace.

One living Trinity, One unseen Light,
All, all is Thine, Thy light
Beholds alike the bounds of depth and height. Amen.

GIBBONS.

63

ST. MATTHEW xxi. 9. Hosanna to the Son of David: blessed is He that cometh in the Name of the LORD.

ST. MARK xi. 10. Blessed be the King of Israel, blessed be the King that cometh in the Name of the LORD.

ST. LUKE xix. 38. Peace in heaven, and glory in the highest places; Hosanna in the highest heavens.

GIBBONS.

64

PSALM xiii. 1. How long wilt Thou forget me, O LORD, for ever? How long wilt Thou hide Thy face from me?

2. How long shall I seek counsel in my soul, and be so vexed in my heart? How long shall mine enemies triumph over me?

3. Consider and hear me, O LORD my GOD; lighten mine eyes, that I sleep not in death.

4. Lest mine enemy say, I have prevailed against him; for if I be cast down, they that trouble me will rejoice at it.

5. But my trust is in Thy mercy, and my heart is joyful in Thy salvation. ·

6. I will sing of the LORD, because He hath dealt so lovingly with me; yea, I will praise the Name of the LORD most Highest. Amen.

BATTISHILL, BOYCE, J. CLARK, GIBBONS, GREENE, LÖHR.

65 M. CAMIDGE, v. 3.
66 DE LACY, OUSELEY, vv. 1-3.
67 B. ROGERS, vv. 1-4, 6.

68

COLOSSIANS iii. 1. If ye be risen again with CHRIST, seek those things which are above, where CHRIST sitteth on the right hand of GOD.

2. Set your affections on heavenly things, and not on earthly things.

3. For ye are dead, and your life is hid with CHRIST in GOD.

4. Whensoever CHRIST, Which is our life, shall shew Himself, then shall ye also appear with Him in glory. So be it.

GIBBONS.

69

PSALM xxiv. 7. Lift up your heads, O ye gates, and be ye lift up, ye everlasting doors: and the King of Glory shall come in.

8, 10. Who is the King of Glory? It is the LORD, strong and mighty: even the LORD of Hosts, He is the King of Glory.

GIBBONS, KING.

70

LORD, grant grace, we humbly beseech Thee, that we, with Thine Angels and Saints, may sing to Thee continually. Holy, Holy, Holy, LORD GOD of Hosts: glory, honour, and power be unto Thee, O GOD, the Creator, O LORD JESUS, the Redeemer, O Holy Spirit, the Comforter. And let every thing that hath breath praise and magnify the same LORD ALMIGHTY. Amen.

GIBBONS.

71

PSALM vi. 1. O LORD, in Thy wrath rebuke me not:
neither chasten me in Thy displeasure.

2. Have mercy upon me, O LORD, for I am weak:
O LORD, heal me, for my bones are vexed.

3. My soul also is sore troubled : but, LORD, how long
wilt Thou punish me ?

4. O save me for Thy mercy's sake.

GIBBONS.

72

THE LAMENTATION.

O LORD, in Thee is all my trust,
  Give ear unto my woeful cry;
Refuse me not, that am unjust,
  But, bowing down Thy heavenly eye,
Behold how I do still lament
  My sins wherein I Thee offend :
O LORD, for them shall I be shent ?
  Sith Thee to please I do intend.

No, no, not so, Thy will is bent
  To deal with sinners in Thine ire,
But when in heart they shall repent
  Thou grant'st with speed their just desire.
To Thee, therefore, still shall I cry,
  To wash away my sinful crime :
Thy blood, O LORD, is not yet dry,
  But that it may help me in time.

Haste Thee, O LORD, haste Thee, I say,
  To pour on me Thy gifts of grace,
That when this life shall fleet away,
  In Heav'n with Thee I may have place :
Where Thou dost reign eternally
  With GOD, Which once Thee down did send,
Where angels sing continually,
  To Thee be praise world without end.   Amen.

GIBBONS,

73

O LORD, increase my faith, strengthen me and confirm me in Thy true faith; endue me with wisdom, charity, and patience, in all my adversity, sweet Saviour. Say Amen.

GIBBONS.

74

O Thou the central orb of righteous love,
Pure beam of the most High, eternal Light
Of this our wintry world, Thy radiance bright
Awakes new joy in faith, hope soars above.

Come, quickly come, and let Thy glory shine,
Gilding our darksome heaven with rays Divine;
Thy saints with holy lustre round Thee move,
As stars about Thy throne, set in the height
Of God's ordaining counsel, as Thy sight
Gives measured grace to each, Thy power to prove.

Let Thy bright beams disperse the gloom of sin,
Our nature all shall feel eternal day,
In fellowship with Thee, transforming day
To souls erewhile unclean, now pure within. Amen.

GIBBONS.

75

PSALM xxx. 4. Sing unto the LORD, O ye Saints of His, and give thanks at the remembrance of His holiness.

5. For His anger endures but for a moment: in His favour is life: weeping may endure for a night, but joy cometh in the morning.

6. And in my prosperity I said, I shall never be moved.

7. LORD, by Thy favour Thou hast made my mountain to stand strong: Thou didst hide Thy face, and I was troubled.

8. I cried unto Thee, O LORD; and, unto the LORD I made supplication.

9. What profit is there in my blood, when I go down into the pit? Shall the dust praise Thee? shall it declare Thy truth?

10. Hear, O LORD, and have mercy upon me: LORD, be Thou my helper.

GIBBONS.

76

See, see, the Word is Incarnate, GOD is made man in the womb of a Virgin. Shepherds rejoice, wise men adore, and Angels sing: Glory be to GOD on high, peace on earth, good will towards men. The law is cancell'd, Jews and Gentiles all converted by the preaching of glad tidings of salvation. The blind have sight, and cripples have their motion, diseases cured, the dead are raised, and miracles are wrought.

Let us welcome such a Guest with Hosanna. The Paschal Lamb is offer'd, CHRIST JESUS made a sacrifice for sin. The earth quakes, the sun is darkened, the powers of hell are shaken, and lo, He is risen up in victory. Sing Hallelujah.

See, O see, the fresh wounds, the goring blood, the pricks of thorns, the print of nails, and in the sight of multitudes, O glorious Ascension. Where now He sits on GOD's right hand, where all the choir of heaven all jointly sings: Glory be to the Lamb that sitteth on the Throne. Let us continue the wonted note with Hosanna. Blessed be He that cometh in the Name of the LORD. With Hallelujah, we triumph in victory: the Serpent's head bruised, CHRIST's Kingdom exalted, and Heaven laid open to sinners. Amen.

GIBBONS.

77

ST. JOHN i. 19. This is the record of John, when the Jews sent Priests and Levites from Jerusalem to ask him, Who art thou ?

20. And he confessed, and denied not; and said plainly, I am not the CHRIST.

21. And they asked him, What art thou then ? Art thou Elias? And he said, I am not. Art thou that Prophet ? And he answered, No.

22. Then said they unto him, What art thou ? that we may give an answer unto them that sent us. What sayest thou of thyself?

23. And he said, I am the voice of him that crieth in the wilderness, Make straight the way of the LORD.

GIBBONS.

78

Proper Preface for Easter Day.

We praise Thee, O Father, for the glorious Resurrection of Thy Son, JESUS CHRIST our LORD. For He is the very Paschal Lamb, Which was offered up for us, and hath taken away the sins of the world. Who by His death hath destroyed death, and by His rising to life again hath restored to us everlasting life.

* Therefore with angels and archangels, and with all the company of Heaven, we laud and magnify Thy glorious Name; evermore praising Thee, and saying, Holy, Holy, Holy, LORD GOD of Hosts, Heaven and earth are full of Thy glory: Glory be to Thee, O LORD most high. Amen.*

GIBBONS.

79 J. L. HOPKINS, NOVELLO.*——*

80

PSALM xliii. 5. Why art thou so heavy, O my soul? and why art thou so disquieted within me?

6. O put thy trust in GOD : for I will yet give Him thanks, Which is the help of my countenance, and my GOD. Amen.

GIBBONS.

81

ISAIAH xxv. 1. O LORD my GOD; I will exalt Thee, I will praise Thy Name; for Thou hast done amazing things; Thy counsels of old are faithfulness and truth.

4. For Thou hast been a defence to the poor and needy in his distress, a refuge from the storm, a shadow from the heat, a shelter against the raging tempest.

8. He will swallow up death in victory: GOD will wipe away tears from off all faces, and He shall vindicate His Saints.

9. Lo, This is our GOD; we have waited for Him, and He will save us : we will rejoice and be glad in His salvation. Amen.

BULL.

82 NARES, vv. 1, 4, 9.

83

Psalm lxxxvi.

Bow Thine ear to me, O Lord :
  Hear my plaint in my distress.
Save my soul, for in Thy Word
  Rests my hope of happiness.
Grace and mercy to me grant,
  Daily thus on Thee to call.
Comfort doth Thy servant want :
  Grant it, Lord, or I must fall.

Thou, O Lord, art good and great,
  And Thy mercy dost dispense
To all those who truly wait
  For Thy love as their defence :
Thou of all the gods alone
  Honour dost and worship claim
All in Heaven and Nature known
  Live to glorify Thy Name.

DOWLAND.

84

Urbs cœlestis, urbs beata,
Super petram collocata,
Urbs in portu satis tuto,
De longinquo te saluto :
Te saluto, te suspiro,
Te affecto, te requiro.

Me receptet Sion illa,
Sion, David urbs tranquilla ;
In hac urbe lux Solennis,
Ver æternum, pax perennis ;
In hac odor implens cœlos,
In hac semper festum melos.

TAYLOR.

85

PSALM vii. 1, 2. O LORD, in Thee have I put my trust; save me from all them that persecute me, and deliver me, lest he devour my soul like a lion while there is none to help.

11. My help cometh of God, Who preserveth all them that are true of heart.

18. I will give thanks unto the Lord, according to His righteousness, and I will praise the Name of the Lord most High.

CARISSIMI and CLARI.

86

PSALM cxxxv. 1. O praise the LORD, laud ye the Name of the LORD; praise it, O ye servants of the LORD;

[2. Ye that stand in the house of the LORD, in the courts of the house of our GOD.]

3. O praise the LORD, for the LORD is gracious; O sing praises unto His Name, for it is lovely.

[4. For why? the LORD hath chosen Jacob unto Himself, and Israel for His own possession.]

5. I know that the LORD is great, and that our Lord is above all gods.

[6. Whatsoever the LORD pleased, that did He in heaven, and in earth, and in the sea, and in all deep places.]

13. Thy Name, O LORD, endureth for ever; so doth Thy memorial, O LORD, from one generation to another.

19. Praise the LORD, ye house of Israel; praise the Lord, ye house of Aaron.

20. Praise the Lord, ye house of Levi; ye that fear the LORD, praise the LORD.

[21. Praised be the LORD out of Sion, Who dwelleth at Jerusalem.]

1. O praise the LORD, laud ye the Name of the LORD; praise it, O ye servants of the LORD.

HUMPHREYS.

87 Goss, vv. 1-3, 19, 20, 1-3.
88 OUSELEY, vv. 5, 6, 11. Hallelujah. Amen.
89 TOURS, vv. 1, 2, 1, 3 5. Amen.

90

ISAIAH i. 2. Hear, O heavens, and give ear, O earth, for the LORD hath spoken : I have nourished and brought up children, and they have rebelled against Me.

4. Ah, sinful nation, a seed of evildoers, children that are corrupters. They have forsaken the LORD, they have provoked the Holy One of Israel unto anger.

16. Wash ye, make you clean ; put away the evil of your doings from before Mine eyes ; cease to do evil ;

17. Learn to do well ; seek judgment, relieve the oppressed, judge the fatherless, plead for the widow.

18. Come now, let us reason together, saith the LORD : though your sins be as scarlet, they shall be as white as snow ; though they be red like crimson, they shall be as wool.

HUMPHREYS.

91

PSALM xlii. 1. Like as the hart desireth the water-brooks, so longeth my soul after Thee, O GOD.

2. My soul is athirst for GOD, yea, even for the living GOD : O when shall I come to appear before the presence of GOD ?

3. My tears have been my meat day and night, while they daily say unto me, Where is now thy GOD ?

4. Now when I think thereupon, I pour out my heart by myself ; for I went with the multitude, and brought them forth into the house of GOD ;

5. In the voice of praise and thanksgiving, among such as keep holy day.

6. Why art thou so full of heaviness, O my soul ? and why art thou so disquieted within me ?

7. O put thy trust in GOD, for I will yet give Him thanks for the help of His countenance.

[14. Why art thou so vexed, O my soul ? and why art thou so disquieted within me ?

15. O put thy trust in GOD, for I will yet thank Him, Which is the help of my countenance, and my GOD.]

HUMPHREYS.

92 T. A. t . Gr ., w t .
5 Or t t , vv. 1 3, 14, 15. Amen.

94

Psalm xxii. 1. O Lord, My God, why hast Thou forsaken Me; and art so far from My health, and from the words of My complaint?

14. I am poured out like water, all My bones are out of joint : My heart also in the midst of My Body is even like melting wax.

19. But be not Thou far from Me, O Lord : Thou art My succour'; haste Thee to help Me.

16. For many dogs are come about Me, and the counsel of the wicked layeth siege against Me.

17. They pierced My hands and My feet, I may tell all My bones : they stand staring and looking upon Me.

18. They part My garments among them, and cast lots upon My vesture.

Humphreys.

95

Psalm lxx. 1. Haste Thee, O God, to deliver me; make haste to help me, O Lord.

2. Let them be ashamed and confounded that seek after my soul ; let them be turned backward, and put to confusion, that wish me evil.

3. Let them for their reward be soon brought to shame, that cry over me, There, there.

4. But let all those that seek Thee be joyful and glad in Thee ; and let all such as delight in Thy salvation say alway, The Lord be praised.

5. As for me, I am poor and in misery; [haste Thee unto me, O God.]

1. Haste Thee, O God, to deliver me ; make haste to help me, O Lord.

6. Thou art my helper and my Redeemer : O Lord, make no long tarrying.

Humphreys.

96 Batten, vv. 1–4. Amen.
97 Ouseley, vv. 1, 2, 3, 6.
98 Sheffield, vv. 1–6. Amen.

99

PSALM xliv.   5. Thou art my King, O GOD, send help unto Jacob.

6. Through Thee will we overthrow our enemies, and in Thy Name will we tread them under that rise up against us.

7. For I will not trust in my bow, it is not my sword that shall help me.

8. But it is Thou that savest us from our enemies, and puttest them to confusion that hate us.

5. Thou art my King, O GOD, send help unto Jacob.

9. We make our boast of GOD all day long, and will praise Thy Name for ever.

CHILD, HUMPHREYS.

100

PSALM xxxix.   5. LORD, let me know mine end, and the number of my days, that I may be certified how long I have to live.

6. Behold, Thou hast made my days as it were a span long, and mine age is even as nothing in respect of Thee ; and verily every man living is altogether vanity.

7. [For man walketh in a vain shadow, and disquieteth himself in vain ;] he heapeth up riches, and cannot tell who shall gather them.

8. And now, LORD, what is my hope ? truly my hope is even in Thee.

12. When Thou with rebukes dost chasten man for sin, Thou makest his beauty to consume away, like as it were a moth fretting a garment : every man therefore is but vanity.

13. Hear my prayer, O LORD, and with Thine ears consider my calling ; hold not Thy peace at my tears.

14. For I am a stranger with Thee, and a sojourner, as all my fathers were.

15. O spare me a little, that I may recover my strength, before I go hence, and be no more seen.

LOCK.

101 Goss, vv. 5–8, 13–15.
102 GRIFFIN, vv. 5 8, 13, 15.
103 HARING, vv. 5 8.
104 SMFE, vv. 5, 6, 15.

105

PSALM cxxii. 1. I was glad when they said unto me, We will go into the house of the LORD.

2. Our feet shall stand in thy gates, O Jerusalem.

3. Jerusalem is built as a city, that is at unity in itself.

4. For thither the tribes go up, even the tribes of the LORD, to testify unto Israel, to give thanks unto the Name of the LORD.

[5. For there is the seat of judgment, even the seat of the house of David.]

†6. O pray for the peace of Jerusalem: they shall prosper that love thee.

7. Peace be within thy walls, and plenteousness within thy palaces.

8. For my brethren and companions' sakes I will wish thee prosperity.

9. Yea, because of the house of the LORD our GOD, I will seek to do thee good.

BUNNETT, †THORNE, TRIMNELL, TUCKER.

106 ATTWOOD, vv. 1, 5, 6, 7. Gloria Patri.

107 CHILD, COBB, KING, MOREIRA, B. ROGERS, vv. 6–9. [Gloria Patri.]

108 ELVEY, vv. 1, 5, 6, 7. Amen.

109 HODGES, TOMKINS, v. 6.

110 J. L. HOPKINS, vv. 1, 5, 6, 3. Hallelujah. Amen.

111 HORSLEY, vv. 1, 4, 6, 3, 7.

112 PERGOLESI, vv. 1, 2, 7.

113 PURCELL, vv. 1–8, 7.

† vv. 6, 7 sometimes sung as a separate Anthem.

114

PSALM cv. 1. O give thanks unto the LORD, and call upon His Name : tell the people what things He hath done for us.

2. O let your songs be of Him, and praise Him : and let your talking be of all His wondrous works.

3. Rejoice in His Holy Name : let the heart of them rejoice that seek the LORD.

ELVEY, TUCKER, T. A. WALMISLEY.

115 †CROFT, W. HAYES, vv. 1–3. Hallelujah.

116 EDWARDS, REA, vv. 1, 2. Amen.

This Anthem is also attributed to BOYCE.

·11·7

PSALM cxliv. 9., I will sing a new song unto Thee, O GOD, and sing praises unto Thee upon a ten-stringed lute.

10. Thou hast given victory unto kings, and hast delivered David Thy servant from the peril of the sword.

11. Save me, and deliver me from the hand of strange children, whose mouth talketh of vanity, and their right hand is a right hand of iniquity.

12. That our sons may grow up as the young plants, and that our daughters may be as the polished corners of the temple.

13. That our garners may be full and plenteous with all manner of store, that our sheep may bring forth thousands and ten thousands in our streets.

[14. That our oxen may be strong to labour, that there be no decay ; no leading into captivity, and no complaining in our streets.]

15. Happy are the people that are in such a case : yea, blessed are the people who have the LORD for their GOD.

WISE.

118 ARMES, vv. 9, 11–15. Amen.

119

LAMENTATIONS i. 4. The ways of Zion do mourn, because none come to the solemn feasts ; all her gates are desolate ; her priests sigh, her virgins are afflicted, and she is in bitterness.

16. For these things I weep ; mine eye runneth down with water.

5. Her adversaries are the chief, her enemies prosper : for the LORD hath afflicted her.

16. For these things I weep ; mine eye runneth down with water.

5. For the multitude of her transgressions, the LORD hath afflicted her.

11. See. O LORD, and consider, for I am become vile.

12. Is it nothing to you, all ye that pass by? Behold and see, if there be any sorrow like my sorrow.

15. The LORD hath trodden under foot all my mighty men in the midst of me: He hath called an assembly against me, to crush my young men: the LORD hath trodden under foot the virgin, the daughter of Judah.

16. For these things I weep: mine eye runneth down with water: because the Comforter that should relieve my soul is far from me.

11. See, O LORD, and consider, for I am become vile.

WISE.

120

2 SAMUEL i. 19. Thy beauty, O Israel, is slain upon thy high places: how are the mighty fallen!

20. Tell it not in Gath, publish it not in the streets of Askelon, lest the daughters of the Philistines rejoice, lest the daughters of the uncircumcised triumph.

21. Ye mountains of Gilboa, let there be no dew, neither let there be rain upon you, nor fields of offerings: for there the shield of the mighty is vilely cast away, the shield of Saul, as though he had not been anointed with oil.

22. From the blood of the slain, from the fat of the mighty, the bow of Jonathan turned not back, and the sword of Saul returned not empty.

23. Saul and Jonathan were lovely and pleasant in their lives, and in their death they were not divided.

24. Ye daughters of Israel, weep over Saul, who clothed you in scarlet, who put on ornaments of gold upon your apparel.

25. How are the mighty fallen in the midst of the battle! O Jonathan, thou wast slain in thine high places.

26. I am distressed for thee, my brother Jonathan: very pleasant hast thou been unto me: thy love to me was wonderful, passing the love of women.

27. How are the mighty fallen, and the weapons of war perished!

WISE.

121

ISAIAH lii. 1. Awake, awake, put on thy strength, O Sion; put on thy beautiful garments, O Jerusalem, thou holy city.

2. Shake thyself from the dust, O Jerusalem, thou holy city: loose thyself from the bands of thy neck, O captive daughter of Sion.

7. How beautiful upon the mountains are the feet of him that bringeth good tidings, that publisheth peace; that bringeth glad tidings of peace, that publisheth salvation; that saith unto Sion, Thy GOD reigneth!

9. Break forth into joy, Hallelujah! sing together, ye waste places of Jerusalem; break forth into joy, Hallelujah! For the LORD hath comforted His people, He hath redeemed Jerusalem.

10. The LORD hath made bare His holy arm in the sight of all nations, and all the ends of the earth shall see the salvation of our GOD. Hallelujah.

WISE.

122

ISAIAH xl. 3. Prepare ye the way of the LORD, make straight in the desert a highway for our GOD.

4. Every valley shall be exalted, and every mountain and hill shall be made low: and the crooked shall be made straight, and the rough places shall be made plain.

5. And the glory of the LORD shall be revealed, and all flesh shall see it together.

6. And the voice said, Cry. What shall I cry? All flesh is grass, and the goodliness thereof is as the flower that is in the field.

8. The grass withereth, the flower fadeth: but the word of the LORD shall stand fast for ever.

9. O Zion, that bringest glad tidings, get thee up into the mountains: O Jerusalem, that bringest glad tidings, lift up thy voice with strength, and say unto Judah, Behold thy GOD.

WISE.

123

1 Corinthians xv. 20. Now is Christ risen from the dead, and He shall take me from among them that sleep.

Job xix. 26, 27. And hereafter shall I be clothed with this my body; and in my flesh shall I see God; Whom I shall see for myself, and mine eyes shall behold, and not another.

(*Sung at the same time as the above.*)

My life is hid in Jesus,
And death is gain to me;
Then, whensoe'er He pleases,
I meet it willingly.

J. M. Bach.

124

Psalm lxxi. 1. In Thee, O Lord, have I put my trust, let me never be put to confusion: but rid me, and deliver me, in Thy righteousness; incline Thine ear unto me, and save me.

4. For Thou, O Lord God, art the thing that I long for: Thou art my hope, even from my youth.

5. Through Thee have I been holden up ever since I was born: Thou art He that took me out of my mother's womb; my praise shall be always of Thee.

[10. Go not far from me, O God: my God, haste Thee to help me.]

18. O what great troubles and adversities hast Thou shewed me; yet didst Thou turn and refresh me: yea, and broughtest me from the deep of the earth again.

20. Therefore will I praise Thee and Thy faithfulness, O God, playing upon an instrument of musick: unto Thee will I sing, O Thou Holy One of Israel.

21. My lips shall be fain when I sing unto Thee: and so will my soul whom Thou hast delivered. Hallelujah.

Purcell.

125 W. S. Bennett. xv. *1 10.

* This verse is sometimes sung as a separate Anthem.

126

St. Luke ii. 10. Behold, I bring you glad tidings of great joy, which shall be to all people.

11. For unto you this day is born a Saviour, Which is Christ the Lord.

10. Glad tidings of great joy, which shall be to all people.

14. Glory be to God on high, and on earth peace, good will towards men. Hallelujah. Amen.

Croce, Greene, Purcell, C. W. Smith.

127

Psalm lxxxvi. 1. Bow down Thine ear, O Lord, and hear me : for I am poor, and in misery.

[2. Preserve Thou my soul, for I am holy : my God, save Thy servant that putteth his trust in Thee.]

3. Be merciful unto me, O Lord : for I will call daily upon Thee.

4. Comfort the soul of Thy servant, for unto Thee, O Lord, do I lift up my soul.

5. For Thou, Lord, art good and gracious, and of great mercy unto all them that call upon Thee.

[6. Give ear, O Lord, unto my prayer, and ponder the voice of my humble desires.

7. In the time of my trouble I will call upon Thee, for Thou hearest me.]

8. Among the gods there is none like unto Thee, [O Lord :] there is none that can do as Thou doest.

[9. All nations whom Thou hast made shall come and worship Thee, O Lord, and shall glorify Thy Name.]

10. For Thou art great, and doest wondrous things : Thou art God alone.

11. Teach me Thy way, O Lord, and I will walk in Thy truth : O knit my heart unto Thee, that I may fear Thy Name.

12. And I will thank Thee, O Lord my God, with all my heart, and will praise Thy Name for evermore.

[13. For great is Thy mercy toward me : and Thou hast delivered my soul from the nethermost hell.

14. O GOD, the proud are risen against me, and the congregations of naughty men have sought after my soul, and have not set Thee before their eyes.]

15. But Thou, O LORD GOD, art full of compassion and mercy: long-suffering, plenteous in goodness and truth,

16. O turn Thee then unto me, and have mercy upon me: [give Thy strength unto Thy servant and help the son of Thine handmaid.]

PURCELL.

128 ATTWOOD, vv. 11–16. Amen.
129 AYRTON, vv. 1, 4, 2, 4, 16, 15.
130 BISHOP, vv. 1, 2. Amen.
131 J. CLARK, vv. 1, 3–5, 9, 10, 14, 16.
132 CROCE, W. H. GLADSTONE, v. 11.
133 CROFT, GREENE, vv. 6–10.
134 CROTCH, vv. 3, *4.
135 CUMMINGS, v. 6 (*O Lord, give ear*).
136 DUPUIS, vv. 1, 4, 5, 8–10.
137 GREENE, J. C. PRING, vv. 1–4. Amen.
138 W. HAYES, vv. 1, 3–5, 12, 13. Hallelujah. Amen.
139 KEETON, vv. 6 (*Give ear*, LORD), 7, 4, 8–10.
140 LUCAS, vv. 1, 3, 11, 12.
141 PATTISON, vv. 6, 7.
142 ROBINSON, vv. 1–3, 6–10. Hallelujah. Amen.
143 WEST, vv. 4–10.

* This verse is sometimes sung as a separate Anthem.

144

PSALM xix. 12. LORD, *who can tell how oft he offendeth? O cleanse Thou me from my secret faults.

13. Keep Thy servant from presumptuous sins, lest they get the dominion over me: so shall I be undefiled, and innocent from the great offence.

14, 15. Let the words of my mouth, and the meditation of my heart, be always acceptable in Thy sight, O LORD, my strength and my Redeemer.

Glory be to the Father, &c. PURCELL.

145 {ATTWOOD, BARNBY, BLAIR,
      CULLEY, KLEIN,   } vv. 14. 15. Amen.}
146 WELDON, vv. 12 (*Who can tell*), 13 15. Amen.

147

PSALM lvi.   1. Be merciful unto me, O GOD, for man goeth about to devour me : he is daily fighting, and troubling me.

2. Mine enemies are daily in hand to swallow me up, for they be many that fight against me, O Thou most Highest.

3. Nevertheless, though I am sometime afraid, yet put I my trust in Thee.

4. I will praise GOD, because of His word : I have put my trust in GOD, and will not fear what flesh can do unto me.

5. They daily mistake my words; all that they imagine is to do me evil.

6. They hold all together, and keep themselves close, and mark my steps, when they lay wait for my soul.

7. Shall they escape for their wickedness ? Thou, O GOD, in Thy displeasure shall cast them down.

10. In GOD's word will I rejoice ; in the LORD's word will I comfort me.

11. Yea, in GOD have I put my trust ; I will not be afraid what man can do unto me.

[12. Unto Thee, O GOD, will I pay my vows ; unto Thee will I give thanks.

13. For Thou hast delivered my soul from death, and my feet from falling, that I may walk before GOD in the light of the living.]   Hallelujah.   Amen.

PURCELL.

148 OUSELEY, vv. 1, 3, 4.
149 CROTCH, OUSELEY, vv. 10–13.   [Amen.]
150 SYDENHAM, vv. 1–3, 11.

151

PSALM cxii.   1. Blessed is the man that feareth the LORD : he hath great delight in His commandments.

2. His seed shall be mighty upon earth, the generation of the faithful shall be blessed.

3. Riches and plenteousness shall be in his house, and his righteousness endureth for ever.

4. Unto the godly there ariseth up light in the darkness; he is merciful, loving, and righteous.

5. A good man is merciful.

[6. He shall never be moved: the righteous shall be had in everlasting remembrance.

7. He will not be afraid of any evil tidings, for his heart standeth fast, and believeth in the LORD.]

9. He hath dispersed abroad; he hath given to the poor; his name shall be exalted with honour. Hallelujah.

PURCELL.

152 BOYCE, vv. 1-3, 6, 7.
153 OUSELEY, vv. 1, 2.
154 WHITFELD, vv. 1-3.

155

THE SONG OF SOLOMON ii. 10. My beloved spake, and said unto me, Rise, my love, my fair one, and come away.

11. For lo, the winter is past, the rain is over and gone.

12. The flowers appear upon the earth. And the time of the singing of birds is come. Hallelujah. And the voice of the turtle is heard in our land.

13. The fig-tree putteth forth her green figs, and the vine with her tender grapes gives a good smell.

10. Rise, my love, my fair one, and come away.

16. My beloved is mine, and I am his. Hallelujah.

PURCELL.

156

PSALM lvii. 8. My heart is fixed, O GOD; I will sing and give praise with the best member that I have.

9. Awake up, my glory; awake, lute and harp; I myself will awake right early.

10. I will give thanks unto Thee, O LORD, among the people; and I will sing unto Thee among the nations.

11. For the greatness of Thy mercy reacheth unto the heavens, and Thy truth unto the clouds.

12. Set up Thyself, O GOD, above the heavens, and Thy glory above all the earth. Hallelujah.

PURCELL.

157 NARES, vv. 9, 12.

158

PSALM cxi.   1. I will give thanks unto the LORD, with my whole heart, secretly among the faithful, and in the congregation.

2. The works of the LORD are great, sought out of all them that have pleasure therein.

3. His work is worthy to be praised, and had in honour, and His righteousness endureth for ever.

4. The merciful and gracious LORD hath so done His marvellous works that they ought to be had in remembrance.

6. He hath shewed His people the power of His works, that He may give them the heritage of the heathen.

7. The works of His hands are verity and judgment ; all His commandments are true.

8. They stand fast for ever and ever, and are done in truth and equity.

9. He sent redemption unto His people ; He hath commanded His covenant for ever ; holy and reverend is His Name.

PURCELL.

159

PSALM cxix.   153. O consider my adversity, and deliver me : for I do not forget Thy law.

154. Avenge Thou my cause, O LORD ; O quicken me, according to Thy word.

155. Health is far from the ungodly : for they regard not Thy statutes.

156. Great is Thy mercy, O LORD ; O quicken me, as Thou art wont.

157. Many there are that trouble me, and persecute me : yet do I not swerve from Thy testimonies.

158. It grieveth me when I see the transgressors ; because they keep not Thy law.

159. Consider, O LORD, how I love Thy commandments : O quicken me, according to Thy loving-kindness.

160. Thy word is true from everlasting : all the judgments of Thy righteousness endure for evermore.

Glory be to the Father, &c.

PURCELL.

160

PSALM lxiii. 1. O GOD, Thou art my GOD: early will I seek Thee.

2. My soul thirsteth for Thee, my flesh also longeth after Thee, in a barren and dry land where no water is.

3. Thus have I looked for Thee in holiness: that I might behold Thy power and glory.

4. For Thy loving-kindness is better than life itself: my lips shall praise Thee.

5. As long as I live will I magnify Thee on this manner, and lift up my hands in Thy Name.

8. Because Thou hast been my helper, therefore under the shadow of Thy wings will I rejoice. Hallelujah. Amen.

[lxviii. 32, 35. Sing unto GOD, O ye kingdoms of the earth: O sing praises unto the LORD; even the GOD of Israel; He will give strength and power unto His people. Blessed be GOD.]

GREENE, W. HAYES, PURCELL.

161 T. JACKSON, vv. 1, 3–5; lxviii. 32, 35. Amen.

162

PSALM cl. 1. O praise GOD in His holiness; praise Him in the firmament of His power.

2. Praise Him in His noble acts; praise Him according to His excellent greatness.

3. Praise Him in the sound of the trumpet; praise Him upon the lute and harp.

4. Praise Him in the cymbals and dances; praise Him upon the strings and pipe.

5. Praise Him upon the well-tuned cymbals; praise Him upon the loud cymbals.

6. Let everything that hath breath praise the LORD.

BLAIR, B. COOKE, DISTIN, GAUL, PURCELL.

163 GOLDWIN, MARTIN, TRIMNELL, WHITFELD, WISE, vv. 1 6. [Hallelujah. Amen.]

164 WELDON, vv. 1 4, 6.

165 R. WOODWARD, vv. 1, 2, 6.

166

PSALM iii. Jehova, quam multi sunt hostes mei, quam multi insurgunt contra me! Quam multi dicunt de animâ meâ, non est ulla salus isti in Deo plane. At Tu, Jehova, clypeus es circa me: gloria mea, et extollens caput meum. Voce meâ ad Jehovam clamanti respondit mihi e monte sanctitatis Suæ maxime. Ego cubui et dormivi, ego expergefeci me, quia Jehova sustentat me. Non timebo a myriadibus populi quas circum disposuerint metatores contra me. Surge, surge, Jehova, fac salvum me, Deus mi: Qui percussisti omnes inimicos meos maxillam, dentes improborum confregisti. Jehova est salus, super populum Tuum sit benedictio Tua maxime.

English Version.

1. O LORD Jehovah, how many are they that vex me, how many arise to seek my hurt.

2. How many say of my soul in derision, It is not for him to find in his GOD salvation.

3. But Thou, Jehovah, like a shield defendest me, Thou art my glory, and the lifter up of my head.

4. With my voice I cry aloud to Jehovah, and He doth hear me, and from His holy mountain He doth answer me.

5. I did lay me down to take rest; I was sleeping, then I awaked; yea, for Jehovah sustaineth me.

6. I will fear not, though of the people ten thousands against me have set themselves as adversaries round about.

7. Rise up, rise up, Jehovah, my help and salvation be.

8. For Thou hast all mine enemies smitten upon the cheek-bone, yea, the teeth of the wicked Thou hast broken.

9. Jehovah doth save us. On Thy people, Thy chosen, for ever be Thy blessing plenteously.

PURCELL.

167

Psm xvii. 1. O Lord our Governour, how excellent is Thy N... ... world' Thou that hast set Thy glory ... the heaven.

2. Out of the mouth of very babes and sucklings hast Thou ordained strength, because of Thine enemies; that Thou mightest still the enemy and the avenger.

3. For I will consider Thy heavens, even the works of Thy fingers; the moon and the stars, which Thou hast ordained.

4. LORD, what is man, that Thou art mindful of him: and the Son of Man, that Thou visitest Him?

5. Thou madest Him lower than the angels, to crown Him with glory and worship.

6. Thou makest Him to have dominion of the works of Thy hands; and Thou hast put all things in subjection under His feet.

7. All sheep and oxen; yea, and the beasts of the field;

8. The fowls of the air, and the fishes of the sea; and whatsoever walketh through the paths of the sea.

9. O LORD our Governour, how excellent is Thy Name in all the world.

Glory be to the Father, &c.

PURCELL.

168 BOYCE, vv. 4-6, 9.
169 GADSBY, PRENDERGAST., vv. 1, 4, 5, 9.
170 P. HAYES, v. 1.
171 KENT, vv. 1, 2, 4, 5, 9. Amen.
172 KENT, vv. 1-6. Hallelujah.
173 STEVENSON, vv. 1-5, 9.

174

ISAIAH xxv. 1. O LORD, Thou art my GOD; I will exalt Thee, I will praise Thy Name; for Thou hast done wonderful things; Thy counsels of old are faithfulness and truth.

4. For Thou hast been a strength to the poor, a strength to the needy in distress, a refuge from the storm, a shadow from the heat.

7. And He will destroy in this mountain the face of the covering cast over all people, and the veil that is spread over all nations.

8. He will swallow up death in victory; and the LORD GOD will wipe away tears from off all faces; and He rebuke

of His people shall He take away from off all the earth :
for the LORD hath spoken it.

1. O LORD, Thou art my GOD; I will exalt Thee, I
will praise Thy Name.

9. And it shall be said in that day, Lo, This is our
GOD; we have waited for Him, and He will save us :
This is the LORD; we have waited for Him, we will be
glad and rejoice in His salvation.   Hallelujah.

PURCELL.

175

PSALM ciii. 1. Praise the LORD, O my soul, and all that
is within me praise His holy Name.

2. Praise the LORD, O my soul, and forget not all His
benefits.

3. Who forgiveth all thy sins, and healeth all thine
infirmities ;

4. Who saveth thy life from destruction; Who crowneth
thee with mercy and loving-kindness.

[6. The LORD executeth righteousness and judgment
for all them that are oppressed with wrong.]

8. The LORD is full of compassion and mercy, long-
suffering, and of great goodness.

9. He will not alway be chiding, neither keepeth He
His anger for ever.

10. He hath not dealt with us after our sins, nor
rewarded us according to our wickednesses.

11. For look how high the heaven is in comparison of
the earth; so great is His mercy toward them that fear
Him.

12. Look how wide also the east is from the west ;
so far hath He set our sins from us.

13. Yea, like as a father pitieth his own children, even
so is the LORD merciful unto them that fear Him.

14. For He knows whereof we are made, He remembereth that we are but dust.

[15. The days of man are but as grass: for he flourisheth
as a flower of the field.

16. For as soon as the wind goeth over it, it is gone ;
and the place thereof shall know it no more.

17. But the merciful goodness of the LORD endureth for ever and ever on them that fear Him.

18. Even upon such as keep His covenant, and think upon His commandments to do them.

19. The LORD hath prepared His seat in heaven : and His Kingdom ruleth over all.

20. O praise the LORD, ye angels of His, ye that excel in strength, ye that fulfil His commandment, and hearken unto the voice of His words.

21. O praise the LORD, all ye His hosts ; ye servants of His, that do His pleasure.]

22. O speak good of the LORD, all ye works of His,* in all places of His dominion. Praise thou the LORD, O my soul.

[cvi. 46. Blessed be the LORD GOD of Israel from this time forth for evermore.]

PURCELL.

176 G. B. ARNOLD, vv. 1, 8, 9, 13, 19.
177 BOYCE, vv. 8, 9, 13, 19–21.
178 CHILD, vv. 1–4, 22. Hallelujah.
179 GARRETT, vv. 1–4 ; cvi. 46. Amen.
180 GREENE, vv. 1, 3, 4, 2, 20–22.* Hallelujah. Amen.
181 HATTON, vv. 13 (*Like as a father*), 14–17, 22.
182 W. HAYES, vv. 1–4, 6, 20–22. Hallelujah. Amen.
183 J. HOPKINS, vv. 8, 9, 11, 13, 15–18, 1–4, 21, 22.
184 BUNNETT, KENT, vv. 19–22.
185 KING, vv. 8–14.

* Ends here.

186

PSALM cxix. 105. Thy word is a lantern unto my feet, and a light unto my paths.

106. I have sworn and am steadfastly purposed to keep Thy righteous judgments.

107. I am troubled above measure : quicken me, O LORD, according to Thy word.

108. Let the free-will offerings of my mouth please Thee, O LORD, and teach me Thy judgments.

109. The ungodly have laid a snare for me ; but yet I swerved not from Thy commandments.

110. Thy testimonies have I claimed as mine heritage for ever : and why ? they are the very joy of my heart. Hallelujah.

PURCELL.

187

PSALM liv. 1. Save me, O GOD, for Thy Name's sake; and avenge me in Thy strength.

2. Hear my prayer, O God, [and hearken unto the words of my mouth.]

3. For strangers are risen up against me, and tyrants, which have not GOD before their eyes, seek after my soul.

4. Behold, GOD is my helper; the LORD is with them that uphold my soul.

[5. He shall reward evil unto mine enemies; destroy Thou them in Thy truth.]

6. An offering of a free heart will I give Thee, and praise Thy Name, O LORD, because it is so comfortable.

7. For He hath delivered me out of all my trouble, and mine eye hath seen His desire upon mine enemies.

PURCELL.

188 BIRD, vv. 1, 2, 4.
189 BOYCE, OUSELEY, vv. 1–3.
190 C. J. FROST, vv. 1, 2, 1.
191 J. L. HOPKINS, vv. 1, 3, 1.
192 B. ROGERS, vv. 1–4. Gloria Patri.

193

PSALM xviii. 30. The way of GOD is an undefiled way; the word of the LORD also is tried in the fire; He is the defender of all them that put their trust in Him.

32. It is GOD that girdeth me with strength of war, and maketh my way perfect.

31. Who is GOD, but the LORD?

34. He teacheth mine hands to fight, and mine arms shall break even a bow of steel.

31. Who hath any strength, except our GOD?

39. Thou hast girded me with strength unto the battle; Thou shalt throw down mine enemies under me.

38. I will smite them, that they shall not be able to stand, but fall under my feet.

50. For this cause will I give thanks unto Thee, O LORD, and sing praises unto Thy Name. Hallelujah.

40. Thou hast made mine enemies also to turn their backs upon me, and I shall destroy them that hate me.

42. I will beat them as small as the dust before the wind, and cast them out as the clay in the streets.

41. They shall cry, but there shall be none to help them ; yea, even unto the LORD shall they cry, but He shall not hear them.

47. The LORD liveth, and blessed be my strong helper ; and praised be the GOD of my salvation.

51. Great prosperity giveth He unto His King.

49. It is He that hath delivered me from my cruel enemies, and setteth me up above mine adversaries ; Thou shalt rid me from the wicked man.

51. Great prosperity giveth He unto His King : and sheweth loving-kindness unto David His Anointed, and unto his seed for evermore. Hallelujah.

PURCELL.

194

PSALM lxxvii. 13. Thy way, O GOD, is holy : who is so great a God as our GOD ?

14. Thou art the GOD that doeth wonders : [and hast declared Thy power among the people.]

15. Thou hast mightily delivered Thy people.

16. The waters saw Thee, O GOD, [the waters saw Thee, and were afraid :] the depths also were troubled.

17. The clouds poured out water, the air thundered : and Thine arrows went abroad.

13. Thy way, O GOD, is holy : who is so great a GOD as our GOD ?

18. The voice of Thy thunder was heard round about : the lightnings shone upon the ground ; the earth was moved, and shook withal.

14. Thou art the God that doeth wonders ;

15. Thou hast mightily delivered Thy people.

13. Thy way, O GOD, is holy : who is so great a God as our GOD ?

[19. Thy way is in the sea, and Thy paths in the great waters : and Thy footsteps are not known.] Hallelujah.

PURCELL.

195 KILWAY, vv. 13, 14, 16, 19.

196

PSALM cvii. 23. They that go down to the sea in ships, [and occupy their business in great waters;]

24. These men see the works of the LORD, and His wonders in the deep.

25. For at His word the stormy wind ariseth, which lifteth up the waves thereof.

26. They are carried up to heaven, and down again to the deep: their soul melteth away because of the trouble.

27. They reel to and fro, and stagger like a drunken man, and are at their wit's end.

28. So when they cry unto the LORD in their trouble, He delivereth them out of their distress.

29. For He maketh the storm to cease, so that the waves thereof are still.

30. Then are they glad, because they are at rest : and so He bringeth them unto the haven where they would be.

31. O that men would therefore praise the LORD for His goodness, and declare the wonders that He doeth for the children of men !

32. That they would exalt Him also in the congregation of the people, and praise Him in the seat of the elders!

31. O praise the LORD for His goodness, and declare the wonders that He doeth for the children of men.

PURCELL, R. WOODWARD.

197 ARTWOOD, vv. 23–26, 28, 31.   Amen.
198 ELVEY, vv. 23–26, 28–31.
199 LOHR, vv. 23–28, 31.

200

PSALM lxxx. 19. Turn Thee again, O LORD GOD of Hosts : shew the light of Thy countenance upon us, and we shall be whole.

4. O LORD GOD of Hosts, how long wilt Thou be angry with Thy people that prayeth ?

5. Thou feedest them with the bread of tears and givest them plenteously of tears to drink.

8, 9. Thou hast brought a vine out of Egypt : Thou hast cast out the heathen, and planted it. and when it had taken root it filled the land.

10. The hills were covered with its shadow, and the boughs thereof were like the goodly cedar-trees.

12. Why hast Thou then broken down her hedge : that all they who pass by pluck off her grapes?

19. Turn Thee again, O Lord God of Hosts: shew the light of Thy countenance upon us, and we shall be whole.

PURCELL.

201

ISAIAH liii. 1. Who hath believed our report? and to whom is the arm of the Lord revealed?

2. For He shall grow up before Him as a tender plant, and as a root out of dry ground : He hath no form nor comeliness; and when we shall see Him, there is no beauty that we should desire Him.

3. He is despised and rejected of men; a Man of sorrows, and acquainted with grief: and we hid as it were our faces from Him ; He was despised, and we esteemed Him not.

4. Surely He hath borne our griefs, and carried our sorrows: yet we did esteem Him stricken and smitten of God, and afflicted.

5. But He was wounded for our transgressions, He was bruised for our iniquities : the chastisement of our peace was upon Him, and with His stripes we are healed.

6. All we like sheep have gone astray; we have turned every one to his own way; and the Lord hath laid on Him the iniquity of us all.

7. He was oppressed, and He was afflicted, yet He opened not His mouth : He is brought as a lamb to the slaughter, and as a sheep before her shearers is dumb, so openeth He not His mouth.

8. He was taken from prison and from judgment ; who shall declare His generation? for He was cut off out of the land of the living : for the transgression of My people was He stricken.

6. All we like sheep have gone astray ; we have turned every one to his own way; and the Lord hath laid on Him the iniquity of us all.

PURCELL.

202

From the Commination Service.

Turn Thou us, O good LORD, and so shall we be turned. Be favourable, O LORD, be favourable to Thy people, who turn to Thee in weeping, fasting, and praying. For Thou art a merciful GOD, full of compassion, long-suffering, and of great pity. Thou sparest when we deserve punishment, and in Thy wrath thinkest upon mercy. Spare Thy people, good LORD, spare them, and let not Thine heritage be brought to confusion. Hear us, O LORD, for Thy mercy is great, and after the multitude of Thy mercies look upon us.

PURCELL.

203

PSALM xxviii. 1. Unto Thee will I cry, O LORD my strength: think no scorn of me, lest, if Thou make as though Thou hearest not, I become like them that go down into the pit.

2. Hear the voice of my humble petitions, when I cry unto Thee; when I hold up my hands towards the mercy-seat of Thy holy temple.

3. O pluck me not away, neither destroy me with the ungodly and wicked doers, [which speak friendly to their neighbours, but imagine mischief in their hearts.]

6. For they regard not in their minds the works of the LORD, nor the operation of His hands; therefore shall He break them down, and not build them up.

7. Praised be the LORD, for He hath heard the voice of my humble petitions.

8. The LORD is the strength of my life; my heart hath trusted in Him, and I am helped; therefore my heart danceth for joy, and in my song will I praise Him. Hallelujah.

PURCELL.

204 Cxr. in vv. 1 3, 6, 7.
205 O   sfii y, vv. 1 3, 7. Hallelujah. Amen.

206

PSALM cxxxiv. 1. Behold now, praise the LORD, all ye servants of the LORD;

2. Ye that by night do stand in the house of the LORD, [even in the courts of the house of our GOD.]

3. Lift up your hands in the sanctuary, and praise the LORD.

4. The LORD that made heaven and earth, give thee blessing out of Zion. Hallelujah. Amen.

ALDRICH, BLOW, CREYGHTON, OAKELEY, B. ROGERS, WHITFELD.

207 G. J. BENNETT, vv. 1, 2, 1. Hallelujah. Amen.
208 PURCELL, vv. 1–4. Gloria Patri.
209 TURLE, v. 4. Hallelujah. Amen.

210

PSALM cvii. 1. O give thanks unto the LORD, for He is gracious, and His mercy endureth for ever.

2. Let them give thanks whom the LORD hath redeemed, and delivered from the hand of the enemy:

3. And gathered them out of the lands, from the east and from the west, from the north and from the south.

4. They went astray in the wilderness out of the way, and found no city to dwell in.

5. Hungry and thirsty, their soul fainted in them.

6. So they cried unto the LORD in their trouble, and He delivered them out of their distress.

8. O that men would therefore praise the LORD for His goodness, and declare the wonders that He doeth for the children of men.

B. ROGERS.

211

PSALM liii. 7. O that the salvation were given unto Israel out of Sion: O that the LORD would deliver His people out of captivity!

8. Then should Jacob rejoice, and Israel should be right glad.

Glory be to the Father. &c

B. ROGERS.

212

Te Deum Patrem colimus,
Te laudibus prosequimur :
Qui corpus cibo reficis,
Cœlesti mentem gratiâ.

Te adoramus, O Jesu!
Te, Fili unigenite,
Te, Qui non dedignatus es
Subire claustra Virginis.

Actus in Crucem, factus es
Irato Deo Victima :
Per Te, Salvator Unice.
Vitæ spes nobis rediit.

Tibi, Æterne Spiritus,
Cujus afflatu peperit
Infantem Deum Maria,
Æternum benedicimus.

Triune Deus, hominum
Salutis Auctor optime,
Immensum hoc mysterium
Ovante linguâ canimus.

B. ROGERS.

213

I wrestle and pray, O JESU, my Saviour, till blessed by
Thee.

(*Sung at the same time as the above.*)

Thou art my GOD, *Almighty* LORD ;
I know by Thy unchanging word,
   Thine is a Father's heart.
Yet I, though dust, for comfort flee,
And find it while I cleave to Thee.

O JESU, Son of GOD, I raise
My voice to Thee in hymns of praise,
   For Thy redeeming grace ;
Increase my faith, and strengthen me,
That I may pray and cleave to Thee !

And while I hail Thy love divine,
O Spirit, make its comforts mine,—
The blessings JESU bought.
Thus, great and undivided Three,
May I for ever cleave to Ye!

J. C. BACH.

214

Gracious LORD GOD, rouse us to watch, that we be prepared, when Thy Son comes, with rejoicing to welcome Him; and Thee, with guileless spirit, to worship; through our Saviour, Thy beloved Son, Thine Anointed. Amen.

J. C. BACH.

215

PSALM xviii. 1. I will love Thee, O LORD, my strength: the LORD is my strong rock, and my defence, my Saviour, my GOD, and my might, in Whom I will trust, my buckler, the horn also of my salvation, and my refuge.

2. I will call upon the LORD, Which is worthy to be praised; so shall I be safe from mine enemies.

3. The sorrows of death compassed me, and the overflowings of ungodliness made me afraid.

4. The pains of hell came about me; the snares of death overtook me.

5. In my trouble I will call upon the LORD, and complain unto my GOD.

6. So shall He hear my voice out of His Holy Temple: and my complaint shall come before Him, it shall enter even into His ears.

7. The earth trembled and quaked, the very foundations also of the hills shook, and were removed, because He was wroth.

13. The LORD also thundered out of heaven, and the Highest gave His thunder, hail-stones, and coals of fire.

16. He shall send down from on high to fetch me, and shall take me out of many waters.

21. Because I have kept the ways of the LORD, and have not forsaken my GOD.

[50. For this cause will I give thanks unto Thee, O LORD, among the Gentiles, and sing praises unto Thy Name.]

J. CLARK.

216 MACFARREN, v. 1.
217 OUSELEY, vv. 1, 2, 50. Amen.

218

Psalm cxviii. 14. The Lord is my strength and my song, and is become my salvation.

15. The voice of joy and health is in the dwellings of the righteous: [the right hand of the Lord bringeth mighty things to pass.]

16. The right hand of the Lord hath the pre-eminence ; the right hand of the Lord bringeth mighty things to pass.

[17. I shall not die, but live, and declare the works of the Lord.

18. The Lord hath chastened and corrected me ; but He hath not given me over unto death.

19. Open me the gates of righteousness, that I may go into them, and give thanks unto the Lord.

20. This is the gate of the Lord, the righteous shall enter into it.

21. I will thank Thee for Thou hast heard me, and art become my salvation.

22. The same stone which the builders refused is become the head-stone in the corner.]

23. This is the Lord's doing : and it is marvellous in our eyes.

24. This is the day which the Lord hath made ; we will rejoice and be glad in it.

25. [Help me now, O Lord ;] O Lord, send us now prosperity.

26. Blessed be He that cometh in the Name of the Lord ; [we have wished you good luck, ye that are of the house of the Lord.

28. Thou art my God, and I will thank Thee ; Thou art my God, and I will praise Thee.]

29. O give thanks unto the Lord, [for He is gracious, and His mercy endureth for ever.] Hallelujah.

J. Clark.

219 Croft, vv. 14, 15, 24–26, 29.
220 Goss, vv. 14–21, 28. Hallelujah. Amen.
221 W. H. Monk, vv. 14, 19, 22, 24. Hallelujah. Amen.
222 Longhurst, vv. 14, 28, 29. Hallelujah.
223 Novello, vv. 14, 15, 24.
224 Oakeley vv. 24 26, 28 29.
225 Reay, vv. 24, 28.
226 H. Smart, vv. 14, 17, 29.

227

PSALM cxlvii. 12. Praise the LORD, O Jerusalem, praise thy GOD, O Sion.

ISAIAH xlix. 23. For kings shall be thy nursing fathers, and queens thy nursing mothers.

PSALM xlviii. 7. As we have heard, so have we seen in the city of our GOD : GOD upholdeth the same for ever.

xxi. 13. Be thou exalted, LORD, in Thine own strength : so we will sing and praise Thy power. Hallelujah.

J. CLARK, PURCELL.

228 GREENE, Psalm cxlvii. 12.

229 PURCELL, Psalm cxlvii. 12 ; Isaiah xlix. 23.

230

PSALM xlvi. 1. GOD is our hope and strength, a very present help in trouble.

2. Therefore will we not fear, though the earth be moved, and though the hills be carried into the midst of the sea.

3. Though the waters thereof rage and swell, and though the mountains shake at the tempest of the same.

[4. The rivers of the flood thereof shall make glad the city of GOD.]

5. GOD is in the midst of her, therefore shall she not be removed : GOD shall help her, [and that right early.

6. The heathen make much ado, and the kingdoms of the earth are moved : but GOD hath shewed His voice, and the earth shall melt away.]

BLOW.

231 ALDRICH, vv. 1–6, 1.

232

PSALM lxxiv. 1. O GOD, wherefore art Thou absent from us so long ? why is Thy wrath so hot against the sheep of Thy pasture ?

2. O think upon Thy congregation, whom Thou hast purchased and redeemed of old.

3. Think upon the tribe of Thine inheritance, and mount Sion wherein Thou hast dwelt.

1. O GOD, wherefore art Thou absent from us so long ?

BLOW.

233 O. SMITH, vv. 1, 2.

234

REVELATION vii. 9. I beheld, and lo, a great multitude, which no man could number, of all nations and kindreds, and people, which stood before the Throne, clothed with white robes, and palms were in their hands.

10. And they cried with a loud voice, saying, Hallelujah ; Salvation to our GOD, Which sitteth on the Throne, and unto the Lamb.

13. And I heard a voice, saying, What are these which are arrayed in white robes ? and whence came they ?

14. These are they which came out of great tribulation, and have washed their robes, and made them white in the Blood of the Lamb.

15. Therefore are they before the Throne of GOD, and serve Him day and night in His temple.

11. And all the angels who stood round the Throne, and the elders, with the four beasts, fell down before the Throne, and worshipped GOD, saying, Hallelujah.

12. Blessing, and glory, and wisdom, and thanksgiving and honour, and power, and might, be unto our GOD for ever and ever. Amen. Hallelujah.

BLOW.

235 BOYCE, v. 12.

236

REVELATION i. 10. I was in the Spirit on the LORD's day.

xix. 1. And I heard a great voice of much people in heaven, saying Hallelujah ; Salvation, and glory, and honour, and power, unto the LORD our GOD.

2, 3. For true and righteous are His judgments : and again they said, Hallelujah.

4. And the four and twenty elders and the four beasts fell down, and worshipped GOD that sat on the Throne, saying, Amen ; and again they said, Hallelujah.

5. And a voice came out of the Throne, saying, Praise our GOD, all ye His servants, and ye that fear Him, both small and great.

6. And I heard as it were the voice of a great multitude, and as the voice of many waters, and as the voice of mighty thunderings, saying, Hallelujah ; for the LORD GOD Omnipotent reigneth.

7. Let us be glad and rejoice, and give honour to Him, for the marriage of the Lamb is come.   Hallelujah.

BLOW.

237

PSALM iii. 1. LORD, how are they increased that trouble me ! many are they that rise against me.

2. Many one there be that say of my soul, there is no help for him in his GOD.

3. But Thou, O LORD, art my defender ; Thou art my worship, and the lifter up of my head.

4. I did call upon the LORD with my voice, and He, heard me out of His holy hill [of Zion].

5. I laid me down and slept, and rose up again, for the LORD sustained me.

6. I will not be afraid for ten thousands of the people, that have set themselves against me round about.

7. Up, LORD, and help me, O my GOD, for Thou smitest all mine enemies upon the cheek-bone ; Thou hast broken the teeth of the ungodly.

[8. Salvation belongeth unto the LORD, and Thy blessing is upon Thy people.]

BLOW.

238 BLOW, v. 7.
239 J. H. CLARKE, vv. 1–5.
240 EBDON, vv. 4, 5.
241 GREENE, vv. 1, 3–5, 8.   Hallelujah.   Amen.
242 KENT, vv. 1–3, 8.
243 PATTISON, vv. 4–8.
244 STEVENSON, vv. 1, 2, 1, 3–6, 8.

245

PSALM xxix. 4. The voice of the LORD is mighty in operation : the voice of the LORD is a glorious voice.

xlvi. 11. The LORD of Hosts is with us : the GOD of Jacob is our refuge.

BLOW.

246

JOB vii. 20. O LORD, I have sinned : what shall I do unto Thee, Thou preserver of men ? O why hast Thou set me up as a mark against Thee, so that I am a burden to myself ?

21. O pardon my transgressions, and take away my sin.

ISAIAH xxxviii. 12. Mine age is departed and removed from me, Thou wilt cut me off with pining sickness.

14. Mine eyes fail with looking upwards, I did mourn as a dove. O LORD, I am oppressed : undertake for me, O LORD my GOD.

JOB iii. 20. O wherefore is light given to him that is in misery, or life to the bitter in soul ;

21, 22. Which long for death, but it cometh not, and rejoice exceedingly when they can find the grave ?

24. For my sighing comes before I eat, and my roarings are poured out like the waters.

BLOW.

247

PSALM lxviii. 4. O sing unto GOD, and sing praises unto His Name : magnify Him that rideth upon the heavens, [as it were upon an horse,] praise Him in His Name JAH, and rejoice before Him.

17. The chariots of GOD are twenty thousand, even thousands of angels, and the LORD is among them, as in the holy place of Sinai.

18. Thou art gone up on high, Thou hast led captivity captive, and received gifts for men : even for Thine enemies, that the LORD GOD might dwell among them.

19. Praised be the LORD daily : even the GOD Who helpeth us, and poureth His benefits upon us.

20. He is our GOD, even the GOD of Whom cometh salvation : GOD is the LORD, by Whom we escape death.

BLOW.

251

PSALM lxix.   1. Save me, O GOD, for the waters are come in, even unto my soul.

[2. I stick fast in the deep mire, where no ground is.]

3. I am weary of crying, my throat is dry : my sight faileth me for waiting so long upon my GOD.

7. And why? for Thy sake have I suffered reproof : shame hath covered my face.

10. I wept and chastened myself with fasting, and that was turned to my reproof.

13. But, LORD, I make my prayer unto Thee, in an acceptable time.

14. Hear me, O GOD, in the multitude of Thy mercy; even in the truth of Thy salvation.

BLOW.

252 JEKYLL, vv. 1–3, 1.
253 NARES, vv. 1, 3, 13, 14.
254 J. C. PRING, vv. 1, 3.

255

Salvator mundi, salva nos, Qui per Crucem et Sanguinem redemisti nos :   auxiliare nobis, Te deprecamur, Deus noster.   BLOW.

English Version.

(From the Office for the Visitation of the Sick.)

O Saviour of the world, Who by Thy Cross and precious Blood hast redeemed us, Save us, and help us, we humbly beseech Thee, O LORD.   Amen.

GOSS, GREATHEED, HAVERGAL, MACFARREN, OUSELEY, PALESTRINA, J. V. ROBERTS.

256

PSALM cxv.   1. Not unto us, LORD, not unto us, but to Thy Name give the praise.

cxlv.   17. For Thou art faithful in all Thy works, and just in all Thy ways.   Hallelujah.   The LORD is faithful in all His works, and just in all His ways.

21. My mouth shall speak of Thy praise, O LORD : and let all flesh give thanks unto Thy holy Name for ever.   Amen.

ATTWOOD.

257

PSALM cxvi. 1. I am well pleased, that the LORD hath heard the voice of my prayer;

2. That He hath inclined His ear unto me; therefore will I call upon Him as long as I live.

3. The snares of death compassed me round about, and the pains of hell gat hold upon me.

4. I have found trouble and heaviness, and I did call upon the Name of the LORD; O LORD, I beseech Thee, deliver my soul.

5. Gracious is the LORD, and righteous; yea, our GOD is merciful.

6. The LORD preserveth the simple; when I was in misery, He delivered me.

7. Turn again then unto thy rest, O my soul, for the LORD hath rewarded thee.

8. For He hath delivered my soul from death, mine eyes from tears, my feet from falling.

9. I will walk before the LORD in the land of the living.

16. I will pay my vows unto the LORD in the sight of His people, in the courts of the LORD's house, even in the midst of thee, O Jerusalem. Hallelujah.

ALDRICH.

258

PSALM xliv. 1. We have heard with our ears, O GOD, our fathers have told us, what Thou hast done in their time of old;

2. How Thou hast driven out the heathen from the land, and planted them in: how Thou hast destroyed the nations, and cast them out.

3. For they gat not the land in possession through their own sword: neither was it their own arm that helped them;

4. But Thy right hand, and Thine arm, and the light of Thy countenance: because Thou hadst a favour unto them.

5. Thou art my King, O GOD: send help unto Jacob.

6. Through Thee will we overthrow our enemies: and in Thy Name will we tread them down that rise up against us. ALDRICH, SULLIVAN.

259 SHOGALL, vv. 1 4.

260

ISAIAH xlii. 1. Behold My Servant, Whom I uphold, Mine Elect, in Whom My soul delighteth, I have put My Spirit upon Him, and He shall bring forth judgment to the Gentiles.

lxii. 11. Say to the daughter of Sion, Behold thy salvation cometh ; behold His reward is with Him, and His work before Him.

ST. LUKE i. 68. Blessed be the LORD GOD of Israel : for He hath visited and redeemed His people.

69. And hath raised up a mighty salvation for us in the house of His servant David.

74, 75. That we, being delivered out of the hands of our enemies, might serve Him without fear, in holiness and righteousness before Him all the days of our life.

ST. MATTHEW xxi. 9. Blessed is He that cometh in the Name of the LORD : Hosanna in the highest. Hallelujah.

GOLDWIN.

261

PSALM xvi. 9. I have set GOD always before me : for He is on my right hand, therefore I shall not fall.

10. Wherefore my heart was glad, and my glory rejoiced : my flesh also shall rest in hope.

11. For why ? Thou shall not leave my soul in hell : neither shalt Thou suffer Thy Holy One to see corruption.

12. Thou shalt shew me the path of life ; in Thy presence is the fulness of joy : and at Thy right hand there is pleasure for evermore. Amen.

BLAKE, BOYCE, H. CLARKE,* GOLDWIN, W. HAYES.

——— Sometimes sung as a separate Anthem.

262 J. W. CALLCOTT, v. 12.

263

PSALM ix. 1. I will give thanks unto Thee, O LORD, with my whole heart : I will speak of all Thy marvellous works.

2. I will be glad and rejoice in Thee : yea, my songs will I make of Thy Name, O Thou most Highest.

3. While mine enemies are driven back, they shall fall and perish at Thy presence.

4. For Thou hast maintained my right and my cause: Thou art set in the throne that judgest right.

11. O praise the LORD Which dwelleth in Sion: shew the people of His doings. Hallelujah.

CROFT.

264

PSALM lxxxviii. 1. O LORD GOD of my salvation, I have cried day and night before Thee: O let my prayer enter into Thy presence, incline Thine ear unto my calling.

2. For my soul is full of trouble, and my life draweth nigh unto hell.

[3. I am counted as one of them that go down into the pit; and I have been even as a man that hath no strength.

4. Free among the dead, like unto them that are wounded, and lie in the grave, and are cut away from Thy hand.]

5. Thou hast laid me in the lowest pit, in a place of darkness, and in the deep.

6. Thine indignation lieth hard upon me, and Thou hast vexed me with all Thy storms.

9. My sight faileth me for very trouble: LORD, I have called daily upon Thee, I have stretched forth my hands unto Thee.

10. Dost Thou shew wonders among the dead, or shall the dead rise up again, and praise Thee?

13. Unto Thee have I cried, O LORD, and early shall my prayer come before Thee. Amen.

[lxxxvi. 15. But Thou, O LORD GOD, art full of compassion and mercy; long-suffering, plenteous in goodness and truth.]

16. O turn Thee then unto me, and have mercy upon me; give Thy strength unto Thy servant, and help the son of Thine handmaid.

CROFT.

269

From the Burial Service.

(1.) St. John. xi. 25, 26. I am the Resurrection and the Life, saith the Lord : he that believeth in Me, though he were dead, yet shall he live ; and whosoever liveth and believeth in Me shall never die.

(2.) Job xix. 25—27. I know that my Redeemer liveth, and that He shall stand at the latter day upon the earth. And though after my skin worms destroy this body, yet in my flesh shall I see God : Whom I shall see for myself, and mine eyes shall behold, and not another.

(3.) Job i. 21. We brought nothing into this world, it is certain we can carry nothing out.

(4.) 1 Timothy vi. 7. The Lord gave, and the Lord hath taken away ; blessed be the Name of the Lord.

(5.) Job xiv. 1, 2. Man that is born of a woman hath but a short time to live, and is full of misery. He cometh up, and is cut down, like a flower; he fleeth as it were a shadow, and never continueth in one stay.

(6.) In the midst of life we are in death : of whom may we seek for succour, but of Thee, O Lord, Who for our sins art justly displeased? Yet, O Lord God most Holy, O Lord most Mighty, O Holy and most Merciful Saviour, deliver us not into the bitter pains of eternal death. Amen.

(7.) Thou knowest, Lord, the secrets of our hearts ; shut not Thy merciful ears to our prayer; but spare us, Lord most Holy, O God most Mighty, O Holy and Merciful Saviour, Thou most worthy Judge Eternal, suffer us not, at our last hour, for any pains of death, to fall from Thee.

(8.) Revelation xiv. 13. I heard a voice from heaven, saying unto me, Write, From henceforth blessed are the dead which die in the Lord : even so saith the Spirit ; for they rest from their labours. Amen.

Boyce, Croft, Goss.

270 Garrett, Goss, Gray, § 8.
271 Macks. 1. 4.
272 Purcell. 7.
273 S. S. Wesley, 5, 6

274

PSALM lxxii.　1. Give the king Thy judgments, O GOD, and Thy righteousness unto the king's son.

2. Then shall he judge Thy people according unto right, and defend the poor.

3. The mountains also shall bring peace, and the little hills righteousness unto the people.

5. They shall fear Thee as long as the sun and moon endureth, from one generation to another.

7. In his time shall the righteous flourish, yea, and abundance of peace, so long as the moon endureth.

8. His dominion shall be also from the one sea to the other, and from the flood unto the world's end.

*[11. All kings shall fall down before Him: all nations shall do Him service.]

18. Blessed be the LORD GOD, even the GOD of Israel, Which only doeth wondrous things;

19. And blessed be the Name of His Majesty for ever: and all the earth shall be filled with His Majesty. Amen, Amen.

CROFT.

275 BOYCE, vv. 1–3, 5, 7, 8, *11. Amen, Amen.
276 GOLDWIN, KELWAY, NARES, vv. 18, 19.

* This verse is sometimes sung as a separate Anthem.

277

PSALM cxvii.　1. O praise the LORD, all ye heathen: praise Him, all ye nations.

2. For His merciful kindness is ever more and more towards us : and the truth of the LORD endureth for ever.* Praise the Lord.　[Amen.]

S. ARNOLD, CROFT, GOLDWIN, T. JACKSON,
KELWAY, OUSELEY, RIGHINI.

278 ALDRICH, vv. 1, 2*.　Hallelujah.
279 BATTEN, WILTON, vv. 1, 2.　Amen.
280 PURCELL, vv. 1, 2.　Hallelujah.　Gloria Patri.

* Ends here.

281

PSALM cxxi. 1. I will lift up mine eyes unto the hills, from whence cometh my help.

2. My help cometh even from the LORD, Who hath made heaven and earth.

3. He will not suffer thy foot to be moved, and He that keepeth thee will not sleep.

4. Behold, He that keepeth Israel, shall neither slumber nor sleep.

5. The LORD Himself is thy keeper, the LORD is thy defence upon thy right hand ;

6. So that the sun shall not burn thee by day, neither the moon by night.

7. The LORD shall preserve thee from all evil, yea, it is even He that shall keep thy soul.

8. The LORD shall preserve thy going out, and thy coming in, from this time forth for evercome. Hallelujah. Amen.

CROFT, G. SMART.

282 WELDON, vv. 1–7.
283 WHITFELD, vv. 1, 2, 5–8. Hallelujah. Amen.

284

ISAIAH xii. 1. O LORD, I will praise Thee: though Thou wast angry with me, Thine anger is turned away, and Thou hast restored me.

2. Behold GOD is my salvation : I will trust and not be afraid : for the LORD JEHOVAH is my strength and my song, and He also is become my salvation.

4. Praise the LORD, and call upon His Name, declare His doings among the people, make mention that His Name is exalted.

5. Sing unto the LORD, for He hath done excellent things : this is known in all the earth.

6. Cry aloud and shout, thou inhabitant of Zion : for great is the Holy One of Israel in the midst of thee.

CROFT, GREENE.

* Sometimes sung as a separate Anthem.

285

PSALM cxix. 97. LORD, what love have I unto Thy law; all the day long is my study in it.

[72. The law of Thy mouth is dearer unto me than thousands of gold and silver.]

98. Thou through Thy commandments hast made me wiser than mine enemies; for they are ever with me.

99. I have more understanding than my teachers, for Thy testimonies are my study.

100. I am wiser than the aged, because I keep Thy commandments.

101. I have refrained my feet from every evil way, that I may keep Thy word.

[103. O how sweet are Thy words unto my throat; yea, sweeter than honey unto my mouth.]

104. Through Thy commandments I get understanding; therefore I hate all evil ways.

[142. Thy righteousness is an everlasting righteousness, and Thy law is the truth.

143. Trouble and heaviness have taken hold upon me, yet is my delight in Thy commandments.]

CROFT.

286 ALLEN, vv. 97, 99, 100, 103, 104.
287 KENT, vv. 97, 72, 103, 142, 143.
288 STEGGALL, vv. 97, 103, 104, 72.

289

PSALM vi. 1. O LORD, rebuke me not in Thine indignation, neither chasten me in Thy displeasure.

2. Have mercy upon me, O LORD, for I am weak: O LORD, heal me, for my bones are vexed.

3. My soul also is sore troubled: but, LORD, how long wilt Thou punish me?

4. Turn Thee, O LORD, and deliver my soul: O save me for Thy mercy's sake. Hallelujah. Amen.]

CROFT.

290 PURCELL, WELDON, vv. 1, 4, 2, 3.

291

PSALM cxxxix. 1. O LORD, Thou hast searched me out, and known me : Thou knowest my down-sitting and mine up-rising ; Thou understandest my thoughts long before.

2. Thou art about my path, and about my bed, and spiest out all my ways.

3. For lo, there is not a word in my tongue, but Thou, O LORD, knowest it altogether.

[4. Thou hast fashioned me behind and before, and laid Thine hand upon me.

5. Such knowledge is too wonderful and excellent for me : I cannot attain unto it.]

6. Whither shall I go then from Thy Spirit ; or whither shall I go then from Thy presence ?

7. If I climb up into heaven, Thou art there : If I go down to hell, Thou art there also.

8. If I take the wings of the morning, and remain in the uttermost parts of the sea ;

9. Even there also shall Thy hand lead me, and Thy right hand shall hold me.

[10. If I say, Peradventure the darkness shall cover me : then shall my night be turned to day.

13. I will give thanks unto Thee, for I am fearfully and wonderfully made : marvellous are Thy works, and that my soul knoweth right well.]

17. How dear are Thy counsels unto me, O GOD : O how great is the sum of them !

18. If I tell them, they are more in number than the sand : when I wake up, I am present with Thee.

23. Try me, O GOD, and seek the ground of my heart : prove me, and examine my thoughts.

24. Look well if there be any way of wickedness in me : and lead me in the way everlasting.

CROFT.

292 BENEDICT, CULLEY, E. J. HOPKINS, NARES, J. S. SMITH, C. WOOD, vv. 23, 24. [Amen.]

293 BROW. vv. 1 10. 9, 1, 13.

294 CROTCH, vv. 17. 23, 24.

Novello's Collection. D

295

Psalm lxviii. 32. Sing unto God, O ye kingdoms of the earth: O sing praises unto the Lord;

33. Who sitteth in the heavens over all [from the beginning]: lo, He doth send out His voice, yea, and that a mighty voice.

34. Ascribe ye the power to God over Israel: His worship, and strength is in the clouds.

[32. O sing praises unto the Lord.]

35. O God, wonderful art Thou in Thy holy places: even the God of Israel; He will give strength and power unto His people; blessed be God. Amen.

CROFT, KELWAY, J. PRING, PURCELL.

296

Psalm xcvi. 1. O sing unto the Lord a new song: sing unto the Lord all the whole earth.

2. Sing unto the Lord, and praise His Name: be telling of His salvation from day to day.

3. Declare His honour unto the heathen, and His wonders unto all people.

4. For the Lord is great, and cannot worthily be praised; He is more to be feared than all gods.

5. As for the gods of the heathen, they are but idols: but it is the Lord that made the heavens.

6. Glory and worship are before Him, power and honour are in His sanctuary.

7. Ascribe unto the Lord, O ye kindreds of the people, ascribe unto the Lord worship and power.

8. Ascribe unto the Lord the honour due unto His Name; bring presents, and come into His courts.

9. O worship the Lord in the beauty of holiness: let the whole earth stand in awe of Him.

*10. Tell it out among the heathen that the Lord is King, and that it is He Who hath made the round world so fast that it cannot be moved, and how that He shall jud th   lt   l

[11. Let the heaven rejoice, and let the earth be glad: let the sea make a noise, and all that therein is.

12. Let the field be joyful, and all that is in it; then shall all the trees of the wood rejoice before the Lord.

13. For He cometh, He cometh to judge the earth, and with righteousness to judge the world, and the people with His truth.

xciii. 5. The waves of the sea are mighty, and rage horribly, but yet the LORD, Who dwelleth on high, is mightier.]   CROFT.

> 297 EBDON, vv. 1, 2, 6, 2.
> 298 GREENE, vv. 1–4, 6.   Amen.
> 299 HANDEL, vv. 1–4, 6, 9, 11; xciii. 5.
> 300 W. HAYES, vv. 9, *10, 11.
> 301 PURCELL, v. 1.   Hallelujah.   vv. 2, 3, 6, 4, 5, 9, 10.   Hallelujah.   Amen.
> 302 SWIFT, vv. 1–3, 1.   Amen.
> 303 THORNE, v. 9.
> 304 TRAVERS, vv. 7–13.   Amen.
>
> * This verse is sometimes sung as a separate Anthem.

305

PSALM xxx. 4. Sing praises to the LORD, O ye saints of His, and give thanks unto Him for a remembrance of His holiness.

5. For His wrath endures but for a moment, and in His favour is life; heaviness may endure for a night, but joy cometh in the morning.

CROFT.

306

PSALM xcvi. 2. Sing unto the LORD, and praise His Name: be telling of His salvation from day to day.

xcii. 4. Thou, LORD, hast made me glad through Thy works: and I will rejoice in giving praise, for the operations of Thy hands.

10. Thou, O GOD, hast shewed us Thy goodness plenteously, and hast let us see our desire upon our enemies.

xxvii. 11. Thou hast been our succour; leave us not, neither forsake us, O GOD of our salvation.

14. So we that are Thy people and sheep of Thy pasture will give Thee thanks for ever; and will alway be shewing forth Thy praise from generation to generation.

CROFT.

307

PSALM xxiv. 1. The earth is the LORD'S, and all that therein is: the compass of the world, and they that dwell therein.

2. For He hath founded it upon the seas, and prepared it upon the floods.

3. Who shall ascend into the hill of the LORD? or who shall rise up in His holy place?

4. Even he that hath clean hands, and a pure heart: and that hath not lift up his mind unto vanity, nor sworn to deceive his neighbour.

5. He shall receive the blessing from the LORD, and righteousness from the GOD of his salvation.

6. This is the generation of them that seek Him, even of them that seek Thy face, O Jacob.

7. Lift up your heads, O ye gates, and be ye lift up, ye everlasting doors, and the King of Glory shall come in.

8. Who is the King of Glory? It is the LORD strong and mighty, even the LORD mighty in battle.

9. Lift up your heads, O ye gates, and be ye lift up, ye everlasting doors, and the King of Glory shall come in.

10. Who is the King of Glory? Even the Lord of Hosts, He is the King of Glory.

CROFT.

308 HEAP, KEARTON, T. F. WALMISLEY, vv. 1–5.
309 J. F BRIDGF, OUSELEY, vv. 3–5.

310

PSALM civ. 1. Praise the LORD, O my soul: O LORD my GOD, Thou art become exceeding glorious, Thou art clothed with majesty and honour.

2. Thou deckest Thyself with light as it were with a garment, and spreadest out the heavens like a curtain.

3. Who layeth the beams of His chambers in the waters, and maketh the clouds His chariot, and walketh upon the wings of the wind.

4. He maketh His angels spirits, and His ministers a flaming fire.

5. He laid the foundations of the earth, that it never should move at any time.

6. Thou coveredst it with the deep, like as with a garment : the waters stand in the hills.

7. At Thy rebuke they flee: at the voice of Thy thunder they are afraid.

8. They go up as high as the hills, and down to the valleys beneath : [even unto the place which Thou hast appointed for them.]

13. Thou waterest the hills from above : the earth is filled with the fruit of Thy works.

14. Thou bringest forth grass for the cattle, and green herb for the service of men.

24. O LORD, how manifold are Thy works : in wisdom hast Thou made them all ; the earth is full of Thy riches.

[31. The glorious Majesty of the LORD shall endure for ever and ever : the LORD shall rejoice in His works.]

33. I will sing unto the LORD as long as I live ; I will praise my GOD while I have my being. Hallelujah.

[34. And so shall my words please Him : my joy shall be in the LORD.

35. As for sinners, they shall be consumed out of the earth, and the ungodly shall come to an end, but *praise thou the LORD, O my soul, praise the LORD. Hallelujah. Amen.]

CREYGHTON.

311 BLOW, v. 35.   * (*Praise thou the* LORD.)
    Hallelujah.
312 CROFT, vv. 1–5, 24, 31.   Hallelujah.
313 CROFT, GOLDWIN, J. PRING, PURCELL,
    vv. 33–35.   [Gloria Patri.]
314 MACFARREN, vv. 24, 13, 14.   Amen.
315 A. H. MANN, 33, 34, 33.
316 T. F. WALMISLEY, vv. 24, 33–35.

317

PSALM xxxi. 1. In Thee, O LORD, have I put my trust; let me never be put to confusion, deliver me in Thy righteousness.

2. Bow down Thine ear to me ; make haste to deliver me.

3. And be Thou my strong rock, and house of my defence, that Thou mayest save me.

4. [For Thou art my strong rock, and my castle:] be Thou also my guide, and lead me for Thy Name's sake.

5. Draw me out of the net that they have laid privily for me, for Thou art my GOD.

6. Into Thy hands I commend my spirit, for Thou hast redeemed me, O LORD, Thou GOD of truth.

WELDON.

318 TOURS, vv. 1-4.   Amen.

319

PSALM cxlvii.   1. O praise the LORD, for it is a good thing to sing praises unto our GOD : yea, a joyful and pleasant thing it is to be thankful.

5. Great is our LORD, and great is His power : yea, and His wisdom is infinite.

6. The LORD setteth up the meek, and bringeth the ungodly down to the ground.

11. But the LORD's delight is in them that fear Him, and put their trust in His mercy.

[cxlviii. 12. Young men and maidens, old men and children, praise the Name of the LORD : for His Name only is excellent, and His praise above heaven and earth.]

WELDON.

320 W. S. BENNETT, vv. 5, 6, 11, 5.
321 CHAMPNEYS v. 1 ; cxlviii. 12.

322

REVELATION iv.   8. Holy, Holy, Holy, LORD GOD ALMIGHTY, Which was, and is, and is to come.

11. Thou art worthy, O LORD, to receive glory, honour and power : for Thou hast created all things, and for Thy pleasure they are and were created.

BISHOP.

323 F. E. GLADSTONE, v. 11.

324

PSALM xxxi.   10. O LORD, have mercy upon me, for I am in trouble.

12, 16. My strength faileth me : but my hope hath been in Thee : I have said, Thou art my GOD.

PERGOLESI.

325

PSALM xliv. 26. Arise and help us, and deliver us for Thy mercy's sake.

MARCELLO.

326

PSALM viii. 1. O LORD our Governour, O how excellent is Thy Name in all the world!

2. Out of the mouth of very babes and sucklings hast Thou ordained strength, because of Thine enemies: that Thou mightest still the fruitless rage of the enemy and the avenger.

4. What is a mortal, O Jehovah, that Thou art mindful of him? and the son of a mortal, that Thou visitest him?

9. O LORD, our Governour, O how excellent is Thy Name in all the world!

MARCELLO.

327

PSALM xc. 1. LORD, Thou hast been our refuge from one generation to another.

2. Before the mountains were brought forth, or ever the earth and the world were made, Thou art GOD from everlasting, and world without end. [And let all the people say, Amen.]

3. Thou turnest man to destruction: again Thou sayest, Come again, ye children of men.

4. For a thousand years in Thy sight are but as yesterday, seeing that is past as a watch in the night.

5. As soon as Thou scatterest them they are even as a sleep, and fade away suddenly like the grass.

9. For when Thou art angry, all our days are gone: we bring our years to an end, as it were a tale that is told.

10. The days of our age are threescore years and ten; and though men be so strong that they come to fourscore years, yet is their strength then but labour and sorrow; so soon passeth it away, and we are gone.

4. For a thousand years in Thy sight are but as yesterday, seeing that is past as a watch in the night.

TURNER.

328 W. HAYES, 1-3, 9, 2.

329

Psalm cx. 1. Dixit Dominus Domino meo : Sede a dextris meis, donec ponam inimicos tuos scabellum pedum tuorum.

2. Virgam virtutis tuæ emittet Dominus ex Sion ; dominare in medio inimicorum tuorum.

3. Tecum principium in die virtutis tuæ in splendoribus sanctorum : ex utero ante luciferum genui te.

4. Juravit Dominus, et non pœnitebit eum : Tu es Sacerdos in æternum secundum ordinem Melchisedech.

5. Dominus a dextris tuis confregit in die iræ suæ reges.

6. Judicabit in nationibus, implebit ruinas, conquassabit capita in terrâ multorum.

7. De torrente in viâ bibet ; propterea exaltabit caput.

Gloria Patri, et Filio, et Spiritui Sancto ; Sicut erat in principio, et nunc, et semper : et in sæcula sæculorum. Amen.

English Version.

Psalm cx. 1. The Lord said unto my Lord : Sit thou on my right hand, until I make thine enemies thy footstool.

2. The Lord shall send the rod of thy power out of Sion : be thou ruler, even in the midst among thine enemies.

3. In the day of thy power shall the people offer thee free-will offerings with an holy worship : the dew of thy birth is of the womb of the morning.

4. The Lord sware, and will not repent : Thou art a Priest for ever after the order of Melchisedech.

5. The Lord upon thy right hand shall wound even kings in the day of His wrath.

6. He shall judge among the heathen ; He shall fill the places with the dead bodies, and smite in sunder the heads over divers countries.

7. He shall drink of the brook in the way : therefore shall He lift up His head.

Glory be to the Father, &c.

LEO.

330 S. William.

331

Psalm lvii. 1. Be merciful unto me, O God, be merciful unto me, for my soul trusteth in Thee ; and under the shadow of Thy wings shall be my refuge, until this tyranny be over-past.

  4. God shall send forth His mercy and truth : my soul is among lions.

  6. Set up Thyself, O God, above the heavens, and Thy glory above all the earth.

Clari and Leo.

332

Psalm cxix. 9. Wherewithal shall a young man cleanse his way? even by ruling himself after Thy word.

  10. With my whole heart have I sought Thee ; O let me not go wrong out of Thy commandments.

  11. Thy words have I hid within my heart, that I should not sin against Thee. .

  12. Blessed art Thou, O Lord ; O teach me Thy statutes.

  13. With my lips have I been telling of all the judgments of Thy mouth.

  14. I have had as great delight in the way of Thy testimonies as in all manner of riches.

  15. I will talk of Thy commandments, and have respect unto Thy ways.

  16. My delight shall be in Thy statutes, and I will not forget Thy word.

King, S. S. Wesley.

    333 Alcock, Elvey, vv. 9, 10, 12.
    [Hallelujah. Amen.]
    334 S. Arnold, vv. 9–11, 13, 16.
    335 Boyce, vv. 9–12, 15, 16.
    336 Cooke, vv. 9 12.
    337 W. Hayes, vv. 12, 9, 10, 13, 16.
    Hallelujah. Amen.

338

PSALM xlii.

As pants the hart for cooling streams,
 When heated in the chase :
So longs my soul for Thee, O GOD,
 And Thy refreshing grace.

For Thee, my GOD, the living GOD,
 My thirsty soul doth pine :
O when shall I behold Thy face ?
 Thou Majesty Divine !

KING, †SPOHR.

† (Adapted from " Calvary," No. 6.)

339

PSALM xxx. 11. Hear, O LORD, and have mercy upon me ; LORD, be Thou my helper.

12. Thou hast turned my heaviness into joy, Thou hast put off my sackcloth, and girded me with gladness.

13. Therefore shall every good man sing of Thy praise without ceasing ; O my GOD, I will give thanks unto Thee for ever and ever. Hallelujah.

GREENE, KING, OUSELEY.

340

PSALM xxv. 1. Unto Thee, O LORD, will I lift up my soul ; my GOD, I have put my trust in Thee : O let me not be confounded, neither let mine enemies triumph over me.

2. For all they that hope in Thee shall not be ashamed ; but such as transgress without a cause shall be put to confusion.

3. Shew me Thy ways, O LORD, and teach me Thy paths.

4. Lead me forth in Thy truth and learn me, for Thou art the GOD of my salvation ; in Thee hath been my hope all the day long.

[5. Call to remembrance, O LORD, Thy tender mercies, and Thy loving-kindness, which have been ever of old.

6. O remember not the sins and offences of my youth, but according to Thy mercy think Thou on me, O LORD, for Thy goodness.

7. Gracious and righteous is the LORD; therefore will He teach sinners in the way.

8. Them that are meek shall He guide in judgment, and such as are gentle, them shall He learn His way.]

KELWAY.

311 BATTISHILL, FARRANT, NARES, vv. 5, 6.
342 KING, OUSELEY, v. 1. [Amen.]
343 PRENDERGAST, vv. 3, 4, 7, 8.

344

PSALM cxi. 1. I will give thanks unto the LORD with my whole heart, secretly among the faithful, and in the congregation.

2. The works of the LORD are great, sought out of all them that have pleasure therein.

3. His work is worthy to be praised, and had in honour: and His righteousness endureth for ever. Hallelujah.

KELWAY.

345

ISAIAH xli. 10. Be not afraid, I am with thee: tremble not, for I am thy GOD. I strengthen thee, for I am thy help; yea, I will uphold thee with the right hand of My righteousness.

Then fear thou not, for thou art called, and named; by redemption thou art saved.

(Sung at the same time as the above.)

LORD, by Thee am I provided;
Thou art mine, I am Thine,
    We are undivided.
I am Thine, for Thou didst lave me,
When the tide, from Thy side,
    Flowed to cleanse and save me.

Thou art mine! my Shepherd, lead me;
Day and night, O my Light,
    Shelter, guard, and feed me.
Never, never, let us sever,
Holding me, clasping Thee,
    Keep me Thine for ever.

Be not afraid, Thou art mine.

J. S. BACH.

346

SACRED CANTATA.—"A STRONGHOLD SURE."

No. 1

A stronghold sure our GOD remains,
A shield and hope unfailing;
In need His help our freedom gains,
O'er all we fear prevailing.
Our old malignant foe would fain work us woe;
With craft and great might he doth against us fight;
On earth is not one like him.

No. 2

Our utmost might is all in vain,
We straight had been rejected,
But for us fights the Perfect Man,
By GOD Himself elected.
Ask then, " Who is He ? "
He must JESUS be,
The GOD by hosts ador'd,
Our great Incarnate LORD,
Who all His foes shall conquer.

(*Sung at the same time as the above.*)

All men born of GOD our Father,
At the last will JESUS gather.
He that JESUS' soldier is,
Serving Him and not another,
Still from strength to strength shall rise.

No. 3

Consider, then, child of GOD, all the wondrous love
that JESUS in His precious death vouchsafes to shew
thee, whereby to fight and conquer Satan's host, this
evil world, and every sin. He calls on thee. Then give
no place within thee to Satan, nor to aught of his. Nor
let thine heart, where God Himself would make His
dwelling, lie waste and empty. Repent thee of thy guilt
with tears, that CHRIST Himself with thee be close
united.

No. 4

Within my heart of hearts, LORD JESUS, make Thy dwelling,
The love of sin drive out, within me now Thyself in light
revealing.
Away, base fear and doubt, away !

No. 5

If all the world with fiends were fill'd,
A host that would devour us,
To fear our hearts need never yield,
For they could not o'erpower us.
The prince of this world
From his throne is hurl'd ;
Why should we then fear,
Though grim he may appear ?
A single word confounds him.

No. 6

Then close beside thy Saviour's blood-besprinkled
banner, my soul, remain, and trust thou that thy Leader
will not fail, but make His triumph thine, and open thee
a way to glory. With joy, then, march to war ! If thou
the word of GOD wilt hear and truly follow, thou shalt
the foe repel, and overthrow him. Thy Saviour is thy
Hope, thy Saviour is thy Strength.

No. 7

How blessed, then, are they who still on GOD are calling ;
More blessed is the heart that Him doth make its own ;
Unconquered it remains, with foes before it falling,
And shall at last be crown'd, when Death is overthrown.

No. 8

That word shall still in strength abide,
Yet they no thanks shall merit,
For He is ever at our side,
Both by His gifts and Spirit.
And should they take our life,
Wealth, name, child, and wife :
Though these were all gone,
Yet will they nought have won,
GOD's Kingdom ours remaineth.

J. S. BACH.

347

SACRED CANTATA.—" BIDE WITH US."

No. 1

Bide with us, for eve is drawing onward, and the day is now declining.

No. 2

Thou Whose praises never end,
  Son of GOD, vouchsafe to hear us ;
While before Thy Throne we bend,
  Let Thy favour still be near us,
Grant, O grant us needful light,
  Through the coming hours of night.

No. 3

O bide with us, Thou Saviour dear,
Forsake us not when eve is near ;
Thy sacred Word, clear guiding light,
O grant it ne'er be quench'd in night.
In this our last and weakest hour,
Inspire us, LORD, with steadfast power,
That undefiled Thy faith we keep,
Until in death secure we sleep.

No. 4

Behold, around us, on every side, is darkness still increasing ; and if we ask whence comes this darkness, hence it comes. 'Tis that, from the least to the greatest, scarce one in righteousness before his GOD is walking, and in the works the Saviour loves, abounding ; and thus, instead of light there is but darkness.

No. 5

LORD, to us Thyself be shewing,
That no more we in ways of sin be going ;
May the light of Thy Word on men be shining,
All to trust in Thee inclining.

No. 6

LORD JESUS CHRIST, Thy power display,
Thou, LORD, Whom other lords obey,
Thy servants with Thy grace defend,
That so their thanks may never end.

                                   J. S. BACH.

348

REVELATION vii. 12. Blessing, glory, and wisdom, and thanks, power, and might, be unto the LORD our GOD for evermore. Amen. Hallelujah.

*PSALM cxlviii. 1. O praise the LORD of heaven, praise Him in the height.

12. O praise the Name of the LORD, His Name is excellent, His praise above heaven and earth.

(Sung at the same time as the above.)

O Father, Thine be praise
    From all in earth and heaven,
To JESUS, Son of GOD,
    Let endless praise be given.

Thy praise, O Holy Ghost,
    Be sounded more and more ;
Th' Eternal Three in One
    We worship and adore.*

PSALM lxvi. 1. O be joyful in GOD, all ye lands, make His praise to be glorious, sing praises unto the honour of His Name.

xcvi. 6. Glory and worship are before Him, power and honour are in His sanctuary.

What tongue can tell Thy greatness, LORD,
    That art in all the world adored,
The world by Thee created ?

Through all this temple praise abounds,
    Unceasing praise to Thee resounds,
By every voice repeated.
            Amen, Amen.
    So is Holy, Holy, Holy, ever ringing
    Where the angel choir are singing.

                                   J. S. BACH.

* ——* Sometimes sung as a separate Anthem.

349

Christians, be joyful, and praise your Salvation,
　　Sing, for to-day your Redeemer is born;
Cease to be fearful, forget lamentation,
　　Haste with thanksgiving to greet this glad morn!
Come, let us worship, and fall down before Him,
Let us with praises united adore Him.

(From the "Christmas Oratorio," No. 1.)　J. S. BACH.

350

St. LUKE ii. 1. Now it came to pass in those days
that there went out a deciee from Cæsar Augustus, that
all the world should be enrolled.

3. And all went to enrol themselves, every one to his
own city.

4. And there also went up Joseph from Galilee, out of
the city of Nazareth, into Judæa, to the city of David,
which is called Bethlehem (for he was of the house and
family of David),

5. To enrol himself, with Mary his betrothed wife,
being great with child.

6. And when they were there, the days were fulfilled
that she should be delivered.

See now the Bridegroom, full of grace,
The Hero of King David's race,
To save and heal the earth,
Doth stoop to mortal birth.

See now the Star of Jacob shining,
　　Its beams delight our eyes,
Up, Zion, and forget thy sad repining,
　　For high thy bliss doth rise.

Prepare thyself, Zion, with tender affection,
The purest, the fairest, this day to receive,
Thou must meet Him with a heart with love
　　o'erflowing,
Haste, then, with ardour the Bridegroom to welcome.

How shall I fitly meet Thee,
    And give Thee welcome due ?
The nations long to greet Thee,
    And I would greet Thee too.
O Fount of Light, shine brightly
    Upon my darken'd heart,
That I may serve Thee rightly,
    And know Thee as Thou art.

(From the " Christmas Oratorio," Nos. 2–5.)   J. S. BACH.

351

ST. LUKE ii. · 7. And she brought forth her first-born
Son, and she wrapped Him in swaddling clothes, and laid
Him in a manger, because there was no room for them in
the inn.

For us to earth He cometh poor,
Our redemption to secure,
And rich in Heaven to make us stand,
All number'd with His angel-band.
        LORD, have mercy !

Who rightly can the love declare,
That fills our tender Saviour's breast ?
Yea, who can understand or share
His grief for man by sin oppress'd ?
Himself the SON of GOD will give,
That we may be redeem'd and live ;
So now for this as Man behold Him born.

Mighty LORD, and King all-glorious,
Saviour true, for man victorious,
Earthly state Thou dost disdain.
He, Who all things doth sustain,
Who all state and pomp supplieth,
In a lowly manger lieth.

Ah ! dearest JESUS, Holy Child,
Make Thee a bed, soft, undefiled,
Within my heart, and there recline,
And keep that chamber ever Thine.

(From the " Christmas Oratorio," Nos. 6 9.) J. S. BACH.

352

St. Luke ii. 8. And there were shepherds in the same country, abiding in the field, keeping watch over their flocks by night.

9. And lo, an angel of the Lord stood by them, and the glory of the Lord shone round about them, and they were sore afraid.

> Break forth, O beauteous heavenly light,
>   And usher in the morning;
> Ye shepherds, shrink not with affright,
>   But hear the angel's warning.
> This Child, now weak in infancy,
> Our confidence and joy shall be;
> The power of Satan breaking,
> Our peace eternal making.

(From the " Christmas Oratorio," Nos. 11, 12.) J. S. Bach.

353

St. Luke ii. 10. And the Angel said to them, Be not afraid; behold, I bring you good tidings of great joy, which shall be to all the people.

11. For to-day is born to you in the city of David, a Saviour, Which is Christ the Lord.

12. And this is the sign to you: Ye shall find a Babe wrapped in swaddling clothes, and lying in a manger.

> Within yon gloomy manger lies
> The Lord Who reigns above the skies:
> Within the stall where beasts have fed
> The Virgin-born doth lay His head.

(From the " Christmas Oratorio," Nos. 13, 16, 17.) J. S. Bach.

354

St. Luke ii. 13. And suddenly there was with the Angel a multitude of the heavenly host, praising God and saying:

14. Glory to God in the Highest, and peace on the earth unto men in whom He is well pleased.

(From the " Christmas Oratorio," Nos. 20, 21.) J. S. Bach.

355

'Tis right that angels thus should sing,
To us this day such joy doth bring;
Come, then, our voices let us raise,
And join with them in songs of praise.

With all Thy Hosts, O LORD, we sing,
And thanks and praise to Thee we bring ;
For Thou, O long-expected Guest,
Hast come at length to make us blest.

(*From the " Christmas Oratorio,"* Nos. 22, 23.) J. S. BACH.

356

Hear, King of angels ! though falter our voices;
O ! when Thy Zion before Thee rejoices,
Let her endeavour be pleasing to Thee.
Hear us, O LORD, when we offer our praises,
Hear when Thy Zion glad thanksgiving raises,
Joying Thy mighty salvation to see.

(*From the " Christmas Oratorio,"* No. 24.) J. S. BACH.

357

ST. LUKE ii. 15. And when the angels were gone
from them into heaven, the shepherds said one to another,
Let us even now go to Bethlehem, and see this
thing which is come to pass, which the LORD hath made
known to us.

He bids us comfort take,
And free His Israel doth make ;
Relief to Zion hither sendeth,
And all our sorrow endeth.
Ye shepherds, see what He hath done ;
Haste, make His glory known.

The LORD hath all these wonders wrought,
His great love these gifts hath bought ;
Then let all Christian men rejoice,
And give Him thanks with cheerful voice.
LORD, have mercy.

(*From the " Christmas Oratorio,"* Nos. 25 28.) J. S. BACH.

358

St. Luke ii. 20. And the shepherds returned, glorifying and praising God for all the things which they had heard and seen, even as it was told unto them.

Rejoice, and sing, your gracious King
As Man is born, and lays aside His glory;
He is ador'd as Christ and Lord,
And every tongue repeats the wondrous story.

(*From the " Christmas Oratorio,"* Nos. 34, 35.)   J. S. Bach.

359 •

Come and thank Him, come and praise Him,
Fall before God's throne of grace;
God's own Son, of His mercy, is our Saviour and
Redeemer;
God's own Son all the foes of man subdueth.

(*From the " Christmas Oratorio,"* No. 36.)   J. S. Bach.

360

Glory be to God Almighty, glory, thanks, and praise be
giv'n :
All the earth doth worship Thee, Thou that wilt our
Father be.
Thou that wilt henceforth grant our utmost longings,
And bring Thy children with joy unto heaven.

(*From the " Christmas Oratorio,"* No. 43.)   J. S. Bach.

361

St. Matthew ii. 1. Now when Jesus was born in Bethlehem, in the land of Judah, in the days of Herod the king, behold, there came wise men from the East to Jerusalem,
2. Saying: Where is the new-born King of the Jews?

See Her within my breast,
For with me He vouchsafes to rest.'

For we have seen His star in the East, and are come
to worship Him.

> Rejoice that you this light behold,
> That doth its kindly beam unfold.
> My Saviour, Thou—Thou art the light
> That shall upon the Gentiles shine :
> Thy beams shall make their darkness bright,
> And they shall surely hail it Thine.
> How pure, how clear that light must be,
> That shines, O LORD, from Thee.
>
> All darkness flies before Thy face,
> The shades of night to day give place :
>   In Thy ways lead us ever,
> That from Thy sight and glorious light
>   Our hearts may wander never.

(*From the " Christmas Oratorio,"* Nos. 44–46.) J. S. BACH.

362

ST. MATTHEW ii. 9. And they, when they had heard
the king, went their way. And lo ! the star which they
had seen in the East went before them, until it came and
stood over where the young Child was.

10. When they saw the star, they rejoiced exceedingly.

11. And coming into the house, they saw the young
Child with Mary His mother ; and falling down, they
worshipped Him ; and having opened their treasures, they
offered Him gold, frankincense, and myrrh.

> Beside Thy cradle here I stand,
>   O Thou that ever livest,
> And bring Thee with a willing hand
>   The very gifts Thou givest.
> Accept me ; 'tis my mind and heart,
>   My soul, my strength, my every part,
> That Thou from me requirest.

(*From the " Christmas Oratorio,* Nos. 58, 59.) J. S. BACH.

363

Come, Jesu, come! I now am weary,
  My strength is gone, my hour is nigh;
I long for peace, all now is dreary;
  O leave me not alone to die.
O come and aid my frail endeavour,
Thou art the only Way, the Truth, and Life, for ever.

*When called by Thee I gain Thy portal,
  Mine will be joys no worlds can give;
There shall I know my pains were mortal,
  There will my soul in glory live.
There I around Thy Throne shall hover,
There, my Redeemer, I shall sing Thy praise for ever.*

                                    J. S. Bach.

—— Sometimes sung as a separate Anthem.

364

St. Matthew xi. 28. Come unto Me, all ye that labour
and are heavy laden, and I will give you rest. †

29. Take My yoke upon you and learn of Me;* for I am
meek and lowly in heart: and ye shall find rest unto your
souls.

30. For My yoke is easy, and My burden is light. Amen.

  † T. Adams, J. S. Bach, Cooper, Couldrey, Elvey,
    *Kingston, Oakeley, J. S. Smith, Wray.

              †* Ends here.

365

SACRED CANTATA.—"GOD GOETH UP."

No. 1

God goeth up with shouting, and the Lord with sound
of the trumpet. Sing praises unto God, O sing praises to
our King and God.

No. 2

To-day the Highest His own triumph hath proclaimed,
For now captivity itself He captive leads.
Who shout for Him? What be they who their trumpets
    sound?
Who hasten in, throng, around Him?
Is it not God's own Host.

Who the honour of His Name,
Health, wealth, praise, strength, and might,
With voices loud are singing,
To Him for evermore an Alleluia bringing?

No. 3

Ten thousand times thousand, His chariot surrounding,
As King of all kings, His loud praises are sounding;
The earth and the heavens before Him bow down;
No longer His foes can withhold Him His Crown.

No. 4

So the LORD, after He with His disciples then had
spoken, was received up into heaven, and sat on the
right hand of GOD.

No. 5

Our JESUS hath for aye
  Redemption's work full ended,
And back He takes His way
  From whence He first descended;
His earthly course now o'er,
  Ye heavens, ope your gates,
Receive Him back once more.

No. 6

He comes, the LORD of lords,
  O'er hell the Prince victorious,
Of grave and death destroyer,
  Of sin subduer glorious,
Who Satan's crew cast down.
  Dominions, hither haste,
Your King uplift and crown.

No. 7

'Tis He Who all alone
  Hath trodden well the winepress;
How full of woes unknown,
  For guilty ones the guiltless,
What pain and grief He bore!
  Ye thrones, O hither haste,
And crown Him yet once more.

No. 8

The Father hath appointed Him a realm eternal,
The hour is come when He may claim His throne
    supernal;
          Though vexed by thousand woes,
          I pause upon my way
          To hail Him as He goes.

No. 9

My spirit Him descries at GOD's right hand, where
    sitting,
He Satan now defies, and sends deliverance fitting
          From weeping, loss, and shame.
          I pause upon my way
          Upgazing, help to claim.

No. 10

A mansion at His side is He for me preparing,
Where I may aye abide, my wedding garment wearing,
          Set free from woe and pain.
          I pause upon my way
          To raise my grateful strain.

No. 11

O JESUS CHRIST, Thou dearest LORD,
Thou Prince of life and glory,
Thou with the Father art ador'd
In heaven where saints surround Thee.
How best can I the victory sing
Won by Thy might, Thou gracious King?
What strains can I be raising,
Thy love and power praising?

Draw us to Thee, that haste we may,
The wings of Faith aye plying;
Help us to turn from earth away,
The land of bondage flying.
My GOD, when may I soar to Thee?
When joy and peace my portion be?
When may I stand before Thee?
When reign with Thee in Glory?

                    J. S. BACH.

366

SACRED CANTATA.—"GOD SO LOVED THE WORLD."

No. 1

That GOD doth love the world, we know,
  Since He hath sent His Son to save us:
Tc Him be faithful here below,
  Then take the endless life He gave us.

To trust in JESUS, our salvation,
Will guard the soul from reprobation:
There is no ill which him can move,
Whom GOD the LORD vouchsafes to love.

No. 2

My heart, ever trusting,
Be joyful with singing,
  For JESUS is here.
Bid sorrow and sighing
Their flight to be taking,
  Now JESUS is near.

No. 3

It is not mine to be highminded.
This thought consoles and makes me glad,
  That me hath JESUS not forgotten.
He sought not out the world for judgment,
Nay, nay, He would for sin and guilt, thus
Reconciling GOD and man, effect atonement.

No. 4

On my behalf was Thy revealing,
This know I well, by faith and feeling,
  And Thou for me amends hast made.
Though now the doom of earth were spoken,
Though Satan wielded power unbroken,
  My praise to Thee should still be paid.

No. 5

On Him believing, thou art free from judgment; but if
unbelieving, thou art now under judgment, as believing
not on the Name of the only Son of God the Father.

J. S. BACH.

367

SACRED CANTATA.—"GOD'S OWN TIME IS THE BEST."

God's own time is the best, yea, is ever best of all. In Him live we, move, and have our being, as long as He wills; and, at His good time, in Him we die, when He wills.

O Lord, incline us to consider, that our days are numbered; make us apply our hearts unto wisdom.

"Set in order thine house, for thou shalt die, and not remain among the living." It is the old decree: Man, thou art mortal.

Yea, come, Lord Jesus, come.

Into Thy hands my spirit I commend, for Thou hast redeemed me, O Lord Thou God of truth.

"Thou shalt be with Me to-day in Paradise."

(Sung at the same time as the above.)

In joy and peace I pass away,
　　When God willeth:
The fears that vex my anxious soul
　　His love stilleth.
Trusting in His promise sure,
In death I sleep calm and secure.

All glory, praise, and majesty,
To Father, Son, and Spirit be,
　　The Holy, Blessed Trinity,
Whose power to us gives victory,
　　Through Jesus Christ. Amen.

　　　　　　　　　　　　　J. S. Bach.

368

Nehemiah x. 39. I will not forsake Thee, O Lord.

Psalm cxviii. 28. Thou art my God, and I will praise Thee.

29. Give thanks unto the Lord, for He is good.

　　　　　　　　　　　　　J. S. Bach.

369

GOD, my King, Thy might confessing,
  Ever will I bless Thy Name;
Day by day Thy Throne addressing,
  Still will I Thy praise proclaim.

All Thy works, O LORD, shall bless Thee,
  Thee shall all Thy saints adore;
Kings supreme shall they confess Thee,
  And proclaim Thy sovereign power.

Full of kindness and compassion,
  Slow to anger, vast in love,
GOD is good to all creation,
  All His works His goodness prove.

Still, JEHOVAH, Thee confessing,
  Shall my tongue Thy praise proclaim;
And may all mankind with blessing,
  Ever hail Thy holy Name.

J. S. BACH.

370

SACRED CANTATA.—"JESU, PRICELESS TREASURE."

No. 1

JESU, priceless treasure,
Source of purest pleasure,
Truest friend to me;
Ah, how long I've panted,
And my heart hath fainted,
Thirsting, LORD, for Thee!
Thine I am, O spotless Lamb,
I will suffer nought to hide Thee,
Nought I ask beside Thee.

No. 2

ROMANS viii. 1. So there is now no condemnation
unto them which are in JESUS CHRIST, them who walk
not by the flesh corruptly, but as the Spirit leads.

No. 3

In Thine arm I rest me,
Foes who would molest me
Cannot reach me here ;
Though the earth be shaking,
Every heart be quaking,
JESUS calms my fear ;
Fires may flash, and thunders crash,
Yea, and sin and hell assail me,
JESUS will not fail me.

No. 4

ROMANS viii. 2. Thus, then, the law of the Spirit of
life in CHRIST abiding, now hath made me free from the
law of sin and death.

No. 5

Death, I do not fear thee,
Though thou standest near me ;
Grave, I calmly spurn thee,
Though to dust thou turn me !
Strong in hope and faith,
Rising up and singing,
I shall, heavenward winging,
Soar, and vanquish Death,
And with the blest
Shall for ever rest.
He that reigns will rend my chains :
Earth may vanish, Heaven may sever,
GOD is GOD for ever !

No. 6

ROMANS viii. 9. Ye are not of the flesh, but of the
Spirit, if in your hearts the Spirit abideth.
If JESU's Spirit be not yours, ye are not His.

No. 7

Hence with earthly treasure,
Thou art all my pleasure
Jesu, all in all to me :

Hence, thou empty glory,
Nought to me thy story,
Told with tempting voice ;
Pain, or loss, or shame, or cross,
Shall not from my Saviour move me,
Since He deigns to love me.

No. 8

ROMANS viii. 10. If therefore CHRIST abide in you,
then is the body dead, because of transgression, but the
Spirit liveth, because of righteousness.

No. 9

Fare thee well, that errest,
Thou that earth preferrest,
Thou wilt tempt in vain ;
Fare thee well, transgression,
Hence, abhorred possession,
Come not forth again.
Past your hour, O pride and power,
Worldly life, thy bonds I sever :
Fare thee well for ever.

No. 10

ROMANS viii. 11. If by His Spirit, GOD, that upraised
JESUS from the dead, dwell in you, He that raised CHRIST
up from the dead shall also quicken your mortal bodies,
by His Spirit that dwelleth within you.

No. 11

Hence, all fears and sadness,
For the LORD of gladness,
JESUS, enters in ;
They who love the Father,
Though the storms may gather,
Still have peace within ;
Yea, whate'er I here must bear,
Still in Thee lies purest pleasure,
JESU, priceless treasure.

J. S. BACH.

371

SACRED CANTATA.—"MY SPIRIT WAS IN HEAVINESS."

No. 1 Symphony.

No. 2

Lord my God, my spirit was in heaviness and deep affliction. But, Lord, Thy consolations have my soul restored.

No. 3

Sighing, weeping, sorrow, need, anxious longing, fear of death, rend my troubled heart in twain: I am torn by grief and pain.

No. 4

Why hast Thou then, O God, in this my need, in this my fear and anguish, thus quite forsaken me? Ah! know'st Thou not Thy child? Ah! hear'st Thou not the mourning of those who to Thyself in faith and truth are bound? Thou hast been my delight, and now I see Thee not. I seek for Thee in ev'ry place; I call, I cry to Thee alone. My grief and woe are full, when Thou, O God, regardest not.

No. 5

Fast my bitter tears are flowing,
　　Find I none to comfort me.
Waves and storms are o'er me going,
　　All this dark and troubled sea
O'er my fainting spirit rolleth;
Mine affliction none consoleth.
Floods of sorrow close me round.
Where can light and help be found?

No. 6

Wherefore grievest thou, O my spirit, and art so unquiet in me hope thou in God, for to Him I will give thanks; for He is the help of my countenance and my God.

No. 7

LORD JESUS, my Repose, my Light, where art Thou
gone?
Behold, O spirit, I am with thee.
With me? but here is only night!
*I am thy faithful Friend, that watcheth in the night, when
evil is abroad.*
Then comfort with Thy light and radiance enter in!
*The hour is coming soon, when, all thy conflicts o'er, thou
shalt a sweet reward secure.*

No. 8

| Come, my Saviour, and restore me,
| *Yea, I come, and will restore thee,*
| Shed Thy grace and gladness o'er me,
| *Shed My grace and gladness o'er thee,*
| O'er this spirit that shall perish,
| *Yea, thy spirit I will cherish,*
| That shall its continual sorrow never vanquish,
| *Nor beneath continual sorrow shalt thou languish,*
| But shall still in sorrow languish.
| *But shalt all thy sorrow vanquish.*
    | Yea, ah yea, I am rejected.
    | *Nay, ah nay, thou art elected.*
    | Nay, ah nay, Thou hatest me.
    | *Yea, ah yea, I care for thee.*
| LORD JESUS, Thou bringest me joy and salvation.
| *Soon thou for thy sorrow shalt find consolation.*
| Come, my Saviour, and restore me,
| *Yea, I come, and will restore thee,*
| Shed Thy grace and gladness o'er me.
| *Shed My grace and gladness o'er thee.*

No. 9

Now again be thou joyful,
O my spirit; thy reward is of thy GOD.
Of what avail our bitter sorrow?
Of what avail our pain and grief?

Of what avail that each new morrow
Still finds our woe beyond relief?
The weight of every cross and care,
We make but greater by despair.
Think not, when high thy trouble swelleth,
That thou by GOD forsaken art,
That He in distant darkness dwelleth,
Who fills with joy thy waiting heart.
The future all thy woe shall end,
Relief and comfort GOD will send.

No. 10

Rejoice, O my spirit, in thy consolation,
For now from thy sorrow thou findest salvation.
The water of grief GOD hath changed into wine,
All sadness is over, and gladness is mine.
Within me there burneth and shineth the pure light of
     love
And of comfort, in spirit and heart,
For JESUS doth my consolation impart.

No. 11

The Lamb that was slain for us is worthy to have all
power, and riches, and wisdom, and strength, and honour,
and glory, and praise. Praise, and honour, and glory,
and power, be to our GOD for evermore and evermore.
Amen. Hallelujah.

J. S. BACH.

372

Now shall the grace, and the strength, and the rule,
and the might of our GOD and His CHRIST be declared;
for he to nought is come, which hath reviled us day and
night † (col.

J. S. BACH.

373

No. 1

O Light everlasting, O Love never failing,
· Our darkness illumine, and draw us to Thee;
May we from Thy Spirit receive inspiration,
And grant us, most Highest, Thy temple to be ;
In Thee may our souls find their peace and salvation.

No. 2

LORD, in our inmost hearts we hold
Thy word the truth to be.
With us Thou dost vouchsafe to dwell,
O knit our hearts to Thee ;
LORD, ever near us be !
If Thou within us but abide,
We need not aught beside.

No. 3

Rejoice, ye souls, elect and holy,
Whom GOD His dwelling deigns to make ;
He doth His great salvation send us,
Unnumber'd mercies still attend us,
And all from GOD'S own hand we take.

No. 4

The LORD doth choose a holy dwelling
Whereon to shed His peace :
His boundless grace our lips would fail in telling,
How He to bless His chosen doth not cease.
It is our Father's everlasting will
To bless His children still.

No. 5

Peace be unto Israel !
Thank the LORD Whose love attends us,
Thank Him Who on us hath thought,
Yea, His love this grace hath brought.
Peace be unto Israel,
Peace and rest our Saviour sends.

J. S. BACH.

374

JESUS, Saviour, I am Thine,
Thou hast bid me call Thee mine;
All things else I count but loss,
Find my glory in Thy cross;
In this only plea confide,
That for sinners Thou hast died.

*O Fount of love unbounded,
    So full, so sweet, so free;
My thoughts are all confounded,
    Whene'er I think of Thee.
For me Thou cam'st from heaven,
    To suffer and to die;
That, purchased and forgiven,
    I might ascend on high.*

(*From* " *The Passion,*" Nos. 19, 21.) J. S. BACH, STEANE.

—— Sometimes sung as a separate Anthem.

375

Though all men should forsake Thee,
    Yet will not I, O LORD;
Though death should overtake me,
    I'll not deny my GOD.
Since sorrow, pain, and anguish
    Thou didst endure for me,
Till I in death shall languish,
    Myself I'll give to Thee.

(*From:* " *The Passion,*" No. 23.) J. S. BACH.

376

O Father, let Thy will be done!
    For all things well Thou doest.
In time of need refusest none,
    But helpest e'en the lowest.
        In deep distress
        Thou still dost bless,
In wrath rememb'rest mercy.
        Who trusts in Thee
        Shall ever be
In perfect peace, from danger free.

(*From* " *The Passion,*" No. 31.) J. S. BACH.

377

Lamb of GOD, I fall before Thee,
   Humbly trusting in Thy Cross;
That alone be all my glory,
   All things else I count but loss.
JESUS, all my consolations
   Flow from Thee, Thou sovereign good,
Hope and Love, and Faith, and Patience,
   All were purchased by Thy Blood.
      (*From " The Passion,"* No. 49.) J. S. BACH.

378

Commit thy ways to JESUS,
   Thy burdens and thy cares;
He from them all releases,
   He all thy sorrow shares.
Who gives the winds their courses,
   And bounds the ocean's shore,
Will suffer not temptation
   To rise beyond thy power.
      (*From " The Passion,"* No. 53.) J. S. BACH.

379

O Thou Whose Head was wounded,
   And pierced with prickly thorn,
Who wast with grief surrounded,
   Thy soul with anguish torn:
Whom once, in light enthroned,
   The angels did adore,
But now with shame art crowned;
   I'll praise Thee evermore!

O may Thy love constrain me,
   To give my heart to Thee,
Let nothing henceforth pain me,
   ut that which paineth Thee.
My joy, my one endeavour,
   Thro' suff'ring, conflict, shame,
To serve Thee, gracious Saviour,
   And magnify Thy Name.
      (*From " The Passion,'* No. 63.) J. S. BACH.

380

If I should e'er forsake Thee,
  Forsake me not, O LORD;
When sorrows overtake me,
  Sustain me by Thy word.
When death and hell assail me,
  And rend my heart in twain,
Then, Saviour, do not fail me,
  For Thou enduredst pain.

    (*From " The Passion,"* No. 72.) J. S. BACH.

381

PSALM cl. 6. Praise ye the LORD.

cxlix. 1. O sing unto the LORD a new song : let the congregation of saints praise Him.

2. Let Israel rejoice in Him that made him : and let the children of Sion be joyful in their King.

4. For the LORD hath pleasure in His people, and helpeth the meek-hearted.

cl. 2. Praise GOD in His noble acts: praise Him according to His excellent greatness. Hallelujah.

                         J. S. BACH.

382

The LORD is risen again :
CHRIST hath broken every chain.
To Him Who gave for us His life,
Who for us endured the strife,
  Sing praises evermore.

He Who for our sins and loss
Made atonement on the Cross,
He reigns in glory now on High ;
He pleads for us, and hears our cry:
  To Him all praise be given.

Hallelujah !
O LAMB of GOD, to Thee we pray ;
Take all our guilt and sin away
  Make us one with Thee

                         J. S. BACH.

383

PSALM cxlix.   1. Sing to the LORD a new-made song :
let the saints in congregation sing and praise Him.
2. O Israel, rejoice in Him that made thee ! let Zion's
children be joyful in their King,
3. And let them praise His holy Name in their
dances : with timbrel and harp united, sing His praises.

Like as a father bendeth
In pity o'er his infant race,
So GOD the LORD befriendeth
The meek and lowly heirs of grace.

That we are frail He knoweth,
Like sheep we go astray :
Like grass the reaper moweth,
We fall and fade away.

Like wind that ever flieth,
We are but passing breath ;
Thus man each moment dieth,
For life must yield to death.

(*Sung at the same time as the above.*)

Almighty GOD ! preserve us still,
Teach us to heed Thy sovereign will ;
In all we do protect us.

Be Thou our shield by day and night,
Make Hope our staff, and Faith our light ;
In all our ways protect us.

How blessed and secure is he
Who placeth all his trust in Thee.

* Praise ye the LORD, His acts are mighty; praise
Him greatly, for His excellence is great. All breathing
life, sing and praise ye the LORD ! Hallelujah. *

J. S. BACH.

Sometimes sung as a separate Anthem.

384

ROMANS viii. 26. The Spirit also helpeth us, for we know not what we should rightly pray for; therefore, the Spirit intercedeth for us with inexpressible groanings.

* 27. The Searcher of hearts ever knoweth the mind dwelling in the Spirit, because He pleads for all the saints, according to the will of GOD.

Look down, Holy Dove ; Spirit bow ;
Descend from heaven and help us now.
Inspire our hearts while humbly kneeling,
To pray with zeal and contrite feeling ;
Prepare us through Thy cleansing power,
For death, at life's expiring hour :
That we may find the grave a portal
To Thee in heaven, and life immortal.
Hallelujah. Hallelujah. *

J. S. BACH.

* —— * Sometimes sung as a separate Anthem.

385

PSALM cxix. 1. Blessed are those that are undefiled in the way, and walk in the law of the LORD.

2. Blessed are they that keep His testimonies, and seek Him with their whole heart.

4. Thou hast charged that we shall diligently keep Thy commandments.

5. O that my ways were made so direct, that I might keep Thy statutes.

18. Open Thou mine eyes, that I may see the wondrous things of Thy law.

15. Then will I talk of Thy commandments, and have respect unto Thy ways.

16. My delight shall be in Thy statutes, and I will not forget Thy word.

171. My lips shall speak of Thy praise, when Thou hast taught me Thy statutes.

172. Yea, my tongue shall sing of Thy word, for all Thy commandments are righteousness.

GREENE.

386

Job xxii. 21, 22. Acquaint thyself with God, and be at peace with Him, and lay up His words in thine heart.

23. If thou return to the Almighty, put away iniquity from thee.

25, 26. Then shall He be thy defence, and thy delight.

27. Thou shalt make thy prayer unto Him, and He will hear thee.

29. The Lord will deliver the righteous, He will save the humble man.

GREENE.

—— Sometimes sung as a separate Anthem.

387

Psalm lxi. 1. Hear my crying, O God, give ear unto my prayer.

2. From the ends of the earth will I call upon Thee, [when my heart is in heaviness.]

3. O set me up upon the rock that is higher than I, for Thou hast been my hope, and a strong tower for me against the enemy.

4. I will dwell in Thy tabernacle for ever, and my trust shall be under the covering of Thy wings.

5. For Thou, O Lord, hast heard my desires, [and hast given an heritage unto those that fear Thy Name.]

6. Thou shalt grant the king a long life, that his years may endure throughout all generations.

7. [He shall dwell before God for ever:] O prepare Thy loving mercy and faithfulness, that they may preserve him.

8. So will I alway sing praise unto Thy Name, [that I may daily perform my vows.] Hallelujah. Amen.

GREENE.

388 Boyce, vv. 1-8.
389 J. L. Hopkins, vv. 1, 2.
390 Travers. vv. 1 3.
391 Turle, vv. 1 3. 8.
392 Weldon, vv. 1 5. Amen.

393

PSALM xlvi. 1. GOD is our hope and strength, a very present help in trouble.

2, 3. Therefore we will not fear, though the earth tremble, though the mountains shake, and the waters rage and swell.

5, 7. For GOD is in the midst of us, therefore shall we not be moved : GOD is our hope and refuge.

8. O behold the works of the LORD.

9. He maketh wars to cease in all the world.

10. He is exalted among the heathen, He is exalted in the earth.

GRFENE.

394

PSALM cxlv. 1. I will magnify Thee, O GOD, my King, and I will praise Thy Name for ever and ever.

2. Every day will I give thanks unto Thee, and praise Thy Name for ever and ever.

3. Great is the LORD, and marvellous, worthy to be praised ; there is no end of His greatness.

4. One generation shall praise Thy works unto another, and declare Thy power.

5. As for me, I will be talking of Thy worship, Thy glory, Thy praise, and wondrous works ;

6. [So that men shall speak of the might of Thy marvellous acts,] and I will also tell of Thy greatness.

[7. The memorial of Thine abundant kindness shall be shewed, and men shall sing of Thy righteousness.

8. The Lord is gracious, and merciful, long-suffering, and of great goodness.

9. The Lord is loving unto every man, and His mercy is over all His works.]

10. All Thy works praise Thee, O LORD, and Thy saints give thanks unto Thee.

[11. They shew the glory of Thy Kingdom, and talk of Thy power ;

12. That Thy power, Thy glory, and mightiness of Thy Kingdom might be known unto men.

13. Thy Kingdom is an everlasting Kingdom, and Thy Dominion endureth throughout all ages.

14. The LORD upholdeth all such as fall, and lifteth up all those that are down.

15. The eyes of all wait upon Thee, O LORD, and Thou givest them their meat in due season.

16. Thou openest Thine hand, and fillest all things living with plenteousness.

17. The LORD is righteous in all His ways, and holy in all His works.

18. The LORD is nigh unto all them that call upon Him, yea, all such as call upon Him faithfully.

19. He will fulfil the desire of them that fear Him ; He also will hear their cry and will help them.

20. The LORD preserveth all them that love Him, but scattereth abroad all the ungodly.

21. My mouth shall speak the praise of the LORD, and let all flesh give thanks unto His holy Name for ever and ever.

lxii. 8. O put your trust in Him alway, ye people; pour out your hearts before Him, for GOD is our hope.

cxliv. 15. Happy are the people that are in such a case : blessed are the people who have the LORD for their GOD.

1 CHRONICLES XXIX. 13. Now, therefore, O GOD, we thank Thee, and praise Thy glorious Name.]

CRAMENT (vv. 1–21), GREENE (vv. 1–6, 10).

395 S. ARNOLD, vv. 10–13.
396 BARRETT, M. SMITH, vv. 15–17.
397 BOYCE, vv. 1–6.
398 CALKIN, vv. 1, 2, 8, 9, 3, 4.
399 DUPUIS, SHAW, vv. 1–3.
400 GIBBONS, vv. 15–21.   Gloria Patri.
401 GOSS, TRAVERS. TUCKER, vv. 1, 2, 15, 16.   Amen.
402 HANDEL, vv. 1, 2, 4, 17, 19, 20; lxii. 8; cxliv. 15; cxlv. 21.
403 P. HAYES, SELBY, vv. 1, 2.   [Hallelujah.]
404 W. HAYES, vv. 3, 4.   Amen.
405 HINE, vv. 1–3, 5, 6, 4.
406 T. ADAMS, R. JACKSON, vv. 15, 16, 21.   Amen.
407 KEETON, vv. 15, 16, 10–12.
408 KENT, vv. 10–16.
409 OUSELEY, vv. 1–4.   Hallelujah.   Amen.
410 PATTISON, vv. 10–13, 15, 16, 10–13.   Amen.
411 ROBERTS, vv. 1–3, 15, 16.   Amen.
412 SYDENHAM. vv. 3, 15, 16, 3, 17; lxii. 8.   Hallelujah. Amen.
413 THORNE, vv. 10, 11, 15, 16,   1 CHRONICLES XXIX. 13.

414

Isaiah lx. 1. Arise, shine, O Zion, for thy light is come, and the glory of the Lord is risen upon thee.

2. Behold, the darkness shall cover the earth, and gross darkness the people : but the Lord shall arise upon thee, and His glory shall be seen upon thee.

3. The Gentiles shall come to thy light, and kings to the brightness of thy rising.

19. The sun shall be no more thy light by day ; neither for brightness shall the moon give light unto thee : but the Lord shall be unto thee an everlasting light, and thy God thy glory.

lxi. 10. I will greatly rejoice in the Lord, my soul shall be joyful in my God ; for He hath clothed me with the garments of salvation, He hath covered me with the robe of righteousness.

Greene.

415

Psalm lv. 1. Hear my prayer, O God,

cxix. 170. And let my supplication come before Thee.

xxxv. 1. Plead Thou my cause, O Lord, with them that strive with me ; fight Thou against them that fight against me.

2. Lay hand upon the shield and buckler ; stand up to help me.

3. Bring forth the spear, and stop the way against them that persecute me.

23. Avenge Thou my cause, my God and my Lord.

xx. 9. Save, Lord, and hear us, O King of Heaven, when we call upon Thee.

lxxi. 14. We will go forth in the strength of the Lord God.

xliv. 6. Through Thee will we overthrow our enemies, and in Thy Name will we tread them under that rise up against us.

cxxiv. 7. Our help standeth in the Name of the Lord our God. Who hath made heaven and earth.

Greene.

416

PSALM xxxiv. I will alway give thanks unto the LORD: His praise shall be ever in my mouth.

cxviii. 28. Thou art my GOD, and I will thank Thee: Thou art my GOD, and I will praise Thee.

lxvi. 18. Praised be GOD, Who hath not cast out my prayer, nor turned His mercy from me.

civ. 33. I will sing unto the LORD as long as I live: I will praise my GOD whilst I have my being.

lxxii. 18. Blessed be the LORD GOD, even the GOD of Israel, Which only doeth wondrous things;

19. And blessed be the Name of His Majesty for ever, and all the earth shall be filled with His Majesty. Amen, Amen.

GREENE.

417

PSALM cxix. 169. Let my complaint come before Thee, O LORD: give me understanding, according to Thy word.

170. Let my supplication come before Thee: deliver me, according to Thy word.

171. My lips shall speak of Thy praise, when Thou hast taught me Thy statutes.

172. Yea, my tongue shall sing of Thy word, for all Thy commandments are righteous.

173. Let Thine hand help me, for I have chosen Thy commandments.

174. I have longed for Thy saving health, O LORD, and in Thy law is my delight.

175. O let my soul live, and it shall praise Thee, and Thy judgments shall help me.

[176. I have gone astray like a sheep that is lost: O seek Thy servant, for I do not forget Thy commandments.]

GREENE.

418 ALLEN, vv. 169–172, 174.
419 BATTEN, BOYCE, vv. 169–172, 175.
420 GREENE, THORNE, vv. 169–172.
421 GREENE, vv. 174 176.
422 READ, vv. 169, 170, 176, 175, 171, 172, 171.

423

Job. v.   8, 9. I will seek unto God, and commit my
cause unto Him : for He doeth great and wondrous things.

10. He giveth rain upon the earth, and sendeth waters
upon the fields.

11. He setteth up the lowly on high, and exalteth them
that mourn.

13. He taketh the wise in their own craftiness, and
carries headlong the counsel of the froward.

14. They meet with darkness, and grope in the noon-
day as in the night.

15. But He saveth the poor from the sword, and from
the hand of the mighty.

17. Behold, happy is the man whom God correcteth.

18. For He maketh sore, and bindeth up ; He woundeth,
and maketh whole.

Greene.

424

Psalm lix.   16. I will sing of Thy power, O God, and
will praise Thy mercy betimes in the morning; for Thou
hast been my defence and refuge in the day of my trouble.

[9. My strength will I ascribe unto Thee, for Thou art
the God of my refuge.]

17. Unto Thee, O my strength, will I sing ; for Thou,
O God, art my refuge, and my merciful God.

lx.   12. Through God will we do great acts ; for it is
He that shall tread down our enemies.

Greene.

425 Sullivan, vv. 16, 9, 17.   Amen.

426

Psalm lxviii.   1. Let God arise, and let His enemies
be scattered.

2. Like as smoke vanisheth, as wax melteth at the fire,
so let them perish and be driven away.

7, 8. O God when Thou wentest forth. the earth
shook. and the heavens dropped at the presence of God,
even the God of Israel.

*32. Sing unto GOD, ye kingdoms of the earth; O sing praises unto the LORD.

20. Sing praises unto Him Who is the GOD of our salvation.*

5, 6. He is a Father of the fatherless : He bringeth the prisoners out of captivity.

35. Blessed be GOD.   Hallelujah.

GREENE.

* —— * Sometimes sung as a separate Anthem.

427

PSALM xlii.   1. Like as the hart desires the waterbrooks, so panteth my soul after Thee, O GOD.

2. My soul is athirst for GOD, yea, even for the living GOD; when shall I come to appear before the presence of GOD ?

8. My GOD, my soul is vexed within me, therefore will I remember Thee.

11. I will say unto the GOD of my strength, why hast Thou forgotten me ?

xliii.   3. O send out Thy light and Thy truth, that they may lead me; and bring me to Thy holy hill, and to Thy dwelling,

4. Even unto the altar of GOD, the GOD of my joy and gladness.

5. Why art thou so vexed, O my soul? and why art thou so disquieted within me ?

6. O put thy trust in GOD, Which is the help of my countenance, and my GOD.   GREENE.

428

PSALM xc.   12. LORD, teach us to number our days, that we may apply our hearts unto wisdom.

13. Turn Thee again, O LORD, at the last, and be gracious unto Thy servants.

14. O satisfy us with Thy mercy, and that soon : so shall we rejoice and be glad all the days of our life.

GREENE.

129 ATTWOOD, v. 13. Amen.
480 SULLIVAN, vv. 13, 14.

431

PSALM lxxix.　5. LORD, how long wilt Thou be angry ? shall Thy jealousy burn like fire for ever ?

6. Pour out Thine indignation upon the heathen, and upon the kingdoms that have not called upon Thy Name.

7. For they have devoured Jacob, and laid waste his dwelling place.

8. O remember not our old sins, but have mercy upon us, and that soon, for we are come to great misery.

9. Help us, O GOD of our salvation, for the glory of Thy Name : O deliver us, and be merciful unto our sins for Thy Name's sake.

[14. So we, that are Thy people, and sheep of Thy pasture, shall give Thee thanks for ever : and will alway be shewing forth Thy praise from generation to generation.]

GREENE.

432 W. HAYES, vv. 5, 8, 9.
433 PURCELL, vv. 5, 8, 9, 14.

434

PSALM lx.　1. O GOD, Thou hast cast us out, and scattered us abroad : Thou hast also been displeased ; O turn Thee unto us again.

2. Thou hast moved the land, and divided it ; heal the sores thereof, for it shaketh.

11. O be Thou our help in trouble, for vain is the help of man.

12. Through GOD will we do great acts; for it is He that shall tread down our enemies.

lxxix.　8. O remember not our old sins, but have mercy upon us, for we are come to great misery.

9. Help us, O GOD of our salvation, for the glory of Thy Name ; O deliver us, and be merciful unto our sins, for Thy Name's sake.

GREENE.

435 PURCELL, vv. 1, 2, 11, 12. Amen.
436 WELDON, vv. 1, 11 ; lxxix. 8, 9; lx. 12.

437

Psalm xxii.   1. My God, my God, look upon Me ; why hast Thou forsaken Me, and art so far from My health, and from the words of My complaint ? ·

2. O my God, I cry in the day time, but Thou hearest not : and in the night season also I take no rest.

3. And Thou continuest holy, O Thou worship of Israel.

7. All they that see Me laugh Me to scorn : they shoot out their lips, and shake their heads ; saying,

8. He trusted in God, that He would deliver Him : let Him deliver Him, if He will have Him.

14. I am poured out like water, and all My bones are out of joint : My heart also in the midst of My Body is even like melting wax.

17. They pierced My hands and My feet ; I may tell all My bones : they stand staring and looking upon Me.

18. They part My garments among them, and cast lots upon My vesture.

xxxviii. 21. But be not Thou far from Me, O Lord.

22. Haste Thee to help Me, O Lord God of My salvation.

GREENE.

488 Benson, Blow, J. L. Hopkins, Reynolds, vv. 1–3.
439 Crotch, vv. 1, 2.

440

Psalm cvii.   1. O give thanks unto the Lord.

2. Let them give thanks whom the Lord hath redeemed, and delivered from the hand of the enemy.

16. For He hath broken the gates of brass.

14, 13. He hath brought them out of darkness, and the shadow of death, and delivered them from their distress.

15. O that men would therefore praise the Lord for His goodness, and declare the wonders that He doeth for the children of men!

22. That they would offer unto Him the sacrifice of thanksgiving, and tell out His works with gladness.

GREENE.

441

PSALM iv. 1. O GOD of my righteousness, hear me when I call : Thou hast set me at liberty when I was in trouble, have mercy upon me, and hearken unto my prayer.

2. O ye sons of men, how long will ye blaspheme mine honour, and have pleasure in vanity?

3. Know this, the LORD hath chosen to Himself the man that is godly.

9. I will lay me down in peace, and take my rest : for it is Thou, O LORD, that makest me to dwell in safety.

5, 4. Offer the sacrifice of righteousness : stand in awe, and sin not and put your trust in the LORD.

GREENE.

442

ISAIAH lxiii. 15. O LORD, look down from heaven, and behold from the habitation of Thy holiness and of Thy glory. Where is Thy zeal and Thy strength? Thy mercies toward me, are they restrained?

16. Doubtless Thou art our Father, though Abraham be ignorant of us, and Israel acknowledge us not ; doubtless Thou art our Father. Thou, O LORD, art our Father, our Redeemer; Thy Name is from everlasting.

GREENE.

443 BATTISHILL, v. 15.

444

PSALM lxviii. 4. O sing unto GOD, sing praises to His Name, and rejoice before Him.

5, 6. He is the Father of the fatherless, He defendeth the cause of the widows, and bringeth the prisoners out of captivity.

19. Praised be the LORD daily: even the GOD Who helpeth us, and poureth His benefits upon us.

20. He is our GOD, even the GOD of Whom cometh salvation : GOD is the LORD by Whom we escape death.

32. Sing unto GOD, O ye kingdoms of the earth : O sing praises unto the LORD. Amen.

GREENE.

445 CALKIN, L. kii 11, v. 19, 20*. 19. Amen.

* Ends here.

446

PSALM cxiii. 1. Praise the LORD, ye servants, O praise the Name of the LORD.

2. Blessed be the Name of the LORD from this time forth for evermore.

3. The LORD'S Name is praised from the rising up of the sun unto the going down of the same.

4. The LORD is high above all heathen, and His glory above the heavens.

5. Who is like unto the LORD our GOD, that hath His dwelling so high, and yet humbleth Himself to behold the things that are in heaven and earth ?

[6. He taketh up the simple out of the dust, and lifteth the poor out of the mire :

7. That He may set him with princes, even with the princes of his people.]

GREENE.

447 BOYCE, vv. 1–5, 1. Amen.
448 WHITFELD, vv. 1, 3, 5–7, 1. Hallelujah. Amen.

449

PSALM xxxviii. 1. Put me not to rebuke, O LORD, in Thine anger, neither chasten me in Thy heavy displeasure.

2. For Thine arrows stick fast in me, and Thy hand presseth me sore.

3. There is no health in my flesh, because of Thy displeasure, neither is there any rest in my bones, by reason of my sin.

4. For my wickednesses are gone over my head, and are like a sore burden too heavy for me to bear.

6. I am brought into so great trouble and misery, that I go mourning all the day long.

9. LORD, Thou knowest all my desire, and my groaning is not hid from Thee.

21. Forsake me not, O LORD my GOD; be not Thou far from me.

22. Haste Thee to help me, O LORD GOD of my salvation.

GREENE.

450 CROFT, vv. 1–3.
451 J. FOSTER, vv. 21, 22.

452

Isaiah xlii. 10. Sing unto the Lord a new song, ye that go down to the sea, the isles, and the inhabitants thereof.

12. Let them give glory unto the Lord, and declare His praise.

13. The Lord shall go forth in His might; He shall prevail against His enemies.

xliii. 16. The Lord, Who maketh a way in the sea, and a path in the mighty waters:

xl. 22. He sitteth upon the circle of the earth; He stretcheth out the heavens as a curtain.

St. Matthew viii. 27. He speaketh the word, and the winds and sea obey His voice.

Isaiah xli. 10. The Lord shall strengthen us with His arm, and uphold us with His right hand.

14. The Lord our God is with us; He is our Redeemer, even the Holy One of Israel. Hallelujah.

Greene.

453

Psalm xxiii. 1. The Lord is my Shepherd, therefore can I want nothing.

2 He shall feed me in green pastures, and lead me forth beside the waters of comfort.

3. He shall convert my soul, and bring me in the paths of righteousness, for His Name's sake.

4. Though I walk through the valley of the shadow of death, I will fear no evil, for Thou art with me.

cxlv. 14. The Lord upholdeth all such as fall, and lifteth up all those that are down.

15. The eyes of all wait upon Thee, O Lord, and Thou givest them their meat in due season.

16. Thou openest Thine hand, and fillest all things living with plenteousness.

21. My mouth shall speak the praise of the Lord, and let all flesh give thanks unto His Holy Name, for ever and ever.

Greene.

454

PSALM xxi. 1. The King shall rejoice in Thy strength, O LORD: exceeding glad shall he be of Thy salvation.

3. Thou hast prevented him with the blessings of goodness, and hast set a crown of pure gold upon his head.

[5. Glory and great worship hast Thou laid upon him.]

lxi. 6. O LORD, grant the king a long life, that his years may endure throughout all generations.

7. He shall dwell before GOD for ever: O prepare Thy loving mercy and faithfulness, that they may preserve him.

cxxxii. 19. As for his enemies, clothe them with shame: but upon himself let his crown flourish. Hallelujah. Amen.

lxxxix. 29. Let Thy mercy, O LORD, continue upon him for evermore, and Thy counsel stand fast with him.

30. Let his seed endure for ever, and his throne as the days of heaven.

c. 1. O be joyful in the LORD, all ye lands.

xcviii. 5. Sing, rejoice, and give thanks. Amen.

[cxviii. 24. This is the day which the LORD hath made: we will rejoice and be glad in it.

xx. 5. We will rejoice in Thy salvation, and triumph in the Name of the Lord our God.]

GREENE.

455 ATTWOOD, CHILD, CROFT, NARES, lxi. 6, 7; cxxxii. 19.
456 GREENE, lxi. 6, 7; lxxxix. 29, 30; cxxxii. 19; cxviii 24; xx. 5.
457 HANDEL, vv. 1, 5, 3. Hallelujah.
458 PURCELL, lxi. 6, 7; cxxxii. 19. Amen.

459

EXODUS xv. 2. The LORD is my strength and my song, and He is become my salvation. He is my GOD, I will exalt Him.

11. Who is like unto Thee, O LORD, among the gods? glorious in holiness, fearful in praises, doing wonders.

13. Thou in Thy mercy hast led forth Thy people which Thou hast redeemed: Thou hast guided them in Thy strength unto Thy holy habitation.

18. The LORD shall reign for ever and ever. Hallelujah. Amen.

GREENE.

460

PSALM cxlvii. 7. O sing unto the LORD with thanksgiving; sing praises upon the harp unto our GOD.

5. Great is our LORD, and great is His power; yea, and His wisdom is infinite.

6. The LORD setteth up the meek, and bringeth the ungodly down to the ground.

11. The LORD delighteth in them that fear Him, and put their trust in His mercy.

12. Praise the LORD, O Jerusalem; praise thy GOD, O Sion.

[13. For He hath made fast the bars of thy gates, and hath blessed thy children within thee.]

GREENE.

461 J. L. HOPKINS, vv. 7, 5, 11, 6, 12, 13. Amen.

462

PSALM lxv. 1. Thou, O GOD, art praised in Sion: unto Thee shall the vow be performed in Jerusalem.

2, 3. Thou that hearest the prayer, be merciful unto our sins.

4. Blessed is the man whom Thou choosest and receivest unto Thee; he shall dwell in Thy court, and shall be satisfied with the pleasures of Thy house, even of Thy holy temple.

5. Thou shalt shew us wonderful things, O GOD of our salvation: Thou art the hope of all the ends of the earth.

7. Thou stillest the raging of the sea, the noise of his waves, and the madness of the people.

9, 12. Thou visitest the earth and blessest it: Thou crownest the year with Thy goodness.

GREENE.

* ——* Sometimes sung as a separate Anthem.

463

PSALM cxliii. 1. Hear my prayer, O LORD, and consider my desire: hearken unto me for Thy truth and righteousness' sake.

2. Enter not into judgment with Thy servant, O LORD: for in Thy sight shall no man living be justified.

[3. For the enemy hath persecuted my soul; he hath smitten my life down to the ground : he hath laid me in the darkness, as the men that have been long dead.

4. Therefore is my spirit vexed within me, and my heart within me is desolate.

5. Yet do I remember the time past, I muse upon all Thy works : yea, I exercise myself in the works of Thy hands.]

7. Hear me, O Lord, and that soon, for my spirit waxeth faint : hide not Thy face from me, lest I be like unto them that go down into the pit.

8. O let me hear Thy loving-kindness betimes in the morning, for in Thee is my trust ; shew Thou me the way that I should walk in, for I lift up my soul unto Thee.

9. Deliver me, O Lord, from mine enemies, for I flee unto Thee to hide me.

10. Teach me to do the thing that pleaseth Thee, for Thou art my God; let Thy loving Spirit lead me forth into the land of righteousness.

11. Quicken me, O Lord, for Thy Name's sake, and for Thy righteousness' sake bring my soul out of trouble.

Travers.

464 Attwood, Whitfeld, v. 2.
465 Croft, Greene, vv. 1–5, 7.
466 Greene, vv. 1, 7, 8, 10, 11.
467 Miller, vv. 1, 2.
468 Purcell, vv. 7–11. Gloria Patri.
469 Stainer, vv. 9–11.
470 T. F. Walmisley, vv. 7, 8, 10. Amen.

471

COLLECT

For the Fifteenth Sunday after Trinity.

Keep, we beseech Thee, O Lord, Thy Church with Thy perpetual mercy : and because the frailty of man without Thee cannot but fall, keep us ever by Thy help from all things hurtful, and lead us to all things profitable to our salvation, through Jesus Christ our Lord. Amen.

Travers.

472 ·

PSALM xlii.   1. As pants the hart for cooling streams, so longs my soul for Thee, O GOD.

3. Tears are my daily food, while thus they say, Where is now thy GOD?

4. Now when I think thereupon, I pour out my heart by myself; for I went with the multitude, and brought them forth into the house of GOD.

5. In the voice of praise and thanksgiving, among such as keep holyday.

6. Why so full of grief, O my soul? why so disquieted within me?

7. Put your trust in GOD, for I will praise Him.

(Chandos Anthem, vi.)   HANDEL.

473

PSALM xxxviii.   21, 15. Forsake me not, O LORD my GOD, in Thee I put my trust.

lxxxvi.   4. Comfort the soul of Thy servant, for unto Thee I lift up my soul.

HANDEL.

474

EXODUS x.   21. He sent a thick darkness over all the land, even darkness which might be felt.

PSALM cv. 36, 37.   He smote all the first-born of Egypt, the chief of all their strength.

lxxviii.   53. But as for His people, He led them forth like sheep.   He brought them out with silver and gold : there was not one feeble person among their tribes.

(From " Israel in Egypt," Nos. 8–10.)   HANDEL.

475

EXODUS xv.   1. I will sing unto the LORD, for He hath triumphed gloriously : the horse and his rider hath He thrown into the sea.

(From " Israel in Egypt," No. 18.)   HANDEL.

476

EXODUS xv. 3. The LORD is a man of war : the LORD is His Name.

4. Pharaoh's chariots and his hosts hath He cast into the sea : His chosen captains also are drowned in the Red Sea.

(From " Israel in Egypt," No. 22.) HANDEL.

477

EXODUS xv. 17. Thou shalt bring them in, and plant them in the mountain of Thine inheritance, in the place, O LORD, which Thou hast made for Thee to dwell in, in the sanctuary, O LORD, which Thy hands have established.

18. The LORD shall reign for ever and ever.

19. For the horse of Pharaoh went in with his chariots and with his horsemen into the sea, and the LORD brought again the waters of the sea upon them ; but the children of Israel went on dry land in the midst of the sea.

18. The LORD shall reign for ever and ever.

(From " Israel in Egypt," Nos. 34–37.) HANDEL.

478

EXODUS xv. 20. And Miriam the prophetess, the sister of Aaron, took a timbrel in her hand, and all the women went out after her with timbrels and with dances. And Miriam answered them,

*21. Sing ye to the LORD, for He hath triumphed gloriously.

18. The LORD shall reign for ever and ever.

21. The horse and his rider hath He thrown into the sea.

18, 21. The LORD shall reign for ever and ever, for He hath triumphed gloriously ; the horse and his rider hath He thrown into the sea. I will sing unto the LORD, for He hath triumphed gloriously: the horse and his rider hath He thrown into the sea.*

(From " Israel in Egypt," Nos. 38, 39.) HANDEL.

* —— * Sometimes sung as a separate Anthem.

479

REVELATION iv. 8. Holy, Holy, LORD GOD ALMIGHTY, Who was, and is, and is to come.

xv. 4. Who shall not glorify Thy Name? for Thou art Holy: Thou only art the LORD.

xix. 6. Hallelujah; for the LORD GOD Omnipotent reigneth.

xi. 15. The kingdom of this world is become the Kingdom of our LORD and of His CHRIST, and He shall reign for ever and ever.

xix. 16. King of Kings, and LORD of Lords. Hallelujah.

HANDEL.

480

ISAIAH lii. 7. How beautiful are the feet of him that bringeth good tidings of salvation; that saith unto Zion, Thy GOD reigneth!

9. Break forth into joy.

(*From " The Messiah,"* Appendix.) HANDEL.

481

PSALM xiii.

How long wilt Thou forget me, LORD?
    Must I for ever mourn?
How long wilt Thou withdraw from me,
    Oh! never to return?

How long shall anxious thoughts my soul,
    And grief my heart oppress?
How long mine enemies insult,
    And I have no redress?

O hear, and to my longing eyes
    Re fore Thy wonted light:
O hear end save me, lest I sleep
    In everlasting night.   HANDEL.

482

PSALM viii.

How excellent Thy Name, O LORD,
In all the world is known.
Above all heavens, O King ador'd,
How hast Thou set Thy glorious Throne.

O sing ye praises to great JEHOVAH ; His power among
the nations, and wondrous works proclaim.

The great JEHOVAH is our awful theme,
Sublime in majesty, in power supreme.
Hallelujah.

(*From " Saul."*)   HANDEL.

483

ST. MATTHEW ii. 1. In the days of Herod the king,
behold, there came wise men from the east to Jerusalem,

2. Saying, Where is He that is born King of the Jews?
for we have seen His star in the east, and have come to
worship Him.

There beneath a lowly shed
They found the Heavenly Infant laid,
Their richest gifts before Him spread,
And humblest adoration paid.

*xx. 18. 19. When the time drew near, that all things
that were written concerning the Son of Man should be
accomplished, that He should be delivered unto the
Gentiles, and be mocked and spit upon, and that they
should scourge Him and put Him to death, and on the
third day He should rise again, then Jesus went up to
Jerusalem.

xxi. 8. And a very great multitude spread their
garments in the way, others cut down branches from the
trees, and spread them in the way.

9. And the multitude that went before, and that
followed after, cried, saying, Hosanna to the Son of
David : Blessed is He that cometh in the Name of the
LORD ; Hosanna in the highest.*

HANDEL.

—— Sometimes sung as a separate Anthem.

484

No. 1

Psalm xi. 1. In the Lord put I my trust: how say
ye then to my soul, she shall flee as a bird unto the hill?

No. 2

    ix.   9. God is a constant sure defence
            Against oppressing rage;
            As troubles rise His needful aids
            In our behalf èngage.

No. 3

    xi.   2. Behold, the wicked bend their bow,
            And ready fix their dart,
            Lurking in ambush to destroy
            The man of upright heart.

No. 4

    xii.   5. But God, Who hears the suff'ring poor,
            And their oppression knows,
            Will soon arise, and give them rest,
            In spite of all their foes.

No. 5

    xi.   6. Snares, fire, and brimstone, on their heads
            Shall in one tempest shower;
            This dreadful mixture His revenge
            Into their cup shall pour.

No. 6

       7. The righteous Lord will righteous deeds
            With signal favour grace,
            And to the upright man disclose
            The brightness of His face.

No. 7

    xiii.   6. Then shall my song, with praise inspir'd,
            To Thee my God ascend,
            Who to Thy servants in distress
            Such bounty didst extend.

                                   Handel.

485

Psalm lxviii. 1. Let God arise, and let His enemies be scattered : let them also that hate Him flee before Him.

2. Like as the smoke vanisheth, so shalt Thou drive them away : and like as wax melteth at the fire, so let the ungodly perish at the presence of God.

3. Let the righteous be glad and rejoice before God, let them also be merry and joyful.

4. O sing unto God, and sing praises unto His Name.

19. Praised be the Lord.

lxxvi. 6. At Thy rebuke, O God, both the chariot and horse are fallen.

lxviii. 35. Blessed be God. Hallelujah.

(*Chandos Anthem*, xi.) Handel.

486

Let the bright Seraphim, in burning row,
Their loud, uplifted angel-trumpets blow.
Let the Cherubic Host, in tuneful choirs,
Touch their immortal harps with golden wires.
*Let their celestial concerts all unite
Ever to sound His praise in endless blaze of light.*

(*From " Samson,"* Nos. 95, 96.) Handel.

* ——— * Sometimes sung as a separate Anthem.

487

Psalm lxxxix. 14. Let Thy hand be strengthened, and Thy right hand be exalted.

15. Let justice and judgment be the preparation of Thy seat, let mercy and truth go before Thy face. Hallelujah. Amen.

Handel.

488

"THE MESSIAH."

No. 1 Overture.

No. 2

ISAIAH xl. 1. Comfort ye, comfort ye My people, saith your GOD.

2. Speak ye comfortably to Jerusalem, and cry unto her, that her warfare is accomplished, that her iniquity is pardoned.

3. The voice of him that crieth in the wilderness, Prepare ye the way of the LORD, make straight in the desert a highway for our GOD.

No. 3

4. Every valley shall be exalted, and every mountain and hill made low, the crooked straight, and the rough places plain.

No. 4

ISAIAH xl. 5. And the glory of the LORD shall be revealed, and all flesh shall see it together, for the mouth of the LORD hath spoken it.

489

No. 5

HAGGAI ii. 6, 7. Thus saith the LORD of Hosts; yet once, a little while, and I will shake the heavens, and the earth, the sea, and the dry land; and I will shake all nations, and the desire of all nations shall come.

MALACHI iii. 1. The LORD, Whom ye seek, shall suddenly come to His temple, even the messenger of the covenant, Whom ye delight in: behold, He shall come, saith the LORD of Hosts.

No. 6

2. But who may abide the day of His coming? and who shall stand when He appeareth? for He is like a refiner's fire.

No. 7

, And He . h purify the sons of Levi, that they may offer unto the Lord an offering in righteousness.

490

No. 8

ISAIAH vii. 14. Behold a virgin shall conceive, and bear a son, and shall call His name Emmanuel.
ST. MATTHEW i. 23. " GOD with us."

No. 9

ISAIAH xl. 9. O thou that tellest good tidings to Zion, get thee up into the high mountain : O thou that tellest good tidings to Jerusalem, lift up thy voice with strength : lift it up, be not afraid : say unto the cities of Judah, Behold your GOD !

lx. 1. O thou that tellest good tidings to Zion, arise, shine, for thy light is come : and the glory of the LORD is risen upon thee.

O thou that tellest good tidings to Zion, arise, say unto the cities of Judah, Behold your GOD ! Behold, the glory of the LORD is risen upon Thee.

* —— * Sometimes sung as a separate Anthem.

491

No. 10

ISAIAH lx. 2, 3. For behold, darkness shall cover the earth, and gross darkness the people : but the LORD shall arise upon thee, and His glory shall be seen upon thee. And the Gentiles shall come to thy light, and kings to the brightness of thy rising.

No. 11

ix. 2. The people that walked in darkness have seen a great light : and they that dwell in the land of the shadow of death, upon them hath the light shined.

No. 12

6. For unto us a Child is born, unto us a Son is given : and the government shall be upon His shoulder; and His Name shall be called Wonderful, Counsellor, The Mighty God, The Everlasting Father, The Prince of Peace.

492

No. 13 Pastoral Symphony.

No. 14

St. Luke ii. 8. There were shepherds abiding in the field, keeping watch over their flocks by night,

9. And lo, the angel of the Lord came upon them, and the glory of the Lord shone round about them, and they were sore afraid.

No. 15

10. And the angel said unto them, Fear not; for, behold, I bring you glad tidings of great joy, which shall be to all people.

11. For unto you is born this day, in the city of David, a Saviour, Which is Christ the Lord.

No. 16

13. And suddenly there was with the angel a multitude of the heavenly host, praising God, and saying,

No. 17

14. Glory to God in the highest, and peace on earth, good-will towards men.

493

No. 18

Zechariah ix. 9, 10. Rejoice greatly, O daughter of Zion! Shout, O daughter of Jerusalem! Behold, thy King cometh unto thee! He is the righteous Saviour, and He shall speak peace unto the heathen.

494

No. 19

Isaiah xxxv. 5. Then shall the eyes of the blind be opened, and the ears of the deaf not stopped

6. Then shall the lame man leap as a hart, and the tongue of the dumb shall sing.

No. 20

xl. 11. He shall feed His flock like a shepherd, and He shall gather the lambs with His arm, and carry them in His bosom, and gently lead those that are with young.

St. Matthew xi. 28. Come unto Him, all ye that labour, ye that are heavy laden, and He will give you rest.

29. Take His yoke upon you, and learn of Him, for He is meek and lowly of heart, and ye shall find rest unto your souls.

No. 21

30. His yoke is easy, and His burden is light.

495

Part II.—No. 22

St. John i. 29. Behold the Lamb of God that taketh away the sins of the world.

No. 23

Isaiah liii. 3. He was despised and rejected of men, a man of sorrows, and acquainted with grief.

*1. 6. He gave His back to the smiters, and His cheeks to them that plucked off the hair: He hid not His face from shame and spitting.

* This verse is usually omitted.

No. 24

Isaiah liii. 4. Surely He hath borne our griefs, and carried our sorrows.

5. He was wounded for our transgressions, He was bruised for our iniquities, the chastisement of our peace was upon Him;

No. 25

And with His stripes we are healed.

No. 26

6. All we like sheep have gone astray; we have turned every one to his own way, and the Lord hath laid on Him the iniquity of us all.

496

No. 27

PSALM xxii. 7. All they that see Him, laugh Him to scorn; they shoot out their lips, and shake their heads, saying:

No. 28

8. He trusted in GOD that He would deliver Him; let Him deliver Him, if He delight in Him.

497

No. 29

PSALM lxix. 21. Thy rebuke hath broken His heart; He is full of heaviness; He looked for some to have pity on Him, but there was no man, neither found He any to comfort Him.

No. 30

LAMENTATIONS i. 12. Behold, and see if there be any sorrow like unto His sorrow.

No. 31

ISAIAH liii. 8. He was cut off out of the land of the living: for the transgressions of Thy people was He stricken.

No. 32

PSALM xvi. 11. But Thou didst not leave His soul in hell, nor didst Thou suffer Thy Holy One to see corruption.

No. 33

PSALM xxiv. 7. Lift up your heads, O ye gates, and be ye lift up, ye everlasting doors, and the King of Glory shall come in.

8. Who is the King of Glory? The LORD strong and mighty, the LORD mighty in battle.

9. Lift up your heads, O ye gates, and be ye lift up, ye everlasting doors, and the King of Glory shall come in.

10. Who is the King of Glory? The Lord of Hosts, He is the King of Glory.

498

No. 34

HEBREWS i. 5. Unto which of the angels said He at any time, Thou art My Son, this day have I begotten Thee?

No. 35

6. Let all the angels of GOD worship Him.

499

No. 36

PSALM lxviii. 18. Thou art gone up on high, Thou hast led captivity captive, and received gifts for men; yea, even for Thine enemies, that the LORD GOD might dwell among them.

No. 37

PSALM lxviii. 11. The LORD gave the word; great was the company of the preachers.

No. 38

ROMANS x. 15. How beautiful are the feet of them that preach the gospel of peace, and bring glad tidings of good things!

No. 39

ROMANS x. 18. Their sound is gone out into all lands, and their words unto the ends of the world.

500

No. 40

PSALM ii. 1. Why do the nations so furiously rage together? and why do the people imagine a vain thing?

2. The kings of the earth rise up, and the rulers take counsel together against the LORD, and against His Anointed.

No. 41

3. Let us break their bonds asunder, and cast away their yokes from us.

Novello's Collection. F

No. 42

4. He that dwelleth in heaven shall laugh them to scorn ; the LORD shall have them in derision.   .

No. 43

9. Thou shalt break them with a rod of iron ; Thou shalt dash them in pieces like a potter's vessel.

No. 44

REVELATION xix. 6. Hallelujah ; for the LORD GOD Omnipotent reigneth.

xi. 15. The kingdom of this world is become the Kingdom of our LORD and of HIS CHRIST ; and He shall reign for ever and ever.

xix. 16. King of Kings, and LORD of Lords. Hallelujah.

501

No. 45

JOB xix. 25. I know that my Redeemer liveth, and that He shall stand at the latter day upon the earth :

26. And though worms destroy this body, yet in my flesh shall I see GOD.

1 CORINTHIANS xv. 20. For now is CHRIST risen from the dead, the firstfruits of them that sleep.

Nos. 46–49

21. Since by man came death, by man came also the resurrection of the dead.

22. For as in Adam all die, even so in CHRIST shall all be made alive.

502

No. 50

1 CORINTHIANS xv. 51, 52. Behold, I shew you a mystery ; we shall not all sleep, but we shall all be changed in a moment, in the twinkling of an eye, at the last trumpet.

No. 51

52. The trumpet shall sound, and the dead shall be raised incorruptible, and we shall be changed.

53. For this corruptible must put on incorruption, and this mortal must put on immortality.

* This verse is usually omitted.

No. 52

54. Then shall be brought to pass the saying that is written, Death is swallowed up in victory.

No. 53

1 CORINTHIANS xv. 55. O death, where is thy sting? O grave, where is thy victory?

56. The sting of death is sin, and the strength of sin is the law.

No. 54

57. But thanks be to GOD, Who giveth us the victory through our LORD JESUS CHRIST.

503

No. 55

ROMANS viii. 31. If GOD be for us, who can be against us?

33. Who shall lay anything to the charge of GOD's elect? It is GOD that justifieth. Who is he that condemneth? It is CHRIST that died, yea rather, that is risen again, Who is at the right hand of GOD, Who makes intercession for us.

Nos. 56-57

REVELATION v. 12. Worthy is the Lamb that was slain, and hath redeemed us to GOD by His Blood, to receive power, and riches, and wisdom, and strength, and honour, and glory, and blessing.

13. Blessing and honour, glory and power, be unto Him that sitteth upon the Throne, and unto the Lamb, for ever and ever. Amen.

HANDEL.

504

PSALM lxxxix.　1. My song shall be alway of the loving-kindness of the LORD : with my mouth will I ever be shewing forth Thy truth, from one generation to another.

5. [O LORD,] the very heavens shall praise Thy wondrous works, and Thy truth in the congregation of the saints.

6. For who is he among the clouds that shall be compared unto the LORD ?

7. And what is he among the Gods that shall be like unto the LORD ?

8. GOD is very greatly to be feared in the council of the saints, and to be had in reverence of all them that are round about Him.

9. O LORD GOD of Hosts, who is like unto Thee ? Thy truth, most mighty LORD, is on every side.

10. Thou rulest the raging of the sea : Thou stillest the waves thereof when they arise.

[11. Thou hast subdued Egypt, and destroyed it; Thou hast scattered Thine enemies abroad with Thy mighty arm.]

12. The heavens are Thine, [the earth also is Thine;] Thou hast laid the foundation of the round world, [and all that therein is.

14. Thou hast a mighty arm; strong is Thy hand, and high is Thy right hand.]

15. Righteousness and equity are the habitation of Thy seat ; mercy and truth shall go before Thy face.

16. Blessed is the people, O LORD, that can rejoice in Thee ; they shall walk in the light of Thy countenance.

[17. Their delight shall be daily in Thy Name, and in Thy righteousness shall they make their boast.]

18. [For] Thou art the glory of their strength, [and in Thy loving-kindness Thou shalt lift up our horns.

19. For the LORD is our defence, the Holy One of Israel is our King.]　Hallelujah.

(Chandos Anthem, vii.)　HANDEL.

505 CR-FI, vv. 16 19.

506 GIIINF. vv 9 12.　Amen.

507 PERUIIT. vv. 1, 5 10 14, 15.　Hallelujah.

508

PSALM c. 1. O be joyful in the LORD, all ye lands: serve the LORD with gladness, and come before His presence with a song.

2. Be ye sure that the LORD He is GOD: it is He that hath made us, and not we ourselves; we are His people, and the sheep of His pasture.

3. O go your way into His gates with thanksgiving, and into His courts with praise: be thankful unto Him, and speak good of His Name.

4. For the LORD is gracious, His mercy is everlasting, and His truth endureth from generation to generation.

Glory be to the Father, &c.

[To FATHER, SON, and HOLY GHOST,
The GOD Whom heaven and earth adore,
From men and from the Angel-host
Be praise and glory evermore. Amen.]

HANDEL (*Chandos Anthem*, ;.), MARTIN, PROUT.

509

PSALM xlv. 1. My heart is inditing of a good matter: I speak of the things which I have made unto the king.

10. King's daughters were among thy honourable women.

10, 12. Upon thy right hand did stand the queen in vesture of gold, and the king shall have pleasure in thy beauty.

ISAIAH xlix. 23. Kings shall be thy nursing fathers, and queens thy nursing mothers.

HANDEL.

510

Sing unto GOD, and high affections raise,
To crown this conquest with unmeasured praise.

(*From* "*Judas Maccabæus*," No. 60.) HANDEL.

511

O lovely peace, with plenty crown'd,
Come spread thy blessings all around,
Let fleecy flocks the hills adorn,
And valleys smile with wavy corn,

To our great GOD be all the honour giv'n,
That grateful hearts can send from earth to heav'n.

Rejoice, O Judah, and in songs divine,
With Cherubin and Seraphin harmonious join.
HALLELUJAH !   AMEN.

(*From "Judas Maccabæus."*)   HANDEL.

512

PSALM XCV.   1. O come, let us sing unto the LORD : let us heartily rejoice in the strength of our salvation.

2. Let us come before His presence with thanksgiving, and shew ourselves glad in Him with psalms.

3. For the LORD is a great GOD, and a great King above all gods.

6. O come, let us worship, and fall down, and kneel before the LORD our Maker.

4. In His hands are all the corners of the earth, and the strength of the hills is His also.

7. For He is the LORD our GOD : and we are the people of His pasture, and the sheep of His hand.

xcvi.   6. Glory and worship are before Him : power and honour are in His sanctuary.

10. Tell it out among the heathen that the LORD is King, and that He made the world so fast, that it cannot be moved.

xcix.   9. O magnify the LORD, and worship Him upon His holy hill, for the LORD our GOD is holy.

xcvii.   10. The LORD preserveth the souls of His saints; He shall deliver them from the hand of the ungodly.

ciii.   11. For look, as high as the heaven is in comparison of the earth, so great is His mercy toward them that fear Him.

xcvii.   11, 12. There is sprung up a light for the righteous, and joyful gladness for such as are true-hearted.   Rejoice in the LORD, ye righteous.

(*Chandos Anthem*, viii.)   HANDEL.

513 AYRTON, vv. 1, 3.
514 AYRTON, vv. 6, 3.
515 NARES, vv. 1. 3, 6. 4.
516 PALESTRINA, vv. 6 (*Come, let us worship*), 7.

517

PSALM CXXXV. **No. 1**

1. O praise the LORD with one consent,
   And magnify His Name;
   Let all the servants of the LORD
   His worthy praise proclaim.

No. 2

2. Praise Him, all ye that in His house
   Attend with constant care;
   With those that to His utmost court
   With humble zeal repair.

No. 3

3. For this our truest interest is,
   Glad hymns of praise to sing,
   And with loud songs to bless His Name,
   A most delightful thing.

No. 4

5. That GOD is great we often have
   By glad experience found;
   And seen how He, with wondrous pow'r,
   Above all gods is crown'd.

No. 5

cxvii. 1. With cheerful notes let all the earth
   To Heav'n their voices raise;
   Let all, inspir'd with godly mirth,
   Sing solemn hymns of praise.

No. 6

2. GOD's tender mercy knows no bounds,
   His truth shall ne'er decay;
   Then let the willing nations round
   Their grateful tribute pay.

No. 7

cxlviii. 1, 2. Ye boundless realms of joy,
   Exalt your Maker's fame;
   His praise your song employ,
   Above the starry frame.

No. 8

Your voices raise, ye Cherubin and Seraphin,
   To sing His praise. Hallelujah.

(*Chandos Anthem, IX.)* HANDEL.

518

PSALM xxvii. 1. The LORD is my light, and my salvation ; whom then shall I fear ? The LORD is the strength of my life, of whom then shall I be afraid ?

3. Though a host of men were laid against me, yet shall my heart not be afraid : though there rose up war against me, yet will I put my trust in Him.

4. One thing have I desired of the LORD, which I will require, that I may dwell in the house of the LORD all the days of my life, to behold the fair beauty of the LORD, and to visit His temple.

7. I will offer in His dwelling an oblation with great gladness; I will sing and speak praises unto the LORD.

xviii. 31. For who is GOD, but the LORD ? or who hath any strength, except the LORD ?

7. The earth trembled and quaked; the very foundations also of the hills shook, and were removed.

13, 14. He cast forth lightnings, and gave His thunder, and destroyed them.

xx. 8. They are brought down, and fallen, but we are risen.

xxxiv. 3. O praise the LORD with me, and let us magnify His Name together.

xxviii. 8. The LORD is my strength, and my shield, my heart hath trusted in Him, and I am helped : therefore my heart danceth for joy, and in my song will I praise Him.

xxix. 4, 9. It is the LORD, that ruleth the sea. The LORD sitteth above the water flood, and the LORD remaineth a King for ever.

xxx. 4. Sing praises unto the LORD, O ye saints of His, and give thanks unto Him for a remembrance of His holiness.

xlv. 18. I will remember Thy Name from one generation to another : therefore shall the people give thanks unto Thee, world without end. Amen.

(*Chandos Anthem*, x.) HANDEL.

519

ISAIAH xlv. 1 b. Thus saith the LORD to Cyrus His anointed, whose right hand I have holden to subdue nations before him : I will go before thee, to loose the strong-knit loins of mighty kings, make straight the crooked places, break in pieces the gates of solid brass, and cut in sunder the bars of iron, for My servant's sake, Israel My chosen. Though thou hast not known Me, I have surnamed thee, I have girded thee, that from the rising to the setting sun, the nations may confess I am the LORD: there is none else: there is no GOD beside Me.

xliv. 28. Thou shalt perform My pleasure to Jerusalem, saying, "Thou shalt be built," and to the Temple, "Thy razed foundation shall again be laid."

23. Sing, O ye heavens, for the LORD hath done it. Earth, from thy centre shout. Break forth, ye mountains, into songs of joy, O forest, and each tree therein, for the LORD hath done it. JEHOVAH hath redeemed Jacob, and glorified Himself in Israel. Hallelujah. Amen.

(*From "Belshazzar,"* Nos. 20, 21.) HANDEL.

—— Sometimes sung as a separate Anthem.

520

PSALM ciii. 20. O praise the LORD, ye angels of His, ye that excel in strength, ye that fulfil His commandment, and hearken to the voice of His words.

21. O praise the LORD, all ye His hosts, ye servants of His that do His pleasure.

11. For as the heaven is high above the earth, so great is His mercy also toward them that fear Him.

13. Like as a father pitieth his own children, even so is the LORD merciful unto them that fear Him.

17. The merciful goodness of the LORD endureth for ever upon them that fear Him, and His righteousness upon children's children.

cxv. 12. The LORD hath been mindful of us, and He shall bless us: even He shall bless the house of Israel, He shall bless the house of Aaron.

cxlv. 21. My mouth shall speak the praise of the LORD: and let all flesh give thanks unto His holy Name for ever and ever. Hallelujah. Amen.

(*Chandos Anthem,* xii.) HANDEL.

521

O Lord, we trust alone in Thee.

HANDEL.

522

No. 1

LAMENTATIONS i. 4. The ways of Zion do mourn, and she is in bitterness : all her people sigh, and hang down their heads to the ground.

2 SAMUEL i. 27. How are the mighty fallen ! he that was great among the nations and prince of the provinces. How are the mighty fallen !

No. 2

JOB xxix. 14. He put on righteousness, and it clothed him : his judgment was a robe and a diadem.

No. 3

JOB xxix. 11. When the ear heard him, then it blessed him : and when the eye saw him, it gave witness of him.

No. 4

2 SAMUEL i. 27. How are the mighty fallen ! he that was great among the nations and prince of the provinces.

No. 5

JOB xxix. 12. He delivered the poor that cried : the fatherless, and him that had no helper.

COLOSSIANS iii. 12. Kindness, meekness, and comfort were in his tongue.

EPHESIANS iv. 8. If there was any virtue, and if there was any praise, he thought on those things.

No. 6

2 SAMUEL i. 27. How are the mighty fallen ! he that was great among the nations and prince of the provinces.

No. 7

PSALM cxii. 6. The righteous shall be had in everlasting remembrance.

DANIEL xii. 3. And the wise will shine as the brightness of the firmament.

Nos. 8-11

ECCLESIASTICUS xliv. 14. Their bodies are buried in peace, but their name liveth for evermore.

Nos. 12, 13

15. The people will tell of their wisdom, and the congregation will shew forth their praise.

WISDOM v. 15. Their reward also is with the LORD, and the care of them is with the Most High.

No. 14

16. They shall receive a glorious kingdom, and a beautiful crown from the LORD's hand. Hallelujah.

PSALM ciii. 17. The merciful goodness of the LORD endureth for ever on them that fear Him: and His righteousness upon children's children.

HANDEL.

523

Waft her, angels, through the skies,
Far above yon azure plain ;
Glorious there, like you to rise,
There, like you, for ever reign.
*Theme sublime of endless praise,
Just and righteous are Thy ways ;
And Thy mercies still endure
Ever faithful, ever sure.*
(*From " Jephtha,"* Nos. 53, 61.) HANDEL.
—— Sometimes sung as a separate Anthem.

524

GENESIS i. 2. When the earth was without form and void, and when darkness covered the face of the deep, the Spirit of GOD moved upon the face of the waters.

3. Let there be light, the Almighty said ; and light was over all.

*O first-created beam ! and Thou, great Word,
Let there be light ! and light was over all !
One heavenly blaze shone round this earthly ball.
To Thy dark servant life by light afford.
From " Samson," No. 16. HANDEL.
—— Sometimes sung as a separate Anthem.

525

I KINGS i. 39, 40. Zadok the priest, and Nathan the prophet, anointed Solomon king. And all the people rejoiced, and said, GOD save the king. Long live the king. May the king live for ever. Hallelujah. Amen.

HANDEL.

526

The LORD that wept for sorrow
  O'er Zion's coming doom ;
Foreknowing of the morrow,
  To break in wrath and gloom ;
What power shall e'er enclose Him
  Within the depths of hell ?
The foes that dare oppose Him,
  Shall they at last prevail ?

(*From " The Passion,"* No. 1.) GRAUN.

527

His spirit is faint. He is fearful, and very heavy, and His soul is full of sorrow ; for darkness is closing round about Him.

(*From " The Passion,"* No. 2.) GRAUN.

528

Whom have I, LORD, but Thee alone,
To hear and heed my dying moan,
  For light, and strength, and consolation ?
Who shall my parting soul receive,
When I am called this world to leave,
  And yield to death's just condemnation ;
When perish wonted pow'r and thought,
If Thou, my GOD, receive me not ?

(*From " The Passion,"* No. 4.) GRAUN.

529

Sadly bendeth earthward our afflicted spirit. O sorrow! For our sins are many, their heavy burden is grievous.

(*From " The Passion,"* No. 7.) GRAUN.

530

From sin's dread power I fain would fly,
And to my LORD betake me ;
When I for help and counsel cry,
Thou, GOD, wilt not forsake me :
Thy gracious Spirit Thou wilt send,
My faltering heart toward Thee to bend,
And wholly Thine to make me.

(From " The Passion," No. 8.) GRAUN.

531

CHRIST unto us hath left an example, that we His foot-steps should follow.

(From " The Passion," No. 10.) GRAUN.

532

To utmost heights of faith I would be rising ;
Both shame and torment, e'en the cross despising.
Not persecution, e'en though death await me,
Shall e'er affright me.

(From " The Passion," No. 11.) GRAUN.

533

Sing and be joyful, ye righteous, for the Word of GOD is unfailing for evermore. As for His commandments, they stand for ever sure.

(From " The Passion," No. 14.) GRAUN.

534

How glorious is the home above,
By love prepared for those that love !
Yet man might ne'er attain it.
O JESU, SAVIOUR, LORD of Lords,
Thy love that gift to me accords,
O send me grace to gain it !
O LORD, grant me once to gaze on heavenly gladness,
Life to brighten, and mine exiled heart to lighten.

(From " The Passion," No. 15.) GRAUN.

535

Behold us here, repentant sinners, O JESUS, lowly laid; with tears the very dust we moisten—the sacred dust that drank Thy Blood. O JESUS, our sighs and tears regard. Thou SAVIOUR, Who makest reconciliation, Who by Thy precious death hast sealed the truth of GOD'S eternal laws, we thank Thee, and adore, and offer Thee ourselves.

(From " The Passion," No. 18.) GRAUN.

536

PSALM lv. 1. Hear my prayer, O GOD, and hide not Thyself from my petition.

2. Take heed unto me and hear me, how I mourn in my prayer, and am vexed.

3. The enemy crieth so, and the ungodly cometh on so fast; for they are minded to do me some mischief, so maliciously are they set against me.

4. My heart is disquieted within me, and the fear of death is fallen upon me.

[5. Fearfulness and trembling are come upon me, and an horrible dread hath overwhelmed me.]

6. And I said, O that I had wings like a dove, then would I flee away and be at rest.

HENLEY.

537 BATTEN, KENT, STROUD, vv. 1, 2, 4, 6.
538 NORRIS, vv. 1, 2, 5, 3, 6.

539

PSALM ci. 1. My song shall be of mercy and judgment; unto Thee, O LORD, will I sing.

2. O let me have understanding in the way of godliness.

3. When wilt Thou come unto me? I will walk in my house with a perfect heart.

cviii. 3. I will give thanks unto Thee, O LORD, among the people; I will sing praises unto Thee among the nations.

4. For Thy mercy is greater than the heavens, and Thy truth reacheth unto the clouds.

Glory be to the Father, &c.

KENT.

540 HILES,

541

ISAIAH xlix. 13. Sing, O [ye] heavens, and be joyful, O earth : break forth into singing, O mountains : for the LORD hath comforted His people, and will have mercy on His afflicted.

14. Let not Sion say, The LORD hath forsaken me, and the LORD hath forgotten me.

lv. 7. Return unto the LORD, and He will have mercy upon you ; and to your GOD, for He will abundantly pardon.

xxx. 18. Therefore will the LORD wait that He may be gracious unto you, and therefore will He be exalted, that He may have mercy upon you : for the LORD is a GOD of judgment : blessed are they that wait for His salvation.

xlix. 13. Break forth into singing, O mountains, for the LORD hath comforted His people, and will have mercy on His afflicted.

KENT.

542 R. WOODWARD, v. 13 (*Sing, O ye heavens*).

543

PSALM xxiii. 1. The LORD is my shepherd, therefore can I want nothing.

2. He shall feed me in a green pasture, and lead me forth beside the waters of comfort.

3. He shall convert my soul, and lead me forth in the paths of righteousness, for His Name's sake.

4. Yea, though I walk through the valley of the shadow of death, I will fear no evil, for Thou art with me ; Thy rod and Thy staff comfort me.

5. Thou shalt prepare a table before me, against them that trouble me : Thou hast anointed my head with oil, and my cup shall be full.

6. But Thy loving-kindness and mercy shall follow me all the days of my life, and I will dwell in the house of the LORD for ever and ever. Amen.

BUNNETT, DYKES, GAUL, KENT, OUSELEY, STANFORD.

544 SHAW, vv. 1-4.
545 ALLEN, STEVENSON, S. S. WESLEY, vv. 1 4, 6.
546 TINNEY, vv. 1, 2.

547

St. Matthew xxv. 31. When the Son of Man shall come in His glory, and all the holy Angels with Him, then shall He sit upon the throne of His glory.

32. Before Him shall be gathered all nations, and He shall separate them one from another.

34. He shall say to them on His right hand, Come, ye blessed of My Father, inherit the Kingdom prepared for you from the foundation of the world.

35. For I was hungry, and ye gave Me meat; I was thirsty, and ye gave Me drink; I was a stranger, and ye took Me in;

36. Naked, and ye clothed Me; I was sick, and ye visited Me; I was in prison, and ye came unto Me.

37. Lord, when saw we Thee an hungered, and fed Thee? or thirsty, and gave Thee drink?

38. When saw we Thee a stranger, and took Thee in? naked, and clothed Thee?

39. Or when saw we Thee sick, or in prison, and came unto Thee?

40. Verily I say unto you, Inasmuch as ye have done it unto one of the least of these My brethren, ye have done it unto Me.

46. The righteous shall go into life eternal. Hallelujah.

Kent.

548

Isaiah lxiii. 1. Who is this that cometh from Edom, with dyed garments from Bozrah? This that is glorious in His apparel, travelling in the greatness of His strength? I that speak in righteousness, mighty to save.

2. Wherefore art Thou red in Thine apparel, and Thy garments like Him that treadeth in the wine-fat?

3. I have trodden the wine-press alone, and of the people there was none with Me: for I will tread them in Mine anger, [and trample them in My fury;] and their blood shall be sprinkled upon my garments, [and I will stain all My raiment.]

4. For the day of vengeance is in Mine heart, and the year of My redeemed is come.

5. And I looked, and there was none to help; and I wondered there was none to uphold: therefore Mine own arm brought salvation [unto Me], and My fury it upheld Me.

6. And I will tread down the people in Mine anger, [and trample them in My fury,] and I will bring down their strength to the earth.

7. I will mention the loving-kindness of the LORD, and the praises of the LORD, and His great goodness towards the house of Israel, which He hath bestowed upon them according to His mercies.

9. For the angel of His presence saved them : in His love and in His pity He redeemed them ; and He bare them, and carried them all the days of old.

*15. Look down from Heaven, and behold from the habitation of Thy holiness and Thy glory.

16. For Thou, O LORD, art our Father, our Redeemer; Thy Name is from everlasting.*

KENT.

—— Sometimes sung as a separate Anthem.
549 OAKELEY, vv. 1-6.

550

PSALM cxxi.

Lo! from the hills my help descends,
  To them I lift mine eyes;
My strength on Him alone depends
  Who form'd the earth and skies.
He, ever watchful, ever nigh,
  Forbids my feet to slide;
Nor sleep nor slumber seals the eye
  Of Israel's guard and guide.

He, at thy hand, array'd in might,
  His shield shall o'er thee spread;
Nor sun by day, nor moon by night,
  Shall hurt thy favour'd head.
Safe shalt thou go, and safe return,
  While He thy life defends,
Whose eyes thy every step discern,
  Whose mercy never ends.

W. HAYES.

551

PSALM cxxxviii. 1. I will give thanks unto Thee, O LORD, with my whole heart, even before the gods will I sing praises unto Thee.

2. I will worship toward Thy holy temple, and praise Thy Name, because of Thy loving-kindness and truth; * for Thou hast magnified Thy Name and Thy word above all things.

[3. When I called upon Thee, Thou heardest me, and enduedst my soul with much strength.]

4. All the kings of the earth shall praise Thee, O LORD: for they have heard the words of Thy mouth.

[5. Yea, they shall sing in the ways of the LORD, that great is the glory of the LORD.

6. For though the LORD be high, yet hath He respect unto the lowly: but He beholdeth the proud afar off.]

7. Though I walk in the midst of trouble, yet shalt Thou refresh me: Thou shalt stretch forth Thy hand upon the furiousness of mine enemies, and Thy right hand shall save me.

8. The LORD shall make good His loving-kindness toward me: yea, Thy mercy, O LORD, endureth for ever; * despise not then the works of Thine own hands. Amen.

W. HAYES.

552 GREENE, vv. 1–3, 6, 7, 4, 5.
553 LONGHURST, vv 1–5, 8.* Amen.
554 OUSELEY, vv. 1, 2.* Hallelujah. Amen.

* Ends here.

555

PSALM l. 1. The LORD, even the most mighty GOD, hath spoken, and called the world, from the rising up of the sun, unto the going down thereof.

2. Out of Sion hath GOD appeared in perfect beauty.

3. Our GOD shall come, and shall not keep silence; there shall go before Him a consuming fire, and a mighty tempest shall be stirred up round about Him.

4. He shall call the heaven from above, and the earth, that He may judge His people.

6. And the heavens shall declare His righteousness; for GOD is Judge Himself

5. Gather My saints together unto Me, those that have made a covenant with Me with sacrifice.

14. Offer unto God thanksgiving, and pay thy vows unto the Most Highest.

15. And call upon Me in the time of trouble: so will I hear thee, and thou shalt praise Me.

[xcviii. 10. With righteousness shall He judge the world, and the people with equity.]

From the Gloria in Excelsis.

Glory be to God on high, and in earth peace, good will towards men. We praise Thee, we bless Thee, we worship Thee, we glorify Thee, we give thanks to Thee for Thy great glory, O Lord God, heavenly King, God the Father Almighty.

W. Hayes.

556 Crotch, vv. 1–4, 6.
557 Dupuis, vv. 1–4, 6 ; xcviii. 10. Hallelujah.
558 Greene, vv. 1, 6, 3, 15.

559

The Festal morn, my God, is come,
That calls me to Thy honour'd dome,
　　Thy Presence to adore :
My feet the summons shall attend,
With willing step Thy courts ascend,
　　And tread the hallow'd floor.

Ev'n now to our transported eyes
Fair Sion's tow'rs in prospect rise :
　　Within her gates we stand,
And, lost in wonder and delight,
Behold her happy sons unite
　　In friendship's firmest band.

Hither from Judah's utmost end,
The heav'n-protected Tribes ascend,
　　Their off'rings hither bring :
Here, eager to attest their joy,
In hymns of praise their tongues employ,
　　And hail th' immortal King.

W. Hayes.

560

Psalm cxlv.

The Lord is good ; fresh acts of grace
  His pity still supplies :
His anger moves with slowest pace,
  His willing mercy flies.

By angels in heav'n of ev'ry degree,
  And saints upon earth all praise be addrest ;
  To God in Three Persons, One God ever blest,
As it has been, now is, and always shall be.

The longing of the poor and meek
  His goodness will supply :
He will revive their fainting hopes,
  Who on His strength rely.

Whate'er our various wants require,
  With open hand He gives,
And so fulfils the just desire
  Of ev'ry thing that lives.

Therefore will we the righteous ways
  Of Providence proclaim :
Will sing the praise of God Most High,
  And celebrate His Name.

By angels in heav'n of every degree,
  And saints upon earth all praise be addrest ;
  To God in Three Persons, One God ever blest,
As it has been, now is, and always shall be.   Amen.

W. Hayes.

561

Psalm xx. 9. Save, Lord, and hear us, O King of heaven, when we call upon Thee.

xxviii. 10. O save Thy people, and give Thy blessing unto Thine inheritance : feed them, and set them up for ever.

xxi. 13. So will we sing, and praise Thy power. Hallelujah.   Amen.

W. Hayes.

562

COLLECT

For the Seventh Sunday after Trinity.

LORD of all power and might, Who art the Author and Giver of all good things: graft in our hearts the love of Thy Name, increase in us true religion, nourish us with all goodness, and of Thy great mercy keep us in the same; through JESUS CHRIST our LORD. Amen.

BARNBY, CHIPP, MASON, SMEE, S. S. WESLEY, D. WOOD.

563

PSALM xli. 1. Blessed is he that considereth the poor and needy; the LORD shall deliver him in the time of trouble.

2. The LORD preserve him, and keep him alive, that he may be blessed upon earth, [and deliver not Thou him into the will of his enemies.]

3. The LORD comfort him when he lieth sick upon his bed : make Thou all his bed in his sickness.

[4. LORD, be merciful unto me : heal my soul, for I have sinned against Thee.

7. All mine enemies whisper together against me.

10. But be Thou merciful unto me, O LORD : raise Thou me up again, and I shall reward them.]

12. When I am in my health, Thou upholdest me, and shalt set me before Thy face for ever. Hallelujah. Amen.

[13. Blessed be the LORD GOD of Israel : world without end.]

BOYCE.

564 ATTWOOD, vv. 1–3, 13. Hallelujah. Amen.
565 C. H. LLOYD, vv. 1–3, 12, 13. Amen.
566 PURCELL, vv. 1 3. Gloria Patri.
567 VERRINDER, vv. 1, 2.
568 WISE, vv. 1, 3, 4, 7, 10, 13. Hallelujah. Amen.

569

Psalm cxxxvii. 1. By the waters of Babylon we sat down and wept, when we remembered thee, O Sion.

2. As for our harps, we hanged them up, upon the trees that are therein.

3. For they that led us away captive, required of us then a song and melody in our heaviness : sing us one of the songs of Sion.

4. How shall we sing the Lord's song, in a strange land ?

5. If I forget thee. O Jerusalem, [let my right hand forget her cunning.]

6. [If I do not remember thee,] let my tongue cleave to the roof of my mouth, yea, if I prefer not Jerusalem in my mirth.

7. Remember the children of Edom, O Lord, in the day of Jerusalem : how they said, Down with it, down with it, even to the ground.

8. O daughter of Babylon, wasted with misery, yea, happy shall he be that rewardeth thee as thou hast served us.

9. Blessed shall he be that taketh Thy children and throweth them against the stones.

Allen, Coleridge-Taylor, O. King,
Macpherson, Purcell.

570 Aldrich, vv. 1–6.

571 Boyce, Stevenson, vv. 1–8.

572 Nares, vv. 1–3, 8.

573

Psalm xxix. 1. Give unto the Lord, O ye mighty, give unto the Lord glory and strength.

2. Give the Lord the honour due unto His Name; worship the Lord with holy worship.

3. It is the Lord, that commandeth the waters; it is the glorious God, that maketh the thunder.

4. The voice of the Lord is powerful ; the voice of the Lord is full of majesty.

10. He shall give strength unto His people, and the blessing of peace.

9. The Lord remaineth a King for ever. Amen.

Boyce.

574

Psalm cxlii. 1. I cried unto the Lord with my voice, yea, even unto the Lord did I make my supplication.

2. I poured out my complaints before Him, and shewed Him of my trouble.

lxxvii. 3. When I am in heaviness, I will think upon God; when my heart is vexed, I will complain.

6. I call to remembrance my song, and in the night I commune with my own heart, and search out my spirits.

7. Will the Lord absent Himself for ever? and will He be no more intreated?

11. I will remember the works of the Lord, and call to mind Thy wonders of old time.

12. I will think also of all Thy works, and my talking shall be of Thy doings.

13. Thy way, O God, is holy: who is so great a God as our God?

Boyce.

575

1 Thessalonians iv. 14. If we believe that Jesus died, and rose again, even so them also which sleep in Jesus will God bring with Him.

15. For this we say unto you by the word of the Lord, that we which are alive and remain unto the coming of the Lord shall not prevent them which are asleep.

16. For the Lord Himself shall descend from heaven with a shout, with the voice of the Archangel, and with the trump of God; and the dead in Christ shall rise first.

17. Then we, which are alive and remain, shall be caught up together with them in the clouds, to meet the Lord in the air; and so shall we ever be with the Lord.

18. Wherefore comfort one another with these words.

Boyce, Bunnett.

576 Goss, vv. 14, 18.
577 Macfarren, v. 14. Amen.

578

1 Kings viii. 13. I have surely built Thee an house to dwell in, a settled place for Thee to abide in for ever.

27. But will God indeed dwell on the earth? Behold, the heaven and heaven of heavens cannot contain Thee; how much less this house that I have builded?

28, 29. Yet have Thou respect unto the prayer of Thy servant, O Lord my God, that Thine eyes may be open toward this house, night and day, even toward the place of which Thou hast said, My Name shall be there.

30. And hearken Thou to the supplication of Thy servant, and of Thy people Israel, when they shall pray toward this place: and hear Thou in Heaven, Thy dwelling-place, and when Thou hearest, forgive.

37. If there be in the land famine, if there be pestilence, whatsoever plague, whatsoever sickness there be;

38. What prayer and supplication soever be made by any man, or by all Thy people Israel, which shall know every man the plague of his own heart, and spread forth his hands towards this house:

39. Then hear Thou in Heaven Thy dwelling-place, hear and forgive.

ix. [1, 2. And it came to pass, when Solomon had finished the building of the house of the Lord, that the Lord appeared unto Solomon.]

3. And the Lord said to Solomon, I have heard thy prayer: I have hallowed this house, which thou hast built. to put My Name there for ever, and Mine eyes and My heart shall be there perpetually. Amen. Hallelujah.

[Psalm xcvi. 9. Come, let us worship the Lord in the beauty of holiness; let the whole earth stand in awe of Him.

6. Glory and worship are before Him: power and honour are in His Sanctuary.]

Boyce.

579 Trimnell. vv. 13, 27 30; ix. 1 3; Psalm xcvi. 9, 6. Hallelujah. Amen.

580

JOB vii. 17, 18. LORD, what is man, that Thou shouldest visit him?

19. How long wilt Thou not depart from me?

20. I have sinned: what shall I do, O Thou preserver of men?

21. Why pardonest Thou not my transgressions, nor takest mine iniquity from me?

xiv. 13. O that Thou wouldest hide me in the grave, till Thy wrath be past.

iii. 17. There the wicked cease troubling; there the weary are at rest. Hallelujah.

BOYCE.

581

PSALM xv. 1. LORD, who shall dwell in Thy tabernacle? or who shall rest upon Thy holy hill?

2. Even he that leadeth an uncorrupt life, and doeth the thing which is right, and speaketh the truth from his heart.

3. He that hath used no deceit in his tongue, nor done evil to his neighbour, and hath not slandered his neighbour.

1. He shall dwell in Thy tabernacle: he shall rest upon Thy holy hill.

4. He that setteth not by himself, but is lowly in his own eyes, and maketh much of them that fear the LORD.

1. He shall dwell in Thy tabernacle.

5. He that sweareth unto his neighbour, and disappointeth him not, though it were to his own hindrance.

1. He shall rest upon Thy holy hill.

6. He that hath not given his money upon usury, nor taken reward against the innocent.

1. He shall rest upon Thy holy hill.

7. Whoso doeth these things shall never fall. Hallelujah. Amen.

BOYCE.

582 ROBERTS, vv. 1-7.
583 B. ROGERS, vv. 1 4, 6, 7.
584 STEWART, vv. 1 7.

585

PSALM xlii.   1. Like as the hart desires the water-brooks, so longeth my soul after Thee, O GOD.

xliii.   2. Thou art the GOD of my strength, why hast Thou put me from Thee ? and why go I so heavily, while the enemy oppresseth me ?

3. O send out Thy light and Thy truth, that they may lead me, and bring me unto Thy holy hill, and to Thy dwelling.

4. And that I may go unto the Altar of GOD, even unto the GOD of my joy and gladness :* and upon the harp will I give thanks unto Thee, O GOD, my GOD.

5. Why art Thou so heavy, O my soul? and why art thou so disquieted within me ?

6. O put thy trust in GOD, for I will yet give Him thanks, Which is the help of my countenance, and my GOD.

BOYCE.

586 ARMES, J. F. BRIDGE, CALKIN, Psalm xliii. 3, 4.*
587 FIELD, Psalm xliii. 3–6.
588 MACFARREN, Psalm xliii. 3.   Amen.

* Ends here.

589

PSALM lxvi.   1. O be joyful in GOD, all ye lands : sing praises unto the honour of His Name, make His praise to be glorious.

2. Say unto GOD, O how wonderful art Thou in Thy works : [through the greatness of Thy power shall Thine enemies be found liars unto Thee.]

3. For all the world shall worship Thee, sing of Thee, and praise Thy Name.

4. O [come hither, and] behold the works of GOD : how wonderful He is in His doing toward the children of men.

6. He ruleth with His power for ever ; His eyes behold the people : and such as will not believe shall not be able to exalt themselves.   Hallelujah.

[7. O praise our GOD, ye people, and make the voice of His praise to be heard.

8. Who holdeth our soul in life, and suffereth not our feet to slip.

9. For Thou, O GOD, hast proved us ; Thou also hast tried us, like as silver is tried.

14. O come hither, and hearken, all ye that fear GOD, and I will tell you what He hath done for my soul.

15. I called unto Him with my mouth, and gave Him praises with my tongue.

16. If I incline unto wickedness with mine heart, the LORD will not hear me.

17. But GOD hath heard me, and considered the voice of my prayer.

18. Praised be GOD, Who hath not cast out my prayer, nor turned His mercy from me.]

BOYCE.

590 †BÜHLER, vv. 7–9, 16, 17, 14, 15, 7–9.
591 CROFT, vv. 1–3, 14–18.
592 CROTCH, vv. 14–18.
593 GREENE, vv. 7, 8, 7, 9, 7, 14, 17, 18.
594 W. HAYES, KING, vv. 1–3.
595 OUSELEY, vv. 7, 8.

† For Latin Version see No. 41.

596

PSALM cxlix. 1. O sing unto the LORD a new song ; let the congregation of saints praise Him.

2. Let Israel rejoice in Him that made Him, and let the children of Zion be joyful in their King.

4. For the LORD hath pleasure in His people, and helpeth the meek-hearted.

5. Let the saints be joyful with glory.

6. Let the praises of GOD be in their mouth, [and a two-edged sword in their hands ;

7. To be avenged of the heathen, and to rebuke the people.]

cl. 6. Let everything that hath breath, praise the LORD.

BOYCE.

597 J. L. HOPKINS, vv. 1. 2, 4, 6, 7. Amen.

598

*PSALM cxviii. 1. O give thanks unto the LORD, for He is gracious, because His mercy endureth for ever.

2. Let Israel now confess, that He is gracious, and that His mercy endureth for ever.*

[3. Let the house of Aaron now confess, that His mercy endureth for ever.

6. The LORD is on my side; I will not fear what man doeth unto me.

7. The LORD taketh my part with them that help me; therefore shall I see my desire upon mine enemies.]

cxlv. 18. The LORD is nigh unto all them that call upon Him, yea, all such as call upon Him faithfully.

lv. 4. My heart was disquieted within me, and the fear of death was fallen upon me.

cvii. 13. But in my trouble I called upon the LORD, and He delivered me out of my distress.

cxvi. 7. Turn again then unto thy rest, O my soul, for the LORD hath rewarded thee.

xxxiv. 3. O praise the LORD with me, and let us magnify His Name together.

lxxxiv. 9. Behold, O GOD, our Defender, and look upon the face of Thine Anointed.

lxi. 7. O prepare Thy loving mercy and faithfulness, that they may preserve Him.

lxxxix. 30. Let His seed endure for ever, and His throne as the days of heaven.

lxi. 8. So will we always sing praise unto Thy Name. Amen. Hallelujah.

BOYCE.

* —— * Sometimes sung as a separate Anthem.

599 CROFT, Psalm cxviii. 1–3, 6, 7.

600

PSALM xxii. 23, 24. O praise the LORD, ye that fear Him; for He hath not despised nor abhorred the low estate of the poor; He hath not hid His face from him, but when he called unto Him He heard him.

26. The poor shall eat, and be satisfied; they that seek after the LORD shall praise Him.

27. All the ends of the world shall remember themselves, and be turned unto the LORD ; and all the kindreds of the nations shall worship before Him.

28. For the kingdom is the LORD'S, and He is the Governour among the people. Hallelujah. Amen.

BOYCE.

601

PSALM v. 1. Ponder my words, O LORD; and consider my meditation.

2. O hearken Thou unto the voice of my calling, my King, and my GOD: for unto Thee will I make my prayer.

3. My voice shalt Thou hear betimes, O LORD : early in the morning will I direct my prayer unto Thee, [and will look up.]

4. For Thou art the GOD that hast no pleasure in wickedness, neither shall any evil dwell with Thee.

5. Such as be foolish shall not stand in Thy sight, for Thou hatest all them that work vanity.

[6. Thou shalt destroy all them that speak leasing : the LORD will abhor both the bloodthirsty and deceitful man.]

7. But as for me, I will come into Thine house, even upon the multitude of Thy mercy, and in Thy fear will I worship toward Thy holy temple.

8. Lead me, O LORD, in Thy righteousness : make Thy way plain before my face.

[11. Destroy Thou them, O GOD ; let them perish in their own imaginations : cast them out in the multitude of their ungodliness.]

12. And let all them that put their trust in Thee rejoice : they shall ever be giving of thanks, because Thou defendest them, they that love Thy Name shall be joyful in Thee.

[13. For Thou, LORD, wilt give Thy blessing unto the righteous : and with Thy favourable kindness wilt Thou defend him as with a shield.] Amen.

BOYCE.

602 { COLBORNE, CULLEY, GADSBY, J. L. HOPKINS, JEFFERYS, SAWYER, } vv. 1, 2. [Amen.]
    SAWYER, vv. 1, 2. [Amen.]
603 GREENE, vv. 1, 2, 8, 11–13.
604 TATTERSALL, vv. 1 3. 13.
605 TRAVERS, vv. 1, 2, 4 6. Hallelujah.
606 T. A. WALMISLEY, vv. 1 3, 7, 12, 13. Amen.
607 WELDON, vv. 1–7, 5.

608

JOB xxviii. 12. O where shall wisdom be found? and where is the place of understanding?

13. Man knoweth not the price thereof; neither is it found in the land of the living.

14. The depth saith, It is not in me ; and the sea saith, It is not with me.

15. It cannot be gotten for gold, neither shall silver be weighed for the price thereof.

18. No mention shall be made of coral, or of pearls, for the price of wisdom is above rubies.

20, 21. Whence then cometh wisdom ? and where is the place of understanding? seeing it is hid from the eyes of all living.

23. GOD understandeth the way thereof, and He knoweth the place thereof.

24. For He looketh to the ends of the earth, and seeth under the whole heaven ;

25. To make the weight for the winds ; and He weigheth the waters by measure.

26. When He made a decree for the rain, and a way for the lightning of the thunder ;

27. Then did He see it, and declare it ; He prepared it, yea, and searched it out.

28. And unto man He said, Behold, the fear of the LORD, that is wisdom ; and to depart from evil is understanding.

BOYCE.

609

PSALM xcvi. 2. Sing unto the LORD, and praise His Name: be telling of His salvation from day to day.

4. For the LORD is great, and cannot worthily be praised : He is more to be feared than all gods.

6. Glory and worship are before Him, power and honour are in His Sanctuary.

11. Let the heavens rejoice, and let the earth be glad : let the sea make a noise, and all that therein is.

13. For He cometh to judge the world with righteousness, and the people with His truth.

10. Tell it out among the heathen that the LORD is King, and that He shall judge the people righteously.

BOYCE.

610

Isaiah xlix. 13. Sing, O heavens, and be joyful, O earth; break forth into singing, O mountains, for the Lord hath comforted His people, and will have mercy upon His afflicted.*

14. But Zion said, The Lord hath forsaken me, and my Lord hath forgotten me.

15. Can a woman forget her sucking child, that she should not have compassion on the son of her womb? Yea, they may forget, yet will I not forget Thee.

li. 1. Hearken to me, ye that follow after righteousness, ye that seek the Lord: look unto the rock whence ye are hewn.

2. Look unto Abraham your father, and unto Sarah that bare you: for I called him alone, and blessed him, and increased him.

3. For the Lord shall comfort Zion, He will comfort all her waste places, and He will make her wilderness like Eden, and her desert like the garden of the Lord; joy and gladness shall be found therein, thanksgiving and the voice of melody. Amen.

Boyce.

* —— * Sometimes sung as a separate Anthem.

611 Lucas, Isaiah xlix. 13; li. 3.

612

Psalm xxx. 4. Sing praises to the Lord, O ye saints of His: give thanks unto Him for a remembrance of His holiness.

xxxiii. 5. He loveth righteousness and judgment: the earth is full of the goodness of the Lord.

xcvi. 8. Ascribe unto the Lord the honour due unto His Name: bring presents, and come into His courts.

xviii. 31. For who is God, but the Lord? or who hath any strength, except our God?

cxiii. 4. The Lord is high above all people, and His glory above the heavens.

xxxii. 12. Be glad, O ye righteous, and rejoice in the Lord: be joyful, all ye that are true of heart. Hallelujah.

Boyce.

613

*Psalm xix. i. The heavens declare the glory of God, and the firmament sheweth His handy-work.

2. One day telleth another, and one night certifieth another.

3. There is neither speech nor language, but their voices are heard among them.*

4. Their sound is gone out into all lands, and their words into the ends of the world.

5. In them hath He set a tabernacle for the sun, which cometh forth as a bridegroom out of his chamber, and rejoiceth as a giant to run his course.

[9. The fear of the Lord is clean and endureth for ever : the judgments of the Lord are true, and righteous altogether.

10. More to be desired are they than gold, yea, than much fine gold : sweeter also than honey, and the honey-comb.

11. Moreover, by them is thy servant taught : and in keeping of them there is great reward.]

*Revelation xv. 3. Great and marvellous are Thy works, Lord God Almighty; just and true are Thy ways, Thou King of saints !

[4. Who shall not fear Thee, O Lord, and glorify Thy name ? for Thou only art holy ; for all nations shall come and worship before Thee ; for Thy judgments are made manifest.]

iv. 11. Thou art worthy, O Lord, to receive glory and honour and power ; for Thou hast created all things, and for Thy pleasure they are and were created.   Hallelujah.
                                                               Boyce.

—— Sometimes sung as a separate Anthem.

614 S. Arnold, Croft, vv. 1–4.   [Hallelujah.]
615 E. G. Monk, Revelation xv. 3, 4.
616 Whitfield, vv. 1–5, 9–11.   Hallelujah.

617

Psalm xciii. i. The Lord is King, and hath put on glorious apparel ; the Lord hath put on His apparel and girded Himself with strength.

2. He hath made the round world so sure that it cannot be moved.

3. Ever since the world began hath Thy seat been prepared; Thou art from everlasting.

4. The floods are risen, O LORD, the floods have lift up their voice, the floods lift up their waves.

5. The waves of the sea are mighty, the waves rage horribly: but yet the LORD, Who dwelleth on high, is mightier.

6. Thy testimonies, O LORD, are very sure: holiness becometh Thine house for ever. Amen.

BLOW, BOYCE, GADSBY, OUSELEY.

618

PSALM xviii. 47. The LORD liveth, and blessed be my strong helper, and praised be the GOD of my salvation.

48. Even the GOD that seeth that I be avenged, and subdueth the people unto me.

49. It is He that delivereth me from my cruel enemies, and setteth me up above mine adversaries: Thou shalt rid me from the wicked man.

50. For this cause will I give thanks unto Thee, O LORD, among the Gentiles, and sing praises unto Thy Name.

51. Great prosperity giveth He to His Anointed, and to His seed for evermore. Amen.

BOYCE.

619

PSALM xxv. 15. Turn Thee unto me, O LORD, and have mercy upon me, for I am desolate and in misery.

16. The sorrows of my heart are enlarged; O bring Thou me out of my troubles.

17. Look upon my adversity and misery, and forgive me all my sin.

18. Consider mine enemies, how many they are, and they bear a tyrannous hate against me.

19. O keep my soul, and deliver me; let me not be confounded, for I have put my trust in Thee.

BOYCE.

620 BLOW, v. 17.
621 BLOW. vv. 18, 19.
622 BOYCE, vv. 15 17, 19.
623 J. L. HOPKINS, LANGDON, 15 17.

624

PSALM xcix. 1. The LORD is King, be the people never so impatient : He sitteth between the Cherubims, be the earth never so unquiet.

[2 The LORD is great in Sion, and high above all people.

3. They shall give thanks unto Thy Name, which is great, and wonderful, and holy.

5. O magnify the LORD our GOD, and fall down before His footstool for He is holy.]

JEREMIAH xlvii. 6. O thou sword of the LORD, put up thyself into thy scabbard, rest and be still.

PSALM xx. 7. Some put their trust in chariots, and some in horses: but we will remember the Name of the LORD our GOD.

cxlvii. 14. He maketh peace in our borders,

xlvi. 9. And causeth wars to cease in all the world.

cvii. 31. O that men would therefore praise the LORD for His goodness, and declare the wonders that He doeth for the children of men.

32. That they would exalt Him also in the congregation of the people, and praise Him in the seat of the elders. Hallelujah.

BOYCE.

625 CROFT, vv. 1–3, 5. Hallelujah.
626 W. KING, vv. 1–3. Hallelujah.

627

PSALM xxxiv. 15. The eyes of the LORD are over the righteous, and His ears are open unto their prayers.

16. But the countenance of the LORD is against them that do evil.

17. The righteous cry, and the LORD heareth them, and delivereth them out of all their troubles.

[19. Great are the troubles of the righteous : but the LORD delivereth him out of all.]

8. O taste and see how gracious the LORD is : blessed is the man that trusteth in Him.

NARES.

628 C. WOOD, vv. 15, 19.

629

Psalm cxxxiii. 1. Behold, how good and joyful a thing it is, brethren, to dwell together in unity.

[2. It is like the precious ointment upon the head, that ran down unto the beard, even unto Aaron's beard, and went down to the skirts of his clothing.]

3. It is like the dew of Hermon, which fell upon the hill of Sion.

4. For there the Lord promised His blessing, and life for evermore.

[c. 4. For the Lord is gracious, His mercy is everlasting: and His truth endureth from generation to generation.

3. O go your way into His gates with thanksgiving, and into His courts with praise: be thankful unto Him, and speak good of His Name.]

cxxii. 7. Peace be within Thy walls, and plenteousness within Thy palaces.

8. For my brethren and companions' sakes, I will wish thee prosperity. Hallelujah. Amen.

[cxxxiv. 6. Lift up your hands in the sanctuary, and praise the Lord.]

Nares.

630 Baildon, Coward, vv. 1, 3, 4.   [Amen.]
631 Battishill, vv. 1, 3, 4; c. 4, 3. Hallelujah. Amen.
632 Blow, Child, H. Clarke, W. H. Gladstone, Jekyll,
    Ouseley, B. Rogers, Whitfeld, vv. 1–4. [Hallelujah.
    Amen.]
633 Ebdon, vv. 1, 3, 4, 1.
634 Stevenson, vv. 1–4 ; cxxxiv. 6 ; cxxii. 7, 8, 7.   Amen.

635

A PRAYER.

Hide not Thou Thy face from us, O Lord, nor cast away Thy servants in Thy displeasure, for we confess our sins unto Thee, and our unrighteousness have we not hid. Lord, lift Thou up the light of Thy countenance upon us; so shall we rejoice and be glad all the days of our life. Amen.

Nares.

636

PSALM xciv. 2. Arise, Thou Judge of the world: reward the proud after their deserving.

3. LORD, how long shall the ungodly triumph?

7. And yet they say, The LORD shall not see it, neither shall the GOD of Jacob regard it.

8. Take heed, ye unwise among the people: O ye fools, when will ye understand?

9. He that planted the ear, shall He not hear? or He that made the eye, shall He not see?

10. Or He that teacheth man knowledge, shall not He punish?

11. The LORD knoweth the thoughts of man, that they are but vain.

xcv. 6. O come, let us worship and fall down, and kneel before the LORD our Maker.

7. For He is the LORD our GOD: His judgments are in all the world.

ciii. 9. He will not alway be chiding, neither keepeth He His anger for ever.

cvii. 8. O that men would therefore praise the LORD for His goodness, and declare the wonders that He doeth for the children of men!

NARES.

637

WISDOM iii. 1. The souls of the righteous are in the hand of GOD, and there shall no torment touch them.

2. In the sight of the unwise they seemed to die: and their departure is taken for misery,

3. [And their going from us to be their destruction:] but they are in peace.

4. For though they be punished in the sight of men, yet is their hope full of immortality.

5. [And having been a little chastised, they shall be greatly rewarded:] for GOD proved them, and found them worthy for Himself.

[6. As gold in the furnace hath He tried them, and received them as a burnt-offering.

7. And in the time of their visitation they shall shine, [and run to and fro like sparks among the stubble.]

8. They shall judge the nations, and have dominion over the people, and their LORD shall reign for ever and ever. Amen.

NARES.

638 CROFT, vv. 1–8.
639 MACFARREN, vv. 1–3.

640

Ave verum corpus, natum
De Mariâ Virgine,
Vere passum, immolatum
In cruce pro homine,
Cujus latus perforatum
Undâ fluxit et sanguine;
Esto nobis præustatum,
Mortis in examine
[O JESU dulcis, O JESU pie,
O JESU, Fili Mariæ, miserere nobis. Amen.]

Paraphrase.

JESU, [Blessed] Word of GOD Incarnate,
Of the [Blessed] Virgin Mary born,
On the Cross Thy sacred Body,
For us men with nails was torn.
Cleanse us, by the blood and water,
Streaming from Thy pierced Side;
Feed us with Thy Body broken,
Now, and in death's agony!
[O JESU, hear us, O JESU, spare us,
O JESU, Blessed Son of Mary,
O grant us, LORD, Thy mercy. Amen.]

(Sometimes sung to the following words.)

Give ear unto me, LORD, I beseech Thee, for I have walked in Thy commandments. Let me be judged with righteous judgment; hold my goings in Thy paths, that my steps may not be moved.

DOCKER, MOZART.

641 GOUNOD ... ... {Ave verum,
{JESU, Blessed Word of GOD.
642 GOUNOD, HOYTE, (Ave verum,
  WHITE (JESU, Word of GOD.
643 GOUNOD ... Ave verum,
  (Word of GOD.

644

Deus, Tibi laus et honor sit.
O cantemus in tympano, et choro adoremus Dominum.
Quem collaudant omnes gentes piæ, bonæ, sapientes.
O reddemus preces nostras.
Ab ortu solis ad occasum, benedictus es, mi Deus.
Incessanter laudamus Te, jubilantes choris festis, exul-
    tantes propter Te.

Ut in templo sancto tuo, sonus cornu perjucundus,
sonus dulcis tibiæ; ita vivant reunite omnes terræ Tuæ
filii, Deus; ita placeat, ut vota nostra Tibi sint grata.
Fac his votis annuas gratiâ Tuâ, Tibi gaudeant corda
nostra, Tibi sacrum nobis munus primarium.

English Version.

Glory, honour, praise, and power,
Be unto GOD for ever.
Praise to Thee, Thou great Creator,
    Praise be Thine from every tongue.
Young and old, Thy praise expressing,
Worship, honour, glory, blessing,
    Laud Thy Name in joyful song.

Praise the LORD! ye heavens, adore Him,
Sun and moon, rejoice before Him,
    Praise Him, all ye stars and light.
Praise His mercy, His salvation,
Heaven and earth and all creation,
    Praise Him, angels in the height.

As the saints in heav'n adore Thee,
As Thine angels bow before Thee,
    And extol Thy boundless love:
We, Thy servants, lowly bending,
Pray Thee, let Thy grace, descending,
    Fit us for the realms above.

Let the realms of all creation
Praise the GOD of our salvation
    For the hope of future joy;
Sound His praise through earth and heaven
For ten thousand blessings given,
    Sound JEHOVAH's praise on high.

                                        MOZART.

645

REQUIEM.

No. 1

1. Dies iræ, dies illa,
   Solvet sæclum in favillâ,
   Teste David cum Sibyllâ.

2. Quantus tremor est futurus,
   Quando Judex est venturus,
   Cuncta stricte discussurus !

No. 2

3. Tuba mirum spargens sonum
   Per sepulchra regionum
   Coget omnes ante thronum.

4. Mors stupebit, et natura,
   Cum resurget creatura,
   Judicanti responsura.

5. Liber scriptus proferetur,
   In quo totum continetur,
   Unde mundus judicetur.

6. Judex ergo cum sedebit,
   Quidquid latet apparebit,
   Nil inultum remanebit.

7. Quid sum miser tunc dicturus ?
   Quem patronum rogaturus,
   Cum vix justus sit securus ?

No. 3

8. Rex tremendæ Majestatis,
   Qui salvandos salvas gratis,
   Salva me, fons pietatis.

No. 4

9. Recordare, Jesu pie,
   Quod sum causa Tuæ viæ.
   Ne me perdas illâ die.

10. Quærens me sedisti lassus ;
    Redemisti crucem passus :
    Tantus labor non sit cassus.

11. Juste Judex ultionis,
    Donum fac remissionis
    Ante diem rationis.

12. Ingemisco, tanquam reus ;
    Culpâ rubet vultus meus :
    Supplicanti parce Deus.

13. Qui Mariam absolvisti,
    Et latronem exaudisti,
    Mihi quoque spem dedisti.

14. Preces meæ non sunt dignæ ;
    Sed Tu bonus fac benigne,
    Ne perenni cremer igne.

15. Inter oves locum præsta,
    Et ab hœdis me sequestra,
    Statuens in parte dextrâ.

No. 5

16. Confutatis maledictis,
    Flammis acribus addictis,
    Voca me cum benedictis.

17. Oro supplex et acclinis,
    Cor contritum quasi cinis ;
    Gere curam mei finis.

No. 6

18. Lacrymosa dies illa,
    Quâ resurget ex favillâ
    Judicandus homo reus ;
    Huic ergo parce, Deus.

19. Pie Jesu, Domine,
    Dona eis requiem ! Amen.

English Version.
No. 1

1. Day of anger, day of mourning !
   See fulfilled the prophet's warning !
   Heaven and earth in ashes burning !

2. Oh, what fear man's bosom rendeth,
   When from heaven the Judge descendeth,
   On Whose sentence all dependeth !

No. 2

3. Wondrous sound the trumpet flingeth,
   Through earth's sepulchres it ringeth ;
   All before the throne it bringeth.

4. Death is struck, and nature quaking,
   All creation is awaking,
   To its Judge an answer making.

5. Lo ! the book exactly worded,
   Wherein all hath been recorded,
   Thence shall judgment be awarded.

6. When the Judge His seat attaineth,
   And each hidden deed arraigneth,
   Nothing unavenged remaineth.

7. What shall I, frail man, be pleading ?
   Who for me be interceding
   When the righteous are mercy needing ?

No. 3

8. King of majesty tremendous,
   Who salvation free doth send us,
   Fount of pity, then befriend us.

No. 4

9. Think, good JESU, my salvation
   Caused Thy wondrous Incarnation ;
   Leave me not to reprobation.

10. Wearily Thy love has sought me,
    By Thy Passion Thou hast bought me—
    Vainly should such suffering call me ?

11. Judge most just, Whose arm avengeth,
    Grant, O grant me Thy forgiveness,
    Ere the dreadful day of judgment approacheth.

12. See me weeping as one guilty,
    With shame owning my transgression :
    In Thy mercy grant remission.

13. Thou to Mary gavest pardon,
    And the dying thief didst answer,
    Even me with hope Thou fillest !

14. Worthless are my prayers and sighing,
    Yet on Thee, good Lord, relying,
    Lest eternal fire receive me,

15. With Thy favoured sheep O place me,
    Nor among the goats abase me,
    But to Thy right hand upraise me.

No. 5

16. When the wicked are confounded,
    Doom'd to flames of woe unbounded,
    Call Thou me, with Thy saints surrounded.

17. Low I kneel, with heart-submission,
    See, like ashes, my contrition,
    Help me in my last condition.

No. 6

18. Day of mourning, day of weeping,
    From the dust of earth returning,
    Man for judgment must prepare him!

19. Spare, O God, in mercy spare us!
    Lord all-pitying! Jesus blest,
    Grant us Thy eternal rest.   Amen.

MOZART.

646

COLLECT

For the Fifth Sunday after Trinity.

Grant, O Lord, we beseech Thee, that the course of this world may be so peaceably ordered by Thy governance, that Thy Church may joyfully serve Thee in all godly quietness; through Jesus Christ our Lord.   Amen.

MOZART.

647

Psalm lxxxix.   1. Misericordias Domini in æternum cantabo.

(*Sometimes sung to the following words.*)

Thou, Lord, art merciful unto all. We praise Thee for Thy mercy.

MOZART.

648

Ne, pulvis et cinis, superbe te geras,
Irati ne Numinis fulmina feras :
Fulmen, et grando, et horrida mors,
Hominis perfidi justa sunt sors.

Nos, pulvis et cinis, timentes, trementes,
  Prostrati ploramus ad Te :
Da lumen, juvamen, ut sancta sequentes
  Mortales erecti sint spe.

Summe Deus, Miserator,
  Da pugnanti gratiam ;
Et fidelis Munerator,
  Da vincenti gloriam.

(Sometimes sung to the following words.)

Psalm xxxi. 10. Have mercy, O Lord, for I am in trouble : mine eye is consumed for very heaviness.

1. In Thee, O Lord, have I put my trust, let me never be put to confusion, make haste to deliver me.

18. O Lord, shew Thy servant the light of Thy countenance.

16. But my hope hath been in Thee. I have said, Thou art my God.

Mozart.

649

Psalm xxxv. 1. Plead Thou my cause, O Lord, with them that strive with me, and fight Thou against them that fight against me.

24. Judge me, O Lord my God, according to Thy righteousness, and let them not triumph over me.

lvii. 10. I will give thanks unto Thee, O Lord, among the people, and I will sing unto Thee among the nations.

11. For the greatness of Thy mercy reacheth unto the heavens, and Thy truth unto the clouds.

Mozart.

650

Splendente Te, Deus, discussa tristis est nox ;
Jam plebis devote canentis una est vox :
Exaudi,precantes, Qui solus omnipotens es ;
Pugnanti est certa, opitulante Te, spes.

En feri hostes, Tartarei postes,
  Infestant nos :
Arenâ stamus, atque pugnamus ;
  Adjuta nos.
Da juventuti, ut fida virtuti,
  Immunis sit ;
Quæ, virulentis non pressa ventis,
  Virens, et florens sit,
  Florens, fructifera sit.
Tu viris lumen, gratumque sis numen,
  Et fortis vis ;
Tu doctor pusillis, tuisque pupillis,
  Servator et tutor sis.

(Sometimes sung to the following words.)

O GOD, when Thou appearest, darkness flies, Thy light
and Thy glory shine forth on the earth, and Thou art
exalted, O LORD, above all gods. We worship Thy glorious
Name, O LORD GOD Almighty. Thou only art my rock and
my salvation, and my defence, and I shall not be moved.
Thou art my salvation and my glory, my refuge, the rock
of my strength, O LORD of all power and might. Our
LORD is exalted above all gods. O praise the LORD, all
ye people, and praise Him, all ye lands. His merciful
kindness endureth for ever. Praise Him in songs of joy.
We praise Thee, O LORD our GOD. We worship Thy
glorious Name, O LORD GOD Almighty. Be Thou
exalted, O GOD, above all heavens, Thy glory above all the
earth. O LORD GOD, when Thou appearest, darkness
flies, for Thou, LORD, art greater than all that are in the
earth, and Thou art exalted, O LORD, above all gods. O
LORD GOD Almighty, we worship Thy glorious Name.

MOZART.

651

Quis Te comprehendat, Te, Altissime; Te, Qui eras,
Qui es, et Qui eris? Me quam felicem, Qui Te meum
esse Patrem corde credere, et Te appelare possum!

Cherubim! Seraphim! Omnes chori Angelorum, hymnum
læti cantate Patri Optimo. Hymnum nostrum vestro
conjungimus.

English Version.

Who can comprehend Thee, Thee, O GOD Most High;
Thee, Who wert, and Who art, and Who art to come?

O what joy, that I to be my very Father may believe
Thee, and may my Father call Thee. Cherubim! Sera-
phim! All ye joyful choirs of angels, praise the Father
Almighty, praise Him!

We, His children, join you, yea, we join you in praising
Him.

MOZART.

652

PSALM cxlii. 1. I cried unto the LORD with my voice,
yea, even unto the LORD did I make my supplication.

2. I poured out my complaints before Him, and shewed
Him of my trouble.

[3. When my spirit was in heaviness Thou knewest my
path: in the way wherein I walked have they privily laid
a snare for me.]

4. I looked also upon my right hand, and saw there
was no man that would know me.

5. I had no place to flee unto, and no man cared for my
soul.

[6. I cried unto Thee, O LORD, and said: Thou art my
hope, and my portion in the land of the living.]

7. Consider my complaint, for I am brought very low.

9. Bring my soul out of trouble, that I may give thanks
unto Thy Name. Amen.

DUPUIS.

653 CROFT, vv. 1 6.
654 LONGHURST, vv. 1 3, 7. 6.

655

PSALM xviii. (*Old Version*).

9. The LORD descended from above,
   And bow'd the heavens most high,
   And underneath His feet He cast
   The darkness of the sky :

10. On cherubs and on cherubims
    Full royally He rode,
    And on the wings of mighty winds
    Came flying all abroad.

P. HAYES.

656

PSALM i.　1. Blessed is the man that hath not walked in the counsel of the ungodly, nor stood in the way of sinners, and hath not sat in the seat of the scornful.

2. But his delight is in the law of the LORD, and in His law will he exercise himself day and night.

3. And he shall be like a tree planted by the water-side, that will bring forth his fruit in due season.

4. His leaf also shall not wither ; and look, whatsoever he doeth, it shall prosper.

5. As for the ungodly, it is not so with them ; but they are like the chaff, which the wind scattereth away from the face of the earth.

6. Therefore the ungodly shall not be able to stand in the judgment : neither the sinners in the congregation of the righteous.

7. But the LORD knoweth the way of the righteous, and the way of the ungodly shall perish.

DISTIN, J. C. PRING.

657 GOSS, vv. 1–5.

658

PSALM ii.　1. Why do the heathen so furiously rage together ? and why do the people imagine a vain thing ?

2. The kings of the earth stand up, and the rulers take counsel together. against the LORD. and against His Anointed, saying.

3. Let us break their bonds asunder, and cast away their cords from us.

4. [But] He that dwelleth in heaven shall laugh them to scorn ; the LORD shall have them in derision.

5. Then shall He speak unto them in His wrath, and vex them in His sore displeasure.

6. Yet have I set My King, upon My holy hill of Zion.

7. I will preach the law, whereof the LORD hath said unto Me, Thou art My Son,, this day have I begotten Thee.

[8. Desire of Me, and I shall give Thee the heathen for Thine inheritance, and the utmost parts of the earth for Thy possession.

9. Thou shalt bruise them with a rod of iron, and break them in pieces like a potter's vessel.

10. Be wise now therefore, O ye kings ; be learned, ye that are judges of the earth.

11. Serve the LORD in fear, and rejoice unto Him with reverence.

12. Kiss the Son, lest He be angry, and so ye perish from the right way ; if His wrath be kindled, (yea, but a little,) blessed are all they that put their trust in Him.

Blessed are all they that put their trust in the LORD. Hallelujah.]

J. C. PRING.

659 KENT, vv. *1–6.*
660 PURCELL, vv. 1–12. Hallelujah.

661

PSALM XXX. 1. I will magnify Thee, O LORD, for Thou hast set me up, and not made my foes to triumph over me.

3. Thou, LORD, hast brought my soul out of hell. Thou hast delivered me from them that go down into the pit.

xcvi. 2. Sing unto the LORD, and praise His Name ; be telling of His salvation from day to day,

xxx. 4. And give thanks unto Him for a remembrance of His holiness. Hallelujah. Amen.

BATTISHILL.

662

PSALM cvi. 45. Deliver us, O LORD our GOD, from among the heathen, that we may give thanks unto Thy Name, and make our boast of Thy praise.

46. Blessed be the Name of the LORD, from everlasting to everlasting : and let all the people say, Amen.

BATTISHILL.

663

PSALM cxxiii. 1. Unto Thee lift I up mine eyes, O Thou that dwellest in the heavens.

cxix. 117. Hold Thou me up and I shall be safe ; yea, my delight shall be ever in Thy statutes.

lv. 1. Hear my prayer, O LORD, and hide not Thyself from my petition.

BATTISHILL.

664

JESU, LORD of life and glory,
    Bend from heav'n Thy gracious ear ;
While our waiting souls adore Thee,
    Friend of helpless sinners, hear.
By Thy mercy, O deliver us, good LORD.

In the solemn hour of dying,
    In the awful Judgment Day,
May our souls, on Thee relying,
    Find Thee still our hope and stay.
By Thy mercy, O deliver us, good LORD.

NAUMANN.

665

ISAIAH lxiii. 1. Who is this that cometh from Edom ? that is glorious in His apparel, travelling in the greatness of His strength ? I that speak in righteousness, mighty to save.

16. Doubtless Thou art our Father, our Redeemer : Thy Name is from everlasting.

ST. MATTHEW xxi. 9. Hosanna to the Son of David : blessed is He that cometh in the Name of the LORD ; Hosanna in the Highest. Amen.

S. ARNOLD.

* * * Sometime sung as a separate Anthem.

666

PSALM lix. 1. Deliver me from mine enemies, O GOD : defend me from them that rise up against me.

9. My strength will I ascribe unto Thee, for Thou art the GOD of my refuge.

ISAIAH xxv. 1. O LORD my GOD, I will exalt Thee and praise Thy Name.

EBDON.

667

GENESIS i. 1. In the beginning GOD created the heaven and the earth ;

2. And the earth was without form, and void; and darkness was upon the face of the deep. And the Spirit of GOD moved upon the face of the waters.

3. And GOD said, Let there be light: and there was light.

4. And GOD saw the light, that it was good, and GOD divided the light from the darkness.

14-16. And GOD said, Let there be lights in the firmament of heaven to divide the day from the night, and to give light upon the earth ; and let them be for signs, and for seasons, and for days, and for years. He made the stars also.

In splendour bright is rising now the sun,
And darts his rays, a joyful happy spouse,
A giant proud and glad to run his measur'd course.
With softer beams and milder light,
Steps on the silver moon through silent night.
The space immense of the azure sky,
A countless host of radiant orbs adorns.
And the sons of GOD announced the fourth day,
In song divine, proclaiming thus His power.

PSALM xix. 1-4. (*Paraphrase.*)

*The heavens are telling the glory of GOD,
The wonder of His work displays the firmament.
To day that is coming speaks it the day :
The night that is gone to following night.
In all the lands resounds the word,
Never unperceived, ever understood.*

(*From the " Creation," Nos. 2, 12-14.*)   F. J. HAYDN.

* Sometimes sung a a separate Anthem.

668

GENESIS i. 11. And GOD said, Let the earth bring forth grass, the herb yielding seed, and the fruit tree yielding fruit after his kind, whose seed is in itself, upon the earth : and it was so.

* With verdure clad, the fields appear delightful to the ravished sense ;
By flowers sweet and gay enhanced is the charming sight,
Here fragrant herbs their odours shed ; here shoots the healing plant ;
With copious fruits the expanded boughs are hung ;
In leafy arches twine the shady groves ; o'er lofty hills majestic forests wave.
*Achieved is the glorious work ; our song let be the praise of GOD.
Glory to His Name for ever. He sole on high exalted reigns. Hallelujah.*

(*From the " Creation,"* Nos. 8, 9, 27B.)   F. J. HAYDN.

* —— * Sometimes sung as a separate Anthem.

669

And the heavenly host, proclaimed the third day, praising GOD, and saying,
Awake the harp, the lyre awake, and let your joyful song resound.
Rejoice in the LORD, the mighty GOD, for He both heaven and earth has clothed in stately dress.

(*From the " Creation,"* Nos. 10, 11.)   F. J. HAYDN.

670

GENESIS i. 31. And GOD saw every thing that He had made, and, behold, it was very good. And the heavenly choir, in song divine, thus closed the sixth day :
Achieved is the glorious work ; the LORD beholds it, and is pleased :
In lofty strains let us rejoice ; our song let be the praise of GOD.

(*From the " Creation,"* Nos. 26, 27).   F. J. HAYDN.

671

On Thee each living soul awaits; from Thee, O LORD,
    all seek their food;
Thou openest Thy hand, and fillest all with good;
But when Thy face, O LORD, is hid, with sudden terror
    they are struck.
Thou tak'st their breath away, they vanish into dust.
Thou sendest forth Thy breath again, and life with vigour
    fresh returns;
Revived earth unfolds new strength and new delights.
Achieved is the glorious work; our song let be the praise
    of GOD.
Glory to His Name for ever. He sole on high, exalted
    reigns. Hallelujah.

(From the "Creation," Nos. 27A, 27B.) F. J. HAYDN.

672

Insanæ et vanæ curæ invadunt mentes nostras.
Sæpe furore replent corda, privata spe.
Quid prodest, O mortalis, conari pro mundanis, si cœlos
negligas? Sunt fausta tibi cuncta, si Deus est pro te.

(Sometimes sung to the following words.)

Distracted with care and anguish,
When hearts despairing languish,
Madly they seek for comfort
Where it doth ne'er abide.
For us no rest remaineth,
If earth our love retaineth,
And heaven we cast aside;
Relief he only gaineth,
And peace at last attaineth,
Whom GOD vouchsafes to guide.

F. J. HAYDN.

673

LORD CHRIST, when Thou hadst overcome the sharpness
of death, Thou didst open the Kingdom of Heaven to all
believers.

F. J. HAYDN.

674

TE DEUM LAUDAMUS.

1. Te Deum laudamus, Te Dominum confitemur.
2. Te æternum Patrem omnis terra veneratur.
3. Tibi omnes Angeli, Tibi Cœli et universæ Potestates:
4. Tibi Cherubin et Seraphin incessabili voce proclamant,
5. Sanctus, Sanctus, Sanctus, Dominus Deus Sabaoth;
6. Pleni sunt cœli et terra majestatis Gloriæ Tuæ.
7. Te gloriosus Apostolorum chorus,
8. Te Prophetarum laudabilis numerus,
9. Te Martyrum candidatus laudat exercitus.
10. Te per orbem terrarum sancta confitetur Ecclesia,
11. Patrem immensæ Majestatis:
12. Venerandum Tuum verum et unicum Filium:
13. Sanctum quoque Paraclitum Spiritum.
14. Tu Rex Gloriæ, Christe:
15. Tu Patris sempiternus es Filius.
16. Tu ad liberandum suscepturus hominem non horruisti Virginis uterum.
17. Tu devicto mortis aculeo aperuisti credentibus regna cœlorum.
18. Tu ad dexteram Dei sedes in Gloria Patris.
19. Judex crederis esse venturus.
20. Te ergo quæsumus, famulis Tuis subveni, quos pretioso sanguine redemisti.
21. Æternâ fac cum Sanctis Tuis in Gloriâ numerari.
22. Salvum fac populum Tuum Domine, et benedic hæreditati Tuæ.
23. Et rege eos et extolle illos usque in æternum.
24. Per singulos dies benedicimus Te:
25. Et laudamus Nomen Tuum in sæculum, et in sæculum sæculi.
26. Dignare Domine die isto sine peccato nos custodire.
27. Miserere nostri Domine: miserere nostri.
28. Fiat misericordia Tua Domine super nos, quemadmodum speravimus in Te.
29. In Te Domine speravi: non confundar in æternum.

GRAUN, F. J. HAYDN.

English Version.

1. We praise thee, O GOD, we acknowledge Thee to be the LORD.
2. All the earth doth worship Thee, the Father everlasting.
3. To Thee all Angels cry aloud, the Heavens, and all the Powers therein.
4. To Thee Cherubin, and Seraphin, continually do cry,
5. Holy, Holy, Holy, LORD GOD of Sabaoth;
6. Heaven and earth are full of the Majesty of Thy Glory.
7. The glorious company of the Apostles praise Thee.
8. The goodly fellowship of the Prophets praise Thee.
9. The noble army of Martyrs praise Thee.
10. The holy Church throughout all the world, doth acknowledge Thee,
11. The Father, of an infinite Majesty;
12. Thine honourable, true, and only Son;
13. Also the Holy Ghost, the Comforter.
14. Thou art the King of Glory, O CHRIST.
15. Thou art the everlasting Son of the Father.
16. When Thou tookest upon Thee to deliver man, Thou didst not abhor the Virgin's womb.
17. When Thou hadst overcome the sharpness of death, Thou didst open the Kingdom of Heaven to all believers.
18. Thou sittest at the right hand of GOD, in the Glory of the Father.
19. We believe that Thou shalt come to be our Judge.
20. We therefore pray Thee, help Thy servants, whom Thou hast redeemed with Thy precious Blood.
21. Make them to be numbered with Thy Saints, in glory everlasting.
22. O LORD, save Thy people, and bless Thine heritage.
23. Govern them, and lift them up for ever.
24. Day by day we magnify Thee,
25. And we worship Thy Name, ever world without end.
26. Vouchsafe, O LORD, to keep us this day without sin.
27. O LORD, have mercy upon us, have mercy upon us.
28. O LORD, let Thy mercy lighten upon us, as our trust is in Thee.
29. O LORD, in Thee have I trusted: let me never be confounded.   HANDEL, HENSCHEL, SULLIVAN.

(The following words are sometimes added.)

O LORD, save the Queen,
And mercifully hear us when we call upon Thee.

675

DEUTERONOMY vii. 9. Know then, the LORD thy GOD is a faithful GOD, Which sheweth mercy to them that love Him, and keep His commandments.

13. He will love thee, and will bless thee, and multiply thee,

19. Whose mighty hand, and Whose arm outstretched, hath brought thee out.

21. The LORD is with thee, a mighty GOD, and terrible.

F. J. HAYDN.

676

Lo, my Shepherd is divine;
Can I want when He is mine?
By the streams that wander slow,
Thro' the meads where flow'rets blow,
He doth lead me to rest,
Still with peace and comfort blest.

F. J. HAYDN.

677

Father, we adore Thee, and worship Thee,
O GOD most high:
Holy LORD, Mighty GOD,
We worship Thee.
Glorify His Name for evermore,
And tell of all His wondrous works:
Holy, mighty, glorious GOD,
We worship Thy Name evermore.

F. J. HAYDN.

678

COLLECT

For the Seventeenth Sunday after Trinity.

LORD, we pray Thee that Thy grace may always prevent and follow us, and make us continually to be given to all good works; through JESUS CHRIST our LORD. Amen.

F. J. HAYDN, ROBERTS.

679

THE PASSION.

No. 1

St. Luke xxiii. 34. "Father, forgive them; for they know not what they do."

Lamb of God! Surely Thou hast borne our sorrows; with Thy stripes we are healed.

Lamb of God! Thou blessest them that persecute Thee, and prayest for them who despitefully use Thee.

Vengeance is Mine, saith the Lord, I will repay.

A lamb before her shearers is dumb, so Thou openest not Thy mouth.

Thou art cut off from the land of the living; for our transgressions art Thou smitten.

Thou art oppressed; Thou art afflicted; O Lamb of God!

But Thou didst no violence, nor was deceit in Thy mouth.

Lamb of God! Thou blessest them that persecute Thee; with Thy stripes we are healed. Thou didst no evil.

Thou, when reviled, reviledst not again; Thou, suffering, threatenedst not.

Thou bearest our sins in Thy Body on the tree.

Thou art not overcome of evil; but Thou overcomest evil with good.

Reviled, Thou blessest, defamed, entreatest, O Lamb of God!

No. 2

St. Luke xxiii. 43. "Verily I say unto Thee, this day shalt thou be with Me in Paradise."

Psalm li. 1. Lord, have mercy on me after Thy great goodness; I acknowledge my transgressions, and my sin is ever before me.

Cast me not away from Thy presence, and take not Thy Holy Spirit from me.

Wash me throughly from my wickedness, and cleanse me from my sin.

Hide Thy face from my sins.

Against Thee only have I sinned, and done this evil in Thy sight.

My sin is ever before me; I acknowledge my transgression.

Thou shalt purge me, and I shall be clean: Thou shalt wash me, and I shall be whiter than snow.

Thou shalt make me hear of joy and gladness, that the bones which Thou hast broken may rejoice.

No. 3

St. John xix. 26, 27. " WOMAN, BEHOLD THY SON. SON, BEHOLD THY MOTHER."

St. LUKE xxiii. 27. There followed Him a great company of people, and of women which also bewailed and lamented Him.

28. But JESUS said . " Weep not, Daughters of Jerusalem, weep not for Me, weep for yourselves and for your children."

JOEL ii. 12. Turn ye unto Me, saith the LORD, with all your heart, and with fasting, and with weeping, and with mourning.

13. Rend your heart, and not your garments, and turn unto the LORD your GOD; for He is gracious and merciful, slow to anger and of great kindness, and repenteth Him of the evil. The LORD your GOD is merciful.

No. 4

St. MATTHEW xxvii. 46. "ELI, ELI, LAMA SABACTHANI ?"

O My GOD, look upon Me, Why hast Thou forsaken Me? Why art Thou so far from My health, and from the words of My complaint? Go not from Me.

All they that see Me laugh Me to scorn.   •

Hide not Thou Thy face from Me.

Thou hast been My succour, leave Me not: forsake Me not, O GOD.

Turn Thee unto Me; for I am desolate and in misery.

My hope hath been in Thee, O LORD. LORD, in Thee have I trusted: I have said, Thou art My GOD.

No. 5

ST. JOHN xix. 28. THAT THE SCRIPTURE MIGHT BE
FULFILLED, JESUS SAITH, "I THIRST."

REVELATION xix. 15. He treadeth the winepress of the
fierceness and wrath of Almighty GOD.

PSALM lxix. 21. Thy rebuke hath broken His heart : He
is full of heaviness.

He looked for some to have pity on Him, but there was
no man : Neither found He any to comfort Him.

22. They gave Him gall to eat ; and when He was
thirsty they gave Him vinegar to drink.

No. 6 .

ST. JOHN xix. 30. " IT IS FINISHED.

vi. 38. He came down from Heaven, not to do His own
will, but the will of Him that sent Him.

HEBREWS x. 5. "Sacrifice and offering Thou wouldest
not, but a body hast Thou prepared Me; in burnt
offerings and sacrifices for sin Thou hast had no pleasure.
Then said I, Lo, I come to do Thy will, O GOD.

PSALM xl. 10. In the volume of the book it is written
of Me that I should fulfil Thy will, O GOD : I am content
to do it ; yea, Thy law is within My heart.

ST. JOHN xvii. 4, 3. Holy Father, righteous Father, I
have finished the work which Thou gavest Me to do ; and
now I come to Thee."

No. 7

ST. LUKE xxiii. 46. " FATHER, INTO THY HANDS I
COMMEND MY SPIRIT."

Into Thy hands, O LORD, I commend My spirit.

Hereby perceive we the love of GOD, that He laid down
His life for us.

He tasted death for every man : He poured out His
soul unto death ; He made intercession for the transgressors.

He died for us, that, whether we wake or sleep, we
should live together with Him.

Thou hast redeemed us, O LORD, Thou GOD of Truth.

No. 8

The Earthquake.

The veil of the temple was rent in twain: the sun was darkened; the earth did quake; the rocks were rent; the graves opened; and many bodies of the saints which slept arose, for truly This was the Son of God, Whose voice then shook the earth.

And yet once more He will shake not only the earth, but also the heaven.

F. J. Haydn.

680

The arm of the Lord is upon them, by the edge of the sword they fell, and the rolling thunder He cast on all; man against man He set them, none can escape His fury, the sword of the Lord devoureth them all. The Lord, He will have mercy; in peace He keepeth Zion.

F. J. Haydn.

681

Psalm cii. 1, 2. Hear my prayer, O Lord, and turn not away Thy face from Thy servant.

lxxix. 5. How long wilt Thou be angry? shall Thine indignation burn for ever?

lxix. 17, 21. Hear me, O Lord! Thy rebuke hath broken my heart.

I looked for some to have pity on me, but there was no man to comfort me.

lxxi. 1. In Thee, O Lord, do I put my trust: Father, have mercy on me, according to Thy holy Word.

M. Haydn.

682

Job. x. 1. My soul is weary of life: I will speak in the bitterness of my soul. I will say unto God, O do not condemn me; shew me why Thou contendest with me.

xiv. 1. Man that is born of a woman is of few days, and full of trouble.

2. He cometh up, and is cut down like a flower; he fleeth as it were a shadow, and continueth not in one stay.

vii. 21. Why pardonest Thou not my transgression? Why take not mine iniquity from me?

xiv. 13. O that Thou wouldest hide me in the grave till Thy wrath be passed!

iii. 17. There the wicked cease from troubling, there the weary are at rest.

v. 17. Behold, happy is the man whom GOD correcteth;

18. For He maketh sore, and bindeth up; He woundeth, and maketh whole.

ISAIAH xii. 2. Therefore I will trust, and not be afraid: for the LORD JEHOVAH is my strength and my song, and He will also become my salvation.

J. C. BECKWITH.

683

ECCLESIASTICUS xliii. 29. The LORD is very great and terrible; marvellous in His power.

28. He is great above all His works.

11. Look upon the rainbow, and praise Him that made it: beautiful it is in the brightness thereof.

12. It compasseth the heaven with a glorious circle, and the hand of the Most High hath bended it.

13. He maketh the snow to fall apace, and sendeth swiftly the lightnings of His judgment.

19, 18. The hoar-frost also He poureth on the ground, and the eye marvelleth at the beauty of the whiteness thereof.

20. When the cold north-wind bloweth, and the water is congealed into ice, it is clothed as with a breast-plate.

ROMANS xi. 33. O how unsearchable are all His works, and His ways are past finding out!

ECCLESIASTICUS xliii. 16. At His sight the mountains are shaken, and at His will the south wind bloweth.

17. The noise of the thunder, the northern storm, and the whirlwind, make the earth tremble.

PSALM lxviii. 4. Sing unto GOD, and sing praises unto His Name: sing unto GOD, and magnify Him that rideth upon the heavens: praise Him in His Name JEHOVAH, yea, and rejoice before Him. Amen.

J. C. BECKWITH.

684

PSALM cxlv. 3. Great is the LORD and marvellous, worthy to be praised; and all generations shall praise His holy Name. Heaven and earth shall praise His Name for ever and ever, and declare His power and majesty. Amen.

RIGHINI.

685

PSALM xxxi. 2. Incline Thine ear to me, O LORD, make haste to deliver me.

vi. 4. O save me for Thy mercies' sake.

HIMMEL.

686

PSALM xcv. 6, 7. O come, let us worship and kneel before the LORD our Maker, for He is the LORD our GOD.

HIMMEL.

687

PSALM cxlvii. 12. Praise the LORD, O Jerusalem: praise thy GOD, O Sion.

cxlviii. 2. Praise Him, all ye angels: praise Him, all His host.

3. Praise Him, sun and moon: praise Him, stars and light.

cvii. 15. O that men would therefore praise the LORD for His goodness, and declare the wonders that He doeth for the children of men! Hallelujah. Amen.

SCOTT.

688

PSALM cxxi. 1. Unto Thee, O LORD, do I lift up mine eyes, from whence cometh my help.

cxxiv. 2. Our help is in the Name of the LORD, Who made heaven and earth.

xliii. 3. O send out Thy light and Thy truth, that they may lead me, and bring me unto Thy holy hill, and to Thy dwelling.

There to the pleasant harp my voice I'll raise

To Thee, O GOD, my GOD, in songs of praise.

WEBBE.

689

Psalm xix. 1. The heavens declare the glory of God, and the firmament sheweth His handywork.

Psalm cxlv. 10. All Thy works praise Thee, O Lord, and Thy saints give thanks unto Thee.

11. They shew the glory of Thy Kingdom, and talk of Thy power:

12. That Thy power, Thy glory, and mightiness of Thy Kingdom, might be known unto men.

13. Thy Kingdom is an everlasting Kingdom, and Thy dominion endureth throughout all ages.

Webbe.

690

Save us, O God, we fix our hope in Thee,
And to Thy shadowing wing for refuge flee.

Psalm xxiii. 4. Though I walk in the valley of the shadow of death, yet will I fear no ill, for Thou art with me.

cxxi. 3. He will not suffer thy foot to be moved: He that keepeth thee shall not sleep.

4. Behold, He that keepeth Israel, shall neither slumber nor sleep.

5. The Lord Himself is thy keeper; the Lord Himself is thy defence upon thy right hand.

6. So that the sun shall not burn thee by day, neither the moon by night.

7. The Lord shall preserve thee from all evil; yea, it is even He that shall keep thy soul.

Save us, O God, we fix our hope in Thee,
And to Thy shadowing wing for refuge flee.

Webbe.

691

Sit Trinitati sempiterna gloria,
Honor, potestas, atque jubilatio;
In Unitate Quæ gubernat omnia
Per universa sæculorum sæcula.

Webbe.

692

PSALM xxvi.   1. Be Thou my judge, O LORD, for I have walked innocently : my trust hath been also in the LORD, therefore I shall not fall.

2. Examine me, O LORD, and prove me : try out my reins and my heart.

3. For Thy loving-kindness is ever before mine eyes, and I will walk in Thy truth.

6. I will wash my hands in innocency, O LORD, and so will I go to Thine Altar ;

7. That I may shew the voice of thanksgiving, and tell of all Thy wondrous works.

lxxxv.   7. Shew us Thy mercy, O LORD : and grant us Thy salvation.   Amen.

J. CORFE.

> 693 BOYCE, vv. 1–3, 6, 7.
> 694 J. H. CLARKE, v. 1.
> 695 DE LACY, vv. 1–3.
> 696 E. J. HOPKINS, vv. 6, 3, 7.

697

COLLECT

For the Sixth Sunday after Trinity.

O GOD, Who hast prepared for them that love Thee such good things as pass man's understanding ; pour into our hearts such love toward Thee, that we, loving Thee above all things, may obtain Thy promises, which exceed all that we can desire : through JESUS CHRIST our LORD.   Amen.

ALLEN, A. S. BAKER, BATSON, J. CORFE, OAKELEY.

698

PSALM v.   1. Ponder my words, O LORD : consider my meditation.

2. O hearken Thou unto the voice of my calling, my King and my GOD, for unto Thee, O GOD, will I make my prayer.

3. My voice shalt Thou hear betimes, O LORD : early in the morning will I direct my prayer unto Thee, and will look up.

7. I will also come into Thine house, even upon the multitude of Thy mercy, and I will worship toward Thy Holy Temple.

vi. 3. My soul also is sore troubled : but, LORD, how long wilt Thou punish me ?

4. Turn Thee, O LORD, and deliver my soul : O save me for Thy mercy's sake.

9. The LORD hath heard my petition, the LORD will receive my prayer. Amen.

J. CORFE.

699 CHERUBINI, Psalm vi. 4, 9.

700

PSALM cxviii. 24. This is the day which the LORD hath made, we will rejoice and be glad in it.

lxviii. 26. Give thanks, O Israel, unto GOD the LORD in the congregation : give thanks unto GOD from the ground of the heart.

xxvii. 1. The LORD is my light, and my salvation, whom then shall I fear? The LORD is the strength of my life, of whom then shall I be afraid?

xxviii. 10. O save Thy people, and give Thy blessing unto Thine inheritance : feed them, and set them up for ever.

xxix. 10. The LORD shall give strength unto His people, the LORD shall give His people the blessing of peace.

lxxii. 18, 19. Blessed be the LORD GOD, even the GOD of Israel, Which only doth wonders : and blessed be the Name of His Majesty for ever and ever. Amen.

J. CORFE.

701

PSALM cxliii. 1. Hear my prayer, O LORD, give ear to my supplications : in Thy faithfulness answer me, and in Thy righteousness.

WINDR.

702

Great God of all, Holy Creator,
    Father and Lord of heaven, earth, and sea,
Humbly we fall adoring before Thee ;
    Receive our prayers, our praises, Most High !
Infinite beauty, power, and skill,
    Shine over all Thy glorious works.
Oh, who can count the stars that fill
    The spacious firmament of heaven ?
Great is Thy love, O Lord, to man ;
    Mercy and holy peace are Thine ;
Grant us, then, grace with thankful voice
    To praise Thy Name in songs of joy.
Great God of all, Holy Creator,
    Receive our prayers and praises, Most High !

Beethoven.

703

Hallelujah to the Father, and the Son of God.
Praise the Lord, ye everlasting choir, in holy songs of
    joy.
Worlds unborn shall sing His glory, the exalted Son of
    God.
Praise the Lord in holy songs of joy.

Another Version.

Hallelujah unto God's Almighty Son.
Praise the Lord, ye bright angelic choirs, in holy songs
    of joy.
Man, proclaim His grace and glory, Hallelujah.
Praise the Lord in holy songs of joy.

Beethoven.

704

Hear my crying, O turn not Thy mercy from me.
Lord, have mercy on us !
Blessed be the Lord God, even the Lord God of Israel.
Have compassion on us !

Beethoven.

705

TE DEUM LAUDAMUS.

We worship, we confess Thee LORD,
Eternal Father, King adored.
All things on Earth with one accord
   Exalt Thy mighty Name.
The Angel choirs their voices raise ;
The Host of Heaven Thy power displays ;
Thee Cherubim, with endless praise,
   And Seraphim, proclaim.

" All Holy, Holy, Holy, Thou !
" Thy glory Earth and Heaven avow :
" LORD GOD of Hosts, to Thee we bow,
   " Our Maker, Life, and Light ! "
To Thee Thy great Apostles cry ;
Thee sainted Prophets magnify ;
With white-robed Martyrs' songs on high
   Doth Thy whole Church unite.

O CHRIST, the Father's only Son,
With Him, and GOD the Spirit, One,
Before Creation's work begun,
   Thou, glorious King, dost reign :
Yet didst not Thou, Redeemer, scorn
To be of lowly Virgin born,
For those their fallen state that mourn,
   Salvation to obtain.

For us Thou laid'st Thy power aside,
For us to conquer Death hast died,
For all who in Thy faith abide,
   And Thee their Saviour own.
Now in GOD's might at His right hand,
Thou sendest forth Thine high command ,
And lo ! Heaven's portals open stand,
   And crowds approach Thy Throne.

Yet once again, for Thou hast said,
Shall be revealed Thy Presence dread,
When Thou, the LORD of quick and dead,
    For judgment shalt descend.
Then hear, LORD JESUS, hear our prayer;
Thy ransomed flock in mercy spare;
Make us with all Thy saints to share   .
    In glory without end.

O Prince and Saviour, still we pray,
Direct, exalt us in Thy way:
That Name we worship day by day,
    May we in Heaven adore.
On us, LORD, let Thy mercy shine
This day, and ever keep us Thine:
In Thee we trust, our King divine,
    And triumph evermore.

BEETHOVEN.

706

When I call upon Thee, O hear me, for Thy mercy's
sake.   Hear my voice, O LORD, and help me.   Have
mercy on us.   O hear our prayer, O hear and spare us.
Hide not Thou Thy face from us.   O hear us.

BEETHOVEN.

707

Great is JEHOVAH the LORD.   The heavens and the
earth proclaim His power and His might.   'Tis heard in
the crash of the storm, in the wild torrent's loud impetuous
roar.   Great is JEHOVAH the LORD; wondrous His power
and might.   At His command the trees put forth their
opening leaves, and valleys wave bright with golden corn;
with lovely flowers the fields are decked, and stars in
splendour fill the vault of heaven.   Heard with dread in
the thunder's deep blast, and seen in flames of lightning.
But chief in His great loving-kindness shines forth
JEHOVAH's boundless might.   In His loving-kindness
shines forth the boundless power of GOD.   Raise your
prayerful hearts on high, and hope for mercy, and trust
in Him

SCHUBERT.

708

THE SONG OF MIRIAM.

No. 1

Strike your timbrels, Hebrew maidens, Miriam bids upraise the lay;
Mighty is the LORD at all times, mightier hail we Him
to-day.

No. 2

Out of Egypt, as a shepherd guards his flock, and shews
the way,
Thou hast led Thy chosen people, fire by night and cloud
by day.
Shepherd, Thou hast led us onward, strong Thine arm,
and keen Thine eye,
At Thy word the sea obedient parts, and leaves a pathway
dry;
At Thy blast the floods congealing stand upright as crystal
walls;
Through the sea's heart pass we dry-shod, trusting in Thy
voice which calls.

No. 3

As we pass the sky grows darker, voices shout, "We will
pursue!"
Armour gleaming, trumpets clanging, Pharaoh's host
bursts on the view;
LORD of Hosts, this hour we perish, help us, LORD, our
Rock, prove true.
  Voices shout, still pressing onward, "We will pursue
and overtake." But hark! What sighings! wailings!
moanings! cursings! Hark! the storm! 'Tis the LORD
in all His fury. Headlong rush the pent-up waves.
Pharaoh's chariots! horse and rider! mighty waters
overwhelm them. Fearfulness and dread upon them fall:
by darkness and horror are they smitten: drown'd the
captains and drown'd the host.

No. 4

Egypt's king! as lead sinks he down beneath the
mighty flood. Earth hath swallowed all.
GOD no more her tide restraining, all her shores the sea
regaining,
Ne'er restoreth king or slave, her sad waste at once both
shroud and grave.

No. 5

Strike your timbrels, Hebrew maidens, Miriam bids upraise the lay,
Mighty is the LORD at all times, mightier hail we Him
to-day.

SCHUBERT.

709

PSALM xxiii. (Paraphrase.) The LORD is my shepherd;
I shall not want. He maketh me to rest in green pastures,
He leadeth me beside still waters, He giveth peace unto my
soul, He leadeth me in paths of goodness, for His Name's
sake. Yea, though I walk through death's dark vale of
shadows, no evil will I fear, for Thou art still with me. Thy
rod and staff, they comfort me. Thou preparest here a table
for me in presence of mine enemies; my head with oil
Thou anointest; my cup runneth over; yea, surely peace
and mercy all my life shall follow me: and I will dwell
with GOD for evermore.

SCHUBERT.

710

COLLECT

For the Sunday called Quinquagesima.

O LORD, Who hast taught us that all our doings
without charity are nothing worth; Send Thy Holy
Ghost, and pour into our hearts that most excellent
gift of charity, the very bond of peace and of all virtues,
without which whosoever liveth is counted dead before
Thee: Grant this for Thine only Son JESUS CHRIST'S
sake. Amen.

HOLDEN, MARSH.

711

PSALM lxxx. 1. Hear, O Thou Shepherd of Israel, Thou that leadest Joseph like a sheep : shew Thyself also, Thou that sittest upon the Cherubims.

[2. Stir up Thy strength, and come, and help us.]

3. Turn us again, O GOD: shew the light of Thy countenance, and we shall be whole.

4. O LORD GOD of Hosts, how long wilt Thou be angry with Thy people that prayeth ?

5. Thou feedest them with the bread of tears, and givest them plenteousness of tears to drink.

[6. Thou hast made us a very strife unto our neighbours, and our enemies laugh us to scorn.]

7. Turn us again, O GOD [of Hosts] : shew the light of Thy countenance, and we shall be whole.

8. Thou hast brought a vine out of Egypt : Thou hast cast out the heathen and planted it.

12. Why hast Thou then broken down her hedge ?

10. The hills were covered with the shadow of it, and the boughs thereof were like the goodly cedar trees.

11. She stretched out her branches unto the sea, and her boughs unto the river.

12. Why hast Thou then broken down her hedge, that all they that go by pluck off her grapes ?

14. Turn Thee again, Thou GOD of Hosts : behold, and visit this vine.

[17. Let Thy hand be upon the man of Thy right hand, and upon the Son of Man, Whom Thou madest so strong for Thine own Self.]

18. And so will not we go back from Thee : O let us live, and we shall call upon Thy Name.

WHITFELD.

712 S. ARNOLD, vv. 1, 4, 5, 17, 18.
713 W. JACKSON, vv. 1-3.
714 PURCELL, vv. 4-7, 18.
715 T. A. WALMISLEY, vv. 1, 7, 4 5, 17, 18.
716 R. WOODWARD, vv. 1, 2, 4, 5, 7, 18.

717

Isaiah xxvi. 4. Trust ye in the Lord for ever: for in the Lord Jehovah is everlasting strength.

Habakkuk iii. 17. Although the fig-tree shall not blossom, neither shall fruit be in the vines; the labour of the olive shall fail, and the fields shall yield no meat; the flock shall be cut off from the fold, and there shall be no herd in the stalls;

18. Yet will I rejoice in the Lord, I will joy in the God of my salvation.

J. S. Smith.

718

Psalm cxiii. 1. Laudate pueri Dominum, laudate Nomen Domini.

2. Sit Nomen Domini benedictum ex hoc nunc, et usque in sæculum.

3. A solis ortu usque ad occasum laudabile Nomen Domini.

4. Excelsus super omnes gentes Dominus, et super cœlos gloria Ejus.

5. Quis sicut Dominus Deus noster, Qui in altis habitat, et humilia respicit in cœlo et in terrâ?

6. Suscitans à terrâ inopem, et de stercore erigens pauperem.

7. Ut collocet eum cum principibus, cum principibus populi sui.

8. Qui habitare fecit sterilem in domo, matrem filiorum lætantem.

Gloria Patri, et Filio, et Spiritui Sancto; sicut erat in principio, et nunc, et semper, et in sæcula sæculorum. Amen.

English Version.

1. O praise the Lord, ye servants, O praise the Name of the Lord.

2. Let the Name of the Lord be blessed, from this time forth and for evermore.

3. From the sun's uprising, even to the going down of the same, His Name be praised.

4. The Lord is high above all nations, and His glory is above the heavens.

5. Who is like the LORD our GOD, He that hath His seat on high, and yet humbleth Himself to regard both heaven and earth ?

6. He doth raise from the dust the lowly man, from the dunghill lifteth He the needy man,

7. That so He may set him with the princes of His people.

8. He maketh her that is childless keep house, yea, to be a mother rejoicing.

Glory to the Father, and to the Son, and to the Holy Ghost ; As it was in the beginning, is now, and ever shall be, to the ages of the ages. Amen.

ZINGARELLI.

719

PSALM lxxxi. 1. Exultate Deo Adjutori nostro : jubilate Deo Jacob.

2. Sumite psalmum, et date tympanum, jucundum psalterium cum citharâ.

[3. Buccinate in neomenia tuba : in insigni die solemnitatis vestræ.] PALESTRINA.

English Version.

1. Sing aloud with gladness unto GOD our Helper. Sing and praise the GOD of Jacob.

2. Come ye with music, strike ye the tabouret, and bring ye the pleasant harp and psaltery.

Another Version.

1. Sing we merrily unto GOD our Strength : make a cheerful noise unto the GOD of Jacob.

2. Take the psalm, bring hither the tabret, the merry harp with the lute.

[3. Blow up the trumpet in the new moon : even in the time appointed, and upon our solemn feast-day.]

S. WESLEY.

720

ECCLESIASTES ii. 11. Omnia vanitas et vexatio spiritûs, præter amare DEUM, et Illi soli servire.

English Version.

All is vanity and vexation of spirit, except to love GOD, and serve Him only. S. WESLEY.

721

Psalm cxiv.   1–3. In exitu Israel de Ægypto, domus
Jacob de populo barbaro, facta est Judæa sanctificatio ejus,
Israel potestas ejus.   Mare vidit, et fugit ; Jordanis con-
versus est retrorsum.

English Version.

1, 2. When Israel came out of Egypt, and the house of
Jacob from the strange people, Judah was his sanctuary,
and Israel his dominion.

3. The sea saw that, and fled : Jordan was driven back.

S. Wesley.

722

St. Luke xxi.   28. Levate capita vestra ; ecce enim
appropinquat redemptio vestra.

English Adaptation.

Psalm xxxii.   12. Lift up your heads, O ye righteous,
and rejoice in the Lord, all ye that are true of heart.

Isaiah xlix.   13. For the Lord hath comforted His
people, and will have mercy on His afflicted.

St. Luke xxi.   28. For, behold, your redemption draweth
nigh.   S. Wesley.

723

Psalm cx.   4. Tu es sacerdos in æternum, secundum
ordinem Melchisedech.

English Version.

4. Thou art a priest for ever, after the order of Melchisedech.   Leo, S. Wesley.

724

Psalm lxi.   1. Hear my crying, O God ; give ear unto
my prayer.

2. From the ends of the earth will I call upon Thee,
when my heart is in heaviness.

lx.   11. O be Thou our help in trouble, for vain is the
help of man.

12. Through God will we do great acts, for it is He
that shall tread down our enemies.

lxi.   8. So will I alway sing praise unto Thy Name, O
Lord most Highest.

Himmel.

725

PSALM cxxxviii. 1. I will exalt Thee, O LORD my GOD; even before the gods will I praise Thee.

Great is our LORD, and great is His goodness, yea, and His mercy endureth for ever.

In time of trouble, O be Thou near me, and I will praise Thy Name in songs of gladness, now and for ever.

I will exalt Thee, Thou LORD of all lords. In time of trouble, O be Thou near me, and I will praise Thy Name in songs of gladness, now and for ever.

I will exalt Thee, O LORD my GOD. Great is the LORD GOD, great is His goodness, yea, and His mercy endureth for ever. O praise His holy Name for ever and ever.

HUMMEL.

726

PSALM cxix. 33. Teach me, O LORD, the way of Thy statutes: and I shall keep it unto the end.

34. Give me understanding, and I shall keep Thy law: yea, I shall keep it with my whole heart.

35. Make me to go in the path of Thy commandments, for therein is my desire.

36. Incline my heart unto Thy testimonies, and not to covetousness.

[37. O turn away mine eyes, lest they behold vanity: and quicken Thou me in Thy way.]

38. O stablish Thy word in Thy servant, that I may fear Thee.

40. Behold, my delight is in Thy commandments: O quicken me in Thy righteousness. Amen.

ATTWOOD, KELWAY, KENT.

727 BOYCE, vv. 33-35, 37, 38, *40.
728 EBDON, vv. 33-35, 37, 40.
729 GRITTON, vv. 33, 34, 33. Amen.
730 B. ROGERS, vv. 33 36, 40.

—— Sometimes sung as separate Anthems.

731

COLLECT

For the Twenty-first Sunday after Trinity.

Grant, we beseech Thee, merciful LORD, to Thy faithful
people pardon and peace: that they may be cleansed from
all their sins, and serve Thee with a quiet mind; through
JESUS CHRIST our LORD.   Amen.

ATTWOOD, W. S. BENNETT, BOOTH, DE LACY,
M. ELVEY, J. V. ROBERTS, H. SMART.

732

COLLECT

For The Epiphany.

O GOD, Who, by the leading of a star, didst manifest
Thy only begotten Son to the Gentiles: mercifully grant
that we, which know Thee now by faith, may after this
life have the fruition of Thy glorious Godhead, through
JESUS CHRIST our LORD.   Amen.

ATTWOOD.

733

PSALM lxviii. 28. Strengthen, O LORD, Thy work,
which Thou hast wrought in us, Thy servants.

29. For Thy temple's sake at Jerusalem, so shall kings
bring presents unto Thee.   Alleluia.

CHERUBINI.

734

§ 1

Lo! star-led chiefs Assyrian odours bring,
And bending Magi seek their infant King.
Mark'd ye, where, hov'ring o'er His radiant Head,
The dove's white wings celestial glory shed?

§ 2

Daughter of Sion, virgin Queen, rejoice!
Clap the glad hand, and lift th' exulting voice!

§ 3

He comes, but not in regal splendour drest,
The haughty diadem, the Tyrian vest;
Not arm'd in flame, all! glorious from afar,
Of hosts the Chieftain, and the LORD of war.
Messiah comes! let furious discord cease.

§ 4

Be peace on earth, before the Prince of Peace!
Messiah comes! let furious discord cease,
Disease and anguish feel His blest control,
And woe, no more, disturb the troubled soul!
May beams of gladness all our hearts illume,
And mercy brood above the distant gloom!
Be peace on earth! Be peace on earth!
(*From " Palestine,"* Nos. 26–29.) CROTCH.

735

§ 1

Lo! Cherub bands the golden courts prepare;
Lo! thrones arise, and every saint is there.
Earth's utmost bounds confess their awful sway,
The mountains worship, and the isles obey.
Nor sun nor moon they need, nor day nor night;
GOD is their Temple, and the Lamb their Light.

§ 2

And shall not Israel's sons exulting come,
Hail the glad beam, and claim their ancient home?
On David's throne shall David's offspring reign,
And the dry bones be warm with life again.

§ 3

Hosanna! Hark! white-robed crowds their deep
    Hosannas raise,
And the hoarse flood repeats the song of praise.
Ten thousand harps attune the mystic song;
Ten thousand thousand saints the strain prolong:

§ 4

" Worthy the Lamb, Omnipotent to save,
" Who died, Who lives, triumphant o'er the grave!"
    Hallelujah. Amen.
(*From " Palestine,"* Nos. 39–43.) CROTCH.

736

ZECHARIAH ix. 9. Behold, thy King cometh unto thee.
COLOSSIANS i. 16. By Him were all things created
that are in heaven and that are in earth. He is the
righteous Saviour.
ZECHARIAH ix. 10. He shall speak peace unto the
heathen.

CROTCH.

737

Holy, Holy, Holy! LORD GOD Almighty!
  Early in the morning our song shall rise to Thee;
Holy, Holy, Holy! Merciful and Mighty,
  GOD in Three Persons: Blessed Trinity!

Holy, Holy, Holy! though the darkness hide Thee,
  Tho' the eye of sinful man Thy glory may not see,
Only Thou art Holy; there is none beside Thee,
  Perfect in power, in love, and purity.

Holy, Holy, Holy! all the saints adore Thee,
  Casting down their golden crowns around the glassy sea;
Cherubim and Seraphim falling down before Thee,
  Which wert, and art, and ever more shalt be.

Holy, Holy, Holy! LORD GOD Almighty!
  All Thy works shall praise Thy Name in earth, and sky,
    and sea;
Holy, Holy, Holy! Merciful and Mighty:
  GOD in Three Persons: Blessed Trinity!

CROTCH.

738

PSALM xcvii. 1. The LORD is King, the earth may be glad thereof: yea, the multitude of the isles may be glad thereof.

2. Clouds and darkness are round about Him: righteousness and judgment are the habitation of His seat.

3. There shall go a fire before Him, and burn up His enemies on every side.

4. His lightnings gave shine unto the world: the earth saw it, and was afraid.

5. The hills melted like wax at the presence of the LORD: at the presence of the LORD of the whole earth.

6. The heavens have declared His righteousness, and all the people have seen His glory.

7. Confounded be all they that worship carved images, and that delight in vain gods: worship Him, all ye gods.

8. Sion heard of it, and rejoiced, and the daughters of Judah were glad, because of Thy judgments, O LORD.

9. For Thou, LORD, art higher than all that are in the earth : Thou art exalted far above all gods.

10. O ye that love the LORD, see that ye hate the thing which is evil.

*The LORD preserveth the souls of His saints; He shall deliver them from the hand of the ungodly.

11. There is sprung up a light for the righteous, and joyful gladness for such as are true-hearted.

12. Rejoice in the LORD, ye righteous, and give thanks for a remembrance of His holiness.

Glory be to the Father, &c.

BARNBY, CROTCH.

739 ARMES, HATTON, vv. 10 (*The LORD preserveth*), 11, 12.
740 S. ARNOLD, vv. 1, 2, 4–6.
741 J. CORFE, vv. 1–4, 6, 8, 12, 6.
742 DOCKER, ELVEY, NAYLOR, vv. 10–12.
743 STEVENSON, vv. 1–3, 5, 4, 6. Amen.

744

LAMENTATIONS v. 1. Remember, O LORD, what is come upon us : consider, and behold our reproach.

3. We are orphans and fatherless.

16. The crown is fallen from our head.

21. Turn us unto Thee, O LORD, and so shall we be turned ; renew our days as of old.

16. Woe unto us, that we have sinned.

17. For this our heart is faint, our eyes are dim.

CROTCH.

745

PSALM lxxxix. 9. Who is like unto Thee, O LORD GOD of Hosts? Thy truth, most mighty LORD, is on every side.

14. Thou hast a mighty arm ; strong is Thy hand, and high is Thy right hand.

50. Praised be the LORD GOD for evermore. Amen.

CROTCH.

746

Above all praise and all majesty, LORD, Thou reignest evermore. Hallelujah.

MENDELSSOHN.

747

A HYMN OF PRAISE.

(Lobgesang.)

No. 1

PSALM cl. 6. All men, all things, all that has life and breath, sing to the LORD. Hallelujah!

3. Praise the LORD with lute and harp, in joyful song extol Him, and let all flesh magnify His might and His glory.

No. 2

ciii. 1. Praise thou the LORD, O my spirit, and my inmost soul, praise His great loving-kindness.

2. Praise thou the LORD, O my spirit, and forget thou not all His benefits.

No. 3

cvii. 2. Sing ye praise, all ye redeemed of the LORD, redeemed from the hand of the foe, from your distresses, from deep affliction; who sat in the shadow of death and darkness. All ye that cry in trouble unto the LORD, sing ye praise, give ye thanks, proclaim aloud His goodness. He counteth all your sorrows in the time of need. He comforts the bereaved with His regard. Sing ye praise, give ye thanks, proclaim aloud His goodness!

No. 4

All ye that cried unto the LORD in distress and deep affliction, He counteth all your sorrows in the time of need.

No. 5

xl. 1. I waited for the LORD, He inclined unto me, He heard my complaint.

4. O blessed are they that hope and trust in the LORD.

No. 6

xviii. 3. The sorrows of death had closed all around me, and hell's dark terrors had got hold upon me, with trouble and deep heaviness.

EPHESIANS v. 14. But said the LORD, "Come, arise from the dead, and awake thou that sleepest, I bring thee salvation."

Isaiah xxi. 11. We called through the darkness.
Watchman, will the night soon pass ?

12. The watchman only said, Though the morning will
come, the night will come also.   Ask ye, enquire ye, ask,
if ye will, enquire ye, return again, ask, Watchman, will
the night soon pass ?

No. 7

Romans xiii. 12. The night is departing, the day is
approaching.   Therefore let us cast off the works of darkness, and let us gird on the armour of light.   The day is
approaching, the night is departing.

No. 8

Let all men praise the Lord,
    In worship lowly bending;
On His most Holy Word,
    Redeem'd from woe, depending.

He gracious is and just,
    From childhood us doth lead ;
On Him we place our trust
    And hope in time of need.

Glory and praise to God,
    The Father, Son, be given,
And to the Holy Ghost,
    On high enthron'd in Heaven.

Praise to the Three-One God ;
    With powerful arm and strong,
He changeth night to day ;
    Praise Him with grateful song.

No. 9

My song shall alway be Thy mercy, singing Thy praise,
Thou only God ; my tongue ever speaks the goodness
Thou hast done unto me.

I wander in night and foulest darkness, and mine
enemies stand threatening around ; yet called I upon the
Name of the Lord, and He redeemed me with watchful
goodness.

No. 10

Ye nations, offer to the LORD glory and might.
Ye monarchs, offer to the LORD glory and might.
Thou heaven, offer to the LORD glory and might.
The whole earth, offer to the LORD glory and might.
O give thanks to the LORD, praise Him, all ye people,
and ever praise His holy Name.
Sing ye the LORD, and ever praise His holy Name.
All that has life and breath, sing to the LORD.
Hallelujah.

MENDELSSOHN.

748

No. 1

PSALM xlii. 1. As the hart pants after the waterbrooks,
so panteth my soul for Thee, O GOD.

No. 2

2. For my soul thirsteth for GOD, yea, for the living
GOD: when shall I come to appear before the presence of
GOD?

No. 3

3. My tears have been my meat day and night, while
they daily say unto me, Where is now thy GOD?
4. Now when I think thereupon I pour out my heart by
myself; for I had gone forth most gladly with the people,
and to lead them forth into JEHOVAH's temple,
5. In the voice of praise and gladness, like as a people
keeping holiday.

No. 4

6. Why, my soul, art thou so vexed? and why art thou
cast down in me?
7. Trust thou in GOD, for I will yet give Him great
thanks for the help of His good countenance.

No. 5

8. My GOD, within me is my soul cast down; therefore
will I remember Thee at the mighty noise of the waters.
9. Deep calleth to deep, at the noise of the water-
spouts; all Thy waves and all Thy billows are gone over
me.

No. 6

10. The LORD hath commanded His kindness in the day-time; in the night did I sing of Him, and made my prayer to the GOD of my life.

11. My GOD, within me is my soul cast down. Why hast Thou Thy servant forgotten? Why go I on thus heavily, while my foe prevails?

No. 7

14. Why, my soul, art thou so vexed? and why art thou cast down in me?

15. Trust thou in GOD; for I will yet give Him great thanks for the help of His good countenance.

xli. 13. Praised be the LORD, the GOD of Israel, from henceforth and for evermore.

MENDELSSOHN.

749

REVELATION xiv. 13. Beati mortui in Domino morientes deinceps; dicit enim Spiritus, ut requiescant a laboribus suis, et opera illorum sequuntur illos.

English Version.

For ever blessed are they which die in the LORD, from henceforth, for ever. Thus the Spirit saith to us; for they do rest from all their labour and sorrow; their works of good and evil shall be requited.

MENDELSSOHN.

750

Da nobis pacem, Domine,
Da nobis perdurare,
Non enim est qui valide
Pro nobis possit stare,
Quam Tu, nostra spes et salus.

English Version.

Grant us Thy peace, Almighty LORD,
Thou Source of every blessing!
Feeble and frail, trust we Thy Word,
All things in Thee possessing:
In Thee is our hope and safety.

MENDELSSOHN.

751

"CHRISTUS."

§ I.—Nos. 1, 2

*St. Matthew ii. 1. When Jesus our Lord was born in Bethlehem, in the land of Judæa, behold, from the east to the city of Jerusalem, there came wise men, and said:

2. Say, where is He born, the King of Judæa? For we have seen His star, and are come to adore Him.*

*Numbers xxiv. 17; Psalm ii. 9. There shall a Star from Jacob come forth, and a sceptre from Israel rise up, and dash in pieces princes and nations.

As bright the star of morning gleams,
So Jesus sheddeth glorious beams
Of light and consolation!
Thy Word, O Lord, radiance darting,
Truth imparting, gives salvation;
Thine be praise and adoration!*

—— Sometimes sung as a separate Anthem.

§ II.—Nos. 3-12

St. Luke xxiii. 1, 2. And the multitude arose, and together they began thus to accuse Him: This Man we have found perverting all the nation, and forbidding to render tribute to Cæsar. He saith He is Jesus, our Master, King of Israel, the Christ, and the Son of the Blessed.

4. Then Pilate said to the priests, the elders, and the people: In Him I find no evil; the Man is faultless.

5. Then cried the people: He stirreth up the Jews, by teaching them in every place, near and far, throughout Judæa, from here to Galilæa.

St. John xviii. 38. Pilate said again: I find in Him no fault at all:

St. Luke xxiii. 16. I therefore will chastise the man, and let Him go.

18. They cried all together: Away with Jesus! Away with Him, and give Barabbas to us!

20. Still, Pilate spake again unto the people, for he was willing to release Jesus.

21. But still they cried: Crucify Him! Crucify Him!

St. John xix. 6. Then unto them said Pilate, Take ye Him and crucify Him, for I cannot find a fault in Him.

7. The Jews answering, said: We have a sacred law, guilty by that law, let Him suffer! He hath made Himself the Son of God the Lord.

§ III.——Nos. 13-15

St. John xix. 16, 17. Then unto them he delivered Him, that they might crucify Him. They then took Jesus, and straightway to Golgotha they led Him.

St. Luke xxiii. 27. There followed after Him a multitude of men and women, bewailing and lamenting for Him.

*St. John xix. 28 Daughters of Zion, weep for your-selves and your children.

29, 30. For surely the days are coming, when they shall exclaim to the mountains, Fall down on us; and to the hills, Hide us.

28. Daughters of Zion, weep for yourselves and your children.*

> * He leaves His heavenly portals,
> Endures the griefs of mortals,
> To raise our fallen race!
> O love beyond expressing,
> He gains for us a blessing,
> He saves us by redeeming grace.
>
> When Thou, O sun, art shrouded,
> By night or tempest clouded,
> Thy rays no longer dart.
> Though earth be dark and dreary,
> If, Jesus, Thou art near me,
> 'Tis cloudless day within my heart.
>
> For death, which sin engenders,
> He full atonement renders,
> If contrite we believe.
> Then humbly bow before Him,
> Let all the earth adore Him,
> Who dies for man that man may live.
>
> MENDELSSOHN.

.—— Sometimes sung as separate Anthems.

752

2 KINGS xix. 16. LORD! bow Thine ear to our prayer.
LAMENTATIONS i. 17. Zion spreadeth her hands for aid,
and there is neither help nor comfort.

(From " Elijah," No. 2.)   MENDELSSOHN.

753

JOEL ii. 12, 13. Ye people, rend your hearts, and not
your garments, for your transgressions; even as Elijah
hath sealed the heavens through the word of GOD.   I
therefore say to ye, Forsake your idols, return to GOD;
for He is slow to anger, and merciful, and kind, and
gracious, and repenteth Him of the evil.

DEUTERONOMY iv. 29. If with all your hearts ye truly
seek Me, ye shall ever surely find Me.   Thus saith our GOD.

JOB xxiii. 3. O that I knew where I might find Him!
that I might even come before His presence!

* PSALM lv. 22. Cast thy burden upon the LORD, and
He shall sustain thee.   He never will suffer the righteous
to fall.

xvi. 8. He is at thy right hand.

cviii. 5. Thy mercy, LORD, is great, and far above the
heavens.

xxv. 3. Let none be made ashamed that wait upon
Thee.*

(From " Elijah," Nos. 3, 4, 15.)   MENDELSSOHN.

—— Sometimes sung as a separate Anthem.

754

PSALM xci. 11. For He shall give His angels charge
over thee, that they shall protect thee in all the ways
thou goest;

12. That their hands shall uphold and guide thee, lest
thou dash thy foot against a stone.

(From " Elijah, No. 7.)   MENDELSSOHN.

755

1 KINGS xviii. 30. Draw near, all ye people : come to me.

36. LORD GOD of Abraham, Isaac, and Israel, this day let it be known that Thou art GOD, and I am Thy servant. O shew to all this people that I have done these things according to Thy word.

37. O hear me, LORD, and answer me, and shew this people that Thou art LORD GOD, and let their hearts again be turned.

PSALM lv. 22. Cast thy burden upon the LORD, and He shall sustain thee. He never will suffer the righteous to fall.

xvi. 8. He is at thy right hand.

cviii. 5. Thy mercy, LORD, is great, and far above the heavens.

xxv. 3. Let none be made ashamed that wait upon Thee.

(*From " Elijah,"* Nos. 14, 15.) MENDELSSOHN.

756

Look down on us from heaven, O LORD ; regard the distress of Thy people ! Open the heavens and send us relief ! Help, help Thy servant, now, O GOD !

(*From " Elijah,"* No. 19.) MENDELSSOHN.

757

ISAIAH xlviii. 1, 18. Hear ye, Israel ; hear what the LORD speaketh : O·hadst thou heeded My command-ments !

liii. 1. Who hath believed our report ? to whom is the arm of the LORD revealed ?

xlix. 7 ; li. 12 ; xli. 10. Thus saith the LORD, the Redeemer of Israel, and His Holy One, to him oppressed by tyrants : I am He that comforteth : Be not afraid, for I am thy GOD, I will strengthen thee.

li. 12, 13. Say, who art thou, that thou art afraid of a man that shall die ; and forgettest the LORD thy Maker, Who hath stretched forth the heavens, and laid the earth's foundations ?

ISAIAH xli. 10. Be not afraid, saith GOD the LORD.

Be not afraid, thy help is near. God, the Lord thy God, saith unto thee " Be not afraid ! "

Psalm xci. 7. Though thousands languish and fall beside thee, and tens of thousands around thee perish; yet still it shall not come nigh thee.

(*From " Elijah*," Nos. 21, 22.) Mendelssohn.

758

*Psalm cxxi. 1. Lift thine eyes to the mountains, whence cometh help.

2. Thy help cometh from the Lord, the Maker of heaven and earth.

3. He hath said, Thy foot shall not be moved: thy keeper will never slumber.*

*4. He watching over Israel slumbers not, nor sleeps.

cxxxviii. 7. Shouldst thou, walking in grief, languish, He will quicken thee.*

(*From " Elijah*," Nos. 28, 29.) Mendelssohn.

—— Sometimes sung as a separate Anthem.

759

Psalm xxxvii. 7, 4. O rest in the Lord ; wait patiently for Him, and He shall give thee thy heart's desires.

5, 1. Commit thy way unto Him, and trust in Him, and fret not thyself because of evil-doers.

* St. Matthew xxiv. 13. He that shall endure to the end, shall be saved.*

(*From " Elijah*," Nos. 31, 32.) Mendelssohn.

—— Sometimes sung as a separate Anthem.

760

1 Kings xix. 11. Behold, God the Lord passed by !

And a mighty wind rent the mountains around, brake in pieces the rocks, brake them before the Lord. But yet the Lord was not in the tempest.

Behold, God the Lord passed by !

And the sea was upheaved, and the earth was shaken. But yet the Lord was not in the earthquake.

12. And after the earthquake there came a fire. But yet the Lord was not in the fire.

And after the fire there came a still small voice. And in that still voice, onward came the Lord.

* ISAIAH vi. 2, 3. Above Him stood the Seraphim, and one cried to another ;

Holy, Holy, Holy is GOD the LORD, the LORD Sabaoth. Now His glory hath filled all the earth.*

(*From " Elijah,"* Nos. 34, 35.) MENDELSSOHN.

—— Sometimes sung as a separate Anthem.

761

ISAIAH liv. 10. For the mountains shall depart, and the hills be removed ; but Thy kindness shall not depart from me ; neither shall the covenant of Thy peace be removed.

ST. MATTHEW xxiv. 13. He that shall endure to the end shall be saved.

(*From " Elijah,"* Nos. 37, 32.) MENDELSSOHN.

762

ST. MATTHEW xiii. 43. Then shall the righteous shine forth as the sun in their heavenly Father's realm.

ISAIAH xxxv. 9, 10. Joy on their head shall be for everlasting, and all sorrow and mourning shall flee away for ever.

* PSALM cxxviii. 1. Blessed are the men who fear Him, they ever walk in the ways of peace.

cxii. 4. Through darkness riseth light to the upright. He is gracious, compassionate ; He is righteous.*

(*From " Elijah,"* Nos. 39, 9.) MENDELSSOHN.

—— Sometimes sung as a separate Anthem.

763

MALACHI iv. 5. Behold, GOD hath sent Elijah the prophet, before the coming of the great and dreadful day of the LORD.

6. And he shall turn the heart of the fathers to the children, and the heart of the children unto their fathers, lest the LORD shall come and smite the earth with a curse.

* ISAIAH xli. 25. But the LORD from the north hath raised one, who, from the rising of the sun, shall call upon His Name and come on princes.

xlii. 1. Behold, My servant and Mine elect, in whom My soul delighteth.

xi. 2. On him the Spirit of GOD shall rest ; the spirit of wisdom and understanding, the spirit of might and of counsel, the spirit of knowledge, and of the fear of the LORD.

xli. 25. Thus saith the LORD, I have raised one from the north, who, from the rising, on My Name shall call.

* ISAIAH lv. 1, 3. O come, every one that thirsteth, O come to the waters : come unto Him. O hear, and your souls shall live for ever.

* ISAIAH lviii. 8. And then shall your light break forth as the light of morning breaketh, and your health shall speedily spring forth then ; and the glory of the LORD ever shall reward you.

PSALM viii. 1. LORD, our Creator, how excellent Thy Name is in all the nations! Thou fillest heaven with Thy glory ' Amen.

(*From " Elijah,"* Nos. 40–42.)   MENDELSSOHN.

* Each of these movements is sometimes sung as a separate Anthem.

764

PSALM lv.

Hear my prayer, O GOD, incline Thine ear,
Thyself from my petition do not hide ;
Take heed to me ; hear how in prayer I mourn to Thee ;
Without Thee all is dark ; I have no guide.

The enemy shouteth—the godless come fast ;
Iniquity, hatred upon me they cast.
The wicked oppress me—ah, where shall I fly ?
Perplexed and bewildered, O GOD, hear my cry !

My heart is sorely pained within my breast,
My soul with deathly terror is oppressed.
Trembling and fearfulness upon me fall,
With horror overwhelmed, LORD, hear me call !

O for the wings of a dove !
Far away, far away would I rove ;
In the wilderness build me a nest,
And remain there for ever at rest.

MENDELSSOHN.

765

PHILIPPIANS ii. 8. For our offences Jesus took upon Him humility, and unto death, even upon the cross became He obedient. GOD, therefore, Him hath exalted, and on Him a name hath bestowed high above every mortal name. Hallelujah.

MENDELSSOHN.

766

PSALM xliii. 1. Judge me, O GOD, and plead my cause against an ungodly nation : O deliver me from deceitful and unjust men.

2. For Thou art the GOD of my strength ; O why dost Thou cast me from Thee ? Wherefore mourn I because the enemy sorely oppresseth me ?

3. Send out Thy light and truth, LORD : O let them lead me, and bring me unto Thy holy hill, and to Thy dwelling-place.

4. And then will I go to the Altar of GOD : to GOD, the GOD of my gladness and joy. I will praise Thee upon the harp, O my GOD.

5. O my soul, why art thou cast downward? and why art thou disquieted within me ?

6. Hope in the LORD, O my soul, for I will praise Him, Who is the health of my countenance, and my gracious LORD and GOD.

MENDELSSOHN.

767

1. Lauda Sion, Salvatorem,
   Lauda Ducem et Pastorem,
      In hymnis et canticis.
   Quantum potes, tantum aude,
   Quia major omni laude,
      Nec laudare sufficis.

2. Laudis thema specialis,
   Panis vivus et vitalis,
      Hodie proponitur ;
   Quem in sacræ mensâ cœnæ
   Turbæ fratrum duodenæ
      Datum non ambigitur.

3. Sit laus plena, sit sonora.
   Sit jucunda, sit decora,
      Mentis jubilatio.

4. Bone Pastor, Panis Vere,
   JESU, nostri miserere,
   Tu nos pasce, nos tuere,
   Tu nos bona fac videre
      In terrâ viventium.

5. Tu, Qui cuncta scis et vales,
   Qui nos pascis hic mortales,
   Tu nos Tibi commensales,
   Cohæredes et sodales
      Fac Sanctorum Civium.   Amen.

(From "Lauda Sion," Nos. 1–3, 8.)   MENDELSSOHN.

768 NAUMANN, § 1.
769 PALESTRINA, § 1, 4.   Amen.

770

SACRED CANTATA.—LAUDA SION.

English Version.

No. 1

Praise JEHOVAH, bow before Him,
Joyful, all ye saints, adore Him,
   In chorus His deeds proclaim.
He is mighty in creation,
He is gracious in salvation,
   Laud and magnify His Name!

No. 2

By His care are we protected,
We are aided and directed,
   We receive our daily bread.
He sustaineth all that liveth,
All that we enjoy He giveth,
   By His hand we all are fed.

No. 3

*Sing of judgment, sing of mercies,
Bless the LORD in joyful verses,
   Praise His Name with holy mirth : *
For He sitteth between the Cherubim ;
Let the people honour and worship Him,
   Ere He cometh to judge the earth.

   * ——* Sometimes sung as a separate Anthem.

No. 4

Ye who from His ways have turned,
Ye who His commands have spurned,
   Now His gracious call obey.
Sinners who despise His grace,
Trembling, fly before His face,
   Like the night before the day.
But the righteous who revere Him
Shall remain for ever near Him,
   Evermore before His face !

No. 5

They that in much tribulation
Wait and long for His salvation,
   Have with Him their dwelling-place.
They with songs of angels blending
Hallelujahs never-ending,
   All their grief forget in joy,
Joy that shall be never-ceasing,
Through the ages still increasing,
   Happiness without alloy.
They that serve the LORD with gladness
In this world of sin and sadness,
     There shall rest
     For ever blest.

No. 6

LORD, at all times I will bless Thee,
And in songs of praise address Thee,
   Yea, and make my boast in Thee.
Let the humble gladly hear me,
Let the godly gather near me,
   And exalt Thy Name with me.

When the poor man succour craved,
From his trouble he was saved;
  When he called he was heard.
Come, ye children, I beseech you,
Hearken when I fain would teach you
  From your hearts to fear the LORD.
Taste and see, the LORD is gracious,
Bounteous as the heavens are spacious,
  Yea, the LORD our GOD is good;
He our cry in pity heareth,
He regardeth him that feareth,
  He doth send us needful food.

No. 7

Save the people who adore Thee,
Make the godless fly before Thee,
  O vanquish and lay them low!
When the wicked gather round us,
Let no hostile arrows wound us,
  Shield us from each raging foe!
LORD, our Saviour, guard and watch us,
Rend the nets outspread to catch us,
  Shield us from each raging foe!

When Thy people were enslaved,
By Thy mercy they were saved;
Thou didst rend their bonds asunder;
Egypt trembled at Thy might.
When through dangers they were guided,
Thou didst lead them;
  When in deserts they resided,
  Thou didst guard them day and night.
  Seas divided, through the waters
Thou didst lead all Israel's sons and daughters.

When they thirsted, rocks were riven;
When they hunger'd, bread was given;
Food of angels fell from heaven;
From the dry ground sprang a well,
On the desert manna fell!

No. 8

Thou didst free them from oppression,
Thou didst give them their possession,
Thou didst pardon their transgression ;
When they were in tribulation,
In the midst of desolation,
They were still Thy chosen nation.

LORD, in mercy still befriend us ;
While we live, Good Shepherd, tend us,
  Guide us through this barren vale !
Hence to verdant pastures lead us,
There beside still waters feed us ;
When we pass dark Jordan's river,
Quench the darts from Satan's quiver,
  Lest the gates of hell prevail.

Hear, O LORD, our supplication ;
Shew Thy mercy in salvation !
Save Thy people, O befriend us !
While we live, Good Shepherd, tend us !
    Till in glory
    We adore Thee ! Amen.

MENDELSSOHN.

771

FESTGESANG.

No. 1

Let all creation praise the Lord,
  Ye nations, bow before Him :
In choral strains, with one accord,
  Extol Him and adore Him.
Ye orbs of day, that roll in light,
Ye distant stars, that gem the night,
    O praise your great Creator !

Angelic hosts, repeat the song,
  Ye prophets clad in glory,
Ye ransom'd tribes, the theme prolong,
  Repeat the wondrous story ;
Ye spirits, who are flaming fires,
Awake your trumpets, strike your lyres,
    O praise your great Creator !

No. 2

Let our theme of praise ascending,
Blent in music's lofty strain,
Soaring through the starry main,
Peal in echoes never ending.
Learning dawned, its light arose,
Thus the truth assailed its foes.

Faith and hope began to banish
Doubt and soul-appalling fear ;
Spreading, shining still more clear,
Error in their beams will vanish.
Learning dawned, its light arose,
Thus the truth assailed its foes.

Mortals roamed without a guide,
Darkness clouded every nation,
Not a ray could be descried,
All was gloom and desolation.
Learning dawned, its light arose,
Thus the truth assailed its foes,
Till the earth with one accord,
Shall adore and praise the LORD.

No. 3

The Word went forth, the Word was Light !
God spake, His radiance darted,
Light made chaotic darkness bright,
And night from day was parted !

In space the starry hosts He hung,
The universe in music sung
Its great Creator's glory ;
Still all these countless orbs above
Hail Him in concert as they move.
His praise, in everlasting song,
Rings through the vast celestial throng.

No. 4

Soon may we join the lay
His heavenly chorus raises,
And st nd, in bright array,
To harp and sing our praises.

Where shining Cherubim
And flaming Seraphim
Their Hallelujahs blend
In strains that never end !

MENDELSSOHN.

772

No. 1

PSALM cxiii. 1. Laudate pueri Dominum, laudate Nomen Domini.

2. Sit Nomen Domini benedictum ex hoc nunc, et usque in sæculum.

No. 2

cxxviii. 1. Beati omnes qui timent Dominum, qui ambulant in viis Ejus.

MENDELSSOHN.

English Version.

No. 1

Ye sons of Israel, thank the LORD, sing praises to His glorious Name ; O praise the LORD Who liveth for ever, sing praises to Him now and for evermore.

No. 2

How blest are they who, rejoiced to seek Him, gladly obey His holy Word ; who in His ways are ever walking.

MENDELSSOHN.

Another Version.

No. 1

PSALM ciii. 21. O praise the LORD, all ye His hosts : ye servants of His that do His pleasure.

cxiii. 2. Blessed be the Name of the LORD, from this time forth for evermore.

No. 2

cxv. 1. Not unto us, O LORD, not unto us, but unto Thy Name give the praise : for Thy loving mercy, and for Thy truth's sake.

MENDELSSOHN.

773

Let our hearts be joyful: the Saviour approacheth
Whom GOD hath proclaimed. The Name of the LORD
shall be praised for evermore. Hallelujah.

MENDELSSOHN.

774

PSALM xiii.

No. 1

LORD, how long wilt Thou forget me,
While in lonely grief I mourn ?
And how long Thy face be hiding,
Wilt Thou never more return ?
LORD, how long must I take counsel,
Having sorrow in my heart ;
Foes relentless rise against me,
And no helper take my part ?

No. 2

LORD, my GOD, behold and hear me,
While I draw this fleeting breath,
On mine eyes shed light and healing,
Lest I sleep the sleep of death,
Lest my foe should triumph, saying,
" I against him have prevailed " ;
Lest he, in my fall exulting,
See me by despair assailed.

No. 3

LORD, Thy truth and loving-kindness
I will trust in evermore ;
Let me praise Thy great salvation,
And Thy wondrous grace adore.

No. 4

LORD, in thankful exultation
To Thy Name I fain would sing.
More than all my soul desireth
Shall Thine endless bounty bring.

MENDELSSOHN.

Another Version.

No. 1

Lord, bow down Thine ear unto me, lend Thy guiding
Father-hand.
Wilt Thou judge by my transgressions, ne'er can I before
Thee stand !
Shall my woe be everlasting, shall my enemies deride ?
Weak and helpless shall I sorrow, never in Thy thoughts
abide ?
O Lord, my God, bow down Thine ear unto me, lend
Thy guiding Father-hand.
Wilt Thou judge by my transgressions, ne'er can I before
Thee stand, never more !

No. 2

Hear Thy child, O Lord eternal, Father, look again on me.
Lend Thy light, O God, unto me, that mine eyes henceforth may see.
Let my foes not triumph o'er me, shield me from their
scornful pride,
Save me from their persecution, let them not Thy power
deride.

No. 3

Lord, we trust Thy loving-kindness, joy unto our hearts
restore,
We will sing, with true devotion, hallow'd praises evermore.

No. 4

Let us ever sing His praises, let us in His love rejoice.

MENDELSSOHN.

775

A PRAYER.

Lord, on our offences in justice look not, but in mercy,
Lord, look upon us. Lord, Who art our Redeemer, O
send us Thine aid. Deliver us, and forgive us now all
our sins in mercy, for Thy great glory and Thy Name's
sake.

Novello's Collection.   I   MENDELSSOHN.

776

Man is mortal; all who live, live by death surrounded;
Who can grant, and who will give aid and grace un-
bounded ?
Man's great Redeemer only!
If we of our misdeeds repent, GOD offended will relent.
Holy and gracious GOD! Holy and mighty GOD!
Merciful and most holy Saviour! O hear us, good LORD.
In death's bitter anguish, let our cry for help be heard!
Hear us, LORD, in mercy, hear.
When the pains of death alarm, Grave and Hell impending,
Whose can be the mighty arm, us from woe defending?
Thine, great Redeemer, only!
Thy streams of mercy most abound where the greatest
sins are found.
Holy and gracious GOD! Holy and mighty GOD!
Merciful and most holy Saviour! O hear us, good LORD.
When Satan assails us, save us by Thy mighty word!
Save us, LORD, in mercy, save!
Sin hath drawn us far from Thee; plunged in desolation,
Where for shelter can we flee, where is our salvation?
In Thee, LORD JESUS, only!
When Thou for sin wast crucified, cleansing blood ran
from Thy Side.
Holy and gracious GOD! Holy and mighty GOD!
Merciful and most holy Saviour! O hear us, good LORD.
Increase us in faith, and grant us endless life with Thee.
Save us, LORD, in mercy, save!

MENDELSSOHN.

777

PSALM xxii. 1. My GOD, my GOD, why, O why hast
Thou forsaken Me? Why art Thou far from helping Me
while I cry?

2. My GOD, I cry to Thee by day, but yet Thou hearest
not, and at night do I take no rest.

3. But Thou, LORD, art holy, Thou Who dwellest in
the praises of Israel.

4. For our fathers trusted in Thee, and as they trusted,
Thou didst deliver them.

5. And they cried to Thee, and were delivered; they trusted in Thee, and were not confounded.

6. But I am a worm, and no man, the scorn of men, and of the people despised.

7, 8. All they that see Me laugh and scorn Me; shoot out their lip, and they shake their head: He trusted in the LORD, that He would send help, and deliver Him, and delight in Him.

14. I am poured out like the water, and My bones they are also all out of joint; My heart is within My Body melted like unto wax.

15. Now My strength is dried up, even like a potsherd, and to My jaws My tongue it cleaveth; Me Thou hast laid in the dust of death.

16. For dogs have compassed My dwelling, and assemblies of the wicked Me have enclosed.

17. My hands and My feet they have pierced with anger.

18. They part My garments among them, and for My vesture they cast lots.

19. Be not far from Me, O LORD GOD: O My strength, hasten Thee to help Me.

20. Deliver Thou My soul from the sword, and My darling from the dog's power.

21. Save Me from the mouth of the lion, from the horns of the unicorn Thou hast heard Me.

22. I will declare Thy Name to My brethren, and in the congregation will I praise Thee.

23. O praise the LORD, all ye that fear Him, and honour Him, all the seed of Jacob; fear Him, all ye that are of the seed of Israel.

24. For He hath not despised nor abhorred the poor in affliction, neither hath He hid His face from him, but when to Him he cried, He heard his voice.

25. Thee will I praise, LORD, in the great congregation, I will pay all my vows in the sight of them that fear Him.

26. The meek shall eat, and shall be satisfied, and they with their hearts shall praise the LORD that seek Him, and your heart shall live for ever.

27, 28. The ends of the world shall remember, and shall turn to the LORD their Maker: all the kindreds of the people shall worship before Him, for the earth is the LORD's, and He rules over the nations.

MENDELSSOHN.

778

No. 1

PSALM cxv.   1, 2. Non nobis, Domine, non nobis, sed Nomini Tuo da gloriam super misericordiâ Tuâ et veritate Tuâ.   Nequando dicant gentes, Ubi est Deus eorum?

No. 2

9. Domus Israel speravit in Domino, adjutor eorum et protector eorum est.

10. Domus Aaron speravit in Domino, adjutor eorum et protector eorum est.

12. Dominus memor fuit nostri et benedixit nobis; benedixit domui Israël, benedixit domui Aaron.

13. Benedixit omnibus qui timent Dominum, pusillis cum majoribus.

No. 3

14. Adjiciat Dominus super vos, super vos, et super filios vestros.

No. 4

17. Non mortui laudabunt Te, Domine, neque omnes qui descendunt in infernum.

18. Sed nos qui vivimus benedicimus Domino, ex hoc nunc et usque in sæculum.

1. Non nobis, Domine, non nobis, sed Nomini Tuo da gloriam super misericordiâ Tuâ et veritate Tuâ.

English Version.

No. 1

PSALM cxv.   1. Not unto us, O LORD, but unto Thy Name give the glory; yea, for Thy mercy's sake and for Thy truth's sake.

2. Why should the heathen say, Where is now their GOD?

No. 2

9. House of Israel, O trust in the LORD your GOD, for He is their succour, their defender and helper.

10. House of Aaron, O trust in the LORD your GOD, for He is their succour, their defender and helper.

12. GOD hath been mindful of us, and He shall bless us: He shall bless the house of Israel, He shall bless the house of Aaron.

13. He shall bless all those that fear the LORD their GOD, both small and great.

No. 3

14. The LORD shall increase you more and more, both you and your children.

15. Ye are the blessed of the LORD, Who made the heaven and the earth.

No. 4

17. The dead praise not Thee, O LORD, neither any that go down into silence.

18. But we will praise the LORD, from this time forth and for evermore.

1. Not unto us, O LORD, but unto Thy Name give the glory: yea, for Thy mercy's sake and for Thy truth's sake.

MENDELSSOHN.

779
"COME, LET US SING."
No. 1

PSALM xcv. 6. O come, let us worship and kneel before the LORD, and bow down to Him; come, bow the knee to the LORD our Maker.

7. For He is our GOD, and we are the flock of His pasture, and the people of His hand.

No. 2

PSALM xcv. 1. Come, let us sing to the LORD with gladness, and let us rejoice in His strength.

2. Come to His presence with a song of thanksgiving, and with tuneful rejoicing.

3. For the LORD is a mighty GOD, and a mighty Ruler over all false idols.

No. 3

PSALM xcv. 4. In His hands are all the corners of the earth, and the strength of the hills is also His.

6. O come, let us worship and kneel before the LORD.

No. 4

Psalm xcv. 5. ·For His is the sea, and He hath fashioned it : and His hands formed and prepared the dry land.

6. O come, let us worship and bow down to Him; come, bow the knee to the Lord.

7. For He is the Lord our God, and we the flock of His pasture, the people of His hand.

No. 5

Psalm xcv. 8. Henceforth, when ye hear His voice entreating, turn not deaf ears, shew not hard hearts, as at Miraba they did, and at Massa in the desert.

9. When your fathers tempted and proved Me, and witnessed My works.

10. After forty years' grief at this disobedient race, I said, 'Tis a people that do err and in their hearts rebel, and that of My statutes are still unmindful.

11. Unto whom I sware in My wrath that they should not behold the land of promise.

8. Henceforth, when ye hear His voice entreating, turn not deaf ears, shew not hard hearts.

No. 6

Psalm xcv. 5. For His is the sea, and He hath fashioned it : His hands have formed and prepared the dry land.

6. O come, let us worship and kneel before the Lord : come, bow the knee to the Lord our Maker.

7. For He is the Lord our God, and we the flock of His pasture.

6. O come, let us worship, and bow down to Him.

MENDELSSOHN.

780

Rejoice, O ye people of earth ; sing and praise the Lord. The Saviour has appeared, Whom the Lord had promised. He His truth and His justice to the world hath proclaimed. Hallelujah.

MENDELSSOHN.

781

Periti autem fulgebunt ut fulgor æthereus : quique multos reddiderunt justos erunt stellarum similes in omnem æternitatem.

English Version.

DANIEL xii. 3. The righteous, living for ever, shall shine as the firmament. They that serve the LORD with faithful spirit, they shall be like the stars of heaven. Our GOD saith : I will exalt them.

MENDELSSOHN.

782

Saviour of sinners, throned in glory ;
Holy Redeemer, adoration, praise,
And might be unto Thee.
Hear us, O hear us.

Holy Redeemer, hear us in mercy,
Save and bless us.
In mercy, LORD, forgive our sins.
LORD, let Thy mercy fall upon us.   Amen.

MENDELSSOHN.

783

PSALM xcviii. 1. Sing to the LORD a new made song, for He hath done wonders.

2. The victory He hath gotten with His own right hand and His arm.

3. The LORD hath made known His salvation; He hath shewed His righteousness to the heathen.

4. He remembereth His truth and mercy towards all the house of Israel; all the earth's nations have beheld His salvation.

5. Sing to the LORD, all the earth; praise His Name and be joyful.

6. Sing with the harp, and praise Him ; with harp and psalm be thankful.

7. With the trumpet and the cornet make a joyful noise to the LORD the King.

8. Let the sea roar, and the fulness thereof, the round world, and they that dwell therein.

9. Let the water-floods be joyful, and let the hills rejoice together in the LORD. He shall come to judgment.

10. He then shall judge the world with righteousness, and the people with truth. He shall judge with truth the world and the people. MENDELSSOHN.

784

Surrexit Pastor Bonus, Qui animam Suam posuit pro ovibus Suis, et pro grege Suo mori dignatus est. Alleluia.

Tulerunt Dominum meum, et nescio ubi posuerunt Eum. Si tu sustulisti Eum, dicito mihi, et ego tollam.

Surrexit Christus, spes mea, præcedet vos in Galilæam. Alleluia.

English Version.

* ST. JOHN X. 11. The Lord is our Good Shepherd, Who layeth down His life for us, the sheep He hath chosen. He bore meekly for us all the bitterness of death. Alleluia.*

ST. JOHN xx. 2. Behold, my LORD hath been taken away by night!

15. O where have you laid our Master's precious Body? If thou hast removed Him, tell me where He is hidden, that I may seek Him.

ST. MATTHEW xxviii. 6. JESUS from death is arisen! to Galilee He goes before you. Alleluia.

MENDELSSOHN.

Another Version.

* PSALM cxxxix 1. O LORD, Thou hast searched me out, and known me : Thou knowest my down-sitting, and mine uprising : Thou understandest my thoughts long before.*

6. O whither shall I go then from Thy Spirit, or whither shall I go then from Thy presence?

7. If I climb up into heaven, Thou art there : If I go down into hell, Thou art there also.

8. If I take the wings of the morning, and remain in the uttermost parts of the sea ;

9. Even there also shall Thy hand lead me, and Thy right hand shall hold me.

cxxxviii. 1 ; lxxxvi. 12. I will give thanks unto Thee, O LORD, and praise Thy Name for ever more.

MENDELSSOHN.

Sometimes said to separate them.

785

Acts iv. 24. LORD, Thou alone art GOD, and Thine are the heavens, the earth, and mighty waters.

25, 26. The heathen furiously rage, LORD, against Thee and Thy CHRIST.

29. Now behold, lest our foes prevail, and grant to Thy servants all strength and joyfulness, that they may preach Thy word.

> * To GOD on high be thanks and praise,
>   Who deigns our bonds to sever;
> His cares our drooping souls upraise,
>   And harm shall reach us never.
> On Him we rest with faith assured,
> Of all that live the mighty LORD,
>   For ever and for ever. *
>
> (*From " St. Paul,"* Nos. 2, 3.)   MENDELSSOHN.
>   *——* Sometimes sung as a separate Anthem.

786

St. Matthew xxiii. 37. Jerusalem, Jerusalem, thou that killest the prophets, and stonest them which are sent unto thee, how often would I have gathered unto Me thy children, and ye would not !

Acts vii. 57, 58. Then they ran upon him with one accord, and cast him out of the city, and stoned him, and cried aloud :

Lev. xxiv. 16. Stone him to death. He blasphemes GOD : and who does so shall surely perish. Stone him to death.

Acts vii. 59, 60. And they stoned him ; and he kneeled down, and cried aloud, " LORD, lay not this sin to their charge. LORD JESUS, receive my spirit." And when he had said this, he fell asleep.

> * To Thee, O LORD, I yield my spirit,
>   Who break'st in love this mortal chain ;
> My life I but from Thee inherit,
>   And death becomes my chiefest gain.
> In Thee I live, in Thee I die
> Content, for Thou art ever nigh.*

* Acts vii. 58 : viii. 1. And the witnesses had laid down their clothes at the feet of a young man whose name was Saul, who was consenting unto his death.

2. And devout men took Stephen, and carried him to his burial, and made great lamentation over him.

* St. James i. 12. Happy and blest are they who have endured; for though the body dies, the soul shall live for ever. *

(*From " St. Paul,"* Nos. 7–11.) MENDELSSOHN.

—— Sometimes sung as a separate Anthem.

<h1 style="text-align:center">787</h1>

ACTS ix. 2. And he journey'd with companions towards Damascus, and had authority and command from the High Priest that he should bring them bound, men and women, unto Jerusalem.

But the LORD is mindful of His own, He remembers His children. Bow down before Him, ye mighty, for the LORD is near us.

ACTS ix. 3. And as Saul journeyed, he came near unto Damascus : when suddenly there shone around him a light from heaven ;

4. And he fell to the earth, and he heard a voice saying unto him, Saul, Saul, why persecutest thou Me ?

5. And he said, LORD, who art Thou ? And the LORD said to him, I am JESUS of Nazareth, Whom thou persecutest.

6. And he said, trembling and astonished, LORD, what wilt Thou have me do ? The LORD said to him, Arise, and go into the city, and there shalt thou be told what thou must do.

* ISAIAH lx. 1. Rise up, arise, rise and shine, for thy light comes, and the glory of the LORD riseth bright upon thee.

2. Behold, now total darkness covereth the kingdoms, and gross darkness the people : but upon thee riseth the mighty LORD, the glory of the LORD appeareth upon thee.

<blockquote>
* Sleepers, wake ! a voice is calling,
It is the watchman on the walls,
Thou city of Jerusalem !
For lo ! the Bridegroom comes ;
Arise, and take your lamps.
    Hallelujah.
Awake ! His Kingdom is at hand ;
Go forth to meet your LORD. ¯
</blockquote>

(*From " St. Paul,"* Nos. 13-16.) MENDELSSOHN.

* Sometimes sung as a separate Anthem

788

ACTS ix. 7. And his companions, which journeyed with him, stood, and they were afraid, hearing a voice, but seeing no man.

8. And Saul arose from the earth; and when his eyes were opened he saw no man. But they led him by the hand, and brought him into Damascus.

9. And he was three days without sight, and did neither eat nor drink.

*PSALM li. 1, 11, 17, 13, 15. O GOD, have mercy upon me, and blot out my transgressions, according to Thy loving-kindness; yea, even for Thy mercy's sake! Deny me not. O cast me not away from Thy presence, and take not Thy Spirit from me, O LORD. O LORD, a broken heart, and a contrite heart is offered before Thee. I will speak of Thy salvation; I will teach transgressors, and all the sinners shall be converted unto Thee. Then open Thou my lips, O LORD, and my mouth shall shew forth Thy glorious praise.

ACTS ix. 10. And there was a disciple at Damascus, named Ananias; to him said the LORD: Ananias,

11. Arise, and enquire thou for Saul of Tarsus, for behold, he prayeth.

15. He is a chosen vessel unto Me the LORD.

16. And I will shew unto him how great things he must suffer for My Name's sake.

*PSALM lxxxvi. 12. I praise Thee, O LORD my GOD, with all my heart for evermore.

13. For great is Thy mercy toward me, and Thou hast delivered my soul from the lowest hell.

NAHUM i. 7; REVELATION vii. 17; ISAIAH liii. 4. The LORD, He is good, He shall dry your tears, and heal all your sorrows.

ISAIAH xl. 8. For His word shall not decay.*

(*From " St. Paul."* Nos. 17-20.) MENDELSSOHN.

. — Sometimes sung as a separate Anthem.

789

ACTS ix. 17. And Ananias went his way, and entered into the house ; and laying his hands upon him, said : " Hear thou, brother Saul, the LORD hath sent me hither, even JESUS that appeared unto thee as thou camest, that thou mightest receive thy sight, and be likewise filled with the Holy Ghost."

18. And there fell from his eyes as though it were scales ; and he received his sight forthwith, and arose, and was baptized.

20. And straightway he preached JESUS in the Synagogues, and said, " I thank GOD, Who hath made me free through CHRIST."

*ROMANS xi. 33. O great is the depth of the riches of wisdom and knowledge of the Father ! How deep and unerring is He in His judgments ! His ways are past our understanding !

36. Sing His glory for evermore. Amen.*

(From " St. Paul," Nos. 21, 22.)   MENDELSSOHN.

——— Sometimes sung as a separate Anthem.

790

REVELATION xi. 15. The nations are now the LORD'S ; they are His CHRIST'S,

xv. 4. For all the Gentiles come before Thee, and shall worship Thy Name.

Now are made manifest Thy glorious law and judgments.

From " St. Paul," No. 23.)   MENDELSSOHN.

791

ACTS ix. 29. And Paul came to the congregation, and preached freely the Name of JESUS CHRIST our LORD.

xiii. 2. Then spake the Holy Ghost, Set ye apart Barnabas and Paul, for the work whereunto I have called them.

3. And when they had fasted and prayed, and laid their hands on them, they sent them away.

*2 CORINTHIANS v. 20. Now then are ambassadors in the Name of Christ, and God beseech you by us.

*ROMANS x. 15. How lovely are the messengers that preach us the gospel of peace !

18. To all the nations is gone forth the sound of their words, throughout all the lands their glad tidings.*

(*From " St. Paul,"* Nos. 24-26.) MENDELSSOHN.

——— Sometimes sung as a separate Anthem.

792

ACTS xiii. 4, 5. So they, being filled with the Holy Ghost, departing thence, delayed not, and preached the Word of GOD with joyfulness.

PSALM lxxxix. 1. I will sing of Thy great mercies, O LORD, my Saviour, and of Thy faithfulness evermore.

*O Thou, the true and only Light,
Direct the souls that walk in night,
And bring them 'neath Thy shelt'ring care,
To find their blest redemption there.
Illumine those who blindly roam,
Oh, call the wand'rer kindly home;
The hearts astray that union crave,
And those in doubt, confirm and save.*

(*From " St. Paul,"* Nos. 27, 29.) MENDELSSOHN.

——— Sometimes sung as a separate Anthem.

793

2 TIMOTHY iv. 17. And they all persecuted Paul on his way : but the LORD stood with him, and strengthened him, that by him the Word might be fully known, and that all the Gentiles might hear.

*REVELATION ii. 10. Be thou faithful unto death, and I will give to thee a crown of life.

JEREMIAH i. 8. Be not afraid, My help is nigh.*

ACTS xx. 17-19, 21. And Paul sent, and called the elders of the Church at Ephesus, and said to them : Ye know how, at all seasons, I have been with you, serving the LORD with all humility and with many tears, testifying the faith toward our LORD JESUS CHRIST.

22. And now, behold ye! I, bound in spirit, now go forth to Jerusalem.

23. Bonds and affliction abide me there.

25. And ye shall see my face no more.

37. And they all wept sore, and prayed :
St. Matthew xvi. 22. Far be it from thy path : these things shall not be unto thee.

Acts xxi. 13. What mean ye thus to weep, and thus to break my heart ? For I am prepared not only to be bound, but also to die at Jerusalem, for the Name of the Lord our Saviour Jesus Christ.

xx. 36. And when he had thus spoken, he kneeled down, and prayed with them all.

38. And they accompanied him unto the ship, and saw his face no more.

* 1 St. John iii. 1. See what love hath the Father bestowed on us in His goodness, that we should be called God's own children.*

(*From " St. Paul,"* Nos. 39-43.) Mendelssohn.

—— Sometimes sung as a separate Anthem.

794

2 Timothy iv. 6, 7. And though he be offered upon the sacrifice of our faith, yet he hath fought a good fight; he hath finished his course ; he hath kept well the faith :

8. Henceforth there is laid up for him a crown of righteousness, which the Lord, the righteous Judge, shall give him at the last great day.

2 Timothy iv. 8. Not only unto him, but to all them that love truly His appearing. The Lord careth for us, and blesseth us; the Lord saveth us.

Psalm ciii. 1. Bless thou the Lord, O my soul, and all within me bless His most holy Name evermore.

20. All ye His angels, bless ye the Lord ; all ye His angels, praise ye the Lord.

(*From " St. Paul,"* Nos. 44, 45.) Mendelssohn.

795

Psalm xc. 1. Thou, Lord, our refuge hast been from age to age.

2. Ere Thou hadst brought forth the mountains, or the earth hadst formed, or the world created, Thou art God from everlasting, world without end. Hallelujah.

Mendelssohn.

796

Veni, Domine, et tardare. Relaxa facinora plebis
Tuæ, et revoca dispersos in terram Tuam. Excita, Domine,
potentiam Tuam, et veni, ut salvos nos facias. Veni,
Domine, et noli tardare.

MENDELSSOHN.

English Version.

Hear us, gracious LORD! Withhold not Thy mercy;
forgive us our trespasses; save Thy people; and all who
stray, assemble beneath Thy shelter. Good LORD, deliver
us from our afflictions, and hear us, Thy servants, who
trust in Thee.

MENDELSSOHN.

Another Version.

PSALM cii. 1. Hear my prayer, O LORD, and let my
crying come unto Thee.

2. Hide not Thy face from me in the time of my trouble,
incline Thine ear to me when I call, O hear me, and that
right soon.

CROFT, C. J. FROST, MENDELSSOHN,
NORRIS, PURCELL.

797

PSALM cxiv. 1, 2. When Israel out of Egypt came,
and the house of Jacob from the strange land, then was
Judah His holy place, Israel His dominion.

3. The sea saw, and fled, and Jordan's stream was
driven back.

4. The lofty mountains skipp'd like rams, and all the
little hills like young sheep.

5, 6. What ailed thee, thou sea, that thou fleddest,
and thou Jordan, that backward thy stream was driven?
ye mountains, that like rams ye were skipping, and all ye
little hills, like young sheep?

7, 8. At the LORD's coming, ye trembled, at the presence
of the God of Jacob: Who turned rocks into standing
water pools, and flint stones into springing fountains.

1, 2. When Israel out of Egypt came, and the house of Jacob from the strange land; then was Judah His holy place, Israel His dominion.

Hallelujah! Sing to the LORD for evermore.

1, 2. When Israel out of Egypt came, then was Judah His holy place.

MENDELSSOHN.

798

PSALM ii. 1. Why rage fiercely the heathen, and the people meditate a vain thing?

2. The kings of the earth, they set themselves up, and the rulers counsel take together, against the LORD, and against His Anointed.

3. Now let us break their bonds asunder, and cast away their cords from us.

4. He that sitteth in the heavens shall laugh them to scorn, and the LORD shall deride them.

5. In wrath He shall speak to them, and shall vex them in His sore displeasure.

6. Yet have I set My King on Zion's holy hill, yea, on My holy hill of Zion.

7. I will declare the law, whereof the LORD hath said unto me: Thou art my Son, Thee this day have I begotten.

8. Ask Thou of Me, and I shall give Thee the heathen for Thine inheritance, earth's utmost parts for Thy possession.

9. Thou shalt break them in pieces with sceptres of iron; like a potter's vessel Thou shalt dash them.

10. O therefore be ye wise, O kings; ye judges of the earth, be instructed.

11. Serve the LORD with fear: rejoice to Him with trembling.

12. Kiss ye the Son, lest He be angry, and ye perish from the right way, for His wrath shall soon rekindle; all who trust in His Name, they are blessed.

Glory be to the Father, &c.

MENDELSSOHN.

* The *Gloria Patri* is usually omitted.

799

COLLECT

For the First Sunday after Easter.

Almighty Father, Who hast given Thine only Son to die for our sins, and to rise again for our justification : grant us so to put away the leaven of malice and wickedness, that we may alway serve Thee in pureness of living and truth ; through the merits of the same Thy Son JESUS CHRIST our LORD. Amen.

EVANS.

800

COLLECT

For the First Sunday after Trinity.

O GOD, the strength of all them that put their trust in Thee, mercifully accept our prayers : and because, through the weakness of our mortal nature, we can do no good thing without Thee, grant us the help of Thy grace, that in keeping Thy commandments we may please Thee, both in will and deed : through JESUS CHRIST our LORD. Amen.

EVANS.

801

EXODUS iii. 7, 8. I know their sorrows, and I am come down to deliver them.

ST. MATTHEW xxi. 9. Hosanna to the Son of David : Hosanna in the highest. Blessed is He that cometh in the Name of the LORD.

ST. LUKE ii. 14. Glory to GOD in the highest, and on earth peace, good will towards men.

STURGES.

802 PERGOLESI, St. Luke ii. 14.

803

EPHESIANS iii. 14, 15. I bow my knee unto the Father of our LORD JESUS CHRIST, of Whom the whole family in heaven and earth is named.

16. That He will grant me, according to the riches of His glory, to be strengthened with might by His Spirit in the inner man. Amen.

BARNBY. J. C. BECKWITH.

804

DANIEL ii.   20. Blessed be GOD for ever and ever; for wisdom and might are His.

21. He changeth the times and the seasons: He removeth kings, and setteth up kings · He giveth wisdom to the wise, and knowledge to them that know understanding.

22. He revealeth the deep and secret things; He knoweth what is in the darkness; and the light dwelleth with Him.   Blessed be the Name of GOD for ever and ever.

BEXFIELD.

805

DANIEL xii.   12, 13. Blessed is he that waiteth.   But go thou thy way till the end be : for thou shalt rest.

BEXFIELD.

806

ST. LUKE xix.   38. Blessed is He that cometh in the Name of the LORD.   Glory in the highest, peace in heaven.

(*From " Israel Restored,*" No. 92.)   BEXFIELD.

807

JEREMIAH xxxi.   10, 12.   He that scattered Israel will gather him, and keep him, as a shepherd doth his flock. His soul shall be as a watered garden.

(*From " Israel Restored,*" No. 19.)   BEXFIELD.

808

PSALM v.   8, 13. Lead me, O LORD, in Thy righteousness, because of mine enemies: make Thy way plain before my face.   For Thou, O LORD, wilt bless the righteous.

cxxxvii.   8. Happy shall he be that rewardeth thee, as thou hast served us.

(*From ' Israel Restored'* Nos. 11, 8.)   BEXFIELD.

809

ISAIAH xxxiii. 2. O LORD, be gracious unto us; we,
O LORD, do wait for Thee.

(From " Israel Restored," No. 12.) BEXFIELD.

810

PSALM lxxxviii. 1. O LORD GOD of my salvation, I have
cried day and night before Thee : O let my prayer enter
into Thy presence ; incline Thine ear unto my calling.

ROMANS xi. 1. Has GOD cast away His people?

ISAIAH liv. 8, 10. In a little wrath I hid My face from
thee for a moment : but with everlasting kindness will I
have mercy on thee, saith the LORD thy Redeemer. The
mountains shall depart, and the hills be removed ; but
My kindness shall not depart from thee, neither shall the
covenant of My peace be removed.

(From " Israel Restored," Nos. 17, 26.) BEXFIELD.

811

In dulci jubilo
Let us our homage shew :
Our heart's joy reclineth
In præsepio,
And like a bright star shineth
Matris in gremio ;
Alpha es et O.

O Jesu parvule !
My heart is sore for Thee !
Hear me, I beseech Thee,
O Puer optime !
My prayer let it reach Thee,
O Princeps gloriæ !
Trahe me post Te !

O Patris caritas !
O Nati lenitas !
Deeply were we stained
Per nostra crimina ;
But Thou hast for us gained
Cælorum gaudia :
O that we were there !

Ubi sunt gaudia, where ?
If that they be not there,
There are angels singing
Nova cantica ;
There the bells are ringing
In Regis curiâ :
O that we were there !

PEARSALL.

812

ADVENT HYMN.

No. 1

In lowly guise thy King appeareth,
With meekness clad thy gates He neareth;
Jerusalem, Hosanna sing!
Meet Him with palms, glad honour doing,
With leafy boughs the path be strewing ;
So shalt thou welcome duly bring.

No. 2

O King indeed, though no man hail Thee !
O Leader true, though armies fail Thee !
O Prince of Peace, supreme in might !
The lords of earth would fain defeat Thee,
When Thou would'st in Thy Kingdom seat Thee ;
Yet Thou to conquer need'st not fight.
Thy realm is not of this world counted ;
Yet, all the realms of earth surmounted,
Thine only shall have lasting sway.
Thy servants, faithful tidings bearing,
Go through the world, and peace declaring
To all mankind, prepare Thy way.

No. 3

When Thou the stormy sea art crossing,
Down sink the waves that high were tossing,
The wind is hush'd, rebuk'd by Thee.
Thou comest, tho' Thine own forsake Thee,
That all may for their Saviour take Thee.
That sin and death may fettered be.

No. 4

Thou LORD of grace and truth unfailing,
O come to us, Thy glory veiling,
   Once more, and calm our troubled life.

No. 5

Need is there for Thyself returning,
To bid mankind Thy peace be learning,
While yet the world is full of strife.

No. 6

O may Thy light with us be dwelling,
Our darkness everywhere dispelling,

No. 7

And quenching strife whene'er it come ;
   That all, of high estate or lowly,
   May live as brethren, true and holy,
Made one within their Father's home.

SCHUMANN.

813

PSALM lxv. 1. Te decet hymnus, Deus, in Sion, et Tibi
reddetur votum in Jerusalem.

2. Exaudi orationem meam, ad Te omnis caro veniet.
Kyrie, eleison. Christe, eleison. Kyrie, eleison.

SCHUMANN.

814

PSALM xli. 1. Blessed is he that considereth the poor
and needy : the LORD shall deliver him in the time of
trouble.

2. The LORD preserve him, [and keep him alive,] that he
may be blessed upon earth.

3. The LORD comfort him, when he lieth sick upon his
bed : make Thou all his bed in his sickness.

xxx. 4. Sing praises unto the LORD, O ye saints of
His, and give thanks unto Him for a remembrance of His
holiness.

T. A. WALMISLEY.

815 F. E. GrAr 1.·. N ·1 .·\. I.
816 Jıkyıt \v. ı, ·.

817

MATTHEW xxi. 9. Blessed is He that cometh in the Name of the LORD, Hosanna in the highest.

O Lamb of GOD, that takest away the sins of the world, Have mercy upon us.

Glory be to the Father, &c.

T. A. WALMISLEY.

818

Father of Heaven, in Whom our hopes confide,
Whose pow'r defends us, and Whose precepts guide,
In life our Guardian, and in death our Friend,
Glory supreme be Thine till time shall end !

T. A. WALMISLEY.

819

PSALM cxxiv. 1. If the LORD Himself had not been on our side, now may Israel say; if the LORD Himself had not been on our side, when men rose up against us ;

2. They had swallowed us up quick, when they were so wrathfully displeased at us.

3. Yea, the waters had drowned us, and the stream had gone over our soul.

4. The deep waters of the proud had gone even over our soul.

5. But praised be the LORD, Who hath not given us over for a prey unto their teeth.

6. Our soul is escaped even as a bird out of the snare of the fowler : the snare is broken, and we are delivered.

7. Our help standeth in the Name of the LORD, Who hath made heaven and earth.

PSALM cxv. 16. All the whole heavens are the LORD's the earth hath He given to the children of men.

17. The dead praise not Thee, O LORD, neither all they that go down into silence.

18. But we will praise the LORD, from this time forth for evermore. Praise the LORD. Hallelujah. Amen.

T. A. WALMISLEY.

823

PSALM lxxxiv. 9. Behold, O GOD our Defender, and look upon the face of Thine anointed.

lxi. 6; xxi. 6. Grant the king a long life, and make him glad with the joy of Thy countenance.

lxxii. 7. In his time let the righteous flourish, and let peace be in all our borders.

cxiii. 2. Blessed be the Name of the LORD from this time forth for evermore. Amen.

T. A. WALMISLEY.

824

PSALM cv. 1. O give thanks unto the LORD.

cxii. 6. The righteous shall be had in everlasting remembrance, and the just shine as the brightness of the firmament.

cvi. 46. Blessed be the LORD GOD of Israel for evermore, and let all the people say, Amen.

T. A. WALMISLEY.

825

ISAIAH li. 3. The LORD shall comfort Zion, He will comfort all her waste places. He will make her wilderness like Eden, and her desert like the garden of the LORD. Joy and gladness shall be found therein, thanksgiving and the voice of melody.

6. Lift up your eyes to the heavens, and look upon the earth beneath. For the heavens shall vanish away like smoke, and the earth shall wax old like a garment; but My salvation shall be for ever.

7. Hearken unto Me, ye that know righteousness; fear ye not the reproach of men; neither be ye afraid of their revilings.

8. My righteousness shall be for ever, and My salvation from generation to generation.

9. Awake, awake, put on strength, O arm of the LORD : awake, as in the ancient days, in the generations of old.

11. The redeemed of the LORD shall return, and come with singing unto Zion, and everlasting joy shall be upon their head ; they shall obtain gladness and joy; sorrow and mourning shall flee away.

T. A. WALMISLEY.

826 J. L. HOPKINS, Ps. 3, 6, 8, 11. Amen.

827

COLLECT

For the Sunday after Ascension Day.

O GOD, the King of Glory, Who hast exalted Thine only Son JESUS CHRIST with great triumph unto Thy Kingdom in Heaven; we beseech Thee, leave us not comfortless, but send to us Thine Holy Ghost to comfort us, and exalt us unto the same place whither our Saviour CHRIST is gone before, Who liveth and reigneth with Thee and the Holy Ghost, one GOD, world without end. Amen.

H. SMART, T. A. WALMISLEY.

828

COLLECT

or the First Sunday after the Epiphany.

O LORD, we beseech Thee mercifully to receive the prayers of Thy people which call upon Thee; and grant that they may both perceive and know what things they ought to do, and also may have grace and power faithfully to fulfil the same; through JESUS CHRIST our LORD. Amen.

ATTWOOD.

829

LAMENTATIONS v. 1. Remember, O LORD, what is come upon us; consider and behold our reproach.

7. Our fathers have sinned, and are not; and we have borne their iniquities.

15. The joy of our heart is ceased, and our dance is turned into mourning.

17. For this our heart is faint; for these things our eyes are dim.

19. Thou, O LORD, remainest for ever; Thy Throne from generation to generation.

T. A. WALMISLEY.

830

PSALM IX. 7. The LORD shall endure for ever: He hath also prepared His seat for judgment.

8. He shall judge the world in righteousness, and minister true judgment unto His people.

9. The LORD will be a defence for the oppressed, even a refuge in the time of trouble.

1. I will give thanks unto Thee, O LORD, and I will sing of all Thy marvellous works.

T. A. WALMISLEY.

831

Holy is the LORD our GOD. Heaven and earth are full of His Glory and Majesty.

NEUKOMM.

832

PSALM CXXX. From the deep I called, LORD, to Thee: O LORD, hear Thou my voice. O let Thine ears consider well the voice of my complaint. If Thou, LORD, wilt be extreme to mark what is done amiss, LORD, who may abide it? But there is mercy, with Thee is mercy, LORD; therefore shalt Thou be feared. My hope is in the LORD, my soul doth wait for Him; I trust in His word; before the morning watch, I say, my soul doth flee to Him. O Israel, trust in the LORD. And Israel He shall redeem from all his sins. For with the LORD is mercy and plenteous redemption.

SPOHR.

833

PSALM xxiii. (Paraphrase.) 1. GOD is my Shepherd, I shall not want. He feedeth me in tender pastures, He leadeth me to quiet waters. He doth restore my fainting soul, and lead me in the paths of righteousness, to magnify His Name. Yea, though the gloomy vale of death I traverse, no evil will I fear, for Thou art at my side. Thy rod and staff, they comfort me. Thou spreadest me a table in the presence of mine enemies, my head with oil Thou hast anointed, my cup is full, and runneth over. Thy loving kindness and Thy mercy shall abide with me, and I will dwell in the House of GOD, yea, ever dwell with Him.

S. OHR.

834

LAMENTATIONS v.   1. Remember, LORD! what Thou hast laid upon us :

2. Our inheritance hast Thou given to strangers.

20. O wherefore, LORD, dost Thou forsake Thy people ? and why dost Thou forget us for ever ?

21. Return unto Thy servants, and their strength do Thou renew as it was in time of old.

⁺GOD of our fathers, hear Thy people,
In sorrow and abasement who implore Thee !
Captive, forsaken, of hope bereft,
We fly to Thee ;
To Thee, O JEHOVAH, Thy children cry in trouble ;
Bow Thine ear, O LORD, and hear, O hear us, while in
       bondage
          We mourn and languish !
Beloved Zion, shall our feet
          No more Thy sacred courts attend ?
Shall praise no more to Israel's GOD
          From grateful hearts and tongues ascend ?
Arise in wrath, Almighty LORD,
          Strike our oppressors down !
To Israel, trusting in Thy word,
          Let mercy still be shown.*

    (*From " The Fall of Babylon,"* Nos. 3, 1a.)   SPOHR.

      * —— * Sometimes sung as a separate Anthem.

835

LORD, before Thy footstool bending,
   Teach us to adore Thy ways,
Heart and voice in rapture blending,
And in strains of joy ascending,
   Swell the hymn of ardent praise,
   Speak Thy goodness, sing Thy praise.

Darkness, long Thy Throne surrounding,
   Veil'd the brightness of Thy Face ;
Now Thy power our foes confounding,
And Thy mercy still abounding,
   Speak the fulness of Thy grace.

Thou Whose temple is Creation,
   Thron'd in everlasting power;
LORD of every land and nation,
We proclaim Thy great salvation.
   And Thy Majesty adore.
(*From " The Fall of Babylon,"* No. 13.) SPOHR.

836

Strike the harp, for the LORD in His might hath descended;
O Judah be glad, thy mourning is ended :
Rejoice, ye redeemed, exulting bring
Thanksgiving and praise to GOD our King!

   * LORD, Thy Arm hath been uplifted, .
     Israel triumphs o'er her foes :
   By Thy mighty pow'r defended,
   By Thy ceaseless love attended,
     Zion shall in peace repose.

   LORD, reveal Thy awful glory,
     As when Egypt felt Thy rod,
   Soon the heathen shall adore Thee,
   And their idols fall before Thee—
     Thou, and Thou alone, art GOD ! *
(*From " The Fall of Babylon,"* Nos. 27, 28.) SPOHR.

    * ——— * Sometimes sung as a separate Anthem.

837

O Zion, how bright are the hopes that attend thee !
   The wilderness now shall its verdure resume,
   The desert rejoicing, with roses shall bloom ;
The LORD is Thy Shepherd, He shall defend thee.

* Give thanks unto GOD, O house of Jacob, and talk of
all His wonderful works. O praise Him, all ye people,
declare His salvation. Shew forth all His loving-kindness
unto Israel; for He is gracious, He alone is mighty.
Hosanna! JEHOVAH reigneth in majesty, in pow'r, and
glory, and He shall reign for evermore. The LORD hath
been thy refuge, O Zion! He hath been Thy salvation
and thy sure defence. Hosanna! JEHOVAH reigneth in

majesty. Give thanks unto GOD, O house of Jacob, and talk of all His wonderful works. Shew forth all His loving-kindness unto Israel. JEHOVAH reigneth! He alone is mighty, alone is holy.*

(*From " The Fall of Babylon*," Nos. 30, 31.)   SPOHR.

* —— * Sometimes sung as a separate Anthem.

838

JEHOVAH, LORD GOD of Hosts, how glorious is Thy Name on earth, and Thy Majesty above the heavens. Through Thee the weak confound the mighty and crush their haughty foes. LORD, by Thy power, and from the mouth of even babes hast Thou, O LORD, ordained praise. O LORD, I ponder on Thy handywork, the heavens, the earth, the moon, and stars, that Thou governest. LORD, what is man, that Thou regardest him, or son of man, that Thou art mindful of him? Thou hast made him but second to the angels. Him hast Thou crowned with glory; Thou makest him to be lord of all creation, and placest all in his dominion, the ox, the lamb, each bird or fish that in the air or in the water moves.

How glorious is Thy Name on earth, and Thy Majesty above the heavens, JEHOVAH, LORD GOD of Hosts. Amen.

SPOHR.

839

O look not down, thou all-glorious Sun, from out thy dwelling so heavenly bright, nor enlighten the path of death which CHRIST our LORD is doomed to tread.

ISAIAH liii. 3. He is despised and rejected of men, a man of sorrows, and acquainted with griefs. He hath carried our sorrows and hath borne our griefs. It hath pleased the LORD to wound Him, He hath put Him to shame. Weep, O weep, ye daughters of Jerusalem! He is numbered with transgressors, He is wounded for our sins. As a lamb to the slaughter, so the Saviour is led to death. Our Shepherd is smitten, and His sheep are scattered abroad: yea, He is bruised for our transgressions! Hide thou thy beams, O Sun! In midnight darkness and sorrow veil the light.

(*From " Calvary*," No. ??.)   SPOHR.

840

JESUS, Heavenly Master!
Thy love forsakes us not in this dark hour,
Shedding around its holy power;
Like some bright star, that, beaming o'er us,
Dispels the shades of death before us.
Think Thou on us when death shall sever,
And guide us hence to rest for ever!

(From "Calvary," No. 28.) SPOHR.

841

SACRED CANTATA.—GOD, THOU ART GREAT!
No. 1

GOD, Thou art great! The heavens are declaring—the
sun in his brightness, the stars in their wandering—Thou
art the Mighty One. The earth sounds Thy praises, in
deep roaring billows, in bright beaming meadows, in all
living creatures; Thou art the Mighty One.

Worlds in boundless orbits rolling,
Great is He Who formed you first;
All ye hosts of heavenly bodies,
Shout your Maker, sound His glory,
Great is He Who formed you first.

No. 2

Thou earth, waft sweet incense o'er thy plains;
Be an altar pouring thanks.
Sound His praise, ye rocky mountains;
Breathe His glory, whispering breezes:
He will be, and is, and was.
God, Thou art great!
The seraphs hail Thee, the worm and dust.
Thou art our Maker, Thou art the loving one.
God, Thou art great!
Thy love is given to men
Who strive to obey their Maker,
And seek their Father.

No. 3

Be dumb, ye sinners, the world is God's, and He is lov'd.

No. 4

Children, pray this love to cherish ; ye whom GOD has made His like. Ye gentle spirits, the world is all your own. The beams of morning, the rays of evening, the day, the night, they both to you bring peace and bliss. Mortals, rejoice, the curse is past, ye now are blessed. and heaven itself e'en now draws near. Mortals, rejoice! ve filled with joy. Earth, be thou now a land with love o'erflowing. So heaven remains ever with thee.

No. 5

Walk ye, walk, ye hundred thousands,
On the face of earth now dwelling;
Walk ye on in love and truth,
Great is GOD, and vast His goodness,
But on loving spirits only will His shadow rest.

No. 6

GOD, Thou art great! so say the heavens : The earth
   proclaims it :
So sing bright Seraphim, and souls of all men.   GOD,
   Thou art great !
Thou art the Mighty One ; the Loving One for evermore.
   Amen.

842   SPOHR.

PSALM LXXXIV.

No. 1.

How lovely are Thy dwellings fair,
   O LORD of Hosts ! how dear
The pleasant tabernacles are
   Where Thou dost dwell so near !

My soul doth long and almost die
   Thy courts, O LORD. to see ;
My heart and flesh aloud do cry,
   O living GOD, for Thee.

There even the sparrow, freed from wrong,
   Hath found a house of rest :
The swallow there, to lay her young,
   Hath built her brooding nest

Even by Thy altars, LORD of Hosts,
  They find their safe abode ;
And home they fly from round the coasts,
  Toward Thee, my King, my GOD !

No. 2

Happy who in Thy house reside,
  Where Thee they ever praise !
Happy, whose strength in Thee doth bide,
  And in their hearts Thy ways.

They pass through Baca's thirsty vale—
  That dry and barren ground—
As through a fruitful watery dale,
  Where springs and showers abound.

They journey on from strength to strength,
  With joy and gladsome cheer,
Till all before our GOD at length
  In Zion do appear.

No. 3

LORD GOD of Hosts, hear now my prayer,
  O Jacob's GOD, give ear;
Thou GOD, our Shield, look on the face
  Of Thy Anointed dear.

For one day in Thy courts to be,
  Is better and more blest,
Than in the joys of vanity
  A thousand days at best.

I in the temple of my GOD
  Had rather keep a door,
Than dwell in tents and rich abode,
  With sin for evermore.

For GOD the LORD, both Sun and Shield,
  Gives grace and glory bright ;
No good from them shall be withheld
  Whose ways are just and right.

No. 4

LORD GOD of Hosts, that reign'st on high !
That man is truly blest
Who only on Thee doth rely,
And in Thee only rest.

SPOHR.

843

THE CHRISTIAN'S PRAYER.

No. 1

In heaven, O JEHOVAH, is fixed Thy Throne ;
No time Thy empire hath bounded—
Thou reignest there, unchanged, alone,
By thousand worlds surrounded !
Thine, Thine are majesty, power, and love ;
Thou lightest the starry host above ;
Thou causest the sun in his course to move :
Life, light, and joy by Thee are given,
Father and Lord of earth and heaven !

No. 2

Thy love is every morning new,
Its blessings all around extending ;
Thy heavenly mercies fall like dew,
In soft and gentle showers descending.
LORD ! LORD ! our hearts would own Thy praise,
In joy or sorrow still the same ;
The tongue that calls Thee Father, sings
For ever hallowed be Thy Name.

No. 3

Thy boundless grace, O GOD, we praise ;
How bright on high its glories blaze,
And stream on all Thy works below !
Let every tongue and nation
Give praise and adoration
To Thee, from Whom all blessings flow.
LORD ! we own Thy sovereign might,
Thy ways how just, Thy laws how right '
May Thy glorious Kingdom come !

No. 4

All-gracious Father, Heaven's high LORD,
 From Thee all good, all joy descendeth :
Earth smiles, the garden of Thy love,
 Where flower with flower in sweetest fragrance blendeth.
O wisdom eternal, unchangeable might,
 All worlds depend upon Thy breath :
Thy words direct our erring footsteps right,
 Even through the night of death.
　　　LORD ! with joyful, thankful hearts
　　　We celebrate Thy boundless love.

No. 5

O may Thy will be done on earth,
As it is done in heaven above !

No. 6

O clothe our valleys with ripening corn,
 Our trees with autumn's produce bending ;
May peaceful flocks our plains adorn,
 O'er sunny hills our vines extending ;
While nature's rich bounties around us are spread,
Give, O give us, we pray Thee, our daily bread !

No. 7

O LORD ! by Heaven's bright armies surrounded,
Thou Whose power is resistless, unbounded,
　　Receive our adorations !
Gracious Father ! bow Thine ear,
Spare Thy sons, in mercy spare ;
　　Hear, O hear their supplications !
How unsearchable Thy love !
　　Boundless as the heaven :
O forgive us, LORD, our sins,
　　As we hope to be forgiven.

Nos. 8 and 9

Thee, LORD, Thy creatures own
GOD of Hosts, and King alone !
With reverence, with trembling, we own Thy power :

Heavenward our wishes, our hopes are ascending,
There shine Thy glories, unfading, unending,
There sin and death are known no more.
O when shall we soar to those regions of light,
Where glories immortal shall burst on our sight,
Thy goodness, Thy greatness, Thy·love to adore ?

*Lead us not into temptation, but deliver us from evil, for
Thou art Lord, and Thou art God our Father.*

*Thine is the Kingdom, and the power, and the glory, for
evermore. Amen.*

SPOHR.

844

"THE LAST JUDGMENT."

PART I.

No. 1 OVERTURE.

No. 2

Praise His awful Name, Who was, and is, and is to
come : praise to Him Who giveth immortality ; all glory
and majesty surround His Throne. Worship and adore
Him ! Praise ! Glory to GOD !

Mighty He cometh to judgment ; for He shall judge the
world in righteousness, and He shall judge His people
with His truth.

Fear thou not, O man, for thy Redeemer liveth. He
that died is risen, and He shall live to all eternity ; and
He shall reign, and shall conquer all His enemies.

Praise His awful Name, &c.

" I know thy works, and thy labour, and thy patience ;
for My sake thou hast endured affliction. Yet thy first
and chiefest duty thou hast forsaken, and thou art fallen
from thy high estate. Repent, repent, and return to thy
first work. Be thou faithful unto death, and I will give
thee a crown of life."

Praise His awful Name, Who was, and is, and is to
come ; praise to Him Who giveth immortality ; all glory
and majesty surround His Throne. He alone is mighty,
and He alone is great. Praise ! Glory to GOD ! Worship
and adore Him. Praise ! Glory to GOD ! Praise ! Glory
to Him, Who was, and is, and is to come ! Praise Him !

No. 3

REVELATION iv. 1. " Come up hither, and I will shew thee what shall be hereafter."

2. And, lo, a Throne was set in Heaven, and on the Throne One stood.

3-5, 8. And a rainbow was round about the Throne; and the Elders knelt before the Throne, clad in white raiment: and on their heads were crowns of gold: and from the Throne came thunderings and lightnings, and voices, crying day and night:

No. 4

" Holy, Holy, Holy, LORD GOD of Hosts! GOD Almighty! Who wast, and Who art, and art to come!"

No. 5

v. 6. Behold the Lamb that was slain!

No 6

Weep no more; behold, He that died is risen, and hath conquered Death and Hell.

No. 7

8. And the Elders fell down before the Lamb, with their harps, and golden urns bearing odours, singing this song of praise:

No. 8

12. "All glory to the Lamb that died, exalted now at GOD's right hand in blessing, in wisdom, in honour, and praise for ever."

No. 9

13. And every creature that is in Heaven, and on the earth, and under the earth, and in the sea, cried aloud, and said:

No. 10

13. "Blessing, honour, glory and power, be unto Him that sitteth upon the Throne, and unto the Lamb for ever!"

No. 11

vii. 9. And, lo, a mighty host of all nations and people stood before the Throne and the Lamb. Of spotless white was every garment: in every hand a palm was borne. They fell before the Throne of God with holy fear.

14. These, who passed through heavy tribulation, have washed their robes and made them white in the Blood of the Lamb.

15. They stand before GOD's Throne, and serve Him day and night.

17. And the Lamb shall lead them to fountains of living waters, and GOD shall wipe away all tears from their eyes.

No. 12

LORD GOD of Heaven and earth, we adore Thee!

Yes, every tear and every sorrow the LORD shall wipe away from their eyes: nor sin, nor death, nor pain, nor sorrow shall there be known. He is our GOD, and we are His people. Hail, our Redeemer! Hail!

Blessing and power be Thine, our Redeemer! Thou art the LORD our GOD, and we are Thy people. Hail, our Redeemer! Hail!

PART II.

No. 13 SYMPHONY.

No. 14

Thus saith the LORD: "The end is near, and all the winds of heaven proclaim its coming. Prepare to meet thy GOD. I will reward thee even as thy works have been, and judge thee as thou hast deserved. To Me is every action known, each secret thought is unveiled before Me.

The day of wrath is near, the Almighty shall reveal His power. The reaper's song is silent in the field, and the shepherd's voice on the mountain. The valleys then shall shake with fear, with dread the hills shall tremble. It comes, the day of terror comes! The awful morning dawns. Thy mighty arm, O GOD, is uplifted. Thou shalt shake the earth and heavens: they shall shrivel as a scroll, when Thou in wrath appearest. For men shall cast away their silver, and count their gold as dross: it shall not save in the great and awful day. Where is now the monarch's might, where all his splendour, where the dreams of earthly greatness? The princes of the earth shall cast their crowns before Thee, and all the power of the mighty shall fail, when Thou, O LORD, shall come to judge the world.

No. 15

Forsake me not in this dread hour, O GOD, most merciful! Thou art my hope, O LORD, give ear unto my prayer! O spare Thy servant, and cast him not away! If Thou forsake me, whither shall I flee? No friend is nigh, no arm to save, but only Thou, Almighty LORD of Hosts. In Thee, O LORD, in Thee alone I trust!

No. 16

DEUTERONOMY iv. 29. "If with your whole hearts ye humbly seek Me, I will be found of you," saith the LORD;

MALACHI iii. 7. "And if ye return to Me sincerely, I will receive you from all the ends of the earth.

2 CORINTHIANS vi. 16. I will be your Father, ye shall be My people": thus saith the LORD.

No. 17

REVELATION xiv. 7. Jehovah now cometh to judgment! Bow down to worship Him Who made the heavens and earth.

No. 18

xiv. 8. Destroyed is Babylon the mighty!

11. The smoke of her torment ascendeth for evermore.

7. The hour of judgment is come! Now is the LORD at hand!

xx. 12, 13. The grave gives up its dead, the sea gives up its dead, the seals are broken, the books are all unclosed, the mighty now tremble before Him!

SYMPHONY.

It is ended!

No. 19

REVELATION xiv. 13. Blest are the departed, who in the LORD are sleeping, from henceforth for evermore: they rest from their labours, and their works follow them.

No. 20

xxi. I saw a new Heaven and a new Earth, by GOD prepared and adorned as a bride. Lo, the house of GOD is with men, and He will dwell among them, and they shall be His people. Nor sun shall be, nor moon: GOD is their sun; there shall His Majesty unclouded rise. No earthly house is there: GOD is their Temple, and their Light.

No. 21

xxii. 12. Behold, He soon shall come in His might arrayed, to give to every one according to his work.

20. "Then come, LORD JESUS!"

No. 22

xv. 3. Great and wonderful are all Thy works, O Thou Almighty GOD! How just and true are all Thy commandments, Jehovah, King of Saints!

4. O LORD, who shall not fear Thee? LORD, who shall not glorify Thee? Thou alone art holy. All nations of the earth shall come and worship before Thy Throne. Hallelujah.

ST. MATTHEW vi. 13. Thine is the Kingdom, the power, and the glory, for ever and evermore. Hallelujah. Amen.

SPOHR.

845

PSALM cxix. 1. Beati omnes quorum via integra est, qui ambulant in lege Domini.

English Version.

Blessed are those that are undefiled in the way, who walk in the law of the Lord.

REISSIGER.

846

PSALM cii. 1. Domine exaudi orationem meam, et clamor meus ad Te veniat.

2. Ne avertas faciem Tuam a me; in quacunque die tribulor, inclina ad me aurem Tuam.

English Version.

1. Hear my prayer, O Lord, and let my crying come unto Thee.

2. Hide not Thy face from me; in the time of my trouble incline Thine ear unto me.

REISSIGER.

847

WISDOM iii. 1. Justorum animæ in manu Dei ṣunt, et non tanget illos tormentum malitiæ.

2, 3. Visi sunt oculis insipientium mori: Illi autem sunt in pace.

BYRD, DONKIN, REISSIGER.

English Version.

WISDOM iii. 1. The souls of the righteous are in the hand of GOD, and there shall no torment touch them.

2, 3. In the sight of the unwise they seemed to die: but they are in peace.

[PSALM cxxvii. 3. For so He giveth His beloved sleep.]

BYRD, ELVEY, E. V. HALL.

848 M. B. FOSTER, vv. 1–3; Psalm cxxvii. 3.

849

Hear us, O Saviour, hear us, JESUS. Thou LORD of mercy and pity, Thou art our guardian and our succour. To Thee we betake us, perishing children of Adam. We turn us to Thee, lamenting and weeping. To Thee we turn us in life's sad and tearful journey. Be Thou, therefore, our deliverer. Look on us in Thy merciful kindness. LORD, hear our entreaties, and shew us benediction in this our misery. ⸺ O hear us, O gracious, O loving and pitying LORD, our Redeemer.

HAUPTMANN.

850

LORD, my GOD; Thou art my salvation; leave me not, O leave me not, withdraw not Thou Thy hand from me; vouchsafe me Thy protection. Thou, O LORD, Thou art my salvation: Thou, O LORD, my GOD.

HAUPTMANN.

851

Source of all light and life divine,
    We now implore Thee.
O LORD, on us Thy light let shine,
    While we adore Thee.
Thou shalt be LORD of all we own,
Send peace to all, from zone to zone,
Extend to us Thy love and mercy,
And with pleasure, let us measure
All the treasure Thou hast given.
All our blessings come from Heaven.

O make our hearts Thy dwelling-place,
    And let us gather
On earth, all wisdom, love, and grace,
    From Thee our Father!
Grant us Thy loving-kindness free,
Let us in trouble look to Thee,
Thou made us, Thou wilt aid us,
Thou wilt surely lead us,
All sustaining,
Where alone true joy is reigning. Amen.

CRESER, HAUPTMANN.

852

PSALM xcix. 2. The LORD is great in Zion, and high above all people.

9. O magnify the LORD our GOD, and worship Him upon His holy hill, for the LORD our GOD is holy. [Hallelujah. Amen.]

_BEST, NOVELLO.

853

PSALM xxxi. 6. In manus Tuas commendo spiritum meum: redemisti me, Domine, Deus veritatis.

(Sometimes sung to the following words.)

PSALM xlii. 1. Like as the hart desireth the water-brooks, so longeth my soul after Thee, O GOD.

6. Why art thou so full of heaviness, O my soul? And why art thou so disquieted within me?

15. O put thy trust in GOD.

NOVELLO.

854

PSALM cxiii. 1. Praise the LORD, ye servants, O praise the Name of the LORD.

cxlvii. 5. Great is our LORD, and great is His power; yea, and His wisdom is infinite.

xlvii. 6. O sing praises unto our GOD, O sing praises unto our King.

7. For GOD is the King of all the earth, O sing ye praises with understanding. Hallelujah. Amen.

NOVELLO.

855

ISAIAH xlii. 10. Sing unto the LORD a new song, and His praise from the ends of the earth !

ST. LUKE ii. 10. For, behold, I bring you good tidings of great joy, which shall be to all people.

11. For unto you is born this day, in the city of David, a Saviour, Which is CHRIST the LORD.

14. Glory to GOD in the highest. Peace on earth, good will towards men.

NOVELLO.

856

PSALM xci. 1. Qui in manu Dei requiescit, et sub umbrâ Domini altissimi sedet.

2. Dixi Domino, Tu defensio meaque arx, O Deus, in Te speravi.

3. Nam liberavit me a venatore et a mortali pernicie ;

4. Super te alarum tegmen expandet, et firma fides erit tua sub pennis Ejus; Verbum Ejus est tanquam clypeus et securum præsidium ;

5, 6. Ideo non formidabis tenebias noctium nec sagittam quæ in die volat; nec contagium quod sub nocte repit ; neque pestem quæ palam spargit mortem.

7. Si mille atque mille cadant ad lævam tuam, milliaque a dextris tuis, tibi mors non propinquabit.

8. Verum tu ipse videbis gaudia tua, et nosces quod munus peccator accipiet.

9. Nam Tu es spes mea, Domine; O Deus, adjutor meus.

10. Non ad te accedet periculum, nec ullum malum unquam domum tuam attinget.

11. Nam angelis cœlorum mandavit super te, ut cus-
todiant te in cunctis viis tuis.

12. Imperavit super te Deus Angelis, et in manibus te
portabunt, ne ad lapidem te lædas.

13. Basiliscum et aspidem calcabis, leones et dracones
superincedes.

14. Ille Me quæsivit et eum adjuvabo. Nomen cog-
novit Meum, quare servabo eum.

15. Ad Me clamabit et exaudiam eum; cum ipso
mœstus ero, et eum eripiam et glorificabo.

16. Huic dabo vivere per longos annos ævumque pro-
ducere, et eum in cœlum vocabo ad Me.

Paraphrase.

He that under the shield of the Highest dwelleth,
alway under the shadow of the Almighty abideth.
I will say to the LORD "My protection, my strong
defence, my GOD, in Thee will I trust." He shall
deliver thee from the snare of the fowler, and from the
noisome pestilence. My GOD, in Thee will I trust. He
shall cover Thee with His feathers, and beneath His wings
thou shalt hide in safety. Like a buckler shall be His
faithfulness. Thou shalt not be affrighted for the terror
of night; for the arrow that in daytime flieth; for the
pestilence that in darkness walketh; for destruction that
at noonday wasteth: a thousand shall fall beside thee,
and ten thousand at thy right hand; but it shall not come
nigh thee. With thine eyes shalt thou behold it, the
reward of the wicked. O LORD my GOD, Thou art my
refuge. The most High is thy habitation, there shall no
evil befall thee, neither shall any plague come nigh thy
dwelling: for the LORD, He shall give His angels charge
over thee, and in all thy ways they shall keep thee. In
their hands they shall bear thee up, lest thou dash thy
foot against a stone. Thou shalt tread on the lion and the
adder, and trample on the young lion and on the dragon.
He hath set his love on Me, and therefore I will deliver
him; he hath known My Name, and therefore I will exalt
him; he shall call on Me, and I will answer him; I will
be with him in trouble. I will deliver him, and to honour
raise him. Him will I satisfy with length of good days,
and shew him salvation that cometh of Me.

MEYERBEER.

857

PSALM xli. 1. Blessed is he that considereth the poor : the LORD will deliver him in the time of trouble.

2. The LORD will preserve him and keep him alive.

3. The LORD will strengthen him upon a bed of languishing : Thou wilt make all his bed in his sickness.

13. Blessed be the LORD GOD of Israel from everlasting, and to everlasting. Amen, and Amen.

W. JACKSON.

858

HOSEA vi. 1. Come, and let us return unto the LORD, (Isaiah lv. 7.) and He will have mercy upon us; and to our GOD, for He will abundantly pardon.

PSALM cxvi. 1. I love the LORD, because He hath heard my voice and my supplication.

2. Because He hath inclined His ear unto me, therefore will I call upon Him as long as I live.

3. The sorrows of death compassed me, the pains of hell gat hold upon me : I found trouble and sorrow.

4. Then called I upon the Name of the LORD.

5. Gracious is the LORD and righteous; yea, our GOD is merciful.

EXODUS xv. 11. Who is like unto the LORD our GOD?

HOSEA vi. 1. Come, and let us return unto the LORD,

ISAIAH lv. 7. And He will have mercy upon us; and to our GOD, for He will abundantly pardon.

HOSEA vi. 1. Come, and let us return unto the LORD. Amen.

W. JACKSON.

859

PSALM xx. 1. The LORD hear thee in the day of trouble : the Name of the GOD of Jacob defend thee.

2. Send thee help from the sanctuary, and strengthen thee out of Sion.

4. Grant thee according to thine own heart, and fulfil all thy counsel.

W. JACKSON.

860

PSALM cl. 1. Praise ye the LORD. Praise GOD in His
sanctuary, praise Him in the firmament of His power.

2. Praise Him for His mighty acts, praise Him
according to His excellent greatness.

3. Praise Him with the sound of the trumpet, praise
Him with the psaltery and harp.

4. Praise Him with the timbrel and dance, praise Him
with stringed instruments and organs.

5. Praise Him upon the loud cymbals, praise Him upon
the high sounding cymbals.

6. Let every thing that hath breath praise the LORD.
Praise ye the LORD.

W. JACKSON.

861

PSALM xliv. 1. We have heard with our ears, O GOD,
our fathers have told us, what work Thou didst in their
days, in the time of old.

9. But Thou hast cast us off, and put us to shame.

26. Arise for our help, and redeem us for Thy mercies'
sake. Amen.

W. JACKSON.

862

PSALM cxx. 1. When I was in trouble I called upon
the LORD, and He heard me.

PSALM lxviii. 19. Praised be the LORD daily, even the
GOD Who helpeth us, and poureth His benefits upon us.

20. He is our GOD, even the GOD of Whom cometh
salvation : GOD is the LORD, by Whom we escape death.

32. Sing unto GOD, O ye kingdoms of the earth, O sing
praises unto the LORD.

T. F. WALMISLEY.

863

COLLECT

For Peace.

O GOD, Who art the author of peace and lover of con-
cord, in knowledge of Whom standeth our eternal life,
Whose service is perfect freedom ; defend us Thy humble

servants in all assaults of our enemies; that we, surely trusting in Thy defence, may not fear the power of any adversaries, through the might of JESUS CHRIST our LORD. Amen.

G. SMART.

864

ACTS viii. 2. Devout men carried Stephen to his burial, and made great lamentation over him.

*PSALM cvi. 13. Precious in the sight of the LORD is the death of His saints.

lxix. 31. Therefore let us praise the Name of GOD with a song, and magnify Him with thanksgiving. Hallelujah. Amen.*

CHAWNER.

——— Sometimes sung as a separate Anthem.

865

O saving Victim, opening wide
 Access to heaven for man below,
Foemen urge us from ev'ry side,
 Give succour, and Thy strength bestow.

ROSSINI.

866

When Thou comest to the judgment, LORD, remember Thou Thy servants; none else can deliver us. Save and bring us to Thy Kingdom, there to worship with the faithful, and for ever dwell with Thee.

ROSSINI.

867

PSALM lxxi. 1. In Thee, O LORD, have I put my trust, let me never be put to confusion; but rid me, and deliver me, in Thy righteousness; incline Thine ear unto me, and save me.

4. For Thou, O GOD, art the thing that I long for: Thou art my hope, even from my youth.

7. O let my mouth be filled with Thy praise, that I may sing of Thy glory and honour all the day long.

cxiii. 3. The LORD's Name is praised, from the rising up of the sun to the going down of the same.

cvi. 46. Blessed be the LORD GOD of Israel from everlasting, and world without end : and let all the people say, Amen.

T. JACKSON.

868

1 ST. JOHN i. 8, 9. If we say that we have no sin, we deceive ourselves, and the truth is not in us : but, if we confess our sins, He is faithful and just to forgive us our sins, and to cleanse us from all unrighteousness.

CALKIN, HARRIS.

869

JEREMIAH x. 24. O LORD, correct me, but with judgment ; not in Thine anger, lest Thou bring me to nothing.

BATES, COWARD, HARRIS.

870

ST. MARK xi. 9. Hosanna ! Blessed is He that cometh in the Name of the LORD.

10. Blessed be the Kingdom of our father David : Hosanna in the highest.

LUCAS.

871

COLLECT

For the Fourth Sunday in Lent.

Grant, we beseech Thee, Almighty GOD, that we, who for our evil deeds do worthily deserve to be punished, by the comfort of Thy grace may mercifully be relieved ; through our LORD and Saviour JESUS CHRIST. Amen.

R. MANN.

872

PSALM lxix. 1. Save me, O GOD, for the waters are come in, even unto my soul.

19. Draw nigh unto my soul. O deliver me, because of mine enemies.

liv. 1. O save me, for Thy Name's sake.

2. Hear my prayer, O GOD, and hearken unto the words of my mouth.

lxi. 1. Hear my crying, O GOD, give ear unto my prayer.

cii. 2. Hide not Thy face from me, O GOD, in the time of my trouble : O hear me, and that right soon.

xviii. 1. I will love Thee, O LORD, my strength ; the LORD is my stony rock, and my defence : my Saviour, my GOD, in Whom I will trust.

4. The pains of hell came about me, the snares of the wicked overtook me.

6. I did call upon the LORD, and He heard my voice.

2. I will call upon the LORD, Which is worthy to be praised.

BALFE.

873

JEREMIAH v. 7. How shall I pardon thee for this, O Jerusalem ! thy children have forsaken Me, and sworn by them that are no gods.

(*From " Jerusalem,"* No. 6.) PIERSON.

874

DANIEL ix. 16. O LORD, according to Thy righteousness, we beseech Thee, let Thine anger and Thy fury be turned away from Thy city Jerusalem, Thy holy mountain.

19. O LORD, hear ; O LORD, forgive, according to Thy righteousness, we beseech Thee.

(*From " Jerusalem,"* No. 16.) PIERSON.

875

REVELATION vii. 13. What are these that are arrayed in white robes ? Whence came they ?

14. These are they which came out of great tribulation, and have washed their robes, and made them white in the Blood of the Lamb.

15. Therefore are they before the Throne of GOD and serve Him day and night in His temple, and He that sitteth on the Throne shall dwell among them.

17. And GOD shall wipe away all tears from their eyes.

(*From " Jerusalem,"* No. 19.) PIERSON.

876

PSALM xxiv. 7. Lift up your heads, O ye gates, and be ye lift up, ye everlasting doors: and the King of Glory shall come in.

8. Who is the King of Glory? the LORD strong and mighty, mighty in battle.

10. The Lord of Hosts, He is the King of Glory.

J. L. HOPKINS.

877

ST. MATTHEW ii. 1. When JESUS was born in Bethlehem in the days of Herod the King, behold, there came wise men from the East unto Jerusalem,

2. Saying, "Where is He that is born King of the Jews? For we have seen His star in the East, and are come to worship Him."

7-9. Then Herod sent them to Bethlehem, and they departed; and lo, the star, which they saw in the East, went before them, till it came and stood over where the young Child was.

11. When they had opened their treasures, they presented unto Him gifts; gold, and frankincense, and myrrh.

REVELATION xv. 3. Great and marvellous are Thy works, LORD GOD Almighty! Just and true are Thy ways, Thou King of Saints!

4. Who shall not fear Thee, O LORD, and glorify Thy Name? for Thou only art holy; for all nations shall come and worship before Thee.

J. L. HOPKINS.

878

JOB xxiii. 3. O that I knew where I might find Him, that I might come even to His seat.

8. Behold, I go forward, but He is not there; and backward, but I cannot perceive Him;

9. On the left hand, where He doth work, but I cannot behold Him; He hideth Himself on the right hand.

ST. JOHN xx. 29. Blessed are they that have not seen, and yet have believed.

W. S. BENNETT

879

LORD, to Thee our song we raise,
Fill our hearts with grateful praise,
Thine Almighty power we own,
Glory give to Thee alone.
Ever, LORD, vouchsafe to bless
The widow and the fatherless.
May this day most happy prove,
Favoured by Thy gracious love,
And Thy richest blessings come
Unto every orphan home.

W. S. BENNETT.

880

PSALM xv. 1. LORD, who shall dwell in Thy tabernacle? or who shall rest upon Thy holy hill?

2. Even he that leadeth an uncorrupt life, and doeth the
thing which is right, and speaketh the truth from his heart.

*1. LORD, who shall dwell in Thy tabernacle? or who
shall rest upon Thy holy hill?

3. He that hath used no deceit in his tongue, nor done
evil to his neighbour, and hath not slandered his
neighbour.

4. He that setteth not by himself, but is lowly in his
own eyes, and maketh much of them that fear the LORD.

LORD, who shall rest on that bright hill
Of holiness divine,
Within the tabernacle's gate,
Where Thou dost dwell with Thine?

5. He that sweareth unto his neighbour, and disappointeth him not, though it were to his own hindrance.

6. He that hath not given his money upon usury, nor
taken reward against the innocent.

7. Whoso doeth these things, shall never fall.

To Father, Son, and Holy Ghost,
The GOD Whom we adore,
Be glory as it was, is now,
And shall be evermore. Amen.

W. S. BENNETT.

* These words are sometimes omitted

881

§ 1

St. Luke i. 68. Blessed be the Lord God of Israel, He hath visited and redeemed His people,

69. And hath raised up a mighty salvation for us in the house of His servant David.

(From " The Woman of Samaria," No. 3.)

§ 2

St. John iv. 13. Whosoever drinketh of this water shall thirst again ;

14. But whosoever drinketh of the water that I shall give him shall never thirst ; but the water that I shall give him shall be in him a well of water, springing up into everlasting life.

Isaiah xii. 3. Therefore with joy shall ye draw water out of the wells of salvation.

xxx. 21. And thine ears shall hear a word behind thee saying, This is the way, walk ye in it.

(From " The Woman of Samaria," Nos. 6, 7.)

§ 3

Psalm cxxxix. 1. O Lord, Thou has searched me out, and known me ; Thou knowest my downsitting, and mine uprising ; Thou understandest my thoughts long before.

3. For, lo, there is not a word in my tongue, but Thou, O Lord, knowest it altogether.

(From " The Woman of Samaria," No. 9.)

§ 4

Jeremiah xxxi. 12. Therefore they shall come and sing in the height of Zion, and shall flow together to the goodness of the Lord, for wheat, and for wine, and for oil, and their soul shall be as a watered garden, and they shall not sorrow any more at all.

(From " The Woman of Samaria," No. 11.)

§ 5

St. John iv. 24. God is a Spirit ; and they that worship Him must worship Him in spirit and in truth.

23. For the Father seeketh such to worship Him.

(From " The Woman of Samaria," No. 12.)

§ 6

ISAIAH ii. 5; ST. JOHN xii. 35. Come, O Israel, let us walk as sons of light, not as children of darkness.

EPHESIANS v. 8. Let us walk in the light of GOD.

(From " The Woman of Samaria," No. 15.)

§ 7

Abide with me, fast falls the eventide,
The darkness deepens ; LORD, with me abide.
When other helpers fail, and comforts flee,
Help of the helpless, then abide with me.

I need Thy presence every passing hour ;
What but Thy grace can foil the tempter's power ?
Who, like Thyself, my guide and stay can be ?
Through cloud and sunshine, LORD, abide with me.

I fear no foe, with Thee at hand to bless ;
Ills have no weight, and tears no bitterness ;
Where is Death's sting ? Where, Grave, thy victory ?
I triumph still, if Thou abide with me.

(From " The Woman of Samaria," No. 17.)

§ 8

PSALM lxxxv. 9. His salvation is nigh them that fear Him, that glory may dwell in our land.

12. Yea, the LORD shall shew loving-kindness, and our land shall give her increase.

(From " The Woman of Samaria," No. 20.)

§ 9

PSALM xviii. 2. I will call upon the LORD, Who is worthy to be praised.

lxxii. 18. And blessed be the LORD GOD of Israel. Amen, Amen.

(From " The Woman of Samaria," Nos. 21, 22.)

W. S. BENNETT.

882

2 CHRONICLES vi. 40. Now my GOD, let, I beseech Thee, Thine eyes be open, and let Thine ears be attent to the prayer that is made in this place.

41. Arise, O LORD GOD, into Thy resting place, Thou and the ark of Thy strength. Let Thy priests be clothed with salvation, and let Thy saints rejoice in goodness.

PSALM lxxix. 13. So we Thy people, and sheep of Thy pasture, will give Thee thanks for ever. We will shew forth Thy praise to all generations.

REVELATION xxi. 3. And I heard a voice out of Heaven, saying, Behold, the tabernacle of GOD is with men, and He will dwell with them, and they shall be His people, and GOD Himself shall be with them, and be their GOD.

W. S. BENNETT.

883

PSALM xiv. 1. The fool hath said in his heart, There is no GOD.

x. 6. There shall no harm happen unto me.

PSALM xxxvii. 37. I went by, and lo, he was gone ; I sought him, but his place could no where be found.

18. The LORD knoweth the days of the godly, and their inheritance shall endure for ever.

W. S. BENNETT.

884

PSALM xliii. 4. I will go unto the Altar of GOD, even the GOD of my joy and gladness.

3. O send out Thy light and Thy truth, that they may lead me : that they may bring me to Thy holy hill, and to Thy dwelling ;

4. That I may go unto the Altar of GOD, even the GOD of my joy and gladness : and on the harp will I give thanks to Thee, O GOD, my GOD.

GAUNTLETT.

885

ECCLESIASTES iii. 20. All go to one place; all are of the dust, and all turn to dust again.

PSALM xxxix. 8. And now, LORD, what is my hope? truly my hope is even in Thee.

ECCLESIASTES xii. 7. The dust shall return to the earth as it was, and the spirit shall return to GOD Who gave it.

2 CORINTHIANS i. 9. We have the sentence of death in ourselves, that we should not trust in ourselves, but in GOD Which raiseth the dead.

v. 1. For we know that if our earthly house were dissolved, we have a building of GOD; a house not made with hands, eternal in the heavens.

1 THESSALONIANS iv. 18. Wherefore comfort one another with these words.

S. S. WESLEY.

886

COLLECT

For the First Sunday in Advent.

Almighty GOD, give us grace that we may cast away the works of darkness, and put upon us the armour of light, now in the time of this mortal life, in which Thy Son JESUS CHRIST came to visit us in great humility; that in the last day, when He shall come again in His glorious Majesty to judge both the quick and dead, we may rise to the life immortal, through Him Who liveth and reigneth with Thee and the Holy Ghost, now and ever. Amen.

S. S. WESLEY.

887

COLLECT

For the Second Sunday in Advent.

Blessed LORD, Who hast caused all Holy Scriptures to be written for our learning; Grant that we may in such wise hear them, read, mark, learn, and inwardly digest them, that by patience, and comfort of Thy holy Word, we may embrace, and ever hold fast the blessed hope of everlasting life, which Thou hast given us in our SAVIOUR JESUS CHRIST. Amen.

S. S. WESLEY.

888

PSALM xcvi.   7. Ascribe unto the LORD, O ye kindreds of the people, ascribe unto the LORD worship and power.

8. Ascribe unto the LORD the honour due unto His Name.

9. Let the whole earth stand in awe of Him.

10. Tell it out among the heathen that the LORD is King, and that He shall judge the people righteously.

9. O worship the LORD in the beauty of holiness.

2, 3. Sing to the LORD, and praise His Name; be telling of His salvation from day to day, His wonders unto all people.

5. As for the gods of the heathen, they are but idols.

cxv.   4. Their idols are silver and gold, even the work of men's hands.

5. They have mouths and speak not; eyes have they, and see not.

6. They have ears, and hear not : noses have they, and smell not.

7. They have hands, and handle not: feet have they, and walk not : neither speak they through their throat.

8. They that make them are like unto them, and so are all such as put their trust in them.

3. As for our GOD, He is in Heaven : He hath done whatsoever pleased Him.

*12. The LORD hath been mindful of us, and He shall bless us : He shall bless the house of Israel, He shall bless the house of Aaron.

13. He shall bless them that fear the LORD, both small and great.

14. Ye are the blessed of the LORD, you and your children.

15. Ye are the blessed of the LORD, Who made heaven and earth.*

S. S. WESLEY.

*   -- Sometimes sung as a separate Anthem.

889

1 PETER i. 3. Blessed be the GOD and Father of our LORD JESUS CHRIST, Which, according to His abundant mercy, hath begotten us again unto a lively hope by the Resurrection of JESUS CHRIST from the dead,

4, 5. To an inheritance incorruptible and undefiled, that fadeth not away, reserved in Heaven for you, who are kept by the power of GOD, through faith unto salvation ready to be revealed in the last time.

15. But as He Which hath called you is holy, so be ye holy in all manner of conversation.

17. Pass the time of your sojourning here in fear.

22. See that ye love one another with a pure heart fervently :

23. Being born again, not of corruptible seed, but of incorruptible, by the word of GOD.

24. For all flesh is as grass, and all the glory of man as the flower of grass. The grass withereth, and the flower thereof falleth away :

·25. But the word of the LORD endureth for evermore. Amen.

S. S. WESLEY.

890

ST. LUKE i. 68. Blessed be the LORD GOD of Israel, for He hath visited and redeemed His people.

69, 70. And hath raised up a horn of salvation for us, as He spake by the mouth of His holy prophets, which have been since the world began.

ISAIAH ix. 6. For unto us a Child is born, unto us a Son is given : and the government shall be upon His shoulder: and His Name shall be called Wonderful, Counsellor, The Mighty GOD, The Everlasting Father, The Prince of Peace.

7. Of the increase of His government and peace, there shall be no end. The zeal of the LORD of Hosts will perform this.

ST. LUKE ii. 14. Glory to GOD on high, and on earth peace, goodwill toward men. Glory to GOD in the highest.

S. S. WESLEY.

891

PSALM li. 11. Cast me not away from Thy presence, and take not Thy Holy Spirit from me.

12. Restore unto me the joy of Thy salvation, and uphold me with Thy Spirit.

17. The sacrifices of GOD are a broken spirit; a broken and a contrite heart Thou wilt not despise, O GOD.

8. Make me to hear joy and gladness, that the bones which Thou hast broken may rejoice.

S. S. WESLEY.

892 BLAIR, CALKIN, v. 17.
893 HORSLEY, vv. 17, 8.

894

PSALM lxxii. 1. Give the king Thy judgments, O GOD: and Thy righteousness unto the king's son.

2. Then shall he judge Thy people according unto right, and defend the poor, and break in pieces the oppressor.

7, 15. In his days shall the righteous flourish : prayer shall be made for him continually.

17. All nations shall call him blessed.

cxxviii. 5. Lo, thus shall the man be blessed, that feareth the LORD.

6. The LORD from out of Sion shall so bless thee, that thou shalt see Jerusalem in prosperity all thy life long.

3. Thy wife shall be as the fruitful vine, upon the walls of thine house.

4. Thy children like the olive-branches, round about thy table.

2. O well is thee, and happy shalt thou be.

7. Yea, thou shalt see thy children's children, and peace upon Israel.

lxxii. 18. Blessed be the LORD GOD, the GOD of Israel, Who only doeth wondrous things.

19. And blessed be His glorious Name for ever : let the whole earth be filled with His glory. Amen, and Amen.

S. S. WESLEY.

895 OUSELEY, vv. 18, 19.

896

PSALM lxvii. 1. GOD be merciful unto us, and bless us, and shew us the light of His countenance, and be merciful unto us :

2. That Thy way may be known upon earth, Thy saving health among all nations.

3. Let the people praise Thee, O GOD, yea, let all the people praise Thee.

4. O let the nations rejoice and be glad; for Thou shalt judge the folk righteously, and govern the nations upon earth.

5. Let the people praise Thee, O GOD; let all the people praise Thee.

6. Then shall the earth bring forth her increase, and GOD, even our own GOD, shall give us His blessing.

7. GOD shall bless us, and all the ends of the world shall fear Him.

Glory be to the Father, &c.

C. F. LLOYD, A. H. MANN, R. ROGERS, TOURS, S. S. WESLEY.

897 PEREZ, v. 1. Hallelujah. Amen.

898

PSALM cxix. 94. I am Thine, O save me, for I have sought Thy commandments.

92. If my delight had not been in Thy law, I should have perished in my trouble.

94. I am Thine, O save me, for I have sought Thy commandments.

S. S. WESLEY.

899

LAMENTATIONS iii. 41. Let us lift up our heart with our hands to GOD in the heavens.

40. Let us search and try our ways, and turn again to the LORD.

ISAIAH lxiii. 16. Thou, O LORD, art our Father, our Redeemer; Thy Name is from everlasting. Doubtless Thou art our Father; Thy Name is from everlasting.

lxiv. 9. Be not wroth very sore, O LORD, neither remember iniquity for ever; behold, see, we beseech Thee, we are all Thy people.

1. O that Thou would'st rend the heavens, that the mountains might flow down at Thy presence.

9. Be not wroth very sore, O LORD, neither remember iniquity for ever.

6. But we are all as an unclean thing; we all do fade as a leaf.

9. See, we beseech Thee, we are all Thy people.

lxiii. 16, 19. Thou, O LORD, art our Father. We are Thine, O LORD. Thy Name is from everlasting.

lxiv. 8. We are the clay, and Thou our potter. We are all the work of Thine hand.

lxiii. 19, 16. We are Thine, O LORD; Thy Name is from everlasting.

PSALM lxxi. 4. Thou, O LORD GOD, art the thing that I long for; Thou art my hope, even from my youth.

5. Through Thee have I been holden up ever since I was born.

10. Go not far from me, O GOD; my GOD, haste Thee to help me.

1. In Thee, O LORD, have I put my trust.

> *Thou Judge of quick and dead,
>   Before Whose bar severe,
> With holy joy, or guilty dread,
>   We all shall soon appear.
>
> Do Thou our souls prepare
>   For that tremendous day,
> And fill us now with watchful care,
>   And teach our hearts to pray.
>
> O may we thus insure
>   A lot among the blest,
> And watch a moment to secure
>   An everlasting rest!*
>
>   C. 3. WESLEY.

                nmetime 1ing a a separate Anthem.

900

ECCLESIASTICUS xliv. 1. Let us now praise famous men, and our fathers that begat us.

2. The LORD hath wrought great glory through them by His great power from the beginning.

3. Such as did bear rule in their kingdoms, men renowned or their power, giving counsel by their understanding, and declaring prophecies.

4. Leaders of the people by their counsels, and by their knowledge of learning meet for the people, wise and eloquent in their instructions.

7. All these were honoured in their generations, and were the glory of their times.

8. There be of them that have left a name behind them, that their praises might be reported.

9. And some there be, which have no memorial; who are perished, as though they had never been born.

10. But these were merciful men, whose righteousness hath not been forgotten.

11. With their seed shall continually remain a good inheritance, and their children are with the covenant.

12. Their seed standeth fast, and their children for their sakes.

13. Their seed shall remain for ever, and their glory shall not be blotted out.

14. Their bodies are buried in peace; but their name liveth evermore.

15. The people will tell of their wisdom, and the congregation will shew forth their praise.

S. S. WESLEY.

901 THORNE, vv. 1, 2, 8, 9, 13-15. Hallelujah.

902

O GOD, Whose nature and property is ever to have mercy and to forgive, receive our humble petitions; and though we be tied and bound with the chain of our sins, yet let the pitifulness of Thy great mercy loose us; for the honour of JESUS CHRIST, our Mediator and Advocate. Amen.

GRAY, S. S. WESLEY.

903

PSALM cvi.   1. O give thanks unto the LORD, for He is gracious, and His mercy endureth for ever.

2. Who can express the noble acts of the LORD, or shew forth all His praise ?

[3. Blessed are they that alway keep judgment, and do righteousness.

4. Remember me, O LORD, according to the favour that Thou bearest unto Thy people: O visit me with Thy salvation.

5. That I may see the felicity of Thy chosen,* and rejoice in the gladness of Thy people, and give thanks with Thine inheritance.

45. Deliver us, O LORD our GOD, and gather us from among the heathen: that we may give thanks unto Thy holy Name, and make our boast of Thy praise.

46. Blessed be the LORD GOD of Israel from everlasting, and world without end : and let all the people say, Amen.]

lxxxvi.   5. For Thou, O LORD, art good and gracious; and of great mercy unto all them that call upon Thee.

9. All nations whom Thou hast made shall come and worship Thee, O LORD, and shall glorify Thy Name.

10. For Thou art great, and doest wondrous things.

From The Communion Service.   For Thou only art holy ; Thou only art the LORD.

PSALM cvi.   3. Blessed are they that alway keep judgment, and do righteousness.   They always are blessed.

S. S. WESLEY.

904 ALDRICH, v. 1.   Hallelujah.
905 BATTEN, CROFT, † GIBBONS, vv. 45, 46.
906 MACFARREN, vv. 4, 5*.
907 W. H. MONK, vv. 3-5.
908 PURCELL, vv. 1, 2, 4, 5, 46.
909 T. A. WALMISLEY, vv. 2, 4, 5.

† Verse 46 is sometimes sung as a separate Anthem.   * Ends here.

910

PSALM lxxxiv.   1. O how amiable are Thy dwellings, Thou LORD of Hosts.

2. My soul hath a desire and longing to enter into the courts of the LORD: my heart and my flesh rejoice in the living GOD.

[3. Yea, the sparrow hath found her an house, and the swallow a nest where she may lay her young, even Thy altars, O LORD of Hosts, my King and my GOD.]

4. Blessed are they that dwell in Thy house, they will be alway praising Thee.

5. Blessed is the man whose strength is in Thee; in whose heart are Thy ways.

6. Who going through the vale of misery use it for a well, and the pools are filled with water.

7. They will go from strength to strength, and unto the GOD of gods appeareth every one of them in Zion.

4. Blessed are they that dwell in Thy house; they will be alway praising Thee.

[8. O LORD GOD of Hosts, hear my prayer; hearken, O GOD of Jacob.

9. Behold, O GOD, our Defender, and look upon the face of Thine anointed.

10. For one day in Thy courts is better than a thousand.]

12. The LORD will give grace and worship, the LORD is a light and defence; and no good thing shall He withhold from them that live a godly life.

13. O LORD GOD [of Hosts], blessed is the man that putteth his trust in Thee.

[cxvi. 15. I will offer to Thee the sacrifice of thanksgiving, and will call upon the Name of the LORD.

16. I will pay my vows unto the LORD, in the sight of all His people : in the courts of the LORD's house, even in the midst of thee, O Jerusalem. Praise the LORD.]

S. S. WESLEY.

911 BARNBY, BUNNETT, RICHARDSON, vv. 1, 2, 4.
    [Hallelujah. Gloria Patri.]
912 BLOW, vv. 1, 2, 5-7.
913 CROTCH, v. 13.
914 GREENE, vv. 1, 2, 4. Psalm cxvi. 15, 16.
915 GREENE, vv. 4, 5, 7-9, 12, 13.
916 PATTISON, vv. 1-5.
917 PAGE, vv. 4, 10.
918 TOURS, vv. 4 7. Amen.

919

*Isaiah xxv. 1. O Lord, Thou art my God; I will exalt Thee, I will praise Thy Name; Thy counsels of old are faithfulness and truth; Thou hast done wonderful things;

4. For Thou hast been a strength to the poor and needy in his distress.*

Psalm xxxiii. 21. For our heart shall rejoice in Him; because we have trusted in His holy Name.

22. Let Thy mercy, O Lord, be upon us, according as we hope in Thee.

Isaiah xxv. 8. He will swallow up death in victory; and the Lord God will wipe tears from off all faces; the rebuke of His people shall He take away from off all the earth: for the Lord hath spoken it.

1 Corinthians xv. 53. For this mortal must put on immortality.

34. Awake to righteousness, and sin not; for some have not the knowledge of God.

Wisdom iii. 9. They that put their trust in Him shall understand the truth.

1 Corinthians xv. 51, 52. We shall not all sleep, but we shall all be changed, in a moment, in the twinkling of an eye, at the last trumpet.

Isaiah xxv. 9. And in that day it shall be said, Lo, This is our God; we have waited for Him, and He will save us; This is the Lord; we have waited for Him, we will be glad and rejoice in His salvation.

S. S. Wesley.

* ———* Sometimes sung as a separate Anthem.

920

Psalm ciii. 1. Praise the Lord, my soul, and all that is within me praise His holy Name.

iii. 5. I laid me down and slept, and rose up again, for the Lord sustained me.

v. 2. O hearken Thou unto the voice of my calling, my King, and my God.

3. Early in the morning will I direct my prayer to Thee, and will look up.

ciii.   1. Praise the LORD, my soul, and all that is within me praise His holy Name.   Praise the LORD, O my soul ; praise the LORD.

v.   3. My voice shalt Thou hear betimes, O LORD ; early in the morning will I direct my prayer to Thee.

1. Give ear to my words, O LORD ; O LORD, give ear unto my prayer.

2. Hearken Thou unto the voice of my cry.

12. Let all them that trust in Thee rejoice ; they shall ever be giving of thanks, because Thou defendest them ; they that love Thy Name shall be joyful in Thee.

3. My voice shalt Thou hear betimes, O LORD ; early in the morning will I direct my prayer to Thee.

1. Give ear to my words, O LORD ; O LORD, give ear.

7. As for me, I will come into Thy house, in the multitude of Thy mercy ; and in Thy fear will I worship toward Thy holy temple.

*8. Lead me, LORD, lead me in Thy righteousness ; make Thy way plain before my face :

iv.   9. For it is Thou, LORD, only that makest me dwell in safety.*

S. S. WESLEY.

—— Sometimes sung as a separate Anthem.

921

PSALM xxxiv.   16. The face of the LORD is against them that do evil, to cut off the remembrance of them from the earth.

18. The LORD is nigh unto them that are of a broken heart, and saveth such as be of a contrite spirit.

19. Many are the afflictions of the righteous ; but the LORD delivereth him out of all.

17. The righteous cry, and the LORD heareth, and delivereth them out of all their troubles.

20. He keepeth all his bones ; not one of them is broken.

21. Evil shall slay the wicked ; and they that hate the righteous shall be desolate.

17. The righteous cry, and the LORD heareth, and delivereth them out of all their troubles.

22. The LORD redeemeth the soul of His servants, and they that trust in Him shall not be desolate.

S. S. WESLEY.

*   * Sometimes sung as a separate Anthem.

922

ISAIAH xxxv.　1. The wilderness and the solitary place shall be glad for them, and the desert shall rejoice and blossom as the rose.

2. It shall blossom abundantly, and rejoice with joy and singing.

4. Say to them of a fearful heart, Be strong, fear not: behold, your GOD, even GOD, He will come and save you.

6. Then shall the lame man leap as an hart, and the tongue of the dumb sing; for in the wilderness shall waters break out, and streams in the desert.

8, 9. And a highway shall be there: it shall be called The way of holiness; the unclean shall not pass over it, but the redeemed shall walk there.

10. And the ransomed of the LORD shall return, and come to Zion with songs, and everlasting joy upon their heads; they shall obtain joy and gladness, and sorrow and sighing shall flee away.

S. S. WESLEY.

923

* ISAIAH xxvi.　3. Thou wilt keep him in perfect peace, whose mind is stayed on Thee.

PSALM cxxxix.　11. The darkness is no darkness with Thee, but the night is as clear as the day; the darkness and light to Thee are both alike.

1 ST. JOHN i.　5. GOD is light, and in Him is no darkness at all.

PSALM cxix.　175. O let my soul live, and it shall praise Thee.*

ST. MATTHEW vi.　13. For Thine is the Kingdom, the power, and the glory, for evermore.

ISAIAH xxvi.　3. Thou wilt keep him in perfect peace, whose mind is stayed on Thee.

S. S. WESLEY.

924 WILLIAMS　·　.

925

Psalm li. 2. Wash me throughly from my wickedness, and forgive me all my sin.

3. For I acknowledge my faults, and my sin is ever before me.

S. S. Wesley.

926

Psalm cxxxvii. 1. (*Paraphrase.*) By the waters of Babylon sat we down and wept, when we our Zion remembered.

2. And our harps, them we hanged on the willows in the midst thereof.

3. There did they ask of us singing, the same that led us captive ; mirth was required of us by them who vexed and spoiled us : Sing to us a song of Zion.

4. How shall we sing the Lord's song, sing it in a land of strangers ?

5. If I think not on thee, Jerusalem, let my right hand forget her cunning.

6. Let my tongue cleave to the roof of my mouth, if thou art not in remembrance, yea, if thou, Jerusalem, art not more to me than all my joy.

7. Lord, remember the children of Edom, in the day of Jerusalem, how they shouted, Destroy it, yea, down to the ground.

8. Daughter of Babylon, set for destruction, happy, who thee repays what on us thou wroughtest.

Goetz.

927

Psalm lxxxiv. 1. O how amiable are Thy dwellings, Thou Lord of Hosts !

2. My soul hath a desire and longing to enter into the courts of the Lord: my heart and my flesh rejoice in the living God.

4. Blessed are they that dwell in Thy house, they will be alway praising Thee.

cxvi. 11. What reward shall I give unto the Lord, for all the benefits that He hath done unto me ?

Novello's Collection. L

lv.   18. In the evening and morning, and at noon-day will I pray, and He shall hear my voice.

cxlv.   2. Every day will I give thanks unto Him, and praise His Name for ever and ever.

cxvi.   12. I will receive the cup of salvation, **and call** upon the Name of the LORD.

13. I will pay my vows now in the presence of all His people : right dear in the sight of the LORD is the death of His saints.

15. I will offer to Him the sacrifice of thanksgiving, and will call upon the Name of the LORD.

16. I will pay my vows unto the LORD, in the sight of all His people : in the courts of the LORD's house, even in the midst of thee, O Jerusalem. Praise the LORD. Amen.

G. T. SMITH.

928

PSALM xxxii.   12. Be glad, O ye righteous, and rejoice in the LORD, and be joyful, all ye that are true of heart !

xxx.   5. For His wrath endures but for a moment, and in His pleasure is life for evermore ; heaviness may endure for a night, but in the morning cometh joy.

xlvii.   1. O clap your hands together, all ye people, sing unto GOD with the voice of melody.   Hallelujah. Amen.

H. SMART.

929

PSALM xc.   1. LORD, Thou hast been our refuge from one generation to another.

2. Before the mountains were brought forth, or ever the world was made, Thou art GOD from everlasting, and world without end.

xxii.   4. Our fathers hoped in Thee, they trusted in Thee, and Thou didst deliver them.

5. They called upon Thee, and were holpen : they put their trust in Thee, and were not confounded.

xxvii.   8. Hearken unto my voice, O LORD, when I cry unto Thee : have mercy upon me, and hear me, O LORD

10. O hide not Thou Thy face from me, nor cast Thy servant away in displeasure.

16. O tarry thou the LORD's leisure : be strong, and He shall comfort thine heart, and put thou thy trust in the LORD.

8. Hearken unto my voice, O LORD, when I cry unto Thee : have mercy upon me, and hear me,

11. For Thou hast been my succour : leave me not, neither forsake me, O GOD of my salvation.

*ISAIAH xlix. 13. Sing, O heavens, and be joyful, O earth ; break forth into singing, O mountains.

li. 3. For the LORD shall comfort ZION, He will comfort all her waste places, He will make her wilderness like Eden, and her desert like the garden of the LORD ; joy and gladness shall be found therein, thanksgiving, and the voice of melody. Hallelujah. Amen.*

H. SMART.

—— Sometimes sung as a separate Anthem.

930

ISAIAH xlii. 10. Sing to the LORD a new song, ye that go down to the sea, the isles, and the inhabitants thereof.

12. Let them give glory unto the LORD, yea, and declare His praise.

JUDITH xvi. 14. All creatures serve Thee : for Thou spakest, and they were made, Thou sentest forth Thy Spirit, and It created them, and there is none that can resist Thy voice.

PSALM lxxvii. 19. The LORD maketh a way in the sea, and a path in the mighty waters.

ST. MATTHEW viii. 27. He speaketh the word, and the wind and the sea obey His voice.

JUDITH xvi. 15. For the mountains shall be moved from their foundations with the waters, the rocks shall melt as wax at Thy presence : yet Thou art merciful to them that fear Thee, and put their trust in Thee, O LORD.

PSALM lxxii. 18. Blessed be the LORD GOD of Israel.

19. And blessed be the Name of His Majesty for ever and ever. Hallelujah. Amen.

H. SMART.

—— Sometimes sung as a separate Anthem.

931

Psalm lxvi. 1. O be joyful in God, all ye lands : sing praises to the honour of His Name, make His praise to be glorious.

7. O praise our God, and make the voice of His praise to be heard.

14. O come hither, and hearken, all ye that fear the Lord, and I will tell you what He hath done for my soul.

8. He holdeth our soul in life, and suffereth not our feet to slip.

1, 7. O be joyful in God, all ye lands : make the voice of His praise to be heard.

H. Smart.

932

St. Luke i. 26, 27. The Angel Gabriel was sent from God unto a city of Galilee, named Nazareth, to a virgin whose name was Mary.

30. And the Angel said unto her, Fear not, Mary, for thou hast found favour with God.

31. And, behold, thou shalt conceive, and bring forth a Son, and shalt call His Name Jesus.

32. He shall be great, and shall be called The Son of the Highest ; and the Lord God shall give to Him the throne of His father David.

33. And He shall reign over the House of Jacob for ever, and of His Kingdom there shall be no end. Amen.

H. Smart.

933

Psalm cxxvi. 3, 4. The Lord hath done great things for us, whereof we are glad.

6. They that sow in tears shall reap in joy.

7. He that goeth forth and weepeth, bearing precious seed, shall doubtless come again with rejoicing, bringing his sheaves with him.

H. Smart.

934

PSALM xxiii. 1. The LORD is my Shepherd, I shall not want.

2. He maketh me to lie down in green pastures : He leadeth me beside the still waters.

3. He restoreth my soul ; He leadeth me in the paths of righteousness, for His Name's sake.

4. Yea, though I walk through the valley of the shadow of death, I will fear no evil : for Thou art with me ; Thy rod and Thy staff, they comfort me.

5. Thou preparest a table before me in the presence of mine enemies : Thou anointest my head with oil ; my cup runneth over.

6. Surely goodness and mercy shall follow me all the days of my life, and I will dwell in the house of the LORD for ever.

G. B. ARNOLD, H. SMART.

935 MACFARREN, vv. 1–4, 6.

936

COLLECT

For the Third Sunday after Trinity.

O LORD, we beseech Thee mercifully to hear us ; and grant that we, to whom Thou hast given an hearty desire to pray, may by Thy mighty aid be defended and comforted in all dangers and adversities ; through JESUS CHRIST our LORD. Amen.

SMEE.

937

COLLECT

For the Thirteenth Sunday after Trinity.

Almighty and merciful GOD, of Whose only gift it cometh that Thy faithful people do unto Thee true and laudable service ; grant, we beseech Thee, that we may so faithfully serve Thee in this life, that we fail not finally to attain Thy heavenly promises ; through the merits of JESUS CHRIST our LORD. Amen.

GOSS.

938

2 Samuel iii. 31. And the king said to all the people that were with him, Rend your clothes, and gird you with sackcloth, and mourn. And the king himself followed the bier.

32. And they buried him. And the king lifted up his voice and wept at the grave; and all the people wept.

38. And the king said unto his servants, Know ye not that there is a prince and a great man fallen this day in Israel?

Goss.

939

Hosea vi. 1. Come, and let us return unto the Lord; for He hath torn and He will heal us; He hath smitten, and He will bind us up.

1 Samuel ii. 6. The Lord killeth and maketh alive: He bringeth down to the grave, and bringeth up.

7. The Lord maketh poor and maketh rich; He bringeth low, and lifteth up.

8. The pillars of the earth are the Lord's, and He hath set the world upon them.

Job v. 17. Behold, happy is the man whom God correcteth;

18. For He maketh sore and bindeth up, He woundeth and His hands make whole.

Hosea vi. 1. Come, and let us return unto the Lord: for He hath torn and He will heal us; He hath smitten, and He will bind us up.

Goss.

940

Baruch iii. 2. Hear, O Lord, and have mercy, for Thou art merciful: and have pity upon us, because we have sinned before Thee.

5. Remember not the iniquity of our forefathers; but think upon Thy power and Thy Name now at this time.

6. For Thou art the Lord our God, and Thee, O Lord will we praise.

Goss.

941

JOEL ii. 21. Fear not, O land, be glad and rejoice; for the LORD will do great things.

22. Be not afraid, ye beasts of the field : for the pastures of the wilderness do spring, for the tree beareth her fruit, the fig-tree and the vine do yield their strength.

23. Be glad, then, ye children of Zion, and rejoice in the LORD your GOD.* Be glad then, O land, and rejoice, (21) for the LORD will do great things.

24, 26. The floors shall be full of wheat, and ye shall eat in plenty, and be satisfied, and praise the Name of the LORD your GOD, that hath dealt so wondrously with you.

23, 21. Be glad then, ye children, and rejoice in the LORD your GOD, for the LORD will do great things.

Goss.

942 C. H. LLOYD, vv. 21–23.*

* Ends here.

943

Colossians ii. 9. In CHRIST dwelleth all the fulness of the Godhead bodily.

10. And ye are complete in Him, Which is the Head of all principality and power ;

11. In Whom also ye are circumcised with the circumcision made without hands, in putting off the body of the sins of the flesh, by the circumcision of CHRIST ;

12. Buried with Him in baptism, wherein also ye are risen with Him, through the faith of the operation of GOD, Who hath raised Him from the dead. Hallelujah.

Goss.

944

PSALM cvi. 1. O give thanks unto the LORD, for He is gracious, and His mercy endureth for ever.

2. Who can express the noble acts of the LORD, or shew forth all His praise ?

cxviii. 22. The same stone which the builders refused, is become the Head-stone in the corner.

23. This is the LORD's doing, and it is marvellous in our eyes.

29. O give thanks unto the LORD, for He i gracious, and His mercy endureth for ever. Hallelujah. Amen.

Goss.

945

ISAIAH xlix. 18. Lift up Thine eyes round about, and behold; all these gather themselves together, and come to Thee. As I live, saith the LORD, thou shalt surely clothe thee with them all, as with an ornament, and bind them on thee, as a bride doth.

22. Thus saith the LORD GOD, Behold, I will lift up Mine hand to the Gentiles, and set up My standard to the people; and they shall bring thy sons in their arms, and thy daughters shall be carried upon their shoulders.

23. And kings shall be thy nursing fathers, and their queens thy nursing mothers; they shall bow down to thee with their face toward the earth, and thou shalt know that I am the LORD, for they shall not be ashamed that wait for Me.

Goss.

946

PSALM cxl. 7. O LORD GOD, Thou strength of my health, Thou hast covered my head in the day of battle.

xxxi. 6. Into Thy hands I commend my spirit; for Thou hast redeemed me, O LORD, Thou GOD of truth. Amen.

Goss.

947

PSALM cxlviii. 1. O praise the LORD of Heaven: praise Him in the height.

2. Praise Him, all ye angels of His; praise Him, all His host.

3. Praise Him, sun and moon; praise Him, all ye stars and light.

4. Praise Him, all ye heavens, and ye waters that are above the heavens.

5. Let them praise the Name of the LORD, for He spake the word, and they were made; He commanded, and they were created.

6. He hath made them fast for ever and ever: He hath given them a law which shall not be broken.

7. Praise the LORD upon earth, ye dragons, and all deeps;

8. Fire and hail, snow and vapours, wind and storm, fulfilling His word;

9. Mountains and all hills, fruitful trees and all cedars;

10. Beasts and all cattle, worms and feathered fowls;

11. Kings of the earth and all people, princes and all judges of the world;

12. Young men and maidens, old men and children, praise the Name of the LORD; for His Name only is excellent, and His praise above heaven and earth.

[cxlv. 10. All Thy works praise Thee, O LORD: and Thy saints give thanks unto Thee.

cl. 6. Let everything that hath breath praise the LORD.]

Goss.

948 ELVEY, vv. 1–3; cxlv. 10. Hallelujah. Amen.
949 GREENE, vv. 1–4; cl. 6: cxlviii. 5; cl. 6. Amen.

950

PSALM civ. 31. The glory of the LORD shall endure for ever: the LORD shall rejoice in His works.

33. I will sing unto the LORD as long as I live; I will sing praise to my GOD while I have my being.

34. My meditation of Him shall be sweet; I will be glad in the LORD.

35. Bless thou the LORD, O my soul. Praise ye the LORD.

Goss.

951

PSALM xxi. 1. The *Queen* shall rejoice in Thy strength, O LORD: exceeding glad shall *she* be of Thy salvation.

2. Thou hast given *her her* heart's desire, and has not denied *her* the request of *her* lips.

5. *Her* honour is great in Thy salvation; glory and great worship shalt Thou lay upon *her*.

xxii. 22. *She* will declare Thy Name unto *her* people: in the midst of the congregation will *she* praise Thee.

xxi. 13. Be Thou exalted, LORD, in Thine own strength: so will we sing and praise Thy power. Amen.

Goss.

952

PSALM cxlvi. 1. Praise the LORD, O my soul; while I live will I praise the LORD : yea, as long as I have any being, I will sing praises unto my GOD.

cxxii. 6. O pray for the peace of Jerusalem; they shall prosper that love thee.

7. Peace be within thy walls, and plenteousness within thy palaces.

8. For my brethren and companions' sakes, I will wish thee prosperity.

9. Yea, because of the house of the LORD our GOD, I will seek to do thee good.

cxxv. 1. They that put their trust in the LORD shall be even as the Mount Sion, which may not be removed, but standeth fast for ever.

2. As the mountains are round about Jerusalem, so the LORD is round about His people, from henceforth, even for ever.

GOSS.

953

NEHEMIAH IX. 5. Stand up, and bless the LORD your GOD for ever and ever : blessed be Thy glorious Name, which is exalted above all blessing and praise.

6. Thou, even Thou, art LORD alone : Thou hast made the heaven, the heaven of heavens, with all their host, the earth, and all things that are therein, the sea, and all that is therein, and Thou preservest them all; and the host of heaven worshippeth Thee.

*ISAIAH lxiii. 15. Look down from heaven, and behold from the habitation of Thy holiness, and of Thy glory.

16. For Thou, O LORD, art our Father, our Redeemer : Thy Name is from everlasting.*

NEHEMIAH ix. 5. Blessed be Thy glorious Name, which is exalted above all blessing and praise.

6. Thou, even Thou, art LORD alone; blessed be Thy holy Name. Thou hast made the heaven, the heaven of heavens, with all their host, the earth, and all things that are therein, the seas, and all that is therein, and Thou preservest them all.

GOSS.

---

* Sometimes sung as a separate Anthem.

954

DEUTERONOMY xxxiii. 26. There is none like unto the GOD of Jeshurun, Who rideth upon the heaven in thy help, and in HIS excellency on the sky.

27. The Eternal GOD is thy refuge, and underneath are the everlasting arms.

28. And Israel shall dwell in safety, and the heavens shall drop down dew.

29. Happy art thou, O Israel; O people, saved by the LORD.

Goss.

955

ISAIAH xxxv. 1. The wilderness and the solitary place shall be glad for them ; and the desert shall rejoice, and blossom as the rose.

2. It shall blossom abundantly, and rejoice even with joy and singing; the glory of Lebanon shall be given unto it, the excellency of Carmel and Sharon ; they shall see the glory of the LORD, and the excellency of our GOD.

3. Strengthen ye the weak hands, and confirm the feeble knees.

4. Say to them that are of a fearful heart, Be strong, fear not : behold, your GOD will come with vengeance, even GOD with a recompense ; He will come and save you.

5. Then the eyes of the blind shall be opened, and the ears of the deaf shall be unstopped.

6. Then shall the lame man leap as an hart, and the tongue of the dumb shall sing ; for in the wilderness shall waters break out, and streams in the desert.

8. And an highway shall be there, and a way, and it shall be called The way of holiness; the unclean shall not pass over it, but it shall be for those : the wayfaring men, though fools, shall not err therein.

9. No lion shall be there, nor any ravenous beast shall go up thereon, it shall not be found there ; but the redeemed shall walk there.

10. And the ransomed of the LORD shall return and come to Zion with songs and everlasting joy upon their heads ; they shall obtain joy and gladness, and sorrow and sighing shall flee away. Amen.

Goss.

956

REVELATION xiv. 4. These are they which follow the Lamb whithersoever He goeth. These were redeemed from among men, being the first-fruits unto GOD and to the Lamb.

5. And in their mouth was found no guile, for they are without fault before the Throne of GOD.

GOSS.

957

MARRIAGE CHORAL.

1. FATHER of Life, confessing
    Thy majesty and power,
 We seek Thy gracious blessing
    To greet the bridal hour.
 The troth in Eden plighted
    The wedded here renew ;
 May they, in Thee united,
    Till death be pure and true.

2. JESU, Redeemer, hear us ;
    Still be the Wedding Guest ;
 Thy gentle presence near us
    Makes common things more blest ;
 E'en care shall be a learning
    Of blessedness divine,
 If Thou wilt still be turning
    The water into wine.

3. Spirit of Love, descending,
    Impart Thy joy and peace ;
 These hopes together blending
    Bless with Thine own increase.
 Athwart the roughened ocean,
    Or on the peaceful tide,
 Thy breath through each emotion
    Their heavenward course shall guide.

4. The Church, Thy bride, hath given
   Her blessing on the vow,
   O ratify from heaven
   Her benison below.
Bless, FATHER, SON, and SPIRIT,
   The union here begun,
That in the life eternal
   It may be ever one.   Amen.
                              GILBERT, TURLE.

958

COLLECT

For the Twentieth Sunday after Trinity.

O Almighty and most merciful GOD, of Thy bountiful goodness keep us, we beseech Thee, from all things that may hurt us ; that we, being ready both in body and soul, may cheerfully accomplish those things that Thou wouldest have done : through JESUS CHRIST our LORD. Amen.
                              OUSELEY, TURLE.

959

PSALM cxviii. 24. This is the day which the LORD hath made, we will rejoice and be glad in it.

xlvi. 11. The LORD of Hosts is with us, the GOD of Jacob is our refuge.

cvii. 1. O give thanks unto the LORD, for He is gracious, and His mercy endureth for ever. Amen.
                              TURLE.

960

PSALM v. 1. Ponder my words, O LORD, consider my meditation.

2. O hearken Thou unto the voice of my calling, my KING and my GOD, for unto Thee will I make my prayer.

REVELATION xxi. 7. He that overcometh shall inherit all things; and I will be his GOD, and he shall be My son.

To Father, Son, and Holy Ghost,
   The GOD Whom heaven and earth adore,
Be glory, as it was of old,
   Is now, and shall be evermore.   HAYNE.

961

Give peace in our time, O LORD, because there is none other that fighteth for us, but only Thou, O GOD. Defend us, Thy humble servants, in all assaults of our enemies.

W. H. CALLCOTT.

962

PSALM lxv. 9. Thou visitest the earth, and blessest it: Thou makest it very plenteous.

12. Thou crownest the year with Thy goodness, and Thy clouds drop fatness.

14. The valleys stand so thick with corn, that they laugh and sing.

W. H. CALLCOTT.

963

GOD, Who cannot be unjust,
Heedeth all that in Him trust ;
Them who call on Him for aid
Anguish shall not make afraid.
Trust Him then, in life, in death ;
He can give thee living breath ;
After death, the life now thine
He can make a life divine.

COSTA.

964

PSALM lxvii. 5. Let the people praise Thee, O LORD, let all the people praise Thee.

6. Then shall the earth yield her increase, and GOD, even our own GOD, shall bless us.

1. God be merciful unto us, and bless us : and cause His face to shine upon us.

(*From* "*Eli*," No. 5.) COSTA.

¹ Sometimes sung as a separate Anthem.

965

FIRST COLLECT
In the Communion Service.

Almighty GOD, unto Whom all hearts be open, all desires known, and from Whom no secrets are hid, cleanse the thoughts of our hearts by the inspiration of Thy Holy Spirit, that we may perfectly love Thee, and worthily magnify Thy holy Name: through CHRIST our LORD. Amen.

BENSON, JEKYLL.

966

PSALM iv. 1. Hear me when I call, O GOD of my righteousness; Thou hast set me at liberty when I was in trouble; have mercy upon me, and hearken unto my prayer.

BENSON, WEST.

967 HUMMEL, v. 1. Gloria Patri.

968

PSALM lxxxv. 4. Turn us, O GOD of our salvation, and let Thine anger cease from us.

10. Mercy and truth are met together: righteousness and peace have kissed each other.

11. Truth shall flourish out of the earth; and righteousness hath looked down from heaven.

12. Yea, the LORD shall shew loving-kindness, and our land shall give her increase.

13. Righteousness shall go before Him, and He shall direct His going in the way.

BENSON.

969 SULLIVAN, vv. 10, 11, 13. Alleluia. Amen.

970

O LORD most holy, O GOD most mighty, O loving Saviour, Thee would we be praising with joyful lips; for Thou hast redeemed us of Thy grace and mercy.

Teach us to know Thee, teach us to love Thee, make us to follow after holiness; so in temptation, and in the hour of sadness, we shall find comfort and help in Thee.

Guide us, O loving Saviour; so in the hour of sadness we shall find comfort and help in Thee. Amen.

ABT.

971

PSALM cvii. 23, 24. They that go down to the sea in ships, that do business in great waters, these behold the works of the LORD, and His wonders in the deep.

cxxi. 8. The LORD will preserve their going out and their coming in; He is with them, and will keep them, for in His hand is every living thing.

cvii. 23, 24. They that go down to the sea in ships, that do business in great waters, these behold the works of the LORD, and His wonders in the deep.

iv. 8. Lie down in peace and sleep: for Thou, O LORD, makest us to dwell in safety.

(From " St. Peter," No. 2.)   BENEDICT.

972

ISAIAH ii. 5. O house of Jacob, come ye, and let us walk in the light of the LORD.

MICAH iv. 2. He will teach us of His ways: for out of Zion shall go forth a law, and the word of the LORD from Jerusalem.

ISAIAH ii. 4. He shall judge among the nations, and rebuke many people.

*2 CHRONICLES xxx. 9. The LORD will not turn His face from them that seek Him,

MICAH vii. 19. But will have compassion, and cast their sins in the depths of the sea.*

(From " St. Peter," Nos. 4, 5.)   BENEDICT.

—— Sometimes sung as a separate Anthem.

973

PSALM xxxi. 19. How great, O LORD, is Thy goodness, which Thou hast laid up for me.

xvi. 12. Thou hast shewn me the path of life, and inclined my heart to Thee to walk in Thy way.

PROVERBS iii. 17. Thy way is the way of pleasantness, and all Thy paths are peace

*Psalm cxix. 105. The Lord be a lamp unto thy feet, and a light unto thy path.
: cxxi. 8. The Lord preserve thee in all the way thou goest. Amen.*

(*From "St. Peter,"* Nos. 7, 8.) Benedict.

* —— * Sometimes sung as separate Anthem.

974

Revelation xv. 4, 3. Who would not fear Thee, O Lord, who would not fear Thee? for great and marvellous are Thy works.

(*From "St. Peter,"* No. 17.) Benedict.

975

Psalm xcv. 1. O come, let us sing unto the Lord,
lxv. 7. Who stilleth the noise of the seas, and the noise of their waves.
cvii. 29. Who maketh the storm a calm, so that the waves thereof are still.

(*From "St. Peter,"* No. 21.) Benedict.

976

Isaiah xxv. 8. He will swallow up death in victory, and the Lord God will wipe away tears from off all faces.
xxxv. 10. And the ransomed of the Lord shall come to Zion with songs and everlasting joy upon their heads; they shall obtain joy and gladness, and sorrow and sighing shall flee away.

(*From "St. Peter,"* No. 43.) Benedict.

977

Isaiah xii. 4. Praise the Lord, call upon His Name, declare His doings amongst the people, make mention that His Name is exalted.
5. Sing unto the Lord, for He hath done excellent things: this is known in all the earth.
6. Cry aloud and shout, thou inhabitant of Zion, for great is the Holy One of Israel.

PSALM civ. 33. I will sing unto the LORD as long as I live, I will sing praises to my GOD while I have my being.

PSALM cxv. 12. The LORD hath been mindful of us : He will bless us.

13. He will bless them that fear the LORD, both small and great.

NEHEMIAH ix. 5. Stand up and bless the LORD your GOD for ever and for ever : and blessed be Thy glorious Name, which is exalted above all blessing and praise.

> Let the people praise Thee, O LORD,
> Let Thy love on all be pour'd.
> GOD to man His blessing give,
> Man to GOD devoted live.
> All below, and all above,
> One in joy, and light, and love.

> > > > BENEDICT.

978

No. 1

PSALM cxxv. 1. All they that trust in Thee, LORD, shall be as Mount Sion : which may not be removed, but stands for ever.

No. 2

PSALM cxxv. 2. Round Jerusalem stand the mountains ; even so the LORD GOD standeth around His people evermore.

3. For the rod of the ungodly shall not rest upon the lot of the righteous, lest, yea, lest the righteous should put forth their hand to wickedness.

No. 3

PSALM cxxv. 4. LORD, do Thou well to those that are good and true of heart.

5. As for all those that turn back to their wickedness, GOD shall lead them forth with the evil doers ; but peace shall be upon Israel.

No. 4

PSALM cxxv. 5. As for all those that turn back to their wicked counsels, GOD shall lead them forth with evil doers ; but peace shall be upon Israel.

> > > HILLER.

979

A SONG OF VICTORY.

No. 1

Tae LORD great wonders for us hath wrought! Sing and be joyful! Mighty is our GOD, and of mighty power, there is none that searcheth or understandeth His judgments.

No. 2

PSALM cxlvii. 12–14. Praise, O Jerusalem, praise the LORD, praise, O Zion, praise thy GOD! He maketh strong the bars of thy gateways. He gives peace within thy borders. The swords of the foemen He hath broken, their cities He hath overthrown.

No. 3

The heathen are fallen in the pit that they made for others, their own foot is taken in the net which they had hidden. They are all brought to nought, they are fallen. We are risen and stand upright. LORD, my rock, my tower, my Redeemer, my shield, my defence, my strength, in Whom I put my trust; yea, although a host cometh against me, yet shall not my heart be affrighted; yea, though war riseth up against me, yet my trust shall be put in Him.

O come and see the works of the LORD, what destruction He bringeth on the earth: He restraineth wars in all the world, He breaketh the bow, He knappeth the spear and burneth the chariots with fire.

No. 4

See, it is written in the book of the righteous, The beauty of Israel hath been slain in her high places: how are the mighty fallen, and the weapons of war are broken. The LORD is like to a foe, He hath increased mourning and grief in the daughter of Judah. I weep and lament; mine eyes are like to rivers of water, my heart within my body is greatly troubled, for I am sore afflicted.

No. 5

PSALM cxxvi. 6. He in tears that soweth, reapeth a joyful harvest.

7. He who now goeth weeping, good seed and precious bearing, returneth with gladness, rich sheaves and plenteous bringing.

No. 6

Mighty is our GOD, and of mighty power, there is none that searcheth His judgments.

No. 7

PSALM cl. 1. Praise ye the LORD in His holiness, praise ye Him in the Firmament of His power.

No. 8

PSALM cl. 2-6. Praise the LORD for His great wonders, praise the LORD. O praise His mighty excellence. Praise ye Him with the trumpet, with lute and harp, and psaltery, with timbrels and dances, with tabors and cymbals, with sounding organ. Hallelujah.

HILLER.

980

ST. LUKE i. 68. Blessed be the LORD GOD of Israel, for He hath visited and redeemed His people. Hallelujah.

ST. LUKE ii. 11. For unto us is born a Saviour, Which is CHRIST the LORD. Hallelujah.

14. Glory to GOD in the highest, peace on earth, and good will towards men. Hallelujah. Amen.

HATTON.

981

PSALM cxliv. 1. Blessed be the LORD my strength, Who teacheth my hands to war, and my fingers to fight:

2. My hope and my fortress, my castle and deliverer, my defender in Whom I trust.

3. LORD, what is man, that Thou hast such respect unto him? or the Son of Man, that Thou so regardest Him.

4. Man is like a thing of nought, his time passeth away like a shadow.

5. [Bow Thy heavens, O LORD, and come down:] touch the mountains, and they shall smoke.

[6. Cast forth Thy lightning. and tear them : shoot out Thine arrows. and consume them.]

7. Send down Thine hand from above, deliver me, and take me out of the great waters, from the hand of strange children;

[8. Whose mouth talketh of vanity, and their right hand is a right hand of wickedness.]

12. That our sons may grow up as the young plants: that our daughters may be as the polished corners of the temple.

13. That our garners may be plenteous with all manner of store.

14. That our oxen be strong to labour, that there be no decay: no leading into captivity, and no complaining in our streets.

15. Happy are the people that are in such a case; yea, blessed are the people who have the LORD for their GOD.

HATTON.

982 PURCELL, vv. 1–8.

983

PSALM cxlv. 1. I will extol Thee, my GOD, O King; and I will bless Thy Name for ever and ever.

8. The LORD is gracious, and full of compassion, slow to anger, and of great mercy.

14. The LORD upholdeth all that fall, and raiseth up all those that be bowed down.

15. The eyes of all wait upon Thee, and Thou givest them their meat in due season.

16. Thou openest Thine hand, and satisfiest the desire of every living thing.

17. The LORD is righteous in all His ways, and holy in all His works.

18, 19. The LORD is nigh unto all them that call upon Him in truth; He also will hear their cry, and will save them.

20. The LORD preserveth all them that love Him, but all the wicked will He destroy.

21. My mouth shall speak the praise of the LORD: and let all flesh bless His holy Name for ever and ever.

HATTON.

984 W. HAYES, vv. 20, 21. Amen.

985

PSALM cxxxviii. 1. I will praise Thee with my whole heart : before the gods will I sing praise unto Thee.

2. I will worship toward Thy holy temple, and praise Thy Name, for Thy loving-kindness and for Thy truth : for Thou hast magnified Thy word above all Thy Name.

3. In the day when I cried Thou answeredst me, and strengthenedst me with strength in my soul.

HATTON.

986

ROMANS xiv. 11. As I live, saith the LORD, every knee shall bow to Me, and every tongue shall confess to GOD.

12. So that every one shall give an account of himself to GOD,

ii. 6. Who will render to every man according to his deeds;

11. For there is no respect of persons with GOD.

viii. 14. For as many as are led by the Spirit of GOD, they are the sons of GOD.

xiv. 7. None of us liveth unto himself, and no man dieth to himself.

8. Whether we live, we live unto the LORD ; and whether we die, we die unto the LORD ; whether we live therefore, or die, we are the LORD'S.

xi. 33. O the depth of the riches, both of the wisdom and knowledge of GOD ! For of Him, and through Him, and to Him are all things ; to Whom be glory for ever. Amen.

CHIPP.

987

JOB. i. 21. The LORD gave and the LORD hath taken away, blessed be the Name of the LORD.

*PSALM cxlv. 17. The LORD is righteous in all His ways, and holy in all His works.

cxxviii. 1. Blessed are all they that fear the LORD, and walk in His ways.*

(From " Job," Nos. 8, 9.)   CHIPP.

*   * Sometimes sung as a separate Anthem.

988

JOB v. 17. Behold, happy is the man whom the LORD correcteth; therefore despise not thou the chastening of the Almighty.

(From " Job," No. 18.) CHIPP.

989

PSALM cxxvi. 6. They that sow in tears shall reap in joy.

Bless the LORD of Israel, O my people, that He hath caused the earth to yield her increase. Bless His holy Name.

To the LORD of the harvest we offer our praise,
To GOD, our deliverer, our voices we raise.
For the famine, dire curse of GOD's anger, is o'er,
And the earth yields her increase again as of yore.
To the LORD of the harvest we offer our praise,
To GOD, our deliverer, our voices we raise.

(From " Naomi," Nos. 10, 13.) CHIPP.

990

PSALM lxviii. 5. GOD is a Father of the fatherless, and defendeth the cause of the widows : even GOD in His holy habitation.

(From " Naomi," No. 15.) CHIPP.

991

PSALM lxviii. 19. Blessed be the LORD, Who daily loadeth us with benefits.

lxv. 11, 13. He crowneth the year with His goodness. The pastures are clothed with flocks; the valleys are covered over with corn; they shout for joy, they also sing.

lxviii. 19. Blessed be the LORD, even the GOD of our salvation.

(From " Naomi," No. 17.) CHIPP.

992

PSALM cxv. 12. The LORD hath been mindful of us, and He shall bless us.

13. He shall bless them that fear Him, both small and great.

15. Ye are the blessed of the LORD, Who made Heaven and earth. [Amen.]

CHIPP, MACFARREN.

993

ECCLESIASTICUS ii. 7. Ye that fear the LORD, wait for His mercy; and go not aside, lest ye fall.

8. Ye that fear the LORD, believe Him; and your reward shall not fail.

9. Ye that fear the LORD, hope for good, and for everlasting joy and mercy.

GREATHEED.

994

PSALM lxxxiv. 10. A day in Thy courts is better than a thousand. I had rather be a doorkeeper in the house of my GOD, than to dwell in the tents of wickedness.

11. For the LORD GOD is a sun and shield, the LORD will give grace and glory, no good thing will He withhold from them that walk uprightly.

12. O LORD of Hosts, blessed is the man that trusteth in Thee.

MACFARREN.

995

ROMANS vi. 4. As Christ was raised from the dead by the glory of the Father, even so we also should walk in newness of life.

5. For if we have been planted together in the likeness of His death, we shall be also in the likeness of His Resurrection.

MACFARREN.

996

St. James i. 12. Blessed is the man that endureth temptation : for when he is tried, he shall receive the crown of life, which the Lord hath promised to them that love Him.

Macfarren, Stainer.

997

Genesis i. 29. God said, Behold, I have given you every herb bearing seed, which is upon the face of all the earth, and every tree, in the which is the fruit of a tree yielding seed ; to you it shall be for meat.

viii. 22. While the earth remaineth, seed time and harvest, and cold and heat, and summer and winter, and day and night shall not cease.

Deuteronomy vii. 9. Know therefore that the Lord thy God, He is God, the faithful God, Which keepeth covenant and mercy with them that love Him and keep His commandments to a thousand generations.

Psalm cxi. 4. He hath made His wonderful works to be remembered : the Lord is gracious and full of compassion.

7. The works of His hands are verity and judgment ; all His commandments are sure.

8. They stand fast for ever and ever, and are done in truth and uprightness.

1. Praise ye the Lord. I will praise the Lord with my whole heart, in the assembly of the upright, and in the congregation.

Macfarren.

998

Psalm xix. 5. He cometh forth as a bridegroom out of his chamber, and rejoiceth as a giant to run his course.

6. He goeth forth from the uttermost part of heaven. Hallelujah. Amen.

Macfarren.

999

JOSHUA i. 9. Be strong and of a good courage : be not afraid, neither be thou dismayed : for the LORD thy GOD is with thee whithersoever thou goest.

MACFARREN.

1000

GALATIANS vi. 9. Let us not be weary in well doing, for in due season we shall reap, if we faint not.

MACFARREN.

1001

JOEL ii. 12. Now, saith the LORD, turn ye even to Me with all your heart, and with fasting, and with weeping, and with mourning ; and

13. Rend your heart, and not your garments, and turn unto the LORD your GOD : for He is gracious and merciful, slow to anger, and of great kindness, and repenteth Him of the evil. [Amen.]

MACFARREN.

1002 ATKINSON, CALKIN, CLIPPINGDALF, COLBORNE, F. E. GLADSTONE, HARRIS, OUSELEY, PYE, SCHARTAU, v. 13.

1003

O Holy Ghost, into our minds
　　Send down Thy Heavenly light,
Kindle our hearts with fervent zeal
　　To serve God day and night.

Thou art the very Comforter,
　　In grief and all distress ;
The heavenly gift of God most high,
　　No tongue can it express.

Such measures of Thy powerful grace
　　Grant to us, LORD, we pray,
That Thou may'st be our Comforter
　　At the last awful day.　　　Amen.

MACFARREN.

1004

PSALM xxvii. 4. One thing have I desired of the LORD, after that will I seek; that I may dwell in the House of the LORD all the days of my life, to behold the beauty of the LORD, and to enquire in His temple.

MACFARREN.

1005

PHILIPPIANS ii. 8. Our LORD JESUS CHRIST humbled Himself, and became obedient unto death, even the death of the Cross.

9. Wherefore GOD hath highly exalted Him, and hath given Him a Name which is above every name.

MACFARREN.

1006

FROM THE LITANY.

*Remember not, LORD, our offences, nor the offences of our forefathers; neither take Thou vengeance of our sins: spare us, good LORD, spare Thy people, whom Thou hast redeemed with Thy most precious Blood, and be not angry with us for ever.

Spare us, good LORD,*
From all blindness of heart, from all deadly sin, and from all the deceits of the world, the flesh, and the devil,
Good LORD, deliver us.

(From " King David," No. 10.) MACFARREN.
1007 PURCELL, TINNEY, * —— *.

1008

PSALM xcviii. 1. O sing unto the LORD a new song, for He hath done marvellous things.

4. And all the ends of the world have seen the salvation of our God.

MACFARREN.

1009

REVELATION xi. 17. We give Thee thanks, O LORD GOD Almighty, Which art, and wast, and art to come; because Thou hast taken to Thee Thy great power, and hast reigned.

xv. 4. Who shall not fear Thee, O LORD, and glorify Thy Name, for Thou only art holy.

Glory be to the Father, &c.

MACFARREN.

1010 J. L. HOPKINS, v. 17.

1011

PSALM cxix. 9. Wherewithal shall a young man cleanse his way? even by ruling himself after Thy word.

10. With my whole heart have I sought Thee; O let me not wander from Thy commandments.

11. Thy word have I hid in my heart, that I might not sin against Thee.

12. Blessed art Thou, O LORD; O teach me Thy statutes.

13. With my lips have I declared all the judgments of Thy mouth.

14. I have rejoiced in the way of Thy testimonies, as much as in all riches.

15. I will meditate in Thy precepts, and have respect unto Thy ways.

16. I will delight myself in Thy statutes: I will not forget Thy word.

MACFARREN.

1012

WISDOM xviii. 14, 15. While all things were in quiet silence, and the night was in the midst of her course; the Almighty Word of the LORD came down from His royal Throne.

PSALM xciii. 1. The LORD is King, He hath put on glorious apparel, He hath girded Himself with strength. Amen, Amen.

MACFARREN.

1013

ISAIAH xxvi. 20. Come, my people, enter thou into thy chambers, shut thy doors about thee: hide thyseif as it were a little moment, until the indignation be over-past.

21. For, behold, the LORD cometh out of His place to punish the inhabitants of the eaith for their iniquity: the earth also shall disclose her blood, and shall no more cover her slain.

WINTLE.

1014

PSALM xxvii. 9. Hide not Thy face far from me: leave me not, neither forsake me, O GOD of my salvation.

14. Wait on the LORD, be of good courage, and He shall strengthen thine heart: wait, I say, on the LORD.

PYE.

1015

PSALM xxv. 5. Lead me in Thy truth and teach me, for Thou art the GOD of my salvation.

6. Remember, O LORD, Thy tender mercies, for they have been ever of old.

7. Remember not the sins of my youth, but according to Thy mercy remember Thou me for Thy goodness' sake.

5. Lead me in Thy truth and teach me, for Thou art the GOD of my salvation. Amen.

PYE.

1016

ISAIAH xxv. 1. O LORD, Thou art my GOD. O LORD, I will exalt Thee. I will praise Thy Name, for Thou hast done wonderful things. Thy counsels of old are faithfulness and truth.

PYE.

1017

All people that on earth do dwell,.
 Sing to the Lord with cheerful voice ;
Him serve with fear His praise forth tell,
 Come ye before Him and rejoice.

Psalm c.   1. O be joyful in the Lord, all ye lands;
serve the Lord with gladness, and come before His
presence with a song.

2. Be ye sure that the Lord He is God : it is He that
hath made us, and not we ourselves ; we are His people,
and the sheep of His pasture.

3. O go your way into His gates with thanksgiving, and
into His courts with praise ; be thankful unto Him, and
speak good of His Name.

4. For the Lord is gracious, His mercy is everlasting,
and His truth endureth from generation to generation.

(Sung at the same time as the above.)

For why ? the Lord our God is good ;
His mercy is for ever sure ;
His truth at all times firmly stood,
And shall from age to age endure.

Glory be to the Father, and to the Son, and to the Holy
Ghost ; as it was in the beginning, is now, and ever shall
be, world without end.   Amen.

(Sung at the same time as the above.)

Praise God from Whom all blessings flow,
Praise Him all creatures here below ;
Praise Him above, Angelic Host,
Praise Father, Son, and Holy Ghost.   Amen.
                                        Pole.

1018

Psalm xxix.   1. Give to the Lord, O ye sons of the
Mighty, O give to the Lord glory and strength.

2. Give to the Lord what is due to His Name, and
worship God in the beauty of holiness.

3. The voice of the LORD is upon the waters, the GOD of glory thundereth.

4, 5. The voice of the LORD resounds with power : His voice, it is full of majesty : it breaketh the cedars of Lebanon.

7. The voice of the LORD riveth asunder the flames of fire.

8. The voice of the LORD shaketh the wilderness of Kadesh.

9. The voice of the LORD makes the deer to start, and layeth the forest bare, and in His temple all declare His glory.

10. The LORD sat enthroned at the flood. The LORD reigns as King for ever.

11. The LORD will give strength to His people. The LORD will give His people the blessing of peace.

SALAMAN.

1019

PSALM vi. 2. Have mercy upon me, O LORD, for I am weak : O LORD, heal me, for my bones are vexed.

3. My soul also is sore troubled : but, LORD, how long wilt Thou punish me ?

4. Turn Thee, O LORD, and deliver my soul : O LORD, save me, for Thy mercies' sake.

xx. 9. Save, LORD, and hear us, when we call upon Thee.

lxxxv. 7. O shew us Thy mercy, and grant us Thy salvation. Amen.

SALAMAN.

1020 WINTER, vv. 2-4.

1021

PSALM lxxxiv. 1. How lovely are Thy habitations, gracious LORD of Hosts.

2. My soul yearneth, yea, it fainteth for Thy hallowed courts, O LORD, where heart and flesh exult in chanting praises of the living GOD.

3. Yea, the sparrow finds a dwelling, to her nest the swallow turns, where she rears her tender young. Also have I found Thine Altars, LORD of Hosts, my King and GOD !

4. Blest are those who dwell with Thee, ever will they praise Thee.

5. How happy are they who are strong in Thee, for with their hearts Thy paths they keep. How happy are they who dwell with Thee, O Lord God of Hosts.

8. O hear my prayer. Give ear, mighty Lord, O Lord God of Jacob.

9. Behold our shield, O God, and regard the face of Thine anointed.

10. For one day in Thy courts, O Lord, is better than a thousand.

11. I would rather humbly stand at the doorway of God's house, than live in tents where evil dwelleth.

12. For a sun and shield is God, He will grace and glory grant, and from the just will He no good withhold.

13. Holy Lord, how blest are those who trust in Thee.

Salaman.

1022

Psalm xvi. 1. Preserve me, O God, for in Thee do I put my trust.

2. O my soul, thou hast said unto the Lord, Thou art my God, my gladness is centred in Thee ;

3. And in the pious of the earth, and in the excellent, in whom is all my delight.

7. I will bless the Lord, Who hath given me counsel.

8. I have set the Lord always before me.

1. Preserve me, O God, for in Thee do I put my trust.

8. Because He is at my right hand, I shall not be moved.

1. Preserve me, O God. Amen.

Salaman.

1023

Psalm lxxxiv. 9. Behold, O God, our defender, and look upon the face of Thine anointed.

lxi. 6. O Lord, grant the *king* a long life (xxi. 6) and make *him* glad with the joy of Thy countenance.

cxxxii. 19. As for *his* enemies, clothe them with shame : but upon *himself* let *his* crown flourish. Amen.

Elvey.

1024

St. Mark xv. 25. And it was the third hour, and they crucified Him.

29. And they that passed by railed on Him.

34. And at the ninth hour Jesus cried with a loud voice, My God, My God, look upon Me; why hast Thou forsaken Me?

St. Matthew xxvii. 43. He trusted in God, that He would deliver Him; let Him deliver Him, if He will have Him.

St. Mark xv. 31. He saved others, Himself He cannot save.

32. Let Christ, the King of Israel, descend from the Cross, that we may see and believe.

St. Luke xxiii. 46. Father, into Thy hands I commend My spirit.

44, 45. There was darkness over all the earth, and the veil of the temple was rent.

St. Mark xv. 39. Truly This was the Son of God.

Elvey.

1025

Revelation vii. 9. I beheld, and lo, a great multitude, which no man could number, [of all nations, and kindreds, and people, and tongues, stood before the Throne,] clothed with white robes, and palms were in their hands.

10. And they cried with a loud voice, saying, Salvation to our God, Which sitteth upon the Throne, and unto the Lamb. Hallelujah.

13. I heard a voice, saying unto me, What are these which are arrayed in white robes? and whence came they?

14. These are they which came out of great tribulation, and have washed their robes, and made them white in the Blood of the Lamb.

11. And all the angels stood round [about] the Throne, and [about] the elders, and the four beasts, and fell down before the Throne, and worshipped God,

12. Saying, [Amen:] Blessing, and glory, and wisdom, and thanksgiving, and honour, and power, [and might,] be unto our God for ever and ever. Amen.

Elvey.

1026 Jordan, vv. 9-12.

1027

PSALM lxxxvi. 1. Bow down Thine ear, O LORD, for I am poor and in misery.

xxv. 17. Look upon my adversity and misery, and forgive me all my sin.

lxxxv. 4. Turn Thee again, O LORD, and let Thine anger cease from us. Amen.

ELVEY.

1028

1 CORINTHIANS xv. 20. CHRIST is risen from the dead. Hallelujah.

ROMANS vi. 10. In that He died, He died unto sin once; but in that He liveth, He liveth unto GOD.

1 CORINTHIANS xv. 20. CHRIST is risen from the dead. Hallelujah.

EI VEY.

1029

ISAIAH xxvi. 1. In that day shall this song be sung in the land of Judah, We have a strong city; salvation will GOD appoint for walls and bulwarks.

2. Open ye the gates, that the righteous nation, which keepeth the truth, may enter in.

3. Thou wilt keep him in perfect peace, whose mind is stayed on Thee: [because he trusteth in Thee.]

4. Trust ye in the LORD for ever: for in the LORD JEHOVAH is everlasting strength.

[13, 14. O LORD our GOD, other gods have had dominion over us, but they are dead, they shall not live; they are deceased, they shall not rise. Of Thee alone, and of Thy Name, will we make mention evermore.]

xxxiii. 2. Be gracious unto us, O LORD, we have waited for Thee: be Thou our salvation in the time of trouble.

5. The LORD is exalted, He dwelleth on high, for He hath filled Zion with judgment and righteousness. Amen.

ELVEY.

1030 \k d, . CORIN. CII i i. xv. 3, 4.
1031 GAl vT) FII, vv. 3, 4, 13, 14, 3.

1032

PSALM lxvi. 1. O be joyful in GOD, all ye lands : sing praises unto the honour of His Name, make His praise to be glorious.

4. O come hither, and behold the works of GOD ; how wonderful He is in His doing toward the children of men.

lxviii. 5. He is a Father of the fatherless :

cxlvii. 3. He healeth those that are broken in heart, and defendeth the cause of the widows.

lxvii. 3. Let the people praise Thee, O GOD ; yea, let all the people praise Thee.

cxlv. 15. The eyes of all wait on Thee, O LORD, and Thou givest them their meat in due season.

16. Thou openest Thine hand, and fillest all things living with plenteousness.

lxvi. 7. O praise our GOD, ye people, and make the voice of His praise to be heard.

cl. 6. Let everything that hath breath praise the LORD. Amen.

ELVEY.

1033

PSALM cxix. 17. O do well unto Thy servant, that I may live, and keep Thy word.

18. Open Thou mine eyes, that I may see the wondrous things of Thy law.

19. I am a stranger upon earth, O hide not Thy commandments from me.

ELVEY.

1034

ISAIAH xii. 4. Praise the LORD, and call upon His Name, declare His doings among the people. Make mention that His Name is exalted.

PSALM lxiii. 5. Thus will I bless Thee while I live. I will lift up my hands in Thy Name.

REVELATION vii. 12. Blessing, and glory, and honour, and power, be unto our GOD, for ever and ever. Hallelujah Amen.

ELVEY.

1035

PSALM cxviii. 24. This is the day which the LORD hath made; we will rejoice and be glad in it.

JEREMIAH l. 20. A sound of battle was heard in the land, and of great destruction.

EZRA viii. 31. But the LORD hath delivered us from the hands of our enemies.

PSALM cxv. 1. Not unto us, O LORD, but unto Thy Name be the glory.

cvii. 8. O that men would praise the LORD for His goodness, and declare the wonders that He doeth for the children of men.

25. We cried unto the LORD, and the LORD saved us from our distress.

8. O that men would praise the LORD, for His goodness, and declare the wonders that He doeth for the children of men.

cxlvii. 14. He maketh peace in our borders, and filleth us with the flour of wheat.

cxviii. 24. This is the day which the LORD hath made; we will rejoice and be glad in it. Amen.

ELVEY.

1036

PSALM lxxxviii. 13. Unto Thee have I cried, O LORD, and early shall my prayer come before Thee.

xiii. 3. Consider, and hear me, O LORD, lighten mine eyes, that I sleep not in death.

vi. 4. Turn Thee, O LORD, and deliver my soul: O save me for Thy mercy's sake. Amen.

ELVEY.

1037

PSALM cxv. 1. Not unto us, O LORD, not unto us, but unto Thy Name give the praise: for Thy loving mercy, and for Thy truth's sake.

2. Wherefore shall the heathen say, Where is now their God? [Hallelujah. Amen.]

ROBINSON.

1038 BANTON. KINGS. T. A. WALMISLEY v. 1

1039.

Behold, a Star appeareth,
Expectant eyes now meeting:
Arise, ye wakeful shepherds,
Your infant LORD be greeting:
Let man self-love abandon,
The Love made man receiving.

Angelic hosts surround us,
From Heaven to earth descending,
Their songs of exultation
With Nature's voices blending.
O tidings sweet and blessed,
Which GOD to man is giving.

(*From " Christmas Eve," No.* 2.)   GADE.

1040

SACRED CANTATA.—"ZION."

§ 1

Hear, O my flock Israel, words from the LORD GOD!

For aloud my sayings shall be sounding, I will tell you dark and mighty words, from of old, from the byegone ages, of the wonders that were wrought by His arm.

He heard the groanings and cries of the children of Israel; He broke the chain of their bondage, and He brought them home for His people.

Hear, O my flock Israel, words from the LORD! Hear Thou, O Israel!

§ 2

THE DEPARTURE FROM EGYPT.

The LORD, the Omnipotent, hath in Egypt, in the field of Zoan, shewn unto His people His mighty power.

He clave in twain the sea, and through the deep He led them, yea, He led them, and as a wall He gathered the waters.

He led them on in the day-time with a cloudy pillar, and all night through with a light of fire; from out the stony rock gushed forth at His command full-flowing rivers: manna dropped like the rain at His word, GOD's heavenly bread was food unto all.

Like as a flock He hath gently led His people by Moses' and Aaron's hand.

§ 3
THE CAPTIVITY IN BABYLON.

But then His flock forsook the commandments of GOD, they scorned the Holy One of Israel, forgat the wonders and the works He had wrought.

GOD the Omnipotent cries unto the earth; from morning until evening He is calling, if we perchance may hearken.

Wasting fire before Him is going, mighty thunder and tempest. GOD the LORD judgeth His people.

As chaff will I scatter them that forsake Me, yea, like as chaff to the winds of the desert.

Hearken! I bid My servant smite them, the King out of Babylon; with the breath of My anger I desolate the land!

So He made them to fall by the heathen, and their mighty foemen bowed them down.

§ 4
THE RETURN

Yet merciful and tender is the LORD, forgiving, and full of goodness; His anger doth not ever burn; He pardons sin, and forgets wickedness, and puts far away displeasure.

He doth lead gently His flock Israel, and bring them to their native land.

Merciful and tender is the LORD, forgiving, and full of goodness.

There shall come a Redeemer, a Saviour, to Zion, for the sons of Jacob, if, turning and repenting, they will seek from the LORD mercy.

Bethlehem Ephratah, Thou art not the least of the towns of Judah, for out of thee shall rise a Ruler of Israel: and His reign is everlasting; from eternity are His goings forth!

Arise and shine O Zion! Thy light comes, and the glory of the Lord surrounds thee.

Lift up thy head, and behold how they gather themselves together; from all countries come thy sons assembling, and at thy side thy daughters shall be nursed and be sheltered: the cedars of Lebanon come unto thee to adorn thy sacred temple.

Thou shalt call thy sheltering walls Salvation; of thy gates shall the name be Praise to GOD !

Never shall thy sun be setting, and never thy moon withdraw herself, for the LORD is thy Light everlasting.

GADE.

1041

All ye who weep, O come unto Me,
    I will comfort you.
All ye who suffer, O come to Me,
    I will console you.
All ye who mourn, O come to Me,
    I am your peace.
All ye who die, O come to Me
    For life eternal.

GOUNOD.

1042

BY BABYLON'S WAVE.

PSALM cxxxvii. (*Paraphrase*).

Here by Babylon's wave
    Though heathen hands have bound us,
Though afar from our land,
    The pains of death surround us;
Sion ! thy memory still
    In our heart we are keeping,
And still we turn to thee,
    Our eyes all sad with weeping.
Through our harps that we hung on the trees,
    Goes the low wind wearily moaning:
Mingles the sad note of the breeze,
    With voice as sad of sigh and groaning

When mad with wine our foe rejoices,
　　When unto their altars they throng,
　　Loud for mirth then they call—" A song !
A song of Sion sing, lift up your voices ! "
O LORD, though the victor command
　　Our captivity sad and lowly,
　　How shall we raise Thy song so holy,
That we sung in our father's land ?
　　Jerusalem, if we forget thee,
Let our hands remember not their power,
And our tongues be silent from that hour,
　　Jerusalem, if we forget thee.

Woe unto thee, Babylon, mighty city,
　　For the day of thy fall is nigh !
For thee no hope, for thee no pity,
　　Though loud thy wail riseth on high !
Then shalt thou, desolate, forsaken,
　　Be torn from thy fanes and thy thrones ;
In that day shall thy babes be taken
　　And dashed against the stones.
Then unto thee, O Babylon the mighty,
　　Be woe ! Be woe ! Be woe !

GOUNOD.

1043

Come unto Him, all ye who labour,
Your LORD will give you rest and peace,
Comfort for all your sorrows : ye weary,
He will give you rest for your souls.
O turn from the pleasures of sin,
And behold your LORD on His Cross,
Who dies for the sins of the world.
He will receive you, He will refresh you,
He will give rest to your souls.
Behold, on His Cross our Redeemer,
Nailed there by our transgressions,
Calls all men to Himself ;
He pleads His Blood,
He shews His streaming wounds,
As He makes intercession : He cries,
" Come ye to Me, and I will save your soul ! "

GOUNOD.

1044

"BETHLEHEM."

Cradled all lowly behold the Saviour Child,
A Being Holy, in dwelling rude and wild.
Ne'er yet was regal state
Of monarch proud and great,
Who grasped a nation's fate,
So glorious as the manger-bed of Bethlehem.

No longer sorrow as without hope, oh earth!
A brighter morrow dawned with that Infant's birth.
Our sins were great and sore,
But these the Saviour bore,
And GOD was wrath no more:
His own Son was the Child that lay in Bethlehem.

Babe weak and wailing, in lowly village stall
Thy glory veiling, Thou cam'st to die for all.
The sacrifice is done, The world's atonement won,
Till time its course hath run.
O JESU, Saviour, Morning Star of Bethlehem!
    Hallelujah. Amen.

GOUNOD.

1045

Hail, gladdening Light, of His pure glory poured,
  Who is the Immortal Father, Heavenly, Blest,
Holiest of Holies, JESU CHRIST, our LORD.

Now we are come to the sun's hour of rest,
  The lights of evening round us shine,
We hymn the Father, Son, and Holy Spirit Divine.

Worthiest art Thou at all times to be sung
    With undefiled tongue,
Son of our GOD, Giver of life, alone:
Therefore in all the world Thy glories, LORD, they
  own. Amen.

FIFID, GOUNOD. MARTIN.

1046

St. Luke xxiii. 28. Filiæ Jerusalem, nolite flere super Me, sed super vos ipsas flete, et super filios vestros.

33. Et venerunt in eum, qui dicitur Calvaria, locum, ibi crucifixerunt Jesum.

St. Matthew xxvii. 39. Prætereuntes autem blasphemabant Eum, moventes capita sua.

St. Luke xxiii. 34. Jesus autem dicebat: Pater, dimitte illis, non enim sciunt quid faciunt.

39. Unus autem de his qui pendebant latronibus,

42. Dicebat ad Jesum: Domine, memento mei, cum veneris in regnum Tuum.

43. Et dixit illi Jesus: Amen dico tibi; Hodie Mecum eris in Paradiso.

St. John xix. 26. Cum vidisset ergo Jesus matrem, et discipulum stantem quem diligebat, dicit matri Suæ: Mulier, ecce filius tuus.

27. Deinde dicit discipulo, Ecce mater tua.

St. Matthew xxvii. 45. Tenebræ factæ sunt super universam terram.

46. Et circa horam nonam clamavit Jesus voce magnâ, dicens:

St. Mark xv. 34. Eloi, Eloi, lama Sabacthani? quod est interpretatum: Deus Meus, Deus Meus, ut quid dereliquisti Me?

St. John xix. 28. Posteà sciens Jesus quia omnia consummata sunt, ut consummaretur scriptura, dixit: Sitio.

29. Vas ergo erat positum aceto plenum, Illi autem spongiam plenam aceto, hyssopo circumponentes, obtulerunt ori Ejus.

30. Cum ergo accepisset Jesus acetum, dixit: Consummatum est.

St. L⸳ ⸳ ⸳ ⸳iii. ⸳⸳. Pater, in ⸳⸳⸳⸳⸳⸳ ⸳⸳⸳⸳ commendo spiritum. M⸳⸳⸳⸳.

English Version.

St. Luke xxiii. 28. Daughters of Jerusalem, weep ye not; weep not for Me, weep for yourselves, and for your children.

33. And when they were come to the place, which is called Calvary, there they crucified Jesus.

St. Matthew xxvii. 39. And they that passed by reviled Him, wagging their heads.

St. Luke xxiii. 34. Then said Jesus, Father, forgive them: for they know not what they do.

39, 42. And one of the malefactors which were hanged said unto Jesus, Lord, remember me when Thou comest into Thy Kingdom.

43. And Jesus said unto him, Verily I say unto thee, This day shalt thou be with Me in Paradise.

St. John xix. 26. When Jesus therefore saw His mother and the disciple standing by, whom He loved, He saith unto His mother, Woman, Behold thy son.

27. Then saith He to the disciple, Behold thy mother.

St. Matthew xxvii. 45. There was darkness over all the land.

St. Mark xv. 34. And at the ninth hour Jesus cried with a loud voice, saying, Eloi, Eloi, lama Sabacthani? which is, being interpreted, My God, My God, why hast Thou forsaken Me?

St. John xix. 28. After this, Jesus, knowing that all things were now accomplished, that the Scripture might be fulfilled, saith: I thirst.

29. Now there was a vessel full of vinegar; and they filled a sponge with vinegar, and put it upon hyssop, and they put it to His mouth.

30. When Jesus therefore had received the vinegar, He said: It is finished.

St. Luke xxiii. 46. Father, into Thy hands I commend My spirit: [and He bowed His head and gave up the ghost].

Gou N D. King.

1017 Eivey, St. Luke xxiii. 28.

1048

"GALLIA."

LAMENTATIONS i. 1. Quomodo sedet sola civitas plena populo! Facta est quasi vidua domina gentium, princeps provinciarum, facta est sub tributo.

2. Plorans ploravit in nocte et lacrymæ ejus in maxillis ejus : non est qui consoletur eam ex omnibus charis ejus, omnes amici ejus spreverunt eam, et facti sunt ei inimici.

4. Viæ Sion lugent eo quod non sint qui veniant ad solemnitatem, omnes portæ ejus destructæ, sacerdotes ejus gementes, virgines ejus squalidæ, et ipsa oppressa amaritudine.

12. O vos omnes, qui transitis per viam, attendite, et videte si est dolor sicut dolor meus.

9. Vide, Domine, afflictionem Meam, quoniam erectus est inimicus.

Jerusalem! Jerusalem! Convertere ad Dominum Deum tuum.

English Version.

1. Solitary lies the city, she that was full of people. How is she widowed, she that was great among nations, princess among the provinces? How is she put under tribute?

2. Sorely she weepeth in darkness. Her tears are on her cheeks ; and no one offereth consolation ; yea, all her friends have betrayed her, they are become her enemies.

* 4. Zion's ways do languish, none come to her solemn feasts. All her gates are desolate : her priests sigh, yea, her virgins are afflicted, and she is in bitterness.

12. Is it nothing to all ye that pass by? Behold, and see if there be any sorrow that is like unto My sorrow.

9. Now behold, O LORD, look Thou on My affliction ; see, the foe hath magnified himself.

Jerusalem, Jerusalem, O turn thee to the LORD thy God, O turn thee unto thy God.*

(101 NOD.

* —' Somet nues sung a o opa are Anthem..

1049

JESU our LORD, Son of GOD, our Redeemer, let all created beings praise Thy Name. May Thy grace and Thy blessing descend on us. LORD, our Redeemer, kindle love anew in our hearts. Let all created beings bless Thy Name. Blessed Word Incarnate, Only Son of the Father, hear us, in pity hear our prayer. Give us strength in our weakness, give us rest from our labours, give us help in our sorrows, give us faith in Thy promise, and the glory of heaven. For our sins, our just sentence was death everlasting, but Thy Cross, LORD, hath saved us. Thou art our life! May we share in Thy victory, may we follow Thy triumph, may we rise in Thy likeness, and reign in Heaven with Thee. JESU, our LORD, Son of GOD, our Redeemer, let all created beings praise Thy Name.

Another Version.

PSALM xliii. 3. Send out Thy light and Thy truth, let them lead me, and let them bring me to Thy holy hill.

4. O GOD, then will I go unto Thy altar; on the harp we will praise Thee, O LORD our GOD.

5. Why, O soul, art thou sorrowful? and why cast down within me? Still trust the loving-kindness of the GOD of thy strength, and my tongue yet shall praise Him Who hath pleaded my cause.

xx. 6. LORD our GOD, Thou wilt save Thine anointed, Thou wilt hear us from Heaven.

7. Though in chariots some put their faith, our trust is in Thee.

8. They are brought down and fallen, but the LORD is our helper, we shall not be afraid.

GOUNOD.

1050

O come near to the Cross whereon hangs our Redeemer. Ye faithful, shed your tears, for your LORD pours His life-blood for the world's salvation! O behold, as ye weep, your LORD hung on His Cross, the spotless Victim; how He bleeds, how He dies, how He drinks to the dregs the bitter cup of sorrow, dying to give us life. Ah, behold!

what a scene to our eyes is unfolded, with scourges He is torn, with thorns and cruel nails and with spear He is wounded, for us thus sacrificed.

Hear us, O Saviour, and pardon all our sins, and give us life in Thee. Thou hast suffered for us : we have planted Thy bitter Cross on Mount Golgotha. O grant us Thy grace, our cold hearts to kindle, and to quicken our faith. Thou hast ransomed our souls from the grave and from hell. Thou hast saved Thy redeemed. LORD, we offer to Thee our grateful love and praises at the foot of the Cross. Who suffer here with Thee, shall reign with Thee in glory, in joy, and love, and peace.

Soon, ah, soon from the grave shall Thy all-quickening Spirit call us to life again. LORD, our Redeemer, O hear Thou our petition, bow Thine ear to our prayer. LORD, grant us life eternal.

GOUNOD.

1051

O day of penitence ! O day of mourning ! Remember how the Incarnate Son of GOD, nailed to His Cross, hung between earth and heaven, was put to death by His own people's hands, to save us all from Satan's iron bondage. He bore with patience all these cruel wrongs ! O come, let us with hearts and voices utter our grief, and weep beside His tomb.

Come, let us kneel, in sorrow and contrition, before the Cross which His pure Blood doth lave. Come, rich and poor, offer Him all your hearts, Who gave Himself the world to save.

Just as the sea by stormy winds is driven, whose angry waves do hoarsely rage and roar; the people with madness to the slaughter are crowding, and shouting, " To death ! To death ! Crucify Him !"

Striving to save Him, Pilate has vainly laboured : His cruel foes thirst for their Victim's Blood. Behold, they crown with thorns His sacred Head, beat Him with scourges, and then smite Him on His cheek.

Come, let us kneel in sorrow and contrition, before the Cross which His pure Blood doth lave. Come, rich and poor, offer Him all your hearts, Who gave Himself the

world to save. Slowly, ah slowly, drag on the fatal hours.
Now having drained His bitter cup of pain, the Lamb of
GOD completes His Sacrifice; into His Father's hands
commends His spirit; cries with loud voice, "It is
finished," and expires. Then, as He died, darkness
obscured the land; in dim eclipse the earth with horror
shook; the temple trembled, the veil was rent in twain.

Come, let us kneel in sorrow and contrition, before the
Cross which His pure Blood doth lave. Come, rich and
poor, offer Him all your hearts, Who gave Himself the
world to save.

GOUNOD.

1052

O sing to GOD your hymns of gladness,
Ye loving hearts, your tribute pay;
Your LORD is born this happy day.
Then pierce the sky with songs of gladness,
Disperse the shades of gloom and sadness;
O sing to GOD your hymns of gladness.
Mark how the Mother lulls to slumber
Her new-born Babe with tenderest love,
And guards her treasure from Above.
O blessed Child, with her who bore Thee,
We, too, will kneel in faith before Thee.
O GOD Incarnate, we adore Thee.
O Word of GOD, for us Incarnate,
By faith we hear Thine angels sing
Their hymns of praise to Thee their King.
We join with them in adoration,
We pour to Thee our supplication,
That Thou wouldst grant us, LORD, salvation.

GOUNOD.

1053

O saving Victim, slain for us,
The gates of Heaven to us unfold;
Fierce wars assail, the foes draw nigh,
Grant succour, give us victory.

GOUNOD, STAINER.

1054

O saving Victim, slain for man,
The gates of heaven to us expand ;
Fierce wars assail, the foes draw nigh ;
Grant succour, give us victory.   Amen.

GOUNOD, TOURS.

1055

No. 1

PSALM cxxx.   1. Out of darkness I called unto Thee, O
LORD ; LORD, my GOD, I pray Thee, hear my crying.

2. Let Thine ears well consider the voice of my supplication.

3. Shouldst Thou be extreme, LORD, to mark our sins,
LORD, my GOD, who may abide it ?

1. Out of darkness I called unto Thee; LORD, my GOD,
I pray Thee, hear Thou my crying.

No. 2

4. There is mercy with Thee; yea, with Thee is mercy,
therefore shalt Thou be feared.

5. Mine eyes are looking unto the LORD, my soul for
Him is waiting.   My hope is even in the LORD GOD, yea,
in His word is my trust.

4. There is mercy with Thee ; yea, with Thee is mercy,
therefore shalt Thou be feared.

No. 3

6, 7. From the watch of morning, even until evening,
trust thou, Israel, in GOD the LORD : for with Him is
mercy, and plenteous redemption.

No. 4

8. And He shall redeem thee, Israel, from all thine
iniquities.   Amen.

(*For Latin Version, see* No. 1614.)   GOUNOD.

1056

PSALM xlii.   1. Sicut cervus desiderat ad fontes aquarum,
ita desiderat anima mea ad Te, Deus.

English Version.

PSALM xlii.   1. As the hart pants after the waterbrooks,
so longeth my soul after Thee, O GOD.

GOUNOD.

1057

PSALM xxx. 4. Sing praises unto the LORD, O ye saints of His, and give thanks unto Him for a remembrance of His holiness.

5. For His wrath endureth but the twinkling of an eye, and in His pleasure is life; heaviness may endure for a night, but joy cometh in the morning.

13. Therefore shall every good man sing of Thy praise without ceasing : O my GOD, I will give thanks unto Thee for ever.

[ISAIAH xxxv. 10. And sorrow and sighing shall flee away.]

GOUNOD.

1058 CRUICKSHANK, vv. 4, 5; Isaiah xxxv. 10.
1059 SWIFT, vv. 4, 5, 4. Amen.

1060

O My vineyard, come tell Me why thy grapes are bitter. What have I done, My people ? Wherein hast thou been wronged ? Did I not bring thee out from the land of the stranger ? Made I thee not to pass through the depths of the sea ? Sent I not food from heaven, and gave meat in abundance ? Did manna ever cease till thou camest to Canaan ? Reply, unthankful race, reply! And thou, for all this love, preparest Me the Cross where-- upon I shall die.

(*From " The Redemption,"* p. 44.) GOUNOD.

1061

Beside the Cross remaining,
  A face the Mother wears
Unresisting, uncomplaining,
  And yet the grief she bears
  Her heart in sunder tears.

Though He claim adoration,
  On the Cross JESUS hangs ;
Her soul, past consolation,
Knowing but lamentation,
  Has a share in His pangs.

While my watch I am keeping,
 Ye that go by, sinners,
Gaze at the Mother weeping,
Torn by anguish unsleeping:
  Ask if any one bears
  Any grief like to hers.

While her watch she is keeping,
 Ye that go by, sinners.
Gaze at the Mother weeping,
Torn by anguish unsleeping:
  Ask if any one bears
  Any grief like to hers.

(From " The Redemption," p. 50.)   GOUNOD.

1062

For us the CHRIST is made a Victim availing,
 Yea, unto death, and the death of the Cross ;
In vain our ancient foe will mankind be assailing.
To Him, Who now has died, shall be triumph unfailing.
 O Death, thou art discrowned, thou gainest only loss.
Faith unswerving, holy Hope, that unconquered remaineth,
 Heavenly Love, ever young ; for them thanks do we
 raise.
Thou, by Whose Death and Passion man unto heaven
 attaineth,
 O CHRIST, Thee we adore, and unto Thee give praise.

(From " The Redemption," p. 73.)   GOUNOD.

1063

From Thy love as a Father,
O LORD, teach us to gather
 That Life will conquer death :
They who seek things eternal
Shall rise to light supernal
 On wings of lowly faith.

(From " The Redemption," p. 109.)   GOUNOD.

1064

Unfold, ye portals everlasting,
With welcome to receive Him ascending on high.
Behold the King of Glory! He mounts up through the
    sky,
    Back to the heavenly mansions hasting.
    Unfold, for lo, the King comes nigh.
But Who is He, the King of Glory?
He Who Death overcame, the LORD in battle mighty.
    But Who is He, the King of Glory?
    Of Hosts He is the LORD ; of angels and of powers :
The King of Glory is the King of the saints.
    Unfold, ye portals everlasting,
With welcome to receive Him ascending on high.
Behold the King of Glory! He mounts up through the
    sky,
    Back to the heavenly mansions hasting.
    Unfold, for lo, the King comes nigh.

        (*From " The Redemption,"* p. 118.)   GOUNOD.

1065

*Lovely appear over the mountain
The feet of them that preach, and bring good news of
    peace.*
Ye mountains, ye perpetual hills, bow ye down.
Over the barren wastes shall flowers now have possession.
Dark shades of ancient days, full of hate and oppression,
In the brightness of joy fade away, and are gone.
†In this age, truly blest more than ages preceding,
Shall the corn never fail from the plentiful ground ;
Under the shining sky shall the lambs gaily bound ;
Void of fear, undisturbed, safely shall they be feeding.
Then the timorous doves, wheresoever they fly,
Shall not fear any more the hawk's merciless cry.†
Lovely appear over the mountains, &c.

        (*From " The Redemption,"* p. 128.)   GOUNOD.

      * Sometimes sung as a separate Anthem.
  † —— † These words are usually omitted.

1066

*The Word is Flesh become : thus begin we the story :
  Full of grace, full of truth, is He.
In the womb of a Virgin did He veil the glory
  Of His eternal Majesty.

He is before the worlds, all light from Him we gather,
  God, holy, just, and true, is He;
And, like the Holy Ghost, is one with God the Father
  In everlasting Trinity.

He has given His flesh, the life of men to nourish,
  Whence we His wondrous love may see.
By His love are we drawn in our inmost souls to cherish
  Blessed hope of immortality.*

By faith salvation comes, and by peace consolation.
Hearken ! let all give ear to the Lord's declaration.

He has said, At My Word have the blind had their sight,
and the lame have been healed; the deaf likewise have
heard ; the dead have from the grave been recalled, and
have risen ; back to life and to light at My summons
returning. He has said to all the unhappy, O come to
Me, all ye that are sad and that weep, and I will give
your souls the rest they long to find.
  He has said,
They are blessed, the poor in spirit, for they have the
  Kingdom of Heaven.
They are blessed that mourn, for they shall have comfort.
They are blessed, they that are meek.
They are blessed that hunger and thirst to be righteous.
They are blessed, they that are kind, pure in heart, seek-
  ing peace, falsely blamed for My sake ; they the earth
  shall inherit, they shall have their reward in Heaven
The Word is Flesh become, &c.

F . . "*Th Red.. ...,*' p. 14 . Gounod

* Sometimes sung as a separate anthem.

1067

Rest and peace eternal, LORD, in mercy give to them :
let light perpetual lighten them alway. Thou, GOD, art
praised in Sion ; to Thee is the vow performed in Jerusalem. O hear Thou my supplication. All flesh cometh
unto Thee, O GOD. Rest and peace eternal, LORD, in
mercy give to them : let light perpetual lighten them
alway.

LORD, have mercy. CHRIST, have mercy.

LORD, have mercy.

(*From " Death and Life,"* p. 7.) GOUNOD.

1068

From the morning watch till the evening, yea, till the
evening, trust thou, Israel, upon the LORD ; for with Him
is mercy found, and loving-kindness ; and with the LORD
is also plenteous redemption ; and He Himself will save
Israel from all his sins and his iniquities freely.

From the morning watch till the evening, yea, till the
evening, trust thou, Israel, upon the LORD.

(*From " Death and Life,"* p. 19.) GOUNOD.

1069

Day of anger, day of mourning,
Earth to ashes shall be turning ;
Thus from prophets are we learning.

O what dread on man attendeth,
When the righteous Judge descendeth,
On Whose sentence all dependeth !

Wondrous sound the trumpet flingeth,
Through earth's sepulchres it ringeth,
All before the Throne it bringeth.

Death and Nature both are quaking,
All Creation is awaking,
At the judgment answer making.

Then brought forward is the writing,
All things byegone now reciting,
And us sinners now indicting.

Comes the Judge then, and is seated;
Each thing secret is repeated;
Just repayment is completed.
                (*From " Death and Life,"* p. 27.)   GOUNOD.

1070

Ah ! what shall we then be pleading,
Who for us be interceding,
When the just are mercy needing ?

King of Majesty tremendous,
Who dost free salvation send us,
Fount of Love, do Thou befriend us.

Think, kind JESUS, our salvation
Caused Thy wondrous Incarnation,
Nor adjudge us reprobation.
                (*From " Death and Life,"* p. 40.)   GOUNOD.

1071

Faint and worn, Thou yet hast sought us,
By Thy suffering Thou hast bought us;
Is such mercy vainly brought us ?

Righteous Judge of retribution,
Grant Thy gift of absolution,
That we come not to confusion.
                (*From " Death and Life,"* p. 52.)   GOUNOD.

1072

LORD, for anguish hear us moaning,
Shameful error see us owning,
Spare Thy suppliants deeply groaning.

Thou to Mary pardon gavest.
Thou the contrite thief savest,
Us to rescue still Thou cravest.

Worthless are our prayers and sighing,
Yet, good LORD, in grace complying,
Grant we know not fires undying.

(From "Death and Life," p. 59.) GOUNOD.

1073

While the wicked are confounded,
Doomed to flames of woe unbounded,
Call us, LORD, by saints surrounded.

Lowly kneel we in submission,
See, like ashes, our contrition,
Feel and care for our condition.

(From "Death and Life," p. 71.) GOUNOD.

1074

Day of weeping, day of mourning,
When from ashes man returning,
Unto judgment must prepare him.
GOD, in mercy spare, O spare him.
Mighty Saviour, JESU blest,
Give him endless peace and rest.

(From "Death and Life," p. 81.) GOUNOD.

1075

O LORD JESU CHRIST, King of Glory, keep Thou free the
souls of all Thy faithful servants, departing this life, from
the pains of hell, and from the lake that burneth ; them
do Thou deliver from the mouth of the lion, that by hell
they be not swallowed ; that they fall not into darkness.

But, LORD, do Thou bring them evermore to the light
eternal, which once to Abraham Thou didst promise, and
Abraham's children.

Sacrifice of prayer and praise we offer Thee, O LORD ;
accept us, LORD, through JESUS CHRIST our Saviour.
Grant that we and all Thy servants everywhere, may
pass from death to life, which once to Abraham Thou
didst promise, and Abraham's children.

(From "Death and Life," p. 87.) GOUNOD.

1076

Holy, Holy, Holy, O Lord God of Hosts.   Full is the
heaven, full is the earth, of Thy glory.   Hosanna in the
highest.

(From " Death and Life," p. 101.)   Gounod.

1077

Mighty Saviour, Jesu blest,
Give them endless peace and rest.   Amen.
(From " Death and Life," p. 108.)   Gounod.

1078

Lamb of God, that takest away our sins, grant them
Thy peace.

Lord, for ever let light eternal lighten them, with all
Thy saints, yea, for ever, for Thou art merciful.   Rest
and peace eternal, Lord, in mercy give to them : let light
perpetual lighten them alway, with all Thy saints, yea,
for ever, for Thou art merciful.

(From " Death and Life," p. 114.)   Gounod.

1079

Revelation xxi.   3. And I heard a great voice from
the Throne, thus saying :

Lo, the tabernacle of God is with men, and He will
dwell with them, and they shall be His people, and God
Himself shall be with them, and God Himself shall be
their God.

(From " Death and Life," p. 161.)   Gounod.

1080

Revelation 4. Yea, and God Almighty then will wipe
away all tears from off their faces.   And death shall be
no more. neither mourning, neither crying, neither shall
there be any sorrow : for the first things are passed away.
(From " Death and Life," p. 168.)   Gounod.

1081

REVELATION xxi. 5. Then said He, on the Throne that was seated:

Lo, all things I make new.

And unto me He said: Write·thou, because these sayings are true and faithful.

6. And unto me He said: Done are they.

I ˜am Alpha and Omega, the beginning and the end. I will give unto him that is athirst of the fountain of the water of life freely.

7. He that overcometh shall inherit these things, and I will be his GOD, and he shall be My son.

3. Lo, the tabernacle of GOD is with men, and He will dwell with them, and they shall be His people, and GOD Himself shall be with them, and He shall be their GOD.

(From " Death and Life," p. 174.) GOUNOD.

1082

Hosanna in the highest places!

(From " Death and Life," p. 184.) GOUNOD.

1083

*PSALM xxi. 1. The king shall rejoice in Thy strength, O LORD: exceeding glad shall he be of Thy salvation.

2. Thou hast given him his heart's desire, and hast not denied him the request of his lips.*

3. Thou shalt prevent him with the blessings of goodness, and shalt set a crown of pure gold upon his head.

5. His honour is great in Thy salvation: glory and great worship shalt Thou lay upon him.

6. For Thou shalt give him everlasting felicity, and make him glad with the joy of Thy countenance.

7. Because he putteth his trust in Thee, and in Thy mercy he shall not miscarry.

13. Be Thou exalted, LORD, in Thine own strength: so will we sing, and praise Thy power. Amen.

E. J. HOPKINS.

—— Sometimes sung as a separate Anthem

1084 CONFI, vv. 1, 5, 7, 13.

1085

2 CORINTHIANS iv. 6. GOD, Who commanded the light to shine out of darkness, hath shined in our hearts. Amen.

PSALM xxxiii. 1. Rejoice in the LORD, O ye righteous, for it becometh well the just to be thankful.

2. Praise the LORD with harp, sing praises unto Him with the lute, and instrument of ten strings.

[3. Sing unto the LORD a new song : sing praises lustily unto Him with a good courage.]

4. For the Word of the LORD is true, and all His works are faithful.

5. He loveth righteousness and judgment : the earth is full of the goodness of the LORD.

9. For He spake and it was done ; He commanded and it stood fast.

[10. The LORD bringeth the counsel of the heathen to nought, and maketh the devices of the people to be of none effect, and casteth out the counsels of princes.]

11. The counsel of the LORD shall endure for ever, and the thoughts of His heart from generation to generation.

17. Behold, the eye of the LORD is upon them that fear Him, and upon them that put their trust in His mercy ;

18. To deliver their souls from death, and to feed them in the time of dearth.

19. Our soul hath patiently tarried for the LORD, for He is our help and our shield.

20. For our heart shall rejoice in Him, because we have hoped in His holy Name.

21. Let Thy merciful kindness, O LORD, be upon us. like as we do put our trust in Thee.

E. J. HOPKINS.

1086 BARNBY, Psalm xxxiii. 21. Amen.
1087 CROFT, KENT, Psalm xxxiii. 1-5. Amen.
1088 ELVEY, Psalm xxxiii. 1, 2.
1089 HINE, Psalm xxxiii. 1, 2, 10, 11, 1. Gloria Patri.
1090 J. L. HOPKINS, Psalm xxxiii. 1, 2, 20, 4. Amen.
1091 HUMPHREYS, Psalm xxxiii. 1, 2, 1, 3, 4.
1092 KING, Psalm xxxiii. 1, 2, 4.
1093 S. ELVEY, Psalm xxxiii. 1, 1, 21. Amen.
1094 C. WESLEY, Psalm xxxiii. 19 My soul, 20, 21.

1095

PSALM lvii. 10. I will give thanks unto Thee, O LORD, among the people, and I will sing unto Thee among the nations.

11. For the greatness of Thy mercy reacheth unto the heavens, and Thy truth unto the clouds.

lxii. 7. In GOD is my health and my glory, the Rock of my might; and in GOD is my trust.

6. He truly is my strength and my salvation; He is my defence, so that I shall not fall.

8. O put your trust in Him alway, ye people, pour out your hearts before Him, for GOD is our hope.

E. J. HOPKINS.

1096

ST. LUKE ii. 15. Let us now go even unto Bethlehem, and see this thing which is come to pass, which the LORD hath made known unto us.

10. For the angel said unto us, Fear not: for, behold, I bring you good tidings of great joy, which shall be to all people.

11. For unto you is born this day, in the city of David, a Saviour, Which is CHRIST the LORD.

E. J. HOPKINS.

1097

PSALM xxxvi. 5. Thy mercy, O LORD, reacheth unto the heavens, and Thy faithfulness unto the clouds.

6. Thy righteousness standeth like the strong mountains, Thy judgments are like the great deep.

10. O continue forth Thy loving-kindness unto them that know Thee, and Thy righteousness unto them that are true of heart.

7. How excellent is Thy mercy, Ô GOD, and the children of men shall put their trust under the shadow of Thy wings. Amen.

E. J. HOPKINS.

1098 BARNBY, vv. 5, 6.
1099 OT c11 ... .. b. 7

1100

Psalm cxx. i. In my distress I cried unto the Lord, and He heard me.

cxxxviii. i. I will praise Thee with my whole heart before the gods. Unto Thee, O Lord, will I sing praise. Amen.

E. J. Hopkins.

1101

St. Luke xxiv. 5. Why seek ye the living among the dead ?

6. He is not here, but is risen; remember how He spake unto you when He was yet in Galilee,

7. Saying, The Son of Man must be delivered into the hands of sinful men, and be crucified, and the third day rise again.

6. He is not here, but is risen.

E. J. Hopkins.

1102 Alexander, vv. 5-7.

1103

Psalm xxxix. 13. Give ear, O Lord, unto my prayer : give ear, and hearken unto my prayer.

xx. 9. O save, Lord, and hear us, King of Heaven, when we call upon Thee. Amen.

Oberthür.

1104

COLLECT

For the Ninth Sunday after Trinity.

Grant to us, Lord, we beseech Thee, the spirit to think and do always such things as be rightful; that we, who cannot do any thing that is good without Thee, may by Thee be enabled to live according to Thy will; through Jesus Christ our Lord. Amen.

Barnby, Longhurst, Stevenson.

1105

St. James iv. 10. Humble thyself in the sight of the Lord, and He shall lift you up.

8. Draw nigh unto God, and He will draw nigh unto thee.

Joel ii. 13. Turn unto Him, for He is gracious and merciful, and slow to anger.

Hebrews xii. 6. Whom the Lord loveth He chasteneth, and scourgeth every son whom He receiveth.

Psalm cxii. 4. Unto the godly there ariseth up light in the darkness.

Longhurst.

1106

Psalm cv. 1. O give thanks unto the Lord; call upon His Name: make known His deeds among the people.

2. Sing unto Him, sing psalms unto Him: talk ye of all His wondrous works.

3. Glory ye in His holy Name: let the heart of them rejoice that seek the Lord.

4. Seek the Lord, and His strength: seek His face evermore.

Dixon.

1107

Tobit xiii. 7. I will extol my God, and my soul shall praise the King of Heaven, and shall rejoice in His greatness.

9, 12. O Jerusalem, the Holy City, blessed shall all be which love thee for ever.

14. O blessed are they which love thee, for they shall rejoice in thy peace.

10. Give praise to the Lord, for He is good: and praise the everlasting King. Amen.

Young.

1108

* JUDITH xvi. 13, 15. O LORD Thou art great and glorious, wonderful in strength, yet Thou art merciful to them that fear Thee.

14. Let all nations serve Thee, for Thou spakest, and they were made, Thou didst send forth Thy Spirit, and it created them, and there is none that can resist Thy voice.*

The Song of the Three Holy Children.

68. O all ye that worship the LORD, bless the GOD of gods, praise Him, and give Him thanks, for His mercy endureth for ever.

YOUNG.

* —— * Sometimes sung as a separate Anthem.

1109

JOEL ii. 1. Blow ye the trumpet in Zion, and sound an alarm in My holy mountain : let all the inhabitants of the land tremble : for the day of the LORD cometh : it is nigh at hand.

LESLIE.

1110

EZEKIEL xxviii. 30. Come, we pray ye, come, and hear what is the word that cometh from the LORD.

ST. MARK x. 16, 14. He took us in His arms, and blessed us, saying, Suffer little children to come unto Me, and forbid them not : for of such is the Kingdom of Heaven.

PSALM viii. 2. Out of the mouths of babes hath He ordained praise.

(From " Immanuel," No. 28.) LESLIE.

1111

PSALM li. 1. O have mercy upon me, O LORD, after Thy great goodness : according to the multitude of Thy mercies do away mine offences.

3. I acknowledge my faults, O my God.

9. L ve ·· n Thy t·· from · , sins.

11. Cast me not away from Thy presence, O my GOD, and take not Thy Holy Spirit from me. O my GOD, have mercy. LORD, have mercy.

LESLIE.

1112

ST. JOHN vi. 47. Verily, verily, I say unto you : He that believeth on CHRIST hath everlasting life.

ST. MATTHEW xi. 28, 30. Come unto Him and He will give you rest, all ye that labour and are heavy laden ; for His yoke is easy, and His burden light.

ST. LUKE iv. 18. The spirit of the LORD is upon Him ; for He hath anointed Him to preach the gospel to the poor ; and He hath sent Him to heal the broken-hearted.

(From " Immanuel," Nos. 23–25.) LESLIE.

——— Sometimes sung as a separate Anthem.

1113

ST. JOHN i. 1. In the beginning was the Word, and the Word was with GOD, and the Word was GOD.

14. And the Word was made flesh, and dwelt among us.

PSALM xlv. 3. Thou art fairer than the children of men : full of grace are Thy lips, because GOD hath blessed Thee for ever.

ST. LUKE i. 68. Blessed be the LORD GOD of Israel, for He hath visited and redeemed His people. Amen.

ALLEN.

1114

ISAIAH xlix. 1, 2. Listen, O isles, unto me ; and hearken, ye people, from far. The LORD hath called me from the womb, and He hath made my tongue like a sharp sword.

MALACHI iv. 6. He shall turn the heart of the fathers to the children, and the heart of the children to their fathers.

ST. MATTHEW iii. 2. Repent ye : for the Kingdom of Heaven is at hand

ALLEN.

1115

St. Luke i. 26, 27. And the angel Gabriel was sent from God unto a. city of Galilee, named Nazareth, to a Virgin of the house of David ; and the Virgin's name was Mary.

28. And the angel came in unto her and said, Hail, thou that art highly favoured, the Lord is with thee : blessed art thou among women. Hallelujah. Amen.

W. H. Monk.

1116

Ephesians iv. 32. Be ye kind one to another.

v. 2. And walk in love, as Christ also hath loved us, and hath given Himself for us, an offering and a sacrifice to God for a sweet-smelling savour.

M. Smith.

1117

Psalm xxxvii. 1. Fret not thyself because of the ungodly, neither be thou envious against the evil doers ;

2. For they shall soon be cut down like the grass, and be withered even as the green herb.

3. Put thou thy trust in the Lord, and be doing good :

4. [Delight thou in the Lord,] and He shall give thee thy heart's desire.

[5. Commit thy way unto the Lord, and put thy trust in Him, and He shall bring it to pass.]

6. He shall make thy righteousness as clear as the light, and thy just dealing as the noon-day.

[8. Leave off from wrath, and let go displeasure ; fret not thyself, else shalt thou be moved to do evil.]

9. Wicked doers shall be rooted out.

10. Yet a little while and the ungodly shall be clean gone ; thou shalt look after his place, and he shall be away.

11. But the meek spirited shall possess the earth, and shall be refreshed in the multitude of peace.

28. For the Lord loveth the thing that is right. He forsaketh not his that be godly, but they are preserved for ever.

[ROMANS xii. 19. Vengeance is Mine, I will repay, saith the LORD.

PSALM xxxvii. 40. The salvation of the righteous cometh of the LORD, Who is also their strength in the time of trouble.

41. And the LORD shall stand by them, and save them; He shall deliver them from the ungodly, and shall save them, because they put their trust in Him.]

M. SMITH.

1118 J. CAMIDGE, vv. 1–6, 8; Romans xii. 19; Psalm xxxvii. 40, 41.
1119 OUSELEY, VINCENT, vv. 40, 41.

1120

PSALM viii. 3. When I consider Thy heavens, the work of Thy fingers, the moon and the stars which Thou hast ordained,

4. What is man, that Thou art mindful of him, and the son of man, that Thou regardest him?

AMPS.

1121

REVELATION xxii. 1. And there was a pure river of water of life, clear as crystal, proceeding out of the Throne of GOD and of the Lamb.

2. In the midst of the street of it, and on either side of the river, was there the tree of life, which bare twelve manner of fruits, and yielded her fruit every month: and the leaves of the tree were for the healing of the nations.

3. And, behold, there shall be no more curse: but the Throne of GOD and of the Lamb shall be in it, and His servants shall serve Him.

4. And they shall see His face, and His Name shall be in their foreheads.

5. And there shall be no night there, and they shall need no candle, nor light of the sun; for the LORD their GOD giveth them light: and they shall reign for ever and ever. Hallelujah. Amen.

1122

EPHESIANS v. 14. Awake thou that sleepest, and arise from the dead, and CHRIST shall give thee light.

PSALM lvii. 9. Awake up, my glory; awake, lute and harp : I myself will awake right early.

ST. JOHN xi. 25, 26. I am the Resurrection and the Life, saith the LORD : he that liveth and believeth in Me shall never die.

REVELATION i. 18. I am He that liveth, and was dead ; and, behold, I am alive for evermore.

ISAIAH xxxviii. 18. The grave cannot praise Thee, death cannot celebrate Thee.

19. The living, the living, he shall praise Thee, as I do this day.

PSALM iii. 5. I laid me down and slept, and rose up again, for the LORD sustained me.

ISAIAH xxv. 9. Lo, This is our GOD ; we have waited for Him, and He will save us: This is the LORD; we have waited for Him, we will be glad and rejoice in His salvation. Hallelujah.

OUSELEY.

1123

PSALM cxxxiv. 1. Behold now, praise the LORD, all ye servants of the LORD ;

2. Ye that by night do stand in the house of the LORD, even in the courts of the house of our GOD.

4. For the LORD is gracious, His mercy is everlasting : and His truth endureth from generation to generation. Glory to GOD on high.

To GOD the Father, GOD the Son,
And GOD the Spirit, Three in One ;
Be honour, praise, and glory given,
By all on earth, and all in heaven. Amen.

OUSELEY.

1124

1 CHRONICLES xxix. 10. Blessed be Thou, LORD GOD of Israel, our Father, for ever and ever.

11. Thine, O LORD, is the greatness, and the power, and the glory, and the victory, and the majesty: for all that is in the heaven and in the earth is Thine; Thine is the Kingdom, O LORD, and Thou art exalted as head over all.

[12. Both riches and honour come of Thee, and Thou reignest over all; and in Thine hand is power and might; and in Thine hand it is to make great, and to give strength unto all.

13. Now therefore, our GOD, we thank Thee, and praise Thy glorious Name.]

PSALM cxxxii. 8. Arise, O LORD, into Thy resting-place, Thou, and the ark of Thy strength.

9. Let Thy priests, O LORD GOD, be clothed with salvation, and let Thy saints rejoice in goodness.

PSALM xcvi. 9. O worship the LORD in the beauty of holiness. Hallelujah.

xliii. 3. O send out Thy light and Thy truth, that they may lead us, and bring us unto Thy holy hill, and to Thy dwelling.

xlii. 5. In the voice of praise and thanksgiving; among all such as keep holy-day. Hallelujah.

REVELATION i. 4. Now unto Him Which is, and was, and is to come; and to the seven spirits which are before His Throne;

5. And to JESUS CHRIST, the faithful witness, the first begotten of the dead; to the King, eternal, immortal, invisible, to the only wise GOD be honour and glory for ever and ever. Hallelujah. Amen.

OUSELEY.

1125 BUNNETT, KENT, vv. 10-13.

1126

NUMBERS xxiv. 5. How goodly are thy tents, O Jacob, and thy tabernacles, O Israel!

6. As the valleys are they spread forth, as gardens by the river's side.

OUSELEY.

1127

I CORINTHIANS xv.   20.   CHRIST is risen from the dead,
and become the first fruits of them that slept.   Hallelujah.

21.   For since by man came death, by man came also
the resurrection of the dead.

22.   For as in Adam all die, even so in CHRIST shall all
be made alive.

PSALM cvii.   15. O that men would therefore praise the
LORD for His goodness, and declare the wonders that He
doeth for the children of men.

16.   For He hath broken the gates of brass, and smitten
the bars of iron in sunder.   Amen.

OUSELEY.

1128

PSALM cxxvii.   1. Except the LORD build the house,
their labour is but lost that build it.

2. Except the LORD keep the city, the watchman
waketh but in vain.

cxxi.   2. My help cometh even from the LORD, Who
hath made heaven and earth.

7. The LORD shall preserve thee from all evil : He shall
preserve thy soul.

8. The LORD shall preserve thy going out and thy
coming in, from this time forth, and even for evermore.
Amen.

OUSELEY.

1129

PSALM lxviii.   26. Give thanks, O Israel, unto GOD the
LORD, in the congregation, from the ground of the heart.

24.   It is well seen, O GOD, how Thou goest ; how Thou,
my GOD and King, goest in the Sanctuary.

25.   The singers go before, the minstrels follow after;
in the midst are the damsels playing with the timbrels.

34. A tile   to the   power   unto God over Israel.   His
worship and strength is in the cloud . Amen

OUSELEY.

1130

MALACHI i. 11. From the rising of the sun, unto the going down of the same, My Name shall be great among the Gentiles; and in every place incense shall be offered unto My Name, [and a pure offering;] for My Name shall be great among the heathen: thus saith the LORD [of Hosts].

GADSBY, KEETON, OUSELEY.

1131

PSALM xlviii. 1. Great is the LORD, and highly to be praised, in the city of our GOD, even upon His holy hill. Amen.

8. We wait for Thy loving-kindness, O GOD, in the midst of Thy temple.

[9. O GOD, according to Thy Name, so is Thy praise unto the world's end. Thy right hand is full of righteousness.

10. Let the mount Sion rejoice, and let the daughter of Judah be glad, because of Thy judgments, O LORD.]

11. Walk about Sion, and go round about her, and tell the towers thereof.

12. Mark well her bulwarks, set up her houses, that ye may tell them that come after.

13. For this GOD is our GOD for ever and ever: He shall be our guide unto death. Amen.

OUSELEY.

1132 CROFT, vv. 8–13.
1133 MACFARREN, vv. 8, 9, 1. Amen.

1134

PSALM cxlvi. 5. Happy is the man that hath the GOD of Jacob for his help, whose hope is in the LORD his GOD;

6. Which made heaven and earth, the sea and all that therein is: Which keepeth truth for ever.

7. Which executeth judgment for the oppressed: Which giveth food to the hungry.

lxviii. 19. Praised be the LORD. Amen.

OUSELEY.

1135

PSALM lxxvi.   1. In Jewry is GOD known, His Name is great in Israel.

2. At Salem is His tabernacle, and His dwelling in Sion.

3. There brake He the arrows of the bow, the shield, the sword, and the battle.

11. Promise unto the LORD your GOD, and keep it, all ye that are round about Him ; bring presents unto Him that ought to be feared.

12. He shall refrain the spirit of princes, and is wonderful among the kings of the earth.   O praise the LORD.   Hallelujah.   Amen.

OUSELEY.

1136 P. HAYES, WHITFELD, vv. 1–3.

1137

REVELATION xx.   4. I saw the souls of them that were beheaded for the witness of JESUS and for the word of GOD.

xiv. 13. I heard a voice from heaven, saying unto me, Write, *Blessed are the dead which die in the LORD; even so saith the Spirit, for they rest from their labours, and their works do follow them.   Amen.

OUSELEY.

1138 ELVEY, xiv. 13 (*Blessed are the dead).
1139 J. L. HOPKINS, PIERSON, xiv. 13.

1140

LAMENTATIONS i.   12. Is it nothing to you, all ye that pass by ?   Behold, and see if there be any sorrow like unto My sorrow, which is done unto Me, wherewith the LORD hath afflicted Me in the day of His fierce anger.

OUSELEY.

1141

2 CHR. . . . . . 1 . I . . . . as the trumpet . . . . to make one . . . and to be heard in praising and thanking the LORD;

And when they lifted up their voice with the trumpets and cymbals, and with instruments of music, and praised the LORD, saying, For He is good, for His mercy endureth for ever; that then the house was filled with a cloud, even the house of the LORD;

14. So that the priests could not stand to minister by reason of the cloud; for the glory of the LORD had filled the house of the LORD. Hallelujah. Amen.

OUSELEY.

1142

PSALM xl. 1. I waited patiently for the LORD, and He inclined unto me, and heard my calling.

2. He brought me also out of the horrible pit, out of the mire and clay, and set my feet upon the rock, and ordered my goings.

3. And He hath put a new song in my mouth, even a thanksgiving unto our GOD.

4. Many shall see it, and fear, and shall put their trust in the LORD.

5. Blessed is the man that hath set his hope in the LORD, and turned not to the proud, and to such as go about with lies.

6. O LORD my GOD, great are the wondrous works which Thou hast done, like as be Thy thoughts which are to us-ward; and yet there is no man that ordereth them unto Thee.

[14. Withdraw not Thou Thy mercy from me, O LORD; let Thy loving-kindness and Thy truth alway preserve me.]

16. Make haste, O LORD, to help me.

[20. As for me, I am poor and needy; but the LORD careth for me.]

21. Thou art my helper and my Redeemer: make no long tarrying, O my GOD. Amen.

OUSELEY.

1143 ATTWOOD, vv. 14, 20, 21.
1144 CROFT. vv. 1, 3. 4.
1145 TINNEY, vv. 1. ', 20.
1146 TOURS, vv. I 4. Amen

1147

Psalm xliii. 1. Judge me, O God, and plead my cause against an ungodly nation : deliver me from the deceitful and unjust man.

2. For Thou art the God of my strength.

3. O send out Thy light and Thy truth, that they may lead me, and bring me unto Thy holy hill, and to Thy dwelling.

Ouseley.

1148

Let all the world in every corner sing
　　　My God and King.
The heavens are not too high
　　　His praise may thither fly.
The earth is not too low
　　　His praises there may grow.
The Church with psalms must shout,
　　　No door can keep them out.
But above all, the heart
　　　Must bear the longest part.

Ouseley.

1149

Lord, be merciful to us sinners, and save us for Thy mercy's sake ; Thou art the great God that hast made and rulest all things : O deliver us for Thy Name's sake. Thou art the great God to be feared above all : O save us that we may praise Thee.　Amen.

Ouseley

1150

Psalm lxxxix. 1. My song shall be alway of the loving-kindness of the Lord : with my mouth will I ever be shewing Thy truth from one generation to another.

19. For the Lord is our defence : the Holy One of Israel is our King.

Ouseley.

1151

PSALM xxxi. 21. O how plentiful is Thy goodness, which Thou hast laid up for them that fear Thee, and that Thou hast prepared for them that put their trust in Thee, even before the sons of men.

22. Thou shalt hide them privily by Thine own presence from the provoking of all men : Thou shalt keep them secretly in Thy tabernacle from the strife of tongues.

23. Thanks be to the LORD. Hallelujah. Amen.

[16. But my hope hath been in Thee, O LORD, my GOD.]

OUSELEY.

1152 PATTISON, vv. 21, 16.

1153

ZEPHANIAH iii. 14. Sing, O daughter of Zion; shout, O Israel ; [be glad and rejoice with all the heart, O daughter of Jerusalem.

15. The King of Israel, even the LORD, is in the midst of thee.]

17. The LORD, thy GOD, in the midst of thee is mighty : He will save [thee], He will rejoice over thee with joy; He will rest in His love, He will joy over thee with singing.

PSALM xlvii. 1. O clap your hands, all ye people; shout unto GOD with the voice of triumph.

2. For the LORD our GOD is terrible; He is a great King over all the earth.

7. Sing ye praises with understanding.

cvi. 48. Blessed be the LORD GOD of Israel from everlasting to everlasting, and let all the people say, Amen. Praise ye the LORD. Hallelujah. Amen.

OUSELEY.

1154 GADSBY, vv. 14, 15, 17.

1155

PSALM cxix. 57. Thou art my portion, O LORD : I have said that I will keep Thy words.

58. I intreated Thy favour with my whole heart : be merciful unto me according to Thy word.

OUSELEY.

1156

1 Chronicles xvi. 23. Sing unto the Lord, all the earth; shew forth from day to day His salvation.

27. Glory and honour are in His presence; strength and gladness are in His house.

36. Blessed be the Lord God of Israel for ever and ever. Amen. Praise the Lord. Hallelujah. Amen.

Ouseley.

1157

Isaiah xlix. 7. Thus saith the Lord, the Redeemer of Israel, and His Holy One, to Him Whom man despiseth, to Him Whom the nation abhorreth, to a servant of rulers, Kings shall see and rise, princes also shall worship, because of the Lord that is faithful, and the Holy One of Israel, and He shall choose Thee.

13. Sing, O heavens, and be joyful, O earth; and break forth into singing, O ye mountains: for the Lord hath comforted His people, and He will have mercy upon His afflicted.

22. Thus saith the Lord, Behold, I will lift up Mine hand to the Gentiles.

23. And kings shall be thy nursing fathers, and queens thy nursing mothers: and thou shalt know that I am the Lord. Hallelujah. Amen.

Ouseley.

1158

Psalm x. 1. Why standest Thou so far off, O Lord, and hidest Thy face in the needful time of trouble?

13. Arise, O Lord God, and lift up Thine hand: forget not the poor.

xiv. 11. Who shall give salvation unto Israel out of Sion? When the Lord turneth again the captivity of His people, then shall Jacob rejoice, and Israel shall be glad. Amen.

Ouseley.

1159

PSALM li. 1. O GOD, have mercy upon me, and blot out my transgressions, according to Thy loving-kindness: yea, even for Thy mercy's sake, deny me not.

11. O cast me not away from Thy presence, O GOD, and take not Thy Holy Spirit from me.

17. O LORD, have mercy upon me, a broken heart and a contrite heart is offered before Thee.

12. O give me the comfort of Thy help again, and stablish me with Thy free Spirit.

lix. 16. For Thou hast been my refuge in the day of my trouble. Amen.

SPARK.

1160

ST. JOHN xiv. 15, 16. If ye love Me keep My commandments, and I will pray the Father, and He shall give you another Comforter;

17. Even the Spirit of Truth, Whom the world cannot receive, because it seeth Him not, neither knoweth Him: but ye know Him, for He dwelleth with you, and shall be in you.

27. Peace I leave with you, My peace I give to you. Let not your heart be troubled, neither let it be afraid.

STEWART.

1161

PSALM xi. 1. In the LORD put I my trust: how say ye then to my soul, that she should flee as a bird unto the hill?

2. For lo, the ungodly bend their bow, and make ready their arrows within the quiver, that they may privily shoot at them which are true of heart.

4. The LORD is in His holy temple: the LORD'S seat is in heaven.

5. His eyes consider the poor, and His eyelids try the children of men.

7. Upon the ungodly He shall rain snares, fire, storm, and tempest: this shall be their portion to drink.

8. For the righteous LORD loveth righteousness: His countenance will behold the thing that is just.

STEWART.

1162

1 KINGS viii. 28. O LORD my GOD, hear Thou the prayer Thy servant prayeth; have Thou respect unto his prayer.

30. [Hear Thou in heaven, Thy dwelling-place:] and when Thou hearest, LORD, forgive.

STEWART.

1163 COULDREY, MALAN, S. S. WESLEY, vv. 28, 30.

1164

PSALM xxi. 1. The king shall rejoice in Thy strength, O LORD; exceeding glad shall he be of Thy salvation.

3. Thou hast prevented him with the blessings of goodness, and set a crown of pure gold upon his head.

lxi. 7. O prepare Thy loving mercy and faithfulness that they may preserve him.

1 KINGS i. 39. And they blew the trumpet: and all the people said, GOD save the King. Long live the King. Hallelujah. Amen.

STEWART.

1165

PSALM lxv. 1. Thou, O GOD, art praised in Sion: and unto Thee shall the vow be performed in Jerusalem.

2. Thou that hearest the prayer, unto Thee shall all flesh come.

3. My misdeeds prevail against me: Thou that hearest the prayer, be merciful unto our sins.

4. Blessed is the man whom Thou choosest, and receivest unto Thee: he shall dwell in Thy courts, and shall be satisfied with the pleasures of Thy house, even of Thy holy temple.

lxviii. 19. Praised be the LORD daily, Who poureth His benefits upon us. Amen.

lxv. 5. Thou shalt shew us wonderful things in Thy righteousness, O GOD of our salvation. Amen.

[9. Thou visitest the earth, and blessest it: Thou makest it very plenteous.]

STEWART.

1166 CORIF, vv. 1. 3, 4, 9.
1167 S. WESLEY vv. 1, 2.

1168

St. Matthew v. 7. Blessed are the merciful, for they shall obtain mercy.

3. Blessed are the poor in spirit, for theirs is the Kingdom of Heaven.

8. Blessed are the pure in heart, for they shall see God.

Hiles, Kearton.

1169 Macfarren, v. 8.

1170

Psalm xlvi. 1. God is our refuge and strength, a very present help in trouble.

2. Therefore will we not fear, though the earth be moved.

3. And though the waters rage and swell, though the mountains shake with the tempest.

4. The river of the flood shall make glad the city of God.

1. God is our refuge and strength, a very present help in trouble.

4, 2. The river of the flood shall make glad the city of God; therefore will we not fear.

9. He maketh wars to cease in all the world; He knappeth the spear in sunder, He breaketh the bow, and burneth the chariot in the fire.

10. Be still then, and know that He is God; He will be exalted among the heathen, He will be exalted in all the world.

11. The Lord of Hosts is with us; the God of Jacob is our refuge.

Hiles.

1171

O God, how wonderful art Thou in Thy judgments.

Psalm cxlv. 9. Thy mercies are over all Thy works.

cxv. 9. O Israel, trust Thou in the Lord: He is our help and shield.

Hiles.

1172

Psalm cxxii.   1. I was glad when they said unto me, Let us go into the house of the Lord.

lxxxiv.   1. How lovely are Thy courts, Lord, my King and my God!

2. My heart and my flesh cry out for Thee, the living God!

xlii.   2. My soul thirsteth for God, yea, for the living God.   When shall I come before His presence, before the presence of God?

3. My tears have been my meat day and night, while they said: "Where is now Thy God?"

xliii.   3, 4. Send out Thy light and truth, O Lord, that they may lead me to Thy holy hill: even to Thine altar, O my God.

xxvii.   4. One thing have I desired of the Lord, to dwell in the house of the Lord for ever, that I may see the fair beauty of the Lord.

Hiles.

* —— * Sometimes sung as a separate Anthem

1173

Psalm cxviii.   1. O give thanks to the Lord, for He is gracious and merciful.

6. The Lord is on my side, therefore I will not fear what man may do unto me.

5. I called on the Lord in my trouble, and the Lord heard me at large.

8. It is better to trust in the Lord, than to put any confidence in man.

9. It is better to trust in the Lord, than to put any confidence in princes.

10–12. The wicked compassed me around, they kept me in on every side, they came about me like bees: but in the Name of the Lord will I overcome them.

14. The Lord is my strength and my song, and is become my salvation.

18. He hath chastened and corrected me: but He hath not given me over unto death.

28, 21. Thou art my God, I will thank Thee. I will exalt Thee, and praise Thy Name: for Thou hast heard me, and art become my salvation.

Hiles.

1174

PSALM xxvii. 1. The LORD is my light; whom then shall I fear? the LORD is my strength; of whom then shall I be afraid?

16. O wait thou still upon the LORD, and He shall comfort thine heart.

5. For in the time of my trouble He shall hide me in His secret place, and set me up on a rock of stone.

7. Therefore will I offer in His dwelling an oblation; yea, I will sing, and speak praises to the LORD.

HILLS.

1175

ISAIAH li. 3. The LORD will comfort Zion, even her waste places. He will make her desert like the garden of the LORD; joy and gladness shall be found there; thanksgiving, and the voice of melody.

REVELATION xxi. 4. The LORD will wipe away tears from off every eye, and there shall be no more death, neither shall there be any pain.

ISAIAH xxv. 8. And the rebuke of His people shall He take away.

lii. 8. Thy watchmen shall lift up the voice; together shall they sing, when the LORD shall bring again Zion.

9. Break forth into singing, for the LORD hath redeemed His people.

HILLS.

1176

PSALM cxix. 9, 11. Wherewithal shall a young man cleanse his way, that he should not sin against Thee?

10. With my whole heart have I sought Thee: O let me not go wrong out of Thy commandments.

9. Wherewithal shall a young man cleanse his way? even by ruling himself after Thy word.

HILLS.

1177

HABAKKUK iii. 3. GOD came from Teman, and the Holy One from Mount Paran. His glory covered the heavens, and the earth was full of His praise.

6. He stood, and measured the earth; He beheld, and drove asunder the nations; and the everlasting mountains were scattered, the perpetual hills did bow: His ways are everlasting. Hallelujah. Amen.

STEGGALL.

1178

JEREMIAH xiii. 15. Hear ye, and give ear; be not proud: for the LORD hath spoken.

16. Give glory to the LORD your GOD, before He cause darkness, and before your feet stumble upon the dark mountains, and, while ye look for light, He turn it into the shadow of death, and make it gross darkness.

STEGGALL.

1179

ECCLESIASTES xii. 1. Remember now thy Creator in the days of thy youth, while the evil days come not, nor the years draw nigh, when thou shalt say, I have no pleasure in them:

2. While the sun, or the light, or the moon, or the stars, be not darkened, nor the clouds return after the rain ·

3. In the day when the keepers of the house shall tremble, and the strong men shall bow themselves, and the grinders cease because they are few, and those that look out of the windows be darkened,

4. And the doors shall be shut in the streets, when the sound of the grinding is low, and he shall rise up at the voice of the bird, and all the daughters of music shall be brought low.

7. Then shall the dust return to the earth as it was, and the spirit shall return unto GOD Who gave it.

8. Vanity of vanities, saith the preacher, all is vanity.

1. Remember now thy Creator in the days of thy youth.

[13. Fear GOD and keep His commandments, for this is the whole duty of man.]

STEGGALL.

1180 W. S. BENNETT, vv. 1. 13.

1181

ECCLESIASTICUS l. 6. He was as the morning star in the midst of a cloud, and as the moon at the full:

7. As the sun shining upon the temple of the Most High, and as the rainbow giving light in the bright clouds.

WISDOM iii. 6. As gold in the furnace hath He tried him, and received him as a burnt offering.

ECCLESIASTICUS l. 22. Therefore bless ye the LORD of all, Which only doeth wondrous things, and dealeth with us according to His mercy.

29. Blessed be the LORD for ever. Amen.

STEGGALL.

1182

PSALM lxxvii. 1. I will cry unto GOD with my voice, even unto GOD will I cry with my voice, and He shall hearken unto me.

3. When I am in heaviness, I will think upon GOD: when my heart is vexed, I will complain.

5. I have considered the days of old, and the years that are past.

6. I commune with my own heart; in the night I search out my spirit.

11, 12. I will remember the works of the LORD, and will call to mind Thy wonders of old time. I will think also of all Thy works. I will remember the works of the LORD, and my talking shall be of Thy doings.

STEGGALL.

1183

PSALM lxviii. 19. Praised be the LORD: even the GOD Who helpeth us, and poureth His benefits upon us.

9. Thou, O GOD, sentest a gracious rain upon Thine inheritance, and refreshedst it when it was weary.

cxlv. 16. Thou openest Thine hand, and fillest all things living with plenteousness.

lxv. 12. Thou crownest the year with Thy goodness: Thy clouds drop fatness.

lxviii. 19. Praised be the LORD: even the GOD Who helpeth us, and poureth His benefits upon us. Hallelujah.

STEGGALL.

1184

COLLECT

For Ascension Day.

Grant, we beseech Thee, Almighty GOD, that like as we do believe Thy only begotten Son our LORD JESUS CHRIST to have ascended into the heavens; so we may also in heart and mind thither ascend, and with Him continually dwell, Who liveth and reigneth with Thee and the Holy Ghost, one GOD, world without end. Amen.

LAHEE.

1185

ST. LUKE XXIV. 1. Now on the first day of the week, very early in the morning, they came to the sepulchre.

2. And they found the stone rolled away from the sepulchre.

3. And they entered in, and found not the Body of the LORD JESUS.

20. But now is CHRIST risen from the dead, and become the first-fruits of them that slept.

21. For since by man came death, by man came also the resurrection of the dead.

22. For as in Adam all die, even so in CHRIST shall all be made alive. Amen.

LAHEE.

1186

PSALM CIV. 1. Praise the LORD, O my soul: O LORD my GOD, Thou art become exceeding glorious; Thou art clothed with majesty and honour.

13. He watereth the hills from above: the earth is filled with the fruit of Thy works.

14. He bringeth forth grass for the cattle, and green herb for the service of men;

15. That He may bring food out of the earth, and wine that maketh glad the heart of man, and oil to make him a cheerful countenance, and bread to strengthen man's heart.

1. Praise the LORD, O my soul.

LAHEE.

1187

Psalm xxiv. 1. The earth is the Lord's, and the fulness thereof; the world, and they that dwell therein.

2. For He hath founded it upon the seas, and established it upon the floods.

3. Who shall ascend into the hill of the Lord, or who shall stand in His holy place?

4. He that hath clean hands and a pure heart, [who hath not lifted up his soul unto vanity, nor sworn deceitfully.]

5. He shall' receive the blessing from the Lord, and righteousness from the God of his salvation.

[6. This is the generation of them that seek Him, that seek thy face, O Jacob.

7. Lift up your heads, O ye gates; be ye lift up, ye everlasting doors, and the King of Glory shall come in.

8. Who is the King of Glory? The Lord mighty in battle.

9. Lift up your heads, O ye gates; lift them up, ye everlasting doors, and the King of Glory shall come in.

10. Who is the King of Glory? The Lord of Hosts, He is the King of Glory.]

TRIMNELL.

1188 Spohr, vv. 1–10.

1189

Psalm xcvii. 1. The Lord is King, the earth may be glad thereof : yea, the multitude of the isles may be glad thereof.

2. Clouds and darkness are round about Him: righteousness and judgment are the habitation of His seat.

10. O ye that love the Lord, see that ye hate the thing which is evil.

12. Rejoice in the Lord, ye righteous, and give thanks.

TRIMNELL.

1190

*Psalm cxxxiv. 1. Behold now, praise ye the Lord, ye servants of the Lord ;

2. Ye that by night stand in the house of the Lord, even in the house of the Lord our God.'

* Sometimes sung as a separate Anthem.

3. Lift up your hands in His holy Temple and praise the LORD.

4. The LORD, that made heaven and earth, give thee blessing out of Sion.

CALKIN.

1191

ST. MATTHEW xxi. 9. Blessed is He that cometh in the Name of the LORD. Hosanna in the highest !
O Lamb of GOD, that takest away the sins of the world,
Have mercy upon us.
O Lamb of GOD, that takest away the sins of the world,
Grant us Thy peace.

CALKIN.

1192

PSALM xxxiv. 1. I will alway give thanks unto the LORD : His praise shall ever be in my mouth.

2. My soul shall make her boast in the LORD : the humble shall hear thereof, and be glad.

3. O praise the LORD with me, and let us magnify His Name together.

4. I sought the LORD, and He heard me : yea, He delivered me out of all my fear.

5. They had an eye unto Him, and were lightened, and their faces were not ashamed.

6. Lo, the poor crieth, and the LORD heareth him : yea, and saveth him out of all his troubles. Amen.

[7. The angel of the LORD tarrieth round about them that fear Him, and delivereth them.

8. O taste, and see, how gracious the LORD is : blessed is the man that trusteth in Him.

9. O fear the LORD, ye that are His saints : for they that fear Him lack nothing.

10. The lions do lack, and suffer hunger : but they who seek the LORD shall want no manner of thing that is good.

11. Come, ye children, and hearken unto me : I will teach you the fear of the LORD.

19. Great are the troubles of the righteous : but the LORD delivereth him out of all.

22. The LORD delivereth the souls of His servants, and all they that put their trust in Him shall not be destitute.

xxxiii. 21. Let Thy merciful kindness, O LORD, be upon us; like as we do put our trust in Thee.]

CALKIN.

1193 J. C. BECKWITH, KING, WHITFELD, vv. 1–3. [Hallelujah.]
1194 BLOW, HUMPHREYS, and TURNER (*conjointly*), vv. 1–4, 6; Psalm xxxiii. v. 21.
1195 BOYCE, vv. 1–3, 6, 9. Hallelujah.
1196 CROFT, vv. 1–4, 7, 8, 1. Hallelujah.
1197 GOSS, A. H. MANN, vv. 8–10.
1198 R. JACKSON, vv. 1–5, 1. Amen.
1199 KEETON, vv. 1, 3, 8–10, 1, 3.
1200 MACFARREN, T. ROGERS, v. 8.
1201 NAYLOR, vv. 3, 6, 7, 3.
1202 OUSELEY, vv. 3, *8, 9, 19, 22. Amen.
1203 PATTISON, vv. 3, 4, 8.
1204 SULLIVAN, vv. 8–11.

* This verse is sometimes sung as a separate Anthem.

1205

PSALM li. (*Paraphrase.*) O GOD, have mercy upon me, according to Thy loving-kindness, and wash me throughly from mine iniquity, and cleanse, O cleanse me from my sin. For I confess mine iniquity, my grievous sin is ever before me. Against Thee only have I transgressed and done so evilly. Behold, in sin I was created, and in iniquity I was conceived. But Thou desirest truth in the inmost heart, and wisdom Thou wilt give to me. With hyssop purge me, I shall be clean; wash me, and then I shall be whiter than snow. And from Thy presence O cast me not away; Thy Holy Spirit take not from me. Restore to me the joy of Thy salvation, and with Thy Spirit free, do Thou uphold me evermore. And then, transgressors shall learn of me Thy righteous ways, and sinners thus shall be converted, LORD, unto Thee. My lips, O LORD, do Thou open, and my mouth shall shew forth Thy praise. Sacrifice Thou desirest not, else would I offer it. The sacrifices of GOD are a broken spirit; a broken spirit and a contrite heart, O GOD, Thou wilt not despise. My lips, O LORD, do Thou open, and my mouth shall shew forth Thy praise.

CALKIN.

1206

PSALM xcvii. 12. Rejoice in the LORD, ye righteous.

8. Zion heard and rejoiced, and the daughters of Judah were glad.

1. The LORD is King, let the earth be glad thereof, yea. let the multitude of the isles be glad thereof.

CALKIN.

1207

PSALM xxxiv. 22. The LORD redeemeth the soul of His servants, and none of them that trust in Him shall be desolate.

CALKIN, MACFARREN.

1208

PSALM lxv. 9. Thou visitest the earth, and blessest it : Thou makest it very plenteous.

10. The river of GOD is full of water : Thou preparest their corn, for so Thou providest for the earth.

11. Thou waterest her furrows, Thou sendest rain into the little valleys thereof: Thou makest it soft with the drops of rain, Thou blessest the increase thereof.

12. Thou crownest the year with Thy goodness, and Thy clouds drop fatness.

13. They shall drop upon the dwellings of the wilderness, and the little hills shall rejoice on every side.

14. The folds shall be full of sheep, the valleys shall stand so thick with corn, they shall laugh and sing.

CALKIN, ELLIOTT.

1209

DANIEL ix. 9. To the LORD our GOD belong mercies and forgivenesses, though we have rebelled against Him ;

10. Neither have we obeyed the voice of the LORD our GOD, to walk in His laws which He set before us.

CALKIN, HARRIS. OUSLEY.

1210

WISDOM iii. 1. The souls of the righteous are in the hand of GOD.

2, 3. In the sight of the unwise they seem to die : their departure is taken for misery, their going from us to be utter destruction : but they are in peace.

v. 14. The hope of the ungodly is like the dust which is blown away with the wind, like a thin froth that is driven away with the storm ; like the smoke which is dispersed with the tempest, and passeth away as the remembrance of a guest that tarrieth but a day.

15. But the righteous live for evermore ; their reward is with the LORD, and the care of them is with the Most High.

16. With His right hand shall He cover them, and with His arm shall He protect them. They shall receive a glorious kingdom, and a beautiful crown from the LORD's hand.

REA.

1211

ISAIAH ix. 2. The light hath shined upon us.

6. For unto us a Child is born, unto us a Son is given, and of His Kingdom there shall be no end.

PSALM xcviii. 1. Sing unto the LORD a new song, for He hath done marvellous things. Alleluia. Amen.

SILAS, VERRINDER

1212

PSALM xliii. 4. I will go to the Altar of GOD, even unto the GOD of my joy and gladness : and upon the harp will I give thanks unto Thee, O GOD, my GOD.

REAY.

1213

PSALM xliv. 23. O LORD, why sleepest Thou ? awake, and be not absent from us for ever.

24. Wherefore hidest Thou Thy face ?

26. Arise, and help us, and deliver us for Thy mercy's sake.

1. We have heard with our ears, O LORD, our fathers have declared unto us, what Thou hast done in their time of old.

REAY.

1214

PHILIPPIANS iv. 4. Rejoice in the LORD alway, and again I say, Rejoice.

5. The LORD is at hand.

PSALM lxxxv. 1. O LORD, Thou hast blessed Thy land, Thou hast turned away the captivity of Jacob.

REAY.

1215

ISAIAH lx. 3. The Gentiles shall come to Thy light, and kings to the brightness of Thy glory.

PSALM xcviii. 4. And all the ends of the earth have seen the salvation of our GOD. Hallelujah.

REAY.

1216

ROMANS v. 5 The love of GOD is shed abroad in our hearts by His Spirit that dwelleth in us.

PSALM ciii. 1. Praise the LORD, O my soul, and all that is within me praise His holy Name.

REAY.

1217

PHILIPPIANS iii. 20, 21. Our conversation is in Heaven; from whence we look for the Saviour, the LORD JESUS CHRIST: Who shall change our vile body, that it may be fashioned like unto His glorious Body.

GILBERT.

1218

REVELATION i. 7. Behold, He cometh with clouds; and every eye shall see Him, and they also which pierced Him; and all the kindreds of the earth shall wail because of Him. Even so, Amen.

MALACHI iv. 1. For, behold, the day cometh, that shall burn as an oven; all that do wickedly shall be stubble; and the day that cometh shall burn them up, saith the LORD of Hosts.

2. But unto you that fear My Name shall the Sun of righteousness arise with healing in His wings ; and ye shall go forth, and grow up.

3. And ye shall tread down the wicked, saith the LORD of Hosts.

GILBERT.

1219

PSALM lxxii. 1. Give the king Thy judgments, O GOD, and Thy righteousness unto the king's son.

2. He shall judge Thy people with righteousness, and Thy poor with judgment.

3. The mountains shall bring peace to the people, and the little hills, by righteousness.

17. His Name shall endure for ever, and all men shall be blessed in Him.

18. Blessed be the LORD GOD, the GOD of Israel, Who only doeth wondrous things.

19. And blessed be His glorious Name for ever, and let the whole earth be filled with His glory.

18. Blessed be the LORD GOD, the GOD of Israel, Who only doeth wondrous things.

BROWN.

1220

PROVERBS viii. 1. Doth not wisdom cry, and understanding put forth her voice ?

4. Unto you, O men, I call : and my voice is to the sons of man.

17. I love them that love me, and those that seek me early shall find me.

32. Now, therefore hearken unto me, O ye children, for blessed are they that keep my ways.

33. Hear instruction, and be wise, and refuse it not.

34. Blessed is the man that heareth me, watching daily at my gates, waiting at the posts of my doors. Amen.

HAKING.

1221

1 TIMOTHY i. 17. Now unto the King eternal, immortal, invisible, the only wise GOD, be honour and glory for ever and ever. Amen.

OAKELEY.

1222

1. Comes, at times, a stillness as of even,
  Steeping the soul in memories of love,
 As when the glow is sinking out of heaven,
  As when the twilight deepens in the grove.

2. Comes, at length, a sound of many voices,
  As when the waves break lightly on the shore,
 As when at dawn the feather'd choir rejoices,
  Singing aloud, because the night is o'er.

3. Comes, at times, a voice of days departed,
  On the dying breath of evening borne,
 Sinks then the trav'ller, faint and weary-hearted,
  " Long is the way," it whispers, " and forlorn."

4. Comes, at last, a voice of thrilling gladness,
  Borne on the breezes of the rising day,
 Saying, " The LORD shall make an end of sadness,"
  Saying, " The LORD shall wipe all tears away."

OAKELEY.

1223

COLLECT

For St. Michael and all Angels.

O everlasting GOD, Who hast ordained and constituted
the services of angels and men in a wonderful order, mercifully grant that as Thy holy angels alway do Thee service
in heaven, so by Thy appointment they may succour and
defend us on earth, through JESUS CHRIST our LORD. Amen.

OAKELEY.

1224

COLLECT

For the Twenty-third Sunday after Trinity.

O GOD, our refuge and strength, Who art the author
of all godliness, be ready, we beseech Thee, to hear the
devout prayers of Thy Church, and grant that those
things which we ask faithfully we may obtain effectually,
through [JESUS CHRIST our LORD. Amen.

OAKELEY.

1225

PSALM cxvii. 1. O praise the LORD, all ye nations, praise Him, all ye people.

2. For His merciful kindness is great towards us, and the truth of the LORD endureth for ever. Praise ye the LORD. Amen.

OAKELEY.

1226

1 ST. JOHN v. 4. Whatsoever is born of GOD overcometh the world : and this is the victory that overcometh the world, even our faith.

7. For there are three that bear record in heaven, the Father, the Word, and the Holy Ghost : and these three are One.

8. And there are three that bear witness in earth, the Spirit, and the water, and the blood : and these three agree in one.

REVELATION iv. 8. Holy, Holy, Holy, LORD GOD ALMIGHTY, Which was, and is, and is to come.

xi. 17. We give Thee thanks, O LORD GOD ALMIGHTY, Which art, and wast, and art to come : because Thou hast taken to Thee Thy great power, and hast reigned.

OAKELEY.

1227

PSALM xiii. 1. LORD, how long wilt Thou forget me? how long wilt Thou hide Thy face in anger from me?

2. How long within my soul shall I seek for counsel, having sorrow in my spirit daily? how long must I see mine enemy over me triumph?

3. Hear my cry, and consider me, LORD, my GOD : O let mine eyes be lightened, lest I sleep in death, lest I slumber in darkness ; have mercy and let mine eyes be lightened, lest slumber of death should o'ertake me :

4. And lest my foe, triumphant, boast he hath prevailed, and they that trouble me rejoice with cruel joy that I am brought low.

5. But I will trust Thy mercy, which Thou hast shown toward me. My heart doth rejoice, for Thou all-gracious art.

6. My mouth shall sing Thy praises for all Thy goodness to me.

BRAHMS.

1228

A saving health to us is brought,
  Of grace and love begotten ;
No more do works avail us aught,
  They pass away forgotten.
Our faith is set in JESUS CHRIST,
Whose death for us hath all sufficed ;
He is our loving Saviour.

BRAHMS.

1229

REQUIEM.

No. 1

ST. MATTHEW v. 4. Blessed are they that mourn, for they shall have comfort.

PSALM cxxvi. 5. They that sow in tears shall reap in joy.

6. Who goeth forth and weepeth, and beareth precious seed, shall doubtless return with rejoicing, and bring his sheaves with him.

ST. MATTHEW v. 4. Blessed are they that mourn, for they shall have comfort.

No. 2

1 PETER i. 24. Behold, all flesh is as the grass, and all the goodliness of man is as the flower of grass. For lo, the grass withereth, and the flower thereof decayeth.

JAMES v. 7. Now therefore be patient, O my brethren, unto the coming of CHRIST. See how the husbandman waiteth for the precious fruit of the earth, and hath long patience for it, until he receive the early rain and the latter rain. So be ye patient.

1 PETER i. 24. Behold, all flesh is as the grass, and all the goodliness of man is as the flower of grass. For lo, the grass withereth, and the flower thereof decayeth.

25. But the LORD'S Word endureth for evermore.

ISAIAH xxxv. 10. The redeemed of the LORD shall return again, and come rejoicing unto Zion. Gladness, joy everlasting upon their head, shall be : joy and gladness, these shall be their portion, and tears and sighing shall flee from them.

No. 3

PSALM xxxix. 4. LORD, make me to know the measure of my days on earth; to consider my frailty, that I must perish.

5. Surely all my days here are as an handbreadth to Thee, and my lifetime is nought to Thee.

6, 5. Verily, mankind walketh in a vain show, and his best state is altogether vanity. He passeth away like a shadow: he is disquieted in vain; he heapeth up riches, and cannot tell who shall gather them.

7. Now, LORD, O what do I wait for? my hope is in Thee.

WISDOM iii. 1. But the righteous souls are in the hand of GOD: nor pain nor grief shall nigh them come.

No. 4

PSALM lxxxiv. 1. How lovely is Thy dwelling-place, O LORD of Hosts!

2. For my soul it longeth, yea, fainteth for the courts of the LORD: my soul and body crieth out, yea, for the living GOD.

4. Blest are they that dwell within Thy house, they praise Thy Name evermore.

1. How lovely is Thy dwelling-place.

No. 5

ST. JOHN xvi. 22. Ye now are sorrowful: howbeit, ye shall again behold Me, and your heart shall be joyful, and your joy no man taketh from you.

ISAIAH lxvi. 13. Yea, I will comfort you, as one whom his own mother comforteth. Look upon Me: ye know that for a little time labour and sorrow were Mine, but at the last I have found comfort.

No. 6

HEBREWS xiii. 14. Here on earth we have no continuing city, we seek one to come.

1 CORINTHIANS xv. 51, 52. I unfold you a mystery; we shall not all sleep when He cometh, but we shall all be changed, in a moment, in the twinkling of an eye, at the sound of the trumpet: for the trumpet shall sound, and the dead shall be raised incorruptible, and we all shall be changed.

54. Then what of old was written? the same shall be brought to pass : for death is swallowed up in victory.

55. Grave, where is thy triumph? Death, O where is thy sting?

REVELATION iv. 11. Worthy art Thou to be praised, LORD of honour and might : for Thou hast earth and heaven created, and for Thy good pleasure all things have their being, and were created. LORD, Thou art worthy to be praised.

No. 7

REVELATION xiv. 13. Blessed are the dead which die in the LORD, from henceforth, saith the Spirit, that they rest from their labours, and that their works do follow after them.

BRAHMS.

1230

PSALM lx. 1. O GOD, Thou hast cast us out, and scattered us abroad : Thou hast also been displeased, O turn Thee unto us again.

2. Thou hast moved the land, and divided it : heal the sores thereof, for it shaketh.

4. Thou hast given a banner to them that fear Thee, that they may triumph because of the truth.

5. Therefore were Thy beloved delivered.

xciv. 12, 13. Blessed is the man whom Thou chastenest, O LORD, and teachest him in Thy law : that Thou mayest give him patience in time of adversity.

xc. 1. LORD, Thou hast been our refuge from one generation to another.

4. For a thousand years in Thy sight are but as yesterday, seeing that is past as a watch in the night.

2. Before the mountains were brought forth, or ever the earth and the world were made, Thou art GOD, from everlasting, and world without end.

17. Prosper Thou the work of our hands upon us : O prosper Thou our handy work.

MENDELSSOHN.

1231

Acts xiv. 23. And when they had ordained them elders in every church, and had prayed with fasting, they commended them to the Lord on Whom they had believed.

Isaiah lxi. 6. They shall be named the Priests of the Lord : men shall call them the Ministers of our God.

8. The Lord will direct their work in truth, and He will make an everlasting covenant with them.

Lord, pour Thy Spirit from on high,
    And Thine ordained servants bless.
Graces and gifts to each supply,
    And clothe Thy Priests with righteousness.
So when their work is finished here,
    They may in hope their charge resign,
So when their Master shall appear,
    They may with crowns of glory shine. Amen.

Thorne.

1232

Behold, the Lord the Ruler is come, and dominion, power, and empire are in His Hand.

Psalm lxxii. 1. Give the king Thy judgments, O God, and Thy righteousness unto the king's son.

Thorne.

1233

Psalm lvii. 1. Be merciful unto me, O God, be merciful unto me : for my soul trusteth in Thee : yea, in the shadow of Thy wings will I make my refuge, until these calamities be overpast.

2. I will cry unto God Most High, unto God that performeth all things for me.

3. He shall send from Heaven, and save me from the reproach of him that would swallow me up. God shall send forth His mercy and His truth.

4. My soul is among lions, and I lie even among them that are set on fire, even the sons of men, whose teeth are spears and arrows, and their tongue a sharp sword

5. Set up Thyself, O GOD, above the heavens, and Thy glory above all the earth.

6. They have prepared a net for my steps; my soul is bowed down: they have digged a pit before me, and are fallen into the midst of it themselves.

5. Set up Thyself, O GOD, above the heavens, and Thy glory above all the earth.

7. My heart is fixed, O GOD, my heart is fixed: I will sing and give praise.

8. Awake up, my glory; awake, lute and harp; I myself will awake right early.

9. I will praise Thee, O LORD, among the people: I will sing unto Thee among the nations.

10. For Thy mercy is great unto the heavens, and Thy truth unto the clouds.

11. Set up Thyself, O GOD, above the heavens: let Thy glory be above all the earth.

THORNE.

1234

1 CORINTHIANS xv. 20. Hallelujah! CHRIST is risen!

ISAIAH xxv. 9. He is the LORD! We will be glad and rejoice in His salvation.

REVELATION i. 5. He is the first begotten of the dead, and the Prince of the kings of the earth.

*Unto Him that loved us, and washed us from our sins in His own Blood,

6. And hath made us kings and priests unto GOD and His Father; to Him be glory and dominion for ever and ever. Amen.

THORNE.

1235 HANCOCK, Revelation i. 5* (*Unto Him*), 6.

1236

ST. JOHN i. 1. In the beginning was the Word, and the Word was with GOD, and the Word was GOD.

14. And the Word was made Flesh, and dwelt among us, (and we beheld His glory, the glory as of the only begotten of the Father,) full of grace and truth.

ST. MARK xi. 9. Hosanna! Blessed is He that cometh in the Name of the LORD.

10. Hosanna in the highest.

THORNE.

1237

PSALM xlvii. 1. O clap your hands together, all ye people; O sing unto GOD with the voice of melody.

2. For the LORD is high, and to be feared: He is the great King upon all the earth.

3. He shall subdue the people under us, and the nations under our feet.

4. He shall choose out an heritage for us, even the worship of Jacob, whom He loved.

5. GOD is gone up with a merry noise, and the LORD with the sound of the trumpet.

6. O sing praises, sing praises unto our GOD; O sing praises, sing praises unto our King.

7. For GOD is the King of all the earth, O sing ye praises with understanding.

8. GOD reigneth over the heathen: GOD sitteth upon His holy seat.

9. The princes of the people are joined unto the people of the GOD of Abraham; for GOD, Which is highly exalted, doth defend the earth, as it were with a shield.

THORNE.

1248

EXODUS xiii. 5. The LORD hath brought us into a land flowing with milk and honey.

9. Let the LORD's law be ever in our mouth, for with a strong hand hath the LORD brought us out of Egypt.

PSALM cxxxvi. 1. O give thanks unto the LORD, for He is gracious, and His mercy endureth for ever.

THORNE.

1249

PSALM lv. 23. O cast thy burden upon the LORD, and He shall nourish thee: He shall not suffer the righteous to fall for ever.

THORNE.

1250

1. In humble faith and holy love,
    The song of saints and martyrs sing;
   That incense which to GOD above
    Blest angels and archangels bring.

2. Three mystic rays in glory shine
    From the tremendous Godhead's Throne,
   These in one source doth faith combine,
    In Three we praise one GOD alone,

3. In this sad vale of tears below,
    Our anchor this of faith and love;
   Till GOD His vision shall bestow,
    In CHRIST's triumphant Church above.

4. To GOD our Father raise the voice,
    Invisible, Immortal King!
   In our Redeemer's strength rejoice;
    And to the sacred Spirit sing. Amen.

GARRETT.

1251

ISAIAH ii. 2. It shall come to pass in the last days, that the mountain of the LORD's house shall be established in the top of the mountains, and shall be exalted above the hills; and all nations shall flow unto it.

3. And many people shall say, Come ye, and let us go up to the mountain of the LORD, to the house of the GOD of Jacob; and He will teach us of His ways, and we will walk in His paths: for out of Zion shall go forth the law, and the word of the LORD out of Jerusalem.

5. O house of Jacob, come ye, and let us walk in the light of the LORD.

NAHUM i. 7. The LORD is good, a stronghold in the day of trouble: and He knoweth them that trust in Him.

ISAIAH ii. 4. The LORD shall judge among the nations, and shall rebuke many people: and they shall beat their swords into ploughshares, and their spears into pruning-hooks: nation shall not lift up sword against nation, neither shall they learn war any more.

xi. 9. They shall not hurt nor destroy in all My holy mountain: for the earth shall be full of the knowledge of the LORD, as the waters cover the sea. Amen.

GARRETT.

1252

PSALM xliii.

Just Judge of Heaven, against my foes
  Do Thou assert my injur'd right,
O set me free, my GOD, from those
  That in deceit and wrong delight.
Since Thou art still my only stay,
  Why leav'st Thou me in deep distress?
Why go I mourning all the day,
  While me insulting foes oppress?

Let me with light and truth be blest,
  Be these my guides to lead the way;
Till on Thy holy hill I rest,
  And in Thy sacred temple pray.
Why then cast down my soul? and why
  So much opprest with anxious care?
On GOD thy GOD for aid rely,
  Who will thy ruin'd state repair.

Then will I there fresh altars raise
  To GOD Who is my only joy,
And well-tun'd harps, with songs of praise,
  Shall all my grateful hours employ.
Why then cast down my soul? and why
  So much opprest with anxious care?
On GOD thy GOD for aid rely,
  Who will Thy ruin'd state repair.

TATE, &c.

1253

PSALM xxxiii.   20–22.

Our soul on GOD with patience waits,
  Our help and shield is He ;
Then, LORD, let still our hearts rejoice,
  Because we trust in Thee.

The riches of Thy mercy, LORD,
  Do Thou to us extend,
Since we, for all we want, or wish,
  Alone on Thee depend.

GARRETT.

1254

PSALM cvii. 8. Praise ye the LORD for His goodness, and declare the wonders that He doeth for the children of men.

cxlv. 15. The eyes of all wait on Thee, O LORD, and Thou givest them meat in due season.

16. Thou openest Thine hand, and fillest all things living with plenteousness.

GARRETT.

1255

PSALM cxlv. 9. The LORD is loving unto every man : and His mercy is over all His works.

10. All Thy works praise Thee, O GOD : and Thy saints give thanks unto Thee.

11. They shew the glory of Thy Kingdom : and talk of Thy power ;

12. That Thy power, Thy glory, and the mightiness of Thy Kingdom, might be known unto men.

13. Thy Kingdom is an everlasting Kingdom : and Thy law is the truth.   Amen.

GARRETT.

1256

ISAIAH xl. 3. The voice of one crying in the wilderness, Prepare ye the way of the LORD, make straight in the desert a highway for our God

4. Every valley shall be exalted, and every mountain and hill made low: the crooked shall be made straight, and the rough places shall be made plain.

5. And the glory of the LORD shall be revealed, and all flesh shall see it together: for the mouth of the LORD hath spoken it.

6. The voice said, Cry. What shall I cry? All flesh is grass, and all the goodliness thereof is as the flower of the field:

8. The grass withereth, the flower fadeth: but the word of our GOD shall stand for ever. Amen.

GARRETT.

1257

PSALM cxxv. 1. They that put their trust in the LORD shall be even as the mount Sion, which may not be removed, but standeth fast for ever.

2. The hills stand about Jerusalem: even so standeth the LORD round about His people, from this time forth for evermore, (xxiv. 6) and delivereth them out of all their troubles.

cxxv. 4. Do well, O LORD, unto those that are good and true of heart.

GARRETT.

1258

JOEL ii. 12. Thus saith the LORD, Turn ye even to Me with all your heart, and with fasting, and with weeping, and with mourning.

HOSEA vi. 1. Come, and let us return unto the LORD: for He hath torn, and He will heal us; He hath smitten, and He will bind us up.

ISAIAH i. 18. Come now, and let us reason together, saith the LORD: though your sins be as scarlet, they shall be as white as snow; though they be red as crimson, they shall be as wool.

19, 20. If ye be willing and obedient, ye shall eat the good of the land: but if ye refuse and rebel, ye shall be devoured with the sword: for the mouth of the LORD hath spoken it.

PSALM ciii. 8, 9. The LORD is full of compassion and mercy, plenteous in goodness, neither keepeth He His anger for ever.

13. Yea, like as a father pitieth his own children, even so is the LORD merciful to them that fear Him.

ii. 12. O blessed are they that trust in Him.

ISAIAH ii. 5. O house of Jacob, come ye, and let us walk in the light of the LORD.

GARRETT.

1259

ROMANS viii. 1. There is no condemnation to them which are in CHRIST JESUS, who walk not after the flesh, but after the Spirit.

9. Now if any man have not the Spirit of CHRIST, he is none of His.

14. For as many as are led by the Spirit of GOD, they are the sons of GOD.

IRONS.

1260

PSALM lxi. 1. Hear my cry, O GOD; attend unto my prayer.

2. From the end of the earth will I cry unto Thee, when my heart is overwhelmed : lead me to the rock that is higher than I.

3. For Thou hast been a shelter for me, and a strong tower from the enemy.

4. I will abide in Thy tabernacle for ever : I will trust in the covert of Thy wings.

5. For Thou, O GOD, hast heard my vows : Thou hast given me the heritage of those that fear Thy Name.

6. Thou wilt prolong the king's life, and his years as many generations.

7. He shall abide before GOD for ever : O prepare mercy and truth, which may preserve him.

8. So will I sing praise unto Thy Name for ever, that I may daily perform my vows.

VERRINDER.

1261

St. Luke ii. 8. There were shepherds abiding in the field, keeping watch over their flocks by night.

Thro' the silent night,
O Father, Lord, be near;
O keep us and our flocks
From danger and from fear.

9. And lo, the angel of the Lord came upon them, and the glory of the Lord shone around about them : and they were sore afraid.

10. And the angel said unto them, Fear not : for, behold, I bring you good tidings of great joy, which shall be to you and all people.

11. For unto you is born this day a Saviour, Which is Christ the Lord.

13. And suddenly there was with the angel a multitude of the heavenly host, praising God, and saying,

14. Glory to God in the highest, and peace on earth, good will towards men. Amen.

Sangster.

1262

Proverbs iii. 13. Happy is the man that findeth wisdom, and the man that getteth understanding.

14. For the merchandise of it is better than silver, and the gain thereof than fine gold.

15. She is more precious than rubies, and all the things thou canst desire are not to be compared unto her.

16. Length of days is in her right hand, and in her left hand riches and honour.

17. Her ways are ways of pleasantness, and all her paths are peace.

ii. 2. If thou incline thine ear unto wisdom, and apply thine heart to understanding ;

3. If thou criest after knowledge, and liftest up thy voice for understanding ;

4. If thou seekest her as silver, and searchest for her as for hid treasures ;

5. Then shalt thou understand the fear of the Lord, and find the knowledge of God.

Prout.

1263 J. F. Bridge, v. 13. 1, 1,

1264

St. Mark xiii. 33. Watch and pray: for ye know not when the time is.

35, 36. Watch ye therefore: lest, coming suddenly, He find you sleeping.

37. I say unto all, Watch.

LOCKETT.

1265

Genesis viii. 21, 22. And the Lord said: While the earth remaineth, seedtime and harvest, cold and heat, summer and winter, day and night shall not cease.

Psalm civ. 24. O Lord, how manifold are Thy works: in wisdom hast Thou made them all; the earth is full of Thy riches.

cxlv. 16. Thou openest Thine hand, and fillest all things living with plenteousness.

lxv. 9, 12. Thou visitest the earth, and blessest it: Thou crownest the year with Thy goodness.

13. The pastures are clothed with flocks; the valleys are covered over with corn; they shout for joy, they also sing.

cxxxvi. 1. O give thanks unto the Lord, for He is good: for His mercy endureth for ever.

25. He giveth food to all flesh, for His mercy endureth for ever

cl. 6. Let every thing that hath breath praise the Lord.

TORRANCE.

1266

I Chronicles xxix. 10. Blessed art Thou, Lord, for ever and ever.

11. Thine, O Lord, is the greatness, and the power, and the glory, and the victory, and the majesty: for all that is in the heaven and in the earth is Thine: Thine is the Kingdom, O Lord, and Thou art exalted as head above all.

12, 14. Both riches and honour come of Thee, and of Thine own have we given Thee.

16. O Lord our God, all we have prepared to build an house for Thine holy Name cometh of Thine hand, and is all Thine own.

1 KINGS viii. 27. But will GOD in very deed dwell on the earth? behold, the heaven and heaven of heavens cannot contain Thee; how much less this house that we have builded?

28. Yet have Thou respect unto the prayer of Thy servants, and to their supplication,

29. That Thine eyes may be open toward this house night and day, even toward the place whereof Thou hast said, My Name shall be there.

ST. JOHN iv. 24, 23. GOD is a Spirit: and they that worship Him must worship Him in spirit and in truth; for such doth the Father seek to worship Him.

PSALM xcvi. 9. O worship the LORD in the beauty of holiness: let the whole earth stand in awe of Him,

xcix. 9. For the LORD our GOD is holy.

TORRANCE.

1267

DEUTERONOMY xxxii. 1. Give ear, O ye heavens, and I will speak; and hear, O earth, the words of my mouth.

*2. My doctrine shall drop as the rain, My speech shall distil as the dew, as the small rain upon the tender herb, and as showers upon the grass: *

3. Because I will publish the Name of the LORD: ascribe ye greatness unto our GOD. Amen.

ARMES.

—— Sometimes sung as a separate Anthem.

1268

PSALM xxxiii. 1. Rejoice in the LORD, O ye righteous: for it becometh well the just to be thankful.

xxi. 1. The king shall rejoice in Thy strength, O LORD: exceeding glad shall he be of Thy salvation.

7. And why? because the king putteth his trust in the LORD.

xxxiii. 3. Sing unto the LORD a new song: sing praises lustily unto Him with a good courage.

4. For the word of the LORD is true, and all His works are faithful.

5. He loveth righteousness and judgment: the earth is full of the goodness of the LORD.

lxxi.   18. O what great troubles and adversities hast Thou shewed me, and yet didst Thou turn and refresh me.

19. Thou hast brought me to great honour, and comforted me on every side.

20. Therefore will I praise Thee and Thy faithfulness, O God ; unto Thee will I sing, O Thou Holy One of Israel.

cxviii.   14. The LORD is my strength and my song, and has become my salvation.

24. This is the day which the LORD hath made, we will rejoice and be glad in it.

29. O give thanks unto the LORD, for He is gracious, and His mercy endureth for ever.   Amen.

ARMES.

1269

PSALM xxvii.   1. The LORD is my light, and my salvation ; whom then shall I fear ? the LORD is the strength of my life, of whom then shall I be afraid ?

2. When the wicked, even mine enemies, and my foes, came upon me to eat up my flesh ; they stumbled and fell.

3. Though an host of men were laid against me, yet shall not my heart be afraid : and though there rose up war against me, yet will I put my trust in Him.

4. One thing have I desired of the LORD, which I will require, even that I may dwell in the house of the LORD all the days of my life, to behold the fair beauty of the LORD, and to visit His temple.

5. For in the time of trouble He shall hide me in His tabernacle : yea, in the secret place of His dwelling shall He hide me, and set me up upon a rock of stone.

6. And now shall He lift up mine head above mine enemies round about me.

7. Therefore will I offer in His dwelling an oblation with great gladness : I will sing, and speak praises unto the LORD.

9. [My heart hath talked of Thee, seek ye my face ·] Thy face, LORD, will I seek.

10. O hide not Thou Thy face from me. nor 'cast Thy servant away ; displeasure.

11. Thou hast been my succour : leave me not. neither forsake me, O God of my salvation.

13. Teach me Thy way, O LORD, and lead me in the right way, because of mine enemies.

14. Deliver me not over into the will of mine adversaries; for there are false witnesses risen up against me, and such as speak wrong.

15. I should utterly have fainted, but that I believe verily to see the goodness of the LORD in the land of the living.

16. O tarry thou the LORD's leisure: be strong, and He shall comfort thine heart; and put thou thy trust in the LORD.

ARMES.

1270 BOYCE, vv. 1, 3–7.
1271 J. H. CLARKE, vv. 1–5, 7.
1272 CROFT, vv. 1–3. Hallelujah.
1278 JORDAN, vv. 1–4, 7. Amen.
1274 LAWES, vv. 1, 5, 4, 10, 15.
1275 OUSELEY, vv. 4, 5, 7. Hallelujah. Amen.
1276 PURCELL, vv. 1, 3, 5–7. Hallelujah.

1277

MICAH iv. 2. Come, and let us go up to the mountain of the LORD: to the house of the GOD of Jacob. He will teach us His ways, we will walk in His paths. For the law shall go forth of Zion, and the word of the LORD from Jerusalem.

BARRETT.

1278

JOEL ii. 12. Turn ye unto Me, saith the LORD, with all your hearts, and with fasting, and with weeping, and with mourning.

13. Rend your hearts, and not your garments, and turn to the LORD your GOD: for He is merciful, kind, and gracious, slow to anger, and of great kindness, and repenteth Him of the evil.

BARRETT.

1279

PSALM cvii. 21. O that men would praise the LORD for His goodness, and for His wonderful works to the children of men.

23. They that go down to the sea ·in ships, that do business in great waters ;

24. These see the works of the LORD, and His wonders in the deep.

25. For He commandeth and raiseth the stormy wind, which lifteth up the waves thereof.

28. Then they cry unto the LORD in their trouble, and He bringeth them out of their distresses.

29. He maketh the storm a calm, so that the waves thereof are still.

21. O that men would praise the Lord for His goodness, and for His wonderful works to the children of men.

BARTHOLOMEW.

1280

ST. LUKE ii. 10. Behold, I bring you good tidings of great joy, which shall be to all people.

11. For unto you is born this day in the city of David, a Saviour, Which is CHRIST the LORD.

Yea, LORD, we greet Thee,
Born this happy morning;
JESU, to Thee be glory given ;
Word of the Father,
Now in flesh appearing :
O come, let us adore Him,
O come, let us adore Him,
O come, let us adore Him, CHRIST the LORD. Amen.

HALL.

1281

Brightest and best of the sons of the morning,
Dawn on our darkness and lend us thine aid ;
Star of the East, the horizon adorning,
Guide where our Infant Redeemer is laid.

Cold on His cradle the dewdrops are shining,
I · li , His head with the beasts of the stall ;
Angel adore Him in slumber reclining,
Maker, and Monarch, and Saviour of all.

Say, shall we yield Him, in costly devotion,
  Odours of Edom and offerings divine ;
Gems of the mountain and pearls of the ocean,
  Myrrh from the forest, and gold from the mine ?

Vainly we offer each ample oblation,
  Vainly with gifts would His favour secure ;
Richer by far is the heart's adoration,
  Dearer to GOD are the prayers of the poor.

HALL.

1282

PSALM cxlvii. 12. Praise the LORD, O Jerusalem : praise thy GOD, O Sion.

13. For He hath made fast the bars of thy gates, and hath blessed thy children within thee.

14. He maketh peace in thy borders, and filleth thee with the flour of wheat.

20. He hath not dealt so with any nation, neither have the heathen knowledge of His laws.

[cl. 6. Praise ye the LORD.]

Praise GOD from Whom all blessings flow,
Praise Him all creatures here below,
Praise Him above, ye heavenly host,
Praise Father, Son, and Holy Ghost.   Amen.

HALL.

1283 W. HAYES, vv. 12-14, 20 ; Psalm cl. 6.
        Hallelujah.   Amen.
1284 BLISS, vv. 12-14, 12.

1285

ISAIAH lxv. 17. Thus saith the LORD, Behold, I create new heavens and a new earth : and the former shall not be remembered nor come into mind.

18. But be ye glad and rejoice for ever in that which I create : for, behold, I create Jerusalem a rejoicing, and her people a joy.

REVELATION xxi. 1. And I saw a new heaven and a new earth : for the first heaven and earth were passed away.

2. And I saw the *Holy City*, New Jerusalem.

ISAIAH vi. 3. Holy, Holy, Holy, is the LORD of Hosts.

REVELATION xxi. 3. And I heard a great voice out of heaven, saying, Behold, the tabernacle of GOD is with men, and He will dwell with them, and they shall be His people, and GOD shall be with them, and be their GOD.

4. And GOD shall wipe away all tears from their eyes: and there shall be no more death, neither sorrow, nor crying, nor any more pain; for the former things are passed away.

ISAIAH vi. 3. Holy, Holy, Holy, is the LORD of Hosts.

1. I saw also the LORD sitting upon a throne, high and lifted up, and His train filled the temple.

2. Above it stood the Seraphin.

3. And one cried unto another, and said, Holy, Holy, Holy, is the LORD of Hosts.

*REVELATION xv. 3. Great and marvellous are Thy works, LORD GOD Almighty; just and true are Thy ways, Thou King of Saints! Alleluia! Amen.

From the Te Deum. To Thee all Angels cry aloud: the Heavens, and all the Powers therein. To Thee Cherubim, and Seraphim continually do cry, Holy, Holy, Holy, is the LORD of Hosts.

PSALM xc. 2. Before the mountains were brought forth, or the earth, or world were made, Thou art from everlasting. Alleluia! Amen.*

(*From "The Holy City,"* Nos. 10, 16.) GAUL.

—— Sometimes sung as a separate Anthem.

1286

ST. MATTHEW xxi. 9. Hosanna to the Son of David. Blessed is He that cometh in the Name of the LORD. Hosanna in the highest.

ST. MARK vii. 37. He hath done all things well:

ST. MATTHEW xi. 5. The blind receive their sight, the lame walk, the lepers are cleansed, and the deaf hear, the dead are raised up, to the poor is the gospel preached, which is salvation to them that believe.

ST. MARK xiii. 31. Heaven and earth shall pass away: but His words shall not pass away.

REVELATION xxii. 14. Blessed are they that do His commandments, for they shall never see death.

GAUL.

1287. HAVERGAL, MACFARREN, T. F. WALMISLEY,

1288

HABAKKUK ii. 20. The LORD is in His holy temple: let all the earth keep silence before Him.

ST. MATTHEW xviii. 20. For thus saith the LORD, where two or three are gathered together in My Name, there am I in the midst of them.

PSALM xcv. 6. O come, let us worship and fall down, and kneel before the LORD our Maker.

PSALM xcvi. 6. Glory and worship are before Him: power and honour are in His sanctuary.

7. Ascribe unto the LORD, O ye kindreds of the people, worship and power.

8. Ascribe unto the LORD the honour due unto His Name : bring presents and come into His courts.

9. O worship the LORD in the beauty of holiness : let the whole earth stand in awe of HIM.

SAUNDERS.

1289 { ELLIOTT, C. H. LLOYD, } { STAINER, THORNE, } v. 20. [Hallelujah. Amen].

1290

ST. LUKE i. 68. Blessed be the LORD GOD of Israel, for He hath visited and redeemed His people.

70. As He declared by the mouth of His holy prophets, and as He promised to our fathers to grant to us, that being delivered from our enemies, we might serve HIM without fear, in holiness and righteousness all the days of our life.

68. Blessed be the LORD GOD of Israel, for He hath visited and redeemed His people.

TURPIN.

1291

PSALM iv. 9. I will lay me down in peace and take my rest, for it is Thou, LORD, only, that makest me to dwell in safety.

v. 3. My voice shalt Thou hear betimes, O LORD ; early in the morning will I direct my prayer to Thee';

4. For Thou art the GOD, that hast no pleasure in wickedness, neither shall any evil dwell with Thee.

iv. 9. I will lay me down in peace and take my rest, for it is Thou, LORD, only, that makest me to dwell in safety.

COLBORNE.

1292 { BATES, CLIPPINGDALE, GADSBY, HILES, } v. 9. [Amen]

1293

PSALM viii. 1. O LORD our Governour, how excellent is Thy Name in all the world! Thou that hast set Thy glory above the heavens.

3. I will consider the heavens, the work of Thy fingers, the moon and the stars which Thou hast ordained.

4. LORD, what is man, that Thou art mindful of him? or the son of man, that Thou so regardest him?

5. Thou hast made him a little lower than the angels, to crown him with glory and honour. Amen.

COLBORNE.

1294

1 CORINTHIANS xv. 49. As we have borne the image of the earthy, we shall also bear the image of the heavenly.

57. Thanks be to GOD.

BARNBY.

1295 •

ST. LUKE ii. 10. Behold, I bring you good tidings of great joy, which shall be to all people.

11. For unto you is born this day in the city of David, a Saviour, Which is CHRIST the LORD.

14. Glory to GOD in the highest, and on earth peace, good will toward men.

O JESU, born of Virgin pure,
  Immortal glory be to Thee,
Whom, with the Father, we adore,
  And Holy Ghost eternally. Amen.

BARNBY.

1296 Goss, vv. 10, 11.

1297

ST. LUKE i. 68. Blessed be the LORD GOD of Israel, for He hath visited and redeemed His people,

69. And hath raised up a mighty salvation for us in the house of His servant David,

70. As He spake by the mouth of His holy Prophets, which have been since the world began.

PSALM xlv. 3. Thou art fairer than the children of men, full of grace are Thy lips, because GOD hath blessed Thee for ever.

ZECHARIAH ix. 9. Sing, O daughter of Zion; shout, O daughter of Jerusalem. Behold, thy King cometh unto thee.

Angels, from the realms of glory,
Wing your flight o'er all the earth :
Ye who sang creation's story,
Now proclaim Messiah's birth;
Come and worship,
Worship CHRIST, the new-born King. Amen.
BARNBY.

1298

ISAIAH lii. 9. Break forth into joy; sing together, ye waste places of Jerusalem, for the LORD hath comforted His people. He hath redeemed Jerusalem.

10. The LORD hath made bare His holy arm in the sight of all His people.

Hymns of praise then let us sing   Hallelujah!
Unto CHRIST our Heavenly King,   Hallelujah!
Who endured the Cross and grave, Hallelujah!
Sinners to redeem and save.   Hallelujah! Amen.
BARNBY.

1299

ISAIAH xlv. 8. Drop down, ye heavens, from above, and let the skies pour down righteousness : let the earth open, and let them bring forth salvation, and let righteousness spring up together.

ST. JOHN i. 14. The Word was made flesh, and dwelt among us (and we beheld His glory, the glory as of the only begotten of the Father), full of grace and truth.

PSALM lxxxv. 9. His salvation is nigh them that fear Him : that glory may dwell in our land.

10. Mercy and truth are met together : righteousness and peace have kissed each other.

11. Truth shall flourish out of the earth : and righteousness hath looked down from heaven. Alleluia. Amen.
BARNBY.

1300 MACFARREN, v. 8. Amen.

1301

St. Matthew xxv. 34. Come, ye blessed of my Father, inherit the Kingdom prepared for you from the foundation of the world.

Psalm lxviii. 32. Praise the Lord, all the whole earth. Amen.

Barnby.

1302

1. Holy night! peaceful night!
Through the darkness beams a light,
Yonder where they sweet vigil keep,
O'er the Babe, Who, in silent sleep
Rests in heavenly peace.

2. Silent night! holiest night!
Darkness flies, and all is light!
Shepherds hear the angels sing—
" Hallelujah! Hail the King!
Jesus the Saviour is here!"

3. Holiest night! peaceful night!
Child of Heaven! O how bright
Thou didst smile when Thou wast born!
Blessed was the happy morn,
Full of heavenly joy.

4. Silent night! holiest night!
Guiding Star, O lend Thy light!
See the eastern wise men bring
Gifts and homage to our King!
Jesus the Saviour is here!

5. Silent night! holiest night!
Wondrous Star! O lend Thy light!
With the angels let us sing
Hallelujah to our King!
Jesus our Saviour is here!

Barnby.

1303

PSALM xcii. 1. It is a good thing to give thanks unto the LORD, and to sing praises unto Thy Name, O most High.

2. To tell of Thy loving-kindness early in the morning, and of Thy truth in the night season.

11. The righteous shall flourish like a palm-tree, and spread abroad like a cedar in Libanus. ·

12. Such as are planted in the house of the LORD shall flourish in the courts of the house of our GOD. ·

[13. They also shall bring forth more fruit in their age, and shall be fat and well-liking.]

14. That they may shew how true the LORD my strength is, and that there is no unrighteousness in Him.

7. Thou, LORD, art most Highest for evermore.

To GOD the Father, GOD the Son,
GOD the Spirit, Three in One,
Praise, honour, might, and glory be,
From age to age eternally. Amen.

BARNBY.

1804 CALKIN, vv. 11–14.

1305

ROMANS xiii. 11. It is high time to awake out of sleep, for now is our salvation nearer than when we believed.

12. The night is far spent, the day is at hand; let us therefore cast off the works of darkness, and let us put on the whole armour of light.

BARNBY.

1806 M. SMITH, v. 12.

1307

PSALM xciv. 1. O LORD GOD, to Whom vengeance belongeth, Thou GOD, to Whom vengeance belongeth, shew Thyself.

2. Arise, Thou Judge of the world, and reward the proud after their deserving.

BARNBY.

1308

PSALM ix. 1. I will give thanks unto Thee, O LORD, with my whole heart; I will speak of all Thy marvellous works.

2. I will be glad and rejoice in Thee; yea, my songs will I make of Thy Name, O Thou most Highest.

cxlv. 15. The eyes of all wait upon Thee, O LORD; and Thou givest them their meat in due season.

16. Thou openest Thine hand, and fillest all things living with plenteousness.

> Therefore unto Him we raise
> Hymns of glory, songs of praise;
> To the Father, and the Son,
> And the Spirit, Three in One,
> Honour, might, and glory be,
> Now, and through eternity.

cxlvii. 5. Great is our LORD, and great is His power; yea, and His wisdom is infinite.

cxlv. 20. He preserveth all them that love Him, but scattereth abroad all the ungodly. Amen.

BARNBY.

1309

PSALM cxxi. 1. I will lift up mine eyes unto the hills, from whence cometh my help.

2. My help cometh even from the LORD, Who hath made heaven and earth.

3. He will not suffer thy foot to be moved.

4. He that keepeth thee shall neither slumber nor sleep.

7, 6. The LORD shall preserve thee, so that the sun shall not burn thee by day, neither the moon by night. Amen.

BARNBY.

1310

King all-glorious, LORD of Hosts Almighty, Thou art revealed in victory, over all the world of light ascended. We pray Thee leave us not comfortless, but send the great Father's promise on us, the Spirit of Truth, Thy Spirit. Alleluia. Amen.

BARNBY.

1311

PSALM cxv. 1. Not unto us, O LORD, not unto us, but unto Thy Name give the praise, for Thy loving mercy.

12. The LORD hath been mindful of us, and He shall bless us.

cxxxvi. 1. O give thanks unto the LORD, for He is gracious, and His mercy endureth for ever.

2. O give thanks unto the GOD of all gods, for His mercy endureth for ever.

3. O thank the LORD of all lords, for His mercy endureth for ever.

BARNBY.

1312 KING, Psalm cxxxvi. 1–3.

1313

O Father blest, Thy Name we sing,
  Whose power the world upholdeth :
And Thee, O CHRIST, of Kings the King,
  Whose love our souls enfoldeth :
And Thee, O Holy Ghost, we praise ;
  O be our Guide through all our days.

O Father, Son, and Holy Ghost,
  The GOD of our salvation,
The Church on earth and heavenly host
  Are one in adoration.
With heart and mind may we adore
  Our gracious GOD for evermore. Amen.

. BARNBY.

1314

PSALM civ. 24. O LORD, how manifold are Thy works : in wisdom hast Thou made them all ; the earth is full of Thy riches.

lxv. 14. The valleys stand so thick with corn, that they laugh and sing.

ciii. 2. Praise the LORD, O my soul, and forget not all His benefits.

BARNBY.

1315

PSALM ciii.   20. O praise the LORD, all ye His angels, ye that excel in strength, ye that fulfil His command-ment, and hearken unto the voice of His words.

21. O praise the LORD, all ye His hosts, ye servants of His that do His pleasure.

22. O speak good of the LORD, all ye works of His, in all places of His dominion.

1. Praise the LORD, O my soul, and all that is within me, praise His holy Name.

lxvii.   7. Praise our GOD, ye people.

lxix.   35. Let heaven and earth praise the LORD. Amen.

BARNBY.

1316 BARNBY, vv. 20, 1. Amen.

1317

O risen LORD ! O CHRIST ascended !
O Prince of Peace ! Thy toils on earth are ended,
And Thou art on Thine everlasting Throne adored.
O hear our songs, O hear our prayers and praises,
          O grant us peace !
Thy pilgrim church still raises
Her ardent gaze to Thee.
          As for Thy rest she longs,
Thou, JESUS King, to Heav'n ascending,
With gifts of peace Thy pierced palms extending,
          Shedd'st worlds of hope and joy.
O risen LORD, O Prince of Peace, to Thee we sing
          Alleluia. Amen.

BARNBY.

1318

ZECHARIAH ii.   10. Sing and rejoice, O daughter of Sion, for lo, I come, and I will dwell in the midst of thee, saith the LORD thy GOD.

13. Be silent, O all flesh, before the LORD, for He is raised up out of His holy habitation.

O come, all ye faithful,
Joyful and triumphant,
O come ye, O come ye to Bethlehem ;
Come and behold Him
Born, the King of Angels;
O come, let us adore Him,
O come, let us adore Him,
O come, let us adore Him, CHRIST the LORD. Amen.

BARNBY.

·1319

Sweet is Thy mercy, LORD ;
Before Thy mercy seat
My soul adoring pleads Thy word,
And owns Thy mercy sweet.

Where'er Thy Name is blest,
Where'er Thy people meet,
There I delight in Thee to rest,
And find Thy mercy sweet.

Light Thou our weary way,
Lead Thou our wand'ring feet ,
That while we stay on earth we may
Still find Thy mercy sweet.

Thus shall the heavenly host
Hear all our songs repeat,
To Father, Son, and Holy Ghost,
Our joy, Thy mercy sweet. Amen.

BARNBY.

1320

TITUS ii. 11. The grace of GOD that bringeth salvation hath appeared to all men.

PSALM xcviii. 4. And all the ends of the world have seen the salvation of our GOD.

ST. MATTHEW xxi. 9. Blessed be He that cometh in the Name of the LORD ; Hosanna in the Highest.

ST. JOHN i. · 4. In Him was life, and the life was the light of men.

BARNBY.

1321

Psalm lxii. 1. My soul truly waiteth still upon God, r of Him cometh my salvation.

2. He verily is my strength and my salvation : He is my defence, so that I shall not greatly fall.

3. How long will ye imagine mischief against every man ? ye shall be slain all the sort of you ; yea, as a tottering wall shall ye be, and like a broken hedge.

4. Their device is only how to put him out whom God will exalt : their delight is in lies ; they give good words with their mouth, but curse with their heart.

5. Nevertheless, * my soul, wait thou still upon God, for my hope is in Him.

6. He truly is my strength and my salvation : He is my defence, so that I shall not fall.

7. In God is my health, and my glory, the rock of my might, and in God is my trust.

8. O put your trust in Him alway, ye people : pour out your hearts before Him, for God is our hope.

9. As for the children of men, they are but vanity : the children of men are deceitful upon the weights, they are altogether lighter than vanity itself.

10. O trust not in wrong and robbery, give not your-selves unto vanity : if riches increase, set not your heart upon them.

11. God spake once, and twice I have also heard the same, that power belongeth unto God ;

12. And that Thou, Lord, art merciful : for Thou rewardest every man according to his work.

[cxlv. 2. Every day will I give thanks unto Thee, and praise Thy Name for ever and ever.

Cobb.

1322 Attwood, vv. 1, 2. 8.
1323 Batten, vv. 1, 2, 12.
1324 Carissimi, vv. 1, 2, 8 ; cxlv. 2.
1325 Greene, vv. 1, 2, 8, 7. Hallelujah. Amen.
1326 Kent, vv. 1, 2, 5, 2, 7, 8. Hallelujah.
1327 E. G. Monk, vv. 1, 2, 1, 8.
1328 Naylor, vv. 1, 6–8.
1329 Rea, vv. 1. 7.
1330 Read. vv. *5 (My soul, wait thou). 6 8.
1331 T. F. Walmisley. vv. *5 (My soul, wait thou), 6, 7.

1332

PSALM cxxx. . 1. Out of the deep have I called unto Thee, O LORD : LORD, hear my voice.

2. O let Thine ears consider well the voice of my complaint.

3. If Thou, LORD, wilt be extreme to mark what is done amiss, O LORD, who may abide it?

4. For there is mercy with Thee, therefore shalt Thou be feared.

5. I look for the LORD; my soul doth wait for Him : in His word is my trust.

6. My soul fleeth unto the LORD before the morning watch, I say, before the morning watch.

7. O Israel trust in the LORD, for with the LORD there is mercy, and with Him is plenteous redemption.

8. And He shall redeem Israel from all his sins.

BUNNETT, NAYLOR.

1333 PRINCE ALBERT, vv. 1–4, 6, 4, 1.
1334 ALCOCK, ALDRICH, CALKIN, HATTON, MOZART,
    J. C. PRING, T. A. WALMISLEY, vv. 1–4 [Amen.]
1335 COLBORNE, vv. 1, 2.
1336 CROFT, vv. 1–8, 7.
1337 F. E. GLADSTONE, vv. 1–5, 7.
1338 E. J. HOPKINS, vv. 1–3, 7, 8. Amen.
1339 PURCELL, vv. 1–7.
1340 VERRINDER, v. 1.

1341

ZEPHANIAH iii. 14. Sing, O daughter of Zion; shout, O Israel; be glad and rejoice with all the heart, O daughter of Jerusalem.

15. The LORD hath taken away thy judgments, He hath cast out thine enemy : the King of Israel, even the LORD, is in the midst of thee : thou shalt not see evil any more.

14. Sing, O daughter of Zion; shout, O Israel; be glad and rejoice with all the heart, O daughter of Jerusalem.

16. In that day it shall be said to Jerusalem. Fear thou not : and to Zion, Let not thine hands be slack.

17. The LORD thy GOD in the midst of thee is mighty; He will save, He will rejoice over thee with joy; He will rest in His love, He will joy over thee with singing.

14. Sing, O daughter of Zion; shout, O Israel; be glad and rejoice with all the heart, O daughter of Jerusalem.

NAYLOR.

1342

REVELATION vii. 12. Blessing, glory, wisdom, and thanks, power and might, be unto our GOD, for evermore.

PSALM cxlviii. 1. O praise the LORD of heaven: praise Him in the height.

12. O praise the Name of the LORD: His Name is excellent, and His praise above heaven and earth.

PSALM cvi. 46. Blessed be the LORD GOD of Israel from everlasting, and world without end: and let all the people say, Amen.

TOURS.

1343

PSALM xcv. 1. O come, let us sing to the LORD: let us heartily rejoice in the strength of our salvation.

2. Let us come before His presence with thanksgiving, and shew ourselves glad in Him with psalms.

1. O come, let us sing to the LORD: let us heartily rejoice in the strength of our salvation.

3. For the LORD is a great GOD, and a great King above all gods.

And now, on this our festal day,
Thy bounteous hand confessing,
Upon Thine Altar, LORD, we lay
The first-fruits of Thy blessing;
By Thee the souls of men are fed
With gifts of grace supernal,
Thou, Who dost give us earthly bread,
Give us the Bread Eternal.

PSALM cxiii. 2. Blessed be the Name of the LORD, from this time forth for evermore.

cvi. 1. O give thanks unto the LORD, for He is gracious, and His mercy endureth for ever.

TOURS.

1344

1 Corinthians v. 7. Christ our Passover is sacrificed for us,

8. Therefore let us keep the feast ; not with the, old leaven, nor with the leaven of malice and wickedness, but with the unleavened bread of sincerity and truth.

Romans vi. 9. Christ being raised from the dead dieth no more : death hath no more dominion over Him.

10. For in that He died, He died unto sin once : but in that He liveth, He liveth unto God.

11. Likewise reckon ye also yourselves to be dead indeed unto sin : but alive unto God through Jesus Christ our Lord.

1 Corinthians xv. 20. Christ is risen from the dead, and become the first fruits of them that slept.

21. For since by man came death, by man came also the resurrection of the dead.

22. For as in Adam all die, even so in Christ shall all be made alive.

Glory be to the Father, &c.

Tours.

1845 J. H. Clarke, Sydenham, 1 Corinthians xv. 20-22. [Amen.]

1846 Elvey, Romans vi. 9.

1847 Goss, E. V. Hall, 1 Corinthians, v. 7, 8. [Hallelujah. Amen.]

1348

Acts xvii. 31. God hath appointed a day, in the which He will judge the world in righteousness by that man whom He hath ordained ; whereof He hath given assurance unto all men, in that He hath raised Him from the dead.

Psalm lxxxv. 10. Mercy and truth are met together : righteousness and peace are met together.

1 Corinthians xv. 57. Thanks be to God, Which giveth us the victory through our Lord Jesus Christ. Amen.

Tours.

1349

Psalm cl. 1. Praise God in His holiness, praise Him in the firmament of His power.

cxlviii. 12. Young men and maidens, old men and children, praise the Name of the Lord.

cxlix. 5. Let the saints be joyful with glory: let them rejoice in their beds.

cl. 6. Let everything that hath breath praise the Lord.

1. Praise God in His holiness. Amen.

Tours.

1350

Isaiah xlix. 13. Sing, O heavens, and be joyful, O earth; and break forth into singing, O mountains.

St. Luke ii. 11. For unto us is born this day, in the city of David, a Saviour, Which is Christ the Lord.

St. Matthew xxi. 9. Hosanna to the Son of David. Blessed is He that cometh in the Name of the Lord. Hosanna in the highest. To God on high be glory, and peace on earth to men.

O come, all ye faithful,
Joyful and triumphant :
O come ye, O come ye to Bethlehem ;
Come and behold Him
Born, the King of Angels ;
O come, let us adore Him,
O come, let us adore Him,
O come, let us adore Him, Christ the Lord. Amen.

Tours.

1351

Genesis viii. 22. While the earth remaineth, seed time and harvest, and cold and heat, and summer and winter, and day and night shall not cease.

Psalm lxvi. 1. O be joyful in God, all ye lands : sing praises unto the honour of His Name, make His praise to be glorious.

Psalm lxv. 10. The river of God is full of water: Thou preparest their corn, for so Thou providest the earth.

11. Thou waterest her furrows, Thou sendest rain into the little valleys thereof: Thou makest it soft with the drops of rain, and blessest the increase of it.

PSALM lxviii. 32. Sing unto GOD, O ye kingdoms of the earth, O sing praises unto the LORD.

TOURS.

1352

PSALM cxvi. 1–7. I am well pleased that the LORD hath heard the voice of my supplication. That He hath inclined His ear to me: as long then as I live will I be calling on Him. The sorrows of death came about me: the pains of hell gat hold upon me. I found affliction and grief, then on the Name of the LORD did I call: O LORD, do Thou deliver my soul. How gracious is the LORD, and how just: yea, our GOD is merciful. He guards the simple folk: I was in misery, He gave me help. To thy rest, then, my soul, do I bid thee be turning: because the LORD hath rewarded thee.

RHEINBERGER.

1353

PSALM xxxiii. 1–4, 9, 12. Rejoice, O ye righteous, in the LORD: yea, for thankfulness becometh you. Praise ye the LORD. Sing to Him a new made song with sound of harp and psaltery. For the word of the LORD is faithful: yea, and all His works are righteous. He did speak, and it was performed: He did charge, and it was created. Blessed are they whom the LORD doth call His own.

RHEINBERGER.

1354

PSALM xx. 1. The LORD give ear to thee in the day of thy trouble; the Name of JEHOVAH be thy defence;

2. From out of His dwelling His help afford thee, and from Sion send His strength for thee.

5. Behold, we will be joyful in Thy salvation, and triumph in the Name of the LORD our GOD.

RHEINBERGER.

1355

PSALM liii. The fool within his heart hath spoken, There is no GOD. Corrupt are they all become in their doings, and no man, none there is that doeth good. GOD out of Heaven mankind regarded : were there any that had understanding, and after GOD were seeking ? They all are turned backward, and none there is that doeth good, ah ! no man. Upon the LORD they have not called. In His wrath He hath despised them. Who gives salvation to Israel out of Sion ? When GOD shall bring His own from captivity, then shall Jacob be in gladness, and Israel shall be joyful.

RHEINBERGER.

1356

PSALM ii. 1-4, 11, 12. Why assemble the heathen, and peoples imagine a vain thing ? Behold, the kings of the earth stand up, and thus their counsel take, against the LORD and against His anointed. Let us then break their bonds asunder, and cast away their yoke. But from Heaven the LORD shall despise them : He shall laugh them to scorn. Serve the LORD with fear : praise ye Him with trembling. They are blessed, all, who put their trust in Him.

RHEINBERGER.

1357

JOEL ii. 12. Thus saith the LORD, turn ye to Me with all your heart, and with fasting, and with weeping, and with mourning;

13. And rend your heart, and not your garments, and turn unto the LORD your GOD : for He is gracious and merciful, slow to anger, and of great kindness, and repenteth Him of the evil.

EZEKIEL xxxiii. 11. Turn ye, turn ye from your evil ways; for why will ye die, O house of Israel ?

PSALM xxv. 16. Turn Thee unto me, and have mercy upon me. for I am desolate and afflicted.

17. The troubles of my heart are enlarged. O bring Thou me out of my distresses.

GOD of my life, to Thee I call,
Afflicted at Thy feet I fall ;
When the great water-floods prevail,
Leave not my trembling heart to fail.

HEBREWS xii. 3. For consider Him that endured such contradiction of sinners against Himself, lest ye be wearied and faint in your minds.

PHILIPPIANS iii. 10, 11. That ye may know Him, and the power of His resurrection, and the fellowship of His sufferings, being made conformable unto His death ; if by any means ye might attain unto the resurrection of the dead.

COBB.

1358

ISAIAH lx. 1. Surge, illuminare, Jerusalem ; quia venit lumen tuum, et gloria Domini super te orta est.

2. Quia ecce, tenebræ operient terram, et caligo populos : super te autem orietur Dominus, et gloria Ejus in te videbitur.

3. Et ambulabunt Gentes in lumine tuo, et reges in splendore ortus tui.

COBB.

English Version.

1. Arise, shine, for thy light is come, and the glory of the LORD is risen upon thee.

2. For, behold, darkness shall cover the earth, and gross darkness the people : but the LORD shall arise upon thee, and His glory shall be seen upon thee.

3. And the Gentiles shall come to thy light, and kings to the brightness of thy rising.

COBB, ELVEY.

1359 A. H. MANN, vv. 1, 2.

1360

O Thou most merciful JESU, of souls the blest Redeemer, grant to us, LORD, this our humble desire : By the agony of Thy sacred and pitiful heart, wash in Thy precious all-cleansing Blood sinners laden with heaviest guilt in their agony and now to-day in the pains of dying. Sacred Heart, once with agony smitten, O have mercy on all passing souls, O have mercy, JESU, on all passing souls !

CHAMPNEYS.

1361

The Hosts of Heaven upraise to GOD
A joyful song of praise.

To Thee my will resigning,
To Thee all cares consigning,
My GOD, I will outpour
Sweet praise in hours of gladness,
E'en too in hours of sadness,
Until life's changing scenes be o'er.

Before I was in being,
Thy love and power, all-seeing,
Encompassed me around.
Thy constant love has sought me
And peace and gladness brought me
Where I but pain and sorrow found.

ZOELLER.

1362

PSALM cxvi.   5. Gracious is the LORD, and righteous :
yea, our GOD is merciful.

6. The LORD preserveth the simple : I was brought low,
and He helped me.

7. Return unto thy rest, O my soul, for the LORD hath
dealt bountifully with thee.

5. Gracious is the LORD and righteous ; yea, our GOD is
merciful.   Amen.

R. JACKSON.

1363

*ISAIAH xl.   9. Alleluia.   O Zion, that bringest good
tidings, get thee up into the high mountain ; O Jerusalem,
that bringest good tidings, lift up thy voice with strength ;
be not afraid ; say to the cities of Judah, Behold your
GOD ! Alleluia. Amen.*

O that Birth, for ever blessèd,
When the Virgin, full of grace,
By the HOLY GHOST conceiving,
Bare the Saviour of our race.

`——*` Sometimes sung as a separate Anthem

And the Babe, the world's Redeemer,
  First revealed His sacred Face,
    Evermore and evermore.

Of the Father's Love begotten
  Ere the worlds began to be,
He is Alpha and Omega,
  He the Source, the ending He,
Of the things that are, that have been,
  And that future years shall see,
    Evermore and evermore.

STAINER.

1364

EXODUS xx. 18. And all the people saw the thunderings and the lightnings, and the noise of the trumpet, and the mountain smoking : and when the people saw it, they removed and stood afar off.

19. And they said unto Moses, Speak thou with us, and we will hear : but let not GOD speak with us, lest we die.

When GOD of old came down from Heaven,
  In power and wrath He came;
Before His feet the clouds were riven,
  Half darkness and half flame.

But when He came the second time,
  He came in power and love :
. Softer than gale at morning prime,
  Hovered His holy Dove.   Amen.

1 JOHN iv. 7. Beloved, let us love one another, for love is of GOD ; and every one that loveth is born of GOD, and every one that loveth knoweth GOD.

12. If we love one another, GOD dwelleth in us, and His love is perfected in us.

Come, LORD, come, Wisdom, Love, and Power,
  Open our ears to hear ;
Let us not miss the accepted hour,
  Save. LORD, by love or fear.   Amen.

Novello's Collection   P

STAINER.

1365

Isaiah lii. 1. Awake, awake! put on thy strength, O Zion; put on thy beautiful garments, O Jerusalem, the holy city: for henceforth there shall no more come unto thee the uncircumcised and the unclean.

2. Shake thyself from the dust; arise, and sit down, O Jerusalem; loose thyself from the bands of thy neck, O captive daughter of Zion.

1. Awake, awake! put on thy strength, O Zion; put on thy beautiful garments. Awake, awake!

7. How beautiful upon the mountains are the feet of him that bringeth good tidings, that publisheth peace, that publisheth salvation; that saith unto Zion, thy God reigneth!

8. Thy watchmen shall lift up the voice; with the voice together shall they sing, for they shall see eye to eye, when the Lord shall bring again Zion.

9. Break forth into joy, sing together, ye waste places of Jerusalem: for the Lord hath comforted His people, He hath redeemed Jerusalem.

10. The Lord hath made bare His holy arm in the eyes of all the nations; and all the ends of the world have seen the salvation of our God.

9. Break forth into joy, sing together, ye waste places of Jerusalem. Hallelujah. Amen.

STAINER.

—— Sometimes sung as a separate Anthem.

1366

Isaiah liv. 7. For a small moment have I forsaken thee; but with great mercies will I gather thee.

8. In a little wrath I hid My face from thee for a moment; but with everlasting kindness will I have mercy on thee, saith the Lord thy Redeemer.

10. For the mountains shall depart, and the hills be removed; but My kindness shall not depart from thee, neither shall the covenant of My peace be removed, saith the Lord that hath mercy upon thee

STAINER.

1367

PSALM liv. 4. Behold, GOD is my helper : The LORD is with them that uphold my soul.

6. An offering of a free heart will I give Thee, and praise Thy Name, O LORD, for it is good.

STAINER.

1368

ISAIAH xlv. 8. Drop down, ye heavens, from above, and let the skies pour down righteousness : let the earth open, and let them bring forth salvation, and let righteousness spring forth together.

ST. LUKE i. 28. Hail, thou that art highly favoured, the LORD is with thee.   Blessed art thou among women.

31. Behold, thou shalt conceive and bring forth a Son, and shall call His Name JESUS.

32. He shall be great, and shall be called The Son of the Highest ;

33. And of His Kingdom there shall be no end.

PSALM xlv. 2. Thou art fairer than the children of men, full of grace are thy lips, because GOD hath blessed thee for ever.   Amen.

STAINER.

1369

REVELATION vii. 13. Hallelujah.   What are these which are arrayed in white robes? and whence came they ?

14. These are they which came out of great tribulation, and have washed their robes, and made them white in the Blood of the Lamb.

15. Therefore are they before the Throne of GOD, and serve Him day and night in His temple : [and He that sitteth on the Throne shall dwell among them.]

16. They shall hunger no more, neither thirst any more ; neither shall the sun light on them, nor any heat.

17. For the Lamb Which is in the midst of the Throne shall feed them, and shall lead them unto living fountains of waters, and GOD shall wipe away all tears from their eyes.

STAINER.

1370 DYKES, vv. 14 17. Amen.

1371

EPHESIANS IV. 30. Grieve not the Holy Spirit of GOD, whereby ye are sealed unto the day of redemption.

31. Let all bitterness, and wrath, and anger, and clamour, and evil speaking, be put away from you, with all malice.

32. And be ye kind one to another, tender-hearted, forgiving one another, even as GOD for CHRIST'S sake hath forgiven you.

STAINER.

1372

ST. MATTHEW xxi. 9. Hosanna in the highest.

ISAIAH lxiii. 1. Who is this that cometh from Edom, with dyed garments from Bozrah? This that is glorious in His apparel, travelling in the greatness of His strength? I that speak in righteousness, mighty to save.

2. Wherefore art Thou red in Thine apparel, and Thy garments like him that treadeth in the winefat?

3. I have trodden the winepress alone; and of the people there was none with Me: I will tread them in Mine anger, and trample them in My fury.

4. For the day of vengeance is in Mine heart, and the year of My redeemed is come.

And when as Judge Thou drawest nigh,
The secrets of all hearts to try;
When sinners meet their awful doom,
And saints attain their heavenly home;

O let us not, for evil past,
Be driven from Thy face at last;
But with the blessed evermore
Behold Thee, love Thee, and adore. Amen.

STAINER.

1373

REVELATION i. 8. I am Alpha and Omega, the beginning and the ending, saith the LORD, Which is, and Which was, and Which is to come, the Almighty.

From The Communion Service. Holy, Holy, Holy, LORD GOD of Hosts. Heaven and earth are full of Thy Glory; Glory be to Thee, O LORD most High. Amen.

STAINER.

1374

Ecclesiasticus li.   13. I desired wisdom openly in my prayer.

14. I prayed for her before the Temple, and will seek her out even unto the end.

15. Even from the flower till the grape was ripe hath my heart delighted in her.   .

iv.   14. They that serve her shall minister unto the Holy One.

St. Matthew ii.   1. When Jesus was born in Bethlehem of Judæa, in the days of Herod the King, behold, there came wise men from the East unto Jerusalem,

2. Saying, Where is He, born King of the Jews? for we have seen His star, and are come to worship Him.

9. And lo, the star, which they saw in the East, went before them, till it came and stood over where the young Child was.

- 10. And when they saw the star, they rejoiced with exceeding great joy. Hallelujah.

> Sing, choirs of angels,
> Sing in exultation,
> Sing, all ye citizens of Heaven above.
> Glory to God, Glory in the Highest.
> O come, let us adore Him,
> O come, let us adore Him,
> O come, let us adore Him, Christ the Lord.
>   Hallelujah.   Amen.

Stainer.

1375

Isaiah vi.   1. I saw the Lord sitting upon a Throne, high and lifted up ; and His train filled the Temple.

2. Above it stood the Seraphim : each one had six wings ; with twain he covered his face, and with twain he covered his feet, and with twain he did fly.

3. And one cried unto another, Holy, Holy, Holy, is the Lord of Hosts ; the whole earth is full of His Glory.

4. And the posts of the door moved at the voice of him that cried. and the house was filled with smoke.

O Trinity! O Unity!
Be present as we worship Thee,
And with the songs that angels sing
Unite the hymns of praise we bring. Amen.

(Sung at the same time as the above.)

3. Holy, Holy, Holy, is the Lord of Hosts; the whole earth is full of His Glory. Amen.

STAINER.

1376

St. John vi. 32, 33. Jesus said unto the people, The Bread of God is He which cometh down from Heaven, and giveth life unto the world.

34. Then said they unto Him, Lord, evermore give us this bread.

35. Jesus said unto them, I am the Bread of Life : he that cometh to Me shall never hunger, and he that believeth on Me shall never thirst. Amen.

STAINER.

1377

Lead, kindly Light, amid the encircling gloom,
    Lead Thou me on :
The night is dark, and I am far from home,
    Lead Thou me on.
Keep Thou my feet ; I do not ask to see
The distant scene ; one step enough for me.

I was not ever thus, nor prayed that Thou
    Shouldst lead me on ;
I loved to choose and see my path ; but now
    Lead Thou me on.
I loved the garish day ; and, spite of fears,
Pride ruled my will : remember not past years.

So long Thy power hath blest me, sure it still
    Will lead me on
O'er moor and fen, o'er crag and torrent, till
    The night is gone ;
And with the morn those angel faces smile,
Which I have loved long since, and lost awhile.

Dunstan, C. L. Naylor, Stainer.

1378

PSALM xxvii. 11. Leave us not, neither forsake us, O GOD of our salvation.

xvi. 12. In Thy presence is the fulness of joy.

ACTS i. 11. Ye men of Galilee, why stand ye gazing up into Heaven? This same JESUS, Which is taken up from you into Heaven, shall so come in like manner as ye have seen Him go into Heaven.

PSALM lxviii. 18. Thou art gone up on high, Thou hast led captivity captive, and received gifts for men: yea, even for Thine enemies, that the LORD GOD might dwell among them. Hallelujah. Amen.

STAINER.

1379

ROMANS xiii. 1. Let every soul be subject unto the higher powers, for there is no power but of GOD: the powers that be, are ordained of GOD.

PSALM cxviii. 19. Open me the gates of righteousness, that I may go into them, and give thanks unto the LORD.

20. This is the gate of the LORD: the righteous shall enter into it.

1. O give thanks unto the LORD, for He is good, and His mercy endureth for ever.

2. Let Israel now say, His mercy endureth for ever.

3. Let the house of Aaron now say, His mercy endureth for ever.

4. Let them that fear the LORD now say, His mercy endureth for ever.

5. In my distress I called upon the LORD, He answered me, and set me in a large place. Hallelujah! Amen!

O King of kings, Thy blessing shed
On our anointed Sovereign's head;
And looking from Thy holy Heaven,
Protect the crown Thyself hast given.

Her may we honour and obey,
Uphold her right and lawful sway:
Remembering that the powers that be,
Are ministers ordained of Thee.

Her with Thy choicest mercies bless,
To all her counsels give success;
In war, in peace, Thy power be seen,
Thy grace be given to our Queen!

And oh! when earthly thrones decay,
And earthly kingdoms fade away,
Grant her a throne in worlds on high,
A crown of immortality.   Amen.

STAINER.

1380

COLOSSIANS iii.   15. Let the peace of GOD rule in your hearts to the which ye are called in one body; and be ye thankful.

16. Let the word of CHRIST dwell in you richly in all wisdom, teaching and admonishing one another in psalms and hymns and spiritual songs, singing with grace in your hearts to the LORD.

17. And whatsoever ye do, in word or deed, do all in the Name of the LORD JESUS, giving thanks unto GOD and the Father by Him.   Amen.

STAINER.

1381

No. 1

1 CHRONICLES xvii.   26. LORD, Thou art GOD:

27. Now, therefore, let it please Thee to bless the house of Thy servant, that it may be before Thee for ever: for Thou blessest, O LORD, and it shall be blessed for ever.

No. 2

2 SAMUEL xxiii.   2. The spirit of the LORD spake by me, and His word was in my tongue.

3. The GOD of Israel said, the Rock of Israel spake to me: He that ruleth over men must be just, ruling in the fear of GOD:

4. And he shall be as the light of the morning, when the sun riseth, even as a morning without clouds; even as the tender grass springing out of the earth by clear shining after rain.

No. 3

1 KINGS viii. 57. The LORD our GOD be with us, as He was with our fathers : let Him not leave us, nor forsake us ;

58. That He may incline our hearts unto Him, to walk in His ways, and to keep His commandments.

60. That all the people of the earth may know the LORD is GOD, there is none else.

No. 4

O LORD, save the Queen ;
And mercifully hear us when we call upon Thee.

GOD save our gracious Queen,
Long live our noble Queen,
Long may she reign !
Send her victorious.
Happy and glorious,
Long to reign over us,
GOD save the Queen !

STAINER.

1382

My Maker, and my King,
To Thee my all I owe,
Thy sovereign bounty is the spring
From whence my blessings flow.

The creature of Thy hand,
On Thee alone I live,
My GOD, Thy benefits demand
More praise than I can give.

Shall I withhold Thy due ?
Shall I ungrateful prove ?
LORD, form this wand'ring heart anew,
And fill it with Thy love.

O let Thy grace inspire
My soul with strength divine ;
Let all my powers to Thee aspire,
And all my days be Thine.

STAINER.

1383

PSALM xlvii. 1. O clap your hands, all ye people; shout unto GOD with the voice of triumph.

2. For the LORD our GOD is terrible; He is a great King over all the earth.

ISAIAH xl. 31. They that wait upon the LORD shall renew their strength: they shall mount up with wings as eagles; they shall run and not be weary; they shall walk, and not faint.

xxvi. 4. Trust ye in the LORD for ever; for in the LORD JEHOVAH is everlasting strength. Amen.

STAINER.

* —— * Sometimes sung as a separate Anthem.

1384 OUSELEY, SEWELL, Isaiah xl. 31.

1385

PSALM cxxii. 6. Rogate quæ ad pacem sunt Hierusalem, et abundantia diligentibus te.

7. Fiat pax in virtute tuâ, et abundantia in turribus tuis.

8. Propter fratres meos et proximos meos loquebar pacem de te.

9. Propter domum Domini Dei nostri quæsivi bona tibi.

STAINER.

1386

ECCLESIASTICUS xxxix. 14. Sing a song of praise, bless the LORD in all His works:

15. Magnify His Name, and shew forth His praise with the songs of your lips, and with harps.

ii. 11. The LORD is full of compassion and mercy, long-suffering, and very pitiful, and forgiveth sins, and saveth in time of affliction. Blessed be the LORD for ever. Amen. Hallelujah.

STAINER.

1387

JOB xxxviii. 7. The morning stars sang together, and all the sons of God shouted for joy.

ST. LUKE ii. 11. For unto you is born this day, in the city of David a Saviour, Which is CHRIST the LORD.

*ISAIAH lxvi. 10. Rejoice ye with Jerusalem, all ye that love her : rejoice, all ye that mourn for her.

12. For thus saith the LORD, I will extend peace to her like a river, and the glory of the Gentiles as a flowing stream.* Amen.

STAINER.

* ——— * Sometimes sung as a separate Anthem.

1388

ST. JOHN ii. 1. There was a marriage in Cana of Galilee ; and the mother of JESUS was there ;

2. And both JESUS was called, and His disciples, to the marriage.

Eternal Word, Who didst endure
　To take our flesh and make it Thine :
Whose bidding blessed the waters pure,
　And changed them into better wine :
The hidden grace again bestow ;
　Bid twain be one in one pure love,
And love, which Thou hast blessed below,
　Glow as new wine in feasts above.

O GOD, we lift our praise to Thee,
　Whose face no sinful man may see ;
To Thee, Who, as the wedding Guest,
　Didst make Thy glory manifest ;
To thee be equal honour done,
　Blessed Spirit, binding souls in one :
So sing we, with the Angel Host,
　To Father, Son, and Holy Ghost.　Amen.

STAINER.

1389

WISDOM v. 15. The righteous live for evermore ; their reward also is with the LORD, and the care of them is with the Most High.

16. Therefore shall they receive a glorious kingdom, and a beautiful crown from the LORD's hand : for with His right hand shall He cover them, and with His arm shall He protect them. Amen.

STAINER.

1390

St. John xx. 13. They have taken away my Lord, and I know not where they have laid Him. "Woman, why weepest thou?" Because they have taken away my Lord, and I know not where they have laid Him.

15. "Woman, why weepest thou? Whom seekest thou?" Sir, if Thou have borne Him hence, tell me where Thou hast laid Him.

16. "Mary!" Master!

1 Corinthians xv. 55. O death, where is thy sting? O grave, where is thy victory?

57. Thanks be to God, Who giveth us the victory through our Lord Jesus Christ. Alleluia. Amen.

Stainer.

1391

Ezekiel xxxvi. 28. Ye shall dwell in the land that I gave to your fathers; and ye shall be My people, and I will be your God.

30. I will multiply the fruit of the tree, and the increase of the field.

34. And the desolate land shall be tilled, whereas it lay desolate in the sight of all that passed by.

35. And they shall say, This land that was desolate is become like the Garden of Eden.

Psalm cxxxvi. 1. Give thanks unto the Lord, His mercy endureth for ever.

O blessed is that land of God,
  Where Saints abide for ever,
Where golden fields spread far and broad,
  Where flows the crystal river.

The strains of all its holy throng
  With ours to-day are blending;
Thrice blessed is that harvest song
  Which never hath an ending. Amen.

Stainer.

1392

2 SAMUEL i. 23. They were lovely and pleasant in their lives, and in death they were not divided; they were swifter than eagles, they were stronger than lions.

WISDOM v. 5. How are they numbered among the children of GOD, and their lot is among the saints!

iii. 6. As gold in the furnace hath He tried them, and received them as a burnt offering.

7. And in the day of their visitation they shall shine, and run to and fro like sparks among the stubble.

ECCLESIASTICUS XXIV. 24. Faint not to be strong in the LORD; that He may confirm you, cleave unto Him; for the LORD Almighty is GOD alone, and beside Him there is no other Saviour.

STAINER.

1393

ZECHARIAH vi. 12. Thus speaketh the LORD of Hosts, saying, Behold the Man Whose name is the Branch:

13. He, even He shall build the Temple of the LORD; and He shall bear the glory, and shall sit and rule upon His Throne; and He shall be a Priest upon His Throne: and the counsel of peace shall be between them both.

Art Thou the CHRIST? Art Thou the Son?
The Father's Image bright?
And see we Him, Whose arm upholds
Earth and the starry height?

Yea, faith can pierce the cloud
Which veils Thy glory now;
We hail Thee, GOD, before Whose Throne
The angels prostrate bow.

Our sinful pride to cure
With that pure love of Thine,
O be Thou born within our hearts,
Most Holy Child Divine. Amen

STAINER.

1394

ISAIAH xxviii. 5. In that day shall the LORD of Hosts be for a crown of glory, and for a diadem of beauty unto the residue of His people.

xxxiii. 2. O LORD, be gracious unto us; we have waited for Thee. Be Thou our salvation in the time of trouble.

xxx. 19. He will be very gracious unto thee at the voice of thy cry; when He shall hear it He will answer thee. Thou shalt weep no more.

(From " The Daughter of Jairus," No. 2.) STAINER.

1395

BARUCH iv. 22. My hope is in the Everlasting, that He will save you; and joy is come unto me from the Holy One, because of the mercy which shall soon come unto you from the Everlasting, our Saviour.

23. I sent you out with mourning and weeping. But GOD will give you to me again with joy and gladness for ever.

*EPHESIANS v. 14. Awake, thou that sleepest, and arise from the dead, and CHRIST shall give thee light.

ROMANS vi. 11. Likewise reckon ye yourselves to be dead indeed unto sin, but alive unto GOD, through JESUS CHRIST our LORD.

EPHESIANS v. 14. Awake, thou that sleepest, and arise from the dead, and CHRIST shall give thee light.

ROMANS vi. 12. Let not sin reign in your mortal body, that ye should obey the lusts thereof. But yield yourselves unto GOD as those that are alive from the dead.

EPHESIANS v. 14. Awake, thou that sleepest, and arise from the dead, and CHRIST shall give thee light.*

(From " The Daughter of Jairus," Nos. 4, 8.) STAINER.

—— Sometimes sung as a separate Anthem.

1396

1. Love Divine! all love excelling,
   Joy of heaven to earth come down,
   Fix in us Thy humble dwelling,
   All Thy faithful mercies crown.

2. Jesu ! Thou art all compassion,
   Pure, unbounded Love Thou art ;
   Visit us with Thy salvation,
   Enter every trembling heart.

3. Come, Almighty, to deliver ;
   Let us all Thy grace receive,
   Hasten to return, and never,
   Never more Thy temple leave.

4. Thee we would be always blessing,
   Serve Thee as Thy Hosts above ;
   Pray, and praise Thee without ceasing,
   Glory in Thy perfect love.

5. *To Him Who left His Throne on high
   Mankind from death to raise,
   To Him, with the Father and the Holy Ghost,
   Be everlasting praise.   Amen.   Hallelujah !*

(*From " The Daughter of Jairus,"* Nos. 9, 10.)   Stainer.

—— Sometimes sung as a separate Anthem.

1397

O thou that weepest,
   Strongly endure :
When woe is deepest
   My love is sure.
Love that forgave thee,
   Granted thee peace,
Is mighty to save thee ;
   How can it cease ?
Hear thou, and know it ;
   Not heaven on high,
Nor waters below it
   Unfathomed that lie ;
Nothing that ranges
   In sorrow and strife ;
No, nor the changes
   Of death and of life ;

No, nor the thunder
　　That echoes above,
Ever shall sunder
　　Thee from My love.
While thou art sighing,
　　Sighing for Me,
See, I am dying,
　　Dying for thee."

*" Come, ye sin-defiled and weary,
　　Ye that mourn in grief distrest ;
Come, ye hopeless, lone and dreary,
　　He will hear you, give you rest.

" Mary, in her deep emotion,
　　Wept, His sacred feet beside ;
Like the inflow of the ocean
　　Pour'd His Love in fullest tide,
Pour'd His sweetest Benediction
　　O'er the sadness of the past,
And the weary in affliction
　　Found her perfect peace at last.

" Come, ye sin-defiled and stricken,
　　At His feet your woes shall cease :
Hark ! the Voice to soothe and quicken
　　Sweetly whispers,—' Go in peace.' "*

(*From " St. Mary Magdalen,"* Nos. 11, 7.)　STAINER.

——— Sometimes sung as a separate Anthem.

1398

ROMANS xii. 1. I beseech you, brethren, by the mercies of GOD, that ye present your bodies a living sacrifice, holy, acceptable unto GOD, which is your reasonable service.

xiv. 7. For none of us liveth to himself, and no man dieth to himself.

8. For whether we live. we live unto the LORD, and whether we die, we die unto the LORD ; whether we live therefore, or whether we die, we are the LORD's.

1 CORINTHIANS iii. 16. Know ye not that ye are the temple of GOD, and that the Spirit of GOD dwelleth in you?

17. The temple of GOD is holy, which temple ye are. Amen.

(From " St Mary Magdalen," Nos. 8, 9.) STAINER.

1399

PSALM xx. 1. The LORD hear thee in the day of trouble: the Name of the GOD of Jacob defend thee;

2. Send thee help from the sanctuary, and strengthen thee out of Sion;

3. Remember all thy offerings, and accept thy burnt sacrifice;

4. Grant thee thy heart's desire, and fulfil all thy mind.

5. We will rejoice in Thy salvation, and triumph in the Name of the LORD our GOD: [the LORD perform all thy petitions.]

6. Now know I that the LORD helpeth His Anointed, and will hear him from His holy Heaven, even with the wholesome strength of His right hand.

7. Some put their trust in chariots and some in horses; but we will remember the Name of the LORD our GOD.

[8. They are brought down and fallen: but we are risen and stand upright.]

9. Save, LORD, and hear us, O King of Heaven, when we call upon Thee.

J. H. CLARKE.

1400 BARKWORTH, vv. 1–4, 9.
1401 BLOW, H. E. FORD, JEKYLL, vv. 1–4.
1402 BLOW, vv. 9, 5. Amen.
1403 BLOW, vv. 5–9.
1404 CROFT, vv. 5–7.
1405 DIXON, vv. 5, 4, 7. Amen.
1406 P. HAYES, v. 1. Amen.
1407 NARES, vv. 1 4 9, 5.

1408

St. John iii. 16. God so loved the world, that He gave His only begotten Son, that whosoever believeth in Him should not perish, but have everlasting life.

[17. For God sent not His Son into the world to condemn the world, but that the world through Him might be saved.]

Romans v. 6. For when we were yet without strength, in due time Christ died for the ungodly.

7. For scarcely for a righteous man will one die, but peradventure for a good man some would even dare to die.

8. But God commendeth His love toward us; in that, while we were yet sinners, Christ died for us.

1. Therefore, being justified by faith, we have peace with God, through our Lord Jesus Christ.

J. H. Clarke.

1409 Goss, Kingston, E. G. Monk, †Stainer, Thorne, Tuckerman, vv. 16, 17. Amen.

† *(From "The Crucifixion," No. 9.)*

1410

Psalm xxv. 7. Gracious and righteous is the Lord: therefore will He teach sinners in the way.

8. Them that are meek shall He guide in judgment: and such as are gentle, them shall He learn His way.

cxviii. 29. O give thanks unto the Lord, for He is gracious, and His mercy endureth for ever.

W. H. Gladstone.

1411

The third Collect at Evening Prayer.

Lighten our darkness, we beseech Thee, O Lord: and by Thy great mercy defend us from all perils and dangers of this night; for the love of Thy only Son, our Saviour, Jesus Christ. Amen.

W. H. Gladstone. Vicars.

1412

These are Thy glorious works, Parent of good,
Almighty; Thine this universal frame,
Thus wondrous fair : Thyself how wondrous then,
Unspeakable ; Who sitt'st above these heavens
To us invisible, or dimly seen
In these Thy lowest works; yet these declare
Thy goodness beyond thought, and power divine.

W. H. GLADSTONE.

1413

JOEL ii. 21. Fear not, O land, be glad and rejoice ; for the LORD will do great things.

23. Be glad, then, ye children of Zion ; be glad and rejoice in the LORD your GOD.

JORDAN.

1414

O Death, how sweet the thought
    That this world's strife is ended,
That all we feared and all we sought
    In one deep sleep are blended.

No more the anguish of to-day,
    To wait the darker morrow ;
No more stern call to do or say,
    To brood o'er sin and sorrow.

O Death, how dear the hope
    That thro' the thickest shade,
Beyond the steep and sunless slope,
    Our treasured store is laid.

The loved, the mourned, the honoured dead
    That lonely path have trod ;
And that same path we too must tread,
    To be with them and GOD.

O Life, thou too art sweet,
    Thou breath'st the fragrant breath
Of those whom ev'n the hope to meet
    Can cheer the gate of death.

Life is the scene their presence lighted ;
    Its every hour and place
Is with the thought of them united,
    Irradiate with their grace.

There lie the duties, small and great,
    That we from them inherit ;
There spring the aims that lead us straight
    To their celestial spirit.

All glorious things or seen or heard,
    By love or justice done ;
The helpful deed, th' ennobling word,
    By this poor life are won.

O Life and Death, like day and night,
    Your guardian task combine ;
Pillar of darkness and of light,
    Lead thro' earth's storm till bright heaven's
        dawn shall shine.

PARRATT.

1415

PSALM ciii. 8. The LORD is full of compassion and mercy, long-suffering, and of great goodness.

9. He will not alway be chiding : neither keepeth He His anger for ever.

ST. MATTHEW v. 7. Blessed are the merciful, for they shall obtain mercy.

(From " Jonah," Nos. 17. 19.) ROBERTS.

—— Sometimes sung as a separate Anthem.

1416

PSALM cxlv. 17. The LORD is righteous in all His ways, and holy in all His works.

21. My mouth shall speak the praise of the LORD : and let all flesh bless His holy Name for ever and ever.

PSALM cxlvii. 11. The LORD taketh pleasure in them that hear Him, in those that hope in His mercy.

ST. LUKE xv. 10. There is joy in the presence of the angels of GOD over one sinner that repenteth. Amen.

(From " Jonah," Nos. 14, 18. 21.) ROBERTS.

1417

No. 1

JUDITH xvi. 13. I will sing unto the LORD a new song : O LORD, Thou art great and glorious, wonderful in strength, and invincible.

BARUCH iii. 6. Thou art the LORD our GOD, and Thee, O LORD, will we praise.

No. 2

WISDOM vi. 1. Hear, O ye kings, and understand ; learn, ye that be judges of the earth.

2. Give ear, ye that rule the people ;

3. For power is given you of the LORD, and sovereignty from the Highest, Who shall try your works, and search out your counsels.

No. 3

ECCLESIASTICUS li. 13. When I was yet young, I desired wisdom openly in my prayer.

WISDOM viii. 21. I prayed unto the LORD and besought Him, and with my whole heart I said :

ix. 1, 4. O GOD of my fathers, LORD of mercy, give me wisdom, and reject me not from among Thy children.

5. For I am a feeble person, and of a short time, and too young for the understanding of judgment and laws.

ECCLESIASTICUS li. 17. I profited therein, therefore will I ascribe the glory unto Him that giveth me wisdom.

No. 4

ECCLESIASTICUS xxiv. 1. Wisdom shall praise herself, and shall glory in the midst of her people.

3. I came out of the mouth of the most High, and covered the earth as a cloud.

12. I took root in an honourable people, even in the portion of the LORD's inheritance.

No. 5

PSALM xciii. (*N.V.*)

1. With glory clad, with strength arrayed,
The LORD, that o'er all nature reigns,
The world's foundations strongly laid,
And the vast fabric still sustains.

2. How surely stablish'd is Thy Throne,
Which shall no change or period see,
For Thou, O Lord, and Thou alone
Art God from all eternity.

No. 6

Proverbs viii. 15. By Me kings reign, and princes decree justice.

No. 7

Tobit xiii. 15. Let my soul bless God the great King.

16. For Jerusalem shall be built up with sapphires and emeralds: Thy walls and towers and battlements with pure gold.

18. And all her streets shall say, Alleluia !

Roberts.

1418

Blessed Jesu, Fount of Mercy,
We, Thy faithful, in Thy Passion,
All Thy sorrows share with Thee.

(*From the " Stabat Mater,"* No. 3.)   Dvořák.

1419

§ 1

Isaiah xi. 1. There shall come forth a rod out of the stem of Jesse, and a Branch shall grow out of his roots:

2, 3. And the Spirit of the Lord shall rest upon Him, and shall make Him of quick understanding in the fear of the Lord; and He shall not judge after the sight of His eyes, nor reprove after the hearing of His ears;

lxi. 1. Because the Lord hath anointed Him to preach good tidings unto the meek; He hath sent Him to bind up the broken-hearted, to proclaim liberty to the captives, and the opening of the prison to them that are bound.

xxv. 8. He will swallow up death in victory; and the Lord God will wipe away tears from off all faces, and the rebuke of His people shall He take away from off all the earth.

From " The Light of the World," No. 1.

§ 2

St. Luke ii. 15. Let us now go even unto Bethlehem, and see this thing which is come to pass, which the Lord hath made known unto us.

(From " The Light of the World," No. 4.)

§ 3

St. Luke i. 42. Blessed art thou among women, and blessed is the fruit of thy womb.

32. He shall be great, and shall be called, The Son of the Highest.

(From " The Light of the World," No. 5.)

§ 4

Isaiah xiv. 7. The whole earth is at rest, and is quiet: they break forth into singing.

xxv. 9. Lo, This is our God; we have waited for Him, and He will save us : This is the Lord ; we have waited for Him, we will rejoice and be glad in His salvation.

(From " The Light of the World," No. 8.)

§ 5

St. Matthew ii. 18. In Rama was there a voice heard, lamentation, and weeping, and great mourning, Rachel, weeping for her children, would not be comforted.

(Sung at the same time as the above.)

Jeremiah iv. 31. Woe is me now, for my soul is wearied because of murderers.

(From " The Light of the World," No. 10.)

§ 6

xxxi. 16, 17. Refrain thy voice from weeping, and thine eyes from tears, for thy work shall be rewarded, saith the Lord. And there is hope in thine end, that thy children shall come again to their own border.

(From " The Light of the World," No. 11.)

§ 7

Isaiah xliv. 3. I will pour My spirit upon thy seed, and My blessing upon thine offspring.

Micah v. 4. He shall stand and feed in the strength of the Lord, in the Majesty of the Name of the Lord His God, for He shall be great unto the ends of the earth.

(From " The Light of the World, No. 13.)

§ 8

ISAIAH lxiii. 16. Doubtless Thou art our Father, though Abraham be ignorant of us, and Israel acknowledge us not: Thou, O LORD, art our Father, our Redeemer; Thy Name is from everlasting.

(From " The Light of the World," No. 15.)

§ 9

ST. MATTHEW v. 45. He maketh the sun to rise on the evil and on the good, and sendeth rain on the just and on the unjust.

(From " The Light of the World," No. 16.)

§ 10

JEREMIAH xxii. 10. Weep ye not for the dead, neither bemoan him.

1 THESSALONIANS iv. 13. Nor sorrow not, even as others which have no hope:

JEREMIAH xxxi. 13. For thus saith the LORD: I will turn their mourning into joy, and make them rejoice from their sorrow.

(From " The Light of the World," No. 19.)

§ 11

ISAIAH xxxviii. 18. The grave cannot praise Thee, death cannot celebrate Thee: they that go down to the pit cannot hope for Thy truth.

19. The living, the living, he shall praise Thee: the father to the children shall make known Thy truth.

(From " The Light of the World," No. 23.)

§ 12

ST. MATTHEW xxi. 9. Hosanna to the Son of David: blessed is He that cometh in the Name of the LORD; Hosanna in the highest.

ST. LUKE xix. 38. Blessed is the King of Israel that cometh in the Name of the LORD: peace in heaven, and glory in the highest

From · The Light of the World,' No. 25.

§ 13

ST. MARK xi. 10. Blessed be the Kingdom of our father David, that cometh in the Name of the LORD.

(From " The Light of the World," No. 27.)

§ 14

ST. LUKE xix. 42. If thou hadst known, O Jerusalem, even thou, at least in this thy day, the things which belong unto thy peace; but now they are hid from thine eyes.

(From " The Light of the World," No. 27.)

§ 15

ST. MATTHEW xxi. 9. Hosanna in the highest! Hosanna to the Son of David.

ST. MARK xi. 9, 10. Blessed be the Kingdom of our father David. Peace in heaven, and glory in the highest. Blessed is He that cometh in the Name of the LORD. Hosanna in the highest.

(From " The Light of the World," No. 28.)

§ 16

4. Yea, though I walk through the valley of the shadow of death, I will fear no evil: for Thou art with me; Thy rod and Thy staff comfort me.

(From " The Light of the World," No. 34.)

§ 17

COLOSSIANS iii. 1. If ye be risen with CHRIST, seek those things that are above.

1 TIMOTHY vi. 12. Fight the good fight of faith, lay hold of eternal life:

HEBREWS xii. 2. Looking unto Him, the Author and Finisher of our faith; Who for the joy that was set before Him endured the Cross, despising the shame, and is set down at the right hand of the Throne of GOD.

(From " The Light of the World," No. 41.)

§ 18

ACTS v. 31. Him hath GOD exalted with His right hand to be a Prince and a Saviour, for to give repentance to Israel, and forgiveness of sins.

REVELATION xii. 10. Now is come salvation, and strength, and the Kingdom of our GOD, and the power of His CHRIST.

GALATIANS i. 4, 5. Who gave Himself for our sins, that He might deliver us from the present evil world, according to the will of GOD and our Father : to Whom be glory for ever and ever.   Amen.

(*From " The Light of the World,"* No. 42.)   SULLIVAN.

1420

1. Brother, thou art gone before us, and thy saintly soul
    is flown
Where tears are wiped from every eye, and sorrow is
    unknown ;
From the burthen of the flesh, and from care and fear
    released,
Where the wicked cease from troubling, and the weary
    are at rest.

2. The toilsome road thou'st travelled o'er, and borne
    the heavy load,
But CHRIST hath taught thy languid feet to reach His
    blest abode.
Thou'rt sleeping now, like Lazarus upon his Father's
    breast,
Where the wicked cease from troubling, and the weary
    are at rest.

3. " Earth to earth " and " dust to dust," the solemn
    priest hath said,
So we lay the turf above thee now, and we seal thy
    narrow bed ;
But thy spirit, brother, soars away among the faithful blest,
Where the wicked cease from troubling, and the weary
    are at rest.

4. And, when the LORD shall summon us whom thou hast
    left behind,
May we, untainted by the world, as sure a welcome find ;
May each, like thee, depart in peace, to be a glorious
    guest,
Where the wicked cease from troubling, and the weary
    are at rest

(*From 'In Martyr or Anthem.* No. 5)   S 'LIVAN.

1421 GOSS, vv. 1. 2.

*The following words are sometimes sung in
continuation of No. 1421.*

We are in our holy rest, undisturbed, and undistressed,
But for those we leave behind, there where rest is hard
to find,
Where the wicked trouble still, good too oft rebuked by ill,
Widow by the low grave-stone, infant with its feeble
moan,
Guideless youth and dowerless maid, under penury's cold
shade,   .
For the long and weary strife, with the cares, and woes,
and sins of life;
These will the hard world to its bosom take, in JESUS'
Name, for JESUS' sake.
Blessing on the meekly great, blessing on the comforters
of the disconsolate !
Blessing on those who live to bless, making them friends
of the mammon of unrighteousness.
Blessing on the merciful, with mercy to be blest,
Where the wicked cease from troubling, and the weary
are at rest.

1422

ISAIAH lxiii. 7. I will mention the loving-kindnesses
of the LORD, and the praises of the LORD, according to
all that the LORD hath bestowed on us.

8. For He said, Surely they are My people, children
that will not lie: so He was their Saviour.

9. In all their affliction He was afflicted, and the angel
of His presence saved them: in His love and in His
pity He redeemed them; and He bare them, and carried
them all the days of old.

14. So didst Thou lead Thy people, to make Thyself a
glorious Name.

15. Look down from Heaven, and behold from the
habitation of Thy holiness and of Thy glory: where is
Thy zeal and Thy strength?

16. Doubtless Thou art our Father. Thou, O LORD, art
our Father, our Redeemer; Thy Name is from everlasting.
Amen.

SULLIVAN.

1423

1 St. John ii. 15. Love not the world, nor the things that are in the world. [If any man love the world, the love of the Father is not in him.

16. For all that is in the world, the lust of the flesh, and the lust of the eyes, and the pride of life, is not of the Father, but is of the world.]

17. For the world passeth away, and the lust thereof : but he that doeth the will of God abideth for ever.

Psalm cvii. 8. O that men would·praise the Lord for His goodness, and declare the wonders that He doeth for the children of men.

2. Let them give thanks whom the Lord hath redeemed.

4, 5. They went astray in the wilderness out of the way : hungry and thirsty, their soul fainted within them.

6. Yet, when they cried unto the Lord in their trouble, He delivered them out of their distress.

8. O that men would therefore praise the Lord for His goodness, and declare the wonders that He doeth for the children of men.

(From " The Prodigal Son," Nos. 8, 15.) Sullivan.

1424 H. E. Ford, vv. 15, 17.
1425 Ousfley, vv., 15–17. Amen.

1426

St. Luke xv. 18, 19. I will arise, and go to my father, and will say unto him, " Father, I have sinned against Heaven, and before thee, and am no more worthy to be called thy son :†make me as one of thy hired servants."

*10. There is joy in the presence of the angels of God over one sinner that repenteth.

Psalm li. 17. The sacrifices of God are a broken spirit ; a broken and contrite heart, O God, Thou wilt not despise.*

(From " The Prodigal Son," Nos. 11, 12.) Sullivan.

—— Sometimes sung as a separate Anthem.

1427 Cecil, Crayton, Harris, Whitield. C. Wood, vv. 18. 19.

† Ends here.

1428

ISAIAH xlviii. 18. O that thou hadst hearkened to My commandments ! Then had thy peace been as a river, and thy righteousness as the waves of the sea.

EZEKIEL xxxiii. 11. Turn ye, turn ye, why will ye die ?

*ST. LUKE xv. 10. There is joy in the presence of the Angels of GOD over one sinner that repenteth.

PSALM ciii. 13. Like as a father pitieth his own children : even, so is the LORD merciful to them that fear Him.

REVELATION vii. 16. They shall hunger no more, neither thirst any more.

17. And GOD shall wipe away all tears from their eyes.*

(*From " The Prodigal Son,"* Nos. 10, 2.) SULLIVAN.

—— Sometimes sung as a separate Anthem.

1429

HEBREWS xii. 11. No chastening for the present seemeth to be joyous, but grievous ; nevertheless, afterward it yieldeth the peaceable fruit of righteousness.

6. For whom the LORD loveth He chasteneth, and scourgeth every son whom He receiveth.

*PSALM xxxiv. 11. Come, ye children, and hearken unto Me ; I will teach you the fear of the LORD.

6. Lo, the poor crieth, and the LORD heareth him ; yea, and saveth him out of all his trouble.

*18. The LORD is nigh unto them that are of a contrite heart, and will save such as be of an humble spirit.

ISAIAH lvii. 18. Thus saith the LORD, I have seen his ways, and will heal him ; and restore comforts unto him and to his mourners.*

*lxiii. 16. Thou, O LORD, art our Father, our Redeemer, Thy Name is from everlasting. Hallelujah. Amen. ʾ

(*From " The Prodigal Son,"* Nos. 16- 18.) SULLIVAN.

* * Sometimes sung as a separate Anthem.

1430

TOBIT viii. 15. O GOD, Thou art worthy to be praised with all pure and holy praise, therefore let the saints praise Thee with all Thy creatures ; and let all Thine angels and Thine elect praise Thee for ever.

16. Thou art to be praised, for Thou hast made these Thy servants joyful. Thou hast dealt with them according to Thy great mercy.

17. Grant them mercy, O LORD, and finish their life in health, with joy ; for Thou hast made these Thy servants joyful.

PSALM xx. 2. The LORD send thee help from the sanctuary, and strengthen thee out of Sion ;

4. Grant thee thy heart's desire, and fulfil all thy mind.

1. The LORD hear thee in the day of trouble : the Name of the GOD of Jacob defend thee. Amen.

GREATHEED, SULLIVAN.

1431

ISAIAH xlix. 13. Sing, O heavens : and be joyful, O earth ; break forth into singing, O mountains : for the LORD hath comforted His people, and will have mercy upon His afflicted.

xxv. 8. He will swallow up death in victory, and the LORD GOD will wipe away tears from off all faces ; and the rebuke of His people shall He take away from off all the earth.

9. Lo, This is our GOD ; we have waited for Him, and He will save us : This is the LORD our GOD, we have waited for Him, we will be glad, and rejoice in His salvation.

PSALM lxxxv. 9. For His salvation is nigh them that fear Him, that glory may dwell in our land.

10. Mercy and truth are met together : righteousness and peace have kissed each other.

11. Truth shall flourish out of the earth, and righteousness hath looked down from Heaven.

xlv. 7. Thy seat, O GOD, endureth for ever : the sceptre of Thy kingdom is a right sceptre. Amen.

SULLIVAN.

1432

My Redeemer, and my LORD,
  I beseech Thee, I entreat Thee,
Guide me in each act and word,
  That hereafter I may meet Thee,
Watching, waiting, hoping, yearning,
With my lamp well trimmed and burning.
If my feeble prayer can reach Thee,
O, my Saviour, I beseech Thee,
Let me follow where Thou leadest,
Let me, bleeding as Thou bleedest,
Die, if dying I may give
Life to one who asks to live;
And more nearly,
Dying thus, resemble Thee.

    *O gladsome Light
    Of the Father immortal,
    And of the celestial
    Sacred and blessed
    JESUS our Saviour!

    Now to the sunset
    Again hast Thou brought us,
    And, seeing the evening
    Twilight, we bless Thee,
    Praise Thee, adore Thee.

    Father, Omnipotent!
    Son, the Life-giver!
    Spirit, the Comforter!
    Worthy at all times
    Of worship and wonder!   Amen.*

(*From " The Golden Legend,"* pp. 63, 47.)   SULLIVAN.

—— Sometimes sung as a separate Anthem.

1433

ISAIAH li. 4. Hearken unto Me, My people, and give ear unto Me, O My nation, for a law shall proceed from Me, and I will make my judgment to rest for a light of the people.

5. My righteousness is near, My salvation is gone forth, and Mine arms shall judge the people; the isles shall wait upon Me, and on Mine arm shall they trust.

6. Lift up your eyes to the heavens, and look upon the earth beneath : for the heavens shall vanish away like smoke, and the earth shall wax old as a garment, and they that dwell therein shall die in like manner. But My salvation shall be for ever, and My righteousness shall not be abolished.

SULLIVAN.

1434

EXODUS xv. 11. Who is like unto Thee, O LORD, glorious in holiness, fearful in praises, doing wonders ?

13. Thou in Thy mercy hast led forth the people which Thou hast redeemed.

17. Thou shalt bring them in, and plant them in the mountain of Thine inheritance, in the place, O LORD, which Thou hast made for Thee to dwell in, in the sanctuary, O LORD, which Thy hands have established.

18. The LORD shall reign for ever and ever.

21. Sing ye to the LORD. Hallelujah. Amen.

SULLIVAN.

1435

ST. MARK xvi. 6. He is risen.

1 CORINTHIANS xv. 57. Thanks be to GOD, Who giveth us the victory, through JESUS CHRIST our LORD.

2 CORINTHIANS v. 15. He died for all, that they which live might not henceforth live unto themselves, but unto Him Who died for them, and rose again. Hallelujah. Amen.

GADSBY.

1436

ZECHARIAH ix. 9, 10. Rejoice greatly, O daughter of Sion ; shout, O daughter of Jerusalem : behold, thy King cometh unto thee. He is the righteous Saviour, and He shall speak peace unto the heathen.

GADSBY.

1437

Psalm cxiii. 2. Blessed be the Name of the Lord, from this time forth for evermore.

5. Who is like unto the Lord our God, that hath His dwelling so high, and yet humbleth Himself to behold the things that are in heaven and earth?

civ. 13. He watereth the hills from above: the earth is filled with the fruit of Thy works.

14. He bringeth forth grass for the cattle, and green herb for the service of men.

cxiii. 2. Blessed be the Name of the Lord, from this time forth for evermore.

Gadsby.

1438

Psalm cxv. 1. Not unto us, O Lord, not unto us, but unto Thy Name give the glory, for Thy mercy, and for Thy truth's sake.

2. Wherefore should the heathen say, Where is now their God?

4. Their idols are silver and gold, the work of men's hands.

8. They that make them are like unto them: so is everyone that trusteth in them.

3. But our God is in the heavens: He hath done whatsoever He hath pleased.

12. The Lord hath been mindful of us, He will bless us.

13. He will bless them that fear the Lord, both small and great.

17. The dead praise not the Lord, neither any that go down into silence.

18. But we will praise the Lord, from this time forth for evermore. Amen.

Gadsby.

1439

Psalm x.   12. Arise, O Lord God, lift up Thine hand : forget not the humble.

xxii.   4. Our fathers hoped in Thee : they trusted in Thee, and Thou didst deliver them.

Psalm iii.   3, 4.

For Thou, O Lord, art my defence ;
 On Thee my hopes rely ;
 Thou art my Glory, and shalt yet
  Lift up my head on high.

Salvation to the Lord belongs,
 He only can defend ;
 His blessing He extends to all
  That on His power depend.

Jekyll.

1440

The Song of Solomon iii.   11. Go forth, ye daughters of Zion, and behold King Solomon with the crown wherewith his mother crowned him in the day of the gladness of his heart.

Psalm lxxxiv.   9. Behold, O Lord, our defender, and look upon the face of Thine anointed.

lxi.   7. Let *her* dwell before Thee for ever.   O prepare Thy loving mercy and faithfulness, that they may preserve *her*.

lxxii.   7. In *her* time let the righteous flourish, and let peace be in all *her* borders :

cxxxii.   18. Upon *herself* let *her* crown flourish.

cxi.   4. The merciful and gracious Lord hath so done His marvellous works that they ought to be had in remembrance.

2 Chronicles xxxiii.   13. And all the people of the land rejoiced and sounded with trumpets : also the singers, with instruments of music, rejoiced.   Hallelujah ! Amen.

Jekyll.

Sometimes sung as a separate Anthem.

1441

PSALM xliii. 3. O send out Thy light and Thy truth, that they may lead me, and bring me unto Thy holy hill, and to Thy dwelling.

xxxi. 18. Shew Thy servant the light of Thy countenance, and save me for Thy mercy's sake.

xxxvii. 30. The righteous shall inherit the land, and dwell therein for ever.

ISAIAH xxxv. 10. And sorrow and sighing shall flee away.

xl. 31. They that wait upon the LORD shall renew their strength; they shall mount up as eagles; they shall run, and not be weary; and shall walk, and not faint.

PSALM ciii. 1. Praise the LORD, O my soul. Amen.

JEKYLL.

1442

PSALM xvi. 1. Preserve me, O GOD : for in Thee have I put my trust.

12. Thou shalt shew me the path of life; in Thy presence is the fulness of joy.

JOB iii. 17. There the wicked cease from troubling; there the weary are at rest.

JEKYLL.

1443

PSALM ciii. 8. The LORD is full of compassion and mercy, longsuffering, and of great goodness.

xxii. 26. The poor shall eat, and be satisfied : they that seek after the LORD shall praise Him : your heart shall live for ever.

JEKYLL.

1444

PSALM xxv. 8. Them that are meek shall be guided in judgment : and such as are gentle, them shall He learn His way.

9. All the paths of the LORD are mercy and truth, unto such as keep His covenant, and His testimonies.

19. O keep my soul, and deliver me: let me not be confounded, for I have put my trust in Thee

JEKYLL.

1445

ISAIAH xxvi. 3. Thou wilt keep him in perfect peace, whose mind is stayed on Thee: because he trusteth in Thee.

19. Thy dead men shall live, together with my dead body shall they arise. Awake and sing, ye that dwell in dust : for thy dew is as the dew of herbs, and the earth shall cast out the dead. Amen.

JEKYLL.

1446 TORRANCE, TRIMNELL, v. 3. [Amen.]

1447

Hail ! Festal Day ! Hail ! ever sacred tide,
Wherein the Bridegroom weds the Church, His Bride.

1. This is the court of GOD ; the craving mind
   Here wealth of Solomon in peace may find.

2. Here David's Son, Who heav'n and earth doth span,
   In this our Mother home, is GOD and Man.

3. Ye have a harmony with heav'n above,
   If but the faith be kept, the bond of love.

4. Here New Jerusalem, all pure and bright,
   Descends from GOD, in bridal vesture dight.

5. The King of Righteousness, within this place,
   From Heav'n bestows the font's baptismal grace.

6. 'Tis here the soul draws nigh to David's shrine,
   Here finds the pledges mystical, divine.

7. This is the Ark of GOD, which goes before
   Our steps, advancing on from shore to shore.

8. Here Jacob's ladder points the heavenly way ;
   Here we ascend to life's eternal day.

POWELL

1448

1. Hail ! Festal Day ! to endless ages known,
   When GOD ascended to His starry Throne.

2. Now with the LORD of new and Heavenly birth
   His gifts return to grace the springing earth.

3. Now glows the year with painted flowers' array,
   And warmer light unbars the gates of day.

4. Now CHRIST from gloomy Hell comes triumphing;
   And field and grove with flowers and leafage spring.

5. The reign of Hell o'erthrown, He mounts on high ;
   Sent forth with joyous praise from sea and sky.

6. Loose now the captives, loose the prison door,
   The fallen from the deep to light restore.

7. A countless people, from death's bondage freed,
   Own Thee Redeemer, following Thy lead.

8. Stainless and strong, and in Thine arms sustained,
   Bear them to GOD, an offspring purely gained.

9. One wreath be Thine, that of Thy labour comes,
   And one, that of Thy ransomed people blooms.

10. Creator and Redeemer, CHRIST our Light,
    The One begotten of the Father's might ;

11. Co-equal, co-eternal, Thou to Whom
    The Kingdom of the world decreed shall come.

12. Thou, looking on our race in darkness laid,
    To rescue man, Thyself true man was made.

POWELL.

1449

O JESU, Victim blest,
  What else but love divine
Could Thee constrain to open thus
  That sacred Heart of Thine?

  O Fount of endless life,
  O Spring of water clear !
O flame celestial, cleansing all
  Who unto Thee draw near !

  Hide me in Thy dear Heart,
  For thither do I fly ;
There seek Thy grace through life, in death
  Thine immortality.

POWELL.

1450

Lead us, Heavenly Father, lead us
   O'er the world's tempestuous sea ;
Guide us, guard us, keep us, feed us,
   For we have no help but Thee,
Yet possessing every blessing
   If our GOD our Father be.

SAVIOUR, breathe forgiveness o'er us,
   All our weakness Thou dost know ;
Thou didst tread this earth before us,
   Thou didst feel its keenest woe :
Lone and dreary, faint and weary,
   Through the desert Thou didst go.

Spirit of our GOD, descending,
   Fill our hearts with heavenly joy,
Love with every passion blending,
   Pleasure that can never cloy ;
Thus provided, pardoned, guided,
   Nothing can our peace destroy.   Amen.
                        POWELL.

1451

O Saving Victim, opening wide
   The gate of Heaven to man below,
Our foes press on from every side,
   Thine aid supply, Thy strength bestow.

To Thy great Name be thanks and praise,
   Immortal Godhead, One in Three ;
O grant us endless length of days,
   In our true native land with Thee.   Amen.
                 MILLER, POWELL.

1452

SON of GOD, for man decreed
To be born the woman's Seed,
Very GOD and Man indeed,
       Hear us, Holy JESU,

God with us, Emmanuel,
Coming here as Man to dwell,
Saving us when Adam fell,
  Hear us, Holy Jesu.

Saviour, full of truth and grace,
Leaving Thine eternal place
To restore our fallen race,
  Hear us, Holy Jesu.

Image of the God unseen,
Still what Thou hadst ever been,
Though in form of Infant mean,
  Hear us, Holy Jesu.

Only Victim we can plead,
Our High Priest to intercede,
Advocate in all our need,
  Hear us, Holy Jesu.

       Powell.

1453.

Psalm cxxxii. 8. Arise, O Lord, into Thy resting-place, Thou, and the ark of Thy strength.

9. Let Thy priests be clothed with righteousness, and let Thy saints sing with joyfulness.†

15. This shall be my rest for ever: here will I dwell, for I have a delight therein.

Genesis xxviii. 16, 17. Surely the Lord is in this place. How dreadful is this place! this is none other but the House of God, and this is the gate of Heaven.

       Agutter, Cobb.

  † Ends here.

1454

Psalm cxxxiv. 1. Behold, now praise the Lord, all ye servants of the Lord:

2. Ye that stand in the house of the Lord, in the courts of the house of our God.

cxxxv. 3. O praise the Lord, for the Lord is gracious: O sing praises unto His Name, for it is lovely.

If to the LORD our hearts we give,
   In purity and love,
Then by our Saviour's death we live
   And dwell with Him above.

cxxviii. 5. Lo! thus shall the man be blessed that
feareth the LORD.

cxxxiv. 1. Now, praise the LORD, all ye servants of
the LORD.

MARTIN.

1455

Come, my soul, while daylight dying,
   Moments flying,
Bring the end to one more day ;
Come to Him, Whose mighty powers
   Rule the hours,
Know no rest, nor change display.

Come, Holy Ghost, Thy grace impart,
And comfort every longing heart.

Glory, honour, praise, thanksgiving,
   To the Living
Mighty, Gracious, Potent One,
   Father, Son, and Holy Spirit,
   Praise and merit
Now, and aye, till time be done. Amen.

MARTIN.

1456

1. Far from my heavenly home,
   Far from my Father's breast,
Fainting I cry, " Blest Spirit, come,
   And speed me to my rest."

2. Upon the willows long,
   My harp hath silent hung ;
How should I sing a cheerful song
   Till Thou inspire my tongue.

3. My spirit homeward turns,
   And fain would thither flee ,
My heart, O Sion, droops and yearns
   When I remember thee.

4. To thee, to thee, I press,
   A dark and toilsome road ;
When shall I pass the wilderness,
   And reach the saints' abode ?

5. GOD, of my life, be near,
   On Thee my hopes I cast :
Oh, guide me through the desert here,
   And bring me home at last. 'Amen.

MARTIN, PAGE, 1, 3-5; VINCENT, 1-5.

1457

ISAIAH lv.   1. Ho, every one that thirsteth, come ye to the waters, and he that hath no money ; come ye, buy, and eat.

2. Wherefore do ye spend money for that which is not bread ? and your labour for that which satisfieth not ? Hearken diligently unto Me, eat ye that which is good, and let your soul delight itself in fatness.

3. Incline your ear, and come unto Me : hear, and your soul shall live.

1. Ho, every one that thirsteth, come ye to the waters, and he that hath no money ; come ye, buy and eat.

7. Let the wicked forsake his way, and the unrighteous man his thoughts : and let him return unto the LORD, and He will have mercy upon him ; and, to our GOD, for He will abundantly pardon.

3. Incline your ear, and come unto Me : hear, and your soul shall live.

12. Then ye shall go out with joy, and be led forth with peace : the mountains and hills shall break forth before you into singing, and all the trees of the fields shall clap their hands. Then ye shall go out with joy, and be led forth with peace : the mountains and hills shall break forth before you into singing.

13. Instead of the thorn shall come up the fir tree, instead of the brier, shall come up the myrtle tree.

1, 12. Ho, every one that thirsteth, come ye, come to the waters : then ye shall go out with joy.

MARTIN.

1458

Veni, Sancte Spiritus,
Et emitte cœlitus
Lucis tuæ radium.

Veni, pater pauperum,
Veni, dator munerum,
Veni, lumen cordium.

Consolator optime,
Dulcis hospes animæ,
Dulce refrigerium ,

In labore requies,
In æstu temperies,
In fletu solatium.

O lux beatissima,
Reple cordis intima
Tuorum fidelium.

Sine tuo numine
Nihil est in homine,
Nihil est innoxium.

Lava quod est sordidum,
Riga quod est aridum,
Rege quod est devium ;

Fove quod est languidum,
Flecte quod est rigidum,
Sana quod est saucium.

Da tuis fidelibus
In te confidentibus
Sacrum septenarium ;

Da virtutis meritum,
Da salutis exitum.
Da perenne gaudium.   Amen

English Version.

Holy Spirit, come, O come,
Send from Thy celestial home
  The glory of Thy Light divine.

Father of the poor, descend,
Bounteous Giver, constant Friend,
  Come into our hearts and shine.

Thou of comforters the Best,
Thou the soul's most joyous Guest,
  Thou, all-quickening, saving One ;

'Mid earth's labour Rest most meet,
'Mid earth's tempest Calm most sweet,
  'Mid earth's tears true Peace alone.

Come then, O most blessed Light,
Come, and fill with radiance bright
  Hearts most faithfully Thine own.

Thy sustaining grace apart,
Every good will fail man's heart,
  Nought therein but ill have sway.

Cleanse Thou all impurity,
Pour Thy dew upon the dry,
  Heal all wounds, all pains allay.

Gently the unyielding bend,
Warmth into the cold heart send,
  Guide the wanderer in Thy way.

On Thy faithful here below,
Trusting in Thy strength, bestow
  This Thy holy sevenfold grace ;

Grant them strength that shall uplift,
Grant salvation's highest gift,
  Ever to behold Thy Face. Amen.

MARTIN.

1459

Holiest, breathe an evening blessing,
  Ere repose our spirits seal ;
Sin and want we come confessing,
  Thou canst save, and Thou canst heal.

Though the night be dark and dreary,
  Darkness cannot hide from Thee ;
Thou art He Who, never weary,
  Watches where Thy children be.

Though destruction walk around us,
  Though the arrow past us fly,
Angel guards from Thee surround us,
  We are safe if Thou art nigh.

Should swift death this night o'ertake us,
  And our couch become our tomb,
May the morn in Heaven awake us,
  Clad in light and deathless bloom.   Amen.

                                   MARTIN.

1460

PSALM c.   1. O come before His presence with singing.
 ciii. 8. The LORD is full of compassion and mercy,
long-suffering, and of great goodness.

9. He will not alway be chiding, neither keepeth He
His anger for ever.

10. He hath not dealt with us after our sins, nor
rewarded us according to our wickednesses.

11. For look how high the heaven is in comparison of
the earth ; so great is His mercy also toward them that
fear Him.

12. Look how wide also the east is from the west ; so
far hath He set our sins from us.

13. Like as a father pitieth his own children, so is the
LORD merciful to them that fear Him

                                   MARTIN.

1461 F. L. GLADSTONE, Psalm ciii. vv. 8, 10–12, 8, 10, 13.

1462

Psalm xxxiii. 1. Rejoice in the Lord, O ye righteous, for it becometh well the just to be thankful.

2. Praise the Lord with harp, sing praises unto Him with the lute, and instrument of ten strings.

Amos v. 8. Seek Him Who maketh the seven stars and Orion, and turneth the shadow of death into the morning, and maketh the day dark with night.

Save us, O Lord, while waking, and defend us while sleeping, that when we are awake we may watch with Christ, and when we sleep we may rest in peace.

> O may my soul on Thee repose,
> And may sweet sleep mine eyelids close:
> Sleep that shall me more vigorous make
> To serve my God when I awake.

Psalm xxxiii. 1. Rejoice in the Lord, O ye righteous. Rejoice, rejoice, and be thankful.

Alleluia! Praise the Lord, rejoice in the Lord, and be thankful.

> Praise God from Whom all blessings flow;
> Praise Him, all creatures here below;
> Praise Him above, Angelic Host,
> Praise Father, Son, and Holy Ghost. Amen.

—— Sometimes sung as a separate Anthem. Martin.

1463

Psalm xci. 1. Whoso dwelleth under the defence of the Most High shall abide under the shadow of the Almighty.

2. I will say unto the Lord, Thou art my hope and my stronghold, my God, in Him will I trust.

4. He shall defend thee under His wings, and thou shalt be safe under His feathers; His faithfulness and truth shall be thy shield and buckler.

1. Whoso dwelleth under the defence of the Most High shall abide under the shadow of the Almighty.

O Jesu, King of Paradise, O keep me in Thy love,
And guide me to that happy land of perfect rest above,
Where loyal hearts and true stand ever in the light,
All rapture through and through, in God's most holy sight.

Martin.

1464

" Highest Omnipotent good LORD,
Glory and honour to Thy Name adored,
And praise and every blessing.
Of everything Thou art the source,
No man is worthy to pronounce Thy Name.

" Praised by His creatures all,
Praised be the LORD my GOD ;
By the great Sun my brother, above all,
Who, by his rays, lights us and lights the day ;
Radiant is he, with his great splendour stored,
Thy glory, LORD, confessing.

" By Sister Moon and stars my LORD is praised,
Where, clear and fair, they in the heavens are raised.

" By Brother Wind, my LORD, Thy praise is said,
By air and clouds, and the blue sky o'erhead,
By which Thy creatures all are kept and fed.

" By one most humble, useful, precious, chaste,
By Sister Water, O my LORD, Thou art praised.

" And praised is my LORD
By Brother Fire—he who lights up the night :
Jocund, robust is he, and strong and bright.

" Praised art Thou, my LORD, by Mother Earth ;
Thou who sustainest her, and governest,
And to her flowers, fruit, herbs, dost colour give, and birth.

" And praised is my LORD
By those who, for Thy love, can pardon give,
And bear the weakness and the wrongs of men.
Blessed are those who suffer thus in peace,
By Thee, the Highest, to be crowned in Heaven."

J. F. BRIDGE.

1465

PSALM xxxvii. 35. Hope thou in the LORD, and keep
His way, and He shall promote thee, that thou shalt
possess the land. When the ungodly shall perish, thou
shalt see it.

36. I myself have seen the ungodly in great power, and
flourishing like a green bay-tree.

37. I went by, and lo he was gone : I sought him, but his place could nowhere be found.

38. Keep innocency, and take heed to the thing that is right : for that shall bring a man peace at the last.

[39. As for the transgressors, they shall perish together ; and the end of the ungodly is, they shall be rooted out.

40. But the salvation of the righteous cometh of the LORD, Who is also their strength in the time of trouble.

41. And the LORD shall stand by them, and save them, He shall deliver them from the ungodly, because they put their trust in Him.]

J. F. BRIDGE.

1466 CALKIN, vv. 38–41.

1467

PSALM xcii. 1. It is a good thing to give thanks unto the LORD : and to sing praises unto Thy Name, O [Thou] Most Highest ;

2. To tell of Thy loving-kindness early in the morning, and of Thy truth in the night season ;

3. Upon an instrument of ten strings, and upon the lute ; upon a loud instrument, and upon the harp.

4. For Thou, LORD, hast made me glad through Thy works : and I will rejoice in giving praise for the operation of Thy hands.

5. O LORD, how glorious are Thy works ! Thy thoughts are very deep.

[6. An unwise man doth not well consider this, and a fool doth not understand it.]

cii. 25. Of old Thou hast laid the foundation of the earth ; and the heavens are the work of Thy hands.

26. They shall perish, but Thou shalt endure ; they all shall wax old as doth a garment ;

27. And as a vesture shalt Thou change them, and they shall be changed ; but Thou art the same, and Thy years shall not fail.

civ. 33. I will sing unto the LORD as long as I live ; I will praise my GOD while I have my being.

J. F. BRIDGF.

1468 KENT, PATTISON, vv. 1 4. Hallelujah. Amen.]
1469 PILCHI L, vv. 1 6. 4 Hallelujah.

1470

JESUS, pro me perforatus,
Condar intra Tuum latus;
Tu, per lympham profluentem,
Tu, per sanguinem tepentem,
In peccata mî redunda,
Tolle culpam sordes munda.

Coram Te, nec justus forem,
Quamvis totâ vi laborem,
Nec si fide nunquam cesso.
Fletu stillans indefesso:
Tibi soli tantum munus;
Salva me, Salvator unus.

Nil in manu mecum fero,
Sed me versus Crucem gero;
Vestimenta nudus oro,
Opem debilis imploro;
Fontem Christi quæro immundus,
Nisi laves, moribundus.

Dum hos artus vita regit;
Quando nox sepulchro tegit;
Mortuos cum stare jubes,
Sedens Judex inter nubes;
JESUS, pro me perforatus,
Condar intra Tuum latus.

English Version.

Rock of Ages, cleft for me,
Let me hide myself in Thee,
Let the water, and the blood,
From Thy riven Side which flowed,
Be of sin the double cure,
Cleanse from guilt and make me pure.

Not the labours of my hands
Can fulfil Thy law's demands;
Could my zeal no respite know,
Could my tears for ever flow,
All for sin could not atone:
Thou must save, and Thou alone.

Nothing in my hand I bring,
Simply to Thy Cross I cling;
Naked, come to Thee for dress;
Helpless, look to Thee for grace;
Foul, I to the Fountain fly;
Wash me, Saviour, or I die.

While I draw this fleeting breath,
When mine eyelids close in death,
When I rise to worlds unknown,
See Thee on Thy Judgment Throne;
Rock of Ages, cleft for me,
Let me hide myself in Thee.

J. F. Bridge.

1471

2 Chronicles ix. 8. Blessed be the Lord thy God, Which delighted in thee to set thee on His Throne, to be King for the Lord thy God; because thy God loved Israel, therefore made He thee King, to do judgment and justice.

J. F. Bridge.

1472

Philippians ii. 8. Christ became obedient unto death, even the death of the Cross.

9. Wherefore God also hath highly exalted Him and given Him a Name which is above every name.

10. That at the Name of Jesus every knee should bow, of things in heaven, and things in earth, and things under the earth.

11. And that every tongue should confess that Jesus Christ is Lord, to the glory of God the Father. Amen.

J. F. Bridge.

1473

1 Thessalonians v. 9. God hath not appointed us to wrath, but to obtain salvation by our Lord Jesus Christ;

10. Who died for us, that, whether we wake or sleep, we should live together with Him.

J. F. Bridge.

1474

PSALM xcvi. 8. Give unto the LORD the glory due unto His Name: bring an offering, and come into His courts.

PROVERBS iii. 9. Honour the LORD with thy substance, and with the first-fruits of all thine increase.

10. So shall thy barns be filled with plenty, and thy presses shall burst out with new wine.

PSALM xcvi. 8. Give unto the LORD the glory due unto His Name.

J. F. BRIDGE.

1475

PSALM cxli. 1. LORD, I call upon Thee, haste Thee unto me, and consider my voice when I cry unto Thee.

2. Let my prayer be set forth in Thy sight as the incense, and let the lifting up of my hands be an evening sacrifice.

[3. Set a watch, O LORD, before my mouth, and keep the door of my lips.

4. O let not mine heart be inclined to any evil thing: let me not be occupied in ungodly works.

9. Mine eyes look unto Thee, O LORD GOD: in Thee is my trust, O cast not out my soul.]

Glory to Thee, my GOD, this night,
For all the blessings of the light;
Keep me, O keep me, King of Kings,
Beneath Thine own Almighty wings. Amen.

J. F. BRIDGE.

1476 BAKER, v. 9.
1477 OUSELEY, WEST, vv. 1, 2. [Amen.]
1478 G. T. SMITH, vv. 1-4, 9.

1479

O most merciful! O most bountiful!
  GOD, the Father Almighty,
By the Redeemer's sweet intercession,
  Hear us, help us, when we cry.

J F. BRIDGE, ELLIOTT.

1480

NEHEMIAH ii. 20. The GOD of Heaven, He will prosper us ; therefore we HIS servants will arise and build :

PSALM cxxvii. 1. Except the LORD build the house, their labour is but lost that build ; except the LORD the city keep, the watchman waketh but in vain.

PSALM cxxiv. 8. Our help is in the Name of the LORD, the LORD Who heaven and earth hath made.

NEHEMIAH ii. 20. The GOD of Heaven will prosper us, therefore will we arise and build. He will prosper us.

J. F. BRIDGE.

1481

PSALM cxxxii. 13. The LORD hath chosen Zion ; He hath desired it for His habitation.

14. This is My rest for ever, here will I dwell, for I have desired it.

16. I will also clothe her priests with salvation, and her saints shall shout aloud for joy.

J. F. BRIDGE.

1482

PSALM xxxvii. 23. The LORD ordereth a good man's going, and maketh his way acceptable to Himself.

24. Though he fall, he shall not be cast away : for the LORD upholdeth him with His hand.

28. For the LORD loveth the thing that is right : He forsaketh not His that be godly, but they are preserved for ever.

J. F. BRIDGE.

1483

MALACHI iv. 2. Unto you that fear My Name shall the Sun of righteousness arise with healing in His wings.

ISAIAH lx. 20. Thy sun shall no more go down : for the LORD shall be thine everlasting Light, and the days of thy mourning shall be ended.

J. F. BRIDGE.

1484

ISAIAH lvii. 15. Thus saith the high and lofty One that inhabiteth eternity, Whose Name is Holy: I dwell in the high and holy place, with him also that is of a contrite and humble spirit, to revive the spirit of the humble, and to revive the heart of the contrite ones.

16. For I will not contend for ever, neither will I be always wroth.

18. I have seen his ways, and will heal him: I will lead him also, and restore comforts unto him and to his mourners.

19. Peace, peace to him that is far off, and to him that is near, saith the LORD.

lv. 6. Seek ye the LORD while He may be found, call ye upon Him while He is near.

7. Let the wicked forsake his way, and the unrighteous man his thoughts: and let him return unto the LORD, and He will have mercy upon him; and to our GOD, for He will abundantly pardon.

J. F. BRIDGE.

1485 BRADLEY, KINSLY, ROBERTS, lv. 6, 7.
1486 VERRINDER, lv. 6.

1487

ACTS xiii. 32. We declare unto you glad tidings, how that the promise which was made unto the fathers, ·

33. GOD hath fulfilled the same unto us their children, in that He hath raised up JESUS again.

J. F. BRIDGE.

1488

ST. JOHN xiv. 1. Let not your heart be troubled, neither let it be afraid. Ye believe in GOD, believe also in Me;

13. And whatsoever ye shall ask in My Name, that will I do, that the Father may be glorified in the Son.

15. If ye love Me, keep My commandments.

16, 17. And I will pray the Father and He shall give you another Comforter, even the Spirit of truth. that He may abide with you for ever.

TRELBATH.

1489

St. John xiv. 2. In my Father's house are many mansions : if it were not so, I would have told you. I go to prepare a place for you.

16, 17. And I will pray the Father, and He shall give you another Comforter, even the Spirit of truth.

18. I will not leave you comfortless : I will come to you.

27. Peace I leave with you, My peace I give unto you : not as the world giveth, give I unto you.

Crament.

1490

Psalm xxix. 1. Bring unto the Lord, O ye mighty, bring young rams unto the Lord : ascribe unto the Lord worship and strength.

2. Give the Lord the honour due unto His Name : worship the Lord with holy worship.

3. It is the Lord that commandeth the waters ; it is the glorious God that maketh the thunder.

4. It is the Lord that ruleth the sea ; the voice of the Lord is mighty in operation, the voice of the Lord is a glorious voice.

9. The Lord sitteth above the water-flood, and the Lord remaineth a King for ever.

10. The Lord shall give strength unto His people : the Lord shall give His people the blessing of peace.

F. E. Gladstone.

1491 S. Arnold, vv. 2-4, 9. Hallelujah. Amen.
1492 W. Hayes, vv. 1-4, 10. Amen.
1493 Kent, C. H. Lloyd, vv. 2-4, 9, 10. Hallelujah. Amen.

1494

Romans viii. 32. He that spared not His own Son, but delivered Him up for us all, how shall He not with Him also freely give us all things ?

34. It is Christ that died, yea rather, that is risen again, Who is even at the right hand of God,

38, 39. Neither death, nor life, nor height. nor depth, shall be able to separate us from the love of God, Which is in Christ Jesus our Lord.

F. E. Gladstone.

1495

1 St. John iv. 9. In this was manifested the love of God towards us, because that God sent His only begotten Son into the world, that we might live through Him.

11. Beloved, if God so loved us, we ought also to love one another.

(*From " Philippi,"* No. 17.)

F. E. Gladstone; C. H. Lloyd.

1496

Lamentations iii. 24. The Lord is my portion, saith my soul; therefore will I hope in Him.

Habakkuk iii. 17. Although the fig tree shall not blossom, neither shall fruit be in the vines; the labour of the olive shall fail, and the fields shall yield no meat; the flock shall be cut off from the fold, and there shall be no herd in the stalls:

18. Yet I will rejoice in the Lord, I will joy in the God of my salvation.

F. E. Gladstone.

1497

Let me be with Thee where Thou art,
  My Saviour, my Eternal Rest:
Then only will this longing heart
  Be fully and completely blest.

Let me be with Thee where Thou art,
  Thy unveiled glory to behold;
Then only will this longing heart
  Cease to be treacherous, faithless, cold.

Page.

1498

Genesis viii. 22. While the earth remaineth, seedtime and harvest shall not cease, saith the Lord.

Psalm xxvii. 7. Therefore will we offer in His dwelling an oblation with great gladness.

Isaiah lvi. 7. Their offerings shall come up with acceptance upon Mine Altar, saith the Lord.

PSALM cxlv. 7. The memorial of His abundant kindness shall be shewed,

cxvi. 16. In the courts of the LORD's house. Alleluia. Amen.

HEAP.

1499

JESU, Lover of my soul,
　Let me to Thy bosom fly,
While the gathering waters roll,
　While the tempest still is high :
Hide me, O my Saviour, hide,
　Till the storm of life be past ;
Safe into the haven guide,
　O receive my soul at last.

Other refuge have I none ;
　Hangs my helpless soul on Thee ;
Leave, ah, leave me not alone,
　Still support and comfort me.
All my trust on Thee is stayed,
　All my help from Thee I bring ;
Cover my defenceless head
　With the shadow of Thy wing. Amen.

ILIFFE.

1500

PSALM cxliii. 1. Hearken, O LORD, to my petition, and incline Thine ear.

7. O LORD, speedily make answer, for my heart is faint.

10, 8. Teach me to do Thy will, shew me the way to walk in, for Thou art my GOD. Thy Spirit is good.

(From "The Rose of Sharon.") MACKENZIE.

1501

PSALM c. 1. Make a joyful noise unto the LORD, all ye lands :

2. Serve the LORD with gladness, come before His presence with a song.

3. Enter into His gates with thanksgiving, and into His courts with praise.

4. For the LORD is good, His mercy is everlasting.

(From "The Rose of Sharon.) MACKENZIE.

1502

Isaiah xlix. 13, 14, 9, 10. Sing, O heavens; and be joyful, O earth: break forth into singing, O mountains: for the Lord hath comforted His people, and had mercy on His afflicted. We said, The Lord hath forsaken them, my Lord hath forgotten them. But He said to the prisoners, Go forth; to them that were in darkness, Shew yourselves. We shall not hunger nor thirst; neither shall the sun smite us: for He that hath mercy shall lead us, even by springs of water shall He guide us.

(From " The Rose of Sharon.") Mackenzie.

1503

Proverbs x. 22. The blessing of the Lord, it maketh rich, and He addeth no sorrow with it.

24. The fear of the wicked, it shall come upon him: but the desire of the righteous shall be granted. Amen.

Mackenzie.

1504

Psalm xxvii. 8. Hearken unto my voice, O Lord, when I cry unto Thee: have mercy upon me and hear me.

10. O hide not Thou Thy face from me, nor cast Thy servant away in displeasure.

11. Thou hast been my succour: leave me not, neither forsake me, O God of my salvation.

16. O tarry thou the Lord's leisure; be strong, and He shall comfort thine heart, and put thou thy trust in the Lord.

Sydenham.

1505 Kent, vv. 8, 10.
1506 West, v. 16.

1507

Spare us, Lord most holy: let us never fall from Thee. For Thou art merciful, Thou alone, mighty to save us.

Sydenham.

1508

PSALM cvii. 1. O give thanks unto the LORD, for He is gracious, and His mercy endureth for ever.

cv. 8. He hath been alway mindful of His covenant and promise, that He made to a thousand generations.

cvii. 9. For He satisfieth the empty soul, and filleth the hungry soul with goodness.

civ. 14. He bringeth forth grass for the cattle, and green herb for the service of men.

13. He watereth the hills from above: the earth is filled with the fruit of His works.

cv. 2. O let your songs be of Him, and praise Him: and let your talking be of all His wondrous works.

cl. 6. Let everything that hath life and breath, praise the LORD.

SYDENHAM.

1509

JEREMIAH xxiii. 5. Behold, the days come, saith the LORD, that I will raise unto David a righteous Branch, and a King shall reign and prosper, [and shall execute judgment and justice in the earth.]

6. In His days Judah shall be saved, and Israel shall dwell safely: and this is His Name whereby He shall be called, The LORD our Righteousness.

ISAIAH lx. 18. Then shalt thou call thy walls Salvation, and thy gates Praise.

liv. 13. And thy children shall be all taught of the LORD, and great shall be the peace of thy children.

v. 17. Then shall the lambs feed after their manner.

xi. 7. The lion shall eat straw like the ox.

6. The wolf and the lamb shall dwell together, and a little child shall lead them.

9. They shall not hurt nor kill in all My holy mountain.

O home of fadeless beauty, of flowers that fear no thorn,
Where they shall dwell as children, who here as exiles
mourn.
The Lamb is all Thy splendour, the Crucified Thy praise,
His laud and benediction Thy ransomed people raise.

Hallelujah. Amen.

H. H. W....W ..D.

1510 THOMAS, xv. 5, 6.

1511

The radiant morn hath passed away,
And spent too soon her golden store ;
The shadows of departing day
　　　　Creep on once more.

Our life is but a fading dawn,
Its glorious noon, how quickly past !
Lead us, O CHRIST, when all is gone,
　　　　Safe home at last,

Where saints are clothed in spotless white,
And evening shadows never fall,
Where Thou, Eternal Light of Light,
　　　　Art LORD of all.

H. H. WOODWARD.

1512

ISAIAH lx. 19. The Sun shall be no more thy light by
day, neither for brightness the Moon by night : but the
LORD thy GOD shall be thine everlasting Light, and thy
GOD thy Glory.

xxxiii. 17. Thine eyes shall see the King in His
beauty : they shall behold the land which is very far off.

O GOD of Saints, to Thee we cry ;
O SAVIOUR, plead for us on high ;
O HOLY GHOST, our Guide and Friend,
Grant us Thy grace till life shall end ;
That with all Saints our rest may be
In that bright Paradise with Thee. Amen.

H. H. WOODWARD.

1513

PSALM lxiii. 23. Thou shalt guide me with Thy
counsel, and after that receive me with glory.

24. Whom have I in heaven but Thee ? and there is
none on earth to compare with Thee. O guide me.

R. ROGERS.

1514

PSALM vii. 18. I will give thanks unto the LORD,
according to His righteousness, and I will praise the
Name of the LORD Most High.

R. ROGERS.

1515

PSALM lxv. 5. Thou shalt shew us wonderful things in Thy righteousness.

9. Thou visitest the earth and blessest it : Thou makest it very plenteous.

10. Thou preparest their corn, for so Thou providest for the earth.

cix. 29. As for me, I will give great thanks unto the LORD with my mouth, and praise Him among the multitude. Amen.

C. J. FROST.

1516

PSALM cxxvi. 1. When the LORD turned again the captivity of Sion, then were we like unto them that dream.

2. Then was our mouth filled with laughter, and our tongue with joy.

3. Then said they among the heathen, the LORD hath done great things for them.

4. Yea, the LORD hath done great things for us already, whereof we rejoice.

5. Turn our captivity, O LORD, as the rivers in the south.

6. They that sow in tears shall reap in joy.

7. He that now goeth on his way weeping, and beareth forth good seed, shall doubtless come again, and bring his sheaves with him.

C. J. FROST, PROUT.

1517 BATTEN, NARES, vv. 1–4. [Gloria Patri.]
1518 BLOW, vv. 1–6. Hallelujah.

1519

Prevent us, O LORD, in all our doings with Thy most gracious favour, and further us with Thy continual help ; that in all our works begun, continued, and ended in Thee, we may glorify Thy holy Name, and finally by Thy mercy obtain everlasting life ; through JESUS CHRIST our LORD. Amen.

PALEY,

1520

PSALM xxxii. 1. Blessed is he whose unrighteousness is forgiven, and whose sin is covered.

i. 3. For he shall be like a tree planted by the water-side.

xxxii. 2. Blessed is he to whom the LORD will not impute sin, and in whose spirit there is no guile. Blessed for ever is he.

11. Great plagues remain for the ungodly. but whoso putteth his trust in the LORD, mercy embraceth him on every side.

12. Be glad, O ye righteous, and rejoice in the LORD : and be joyful, all ye that are true of heart. Amen.

PARRY.

1521 OUSELEY, vv. 1, 2, 11.

1522

PSALM cxix. 1. Blessed are the undefiled in the way, who walk in the law of the LORD.

2. Blessed are they that keep His testimonies, and that seek Him with the whole heart.

li. 10. Create in me a clean heart, O GOD, and renew a right spirit within me.

REVELATION ii. 10. Be thou faithful unto death, and I will give thee a crown of life.

SEWELL.

1523

PSALM cxviii. 24. This is the day which the LORD hath made : we will rejoice and be glad in it.

1 CORINTHIANS xv. 20. For now is CHRIST risen from the dead, and become the firstfruits of them that slept.

21. For since by man came death, by man came also the resurrection of the dead.

22. For as in Adam all die, even so in CHRIST shall all be made alive.

57. Thanks be to GOD, Which giveth us the victory through our LORD JESUS CHRIST. Hallelujah. Amen.

S. C. COOKE. SEWELL.

1524

ISAIAH lii. 9. Break forth into joy, sing together, ye
waste places of Jerusalem: for the LORD hath comforted
His people, He hath redeemed Jerusalem.

10. The LORD hath made bare His holy arm in the
eyes of all the nations: and all the ends of the earth
shall see the salvation of our GOD.

XI. 6. For unto us a Child is born, unto us a Son is
given: and the government shall be upon His shoulder;
and His Name shall be called Wonderful, Counsellor, The
Mighty GOD, The Everlasting Father, The Prince of Peace.

ISAIAH lii. 9. Break forth into joy. Hallelujah.

SEWELL.

1525 PALESTRINA, PRENTICE, vv. 9, 10.

1526

Art thou weary, art thou languid,
   Art thou sore distrest?
" Come to Me," saith One, " and coming,
    Be at rest."

Hath He marks to lead me to Him.
   If He be my Guide?
" In His Feet and Hands are Wound-prints,
    And His Side."

Hath He diadem as Monarch
   That His brow adorns?
" Yea, a Crown, in very surety,
    But of Thorns."

If I find Him, if I follow,
   What His guerdon here?
" Many a sorrow, many a labour,
    Many a tear."

If I still hold closely to Him,
   What hath He at last?
" Sorrow vanquished, labour ended,
    Jordan past."

If I ask Him to receive me,
   Will He say me nay?
" Not till earth, and not till heaven
    Pass away."

Finding, following, keeping, struggling,
   Is He sure to bless?
" Angels, Martyrs, Prophets, Virgins,
   Answer, Yes! "

C. H. LLOYD.

1527

HEBREWS iv. 16. Let us come boldly unto the throne of grace, that we may obtain mercy, and find grace to help in time of need.

C. H. LLOYD.

1528

I CHRONICLES xxix. 14. Who are we, O LORD, that we should be able to offer so willingly after this sort? For all things come of Thee, and of Thine own have we given Thee.

C. H. LLOYD.

1529

Come unto CHRIST, ye mourners,
   And He will give you rest;
Come with your sins and sorrows
   To His all-pitying breast.

Come to the arms that love you,
   Out-stretched upon the Cross,
Come to the patient Saviour,
   That knows your grief and loss.

Behold Him gently knocking
   Without the fast-closed door;
Have ye no word of welcome,
   And must He knock no more?

O come and open quickly,
   Before He turn away;
And through the doorway streaming
   Shall shine the light of day.

Come unto CHRIST, ye mourners,
   And find in Him your peace;
For He is consolation.
   And He has sure release

Come to the love unending,
The perfect sympathy ;
And He shall be your solace
To all eternity.

SOMERSET.

1530

There is a green hill far away,
Without a city wall,
Where the dear LORD was crucified,
Who died to save us all.

We may not know, we cannot tell
What pains He had to bear,
But we believe it was for us
He hung and suffered there.

He died that we might be forgiven,
He died to make us good,
That we might go at last to Heaven,
Saved by His precious Blood.

There was no other good enough
To pay the price of sin ;
He only could unlock the gate
Of Heaven, and let us in.

O dearly, dearly has He loved,
And we must love Him too,
And trust in His redeeming Blood,
And try His works to do.

GOUNOD, SOMERSET.

1531

ST. LUKE ii. 15. Let us now go even unto Bethlehem, and see this thing which is come to pass, which the LORD hath made known unto us.

16. And they came with haste, and found Mary, and Joseph, and the Babe lying in a manger.

20. And the shepherds returned, glorifying and praising GOD for all the things that they had heard and seen, as it was told unto them.

This is He Whom seers in old time
Chanted of with one accord ;
Whom the voices of the Prophets
Promised in their faithful word :
Now He shines, the long expected :
Let creation praise its LORD
Evermore and evermore. Amen.

FIELD.

1532

No. 1

PSALM CXXX. (*Paraphrase*). Out of darkness call I unto Thee, LORD; LORD, hearken to my calling. O be Thine ears attentive, when I make my supplication, and hear Thou me.

No. 2

If Thou, LORD, shouldst number transgressions, who shall abide it ? But with Thee is forgiveness, that we may fear Thee.

No. 3

I wait for the LORD, my soul doth wait for Him, and my hope is in His word. Yea, my soul is looking for the LORD, far more than watchmen look for the morning.

No. 4

Israel, hope thou in the LORD, for with the LORD there is mercy, and full redemption with Him.

No. 5

And He shall Israel His people from all their sins deliver. Amen.

HENSCHEL.

1533

PSALM XXXI. 26. O love the LORD, all ye His saints: for the LORD preserveth them that are faithful, and plenteously rewardeth the proud doer.

27. Be strong, and He shall establish your heart, [all ye that put your trust in the LORD]

A H. MANN.

1534 ꜱʀ ... ... v.. 26. 27. Amen.]

1535

PSALM cxviii. 19. Open ye me the gates of righteousness, that I may go into them and give thanks unto the LORD.

20. This is the gate of the LORD, the righteous shall enter into it.

ZECHARIAH ii. 10. For thus saith the LORD, I will dwell in the midst of thee for ever.

ISAIAH lx. 9. Surely the isles shall wait for Me, and the ships of Tarshish first, to bring their sons from far, their silver and gold with them, unto the Name of the LORD your GOD, and to the Holy One of Israel, because He hath glorified thee.

10. And the sons of strangers shall build up thy walls, and their kings shall minister unto thee ; for in My wrath I smote thee, but in My favour I will have mercy upon thee.

lxii. 6. I have set watchmen upon thy walls, O Jerusalem, which shall never hold their peace, day or night. Ye, that make mention of the LORD, keep not still silence.

1 KINGS ix. 3. Mine eyes and Mine heart shall be there perpetually.

PSALM cxviii. 20. This is the gate of the Lord, the righteous shall enter into it.

A. H. MANN.

1536

PSALM xliii. 4. I will go unto the Altar of GOD, even the GOD of my joy and gladness.

cxvi. 15. I will offer to Thee the sacrifice of thanksgiving, and will call upon the Name of the LORD.

12. I will receive the cup of salvation, and call upon the Name of the LORD.

> * O blest memorial of our dying LORD,
> Who living bread to men doth here afford ;
> O may our souls for ever feed on Thee,
> And Thou, O CHRIST, for ever precious be.
>
> O CHRIST, Whom now beneath a veil we see,
> May what we thirst for soon our portion be ;
> To gaze on Thee, unveiled, and see Thy Face,
> The vision of Thy glory and Thy grace. Amen.*

W. A. FROST.

—— Sometime sung as a separate Anthem.

1537

O for a closer walk with GOD,
  A calm and heavenly frame ;
A light to shine upon the road
  That leads me to the Lamb.

What peaceful hours I once enjoyed :
  How sweet their memory still :
But they have left an aching void
  The world can never fill.

Return, O Holy Dove, return,
  Sweet messenger of rest :
I hate the sins that made Thee mourn,
  And drove Thee from my breast.

The dearest idol I have known,
  Whate'er that idol be,
Help me to tear it from Thy Throne,
  And worship only Thee.

So shall my walk be close with GOD,
  Calm and serene my frame ;
So purer light shall mark the road
  That leads me to the Lamb.   Amen.

M. B. FOSTER,

1538

ST. JOHN xiv. 27. Peace I leave with you, My peace
I give unto you : not as the world giveth, give I unto you.
Let not your heart be troubled, neither let it be afraid.

xvi. 6. Because I have said these things unto you,
sorrow hath filled your heart.

33. Be of good cheer ; I have overcome the world.

King! King! lo, we adore Thee,
Raising the song of Thy triumph before Thee,
  Lord Divine.
Fled are the shadows that circled Thy dying,
Past are the pangs of the scorn and denying.
  Glory be Thine.

King! King! ever Thou hearest,
Veiled from our eyes, yet we know Thou art nearest,
  Through the long day.
Hear Thou the voice of our glad supplication,
Come, Thou Bestower of life and salvation,
  Humbly we pray.

TINNEY.

1539

DANIEL xii. 1. At that time shall Michael stand up,
the great prince which standeth for the children of Thy
people: and at that time Thy people shall be delivered,
every one that shall be found written in the Book.

3. And *they that be wise shall shine as the brightness
of the firmament; and they that turn many to righteousness as the stars for ever and ever.

MALACHI iii. 17. And they shall be Mine, saith the
LORD of Hosts, in that day when I make up My jewels.

King of Saints, to Whom the number
  Of Thy starry host is known,
Many a name, by man forgotten,
  Lives for ever round Thy Throne.
There are told Thy hidden treasures;
  Number us, O LORD, with them,
When Thou makest up the jewels
  Of Thy living diadem. Amen.

MEE.

1540 ARMES, Daniel xii. v. 3 (*They that be wise*).

1541

REVELATION vi. 9. I saw under the altar the souls of them that were slain for the word of GOD.

10. And they cried with a loud voice, How long, O LORD, holy and true, dost Thou not judge and avenge our blood on them that dwell on the earth ?

11. And white robes were given unto every one of them ; and it was said unto them, that they should rest yet for a little season, until their fellow-servants also and their brethren should be fulfilled.

From the Burial Service. Almighty GOD, with Whom the souls of the faithful are in joy and felicity, we give Thee hearty thanks, for that it hath pleased Thee to deliver these our brethren out of the miseries of this sinful world, beseeching Thee that it would please Thee shortly to accomplish the number of Thine elect, and to hasten Thy Kingdom ; that we, with all those that are departed in the true faith of Thy holy Name, may have our perfect consummation and bliss, in Thy eternal and everlasting glory.

MEE.

1542

ST. MATTHEW xxv. 5. Moram faciente sponso, dormitaverunt omnes et dormierunt.

6. Mediâ nocte clamor factus est, Ecce sponsus venit, exite obviam ei.

From the Litany. In horâ mortis et in die judicii, Libera nos, Domine. Amen.

(For English Version see No. 1805.) MEE.

1543

COLOSSIANS iii. 1 If ye then be risen with CHRIST, seek those things which are above, where CHRIST sitteth on the right hand of GOD.

2. Set your affection on things above, not on things on the earth.

3. For ye are dead, and your life is hid with CHRIST in GOD.

4. When Christ Who is our life shall appear, then shall ye also appear with Him in glory.

1. If ye then be risen with CHRIST, seek those things which are above, where CHRIST sitteth on the right hand of GOD. Hallelujah. Amen.

STANFORD.

1544 NAYLOR, vv. 1–4.

1545

PSALM cxii. 6. In memoriâ æternâ erit justus; ab auditione malâ non timebit.

cxlviii. 7, 11. Laudate Dominum de terrâ, reges terræ, et omnes populi, principes, et omnes judices terræ.

STANFORD.

1546

PSALM cii. 15, 16. The heathen shall fear Thy Name, O LORD : and all the kings of the earth shall fear Thy Majesty ; when the LORD shall build up Sion, and when His glory shall appear.

BARUCH iv. 36. O Jerusalem, look about thee toward the east, and behold the joy that cometh unto thee from GOD.

37. Lo, thy sons come, whom thou sentest away, they come gathered together from the east to the west by the word of the Holy One, rejoicing in the glory of GOD.

PSALM cii. 15, 16. The heathen shall fear Thy Name, O LORD : and all the kings of the earth shall fear Thy Majesty ; when the LORD shall build up Sion, and when His glory shall appear.

(*From "The Three Holy Children,"* No. 6.) STANFORD.

1547

ISAIAH xliii. 10. Ye are My witnesses and My servants whom I have chosen : that ye may know and believe Me, and understand that I am He. Before Me was no GOD formed, neither shall be after Me.

11. I, even I, am the LORD ; and beside Me there is no Saviour.

10, 11. That ye may know and believe Me, and understand that I am He. I, even I, am the LORD.

(*From "The Three Holy Children.* No. 13.) STANFORD.

1548

Song of the Three Children. 29. Blessed art Thou, O LORD GOD of our fathers: and to be praised and exalted above all for ever.

30. And blessed is Thy glorious and holy Name: and to be praised and exalted above all for ever.

31. Blessed art Thou in the temple of Thy holy glory: and to be praised and exalted above all for ever.

35. O all ye works of the LORD, bless ye the LORD: praise and exalt Him above all for ever.

36. O ye heavens, bless ye the LORD: praise and exalt Him above all for ever.

37. O ye angels of the LORD, bless ye the LORD: praise and exalt Him above all for ever.

38. O ye waters above the heaven, bless ye the LORD: praise and exalt Him above all for ever.

39. O all ye powers of the LORD, bless ye the LORD: praise and exalt Him above all for ever.

40. O ye sun and moon, bless ye the LORD: praise and exalt Him above all for ever.

41. Ye stars of heaven, bless ye the LORD: praise and exalt Him above all for ever

42. Ye showers and dew, bless ye the LORD: praise and exalt Him above all for ever.

43. O ye winds of GOD, bless ye the LORD: praise and exalt Him above all for ever.

PSALM cxlviii. 7. Praise the LORD upon earth: ye dragons, and all deeps;

8. Fire and hail, snow and vapours: wind and storm, fulfilling His word;

9. O ye mountains and all hills, fruitful trees and all cedars.

Song of the Three Children. 58. O ye fowls of the air, bless ye the LORD;

59. O ye beasts and cattle, bless ye the LORD;

60, 62. O ye children of men, O ye priests of the LORD, praise Him and exalt Him for ever.

68. All that worship the LORD, bless ye the LORD. Ye that worship the LORD, O praise the LORD.

PSALM cxlviii. 12. For His Name only is excellent, and His praise above heaven and earth. Hallelujah.

(*From "The Three Holy Children,* Nos. 16, 17.) STANFORD.

1549

RESURRECTION HYMN.

Rise again, yes, rise again wilt thou,
  My dust, though buried now!
    To life immortal
Is this brief rest the portal:
        Hallelujah!

For the seed is sown again to bloom
  Whene'er the LORD shall come,
    His harvest reaping
In us who now are sleeping:
        Hallelujah!

Day of praise, of joyful tears the day,
  Thou of my GOD the day,
    When shall I number
My destined years of slumber,
        Thou wakenest me!

Then shall we be like to those that dream,
  When on us breaks the beam
    Of that blest morrow;
The weary pilgrim's sorrow
        Is then no more.

Then into the Holiest Place leads me
  My Saviour, there to rest
    With Him for ever.
Praise His Name Who doth deliver!
        Hallelujah! Amen!

                      STANFORD.

1550

*1. Awake, my heart, upraising
  Our Maker's pow'r amazing,
  Who all good gifts bestoweth,
  From Whom all comfort floweth

2. With godlike grace and holy
   Thou clothest me, the lowly ;
   " Sleep," say'st Thou, "free from sorrow,
   Thy sun shall rise to-morrow."*

3. Yea, truly hast Thou spoken,
   On me the day hath broken !
   Thou, Lord, alone dost make me
   Once more to life betake me.

4. O hear my grateful pray'r,
   Who know'st my inmost care ;
   And may a glad fruition
   Answer my heart's petition !   •

5. Thy gracious work be ending,
   To me, kind Father, sending
   An angel to be near me
   In loving arms to bear me.

†6. All glory, praise, and merit,
   To Father, Son, and Spirit,
   Whose might all else excelleth
   That in the wide world dwelleth.

7. Would'st Thou but rule for ever
   Each falt'ring, weak endeavour,
   Through paths of peace direct me
   And evermore protect me !

8. Thy boundless grace be given
   To guide my steps to heaven,
   Thy word, a feast unending,
   My weary way attending.

9. All glory, thanks, and merit,
   To Father, Son, and Spirit,
   Whose might all else excelleth
   That in the wide world dwelleth.

STANFORD.

* . ' Som et? it e sung as a separate Anthem..
† Ih e ver . . . ng at the same time as v.

1551

REVELATION xiv. 13. Blessed are the dead that die in the LORD, [from henceforth and for ever:] for they rest from their labours and their works follow them.

SPOHR, STANFORD.

1552

PSALM xlvi. 1. GOD is our hope and strength, a very present help in trouble.

2. Therefore will we not fear, though the earth be moved, and though the hills be carried into the midst of the sea.

3. Though the waters rage and swell, and the mountains shake at the tempest of the same.

1. GOD is our hope and strength, a very present help in trouble.

4. The rivers of the flood thereof shall make glad the city of GOD, the Holy Place of the Most Highest.

5. GOD is in the midst of her, therefore shall she not be removed : GOD shall help her, and that right early.

6. The heathen make much ado, and the kingdoms are moved : but GOD hath shewed His voice, and the earth shall melt away.

7. The LORD of Hosts is with us ; the GOD of Jacob is our refuge.

8. O come hither, and see the works of the LORD, what destruction He hath brought upon the earth.

9. He maketh wars to cease in all the world ; He breaketh the bow, and knappeth the spear in sunder, and burneth the chariots in the fire.

10. Be still, then, and know that I am GOD : I will be exalted among the heathen, I will be exalted in the earth.

1. GOD is our hope and strength, a very present help in time of trouble. Hallelujah.

11. The LORD of Hosts is with us ; the GOD of Jacob is our refuge.

STANFORD.

1553

ISAIAH xxv. 1. O LORD, Thou art my GOD; I will exalt Thee, I will praise Thy Name; for Thou hast done wonderful things; Thy counsels of old are faithfulness and truth.

[9. Lo, This is our GOD; we have waited for Him, and He will save us: This is the LORD; we have waited for Him, we will be glad and rejoice in His salvation.]

PSALM cxviii. 28. Thou art my GOD, and I will praise Thee: Thou art my GOD, I will exalt Thee.

29. O give thanks unto the LORD, for He is gracious: His mercy endureth for ever. Amen.

C. F. LLOYD.

1554 BUNNETT, vv. 1, 9.

1555

WISDOM iii. 1. The souls of the righteous are in the hand of GOD, and there shall no torment touch them.

2, 3. In the sight of the unwise they seem to die, and their departure is taken for misery, but they are in peace.

4. For though they be punished in the sight of men, yet is their hope full of immortality.

5, 6. For GOD hath proved them, and found them worthy for Himself. As gold in the furnace hath He tried them, and found them worthy for Himself.

v. 5. They are numbered among the children of GOD, and their lot is among the Saints.

[Job iii. 17. There the wicked cease from troubling, and the weary be at rest.]

WILLIAMS.

1556 OUSELEY, vv. 2, 3.
1557 H. H. WOODWARD, vv. 1-3 ; JOB. iii. 17.

1558

PSALM lxxxvi. 9. All nations, whom Thou hast made, shall come and worship before Thee, O LORD.

PSALM cxvii. (*Old Version*).

From all that dwell below the skies
Let the Creator's praise arise:
Let the Redeemer's Name be sung
Through every land, by every tongue.

Eternal are Thy mercies, LORD,
Eternal truth attends Thy Word ;
Thy praise shall sound from shore to shore,
Till suns shall rise and set no more.   Amen.

SELBY.

1559 T. A. WALMISLEY, Psalm cxvii.

1560

PSALM cvii.   8. O that men would praise the LORD for His goodness, and declare the wonders that He doeth for the children of men.

civ.   13. He watereth the hills from above : the earth is filled with the fruit of Thy works.

14. He bringeth forth grass for the cattle, and green herb for the service of men.

ZECHARIAH ix.   17. For how great is His goodness and how great is His beauty !   Coin shall make the young men cheerful.   Hallelujah !   Amen.

J. C. BRIDGE.

1561

HABAKKUK iii.   17. Although the fig tree shall not blossom, neither shall fruit be in the vines ; the labour of the olive shall fail, and the fields shall yield no meat ; the flock shall be cut off from the fold, and there shall be no herd in the stalls :

18. Yet will I rejoice in the LORD, I will joy in the GOD of my salvation.

19. The LORD GOD is my strength, and He will make my feet like hind's feet, and He will make me to walk upon mine high places.

(*From " The Widow of Zarephath,"* Pt. 1, No. 7.) GRAY.

1562

ISAIAH xliii.   1, 25. Thus saith the LORD that created thee, Fear not : for I have redeemed thee, I have called thee by name ; thou art Mine.   Thus saith the Lord Who created thee, Fear not : for I, even I, am He that blotteth out thy transgressions for Mine own sake, and will not remember thy sins.

2. When thou passest through the waters, I will be with thee ; and through the rivers, they shall not overflow thee : when thou walkest through the fire, thou shalt not be burned ; neither shall the flame kindle upon thee.

25. Thus saith the LORD Who created thee, Fear not : For I, even I, am He that blotteth out thy transgressions for Mine own sake, and will not remember thy sins. I am thy helper.

(*From "The Widow of Zarephath,"* Pt. 2. No. 3.)   GRAY.

1563

PSALM xxx. 12. Thou hast turned my heaviness into joy : Thou hast put off my sackcloth and girded me with gladness.

13. Therefore shall every good man sing of Thy praise without ceasing : O my God, I will give thanks unto Thee for ever.

ISAIAH xxvi. 19. Awake, and sing, ye that dwell in dust : for thy dew is as the dew of herbs, and the earth shall cast out the dead. Awake, and sing, ye that dwell in the dust.

I CORINTHIANS xv. 57. Thanks be to God, Which giveth us the victory through our LORD JESUS CHRIST. Amen.

(*From "The Widow of Zarephath,"* Pt. 2, No. 7.)   GRAY.

1564

PSALM xxiv. 3. Who shall ascend into the hill of the LORD ? or who shall rise up in His holy place ?

4. He that hath clean hands, and a pure heart : that hath not lift up his mind unto vanity, nor sworn to deceive his neighbour.

5. He shall receive the blessing from the LORD.

Hail the day that sees Him rise   Alleluia !
Glorious to His native skies ;   Alleluia !
CHRIST, the Lamb for sinners given Alleluia !
Enters now the highest heaven.   Alleluia !

There for Him high triumph waits ; Alleluia !
Lift your heads, eternal gates ;   Alleluia ! '
He hath conquered death and sin.   Alleluia !
Take the King of Glory in !   Alleluia ! Amen.

GRAY.

1565

1. God {that \ Who} madest earth and heaven,
     Darkness and light;
   Who the day for toil hast given,
     For rest the night;
   May Thine Angel-guards defend us,
   Slumber sweet Thy mercy send us,
   Holy dreams and hopes attend us,
     This livelong night.

2. Guard us waking, guard us sleeping,—
     And, when we die,
   May we in Thy mighty keeping
     All peaceful lie:
   When the last dread call shall wake us,
   Do not Thou, our God, forsake us,
   But to reign in glory take us
     With Thee on high. Amen.

> Davies, Fisher, Löhr, C. L. Naylor.

1566 Hummel, v. i. (God *that madest*.)

1567

Isaiah li. 9. Awake, awake, put on strength, O arm of the Lord; awake!

10. Art Thou not it that hath dried the sea, the waters of the great deep; that hath made the depths of the sea a way for the ransomed to pass over?

11. Therefore the redeemed of the Lord shall return, and come with singing unto Zion: and everlasting joy shall be upon their head: they shall obtain gladness and joy, and sorrow and mourning shall flee away.

> Borton.

1568

Psalm lxxxv. 7. Shew us Thy mercy, O Lord, and grant us Thy salvation.

8. I will hearken what the Lord God will say concerning me: for He shall speak peace unto His people, and to His saints, that they turn not again.

9. For His salvation is nigh them that fear Him, that glory may dwell in our land.

> Swift.

1569 Brow, v. 7.

1570

GENESIS ii. 8. And the LORD GOD planted a garden eastward in Eden ; and there He put the man whom He had formed.

9. And out of the ground made the LORD GOD to grow every tree that is pleasant to the sight, and good for food ; the tree of life also in the midst of the garden.

LEVITICUS xxvi. 3. If ye walk in My statutes, and keep My commandments, and do them ;

4. Then I will give you rain in due season, and the land shall yield her increase, and the trees of the field shall yield their fruit.

JEREMIAH v. 24. Let us now fear the LORD our GOD, that giveth rain, both the former and the latter, in his season : He reserveth unto us the appointed weeks of the harvest.

ST. MARK iv. 26. So is the Kingdom of GOD, as if a man should cast seed into the ground ;

27. And should sleep, and rise night and day, and the seed should spring and grow up, he knoweth not how.

28. For the earth bringeth forth fruit of herself; first the blade, then the ear, after that the full corn in the ear.

29. But when the fruit is brought forth, immediately he putteth in the sickle, because the harvest is come.

REVELATION xiv. 15, 16. Thrust in thy sickle, and reap : for the time is come for thee to reap ; for the harvest of the earth is ripe. And the earth was reaped.

xxii. 14. Blessed are they that do His commandments, that they may have right to the tree of life, and may enter in through the gates into the city.

5. And there shall be no night there ; and they need no candle, neither light of the sun ; for the LORD GOD giveth them light : and they shall reign for ever and ever.

CRASTON.

1571

PSALM xliii. 4. I will go to the Altar of GOD, unto GOD, my exceeding joy : yea, upon the harp will I praise Thee, O GOD my GOD.

MILLER.

1572

Isaiah xxxii. 18. My people shall dwell in a peaceable habitation, in sure dwellings, and in quiet resting places.

20. O blessed are ye that sow beside all waters.

xxvi. 3. For Thou wilt keep him in perfect peace, whose mind is stayed on Thee.

i. 18. Come now, and let us reason together, saith the Lord : yea, though your sins be as scarlet, though they be red like crimson, yet shall they be white as snow.

19. If ye be willing and obedient, ye shall eat the good of the land.

Leviticus xxvi. 1. For I am the Lord your God :

12. And I will walk among you, and I will be your God, and ye shall be My people.

9. For I will have respect to you, and will make you fruitful and multiply you, and I will make My covenant with you, thus saith the Lord.

Exodus xv. 11. Who is like unto Thee, O Lord, among the gods ?

Psalm cl. 3. Praise the Lord in the sound of the trumpet : praise the Lord upon the lute and harp.

cxlv. 2. And I will praise Thy Name, O Lord, for evermore.

Wareing.

1573

Psalm lxviii. 32. Sing praises to God, O ye kingdoms of the earth, O sing praises to the Lord,

xlviii. 14. For this God is our God for ever and ever.

St. John iv. 35. Behold, I say unto you, Lift up your eyes and look upon the fields, for they are white already to harvest. Sing praises unto God our King : rejoice, give thanks ;

Joel iii. 13. For the harvest is ripe, and the presses are filled.

Zephaniah ii. 11. The isles of the heathen shall worship Him. For our God hath not forsaken us, but hath had mercy upon us. Sing unto God, praise Him, and magnify His Name for ever. Hallelujah.

Wareing.

1574

PSALM civ. 33. I will sing unto tne LORD as long as I live : I will praise my GOD while I have my being.

c. 4. For the LORD is · gracious, His mercy is everlasting.

civ. 34. My meditation of Him shall be sweet : my joy shall be in the LORD. Amen.

WAREING.

1575

SAVIOUR, again to Thy dear Name we raise
With one accord our parting hymn of praise ;
We stand to bless Thee ere our worship cease ;
Then, lowly kneeling, wait Thy word of peace.

Grant us Thy peace, LORD, through the coming night ;
Turn Thou for us its darkness into light ;
From harm and danger keep Thy children free,
For dark and light are both alike to Thee.

Grant us Thy peace throughout our earthly life,
Our balm in sorrow, and our stay in strife ;
Then, when Thy voice shall bid our conflict cease,
Call us, O LORD, to Thine eternal peace.　　　Amen.

TARRANT.

1576

PSALM lxxxviii. 1. Domine Deus salutis meæ in die clamavi et nocte coram Te : intret in conspectu Tuo oratio mea ; inclina aurem Tuam ad precem meam :

2. Quia repleta est malis anima mea, et vita mea inferno approquinquavit.

10. Numquid mortuis facies mirabilia, aut medici suscitabunt et confitebuntur Tibi ?

PSALM vi. 9. Exaudivit Dominus deprecationem meam.

PSALM cxxx. 5. Sustinuit anima mea in verbo ejus, speravit anima mea in Domino.

English Version.

PSALM lxxxviii. 1. O LORD GOD of my salvation, I nave cried day and night before Thee : let my prayer come before Thee : incline Thine ear unto my cry.

2. For my soul is full of trouble, and my life draweth nigh to the grave.

10. Dost Thou shew wonders among the dead ? shall the dead rise up again and praise Thee ?

PSALM vi. 9. The LORD hath heard my supplication : the LORD will receive my prayer.

PSALM cxxx. 5. I look for the LORD, my soul doth wait for Him ; in His word is my trust.   Amen.

E. FORD.

1577

PSALM cxlvii. 12. Praise the LORD, O Jerusalem : praise thy GOD, O Sion.

13. For He hath made fast the bars of thy gates, and hath blessed thy children within thee.

14. He maketh peace in thy borders, and filleth thee with the flour of wheat.

7, 9. O sing unto the LORD with thanksgiving : sing praise upon the harp. Sing praise to our GOD, Who covereth the heaven with clouds, and prepareth rain for the earth, and maketh the grass to grow upon the mountains, and herb for the use of men.

5. Great is our LORD, and great is His power : yea, and His wisdom is infinite.

Therefore unto Him we raise
Hymns of glory, songs of praise,
To the Father, and the Son,
And the Spirit, Three in One,
Honour, might, and glory be
Now, and through eternity.   Amen.

W. G. WOOD.

1578

Love, that caused us first to be,
Love, that bled upon the tree,
Love, that draws us lovingly :
     We beseech Thee, hear us.

Teach us what Thy love has borne,
That, with loving sorrow torn,
Truly contrite we may mourn :
    We beseech Thee, hear us.

Grant us love, Thy love to own,
Love to live for Thee alone,
And the power of grace make known
    We beseech Thee, hear us.

O Great Absolver, grant my soul may wear
The lowliest garb of penitence and prayer,
That in the Father's House my glorious dress
May be the garment of Thy righteousness.

Yea, Thou wilt answer for me, Righteous LORD,
Thine all the merit, mine the great reward ;
Thine the sharp thorns, mine the golden crown,
Mine the life won, Thine the life laid down.

Lead us daily nearer Thee,
Till at last Thy face we see,
Crowned with Thine own purity :
    We beseech Thee, hear us.
                  GREGORY.

1579

Sweet SAVIOUR, bless us ere we go ;
  Thy word into our minds instil,
And make our lukewarm hearts to glow
  With lowly love and fervent will.
Through life's long day and death's dark night,
O gentle JESUS, be our Light.

The day is done, its hours have run,
  And Thou hast taken count of all,
The scanty triumphs grace hath won,
  The broken vow, the frequent fall.
Through life's long day and death's dark night,
O gentle JESUS, be our Light.

Grant us, dear LORD, from evil ways
  True absolution and release ;
And bless us more, than in past days,
  With purity and inward peace.
Through life's long day and death's dark night,
O gentle JESUS, be our Light.

For all we love, the poor, the sad,
  The sinful, unto Thee we call ;
O let Thy mercy make us glad :
  Thou art our JESUS, and our All.
Through life's long day and death's dark night,
O gentle JESUS, be our Light.

GREGORY.

1580

ISAIAH xxxiii. 5. The LORD is exalted, for He dwelleth
on high : He hath filled Zion with judgment and righteousness.

9. The earth mourneth and languisheth.

10, 5. Now will I rise, saith the LORD, now will I be
exalted, now will I lift up Myself, for He dwelleth on high.

WEST.

1581

PSALM lxxxiv.

O LORD of Hosts, my King and GOD,
  How lovely is the place
Where Thou, enthroned in glory, shew'st
  The brightness of Thy face.

O LORD of Hosts, my King and GOD,
  How highly blest are they
Who in Thy temple always dwell,
  And there Thy praise display.

To Father, Son, and Holy Ghost,
  The GOD Whom we adore,
Be glory, as it was, is now,
  And shall be evermore. Amen.

BOUNDY.

1582

O Rex Gloriæ, Domine virtutum, Qui Triumphator hodie super omnes cœlos ascendisti. Ne derelinquas nos orphanos, sed mitte promissum Patris in nos, Spiritum veritatis. Alleluia.

English Version.

O King of Glory, LORD of power and might, Who hast this day as Conqueror ascended into the highest heavens. Leave us not comfortless, but send the promise of the Father upon us, even the Spirit of truth. Alleluia.

ANONYMOUS.

1583

OFFERTORY SENTENCES.

No. 1

ST. MATTHEW v. 16. Let your light so shine before men, that they may see your good works, and glorify your Father Which is in Heaven.

No. 2

ST. MATTHEW vi. 19, 20. Lay not up for yourselves treasure upon the earth; where the rust and moth doth corrupt, and where thieves break through and steal : but lay up for yourselves treasures in Heaven, where neither rust nor moth doth corrupt, and where thieves do not break through and steal.

No. 3

ST. MATTHEW vii. 12. Whatsoever ye would that men should do unto you, even so do unto them ; for this is the Law and the Prophets.

No. 4

ST. MATTHEW vii. 21. Not every one that saith unto Me, Lord, Lord, shall enter into the Kingdom of Heaven ; but he that doeth the will of My Father Which is in Heaven.

No. 5

ST. LUKE xix. 8. Zacchæus stood forth, and said unto the LORD. Behold, LORD, the half of my goods I give to the poor : and if I have done any wrong to any man, I restore four-fold.

No. 6

1 CORINTHIANS ix. 7. Who goeth a warfare at any time of his own cost ?   Who planteth a vineyard, and eateth not of the fruit thereof ?   Or who feedeth a flock, and eateth not of the milk of the flock.

No. 7

1 CORINTHIANS ix.   11. If we have sown unto you spiritual things, is it a great matter if we shall reap your worldly things?

No. 8

1 CORINTHIANS ix.   13, 14. Do ye not know, that they who minister about holy things live of the sacrifice ; and they who wait at the altar are partakers with the altar ? Even so hath the LORD also ordained, that they who preach the Gospel should live of the Gospel.

No. 9

2 CORINTHIANS ix.   6, 7. He that soweth little shall reap little ; and he that soweth plenteously shall reap plenteously.   Let every man do according as he is disposed in his heart, not grudgingly, or of necessity ; for GOD loveth a cheerful giver.

No. 10

GALATIANS vi.   6, 7. Let him that is taught in the Word minister unto him that teacheth, in all good things. Be not deceived, GOD is not mocked : for whatsoever a man soweth that shall he reap.

No. 11

GALATIANS vi.   10. While we have time, let us do good unto all men ; and specially unto them that are of the household of faith

No. 12

1 TIMOTHY vi.   6, 7. Godliness is great riches, if a man be content with that he hath : for we brought nothing into the world, neither may we carry anything out.

No. 13

1 TIMOTHY vi. 17. Charge them who are rich in this world, that they be ready to give, and glad to distribute; laying up in store for themselves a good foundation against the time to come, that they may attain eternal life.

No. 14

HEBREWS vi. 10. GOD is not unrighteous, that He will forget your works, and labour that proceedeth of love; which love ye have shewed for His Name's sake, who have ministered unto the saints, and yet do minister.

No. 15

HEBREWS xiii. 16. To do good, and to distribute, forget not; for with such sacrifices GOD is well pleased.

No. 16

1 ST. JOHN iii. 17. Whoso hath this world's good, and seeth his brother have need, and shutteth up his compassion from him, how dwelleth the love of GOD in him?

No. 17 ˙

TOBIT iv. 7. Give alms of thy goods, and never turn thy face from any poor man; and then the face of the LORD shall not be turned away from thee.

No. 18

TOBIT iv. 8, 9. Be merciful after thy power. If thou hast much, give plenteously: if thou hast little, do thy diligence gladly to give of that little: for so gatherest thou thyself a good reward in the day of necessity.

No. 19

PROVERBS xix. 17. He that hath pity upon the poor lendeth unto the LORD: and look, what he layeth out, it shall be paid him again.

No. 20

PSALM xli. 1. Blessed be the man that provideth for the sick and needy · the LORD shall deliver him in the time of trouble.

1584

KYRIE ELEISON.

Kyrie, eleison; Christe, eleison; Kyrie, eleison.

English Version.

LORD, have mercy upon us; CHRIST, have mercy upon us; LORD, have mercy upon us.

1585

GLORIA IN EXCELSIS.

Gloria in excelsis Deo, et in terra pax hominibus bonæ voluntatis. Laudamus Te, Benedicimus Te, Adoramus Te, Glorificamus Te, Gratias agimus Tibi propter magnam gloriam Tuam, Domine Deus, Rex cœlestis, Deus Pater Omnipotens.

Domine Fili Unigenite, Jesu Christe; Domine Deus, Agnus Dei, Filius Patris, Qui tollis peccata mundi, miserere nobis; Qui tollis peccata mundi, suscipe deprecationem nostram; Qui sedes ad dexteram Patris, miserere nobis.

Quoniam Tu solus sanctus, Tu solus Dominus, Tu solus altissimus, Jesu Christe, cum Sancto Spiritu, in gloria Dei Patris. Amen.

English Version.

Glory be to GOD on high, and in earth peace, good will towards men. We praise Thee, we bless Thee, we worship Thee, we glorify Thee, we give thanks to Thee for Thy great glory, O LORD GOD, Heavenly King, GOD the Father Almighty. O LORD, the only-begotten Son JESU CHRIST; O LORD GOD, Lamb of GOD, Son of the Father, that takest away the sins of the world, have mercy upon us. Thou that takest away the sins of the world, have mercy upon us. Thou that takest away the sins of the world, receive our prayer. Thou that sittest at the right hand of GOD the Father, have mercy upon us. For Thou only art Holy; Thou only art the LORD; Thou only, O CHRIST, with the Holy Ghost, art most high in the glory of GOD the Father. Amen.

1586

CREDO IN UNUM DEUM.

Credo in unum Deum Patrem Omnipotentem, factorem cœli et terræ, visibilium omnium et invisibilium.

Et in unum Dominum Jesum Christum, Filium Dei unigenitum, et ex Patre natum ante omnia sæcula, Deum de Deo, Lumen de Lumine, Deum verum de Deo vero, Genitum non factum, Consubstantialem Patri, per Quem omnia facta sunt, Qui propter nos homines et propter nostram salutem descendit de cœlis, Et incarnatus est de Spiritu Sancto ex Maria Virgine, Et homo factus est : Crucifixus etiam pro nobis sub Pontio Pilato. Passus et sepultus est, Et resurrexit tertia die, secundum Scripturas, Et ascendit in cœlum, sedet ad dexteram Patris, et iterum venturus est cum gloriâ judicare vivos et mortuos ; cujus regni non erit finis.

Et in Spiritum Sanctum, Dominum et Vivificantem, Qui ex Patre Filioque procedit, Qui cum Patre et Filio simul adoratur et conglorificatur, Qui locutus est per Prophetas. Et unam Sanctam Catholicam et Apostolicam Ecclesiam. Confiteor unum Baptisma in remissionem peccatorum, et expecto resurrectionem mortuorum, et vitam venturi sæculi. Amen.

English Version.

I believe in one GOD the Father Almighty, Maker of heaven and earth, And of all things visible and invisible :

And in one LORD JESUS CHRIST, the only-begotten Son of GOD, Begotten of His Father before all worlds, GOD of GOD, Light of Light, Very GOD of very GOD, Begotten, not made, Being of one substance with the Father ; By Whom all things were made : Who for us men, and for our salvation came down from heaven, And was incarnate by the Holy Ghost of the Virgin Mary, And was made man, And was crucified also for us under Pontius Pilate. He suffered and was buried, And the third day He rose again according to the Scriptures, And ascended into heaven, And sitteth on the right hand of the Father. And He shall come again with glory to judge both the quick and the dead : Whose Kingdom shall have no end.

And I believe in the Holy Ghost, The LORD and Giver of life, Who proceedeth from the Father and the Son, Who with the Father and the Son together is worshipped and glorified, Who spake by the Prophets. And I believe one Catholick and Apostolick Church. I acknowledge one Baptism for the remission of sins, And I look for the Resurrection of the dead, And the life of the world to come. Amen.

1587

SANCTUS.

Sanctus, Sanctus. Sanctus, Dominus Deus Sabaoth. Pleni sunt cœli et terra Gloriâ Tuâ.
Hosanna in excelsis.

English Version.

Holy, Holy, Holy, LORD GOD of Hosts. Heaven and earth are full of Thy Glory.
Hosanna in the highest.

1588

BENEDICTUS.

Benedictus Qui venit in Nomine Domini.
Hosanna in excelsis.

English Version.

Blessed is He Who cometh in the Name of the LORD.
Hosanna in the highest.

Another Version.

He is blessed that cometh, O LORD, in Thy holy Name.
Hosanna in the highest.

1589

AGNUS DEI.

Agnus Dei, Qui tollis peccata mundi
      Miserere nobis.
Agnus Dei, Qui tollis peccata mundi,
      Dona nobis pacem.

English Version.

O Lamb of God, that takest away the sins of the world,
      Have mercy upon us.
O Lamb of God, that takest away the sins of the world,
      Grant us Thy peace.

APPENDIX.

1590

Misericordias Domini in æternum cantabo.
Misericordiâ Domini cuncta creata sunt.
Misericordiâ Domini plena est terra.
Misericordiâ Domini quia non sumus consumpti.

JOSQUIN DE PRÈS.

1591

Almighty GOD, Who hast me brought
  In safety to the present day,
Keep me from sin in heart and thought,
  And teach me what to do and say.

T. FORDE.

1592

PSALM xlvii.

O all ye people, clap your hands,
  And make a cheerful noise,
With acclamations to your GOD
  Declare your inward joys.

His high perfections proclaim
  Him greatly to be feared;
This King of all the world commands
  Your honour and regard.

In a triumphant state our LORD
  Is gone above the skies.
Trumpets proclaim our joys,
  And all applaud His victories.

Sing cheerful praises to our GOD,
  Sing praises to our King;
He is LORD of all the earth,
  His praise with understanding sing.

GOD o'er the heathen people reigns,
  And in that Throne is placed
Where He in glory sits, and thence
  Shall judge the world at last.

PURCELL.

1593

Psalm xxii. 23. O praise the Lord, all ye that fear Him : magnify Him, all ye of the seed of Jacob, and fear Him, ye seed of Israel.

cvii. 2. Let them give thanks whom the Lord hath redeemed : and delivered from the hand of the enemy.

xx. 5. We will rejoice in Thy salvation, and triumph in the Name of the Lord our God.

6. Now know I, that the Lord helpeth His Anointed, and will hear Him from His holy heaven : with the saving strength of His right hand.

7. Some put their trust in chariots, and some in horses : but we will remember the Name of the Lord our God.

8. They are brought down, and fallen : but we are risen, and stand upright.

*9. Save, Lord, and hear us, O King of heaven : when we call upon Thee.

xxi. 13. Be Thou exalted, Lord, in Thine own strength : so will we sing and praise Thy power.*

CROFT.

—— Sometimes sung as a separate Anthem.

1594

Jesus, now will we praise Thee,
Thus far in safety brought,
And grateful anthems raise Thee
For all that Thou hast wrought.

Thy gift are we possessing
In this glad op'ning year :
How full of grace and blessing
Its advent doth appear.
Through Thee from ill defended
The old year have we ended.

We would to Thee be living
Throughout the coming year ;
O receive to Thee be given
Thou in all our lifetime here.

O grant us, mighty LORD, this year when ending,
To find its closing hours, like this beginning, blest,
   Its course, let nought of ill molest;
Then heart and voice shall heavenward go,
Because our blessings overflow,
   In wonted Hallelujahs blending.

LORD, Thy defence, Thy favour do we need in all our
works: when we begin, and when we end. Of life and
death the issues are with Thee; and of our days Thou
dost record the number; Thine eye beholdeth every
place; Thou countest all our joys, and knowest all our
sorrows: Ah! send of each whatsoe'er Thou seest fit, as
much as in Thy mercy Thou appointest.

What time as we in peace are living.
And health and wealth from Thee receiving,
Then let the soul retain Thy Word that bringeth joy.
That saving Word possessing,
On earth we have Thy blessing
And shall be Thine on High.

What though our foe, by night and day
His harmful watch doth lay,
And to our ruin would enslave us,
Thou hast the will, Almighty GOD, to save us,
When we for succour unto Thee are calling:
And Satan shall beneath our feet be falling.

And Thou to us Thy grace wilt give,
Thy chosen people here to live;
And after earthly pain and sadness,
To take our flight to heavenly gladness.

To Thee alone be glory,
To Thee alone be praise,
Thy Passion's moving story
Shall govern all our ways,
Till, freed from earthly sadness,
We take our heavenward flight,
To dwell with peace and gladness
In GOD's most holy sight.

To all men shall Thy pleasure
Their good and evil measure: .
On Thee then safely staying,
Let Christian people sing,
With hearts and voices praying
That good this year may bring.

J. S. BACH.

1595

PSALM xvii.   1. Hear, O LORD, and consider my complaint; give ear unto my prayer, that goeth not out of feigned lips.

5, 8, 9. O hold up my goings in Thy paths: and hide me under the shadow of Thy wings; hide me from the ungodly that trouble me to take away my soul.

16. As for me, I will behold Thy presence in righteousness; and when I awake up after Thy likeness, I shall be satisfied with it.

9. Mine enemies compass me round about to take away my soul.

13. Up, LORD, disappoint them, and cast them down.

GREENE.

1596

PSALM lxvi.   7. O praise our God, ye people.
cxlviii.   12. Young men and maidens, old men and children, praise the Name of the LORD: for HIS Name only is excellent, and His praise above heaven and earth.

BOYCE.

1597

PSALM lvii.   10. I will give thanks unto Thee, O LORD, among the people; and I will sing unto Thee among the nations.

11. For the greatness of Thy mercy reacheth unto the heavens, and Thy truth unto the clouds.

MOZART.

1598

In constant order works the LORD:
His several wonders all, by rule, and in their time,
Appear, when called by His eternal power.
Can things create urge onward their Creator?
When He commands, can they delay Him?
In constant order works the LORD.
The morn awakes, the noonday glows, the light declines; then follows restful evening.
The winter yields, the spring returns, the autumn comes, the fruitage swells and ripens.
The maiden blooms, a spring is hers, her bloom decays; transformed is life thereafter.
Can things create urge onward their Creator?
At daybreak assemble the menacing clouds
To master the sun as he rises;
The buds shrivel up with the chill of the rime;
The maiden of roughness and strength is afraid: yet stands His appointment.
The day has its course, the rime dissolves, and love prevails.
When He commandeth, who can stay Him?
In constant order works the LORD.
The gloominess of night will hang on the soul and hide the light of GOD:
Distress will weigh on tender spirits and weaken pious trust in GOD;
So terror will seize on a people, and break their growing manhood down.
The pure and good, the true and just, with evil must to battle go; yet shall in battle conquer and endure.

Then let me learn to trust Thee,
On Thee in faith to wait,
To fear not, and to sin not,
How sore soe'er my strait.

Not now, and not to-morrow,
But when it pleases Thee,
O Father, comes salvation
To all men, yea, to me.

All praise to God, Whose wondrous power
His children guides in danger's hour,
Whose work, though men to mar it strive,
In ageless glory shall survive.

Uplift the heart, the spirit raise
To Him Whom light and darkness praise.
When storms are loud, when waves are strong,
Then thank Him, as in festal song ;
Thy joyful thanks to Him belong.
    All praise to God.

WEBER.

1599

Where Thou reignest, King of Glory,
  Throned in everlasting light,
In Thy courts no more is needed
  Sun by day, nor moon by night.

Soon may we those portals enter,
  When this earthly strife is o'er,
There to reign with saints and angels,
  In Thy presence evermore.

Praise to God, th'eternal Father,
  Praise to God, th'eternal Son,
Praise to God, th'eternal Spirit,
  One in Three, and Three in One.

Honour, praise, thanksgiving, blessing,
  Now and evermore be done ;
God most holy, we adore Thee,
  Ever-blessed Trinity.

SCHUBERT.

1600

PSALM lxxxvi. 1. Bow down Thine ear to me, O LORD,
and hear me : for I am poor and in misery.

3. Be merciful unto me, O LORD : for I will call daily
upon Thee.

5. For Thou, LORD, art good and gracious : and of
great mercy unto all them that call upon Thee.

PSALM xli. 1. Blessed is he that considereth the poor and needy: the LORD shall deliver him in the time of trouble.

13. Blessed be the LORD GOD of Israel: world without end. Amen.

BEALE.

1601

ACTS ii. 1. And when the day of Pentecost was fully come, they were all with one accord in one place.

2. And suddenly there came a sound from heaven as of a rushing mighty wind, and it filled all the house where they were sitting.

3. And there appeared unto them cloven tongues like as of fire, and it sat upon each of them.

4. And they were all filled with the Holy Ghost, and began to speak with other tongues, as the Spirit gave them utterance.

16. But this is that which was spoken by the prophet Joel;

17. And it shall come to pass in the last days, saith GOD, I will pour out of My Spirit upon all flesh : and your sons and your daughters shall prophesy, and your young men shall see visions, and your old men shall dream dreams :

21. And it shall come to pass, that whosoever shall call on the Name of the LORD shall be saved.

C. W. SMITH.

1602

Hear us, LORD ! We bless the Name of our Redeemer ! and all His great and wondrous mercies now and ever glorify !

To Him be glory evermore. Amen.

Novello's Collection.   S

ROSSINI.

1603

The fostering earth, the genial showers,
　　And ripening rays their work have done;
The seed consigned'to nature's powers
　　Has borne its fruit, the harvest's won.
Still in its buoyant pride it stands,
　　And tempts the busy reaper's hands:
Soon as the loaded waggon heaves,
　　Rocked by the weight of fruitful sheaves,
　　　Sing we the Harvest Home.

From field to field the work goes on,
　　From morn to eve we strive and toil,
Nor pause nor rest till we have won,
　　And gathered all the golden spoil.
For surely 'tis the noblest prize
　　The toil of man to man supplies:
Then, while the loaded waggon heaves,
　　Rocked by the weight of fruitful sheaves,
　　　Sing we the Harvest Home.

And now our task is nearly o'er,
　　The last rich sheaf is made secure,
Once more we pile the gathered store
　　And make the year's great labour sure;
And they that glean may freely go
　　And gather up the overflow.
Shout while the loaded waggon heaves,
　　Sing to the sway of fruitful sheaves,
　　　Sing to the Harvest Home.

J. L. Hopkins.

1604

Psalm cvi.　1. O give thanks unto the Lord, and call upon His Name: tell the people what things He hath done.

lxxv.　8. God is the Judge: He putteth down one, and setteth up another.

cxviii.　23. This is the Lord's doing, and it is marvellous in our eyes.

24. This is the day which the Lord hath made: we will rejoice and be glad in it.

Turle.

1605

*SONG OF SOLOMON ii. 11, 12. Lo, the winter is past ; the rain is over and gone. The flowers appear upon the earth, and the time of the singing birds is come. Praise the LORD.

[PSALM cxviii. 24. This is the day which the LORD hath made: we will rejoice and be glad in it. Alleluia. Amen.]*

DEUTERONOMY xxxii. 2. My speech shall distil as the dew, as the small rain upon the tender herb, and as showers upon the grass.

ST. MATTHEW vi. 28, 29. Consider the lilies of the field how they grow: they toil not, neither do they spin ; and yet I say to you, That Solomon in all his glory was not arrayed like one of these. Consider the lilies of the field.

FAREBROTHER.

1606 GADSBY. *———*

1607
"CHRISTMAS EVE."
NO. 1.

Hear, ye hosts of angels,
Speed on wings unresting,
GOD Himself commands you !
Fly, from heaven descending,
Earthward is your mission :
Sing in exultation,
CHRIST the LORD to honour.

NO. 2.

Behold, a Star appeareth,
Expectant eyes now meeting :
Arise, ye wakeful shepherds,
Your infant LORD be greeting :
Let man self-love abandon,
The Love made Man receiving.

(Sung at the same time as the above.)
Angelic hosts surround us,
From Heaven to earth descending,
Their songs of exultation
With Nature's voices blending.
O tidings sweet and blessed,
Which GOD to man is giving.

No. 3.

O ! with pure devotion
May each heart be filled ;
Haste to yonder cradle,
Worship ye the Child.

Long-desired salvation
Comes to bless mankind ;
Our GOD's loving-kindness
Yours it is to find.

Lo, the night of evil
Soon will pass away ;
Full and free redemption
·Brings a brighter day.

Worship ye !
Praise to the Newly-born
Here do we bring,
Praise to our LORD do we sing.

No. 4.

When onward I am gazing,
I read distress and wrath ;
I hear the tramp of nations,
Destruction round their path.

But now a cheerful morning
O'erspreads the weary earth,
Once more is hope up-springing,
To greet the Saviour's birth.

*Forget, O man, thy sorrow,
Break off the chains of sin ;
All they that live to JESUS,
True life in heaven shall win.*

GADE.

This verse is sometimes sung a a separate Anthen

1608

PSALM cxlvii. 7. Sing unto the LORD with thanksgiving; sing praise upon the harp unto our GOD:

8. Who covereth the heaven with clouds, Who prepareth rain for the earth, Who maketh grass to grow upon the mountains.

9. He giveth to the beast his food, and to the young ravens which cry.

11. The LORD taketh pleasure in them that fear Him, in those that hope in His mercy.

12. Praise the LORD, O Jerusalem; praise thy GOD, O Zion.

14. He maketh peace in thy borders, and filleth thee with the finest of the wheat.

12. Praise the LORD, O Jerusalem; praise thy GOD, O Zion. Hallelujah. Amen.

SYDENHAM.

1609

PSALM xxvii. 1. (*Bible Version.*) The LORD is my light and my salvation; whom shall I fear? the LORD is the strength of my life; of whom shall I be afraid?

xviii. 35. Thou hast given me the shield of Thy salvation: and Thy right hand hath holden me up, and Thy gentleness hath made me great.

SYDENHAM.

1610

PSALM cxix. 33. (*Bible Version.*) Teach me, O LORD, the way of Thy statutes; and I shall keep it unto the end.

34. Give me understanding, and I shall keep Thy law; yea, I shall observe it with my whole heart.

35. Make me to go in the path of Thy commandments; for therein do I delight.

36. Incline my heart unto Thy testimonies, and not to covetousness.

40. Behold, I have longed after Thy precepts: quicken me in Thy righteousness.

ELVEY.

1611

PSALM cxlv. 15. The eyes of all wait on Thee, O
LORD, and Thou givest them their meat in due season.

16. Thou openest Thine hand, and fillest all things
living with plenteousness.

cxlvii. 14. He maketh peace in thy borders, and filleth
thee with the flour of wheat.

cxlv. 1. I will magnify Thee, O LORD, and will praise
Thy Name for ever and ever. Hallelujah. Amen.

ELVEY.

1612

PSALM lxxiii. 25. Whom have I in heaven but Thee?
and there is none upon earth that I desire beside Thee.

26. My flesh and my heart faileth : but GOD is the
strength of my heart, and my portion for ever.

27. For, lo, they that are far from Thee shall perish.

28. But it is good for me to draw near to GOD; I have put
my trust in the LORD GOD, that I may declare all Thy works.

ELVEY.

1613 WEST, vv. 25, 26.

1614

PSALM cxxix.

No. 1.

De profundis clamavi ad Te, Domine : Domine, exaudi
vocem meam, fiant aures Tuæ intendentes in vocem
deprecationis meæ. Si iniquitates observaveris, Domine :
Domine, quis sustenebit ?

No. 2.

Quia apud Te propitiatio est, et propter legem Tuam
sustinui Te, Domine. Sustinuit anima mea, in verbo
Ejus, speravit anima mea in Domino.

No. 3.

A custodiâ matutinâ usque ad noctem, speret Israel in
Domino. Quia apud Dominum misericordia et copiosa
apud Eum redemptio.

No. 4.

Et Ipse redimet Israel ex omnibus iniquitatibus ejus.
Amen.   GOUNOD.

For English Version, see No. 105.

1615

Lo ! the children of the Hebrews took boughs of trees
and olive branches, and they went forth to meet the LORD :
and shouted with loud voices,

ST. MATTHEW xxi. 9. Hosanna to the Son of David.
Blessed be He that cometh in the Name of the LORD :
Hosanna in the highest !

GOUNOD.

1616

SAVIOUR of men, we know that for ever Thou livest :
We know that to the dead resurrection Thou givest :
Yea, all them that are sleeping, from the grave Thou wilt
  bring,
So that, to life restored, we shall see Thou art glorious,
When as Death, over whom this day Thou art victorious,
  Has fled before the LORD and King.

(*From " The Redemption,"* p. 77.)   GOUNOD.

1617

PSALM iv. 1. Hear me when I call, O GOD of my
righteousness: Thou hast set me at liberty when I was
in trouble; have mercy upon me, and hearken unto my
prayer.

7. LORD, lift Thou up the light of Thy countenance
upon us.

9. I will lay me down in peace, and take my rest : for
it is Thou, LORD, only, that makest me dwell in safety.

C. KING HALL.

1618 DISTIN, vv. 1, 9.

1619

PSALM xiii. 5. O LORD, my trust is in Thy mercy :
and my heart is joyful in Thy salvation.

6. I will sing of the LORD, because He hath dealt so
lovingly with me.

5. O LORD, my trust is in Thy mercy.

C. KING HALL.

1620

PSALM xxv.   1. To Thee do I lift up my soul; my GOD,
I have hoped in Thee, and shall not be confounded.

2. Neither shall mine enemies laugh me to scorn ; for
all they that hope in Thee shall not be confounded.

3. Shew me Thy ways, O LORD ; teach me Thy paths.

C. KING HALL.

1621

PSALM ciii.   20. O praise the LORD, ye angels of His,
ye that excel in strength : ye that fulfil His commandment.

21. O praise the LORD, all ye His hosts ; ye servants
of His that do His pleasure.

xxxiv.   7. The angel of the LORD encampeth round
about them that fear Him : and delivereth them.

REVELATION vii.   11. And all the angels stood round
about the throne, and worshipped GOD.

12. Saying, Amen : Blessing, and glory, and wisdom,
and thanksgiving, and honour, and power, and might, be
unto our GOD for ever and ever.   Amen.

W. G. WOOD.

1622

PSALM cxlv.   10. All Thy works praise Thee, O LORD :
and Thy saints give thanks unto Thee.

11, 12. They shew the glory of Thy kingdom, and talk
of Thy power; that Thy power, Thy glory, and mightiness
of Thy kingdom might be known unto men.

13. Thy kingdom is an everlasting kingdom, and Thy
dominion endureth throughout all ages.

8. The LORD is gracious and merciful; long-suffering,
and of great goodness.

9. The LORD is loving unto every man, and His mercy
is over all his works.

21. My mouth shall speak the praise of the LORD : and
let all flesh give thanks unto His holy Name for ever
and ever.   Amen.

BARNBY.

1623 BARNBY, xxiv. 12.

1624

PSALM lvii. 9. Awake up, my glory; awake, lute and harp; I myself will awake right early.

cxviii. 24. This is the day which the LORD hath made: we will rejoice and be glad in it.

lvii. 9. Awake up, my glory; awake, lute and harp; I myself will awake right early.

I CORINTHIANS xv. 20. For now is CHRIST risen from the dead, and become the first-fruits of them that slept.

57. Thanks be to GOD, Which giveth us the victory through our LORD JESUS CHRIST.

> All praise be Thine, O risen LORD,
> From death to endless life restored;
> All praise to GOD the FATHER be,
> And HOLY GHOST eternally. Amen.

BARNBY.

1625

I ST. JOHN iv. 11. Beloved, if GOD so loved us, we ought also to love one another.

21. And this commandment have we from Him, That he who loveth GOD love his brother also.

BARNBY.

1626

> Christians, awake, salute the happy morn,
> Whereon the SAVIOUR of mankind was born;
> Rise to adore the mystery of love,
> Which hosts of angels chanted from above;
> With them the joyful tidings first begun
> Of GOD Incarnate, of the Virgin's Son.
>
> Oh! may we keep and ponder in our mind
> GOD's wondrous love in saving lost mankind;
> Trace we the Babe, Who hath retrieved our loss,
> From the poor manger to the bitter Cross;
> Tread in His steps, assisted by His grace,
> Till man's first heavenly state again takes place.

Then may we hope, the angelic hosts among,
To join, redeemed, a glad triumphant throng.
He That was born upon this joyful day
Around us all His glory shall display;
Saved by His love, incessant we shall sing
Eternal praise to heaven's Almighty King.   Amen.

BARNBY.

1627

HAIL TO THE CHRIST!

No pomp of earthly kingdom,
   No worldly grandeur then,
Hailed Thy coming, Son of Mary,
   To a world of weary men;
But sweet angelic voices
   Sang the song that ne'er shall cease
The song that down the ages
   Brings everlasting peace.

No bounds of space now fetter
   The memory of Thy birth;
To-day the gladsome news rings out
   Through all the awakened earth;
The glorious tidings joyously,
   Now countless mortals sing,
On us a SAVIOUR is bestowed,
   To us is born a King.

Then let mankind their voices raise
   In thankful praise to Thee,
Hail to Thee, Son of Mary,
   For Thou hast made us free!
Hail to Thee, Babe of Bethlehem,
   On this Thy natal day,
Thy sacrifice of boundless love
   Thy saints shall laud for aye.

BARNBY.

1628

From the Order for Holy Communion.

Lift up your hearts.
 We lift them up unto the LORD.
Let us give thanks unto our LORD GOD.
 It is meet and right so to do.

It is very meet, right, and our bounden duty, that we should at all times, and in all places, give thanks unto Thee, O LORD, Holy Father, Almighty, Everlasting GOD.

Therefore with Angels and Archangels, and all the company of heaven, we laud and magnify Thy glorious Name; evermore praising Thee, and saying, Holy, Holy, Holy, LORD GOD of Hosts, heaven and earth are full of Thy glory: Glory be to Thee, O LORD, most High. Amen.

BARNBY.

1629

LORD of the harvest, Thee we hail;
Thine ancient promise doth not fail;
The varying seasons haste their round,
With goodness all our years are crown'd :
 Our thanks we pay,
 This holy day;
O let our hearts in tune be found.

If Spring doth wake the song of mirth;
If Summer warms the fruitful earth;
When Winter sweeps the naked plain,
Or Autumn yields its ripened grain;
 Our thanks we pay,
 This holy day,
O let our hearts in tune be found.

But chiefly when Thy liberal Hand
Bestows new plenty o'er the land,
When sounds of music fill the air,
As homeward all their treasures bear ;
    We too will raise
    Our hymn of praise,
For we Thy common bounties share.

LORD of the harvest, all is Thine ;
The rains that fall, the suns that shine,
The seed once hidden in the ground,
The skill that makes our fruits abound ;
    New every year
    Thy gifts appear ;
New praises from our lips shall sound :

Immortal honour, endless fame,
Attend the Almighty Father's Name ;
Like honour to the Incarnate Son,
Who, for lost man, redemption won ;
    And equal praise
    We thankful raise
To Thee, Blest Spirit, with Them One.   Amen.
                    BARNBY.

1630

1. O Perfect Love, all human thought transcending,
    Lowly we kneel in prayer before Thy Throne,
That theirs may be the love that knows no ending,
    Whom Thou for evermore dost join in one.

2. O Perfect Life, be Thou their full assurance
    Of tender charity and stedfast faith,
Of patient hope and quiet brave endurance,
    With child-like trust that fears nor pain nor death.

3. Grant them the joy that brightens earthly sorrow,
    Grant them the peace which calms all earthly strife,
And to life's day the glorious unknown morrow,
    That dawns upon eternal love and life.   Amen.
            BARNBY, BRITON, HILL.

1631

Our Father, which art in heaven, Hallowed be Thy
Name. Thy kingdom come. Thy will be done in earth,
As it is in heaven. Give us this day our daily bread.
And forgive us our trespasses, As we forgive them that
trespass against us. And lead us not into temptation;
But deliver us from evil: For Thine is the kingdom, The
power, and the glory, For ever and ever. Amen.

BARNBY.

1632

PSALM cxlvii. 7. Sing to the LORD with thanksgiving,
sing to the LORD with harp.

cv. 2. O let your songs be of Him, and praise Him;
and let your talking be of all His wondrous works.

cxlvii. 7. Sing to the LORD with thanksgiving, sing to
the LORD upon the harp, sing praise to our GOD.

8. Who covereth the heaven with clouds, and prepareth
rain for the earth. Sing praise to our GOD, Who maketh
the grass to grow upon the mountains, and herb for the
use of men.

7. Sing to the LORD with thanksgiving, sing to the
LORD with harp.

Father, blessing every seed-time,
And refreshing all the soil,
Ripening the gracious harvest
For which all Thy servants toil:
O Thou Source of every blessing
Showered daily from above,
Hearken to our lips confessing
Our thanksgiving for Thy love. Amen.

BARNBY.

1633

THE FIRST CHRISTMAS.

(*A*.)—"THE ANNUNCIATION."

Mary sat at even
In her garden's shade,
And the evening sunlight
Round about her played.

Suddenly from heaven
　　Came an angel fair,
To her threshold flying,
　　Halting gently there.

Mary, pale and trembling,
　　To the angel said :
" What can be thy message
　　To me, Mary, maid ? "

And the angel answered :
　　" Hearken unto me,
Thou that art a maiden
　　Shalt a mother be !

" Blessed among women,
　　Thou shalt bear a Son,
And the Lord will give Him
　　Father David's throne."

Mary knelt at even,
　　Praying to the Lord :
" Be it to me, Father,
　　According to Thy word."

(*B.*)—" The Message to the Shepherds."

Beside their flocks the shepherds watched
　　That holy Christmas night,
When lo ! the angel of the Lord
　　Shone on their dazzled sight.

" Fear not," he cried, " of joy and peace
　　Glad tidings do I bring,
In Bethlehem, a new-born Babe,
　　Lies Christ your heavenly King."

" And this shall be a guiding sign
　　To you and nations all,
The holy Babe you there shall find,
　　Laid in a humble stall."

And suddenly the hosts of heav'n
  Shone on their wond'ring eyes,
And raised a song of holy praise
  That echoed through the skies.

Then marvelled all the shepherds sore,
  What was this wondrous thing;
To Bethlehem they took their way,
  And there they found their King."

(C.)—" Cradle Song of the Blessed Virgin."

Sleep, my Babe, and o'er Thee
  Angels vigil keep;
Silent they adore Thee,
  Sleep, my Baby, sleep.

Jesu, sleep, Thy mother
  Holds Thee in her arm;
May the love she bears Thee
  Shield Thee safe from harm.

Sleep, my Babe, still dreaming
  Of Thy home above;
Whence Thou cam'st to save us
  By Thy Father's love.

Earthly pomp may tempt Thee,
  Earthly sin assail;
But the Tempter's legions
  Shall in terror quail.

Thou shalt suffer torment,
  Thou Thy life shalt give;
Thou shalt die for sinners,
  That the sinners live.

Jesu, Thou shalt triumph,
  Glorious Thou shalt rise;
Thou shalt come to judge us,
  Thronèd in the skies.

Sleep, my Babe, and o'er Thee
  Angels vigil keep;
Silent they adore Thee,
  Sleep, my Baby, sleep.

(D.)—" GLORIA IN EXCELSIS."

Glory to GOD in the highest,
  Glory to GOD let us sing;
Glory to GOD in His Heaven,
  Glory to JESUS, our King.

Glory to GOD in the highest,
  Peace on this earth here below;
JESUS has come to redeem us,
  To free us from sin and from woe.

As love is the law in the heavens,
  So love shall be law upon earth;
By love shall each man be a free-man,
  Born anew by the heav'nly birth.

Glory to GOD in the highest,
  Glory to GOD let us sing;
Glory to GOD in His Heaven,
  Glory to JESUS, our King.   Amen.

BARNBY.

1634

JEREMIAH X. 10. The LORD is the true GOD, He is
the living GOD, and our everlasting King; at His wrath
the earth shall tremble.   Amen.

BARNBY.

1635

PSALM lxv. 9. Thou visitest the earth and blessest it:
Thou makest it very plenteous.

11. Thou waterest her furrows, Thou sendest rain into
the little valleys thereof: Thou makest it soft with the
drops of rain, and blessest the increase of it.

12. Thou crownest the year with Thy goodness, and
Thy clouds drop fatness.

ISAIAH XXV. 1. O LORD, Thou art my GOD; I will
exalt Thee, I will praise Thy Name.   Thou art my GOD,
and I will praise Thee: Thou art my GOD, I will exalt
Thee; for Thou hast done wonderful things; Thy counsels
of old are faithfulness and truth.

PSALM cvi. 1. O give thanks unto the LORD, for He is
gracious: His mercy endureth for ever.

BARNBY.

1636

While Shepherds watched their flocks by night,
  All seated on the ground,
The angel of the LORD came down,
  And glory shone around.

"Fear not," said he, for mighty dread
  Had seized their troubled mind,
"Glad tidings of great joy I bring
  To you and all mankind.

"To you, in David's town, this day,
  Is born of David's line
A SAVIOUR, Who is CHRIST the LORD,
  And this shall be the sign:

"The Heavenly Babe ye there shall find
  To human view displayed,
All meanly wrapped in swathing-bands,
  And in a manger laid."

Thus spake the seraph, and forthwith
  Appeared a shining throng
Of angels, praising GOD, who thus
  Addressed their joyful song:

"All glory be to GOD on high,
  And in the earth be peace;
Good-will henceforth from heaven to men
  Begin and never cease!" [Amen.]

BARNBY, BEST, ELVEY, MARTIN.

1637

ISAIAH lv. 12. Ye shall go out with joy, and be led forth with peace: the mountains and hills shall break forth before you into singing, and all the trees of the fields shall clap their hands.

ST. JOHN iv. 35. Lift up your eyes, and look upon the fields, for they are white already to harvest.

JOEL iii. 13. For the harvest is ripe and the presses are filled.

ISAIAH xxxii. 20. O blessed are ye that sow beside all waters.

i. 19. If ye be willing and obedient, ye shall eat the good of the land: for I am the LORD thy GOD.

BARNBY.

1638

Our GOD is LORD of the harvest ;
The whole earth is His, and the fruits of the earth.
Then praise the LORD for His power and His goodness.

O LORD GOD, LORD of the harvest,
We praise Thee with heart and with voice,
The treasures of earth and the treasures of heaven
Are Thine, and to Thee all praise shall be given.
Then thank ye the LORD, our Father above,
For He giveth food to His creatures in love.
O LORD GOD, Father above,
We thank Thee for all Thy love.
For seed-time and harvest, for sunshine and showers,
Rich fruits, ripe grain, and sweet smelling flowers.

Amen.

MUNDELLA.

1639

Blessed city, heavenly Salem,
  Vision dear of peace and love,
Who of living stones art builded
  In the height of heaven above,
And, with angel hosts encircled,
  As a bride dost earthward move ;

To this temple, where we call Thee,
  Come, O LORD of Hosts, to-day ;
With Thy wonted loving-kindness
  Hear Thy servants, as they pray ;
And Thy fullest benediction
  Shed within its walls alway.

Here vouchsafe to all Thy servants
  What they ask of Thee to gain,
What they gain from Thee for ever
  With the Blessed to retain,
And hereafter in Thy glory
  Evermore with Thee to reign.

REVELATION xxi. 23. And the city had no need of the sun, neither of the moon, to shine in it, for the glory of GOD did lighten it, and the LAMB is the Light thereof.

27. And there shall in no wise enter into it anything that defileth, but they which are written in the LAMB'S book of life.

> Laud and honour to the FATHER,
> Laud and honour to the SON,
> Laud and honour to the SPIRIT,
> Ever THREE, and ever ONE,
> Consubstantial, Co-eternal,
> While unending ages run. Amen.
>
> FISHER.

1640

PSALM cxlv. 1. (*Bible Version.*) I will extol Thee, my GOD, O King; and I will bless Thy Name for ever and ever.

3. Great is the LORD, and greatly to be praised; and His greatness is unsearchable.

8. The LORD is gracious, and full of compassion; slow to anger, and of great mercy.

9. The LORD is good to all; and His tender mercies are over all His works.

10. All Thy works shall praise Thee, O LORD; and Thy saints shall bless Thee.

11. They shall speak of the glory of Thy kingdom, and talk of Thy power.

13. Thy kingdom is an everlasting kingdom, and Thy dominion endureth throughout all generations. Hallelujah! Amen. HUDSON.

1641

ST. MATTHEW xxviii. 2. Behold, the angel of the LORD descended from heaven,

5, 6. And the angel said, He is not here: for He is risen, as He said.

1 CORINTHIANS xv. 20. CHRIST is risen from the dead, and become the first-fruits of them that slept.

[EPHESIANS v. 14. Awake, thou that sleepest, arise from the dead, and CHRIST shall give thee light.]

ROMANS vi. 9. CHRIST being raised from the dead dieth no more: death hath no more dominion over Him.

1 CORINTHIANS xv. 55. O death, where is thy sting? O grave, where is thy victory?

PSALM xlvii. 1. O sing unto GOD with the voice of melody.

cxlv. 3. Great is the LORD, and marvellous, worthy to be praised.

cxiii. 2. Let the Name of the LORD be blessed from this time forth for evermore. Amen.

TOURS.

1642 J. V. ROBERTS, 1 Cor. xv. 20; Ephes. v. 14.

1643

ACTS ii. 17. It shall come to pass in the last days, saith GOD, I will pour out My Spirit upon all flesh: and your sons and your daughters shall prophesy, and your young men shall see visions, and your old men shall dream dreams.

18. And on My servants and on My handmaidens will I pour out in those days of My Spirit.

21. And it shall come to pass, that whosoever shall call upon the Name of the LORD shall be saved.

PSALM lxxii. 6. He shall come down like the rain into a fleece of wool, even as the drops that water the earth.

HABAKKUK ii. 14. The earth shall be full of the knowledge of the LORD, as the waters cover the sea. Amen.

TOURS.

1644

O joyful Light, of the Holy Glory,
Of the everlasting Father
Which is in Heaven, holy and blessed,
    JESUS CHRIST our LORD.

We are come unto the going down of the sun,
And at eventide we have seen Light,
Therefore we give thanks and glory to the Father, and to
    the Son, and to the Holy Spirit of GOD.

Worthy art Thou at all times to be praised by holy voices,
    Son of GOD, that givest life!
Therefore doth the world glorify Thee. Amen.

TOURS.

1645

PSALM xxxiii. 1, 4. Rejoice in the LORD, O ye righteous: for the Word of the LORD is true, and all His works are faithful.

civ. 13. He watereth the hills from above: the earth is filled with the fruit of His works.

14. He bringeth forth grass for the cattle, and green herb for the service of men.

cxlv. 3. Great is the LORD, and marvellous, worthy to be praised: there is no end of His greatness.

Heaven and earth shall praise His Name for ever and ever: and declare His power and majesty. Amen.

TOURS.

1646

1 SAMUEL ii. 8. The pillars of the earth are the LORD'S, and, He hath set the world upon them.

9. He will keep the feet of His saints, and the wicked shall be silent in darkness; for by strength shall no man prevail.

TOURS.

1647

§ 1.

1 TIMOTHY iii. 16. GOD was made manifest in the flesh, justified in the Spirit, seen of Angels, preached unto the Gentiles, believed on in the world, received up into glory.

§ 2.

LORD, Thou hast come in lowly manger lying,
　Born of a Virgin-mother, meek and mild;
Yet ever there the light of life undying
　Beamed from the brow of Mary's new-born Child.

LORD of all Lords! co-equal, co-eternal,
　Only begotten Son of GOD most high;
Stripped of Thy might and majesty supernal
　Thou camest down to live on earth, and di .

Thou, the All-good, Almighty, and All-knowing,
    Sinless, yet burdened with the sinner's ban
Daily in wisdom and in stature growing,
    By Thine own growth didst know the mind of man.

Then, knowing all, and bearing all, yet shrinking
    From the smallest taint of mortal guilt and sin,
Thou, the full cup of sin and sorrow drinking,
    Dying, for us didst life eternal win.

§ 3.

Thus Thou hast come, redeeming and life-giving,
    Now by the Father's Throne with glory crowned,
Thou, by the sinner still an ever-living
    Friend, Intercessor, Advocate, art found.

§ 4.

1 THESSALONIANS iv. 16. For the LORD Himself. shall descend from heaven with a shout, with the voice of the archangel, and with the trump of GOD; and the dead in CHRIST shall rise first.

REVELATION i. 7. Behold, He cometh with clouds, and every eye shall see Him.

LORD, Thou art coming, not as shepherds found Thee—
    Lowly and meek, and in a manger laid;
Angels, and saints, and seraphs shall surround Thee ·
    Honour to Thee by heaven and earth be paid.

§ 5.

When Thou shalt come, the Judge of all creation,
    When we behold Thy glory face to face,
Be to us still the GOD of our salvation,
    Save us, good LORD, by Thy redeeming grace.

When the Archangel's shout, the loudly-pealing
    Trumpet of GOD shall bid the dead arise,
Through the rent clouds, the throne of GOD revealing,
    May we look up to Thee with tearless eyes.

§. 6.

1 TIMOTHY ii. 5. There is one GOD, and one Mediator between GOD and man : the man CHRIST JESUS.

HEBREWS vii. 25. He is able also to save them to the uttermost, that come to GOD by Him, seeing He ever liveth to make intercession for them.

Thou Who hast come to pardon and deliver,
   Thou Who still pleadest in our Father's home,
Be to us now of life divine the Giver,
   Then come again, LORD JESUS, quickly come!

(*From " The Two Advents.*") GARRETT.

1648

EPHESIANS ii. 4, 5. GOD, Who is rich in mercy, for His great love wherewith He hath loved us, even when we were dead in sins, hath quickened us together with CHRIST;

6. And hath raised us up together, and made us sit together in heavenly places in CHRIST JESUS.

GARRETT.

1649

ST. LUKE xxiv. 34. The LORD is risen!

PSALM cxviii. 24. This is the day which the LORD hath made; we will rejoice and be glad in it.

ROMANS vi. 9. CHRIST being raised from the dead dieth no more ; death hath no more dominion over Him.

10. For in that He died, He died unto sin once : but in that He liveth, He liveth unto GOD.

11. Likewise reckon ye also yourselves to be dead indeed unto sin, but alive unto GOD through JESUS CHRIST our LORD.

COLOSSIANS iii. 1. If ye then be risen with CHRIST, seek those things which are above, where CHRIST sitteth on the right hand of God. Amen.

GARRETT.

1650

PSALM xxxvi. 5. Thy mercy, O LORD, reacheth unto the heavens, and Thy faithfulness unto the clouds.

6. Thy righteousness standeth like the strong mountains: Thy judgments are like the great deep.

7. Thou preservest man and beast. How excellent is Thy mercy, O GOD; therefore the children of men shall put their trust under the shadow of Thy wings.

8. They shall be satisfied with the plenteousness of Thy house: and Thou shalt give them drink of Thy pleasures as out of the river.

9. For with Thee is the well of life: and in Thy light shall we see light. Amen.

GARRETT.

1651

PSALM lxviii. 1. Let GOD arise, and let His enemies be scattered: let them also that hate Him flee before Him.

2. Like as the smoke vanisheth, so shalt Thou drive them away: and like as wax melteth at the fire, so let the ungodly perish at the presence of GOD.

3. But let the righteous be glad, and rejoice before GOD: yea, let them exceedingly rejoice; let them also be merry and joyful.

32. Sing unto GOD, sing praises unto His Name; O sing praises, ye kingdoms of the earth.

34, 35. Ascribe ye the power to GOD, even the GOD of Israel. Blessed be GOD.

TRIMNELL.

1652

ISAIAH xlix. 13. Sing, O heavens; be joyful, O earth; and break forth into singing, O mountains.

14. Let not Zion say, The LORD hath forsaken me, and the LORD hath forgotten me.

13. For the LORD hath comforted His people and will have mercy on His afflicted.

lii. 9. Break forth into joy; sing together, ye waste places of Jerusalem, for the LORD hath comforted His people. He hath redeemed Jerusalem. Amen.

TRIMNELL.

1653

Psalm cxxxiii. 1. Behold, brethren, how good and joyful a thing it is, to dwell together in unity!

cxxii. 3. Jerusalem is built as a city, that is at unity in itself.

8. For our brethren and companions' sakes, I will wish thee prosperity.

9. Yea, because of the house of the Lord our God : we will seek to do thee good.

cxxi. 8. The Lord preserve thy going out, and thy coming in, from this time forth for evermore.

CALDICOTT.

1654

COLLECT

For the Second Sunday after the Epiphany.

Almighty and everlasting God, Who dost govern all things in heaven and earth; mercifully hear the supplications of Thy people, and grant us Thy peace all the days of our life; through Jesus Christ our Lord. Amen.

ALLEN, J. S. SMITH.

1655

1 Corinthians xv. 20. Now is Christ risen from the dead, and become the first-fruits of them that slept.

1 Thessalonians v. 11, 16. Wherefore comfort yourselves together, and rejoice evermore.

1 Corinthians xv. 21. For since by man came death, by man came also the resurrection of the dead.

23. But every man in his own order : Christ the first-fruits; afterward they that are Christ's at His coming.

51, 52. Behold, I shew you a mystery; We shall not all sleep, but we shall all be changed, in a moment, in the twinkling of an eye, at the last trump : for the trumpet shall sound, and the dead shall be raised incorruptible, and we shall all be changed.

Revelation xii. 10. Hallelujah. Now is come salvation and strength, and the Kingdom of God, and the power of His Christ. Hallelujah.

ALLEN.

1656

PSALM li. 1. (*Bible Version.*) Have mercy upon me, O GOD, according to Thy loving-kindness. Blot out my transgressions.

3. For I acknowledge my transgressions : and my sin is ever before me.

10. Create in me a clean heart, O GOD ; and renew a right spirit within me.

1. According to Thy loving-kindness, have mercy upon me, O GOD.

PYE.

1657

PSALM cxvii. Praise ye the LORD, all ye nations, laud ye Him, all ye peoples; laud ye and praise ye the LORD.

For loving-kindness and judgment sheweth He to us for evermore. Hallelujah.

FRANZ.

1658

ISAIAH lx. 1. Arise, shine, for thy light is come : and the glory of the LORD is risen upon thee.

2. For, behold, darkness shall cover the earth : and gross darkness the people ; but the LORD shall arise upon thee, and His glory shall be seen upon thee.

3. And the Gentiles shall come to thy light, and kings to the brightness of thy rising.

11. Thy gates shall be open continually : they shall not be shut day nor night ;

14. And they shall call thee The city of the LORD, The Sion of the Holy One of Israel.

18. Violence shall no more be heard in thy land : wasting nor destruction within thy borders ; but thou shalt call thy walls Salvation, and thy gates Praise.

19. The sun shall be no more thy light by day : neither for brightness shall the moon give light unto thee ; but the LORD shall be unto thee an everlasting light, and thy GOD thy glory. Glory be to the FATHER, &c.

[ZECHARIAH ii. 10. Sing and rejoice, O daughter of Zion : for, lo, I come, and I will dwell in the midst of thee, saith the LORD.

11. And many nations shall be joined to the LORD in that day, and shall be My people : and I will dwell in the miast of thee, and thou shalt know that the LORD of Hosts hath sent Me unto thee.]

J. HOPKINS.

1659 C. F. LLOYD, Isaiah lx. 1–3.
1660 BUNNETT, Isaiah lx. 1–3 ; Zech. ii. 10, 11.

1661

ISAIAH xlii. 10. Sing unto the LORD a new song, and His praise from the end of the earth, ye that go down to the sea, and all that is therein : the isles and all the inhabitants thereof.

11. Let the wilderness and the cities thereof lift up their voice : the villages that Kedar doth inhabit : let the inhabitants of the rock sing, let them shout from the top of the mountains.

12. Let them give glory unto the LORD, and declare His praise in the islands.

Glory be to the FATHER, &c.

J. HOPKINS

1662

PSALM xxiv. 1. The earth is the LORD'S, and the fulness thereof.

ACTS xiv. 17.· He giveth us rain from heaven, and fruitful seasons, filling oui hearts with food and gladness.

PSALM lxv. 14. The valleys also shall stand so thick with corn, that they shall laugh and sing.

ST. JOHN vi. 33. The Bread of GOD is He which cometh down from heaven, and giveth life unto the world.

34. LORD, evermore give us this bread.

51. If any man eat of this bread, he shall live for ever;

REVELATION xix. 9. Blessed are they which are called unto the marriage supper of the Lamb. Alleluia. Amen.

J. HOPKINS.

1663

PSALM vi. 1. O LORD, rebuke me not in Thine indignation : neither chasten me in Thy displeasure.

2. Have mercy upon me, O LORD, for I am weak : O LORD, have mercy.

LAHEE.

1664

ZEPHANIAH iii. 14. Sing, O daughter of Zion; shout, O Israel;

17. The LORD thy GOD in the midst of thee is mighty; He will save, He will rejoice over thee with joy; He will rest in His love, He will joy over thee with singing.

REA.

1665

"PAST AND FUTURE."

1. Adown the river year by year
   The fragile bark flies fast;
   And still a fond reverted gaze
   Goes back to days long past.

2. Long, long ago the voices loved
   Have breathed their last farewell;
   And yet their tones within the heart
   Still unforgotten dwell.

3. But soon a golden ray shall dart
   Across the eastern sky,
   To bid the weary earth rejoice;
   At last her LORD draws nigh.

4. O time, fly fast! O ages, end!
   That He, Whom we adore,
   May gather round Himself His own
   For ever, evermore. Amen.

OAKELEY.

1666

Strong Son of GOD, immortal Love,
   Whom we that have not seen Thy face,
   By faith, and faith alone, embrace,
Believing where we cannot prove ;

Thine are these orbs of light and shade ;
   Thou madest life in man and brute ;
   Thou madest Death ; and lo, Thy foot
Is on the skull which Thou hast made.

Thou wilt not leave us in the dust ;
   Thou madest man, he knows not why,
   He thinks he was not made to die ;
And Thou hast made him : Thou art just.

Our little systems have their day ;
   They have their day, and cease to be ;
   They are but broken lights of Thee,
And Thou, O Lord, art more than they.

OAKELEY.

1667

   1. The day-beam dies
      Behind yon cloud ;
   The wintry wind
      Is wailing loud
        In sore distress
        And weariness.
O GOD, our GOD, be with us now,
For Thou canst save, and only Thou ;
And, when the world is dark and drear,
The heart is bright, if Thou art near.

   2. Lo ! darts a ray
      Across the gloom,
   A message, from
      Beyond the tomb,
        Of peace and love
        In heaven above ;
For Thou, O GOD, our GOD, art nigh,
Though all that is must fade and die ;
And, when the world is dark and drear,
The heart is bright, if Thou art near.

3. Each passing year
    Demands its due,
And calls away
    The loved, the true;
    And we are left
    Alone, bereft.
But we and they shall meet at last,
When all this troubled dream is past;
And, let the world be dark and drear,
The heart is bright, for Thou art near. Amen.

OAKELEY.

1668

Eternal Source of every joy,
Well may Thy praise our lips employ,
When in Thy temple we appear,
Whose goodness crowns the circling year.
The flow'ry spring at Thy command
Embalms the air and paints the land;
The summer rays with vigour shine,
To bless the corn and cheer the vine.

Thy hand in autumn richly pours
Through all our coasts redundant stores;
And winter, softened by Thy cares,
No more a face of horror wears,
The seasons, months, and weeks, and days,
Demand successive songs of praise;
Still be the cheerful homage paid,
With opening light and evening shade.

BRANDEIS.

1669

Father, hear the prayer we offer!
    Not for ease that prayer shall be,
But for strength, that we may ever
    Live our lives courageously.

Not for ever by still waters
    Would we idly quiet stay,
But would smite the living fountains,
    From the rocks along our way.

Be our Strength in hours of weakness,
  In our wanderings be our Guide;
Through endeavour, failure, danger,
  Father,. be Thou at our side.
                        BRANDEIS.

1670

The strong foundations of the earth
  Of old by Thee were laid;
Thy hands, O LORD, the arch of heaven
  With wondrous skill have made.
While Thou for ever shalt endure,
  They soon shall pass away,
And, like a garment often worn,
  Shall tarnish and decay.

Like that when Thou ordain'st their change,
  To Thy command they bend;
But Thou continuest still the same,
  Nor have Thy years an end.
Thou to the children of Thy Name
  Shall lasting quiet give;
Whose happy race, securely firm,
  Shall in Thy presence live.
                        BRANDEIS.

1671

Think not that they are blest alone
  Whose days a peaceful tenour keep,
The GOD Who rules on high has shown
  A blessing for the eyes that weep.

The light of smiles shall fill again
  The lids that now o'erflow with tears,
And weary hours of pain and woe
  Are earnests of serener years.

O there are days of hope and rest
  For every dark and troubled night,
And grief may bide an evening guest,
  But joy shall come with morning light.
                        BRANDEIS.

1672

To bless Thy chosen race,
　In mercy to incline,
And cause the brightness of Thy face
　On all Thy saints to shine.

That so Thy wondrous way
　May through the world be known,
While distant lands their tribute pay,
　And Thy salvation own.

O let them shout and sing
　With joy and pious mirth;
For Thou, the righteous Judge and King,
　Shalt govern all the earth.

Let differing nations join
　To celebrate Thy fame;
Let all the world, O LORD, combine
　To praise Thy glorious Name.

Then GOD upon our land
　Shall constant blessing shower,
And all the world in awe shall stand
　Of His relentless power.

　　　　　　　　　　BRANDEIS.

1673

While with ceaseless course the sun
　Hasted through the former year,
Many souls their race have run,
　Never more to meet us here;
Fixed in an eternal state,
　They've done with all below,
We a little longer wait,
　How little none can know.

·As the winged arrow flies,
　Speedily the mark to find,
As the lightning from the skies
　Darts and leaves no trace behind

Swiftly thus our fleeting days
  Bear us down life's rapid stream,
Upward, LORD, our spirits raise,
  All below is but a dream.

Thanks for mercies past receive,
  Pardon of our sins renew,
And teach us henceforth how to live,
  With eternity in view.
Bless Thy Word to young and old,
  Fill us with a Saviour's love;
And then when life's short tale is told,
  May we dwell with Thee above.

BRANDEIS.

1674

PSALM xcvii. 10. O ye that love the LORD, see that ye hate the thing which is evil : [the LORD preserveth the souls of His saints, He shall deliver them from the hand of the ungodly.]

  To FATHER, SON, and HOLY GHOST,
  The GOD Whom heaven and earth adore,
  From men and from the angel-host
  Be praise and glory evermore. Amen.

ELLIOTT.

1675 COLERIDGE-TAYLOR, C. F. LLOYD, Ps. xcvii. 10.   Amen.

1676

LEVITICUS xxvi. 3. If ye walk in My statutes, and keep My commandments, and do them ;

4. Then I will give you rain in due season, and the land shall yield her increase.

PSALM xix. 8. The statutes of the LORD are right, rejoicing the heart : the commandments of the LORD are pure, enlightening the eyes.

cxix. 33. Teach me, O LORD, the way of Thy statutes : and I shall keep it unto the end.

Novello's Collection.   T   CLIPPINGDALE.

1677

PSALM xxi. 13. Be Thou exalted, LORD, in Thine own strength : so will we sing and praise Thy power.

xxii. 19. Be not Thou far from me, O LORD : hasten Thou to help me.

xliii. 5. Why art thou cast down, O my soul? why art thou disquieted within me ? hope thou in GOD : for I shall yet praise Him for the help of His countenance. Sing praises unto the LORD. Hope thou in GOD.

BAYLEY.

1678

PSALM ciii. 12. (*Bible Version.*) Bless thou the LORD, my inmost soul : sing praise unto His holy Name, forget not all His benefits.

4. He crowneth thee with loving-kindness and tenderest mercy.

11. For as the heaven is high above the earth, so great is His mercy towards them that fear Him.

1. Sing praise to the LORD. Bless thou the LORD.

13. Like as a father pitieth his children, so doth the LORD have pity on all them that live in His fear, and delivereth them. The LORD hath pity on them that fear Him.

19. The LORD hath prepared His throne in the heavens : His kingdom ruleth over all.

1. Bless thou the LORD.

BAYLEY.

1679

LAMENTATIONS iii. 22. It is of the LORD'S mercies we are not consumed, because His compassions fail not.

THORNE.

1680

PSALM xlvii. 1. O clap your hands together, all ye people : O sing unto GOD with the voice of melody.

6. O sing praises, sing praises unto our GOD : O sing praises, sing praises unto our King.

7. For GOD is the King of all the earth : sing ye praises with understanding.

civ. 24. O LORD, how manifold are Thy works: in wisdom hast Thou made them all ; the earth is full of Thy riches.

cxlv. 14. The LORD upholdeth all such as fall, and lifteth up all those that are down.

15. The eyes of all wait upon Thee, O LORD : and Thou givest them their meat in due season.

16. Thou openest Thine hand, and fillest all things living with plenteousness.

cvii. 8. O that men would therefore praise the LORD for His goodness : and declare the wonders that He doeth for the children of men !

cxviii. 28. Thou art my GOD, and I will thank Thee : Thou art my GOD, and I will praise Thee.

29. O give thanks unto the LORD, for He is gracious : and His mercy endureth for ever. Amen.

BUNNETT.

1681

ST. MARK xvi. 2. On the first day of the week, they came unto the sepulchre, at the rising of the sun.

ST. MATTHEW xxviii. 2. And, behold, there was a great earthquake : for the Angel of the LORD had rolled away the stone from the door, and sat upon it.

3. His countenance was like lightning, and his raiment white as snow.

5. And the Angel said unto the women, Fear not ye, for I know that ye seek JESUS Which was crucified.

6. He is not here, for He is risen. Hallelujah ! Amen.

8. And they departed quickly with fear and great joy ; and did run to bring His disciples word.

ST. LUKE xxiv. 34. The LORD is risen indeed. Hallelujah ! LOTT.

1682

PSALM cxxii. 1. I was glad when they said unto me : We will go into the house of the LORD.

2. Our feet shall stand in Thy gates, O Jerusalem.

lxxxiv. 10. For one day in Thy courts is better than a thousand.

11. I had rather be a door-keeper in the house of my GOD, than to dwell in the tents of ungodliness.

13. O LORD GOD of hosts : blessed is the man that putteth his trust in Thee. GAUL.

1683

1. No shadows yonder!
    All light and song!
Each day I wonder
    And say, " How long
Shall time me sunder
    From that dear throng?"

2. No weeping yonder!
    All fled away!
While here I wander
    Each weary day,
And sigh as I ponder
    My long, long stay.

3. No partings yonder!
    Time and space never
Again shall sunder,
    Hearts cannot sever :
Dearer and fonder
    Hands clasp for ever.

4. None wanting yonder!
    Bought by the Lamb,·
All gather'd under
    The ever-green palm—
Loud as night's thunder
    Ascends the glad psalm.

(*From " The Holy City,*" No. 2.)   GAUL.

1684

ECCLESIASTES xii. 1. Remember now thy Creator in the days of thy youth, while the evil days come not, nor the years draw nigh, when thou shalt say, I have no pleasure in them.

14. For GOD shall bring every work into judgment, with every secret thing, whether it be good, or whether it be evil.

GAUL.

1685

ISAIAH xlix. 13. Sing, O Heavens, and be joyful, O earth.
ST. LUKE i. 68, 69. For the LORD hath visited His people; and hath raised up a mighty salvation for us in the house of His servant David.

> Hark! the herald-angels sing
> Glory to the new-born King,
> Peace on earth, and mercy mild,
> GOD and sinners reconciled.
> Joyful, all ye nations, rise,
> Join the triumph of the skies:
> With the angelic host proclaim,
> "Christ is born in Bethlehem."
> > Hark! the herald-angels sing
> > Glory to the new-born King.

ST. LUKE ii. 14. Glory to GOD in the highest, and on earth peace; goodwill toward men. Glory to GOD.

GAUL.

1686

PSALM cxlv. 15. The eyes of all wait on Thee, O LORD: and Thou givest them their meat in due season.
BENEDICITE. 26. O ye children of men, bless ye the LORD: praise Him, and magnify Him for ever.
PSALM lxv. 9. Thou visitest the earth and blessest it: Thou makest it very plenteous.
BENEDICITE. 18. O let the earth bless the LORD: yea, let it praise Him, and magnify Him for ever.
PSALM lxv. 14. The valleys stand so thick with corn that they laugh and sing.
BENEDICITE. 1. O all ye works of the LORD, bless ye the LORD: praise Him and magnify Him for ever. Bless Him, and praise Him for ever.

> Sower Divine! sow the good seed in me,
> > Seed for eternity, Sower Divine.
> Sower Divine! stay not Thy hand, but sow:
> > Then shall the harvest grow, Sower Divine.
> Sower Divine! Let not this field be dry;
> > Refresh it from on high, Sower Divine.
> Water this heart of mine, Sower Divine.   GAUL.

1687

At the Lamb's high feast we sing,
Praise to our victorious King,
Who hath washed us in the tide
Flowing from His piercèd Side ;
Praise we Him, Whose love Divine
Gives His Sacred Blood for wine,
Gives His Body for the feast,
CHRIST the Victim, CHRIST the Priest.

Mighty Victim from the sky,
Hell's fierce powers beneath Thee lie ;
Thou hast conquered in the fight,
Thou hast brought us life and light ;
Now no more can death appal,
Now no more the grave enthral ;
Thou hast opened Paradise,
And in Thee Thy saints shall rise.

Easter triumph, Easter joy,
Sin alone can this destroy ;
From sin's power do Thou set free
Souls new-born, O LORD, in Thee.
Hymns of glory and of praise,
Risen LORD, to Thee we raise ;
Holy Father, praise to Thee,
With the Spirit, ever be.   Amen.

E. V. HALL.

1688

CHRIST the LORD is risen to-day ;
Christians, haste your vows to pay ;
[Offer ye your praises meet
At the Paschal Victim's feet.]
For the sheep the LAMB hath bled,
Sinless in the sinner's stead ;
" CHRIST is risen," to-day we cry ;
Now He lives no more to die.

CHRIST, the Victim undefiled,
Man to GOD hath reconciled ;
Whilst in strange and awful strife
Met together Death and Life :

Christians, on this happy day,
Haste with joy your vows to pay;
" CHRIST is risen," to-day we'cry;
Now He lives no more to die.

CHRIST, Who once for sinners bled,
Now the first-born from the dead,
Throned in endless might and power,
Lives and reigns for evermore.
Hail, Eternal Hope on high !
Hail, Thou King of victory !
Hail, Thou Prince of Life adored ! ,
Help and save us, gracious LORD.
   Hallelujah. Amen.   E. V. HALL.

1689

Come, ye faithful, raise the anthem,
 Cleave the skies with shouts of praise ;
Sing to Him Who found the ransom,
 Ancient of eternal days,
GOD of GOD, the WORD Incarnate,
 Whom the heaven of heaven obeys.

Ere He raised the mighty mountains,
 Formed the seas, or built the sky,
Love eternal, free, and boundless,
 Moved the LORD of Life to die,
Fore-ordained the Prince of princes
 . For the throne of Calvary.

There, for us and our redemption,
 See Him all His Life-blood pour !
There He wins our full salvation,
 Dies that we may die no more ;
Then, arising, lives for ever,
 Reigning where He was before.

Bring your harps, and bring your odour
 · Sweep the string and pour the lay ;
Let the earth proclaim His praises,
 King of that celestial day ;
He the LAMB once slain is worthy,
 Who was dead, and lives for aye.
   Hallelujah. Amen.   E. V. HALL.

1690

Hark the glad sound! the Saviour comes,
　The Saviour promised long;
Let every heart prepare a throne,
　And every voice a song.

He comes, the prisoners to release
　In Satan's bondage held;
The gates of brass before him burst,
　The iron fetters yield.

He comes, the broken heart to bind,
　The bleeding soul to cure,
And with the treasures of His grace
　To bless the humble poor.

Our glad hosannas, Prince of peace,
　Thy welcome shall proclaim;
And heaven's eternal arches ring
　With Thy belovèd Name.　Amen.

E. V. Hall.

1691

O worship the King All-glorious above;
O gratefully sing His power and His love;
Our Shield and Defender, the Ancient of days,
Pavilioned in splendour, and girded with praise.

O tell of His might, O sing of His grace,
Whose robe is the light, Whose canopy space;
His chariots of wrath the deep thunder clouds form,
And dark is His path on the wings of the storm.

The earth with its store of wonders untold,
Almighty, Thy power hath founded of old;
Hath stablished it fast by a changeless decree,
And round it hath cast, like a mantle, the sea.

Thy bountiful care what tongue can recite?
It breathes in the air, it shines in the light;
It streams from the hills, it descends to the plain,
And sweetly distils in the dew and the rain.

Frail children of dust, and feeble as frail,
In Thee do we trust, nor find Thee to fail;
Thy mercies how tender! how firm to the end!
Our Maker, Defender, Redeemer, and Friend.

O measureless Might, ineffable Love!
While angels delight to hymn Thee above,
Thy ransomed creation, though feeble their lays,
With true adoration shall sing to Thy praise. Amen.

E. V. HALL.

1692

Praise, my soul, the King of heaven,
To His feet thy tribute bring;
Ransomed, healed, restored, forgiven,
Evermore His praises sing;
Alleluia! Alleluia!
Praise the everlasting King.

Praise Him for His grace and favour
To our fathers in distress;
Praise Him still the same as ever,
Slow to chide and swift to bless:
Alleluia! Alleluia!
Glorious in His faithfulness.

Father-like, He tends and spares us,
Well our feeble frame He knows;
In His hands He gently bears us,
Rescues us from all our foes;
Alleluia! Alleluia!
Widely yet His mercy flows.

Angels in the height, adore Him;
Ye behold Him face to face;
Saints triumphant, bow before Him,
Gathered in from every race;
Alleluia! Alleluia!
Praise with us the GOD of grace. Amen.

E. V. HALL.

1693

Praise, O praise our GOD and King,
Hymns of adoration sing;
  For His mercies still endure
  Ever faithful, ever sure.

Praise Him that He made the sun
Day by day his course to run;
  For His mercies still endure
  Ever faithful, ever sure;

And the silver moon by night,
Shining with her gentle light;
  For His mercies still endure
  Ever faithful, ever sure.

Praise Him that He gave the rain
To mature the swelling grain;
  For His mercies still endure
  Ever faithful, ever sure;

And hath bid the fruitful field
Crops of precious increase yield;
  For His mercies still endure
  Ever faithful, ever sure.

Praise Him for our harvest-store,
He hath filled the garner-floor;
  For His mercies still endure
  Ever faithful, ever sure;

And for richer Food than this,
Pledge of everlasting bliss;
  For His mercies still endure
  Ever faithful, ever sure.

.Glory to our bounteous King;
Glory let creation sing,
  Glory to the FATHER, SON,
  And blest SPIRIT, Three in One.   Amen.

E. V. HALL.

1694

PSALM lxxxi. 1. Sing we merrily to GOD our strength : make a cheerful noise to the GOD of Jacob.

2. Take the psalm, bring hither the tabret : the merry harp with the lute.

3. Blow up the trumpet in the new moon : even in the time appointed, and upon our solemn feast-day.

1. Sing we merrily to GOD our strength : make cheerful noise to the GOD of Jacob.

Praise, O praise our GOD and King ;
Hymns of adoration sing ;
For His mercies still endure
Ever faithful, ever sure.
Glory to our bounteous King ;
Glory let creation sing ;
Glory to the FATHER, SON,
And blest SPIRIT, Three in One.
Hallelujah. Amen.　　E. V. HALL.

1695

The Day of Resurrection !
Earth, tell it out abroad ;
The Passover of gladness,
The Passover of GOD !
From death to life eternal,
From earth unto the sky,
Our CHRIST hath brought us over
With hymns of victory.

Our hearts be pure from evil
That we may see aright
The LORD in rays eternal
Of resurrection-light ;
And, listening to His accents,
May hear so calm and plain
His own " All hail," and, hearing,
May raise the victor strain.

Now let the heavens be joyful,
And earth her song begin,
The round world keep high triumph,
And all that is therein ;

> Let all things seen and unseen
>   Their notes of gladness blend,
> For CHRIST the LORD is risen,
>   Our Joy that hath no end.   Amen.
> E. V. HALL.

1696

PSALM cxviii. 24. This is the day which the LORD hath made : we will rejoice and be glad in it.

1 CORINTHIANS xv. 20. For now is CHRIST risen from the dead and become the first-fruits of them that slept.

21. For since by man came death, by man came also the resurrection of the dead.

22. For as in Adam all die, even so in CHRIST shall all be made alive.

PSALM cxviii. 24. This is the day which the LORD hath made : we will rejoice and be glad in it.

> JESUS CHRIST is risen to-day,   Alleluia !
> Our triumphant holy day,   Alleluia !
> Who did once, upon the Cross, Alleluia !
> Suffer to redeem our loss.   Alleluia ! Amen.
> E. V. HALL.

1697

PSALM lxv. 1. Thou, O GOD, art praised in Sion : and unto Thee shall the vow be performed in Jerusalem.

2. Thou that hearest the prayer, unto Thee shall all flesh come

9. Thou visitest the earth, and blessest it : Thou makest it very plenteous.

10. Thou preparest their corn, for so Thou providest for the earth.

1. Thou, O GOD, art praised in Sion : and unto Thee shall the vow be performed in Jerusalem.

> Come, ye thankful people, come,
> Raise the song of Harvest-home ;
> All is safely gathered in,
> Ere the winter storms begin ;
> GOD, our Maker, doth provide
> For our wants to be supplied ;
> Come to GOD's own Temple, come :
> Raise the song of Harvest-home.   Amen.
> E. V. HALL.

1698

When GOD of old came down from heaven,
  In power and wrath He came ;
Before His feet the clouds were riven,
  Half darkness and half flame :

But, when He came the second time,
  He came in power and love ;
Softer than gale at morning prime
  Hovered His holy Dove.

The fires, that rushed on Sinai down
  In sudden torrents dread,
Now gently light, a glorious crown,
  On every sainted head.

And as on Israel's awe-struck ear
  The voice exceeding loud,
The trump, that angels quake to hear,
  Thrilled from the deep, dark cloud ;

So when the Spirit of our GOD
  Came down His flock to find,
A voice from heaven was heard abroad,
  A rushing, mighty wind.

It fills the Church of GOD ; It fills
  The sinful world around ;
Only in stubborn hearts and wills
  No place for It is found.

Come LORD, come Wisdom, Love, and Power,
  Open our ears to hear ;
Let us not miss the accepted hour ;
  Save, LORD, by love or fear.   Amen.

E. V. HALL.

1699

REVELATION v.   12. Worthy is the Lamb that was
slain to receive power, and riches, and wisdom, and
strength, and honour, and glory, and blessing.

  xix.   1. Alleluia ; Salvation, and glory, and honour,
and power, unto the LORD our GOD.

7. Let us be glad and rejoice, and give honour to Him, (vii. 10.) saying, Salvation to our GOD which sitteth upon the throne, and unto the Lamb.

xvii. 14. And they that are with Him are called, and chosen, and faithful.

vii. 16. They shall hunger no more, neither thirst any more; neither shall the sun light on them, nor any heat.

17. For the Lamb which is in the midst of the throne shall feed them, and shall lead them unto living fountains of waters : and GOD shall wipe away all tears from their eyes.

xix. 1. Alleluia ; Salvation, and glory, and honour, and power, unto the LORD our GOD. Amen.

BARNETT.

1700

1 ST. JOHN iv. 7. Beloved, let us love one another : for love is of GOD ; and every one that loveth is born of GOD, and knoweth GOD.

16. GOD is love ; and he that dwelleth in love dwelleth in GOD, and GOD in him.

COBB.

1701

REVELATION i. 10. I heard a great voice, as of a trumpet,

11. Saying, I am Alpha and Omega, the first and the last.

12. And I turned to see the voice that spake with me.

17. And when I saw Him, I fell at His feet as dead. And He laid His right hand upon me, saying unto me, Fear not ; I am the first and the last :

18. I am He that liveth, and was dead ; and, behold, I am alive for evermore.

Alleluia ! Hosanna in the highest. Amen.

COBB.

1702

St. Luke xxiv. 5. Why seek ye the living among the dead?

St. Matthew xxviii. 6. He is not here: but is risen, as He said. Come, see the place where the Lord lay.

St. John xi. 25. Jesus said, I am the resurrection and the life: He that believeth in Me, though he were dead, yet shall he live:

26. And whosoever liveth and believeth in Me shall never die.

1 Corinthians xv. 57. Thanks be to God, Who giveth us the victory through our Lord Jesus Christ. Amen.

Peel.

1703

Psalm xvi. 11. (*Bible Version.*) Thou shalt shew me the path of life, in Thy presence is the fulness of joy: and at Thy right hand there is pleasure for evermore.

lxxiii. 24. Thou shalt guide me with Thy counsel, and afterward receive me to glory.

Bowdler.

1704

Psalm cxxxvii. 1. By the waters of Babylon we sat down and wept, when we remembered thee, O Sion.

2. As for our harps, we hanged them up, upon the trees that are therein.

3. For they that led us away captive, required of us then a song and melody in our heaviness: sing us one of the songs of Sion.

4. How shall we sing the Lord's song, in a strange land?

7. Remember the children of Edom, O Lord, in the day of Jerusalem: how they said, Down with it, down with it, even to the ground.

8. O daughter of Babylon, wasted with misery, yea, happy shall he be that rewardeth thee as thou hast served us.

J. H. Clarke.

1705

GENESIS xxxii. 24. And Jacob was left alone; and there wrestled a man with him until the breaking of the day.

26. And he said, Let me go, for the day breaketh. And he said, I will not let Thee go, except Thou bless me.

> Come, O Thou Traveller unknown,
>   Whom still I hold, but cannot see,
> My company before is gone,
>   And I am left alone with Thee;
> With Thee all night I mean to stay,
>   And wrestle till the break of day.

27. And He said unto him, What is thy name? And he said, Jacob.

28. And He said, thy name shall be called no more Jacob, but Israel: for as a prince hast thou power with GOD and with men, and hast prevailed.

> In vain Thou strugglest to get free,
>   I never will unloose my hold;
> Art Thou the Man that died for me?
>   The secret of Thy love unfold.
> Wrestling, I will not let Thee go,
>   Till I Thy Name, Thy Nature know.

29. And Jacob asked Him, and said, Tell me, I pray Thee, Thy Name. And He said, Wherefore is it that thou dost ask after My Name? And He blessed him there.

> 'Tis Love! 'tis Love! Thou diedst for me!
>   I hear Thy whisper in my heart!
> The morning breaks, the shadows flee!
>   Pure universal Love Thou art!
> In vain I have not wept nor strove;
>   Thy Nature and Thy Name is Love.

STAINER.

1706

St. Matthew xx. 30. Behold, two blind men sitting by the way-side, when they heard that Jesus passed by, cried out, saying, Have mercy upon us, O Lord, Thou Son of David.

31. And the multitude rebuked them, because they should hold their peace : but they cried out the more, saying, Have mercy on us, O Lord, Thou Son of David, have mercy.

32. And Jesus stood still and called them, and said, What will ye that I shall do unto you?

33. They said, Lord, that our eyes may be opened.

34. So Jesus had compassion on them, and touched their eyes : and immediately their eyes received sight, and they followed Him.

> O lift the veil, Thou God of Love,
>   That dims our blinded sight,
> The darkness from our souls remove,
>   And pour on us Thy light.
> Do Thou our path to Thee direct,
>   And guide us with Thy grace,
> Till near Thy Throne, 'midst Thine elect,
>   We see Thee face to face.   Amen.
>
> Stainer.

1707

Proverbs iii. 9. Honour the Lord with thy substance, and with the first-fruits of all thine increase.

10. So shall thy barns be filled with plenty, and thy presses shall burst out with new wine.

19. The Lord by wisdom hath founded the earth; by understanding He established the heavens.

20. By His knowledge the depths are broken up, and the clouds drop down the dew.

Deuteronomy xxxiii. 27. The eternal God is thy refuge, and underneath are the everlasting arms :

28. Israel shall dwell then alone in safety : the fountain of Jacob shall be upon a land of corn and wine; also his heaven shall drop down dew.

29. Happy art thou, O Israel, happy art thou! who is like unto thee, O people, happy art thou! saved by the Lord, the shield of thy help, the sword of thy excellency! Hallelujah!   Stainer.

1708

LAMENTATIONS i. 12. Is it nothing to you, all ye that
pass by? Behold and see if there be any sorrow like
unto My sorrow which is done unto Me, wherewith the
LORD hath afflicted Me in the day of His fierce anger.

From the Throne of His Cross, the King of grief
Cries out to the world of unbelief:
Oh! men and women afar and nigh,
Is it nothing to you, all ye that pass by?

I laid My eternal power aside,
I came from the Home of the Glorified,
A Babe, in a lowly cave to lie;
Is it nothing to you, all ye that pass by?

I wept for the sorrows and pains of men,
I healed them, and helped them, and loved them—but
     then
They shouted against Me—Crucify!
Is it nothing to you, all ye that pass by?

Behold Me and see: pierced thro' and thro'
With countless sorrows—and all is for you;
For you I suffer, for you I die,
Is it nothing to you, all ye that pass by?

Oh! men and women, your deeds of shame,
Your sins without reason and number and name;
I bear them all on the Cross on high;
Is it nothing to you, all ye that pass by?

Is it nothing to you that I bow My Head?
And nothing to you that My Blood is shed?
O perishing souls to you I cry,
Is it nothing to you, all ye that pass by?

O come unto Me—by the woes I have borne,
By the dreadful scourge, and the crown of thorn,
By these, I implore you to hear My cry,
Is it nothing to you, all ye that pass by?

O come unto Me—this awful price,
Redemption's tremendous sacrifice—
Is paid for you—Oh! why will ye die?
Is it nothing to you, all ye that pass by?

          (*From " The Crucifixion,' Nos. 17, 18.*)   STAINER.

1709

ECCLESIASTICUS iv. 31. Let not thine hand be stretched out to receive, and shut when thou should'st repay.

xxxv. 10. Give unto the Most High according as He hath enriched thee.

iv. 4. Reject not the supplication of the afflicted, neither turn thy face from a poor man.

vii. 35. Be not slow to visit the sick, for that shall make thee to be beloved.

> LORD, shower upon us from above
> The sacred gift of mutual love;
> Each other's wants may we supply,
> And reign together in the sky.

xviii. 25. When thou hast enough, remember the time of hunger; and when thou art rich, think upon poverty and need.   STAINER.

1710

> Lo! summer comes again,
> And after springtide rain,
> The quickening sunbeams flood the world with light:
> See, high in night's clear skies,
> The joy of longing eyes,
> The moon of harvest shines serenely bright.
>
> O LORD of Heaven and earth,
> Who givest joy and mirth,
> Open our lips to show Thy wondrous praise:
> Our hearts are dull and cold,
> We leave Thy love untold,
> O give us strength our anthems glad to raise.
>
> Each month we sow or reap,
> Each hour we toil or sleep,
> Thou givest life and joy, and Thou alone:
> O grant to each and all,
> When death's dark shadows fall,
> To stand true workers round our Master's Throne.
>
> So life's long task-work o'er,
> Set free for evermore,
> We shall sit down at Thy great Harvest Feast;
> Reaper and sower met,
> The burning heat forget,
> And taste GOD's love, the greatest as the least

Yea, LORD, Thou too dost claim
The sower's mystic name ;
Thou sendest forth Thy reapers to the field ;
O be it theirs to bear
The full corn in the ear,
When Thy true seed its hundred-fold shall yield.

Root out the evil tares,
Earth's vexing grief and cares,
Bind the hot blasts that wither and destroy ;
And when the hour is come
To bring the full sheaves home,
Bid men and angels share Thy Harvest joy.   Amen.

STAINER.

1711

PSALM lxxxv.   10. Mercy and truth are met together :
righteousness and peace have kissed each other.
11. Truth shall flourish out of the earth, and righteousness hath looked down from heaven.

*This day the heavens and earth are one,
For CHRIST is born to-day.
This day is God to earth abased,
And man in heaven securely raised,
For CHRIST is born to-day.

The GOD that dwells above the skies
In unseen majesty,
This day is seen in fleshly guise
Of human frailty.

Therefore to Him our songs we raise,
Songs of glory, songs of praise.
For CHRIST is born to-day.
To GOD on high be glory given,
Be peace divine on earth,
The peace that comes to us from heaven
By this Thy wondrous birth.

Saviour, to Thee our joyful hymns we raise ;
Thine the glory. Thine the praise.   Hallelujah.   Amen.

STAINER.

From the Offices of the Greek Church

1712

SEVEN OF THE GREATER ANTIPHONS.

No. 1.—*O Sapientia.*

O Wisdom, which camest out of the mouth of the Most High, mightily and sweetly ordering all things: Come, and shew us the way of understanding.

No. 2.—*O Adonai.*

O Lord and Ruler of the House of Israel, Who appearedst unto Moses in a flame of fire in the bush, and gavest unto him the Law in Sinai: Come, and redeem us with an outstretched arm.

No. 3.—*O Radix Jesse.*

O Root of Jesse, Who standest for an ensign of the people, at Whom kings shall shut their mouths, unto Whom the Gentiles shall pray: Come, and deliver us, and tarry not.

No. 4.—*O Clavis David.*

O Key of David, and sceptre of the House of Israel, Thou that openest and no man shutteth, and shuttest and no man openeth: Come, and bring the prisoner out of his prison-house, who sitteth in darkness and in the shadow of death.

No. 5.—*O Oriens.*

O Dayspring! Brightness of the everlasting Light, and Sun of Righteousness: Come, and enlighten them that sit in darkness and in the shadow of death.

No. 6.—*O Rex Gentium.*

O King and Desire of all nations, Thou Corner-stone, Who hast made both one: Come, and save man, whom Thou formedst from the clay.

No. 7.—*O Emmanuel.*

O Emmanuel, our King and Lawgiver, Hope of all nations, and their Saviour: Come, and save us, O Lord our God.

STAINER.

1713

Alleluia ! The nallowed day hath shined upon us.
Come, ye nations, adore the LORD, for to-day a great
Light hath descended on the earth. Alleluia.

  Hark ! the hosts of heaven are singing,
  Come, ye nations, and adore Him.

  Hark ! the hosts of heaven are singing
  Praises to their new-born LORD,
  Strains of sweetest music flinging,
  Not a sound or word unheard :
  This the day of days most holy,
  Day in which new joys were given ;
  Not in part alone, but wholly
  To the wide world under heaven.

          STAINER.

1714

There was silence in Bethlehem's fields that night,
 Where the shepherds their flocks were keeping ;
The stars calmly shone from their beautiful height,
 The sheep on the hills lay a-sleeping.
And the quiet that fell on that wondrous hour,
 From all others was strangely parted,
And Hope that for years had been robbed of her power
 Was the Hope of the weary-hearted.

How dreary the ages of strife passed away,
 Since the word of His coming was spoken !
Still, still the deep darkness that reigns ere the day
 And quietness almost unbroken,
Through darkness and silence, Peace hasted to earth,
 Where sheep on the hills lay a-sleeping,
And the angels declared the wonderful birth,
 The end of her sorrow and weeping.

Then suddenly came to this angel most bright,
 A host of the heavenly chorus,
And a glory broke forth more dazzling to sight
 Than the sun which at noonday burns o'er us ;
The silence was over, the hope long deferred,
 The waiting for CHRIST and His glory,
When the angels sang out, and the listeners heard
 The tidings they brought in their story. STAINER.

1715

THE STORY OF THE CROSS.

I. THE QUESTION.

In His own raiment clad—
 With His blood dyed';
Women walk sorrowing
   By His side.

Heavy that Cross to Him,
 Weary the weight—
One who will help Him, waits
   At the gate.

See! they are travelling
 On the same road—
Simon is sharing with
   Him the load.

Oh, whither wandering
 Bear they that tree?
He who first carries it —
   Who is He?

II. THE ANSWER.

Follow to Calvary—
 Tread where He trod—
He Who for ever was
   Son of GOD.

You who would love Him stand,
 Gaze at His Face;
Tarry awhile on your
   Earthly race.

As the swift moments fly
 Through the Blest Week
Read the great story the
   Cross will speak.

Is there no beauty to
 You who pass by
In that lone Figure which
   Marks that sky?

III. The Story of the Cross.

On the Cross lifted
  Thy Face we scan—
Bearing that Cross for us,
    Son of Man.
Thorns form Thy diadem,
  Rough wood Thy throne —
For us Thy blood is shed—
    Us alone.
No pillow under Thee
  To rest Thy Head—
Only the splintered Cross
    Is Thy bed.
Nails pierce Thy Hands and Feet,
  Thy Side the spear ;
No voice is nigh to say
    Help is near.
Shadows of midnight fall
  Though it is day—
Thy friends and kinsfolk stand
    Far away.
Loud is Thy bitter cry ;
  Sunk on Thy Breast
Hangeth Thy bleeding Head
    Without rest.
Loud scoffs the dying thief
  Who mocks at Thee—
Can it, my Saviour, be
    All for me ?
Gazing afar from Thee,
  Silent and lone,
Stand those few weepers, Thou
    Callest Thine own.
I see Thy title, Lord,
  Inscribed above—
" Jesus of Nazareth,"
    King of Love !
What, Oh my Saviour !
  Here didst Thou see,
Which made Thee suffer and
    Die for me ?

IV. The Appeal from the Cross.

Child of My grief and pain—
  Watched by My love—
I come to call thee to
        Realms above.

I saw thee wandering
  Far off from Me :
In love I seek for thee—
        Do not flee.

For thee My blood I shed—
  For thee alone :
I came to purchase thee—
        For Mine own. .

Weep not for My grief,
  Child of My love—
Strive to be with Me in
        Heaven above.

V. Our Cry to Jesus.

Oh, I will follow Thee,
  Star of my soul,
Thro' the deep shades of life
        To the goal.

Yes, let Thy Cross be borne
  Each day by me—
Mind not how heavy, if
        But with Thee.

Lord, if Thou only wilt
  Make us Thine own,
Give no companion, save
        Thee alone.

Grant thro' each day of life
  To stand by Thee ;
With Thee, when morning breaks,
        Ever to be.   Amen.

STAINER, M. B. FOSTER, ROBERTS, SOMERVELL.

1716

" Come unto Me, ye weary,
  And I will give you rest."
O blessèd voice of JESUS,
  Which comes to hearts opprest :
It tells of benediction,
  Of pardon, grace, and peace,
Of joy that hath no ending,
  Of love that cannot cease.

" Come unto Me, ye wanderers,
  And I will give you light."
O loving voice of JESUS,
  Which comes to cheer the night ;
. Our hearts were filled with sadness,
  And we had lost our way ;
But He has brought us gladness
  And songs at break of day.

" Come unto Me, ye fainting,
  And I will give you life.'
O cheering voice of JESUS
  Which comes to aid our strife ;
The foe is stern and eager,
  The fight is fierce and long ;
But He has made us mighty,
  And stronger than the strong.

" And whosoever cometh,
  I will not cast him out."
O welcome voice of JESUS,
  Which drives away our doubt ;
Which calls us very sinners,
  Unworthy though we be,
- Of love so free and boundless,
  To come, dear LORD, to Thee.

                              JORDAN.

1717

PSALM xxxvii. 23. (*Bible Version.*) The steps of a good
man are ordered by the LORD : and he delighteth in His way.
  24. He shall not be cast down : for the LORD upholdeth
him with His hand.   CAMBRIDGE.

1718

HOLY GHOST to earth descending,
Unto all Thy love commending,
Grace to them and us extending,
　Now Thy wondrous work begin.

CHRIST, Who by Thy Cross hast bought us,
Thou, Who free redemption wrought us,
Come, and make them pure within,
Cleanse their souls from stain of sin.

Let songs resound, our thankful joy confessing,
And let us wish them health and wealth and blessing.

Powers that dwell in heavenly places,
Plant within them Christian graces,
Turn away from sin their faces,
　Standing alway at their side.

Teach them both from life to gather
Trust in GOD, their loving Father;
While their hearts in Him confide,
Grief will cease, and joy abide.

Let songs resound, our thankful joy confessing,
And let us wish them health and wealth and blessing.
Both Heaven and earth our voices hear delighted :
O sing ye Alleluia, all united.　Alleluia.

DVOŘÁK

1719

ST. LUKE xxiv.　49. Behold, I send the promise of My
Father upon you : but tarry ye in the city of Jerusalem,
until ye be endued with power from on high.

PSALM xlviii. 8. We wait for Thy loving-kindness, O GOD : in the midst of Thy temple.

13. For this GOD is our GOD for ever and ever: He shall be our guide unto death.

lxviii. 19. Praised be the LORD daily: even the GOD Who helpeth us, and poureth His benefits upon us.

J. V. ROBERTS.

1720

REVELATION i. 8. I am Alpha and Omega, the beginning and the ending, saith the LORD, Which is, and Which was, and Which is to come, the Almighty.

xv. 4. Who shall not fear Thee, and glorify Thy Name, O LORD? for Thou only art holy.

ST. MATTHEW vi. 13. For Thine is the kingdom, and the power, and the glory, for ever. Amen.

From the Communion Service. Holy, Holy, Holy, LORD GOD of Hosts, Heaven and earth are full of Thy Glory; Glory be to Thee, O LORD most High. Amen.

O Father, Thine be praise
From all in earth and heaven;
To JESUS, Son of GOD,
Let endless praise be given.
Thy praise, O Holy Ghost,
Be sounded more and more,
Th' Eternal Three in One,
We worship and adore.

J. V. ROBERTS.

1721

PROVERBS xiv. 26. In the fear of the LORD is strong confidence, and His children shall have a place of refuge.

27. The fear of the LORD is a fountain of life, to depart from the snares of death.

J. V. ROBERTS.

1722

*Jesu, priceless treasure,
Source of purest pleasure,
Truest friend to me;
Ah, how long I've panted,
And my heart hath fainted,
Thirsting, Lord, for Thee!
Thine I am, O spotless Lamb,
I will suffer nought to hide Thee,
Nought I ask beside Thee.

(Sung at the same time as the above.)

In Thine arm I rest me,
Foes who would molest me
Cannot reach me here;
Though the earth be shaking,
Every heart be quaking,
Jesus calms my fear;
Fires may flash and thunders crash,
Yea, and sin and hell assail me,
Jesus will not fail me.*

Romans viii. 1. There is therefore now no condemnation to them which are in Christ Jesus, who walk not after the flesh, but after the Spirit.

33. Who shall lay any thing to the charge of God's elect? It is God that justifieth.

34. Who is he that condemneth? It is Christ that died, yea rather, that is risen again, Who is even at the right hand of God, Who also maketh intercession for us.

Hence, all fears and sadness,
For the Lord of gladness,
Jesus, enters in;
They who love the Father,
Though the storms may gather,
Still have peace within;
Yea, whate'er I here must bear,
Still in Thee lies purest pleasure,
Jesu, priceless treasure.

J. V. Roberts.

—* Sometimes sung as a separate Anthem.

1723

St. John xiv. 27. Peace I leave with you, My peace I give unto you : not as the world giveth, give I unto you. Let not your heart be troubled, neither let it be afraid.

xvi. 6. Because I have said these things unto you, sorrow hath filled your heart.

33. But be of good cheer; I have overcome the world.

xiv. 27. Peace I leave with you, My peace I give unto you.

J. V. Roberts.

1724

Psalm xxv. 3. Shew me Thy ways, O Lord, and teach me Thy paths.

4. Lead me forth in Thy truth and learn me, for Thou art the God of my salvation ; in Thee hath been my hope all the day long.

5. Call to remembrance, O Lord, Thy tender mercies : and Thy loving-kindnesses, which have been ever of old.

6. According to Thy mercy think Thou on me, for Thy goodness.

J. V. Roberts.

1725

Proverbs iii. 26. The Lord shall be thy confidence, and shall keep thy foot from being taken.

5. Trust in the Lord with all thine heart ; and lean not unto thine own understanding.

6. In all thy ways acknowledge Him, and He shall direct thy paths.

23. Then shalt thou walk in thy way safely, and thy foot shall not stumble.

24. When thou liest down, thou shalt not be afraid : yea, thou shalt lie down, and thy sleep shall be sweet.

26. The Lord shall be thy confidence, and shall keep thy foot from being taken.

5. Trust in the Lord with all thine heart ; and lean not unto thine own understanding.

5, 26. Trust in the Lord with all thine heart : the Lord shall be thy confidence.

J. V. Roberts.

1726

PROVERBS iv. 18. The path of the just is as the shining light, that shineth more and more unto the perfect day.

J. V. ROBERTS.

1727

ISAIAH xiv. 7. The whole earth is at rest, and is quiet: they break forth into singing.

xxv. 9. Lo, This is our GOD; we have waited for Him, and He will save us: This is the LORD; we have waited for Him, we will be glad and rejoice in His salvation.

ST. LUKE ii. 15. Let us now go even unto Bethlehem, and see this thing which is come to pass, which the LORD hath made known unto us.

10. For the angel said, Fear not: for, behold, I bring you good tidings of great joy, which shall be to all people.

11. For unto you is born this day, in the city of David, a Saviour, Which is CHRIST the LORD.

Beside Thy cradle here I stand,
O Thou that ever livest,
And bring Thee with a willing hand
The very gifts Thou givest.
Accept me; 'tis my mind and heart,
My soul, my strength, my every part,
That Thou from me requirest.

All darkness flies before Thy face,
The shades of night to day give place;
In Thy ways lead us ever,
That from Thy sight and glorious light,
Our hearts may wander never.

J. V. ROBERTS.

1728

PSALM cxxxix. 23. Try me, O GOD, and seek the ground of my heart: prove me, and examine my thoughts.

24. Look well if there be any way of wickedness in me.

v. 8. Make Thy way plain before my face, (cxxxix. 24) and lead me in the way everlasting.

J. V. ROBERTS.

1729

PSALM li. 1. Have mercy upon me, O GOD, after Thy great goodness: according to the multitude of Thy mercies do away mine offences.

2. Wash me throughly from my wickedness, and cleanse me from my sin.

3. For I acknowledge my faults, and my sin is ever before me.

[8. Thou shalt make me hear of joy and gladness: that the bones which Thou hast broken may rejoice.]

9. Turn Thy face from my sins, and put out all my misdeeds.

10. Make me a clean heart, O GOD, and renew a right spirit within me.

[11. Cast me not away from Thy presence, and take not Thy holy Spirit from me.]

17. The sacrifice of GOD is a troubled spirit: a broken and contrite heart, O GOD, shalt Thou not despise.

SHAW.

1730 WHITE, vv. 1, 8.
1731 BATSON, vv. 10, 11.

1732

ST. MATTHEW xxviii. 1. As it began to dawn toward the first day of the week, came Mary Magdalene and the other Mary to see the Sepulchre.

2. For behold, there was a great earthquake: and the angel of the LORD descended from heaven, and came and rolled back the stone from the door, and sat upon it.

3. His countenance was like lightning, and his raiment white as snow:

4. And for fear of him the keepers did shake, and became as dead men.

5. And the angel answered and said unto the women, Fear not ye: for I know that ye seek JESUS, Which was crucified.

6. He is not here: for He is risen, as He said. Come, see the place where the LORD lay.

7. And go quickly, and tell His disciples that He is risen from the dead.

JESUS CHRIST is risen to-day,   Hallelujah !
Our triumphant holy day,   Hallelujah !
Now above the sky He's King,   Hallelujah !
Where the angels ever sing   Hallelujah !

1 CORINTHIANS XV. 20. CHRIST is risen from the dead.
Amen.

MARTIN.

1733

ISAIAH xlix. 23. Kings shall be thy nursing fathers,
and their queens thy nursing mothers : and thou shalt
know that I am the LORD.

TE DEUM. We praise Thee, O GOD.

PSALM lxi. 6. Thou shalt grant the *Queen* a long life :
that *her* years may endure throughout all generations.

7. *She* shall dwell before GOD for ever : O prepare Thy
loving mercy and faithfulness that they may preserve *her*.

TE DEUM. We praise Thee, O GOD.

PSALM lxxii. 7. In *her* time let the righteous flourish :
and let peace be in all our borders.

TE DEUM. We praise Thee, O GOD.

MARTIN.

1734

ECCLESIASTICUS xxxix. 15. Magnify His Name, and
shew forth His praise with the songs of your lips, and
with harps.

PRAYER OF MANASSES. For He is a most high LORD.

PSALM xxxiv. 3. O praise the LORD with me : let us
magnify His Name together. (He is a most high LORD).

4. I sought the LORD, and He heard me : yea, He
delivered me out of my fear.

PRAYER OF MANASSES. He is a most high LORD : of
great compassion, longsuffering, very merciful, and
repenteth of the evil of men.

PSALM xxxiv. 3. O praise the LORD with me : let us
magnify His Name together.

ECCLESIASTICUS xxxix. 15. Magnify His Name, and
shew forth His praise with the songs of your lips, and
with harps.

Praise the LORD! ye heavens, adore Him,
   Praise Him, Angels, in the height;
Sun and moon, rejoice before Him,
   Praise Him, all ye stars and light:
Praise the LORD! for He hath spoken,
   Worlds His mighty voice obeyed;
Laws, which never shall be broken,
   For their guidance He hath made.

Praise the LORD! for He is glorious;
   Never shall His promise fail;
GOD hath made His saints victorious,
   Sin and death shall not prevail.
Praise the GOD of our salvation;
   Hosts on high, His power proclaim;
Heaven and earth, and all creation,
   Laud and magnify His Name!

MARTIN.

1735

ZEPHANIAH i. 14. The Great Day of the LORD is near, it is near, and hasteth greatly, even the voice of the day of the LORD.

ii. 3. Seek ye the LORD, all ye meek upon earth, which have wrought His judgment; seek righteousness, seek meekness: it may be we shall be hid in the day of the LORD's anger.

i. 14. The Great Day of the LORD is near.

MARTIN.

1736

ISAIAH xlii. 1. Behold My Servant, Whom I uphold, mine Elect, in Whom My soul delighteth, I have put My Spirit upon Him, and He shall bring forth judgment to the Gentiles.

lxii. 11. Tell ye the daughter of Sion, Behold thy salvation cometh; behold, His reward is with Him, and His work before Him.

ST. LUKE i. 68. Blessed be the LORD GOD of Israel: for He hath visited and redeemed His people.

ST. MATTHEW xxi. 9. Blessed is He that cometh in the Name of the LORD. To God on high be glory, to God on high in heaven, and peace on earth. Hallelujah.

J. F. BRIDGE.

1737

REVELATION xv. 3. Great and marvellous are Thy works, LORD GOD ALMIGHTY; just and true are Thy ways, Thou King of saints.

JEREMIAH v. 24. Let us now fear the LORD our GOD.

He reserveth unto us the appointed weeks of the harvest. Let us now fear the LORD our GOD.

ACTS xiv. 17. He giveth us rain from heaven, and fruitful seasons, filling our hearts with food and gladness.

JEREMIAH v. 24. Let us now fear the LORD our GOD.

PSALM cxxxvi. 3. O thank the LORD of all lords: for His mercy endureth for ever.

25. Who giveth food to all flesh: for His mercy endureth for ever. Amen.

J. F. BRIDGE.

1738

"HE GIVETH HIS BELOVED SLEEP."

What would we give to our beloved?
The hero's heart to be unmoved,
　The poet's star-tuned harp to sweep,
The patriot's voice to teach and rouse,
The monarch's crown to light the brows?
　"He giveth His beloved sleep."

O earth, so full of dreary noises!
O men, with wailing in your voices!
　O delved gold, the wailer's heap!
O strife, O curse, that o'er it fall!
GOD strikes a silence through you all,
　And "giveth His beloved sleep."

His dews drop mutely on the hill,
His cloud above it saileth still,
　Though on its slopes men sow and reap:
More softly than the dew is shed,
Or cloud is floated overhead,
　"He giveth His beloved sleep."

J. F. BRIDGE.

1739

EZEKIEL xxxiv. 15. I will feed My flock, and I will cause them to lie down, saith the LORD GOD.

27, 28. And the tree of the field shall yield her fruit, and the earth shall yield her increase, and they shall be safe in their land ; they shall dwell safely, and none shall make them afraid.

30. Thus shall they know that I the LORD their GOD am with them, and that they are My people, saith the LORD GOD.   J. F. BRIDGE.

1740

ISAIAH xlii. 10. Sing unto the LORD a new song, and His praise from the end of the earth, ye that go down to the sea, and all that is therein ; the isles, and the inhabitants thereof.

PROVERBS ix. 10. The fear of the LORD is the beginning of wisdom : and the knowledge of the Holy One is understanding.

11. By wisdom thy days shall be multiplied, and the years of thy life shall be increased.

WISDOM vii. 25, 26. For she is a breath of the power of GOD, a pure stream flowing from the glory of the Almighty, and the image of His goodness.

PSALM cxlv. 8. The LORD is gracious, and full of compassion ; slow to anger, and of great mercy.

9. The LORD is good to all : and His tender mercies are over all His works.

13. Thy kingdom is an everlasting kingdom, and Thy dominion endureth throughout all generations.

J. F. BRIDGE.

1741

Sunset and evening star,
   And one clear call for me !
And may there be no moaning of the bar   .
   When I put out to sea.
But such a tide as moving seems asleep,
   Too full for sound and foam,
When that which drew from out the boundless deep
   Turns again home.

Twilight and evening bell,
And after that the dark !
And may there be no sadness of farewell
When I embark.
For though from out our bourne of Time and Place,
The flood may bear me far,
I hope to see my Pilot face to face
When I have crost the bar.

J. F. BRIDGE, H. H. WOODWARD.

1742

PROVERBS x. 22. The blessing of the LORD, it maketh
rich, and He addeth no sorrow with it.

PSALM cxxix. 8. The LORD prosper you : we wish you
good luck in the Name of the LORD.

J. F. BRIDGE.

1743
THE CRADLE OF CHRIST
(STABAT MATER SPECIOSA).

No. 1.

Full of beauty stood the Mother,
By the manger, blest o'er other,
Where her little One she lays:
For her inmost soul's elation,
In its fervid jubilation,
Thrills with ecstasy of praise.

O what glad, what rapturous feeling
Filled that blessed Mother, kneeling
By the Sole-Begotten One!
How, her heart with laughter bounding,
She beheld the work astounding,
Saw His birth, the glorious SON.

No. 2.

Who is he, that sight who beareth,
Nor CHRIST'S Mother's solace shareth,
In her bosom as He lay:
Who is he, that would not render
Tend'rest love for love so tender,
Love, with that dear Babe at play ?

For the trespass of her nation
She with oxen saw His station
　　Subjected to cold and woe:
Saw her sweetest Offspring's wailing,
Wise men Him with worship hailing,
　　In the stable, mean and low.

No. 3.

JESUS lying in the manger,
Heavenly armies sang the Stranger,
　　In the great joy bearing part;
Stood the old man with the maiden,
No words speaking, only laden
　　With this wonder in their heart.

No. 4.

JESUS, fount of life still flowing,
Let me, with her rapture glowing,
　　Learn to sympathise with Thee:
Let me raise my heart's devotion,
Up to CHRIST with pure emotion,
　　That accepted I may be.

SAVIOUR, let me win this blessing,
Let Thy sorrow's deep impressing
　　In my heart engraved remain:
Since Thou didst, from heaven descending,
Deign to bear the manger's tending,
　　O divide with me Thy pain.

Keep my heart its gladness bringing,
To Thee, SAVIOUR, ever clinging,
　　Long as this my life shall last;
Love like that Thine own love, give it,
On Thy Holy Name to rivet,
　　Till this exile shall be past.

No. 5.

Virgin, peerless of condition,
Be not wroth with my petition,
　　Let me clasp thy little Son:
Let me bear that Child so glorious,
Him, whose Birth, o'er Death victorious,
　　Will'd that Life for man was won.

·.No. 6.

All who love this stable truly,
And the shepherds watching duly,
  Tarry there the live-long night:
Pray we that by JESU'S merit,
His elected may inherit
  Their own country's endless light.

J. F. BRIDGE.

Latin Hymn, "Stabat Mater speciosa," Giacopone (13th century).
Translated by Rev Dr. NEALE (1866).

1744

JONAH ii. 7. When my soul fainted within me I remembered the LORD: and my prayer came in unto Thee, into Thy holy temple.

6. I went down to the bottoms of the mountains; the earth with her bars was about me for ever: yet hast Thou brought me up from corruption, O LORD my GOD.

9. I will sacrifice unto Thee with the voice of thanksgiving: and I will pay that I have vowed. Salvation is of the LORD. Alleluia.

J. F. BRIDGE.

1745

ST. LUKE ii. 10. Behold, I bring you good tidings of great joy, which shall be to all people.

11. For unto you is born this day, in the city of David, a Saviour, Which is CHRIST the LORD.

ROMANS x. 15. How beautiful are the feet of them that preach the gospel of peace, and bring glad tidings of good things!

ST. LUKE ii. 14. Glory to GOD in the highest, and on earth peace, good-will toward men. Glory to GOD in the highest.

CRAMENT.

1746

1 CORINTHIANS xv. 20. CHRIST is risen from the dead, and become the first-fruits of them that slept.

ROMANS vi. 10. For in that He died, He died unto sin once: but in that He liveth, He liveth unto GOD.

COLOSSIANS iii. I. If ye then be risen with CHRIST, seek those things which are above, where CHRIST sitteth on the right hand of GOD.

4. When CHRIST, Who is our life, shall appear, then shall ye also appear with Him in glory.

[ROMANS vi. II. Likewise reckon ye yourselves to be dead indeed unto sin, but alive unto GOD through JESUS CHRIST our LORD.]

Hymns of praise then let us sing   Alleluia!
Unto CHRIST, our heavenly King,   Alleluia!
Who endured the Cross and grave, Alleluia!
Sinners to redeem and save.   Alleluia! Amen.

CRAMENT.

1747 AITKEN, 1 Cor. xv. 20; Romans vi. 10; Col. iii. 1;
      Romans vi. 11; 1 Cor. xv. 20. Hallelujah. Amen.
1748 J. V. ROBERTS, Col. iii. 4.

1749

ISAIAH lv. I. Ho, every one that thirsteth, come ye to the waters, and he that hath no money; come ye, buy, and eat; yea, come, buy wine and milk without money and without price.

6. Seek ye the LORD while He may be found, call ye upon Him while He is near:

7. Let the wicked forsake his way, and the unrighteous man his thoughts; and let him return unto the LORD, and He will have mercy upon him; and to our GOD, for He will abundantly pardon.

I. Ho, every one that thirsteth, come ye to the waters.

REVELATION xxii. 17. And the Spirit and the Bride say, Come. And let him that heareth say, Come. And let him that is athirst come. And whosoever will, let him take the water of life freely.

ISAIAH lv. I. Ho, every one that thirsteth, come to the waters.

CRAMENT.

1750

PSALM cxiii. 1. Praise the LORD, ye servants : O praise the Name of the LORD.

3. The LORD'S Name is praised : from the rising up of the sun, unto the going down of the same.

xxxiv. 15. The eyes of the LORD are over the righteous : and His ears are open unto their prayers.

17. The righteous cry, and the LORD heareth them : and saveth them out of all their troubles.

3. O praise the LORD with me : and let us magnify His Name together.

8. Blessed is the man that trusteth in Him.

CRAMENT.

1751

ISAIAH xl. 3. Prepare ye the way of the LORD, make straight in the desert a highway for our GOD.

4. Every valley shall be exalted, and every mountain and hill made low : the crooked shall be made straight, and the rough places plain.

5. And the glory of the LORD shall be revealed, and all flesh shall see it together : for the mouth of the LORD hath spoken it.

CRAMENT.

1752

PSALM xxvi. 8. LORD, I have loved the habitation of Thy house, and the place where Thine honour dwelleth.

v. 8. Lead me, O LORD, in Thy righteousness ; make Thy way plain before my face.

xix. 14, 15. Let the words of my mouth, and the meditation of my heart, be alway acceptable in Thy sight, O LORD, my strength and my Redeemer.

> Guide me, O Thou great Redeemer,
>   Pilgrim through this barren land ;
> I am weak, but Thou art mighty,
>   Hold me with Thy powerful hand ;
>   Bread of heaven,
> Feed me now and evermore.

IILIFFE.

1753

St. Luke i. 68. Blessed be the Lord God of Israel :
for He hath visited and redeemed His people ;

69. And hath raised up a mighty salvation for us : in
the house of his servant David ;

70. As He spake by the mouth of His holy Prophets :
which have been since the world began.

71. That we should be saved from our enemies : and
from the hands of all that hate us.

72. To perform the mercy promised to our forefathers :
and to remember His holy Covenant ;

73. To perform the oath which He sware to our fore-
father Abraham : that he would give us :

74. That we being delivered out of the hand of our
enemies : might serve Him without fear ;

75. In holiness and righteousness before Him : all the
days of our life.

76. And thou, Child, shalt be called the prophet of the
Highest : for thou shalt go before the face of the Lord to
prepare His ways ;

77. To give knowledge of salvation unto His people :
for the remission of their sins.

78. Through the tender mercy of our God : whereby
the day-spring from on high hath visited us ;

79. To give light to them that sit in darkness, and in
the shadow of death ; and to guide our feet into the way
of peace.

Glory be to the Father, &c.

Heap.

1754 Gaul, *vv.* 68, 69, 76—79.

1755

Psalm iii. 4. I cried unto the Lord with my voice ;
and He heard me out of His holy hill.

5. I laid me down and slept, and rose up again : for the
Lord sustained me.

Heap.

1756

Lᴏʀᴅ of life and light and glory,
Gᴏᴅ of our world-empire's story,
  Low we bow before Thy throne.
Thou of good things art the Giver,
Thou from evil dost deliver,
  Praise is Thine, and Thine alone.

King of kings, protect this nation,
Lᴏʀᴅ of lords, be our salvation,
  In the stress of trouble's day.
O Most High, on Thee relying,
Now and ever ill defying,
  We securely rest for aye.   Amen.
(From a " Jubilee Ode," No. 5.)   Mᴀᴄᴋᴇɴᴢɪᴇ.

1757

O Holy Babe! O Majesty Divine!
  To Thee the psalm we sing,
  And wake to praise the sounding string :
Thy light has come, dear Zion, rise and shine.
            (From "Bethlehem.")   Mᴀᴄᴋᴇɴᴢɪᴇ.

1758

Isᴀɪᴀʜ xlix. 10.   We shall not hunger nor thirst :
neither shall the sun smite us ; for He that hath mercy
shall lead us, even by springs of water shall He guide us.
      (From " The Rose of Sharon.")   Mᴀᴄᴋᴇɴᴢɪᴇ.

1759

Rᴇᴠᴇʟᴀᴛɪᴏɴ i.   3. Blessed is he that readeth, and they
that hear the words of this prophecy.   These things saith
the First and the Last, which was dead, and is alive.
  ii.   7. To him that overcometh will I give to eat of the
Tree of Life, which is in the midst of the Paradise of Gᴏᴅ.
  iii.   5. He shall be clothed in white raiment, and I
will confess his name before My Father and His holy
angels.
      (From " The Rose of Sharon.)   Mᴀᴄᴋᴇɴᴢɪᴇ.

1760

1 St. John iii. 2. Beloved, now are we the sons of God, and it doth not yet appear what we shall be : but we know that when He shall appear, we shall be like Him, for we shall see Him as He is.

St. Matthew v. 8. Blessed are the pure in heart ; for they shall see God.

1 St. John iii. 3. Every man that hath this hope in Him purifieth himself, even as He is pure.

2 Corinthians iii. 18. They all, with open face beholding the glory of the Lord, are changed into the same image from glory to glory, even as by the Spirit of the Lord.

St. Matthew v. 8. Blessed are the pure in heart ; for they shall see God.

Keeton.

1761 Thorne, 1 St. John iii. 2, 3.

1762

Isaiah lxi. 10. I will greatly rejoice in the Lord, my soul shall be joyful in my God ; He hath clothed me with the garments of salvation, He hath covered me with the robe of righteousness.

11. As the earth bringeth forth her bud, and as the garden causeth the things that are sown in it to spring forth, so the Lord God will cause righteousness and praise to spring forth before all nations. [Hallelujah! Amen.]

Cruickshank, Keeton.

1763

Revelation i. 5, 6. Unto Him that loveth us, and loosed us from our sins by His blood, unto Him be the glory and the dominion for ever and ever. Amen.

Keeton.

1764

1. Far from their home, our fallen race
   In sinful darkness laid;
   And, knowing not the way to life,
   In hopeless wand'rings strayed.

2. In wondrous love, th' Incarnate GOD
   Descends from highest heaven,
   Those exiles home again to call,
   Himself to exile giv'n.

3. He comes, to feeble knees a staff,
   And strength to sinking soul;
   Himself the Way, Himself the Light,
   Himself the Life and Goal.

4 Eternal GOD, within the veil
   Of human flesh confined,
   Oh, may Thy truth its beams unfold
   To ev'ry faithful mind.

5. All praise to Thee, through Whom alone
   Our stains of guilt are lost,
   Like praise be to the Father given,
   And to the Holy Ghost.   Amen.

H. H. WOODWARD.

1765

ZECHARIAH ix.   9. Rejoice greatly, O daughter of Sion:
behold, thy King cometh unto thee: He is just, and
having salvation.

ST. MATTHEW xxi.   9. Hosanna to the Son of David.
Blessed is He that cometh in the Name of the LORD.

MALACHI iii.   2. But who may abide the day of His
coming? and who shall stand when He appeareth?

PSALM xx.   9. Save, LORD, and hear us, O King of
heaven, when we call upon Thee.

H. H. WOODWARD.

1766

The day Thou gavest, LORD, is ended,
   The darkness falls at Thy behest;
To Thee our morning hymns ascended,
   Thy praise shall hallow now our rest.

We thank Thee that Thy church unsleeping,
  While earth rolls onward into light,
Through all the world her watch is keeping,
  And rests not now by day or night.

As o'er each continent and island
  The dawn leads on another day,
The voice of prayer is never silent,
  Nor dies the strain of praise away.

The sun that bids us rest is waking
  Our brethren 'neath the western sky,
And hour by hour fresh lips are making
  Thy wondrous doings heard on high.

So be it, LORD ; Thy Throne shall never,
  Like earth's proud empires, pass away ;
But stand, and rule. and grow for ever,
  Till all Thy creatures own Thy sway.   Amen.
                              H. H. WOODWARD.

1767

JOB xii. 2. Hear My words, ye people ; give ear unto Me, all ye that have knowledge.

4. Let us choose to us judgment : let us know among ourselves what is good.

xxxvi. 5. Behold, GOD is mighty, and despiseth not any : He is mighty in strength and in wisdom.

26. Behold, He is great, and we know Him not : neither can the number of His years be searched out.

PSALM xi. 4. The LORD'S seat is in heaven.

xcii. 2. Clouds and darkness are round about Him : righteousness and judgment are the habitation of His seat.

civ. 2. He decketh Himself with light as with a garment, and spreadeth out the heavens like a curtain.

3. He layeth the beams of His chambers in the waters, and maketh the clouds His chariots, and walketh upon the wings of the wind.

xviii. 9. He bowed the heavens and came down : and it was dark under His feet.

10. He rode on the cherubim, and did fly, and came flying upon the wings of the wind.

xi. 4. The LORD'S seat is in heaven.

ciii. 19. His kingdom ruleth over all.

xxxiii. 17. Behold the eye of the LORD is on them that fear Him: and upon them that put their trust in His mercy.

18. To deliver their soul from death: and to feed them in a time of dearth.

19. Our soul hath patiently tarried for the LORD, for He is our help and our shield.

lxxii. 12. He delivereth the poor in his affliction, the fatherless and him that hath none to help him.

ISAIAH lxi. 1, 2. He shall bind up the broken-hearted, and proclaim liberty to the captives, and comfort to those that mourn.

3. He shall give them beauty for ashes: the garment of praise for the spirit of heaviness.

11. For as the earth bringeth forth her bud, and as the garden causeth things that are sown to spring forth; so the LORD GOD will cause righteousness and peace to spring forth before all nations.

PSALM ciii. 8. The LORD is full of compassion and mercy.

10. He hath not dealt with us after our sins: nor rewarded us according to our wickedness.

11. For look how high the heaven is in comparison of the earth: so great is His mercy also toward them that fear Him.

12. Look how wide also the east is from the west: so far hath He set our sins from us.

> O praise ye the LORD!
>   Praise Him in the height;
> Rejoice in His Word,
>   Ye angels of light;
> Ye heavens, adore Him
>   By Whom ye were made,
> And worship before Him,
>   In brightness arrayed.
>
> O praise ye the LORD!
>   Praise Him upon earth,
> In tuneful accord,
>   Ye sons of new birth;
> Praise Him Who hath brought you
>   His grace from above,
> Praise Him Who hath taught you
>   To sing of His love.

O praise ye the LORD!
  Thanksgiving and song
To Him be outpoured
  All ages along:
For love in creation,
  For heaven restored,
For grace of salvation
  O praise ye the LORD! Amen.

PARRY.

1768

BARUCH v. 1. Put off, O Jerusalem, the garment of thy mourning, put on the comeliness of glory that cometh of GOD for ever.

3. For He will show thy brightness unto every nation under heaven.

4. Thy name shall be called the peace of righteousness, the glory of GOD's worship.

6. He bringeth thy people, exalted with glory, rejoicing in the remembrance of GOD.

9. And He shall lead Israel with joy in the light of His glory, with mercy and righteousness that cometh from Him.

(From "Judith.") PARRY.

1769

I do not ask, O LORD, that life may be
      A pleasant road;
I do not ask that Thou wouldst take from me
      Aught of its load;
I do not ask that flowers should always spring
      Beneath my feet;
I know the poison and the sting too well,
      Of things too sweet.
For one thing only, LORD, dear LORD, I plead;
      Lead me aright.
Tho' strength should falter, and tho' hearts should bleed,
Lead me aright, dear LORD, I plead,
      Through peace to Light.

J. H. ROBERTS.

1770

PSALM xl. 14. Withdraw not Thou Thy mercy from me, O LORD : let Thy loving-kindness and Thy truth alway preserve me.

21. Thou art my helper and redeemer : make no long tarrying, O my GOD.

KEARTON.

1771

From the Litany.

'O LORD, shew Thy mercy upon us,
    And grant us Thy salvation.
O LORD, save the *Queen ;*
    Who putteth *her* trust in Thee.
Send *her* help from Thy holy place,
    And evermore mightily defend *her*.
Let *her* enemies have no advantage against *her ;*
    Let not the wicked approach to hurt *her*.
O LORD, save Thy people,
    And bless Thine inheritance.
Give peace in our time, O LORD,
    Because there is none other that fighteth for us, but
only Thou, O GOD.
O LORD, hear our prayer
    And let our cry come unto Thee.*

Collect for the Fifth Sunday after Trinity.

Grant, O LORD, we beseech Thee, that the course of this world may be so peaceably ordered by Thy governance, that Thy Church may joyfully serve Thee in all godly quietness ; through JESUS CHRIST our LORD. Amen.

(*From " A Hymn of Thanksgiving," No.* 3.) C. H. LLOYD.

* —— * Sometimes sung as a separate Anthem.

1772

ISAIAH xxv. 1. O LORD, Thou art my GOD ; I will exalt Thee, I will praise Thy Name ; for Thou hast done wonderful things ; Thy counsels of old are faithfulness and truth,

4. For Thou hast been a strength to the poor, a strength to the needy in his distress, a refuge from the storm, a shadow from the heat.

1. O LORD, Thou art my GOD; I will exalt Thee, I will praise Thy Name.

8. He will swallow up death in victory; and the LORD GOD will wipe away tears from all eyes: and the rebuke of His people shall He take away from off all the earth; for the LORD hath spoken it.

9. And it shall be said in that day, Lo, this is our GOD; we have waited for Him, and He will save us: this is the LORD; we have waited for Him, we will be glad and rejoice in His salvation. Hallelujah! Amen.

C. H. LLOYD.

1773

REVELATION xxi. 4. GOD shall wipe away all tears from their eyes; there shall be no more death, neither sorrow, nor crying, neither shall there be any more pain.

FIELD.

1774

Lord of our life, and GOD of our salvation,
Star of our night, and Hope of every nation,
Hear and receive Thy Church's supplication,
    LORD GOD Almighty.

See round Thine ark the hungry billows curling;
See how Thy foes their banners are unfurling;
LORD, while their darts envenomed they are hurling,
    Thou canst preserve us.

LORD, Thou canst help when earthly armour faileth,
LORD, Thou canst save when deadly sin assaileth,
LORD, o'er Thy Church nor death nor hell prevaileth;
    Grant us Thy peace, LORD.

Grant us Thy help till foes are backward driven,
Grant them Thy truth, that they may be forgiven,
Grant peace on earth, and, after we have striven,
    Peace in Thy heaven. Amen.

FIELD.

1775

St. John iv. 13. Whosoever drinketh of this water shall thirst again;

14. But whosoever drinketh of the water that I shall give him shall never thirst; but the water that I shall give him shall be in him a well of water, springing up into everlasting life. Whosoever drinketh of this water shall never thirst. Amen.

Field.

1776

Psalm cxviii. 24. This is the day which the Lord hath made, we will rejoice and be glad in it.

Romans vi. 9. Christ being raised from the dead dieth no more; death hath no more dominion over Him.

10. For in that He died, He died unto sin once; but in that He liveth, He liveth unto God.

Psalm cxviii. 24. This is the day which the Lord hath made, we will rejoice and be glad in it.

cxlv. 8, 9. The Lord is gracious and merciful, long-suffering, and of great goodness: and His mercy is over all His works.

1 Corinthians xv. 57. Thanks be to God, Which giveth us the victory, through Jesus Christ our Lord.

All praise be Thine, O risen Lord,
From death to endless life restored;
All praise to God the Father be,
And Holy Ghost eternally.

Marchant.

1777

Hebrews ix. 24. Christ is not entered into the holy places made with hands, which are the figures of the true; but into heaven itself, now to appear in the presence of God for us.

xii. 12. Wherefore lift up the hands which hang down, and strengthen the feeble knees.

14. Follow peace with all men, and holiness, without which no man shall see the Lord. Alleluia. Amen.

Faning.

1778

St. Matthew xxviii. 1. As it began to dawn toward the first day of the week, came Mary Magdalene and the other Mary to see the sepulchre.

2. And, behold, there was a great earthquake: for the angel of the Lord descended from heaven and rolled back the stone from the door, and sat upon it.

3. His countenance was like lightning, and his raiment white as snow:

4. And for fear of him the keepers did shake, and became as dead men.

5. And the angel answered and said unto the women, Fear not ye: for I know that ye seek Jesus, Which was crucified.

St. Luke xxiv. 6. He is not here; remember how He spake unto you when He was yet in Galilee. Fear not ye: He is not here; He is risen.

Alleluia! Alleluia! Hearts and voices heavenward raise;
Sing to God a hymn of gladness, sing to God a hymn of praise;
He, Who on the Cross a Victim for the world's salvation bled,
Jesus Christ, the King of glory, now is risen from the dead. Alleluia. Amen.

M. B. Fostfr.

1779

1 Corinthians ii. 9. Eye hath not seen, nor ear heard, neither have entered into the heart of man, the things which God hath prepared for them that love Him.

10. But God hath revealed them unto us by His Spirit.

St. Luke xxiv. 6. Remember how He spake unto you.

St. John xiv. 18. I will not leave you comfortless · I will come unto you.

1 Thessalonians iv. 18. Wherefore comfort one another with these words.

1 Corinthians ii. 9. Eye hath not seen, nor ear heard, neither have entered into the heart of man, the things which God hath prepared for them that love Him. Amen.

M. B. Fvster

1780

Isaiah li. 7. Hearken unto Me, ye that know right-eousness.

6. Lift up your eyes to the heavens, and look upon the earth beneath : for the heavens shall vanish away like smoke, and the earth shall wax old like a garment : but My salvation shall be for ever.

xxv. 9. Lo, this is our God ; we have waited for Him, and He will save us : This is the Lord ; we have waited for Him, we will be glad and rejoice in His salvation.

1 Corinthians xv. 55, 54. O death, where is thy sting ? Death is swallowed up in victory.

57. Thanks be to God, Which giveth us the victory through our Lord Jesus Christ. Alleluia. Amen.

M. B. Foster.

1781

Colossians iii. 1. If ye then be risen with Christ, seek those things which are above, where Christ sitteth on the right hand of God.

2. Set your affection on things above, not on things on the earth.

Lift up your hearts.

Psalm xlvii. 6. O sing praises, sing praises unto our God; sing praises, sing praises unto our King.

7. For God is the King of all the earth ; sing ye praises with understanding.

M. B. Foster.

1782

Lamentations i. 12. Is it nothing to you, all ye that pass by ?

Isaiah liii. 5. He was wounded for our transgressions, He was bruised for our iniquities.

St. John iii. 16. God so loved the world, that He gave His only begotten Son, that whosoever believeth in Him should not perish, but have everlasting life.

M B. Foster.

1783

ST. JOHN xiv.   1. Let not your heart be troubled, neither let it be afraid : ye believe in GOD, believe also in Me.

2, 3. In my Father's house are many mansions : I go to prepare a place for you, that where I am, there ye may be also.   In my Father's house are many mansions : if it were not so, I would have told you.

1. Let not your heart be troubled, neither let it be afraid : ye believe in GOD, believe also in Me.

ST. MATTHEW xi.   30. For My yoke is easy, and My burden is light.

28. Come unto Me, all ye that labour and are heavy laden, and I will give you rest.

M. B. FOSTER.

1784

PSALM xlv.   1. My heart is inditing of a good matter : I speak of the things which I have made unto the king.

8. Thou hast loved righteousness and hated iniquity : wherefore GOD, even thy GOD, hath anointed thee with the oil of gladness above thy fellows.

cxviii.   23. This is the LORD's doing : and it is marvellous in our eyes.

cxix.   65. O LORD, Thou hast dealt graciously with Thy servant : according to Thy word.

lxxxiv.   11. For the LORD GOD is a light and defence : and no good thing shall He withhold from them that live a godly life.

ciii.   1. Praise the LORD, O my soul : and all that is within me praise His holy Name.

2. Praise thou the LORD, O my soul : and forget not all His benefits ;

[3. Who forgiveth all thy sin : and healeth all thine infirmities ;]

4. Who saveth thy life from destruction, and crowneth thee with mercy and loving-kindness.

M. B. FOSTER.

1786

Psalm xcv. 1. O come, let us sing unto the Lord : let us heartily rejoice in the strength of our salvation.

lxxxv. 10. Mercy and truth are met together : righteousness and peace have kissed each other.

11. Truth shall flourish out of the earth, and righteousness hath looked down from heaven.

cxiii. 5. Who is like unto the Lord our God, that hath His dwelling so high : and yet humbleth Himself to behold the things that are in heaven and earth.

cvii. 1. O give thanks unto the Lord, for He is gracious, and His mercy endureth for ever.

2. Let them give thanks whom the Lord hath redeemed.

1. O give thanks unto the Lord, for He is gracious, and His mercy endureth for ever and ever. Alleluia. Amen.

M. B. Foster.

1787

Psalm lxxi. 17. O God, who is like unto Thee ? There is not one that can do as Thou doest. Great things are they that Thou hast done.

lxv. 13. The pastures are filled with flocks, the valleys are covered over with corn ; they shout for joy, they also sing.

9. Thou visitest the earth : Thou makest it very plenteous.

lxxi. 17. O God, who is like unto Thee ? There is not one that can do as Thou doest. Great things are they that Thou hast done.

cxlv. 16. Thou openest Thine hand, and fillest all things living with plenteousness.

lxv. 12. Thou crownest the year with Thy goodness.

cvii. 43. Whoso is wise will ponder these things : and they shall understand the loving-kindness of the Lord.

ciii. 1. Praise the Lord, O my soul, and all that is within me, praise His holy Name.

2. Praise thou the Lord, O my soul, and forget not all His benefits.

3, 4. Who saveth thy life from destruction, and crowneth thee with mercy and loving-kindness: Who satisfieth thy mouth with good things.

1. Praise the LORD, O my soul, and all that is within me, praise His holy Name. Praise the LORD. Praise thou the LORD, O my soul !

M. B. FOSTER.

1788

PSALM cxlv. 15. The eyes of all wait upon Thee, O LORD : and Thou givest them their meat in due season.

16. Thou openest Thine hand : and fillest all things living with plenteousness.

civ. 29. When Thou hidest Thy face they are troubled : when Thou takest away their breath they die, and are turned again to their dust.

30. When Thou lettest Thy breath go forth they shall be made : and Thou shalt renew the face of the earth.

cxlv. 15. The eyes of all wait upon Thee, O LORD : and Thou givest them their meat in due season.

cvii. 43. Whoso is wise will ponder these things : and they shall understand the loving-kindness of the LORD. Amen.

M. B. FOSTER.

1789

ROMANS xiii. 12, 11. The night is far spent, the day is at hand ; let us therefore cast off the works of darkness, and let us put on the whole armour of light. It is high time to awake out of sleep.

ST. LUKE xxiii. 29, 30. For, behold, the days are coming, in the which they shall say to the mountains, Fall on us ! to the hills, Cover us !

ST. MARK xiii. 33, 36. Take ye heed, watch and pray: ye know not when the time is, lest, coming suddenly, He find you sleeping. Awake ! Awake !

ROMANS xiii. 12, 11. The night is far spent, the day is at hand ; let us therefore cast off the works of darkness, and let us put on the whole armour of light. It is high time to awake out of sleep. Awake ! Awake !

M. B. FOSTER.

1790

St. Luke ii. 8. There were shepherds abiding in the field, keeping watch over their flocks by night.

9. And lo, the angel of the Lord came upon them, and the glory of the Lord shone round about them : and they were sore afraid.

10. And the angel said unto them, Fear not : for, behold, I bring you good tidings of great joy, which shall be to all people.

11. For unto you is born this day, in the city of David, a Saviour, Which is Christ the Lord.

[13. And suddenly there was with the angel a multitude of the heavenly host, praising God, and saying,]

14. Glory to God in the highest, and on earth peace : goodwill toward men.

[15. And it came to pass, as the angels were gone away from them into heaven, the shepherds said one to another, Let us now go even unto Bethlehem, and see this thing which is come to pass, which the Lord hath made known unto us.]

Shepherds in the field abiding,
   Watching o'er your flocks by night,
God with man is now residing,
   Yonder shines the Heavenly Light :
     Come and worship !
   Worship Christ, the new-born King !

Saints and angels join in praising
   Thee, the Father, Spirit, Son,
Evermore their voices raising
   To the Eternal Three in One ;
     Come and worship !
   Worship Christ, the new-born King !

M. B. Foster.

1791 M. B. Foster, St. Luke ii. 8–11, 14, 15.
1792 Vincent, St. Luke ii. 8–11, 13, 14.

1793

St. Mark xvi. 1. (*Revised Version.*) When the sabbath was past, Mary Magdalene, and Mary the mother of James, and Salome, bought spices, that they might come and anoint Jesus.

2. And very early on the first day of the week, they came to the tomb when the sun was risen.

St. Luke xxiv. 2. And they found the stone rolled away from the tomb.

3. And they entered in, and found not the body of the Lord Jesus.

4. While they were perplexed thereabout, behold, two men stood by them in dazzling apparel.

5, 6. And as they were affrighted, and bowed down their faces to the earth, they said unto them, Why seek ye the living among the dead? He is not here, but is risen.

> Ye children of the light,
>   Arise with Him, arise,
> See how the Daystar bright
>   Is shining in the skies.

> Leave, in the grave beneath,
>   The old things passed away,
> Buried with Him in death,
>   Oh, live with Him to-day.

> We sing Thee, Lord Divine,
>   With all our hearts and powers,
> For we are ever Thine,
>   And Thou art ever ours.

M. B. Foster.

1794

St. Luke xxiv. 5, 6. Why seek ye the living among the dead? He is not here; He is risen.

Romans vi. 9. Christ being raised from the dead dieth no more: death hath no more dominion over Him.

10. For in that He died, He died unto sin once: but in that He liveth, He liveth unto God. Alleluia!

1 CORINTHIANS xv. 57. [*Hallelujah!] Thanks be to GOD, Which giveth us the victory through our LORD JESUS CHRIST. Alleluia! Amen.

[2 CORINTHIANS v. 15. He died for all, that they which live might not henceforth live unto themselves, but unto Him Who died for them, and rose again.] M. B. FOSTER.

1795 GRITTON,* 1 Cor. xv. 57; 2 Cor. v. 15; Hallelujah.

1796

PSALM xxxvi. 7. (*Bible Version.*) How excellent is Thy loving-kindness, O GOD.

lxv. 9. Thou visitest the earth and maketh it soft with showers.

11. Thou crownest the year with Thy goodness, and Thy paths drop fatness.

12. They drop upon the pastures of the wilderness, and the little hills are girded with joy.

13. The valleys also are covered over with corn, they shout for joy and sing.

GENESIS xxvii. 28. GOD hath given me of the dew of heaven: and the fatness of the earth, and plenty of corn and wine.

DEUTERONOMY vii. 13. He will love thee and bless thee, He will also bless the fruit of thy land, thy corn and thy wine.

PSALM xxxvi. 7. How excellent is Thy loving-kindness.

lxv. 9. Thou visitest the earth, and maketh it soft with showers.

13. The hills are girded with joy, the valleys are covered with corn, they shout for joy and sing.

xxxvi. 7. How excellent is Thy loving-kindness. O GOD.

(*From "Ruth."*) COWEN.

1797

1. Who is this, so weak and helpless,
   Child of lowly Hebrew maid,
Rudely in a stable sheltered,
   Coldly in a manger laid?
      'Tis the LORD of all creation,
         Who this wondrous path hath trod;
      He is GOD from everlasting,
         And to everlasting GOD.

2. Who is this?—a Man of Sorrows,
   Walking sadly life's hard way,
Homeless, weary, sighing, weeping,
   Over sin and Satan's sway?
      'Tis our GOD, our glorious Saviour,
      Who above the starry sky
   Now for us a place prepareth,
      Where no tear can dim the eye.

3. Who is this? behold Him shedding
   Drops of blood upon the ground.
Who is this? despised, rejected,
   Mock'd, insulted, beaten, bound?
      'Tis our GOD, Who gifts and graces
      On His Church now poureth down;
   Who shall smite in holy vengeance
      All His foes beneath His throne.

4. Who is this that hangeth dying,
   While the rude world scoffs and scorns;
Numbered with the malefactors,
   Torn with nails and crowned with thorns?
      'Tis the GOD Who ever liveth
      'Mid the shining ones on high,
   In the glorious golden city
      Reigning everlastingly.   Amen.

RAYNER.

1798

PSALM lxv.   11, 13. (*Bible Version.*) Thou crownest the
year with Thy goodness.   The pastures are clothed with
flocks; the valleys also are covered over with corn: they
shout for joy, they also sing.   Thou crownest the year
with Thy goodness.

GENESIS viii.   22. While the earth remaineth, seed-
time and harvest, and cold and heat, and summer and
winter, and day and night shall not cease.

BOOTH.

1799

PSALM iii. 4. I did call upon the LORD with my voice: and He heard me from out of His holy hill.

iv. 9. I will lay me down, and take my rest: for it is Thou, LORD, only that makest me dwell in safety.

xxx. 13. Therefore shall every good man sing of Thy praise without ceasing: O my GOD, I will give thanks unto Thee for ever.

iii. 5. I laid me down and slept, and rose up again: for the LORD sustained me.

xxx. 13. I will give thanks unto Thee for ever.

MOIR.

1800

ST. LUKE i. 68. Blessed be the LORD GOD of Israel, for He hath visited and redeemed His people;

69. And hath raised up a mighty salvation for us in the house of His servant David;

70. As He spake by the mouth of His holy Prophets, which have been since the world began.

ii. 14. Glory to GOD in the highest, and on earth peace, goodwill towards men.

Sing, choirs of Angels,
Sing in exultation,
Sing, all ye citizens of heaven above:
"Glory to GOD
In the highest!"
O come, let us adore Him,
O come, let us adore Him,
O come, let us adore Him, CHRIST the LORD.

Yea, LORD, we greet Thee,
Born this happy morning;
JESU, to Thee be glory given;
Word of the Father,
Now in flesh appearing;
O come, let us adore Him,
O come, let us adore Him,
O come, let us adore Him, CHRIST the LORD. Amen.

WILLIAMS.

1801

To Thee, O LORD, our hearts we raise,
In hymns of adoration ;
To Thee bring sacrifice of praise,
With shouts of exultation.
Bright robes of gold the fields adorn,
The hills with joy are ringing ;
The valleys stand so thick with corn
That even they are singing.

Oh ! blessèd is that land of GOD
Where saints abide for ever ;
Where golden fields spread far and broad
Where flows the crystal river.
The strains of all its holy throng
With ours to-day are blending ;
Thrice blessèd is that harvest song
Which never hath an ending !

WILLIAMS.

1802

GENESIS viii. 22. While the earth remaineth, seed-time and harvest, summer and winter, day and night shall not cease.

PSALM lxvi. 1. O be joyful in GOD, all ye lands : sing praises unto the honour of His Name, make His praise to be glorious.

lxv. 10. The river of GOD is full of water, for so Thou providest for the earth.

11. Thou waterest her furrows, Thou sendest rain into the little valleys thereof : Thou makest it soft with the drops of rain, and blessest the increase of it.

GENESIS viii. 22. While the earth remaineth, seed-time and harvest, summer and winter, day and night shall not cease.

PSALM lxvi. 1. O be joyful in GOD, all ye lands : sing praises unto the honour of His Name, make His praise to be glorious.

WILLIAMS.

1803

PSALM lxxxi. 1. Sing we merrily unto GOD our strength: make a cheerful noise unto the GOD of Jacob.

2. Take the psalm, bring hither the tabret: the merry harp with the lute.

3. Blow up the trumpet in the new moon: even in the time appointed, and upon our solemn feast-day.

cxlviii. 12. Young men and maidens, old men and children, praise the Name of the LORD: for His Name only is excellent, and His praise above heaven and earth.

13. He shall exalt the horn of His people, all His saints shall praise Him: even the children of Israel, even the people that serveth Him. Hallelujah. Amen.

lxxxi. 1. Sing we merrily unto GOD our strength. Hallelujah.

DOCKER.

1804

HEBREWS i. 1. GOD, Who at sundry times and in divers manners spake in time past unto the fathers by the prophets, (2.) Hath in these last days spoken unto us by His Son.

PSALM lxxxv. 10. Mercy and truth are met together: righteousness and peace have kissed each other.

11. Truth shall flourish out of the earth, and righteousness hath looked down from heaven.

12. Yea, the LORD will show loving-kindness.

ST. LUKE ii. 11. For unto us is born this day a Saviour, Which is CHRIST the LORD.

> Immortal Babe, Who this dear day
> Didst change Thine heaven for our clay,
> And didst with flesh Thy Godhead veil,
> Eternal Son of GOD, all hail! MEE.

1805

ST. MATTHEW xxv. 5. While the Bridegroom's coming tarried, all of them slumbered deeply.

6. Loudly at midnight came the summons dread, Lo, the Bridegroom cometh, O go ye forth to Him straightway.

> In the hour of dying,
> When we rise at the Judgment Day,
> O deliver us, good LORD. Amen. MEE.

For Latin Version, see No. 1541.

1806

ST. MATTHEW xxviii.   1, 6. As it began to dawn toward
the first day of the week, came Mary Magdalene and the
other Mary to see the Sepulchre, where the LORD lay.

2, 5, 6. The angel of the LORD descended from heaven,
and said, Fear not ye: For I know that ye seek JESUS.
He is not here, for He is risen.   Hallelujah.   Amen.

PSALM lxviii.   32. Sing unto GOD, O ye kingdoms of
the earth.

From the LITANY.   By Thy glorious Resurrection,
Good LORD, deliver us.   Hallelujah.   Amen.

PSALM lxviii.   32. O sing praises, sing praises unto the
LORD.   Hallelujah.   Amen.

VINCENT.

1807

ST. MATTHEW ix.   13. I came not to call the righteous,
but sinners to repentance.

ST. LUKE xv.   10. There is joy in the presence of the
angels of GOD over one sinner that repenteth.

1 TIMOTHY i.   15. Faithful is the saying, and worthy of
all acceptation, that CHRIST JESUS came into the world
to save sinners.   Amen.

VINCENT.

1808

REVELATION vii.   2, 3. And I saw another angel
ascending from the east, having the seal of the living
GOD; and he cried with a loud voice to the four angels,
saying, Hurt not the earth, neither the sea, nor the trees, till
we have sealed the servants of our GOD in their foreheads.

9. And lo, a great multitude, which no man could
number, of all nations, and kindreds, and people, and
tongues, stood before the Throne, and before the Lamb,
clothed with white robes, and palms were in their hands;

10. And cried with a loud voice, saying, Salvation to our
God Which sitteth upon the Throne, and unto the Lamb.

12. Amen: Blessing and glory, and wisdom, and
thanksgiving, and honour, and power, and might, be unto
our GOD for ever and ever.   Amen.

STANFORD.

1809

ROMANS x. 9. If thou shalt confess with thy mouth the LORD JESUS, and shalt believe in thine heart that GOD hath raised Him from the dead, thou shalt be saved.

11. Whosoever believeth on Him shall not be ashamed.

12. For the same LORD over all is rich unto all that call upon Him.

13. For whosoever shall call upon the Name of the LORD shall be saved.

STANFORD.

1810

ST. LUKE i. 28. Hail, thou that art highly favoured, the LORD is with thee. Blessed art thou among women.

29. And when she saw Him, she was troubled at His saying, and cast in her mind what manner of salutation this should be.

30. And the angel said unto her, Fear not, Mary, for thou hast found favour with GOD.

31. And, behold, thou shalt conceive and bring forth a Son, and shalt call His Name JESUS.

32. He shall be great, and shall be called The Son of the Highest; and the LORD GOD shall give unto Him the throne of His father David.

33. And He shall reign over the House of Jacob for ever; and of His Kingdom there shall be no end.

CARNALL.

1811 C. KING HALL, vv. 30–33. Hallelujah. Amen.

1812

ST. MATTHEW xxviii. 1. In the end of the Sabbath, as it began to dawn toward the first day of the week, came Mary Magdalene and the other Mary to see the Sepulchre.

2. And, behold, there was a great earthquake: for the angel of the LORD descended from heaven, and came and rolled back the stone from the door, and sat upon it.

3. His countenance was like lightning, and his raiment white as snow :

4. And for fear of him the keepers did shake, and became as dead men.

5. And the angel answered and said unto the women, Fear not ye : for I know that ye seek JESUS, Which was crucified.

6, 7. He is not here : for He is risen from the dead : and, behold, He goeth before you into Galilee ; there shall ye see Him ; lo, I have told you.

1 CORINTHIANS xv. 55. O death, where is thy sting ? O grave, where is thy victory ?

56. The sting of death is sin, and the strength of sin is the law.

57. But thanks be to GOD, Which giveth us the victory through our LORD JESUS CHRIST.

CARNALL.

1813

PSALM civ. 23. Man goeth forth to his work, and to his labour, until the evening.

24. O LORD, how manifold are Thy works : in wisdom hast Thou made them all, the earth is full of Thy riches.

25, 27. So is the great and wide sea : wherein are small and great beasts. These wait all upon thee.

21. The lions, roaring after their prey, do seek their meat from GOD.

22. The sun ariseth, and they get them away together, and lay them down in their dens.

cxlvii. 12. Praise the LORD, O Jerusalem : praise thy GOD, O Sion.

8. Who covereth the heaven with clouds, and prepareth rain for the earth : and maketh the grass to grow upon the mountains, and herb for the use of men.

14. He maketh peace in thy borders : and filleth thee with the flour of wheat.

12. Praise the LORD, O Jerusalem : praise thy GOD, O Sion. Praise the LORD.

CARNALL.

1814

PSALM xvi. 10. My heart was glad and my glory rejoiced : my flesh also shall rest in hope.

11. For Thou wilt not leave my soul in hell : neither wilt Thou suffer Thine Holy One to see corruption.

12. Thou wilt shew me the path of life : in Thy presence is the fulness of joy : at Thy right hand there are pleasures for evermore.

10. My heart was glad and my glory rejoiced : my flesh also shall rest in hope.

JOB xiv. 12. Man lieth down, and riseth not : till the heavens be no more, they shall not awake, nor be raised out of their sleep.

xvi. 22. When a few years are come, then I shall go the way whence I shall not return.

1 CORINTHIANS xv. 20. For now is CHRIST risen from the dead, and become the first-fruits of them that slept.

22. For as in Adam all die, even so in CHRIST shall all be made alive.

25. For He must reign, till He hath put all His enemies under His feet.

26. The last enemy that shall be destroyed is death.

20. For now is CHRIST risen from the dead, and become the first-fruits of them that slept.

23, 24. For every man in his own order : CHRIST the first-fruits ; afterward they that are CHRIST'S at His coming. Then cometh the end.

CARNALL.

1815

PSALM xxxii. 1. Blessed is he whose unrighteousness is forgiven, and whose sin is covered.

2. Blessed is the man unto whom the LORD imputeth no sin, and in whose spirit there is no guile.

1. Blessed is he whose unrighteousness is forgiven, and whose sin is covered. Amen.

SELBY.

1816

PSALM lxiii. 1. O GOD, Thou art my GOD: early will I seek Thee.

2. My soul thirsteth for Thee, my flesh also longeth after Thee: in a barren and dry land where no water is.

3. Thus have I looked for Thee in holiness. that I might behold Thy power and glory.

4. For Thy loving-kindness is better than the life itself: my lips shall praise Thee.

5. As long as I live will I magnify Thee on this manner: and lift up my hands in Thy Name.

SELBY.

1817

PSALM lxv. 1. Thou, O GOD, art praised in Sion: and unto Thee shall the vow be performed in Jerusalem.

2. Thou that hearest the prayer: unto Thee shall all flesh come.

12. Thou crownest the year with Thy goodness: and Thy clouds drop fatness.

13. They shall drop upon the dwellings of the wilderness: and the little hills shall rejoice on every side.

14. The folds shall be full of sheep: the valleys also shall stand so thick with corn that they shall laugh and sing.

12. Thou crownest the year with Thy goodness.

lxxii. 18. Blessed be the LORD GOD, even the GOD of Israel: Which only doeth wondrous things.

19. And blessed be the Name of His Majesty for ever: and all the earth shall be filled with His Majesty. Amen. Amen.

SELBY.

1818

PSALM xlvi. 1. (*Bible Version.*) GOD is our refuge and strength, a very present help in trouble.

2. Therefore will we not fear, though the earth be removed, and though the mountains be carried into the midst of the sea;

3. Though the waters thereof roar and be troubled, though the mountains shake with the swelling thereof.

4. There is a river, the streams whereof shall make glad the city of GOD.

5. GOD is in the midst of her; she shall not be moved; GOD shall help her, and that right early.

7. The LORD of hosts is with us; the GOD of Jacob is our refuge. Amen.

FOOTE.

1819

1 CORINTHIANS XV. 1, 3, 4. I declare to you the gospel which I preached, which ye also have received, and wherein ye stand; how that CHRIST died for our sins, and was buried, and rose again the third day according to the Scriptures.

ISAIAH XXV. 8. He will swallow up death in victory; and the LORD GOD will wipe away all tears from off all faces; and the rebuke of His people shall He take away from the earth: for the LORD hath spoken it.

9. And it shall be said in that day, This is our GOD; we have waited for Him, He will save us: this is the LORD; we have waited for Him, we will be glad and rejoice in His salvation.

> The strife is o'er, the battle done;
> The Victor's triumph now is won;
> O let the song of praise be sung.
> Alleluia! Amen.

CRUICKSHANK.

1820

PSALM lvii. 8. My heart is fixed, O GOD, my heart is fixed: I will give thanks.

9. Awake up, my glory; awake, lute and harp: I myself will awake right early.

cviii. 4. For Thy mercy reacheth unto the heavens : and Thy faithfulness unto the clouds.

5. Set up Thyself, O GOD, above the heavens : and Thy glory o'er all the earth.

6. That Thy beloved may be delivered, let Thy hand save them, and hear Thou me.

lvii. 8. My heart is fixed, O GOD, my heart is fixed : I will give thanks.

9. Awake up, my glory; awake, lute and harp : I myself will awake right early.

> Awake, my soul, and with the sun
> Thy daily stage of duty run ;
> Shake off dull sloth, and early rise
> To pay thy morning sacrifice.
>
> Praise GOD, from Whom all blessings flow,
> Praise Him, all creatures here below,
> Praise Him above, Angelic host,
> Praise FATHER, SON, and HOLY GHOST.   Amen.

CRUICKSHANK.

1821

ST. MATTHEW ii. 1. Now when JESUS was born in Bethlehem of Judæa in the days of Herod the king, behold, there came wise men from the east unto Jerusalem.

2. Saying, Where is He that is born the King of the Jews ? for we have seen His star, and are come to worship Him.

9. And, lo, the star went before them, till it came and stood over where the young Child was.

10. And when they saw the star, they rejoiced with exceeding great joy.

ST. LUKE xix. 38. Blessed be the King that cometh in the Name of the LORD : peace in heaven and glory in the highest.

*Hark ! the herald-angels sing
Glory to the new-born King,
Peace on earth, and mercy mild,
GOD and sinners reconciled.
Joyful, all ye nations, rise,
Join the triumph of the skies ;
With the angelic host proclaim,
" CHRIST is born in Bethlehem."
   Hark ! the herald-angels sing
   Glory to the new-born King.

[Hail, the heaven-born Prince of peace !
Hail, the sun of righteousness !
Light and life to all He brings,
Risen with healing in His wings.
 Mild He lays His glory by,
Born that man no more may die,
Born to raise the sons of earth,
Born to give them second birth.
   Hark ! the herald-angels sing
   Glory to the new-born King.*]
       CRUICKSHANK.

1822 *E. V. HALL, *Hark ! the herald-angels sing.*

1823

O Saving Victim, opening wide
The gate of heaven to man below,
Our foes press on from every side,
Thine aid supply, Thy strength bestow.

All praise and thanks to Thee ascend
For evermore, Blest One in Three ;
O grant us life that shall not end
In our true native land with Thee.   Amen.
       CRUICKSHANK.

1824

PSALM xcviii. 1. O sing unto the LORD a new song :
for He hath done marvellous things.

2. With His own right hand, and with His holy arm :
hath He gotten Himself the victory.

3. The LORD declared His salvation : His righteousness hath He shewed in the sight of the heathen.

4. He hath remembered His mercy and truth toward the house of Israel . and all the ends of the world have seen the salvation of our GOD.

1. O sing unto the LORD a new song : for He hath done marvellous things.

2. With His own right hand, and with His holy arm : hath He gotten Himself the victory.

4. And all the ends of the world have seen the salvation of our GOD.

lxxxv. 9. His salvation is nigh them that fear Him : that glory may dwell in our land.

12. Yea, the LORD shall shew loving-kindness : and our land shall yield her increase.

13. Righteousness shall go before Him : and He shall direct His going in the way.

xcviii. 5. Shew yourselves joyful before the LORD, all ye lands : sing, rejoice, and give thanks.

xcvii. 10. For the LORD preserveth the souls of His saints : He shall deliver them from the hand of the ungodly.

xcviii. 5. Shew yourselves joyful before the LORD, all ye lands ; sing, rejoice, and give thanks.

1. O sing unto the LORD a new song.

CRUICKSHANK.

1825

REVELATION xii. 7, 8. There was war in heaven : Michael and his angels fought against the dragon ; and the dragon fought and his angels, and prevailed not ; neither was their place found any more in heaven.

10. And I heard a loud voice saying in heaven, Now is come salvation, and strength, and the kingdom of our GOD, and the power of His CHRIST : for the accuser of our brethren is cast down, which accused them before our GOD day and night.

11. And they overcame him by the blood of the Lamb, and by the word of their witness ; and they loved not their lives unto the death.

12. Therefore rejoice, ye heavens, and ye that dwell in them.

CRUICKSHANK.

1826

PSALM xxxiv. 7. (*Bible Version.*) The angel of the LORD encampeth round about them that fear Him, and delivereth them.

9. O fear the LORD, ye His saints : for there is no want to them that fear Him. O fear the LORD, ye His saints : He delivereth you. GRAY.

1827

PSALM xvi. 12. Thou shalt shew me the path of life : in Thy presence is the fulness of joy : and at Thy right hand there is pleasure for evermore.

ST. MATTHEW vii. 14. Strait is the gate, and narrow the way, which leadeth unto life, and few there be that find it. GRAY.

1828

REVELATION xxi. 14. And the wall of the city had twelve foundations, and in them the names of the twelve apostles of the Lamb.

23. And the city had no need of the sun, neither of the moon, to shine in it : for the glory of GOD did lighten it, and the Lamb is the light thereof.

24. And the nations of them which are saved shall walk in the light of it : and the kings of the earth do bring their glory and honour into it.

25. And the gates of it shall not be shut at all by day : for there shall be no night there.

xxii. 5. And they need no candle, neither light of the sun ; for the LORD GOD giveth them light ; and they shall reign for ever and ever. Hallelujah. O. KING.

1829

BARUCH v. 5. Arise, O Jerusalem, and stand on high, and look about toward the east, and behold thy children gathered from the west unto the east by the Word of the Holy One, rejoicing in the remembrance of GOD.

9. For GOD shall lead Israel with joy in the light of His glory with the mercy and righteousness that cometh from Him. O. KING.

1830

ST. JAMES i. 12. Blessed is the man that endureth temptation; for when he is tried, he shall receive the crown of life.

O. KING

1831

PSALM ciii. 2. Bless thou the LORD, O my soul: and forget thou not all His benefits.

cv. 2. O let your songs be of Him and praise Him: and your talking of His wondrous works.

cxxvi. 6. They that sow in tears shall reap in joy.

ciii. 2. Bless thou the Lord, O my soul: and forget thou not all His benefits. Amen.

O. KING.

1832

ISAIAH lii. 9. Break forth into joy, sing together, ye waste places of Jerusalem: for the LORD hath comforted His people.

JOEL ii. 22. Be not afraid, ye beasts of the field, for the pastures of the wilderness do spring, the tree beareth her fruit, the fig tree and the vine do yield their strength.

23. Be glad then, ye children of Zion.

ISAIAH lii. 9. Break forth into joy, ye waste places of Jerusalem.

JOEL ii. 24, 26. The floors shall be full of wheat, and ye shall eat in plenty and be satisfied. The folds shall be full of sheep, and ye shall eat and be satisfied, and praise the Name of the LORD your GOD, that hath dealt so wondrously with you.

ISAIAH lii. 9. Break forth into joy, sing together, ye waste places of Jerusalem: for the LORD hath comforted his people. Break forth into joy, ye waste places of Jerusalem. Amen.

O. KING.

1833

HEBREWS ii. 10. For it became Him, for Whom are all things, and by Whom are all things, in bringing many sons unto glory, to make the captain of their salvation perfect through suffering.

PHILIPPIANS ii. 9. Wherefore GOD also hath highly exalted Him, and hath given Him a name which is above every name :

10. That at the name of JESUS every knee should bow;

11. And that every tongue should confess that JESUS CHRIST is LORD, to the glory of GOD the Father. Amen.

O. KING.

1834

ISAIAH ix. 2. Hallelujah! The light hath shined upon us.

ST. MATTHEW ii. 2. For we have seen His star, and are come to adore Him.

ISAIAH lx. 3. The Gentiles shall come to Thy light, and kings to the brightness of Thy glory.

ix. 2. The people that walked in darkness have seen a great light : and they that dwell in the land of the shadow of death, upon them hath the light shined.

Hosanna in the highest. Amen.

O. KING.

1835

Hark! hark! what news the angels bring,
Glad tidings of a new-born King.
Who is the SAVIOUR of mankind
In Whom we may salvation find ?

This is the day, the blessed morn,
The SAVIOUR of mankind was born,
Born of a Maid, a Virgin pure,
Born without sin, from guilt secure.

If angels sing at CHRIST His birth,
Sure we have greater cause for mirth ;
For why? it was that for our sake,
CHRIST did our human nature take.

Sweet CHRIST, Thou didst Thyself debase
Thus to descend to human race,
And leave Thy Father's Throne above,
LORD, what could move Thee to thus love ?

May we contemplate and admire,
And join with the celestial choir :
Lift up your voice above the sky,
All glory be to GOD on high.   O. KING.

1836

PSALM xiii. 1. How long wilt Thou forget me, O LORD, for ever : how long wilt Thou hide Thy face from me ?

2. How long shall I seek counsel in my soul, and be so vexed in my heart : how long shall mine enemies triumph over me ?

1. How long wilt Thou forget me, O LORD, for ever : how long wilt Thou hide Thy face from me ?

5. But my trust is in Thy mercy : and my heart is joyful in Thy salvation.

O. KING.

1837

PSALM cxlv. 1. I will magnify Thee, O GOD, my King : and I will praise Thy Name for ever and ever.

2. Every day will I give thanks unto Thee, and praise Thy Name.

3. Great is the LORD, and marvellous, worthy to be praised : there is no end of His greatness.

xxviii. 8. The LORD is my strength and my shield, my heart hath trusted in Him : therefore my heart danceth for joy, and in my song will I praise Him.

cxlv. 1, 2. I will magnify Thee. Every day will I give thanks unto Thee, and praise Thy Name.

15. The eyes of all wait upon Thee, O LORD : and Thou givest them meat in due season.

civ. 29. When Thou hidest Thy face they are troubled : when Thou takest away their breath they die, and are turned again to their dust.

30. When Thou lettest Thy breath go forth they shall be made : and Thou shalt renew the face of the earth.

33. I will sing as long as I live : and praise my GOD while I have my being.

cxlv. 1. I will magnify Thee, O GOD, my King : and I will praise Thy Name for ever and ever.

2. Every day will I give thanks unto Thee and praise Thy holy Name for ever.

O. KING.

1838

JESUS CHRIST is risen to-day, Hallelujah !

I CORINTHIANS xv. 57. Thanks be to GOD, Who giveth us the victory. Hallelujah.

REVELATION xii. 10. Now is come salvation, and strength, and the kingdom of our GOD, and the power of His CHRIST.

xi. 15. And He shall reign for ever and ever.

PSALM xxiii. 4. Yea, though I walk through the valley of the shadow of death, I will fear no evil.

REVELATION xii. 10. Now is come salvation, and strength, and the kingdom of our GOD.

ISAIAH li. 3. The LORD will comfort Zion, even her waste places ; and will make her desert like the garden of the LORD ; joy and gladness shall be found there, thanksgiving, and the voice of melody.

I CORINTHIANS xv. 55. O death, where is thy sting ? O grave, where is thy victory ?

Death is conquered, man is free, Hallelujah !
CHRIST has won the victory, Hallelujah !
Now above the sky He's King, Hallelujah !
Where the angels ever sing. Hallelujah ! Amen.

O KING.

1839

PSALM lxxxiv. 1. O how amiable are Thy dwellings, Thou LORD of hosts !

2. My soul hath a desire and longing to enter into the courts of the LORD : my heart and my flesh rejoice in the living GOD.

3. Yea, the sparrow hath found her an house, and the swallow a nest where she may lay her young : even Thy altars, O LORD of Hosts, my King and my GOD.

4. Blessed are they that dwell in Thy house : they will be alway praising Thee.

5. Blessed is the man whose strength is in Thee : in whose heart are Thy ways.

6. Who going through the vale of misery use it for a well : and the pools are filled with water.

4. Blessed are they that dwell in Thy house : they will be alway praising Thee. Amen. O. KING.

1840 WEST, vv. 1 3.

1841

The star that now is shining
  In skies so blue and bright,
Shone ages since on shepherds
  Who watched their flocks by night.

When lo! a white-winged angel
  The watchers stood before,
And told how CHRIST was born on earth,
  For mortals to adore;

And suddenly in the heavens
  Appeared an angel-band
(The while in reverent wonder
  The Syrian shepherds stand).

And all the bright host chanted
  Words that will never cease
Glory to GOD in the highest,
  On earth, good-will, and peace.

Hark! hark, my soul! angelic songs are swelling
  O'er earth's green fields, and ocean's wave-beat shore:
How sweet the truth those blessèd strains are telling
  Of that new life when sin shall be no more.
Angels of JESUS, angels of light,
Singing to welcome the pilgrims of the night!

Beside a humble manger
  Was the maiden Mother mild,
And in her arm her Son divine,
  A new-born Infant, smiled.

The star that shone in Bethlehem
  Shines still and shall not cease,
And still we hear the tidings
  Of Glory and of Peace.

Angels! sing on, your faithful watches keeping,
  Sing us sweet fragments of the songs above;
Till morning's joy shall end the night of weeping,
  And life's long shadows break in cloudless love.
Angels of JESUS, angels of light,
Singing to welcome the pilgrims of the night!

O. KING.

1842

WISDOM xviii. 14, 15. While all things were in quiet silence, and the night in the midst of her course; the Almighty Word of the LORD came down from His royal Throne.

ISAIAH ix. 2. The light hath shined upon us.

ST. MATTHEW ii. 2. For we have seen His star and are come to adore Him.

> The strain upraise of joy and praise,
> To the glory of their King
> Shall the ransomed people sing
> > Hallelujah!
> And the choirs on high
> Shall re-echo through the sky
> > Hallelujah!

(Sung at the same time as the above.)

> Sing, choirs of angels,
> Sing in exultation,
> Sing, all ye citizens of heaven above:
> " Glory to GOD
> In the highest ";
> O come, let us adore Him,
> O come, let us adore Him,
> O come, let us adore Him, CHRIST the LORD.

O. KING.

1843

PSALM xlvi. 1. GOD is our hope and strength : a very present help in trouble.

2. Therefore will we not fear, though the earth be moved : and though the hills be carried into the midst of the sea.

3. Though the waters thereof rage and swell : and though the mountains shake at the tempest of the same.

7. The LORD of hosts is with us : the GOD of Jacob is our refuge.

BAILS.

1844

PSALM civ.   1. Hear my prayer, O LORD, and let my crying come unto Thee.

2. Hide not Thy face from me in the time of my trouble: incline Thine ear unto me when I call: O hear me, and that right soon.

(Sung at the same time as the above.)

HEBREWS xi.   6. He that cometh to GOD must believe that He is, and that He is a rewarder of them that diligently seek Him.

BATES.

1845

PSALM civ.   33. I will sing unto the LORD as long as I live: I will sing praises to my GOD while I have my being.

34. My meditation of Him shall be sweet.

BATES.

1846

ST. MARK xvi.   1. And when the Sabbath was past, Mary Magdalene, and Mary the mother of James, and Salome, had bought sweet spices, that they might come and anoint Him.

2. And very early in the morning of the first day of the week, they came unto the sepulchre at the rising of the sun.

5. And entering into the sepulchre, they saw a young man sitting on the right side, clothed in a long white garment; and they were affrighted.

6. And he saith unto them, Be not affrighted: Ye seek JESUS of Nazareth, Which was crucified: He is risen; He is not here.

7. But go your way, tell His disciples that He goeth before you into Galilee: there shall ye see Him, as He said unto you.

ROMANS vi.   9. CHRIST being raised from the dead dieth no more; death hath no more dominion over Him.

10. For in that He died, He died unto sin once: but in that He liveth, He liveth unto GOD.

St. Matthew xi. 28. Come unto Him, all ye that labour, and He will give you rest for your souls.

1 Corinthians xv. 57. Thanks be to God, Which giveth us the victory through our Lord Jesus Christ.

Romans vi. 9. For Christ being raised from the dead dieth no more.

Wareing.

1847

St. John xiv. 15. If ye love Me, keep My commandments.

16, 17. And I will pray the Father, and He shall give you another Comforter, that He may abide with you for ever, even the Spirit of truth ; [whom the world cannot receive, because it seeth Him not, neither knoweth Him : but ye know Him ; for He dwelleth with you and shall be in you.]

18. I will not leave you comfortless : I will come to you.

19. Yet a little while, and the world seeth Me no more ; but ye see Me : because I live, ye shall live also.

[20. At that day ye shall know that I am in My Father, and ye in Me, and I in you.

21. He that hath My commandments, and keepeth them, he it is that loveth Me : and he that loveth Me shall be loved by my Father, and I will love him, and will manifest Myself to him.]

Wareing.

1848 Bunnett, Huntley, vv. 15—17.
1849 Steane, vv. 18—21. Amen.

1850

Psalm xcvii. 10. O ye that love the Lord, see that ye hate that which is evil.

xxxvii. 4. Delight ye in the Lord your God : and He will give you your heart's desire.

xcvii. 11. Light is sown for the righteous : and joyful gladness for such as are true-hearted.

Wareing.

1851

Psalm xxiii. 1. (*Bible Version.*) The Lord is my Shepherd, I shall not want.

2. He maketh me to lie down in green pastures : He leadeth me beside the waters of comfort.

3. He leadeth me in the paths of righteousness, for His Name's sake.

4. Yea, though I walk through the valley of the shadow of death, I will fear no evil : for Thou art with me.

6. Yea, surely goodness and mercy shall follow me all the days of my life.   Wareing.

1852

St. Luke ii. 8. There were shepherds abiding in the field, keeping watch over their flocks by night,

9. And lo, the angel of the Lord came upon them, and the glory of the Lord shone round about them, and they were sore afraid.

10. And the angel said unto them, Fear not ; for, behold, I bring you good tidings of great joy.

11. For unto you is born this day, in the city of David, a Saviour, Which is Christ the Lord.

15. And the shepherds said one to another, Let us now go even unto Bethlehem, and see this thing which is come to pass.

11. For unto us is born this day, in the city of David, a Saviour, Which is Christ the Lord.

St. Matthew ii. 6. Thou Bethlehem, in the land of Judah, art not the least among the princes of Judah : for out of thee shall come a Governour, that shall rule My people Israel.

xxi. 9. Glory to God.   Hosanna in the highest.

> Hark ! the herald-angels sing
> Glory to the new-born King,
> Peace on earth, and mercy mild,
> God and sinners reconciled.
> Joyful, all ye nations, rise,
> Join the triumph of the skies ;
> With the Angelic host proclaim,
> "Christ is born in Bethlehem."
> Hark ! the herald-angels sing
> Glory to the new-born King.   Amen.
>   Wareing.

1853

Light of the World, we know Thy praise
The angels and archangels raise,
    And all the host of heaven,
More worthily than our faint hymns,
Whose jarring sound that glory dims,
    Which GOD to Thee has given.

But Thou didst not disdain to take
Our low estate, or e'en to make
    The tomb Thy resting-place ;
So Thou might bring into our night
The dawn of Thine eternal Light
    To shine upon our face.

Nor death, nor hell, nor sin, is LORD,
But Thou, O Son of GOD. Thy Word
    Is now our sovereign law.
Therefore we thank Thee, and we pray
Thy Light may shine unto the Perfect Day
    On us for evermore.

(From " The Light of Life," No. 16.) ELGAR.

1854

PSALM cxviii. 19. *(Bible Version.)* Open to me the gates of righteousness : I will go into them, and I will praise the LORD :

20. This gate of the LORD, into which the righteous shall enter.

21. I will praise Thee : for Thou hast heard me, and art become my salvation.

22. The stone which the builders refused is become the head stone of the corner.

23. This is the LORD'S doing ; it is marvellous in our eyes.

24. This is the day which the LORD hath made ; we will rejoice and be glad in it. Amen.

ADIAM.

1855

Isaiah ix. 6. Unto us a Child is born, unto us a Son is given; and the government shall be upon His shoulder: and His Name shall be called Wonderful, Counsellor, The Mighty God, The Everlasting Father, The Prince of Peace.

Psalm lxxxv. 9. Surely His salvation is nigh them that fear Him; that glory may dwell in our land.

10. Mercy and truth are met together; righteousness and peace have kissed each other.

Adlam.

1856

St. John i. 1. In the beginning was the Word, and the Word was with God, and the Word was God.

4, 9. In Him was life; and the life was the light of men: the Light, which lighteth every man that cometh into the world. In Him was life.

14. And the Word was made flesh, and dwelt among us, (and we beheld His glory, the glory as of the only begotten of the Father,) full of grace and truth.

St. Luke ii. 14. Glory to God in the highest, and on earth peace, goodwill toward men.

> O Heavenly Wisdom, Light Divine,
> Within our bosoms burn and shine;
> That we with heart and voice may bring
> Meet praise to Thee, our new-born King.
> For Thou didst leave Thy throne above,
> A token of the Father's love,
> The souls from sin and death to free,
> Who trust in humble faith on Thee.

St. Luke i. 68. Blessed be the Lord God of Israel. for He hath visited and redeemed His people,

69. And hath raised up a mighty salvation for us in the house of His servant David.

Tozer.

1857

HARVEST HYMN.

LORD of the rich and golden grain,
  Our hearts pour forth glad thanks again,
Loud praise goes up from fruitful field,
  Where crops a blest abundance yield ;
As here within Thy sacred shrine,
  We offer up these gifts of Thine,
O grant the pastures fair to see,
  And garners even plenteous be.

Behold, O LORD, Thyself hath said—
  " Each herb I give for daily bread,
While earth remains there shall not cease,
  Seed-time and harvests' blest increase ;
So thick with corn the valleys stand,
  They laugh and sing on either hand,"
Thus in one glad harmonious lay,
  Proclaim Thy power from day to day.

Oh ! Heavenly Husbandman on high,
  Refresh our souls long parch'd and dry,
The seed which Thou hast planted there,
  For Thine own garden sweet prepare ;
That, at the Resurrection morn,
  When angels reap the ripen'd corn,
Our quicken'd souls salvation win,
  With the good sheaves safe gather'd in.

TOZER

1858

Weary of earth and laden with my sin,
I look at heaven and long to enter in ;
But there no evil thing may find a home,
And yet I hear a voice that bids me, " Come.'

So vile I am, how dare I hope to stand
In the pure glory of that holy land ?
Before the whiteness of that Throne appear .
Yet there are Hands stretched out to draw me near.

The while I fain would tread the heavenly way,
Evil is ever with me day by day;
Yet on mine ears the gracious tidings fall,
" Repent, confess, thou shalt be loosed from all."

It is the voice of JESUS that I hear,
His are the Hands stretched out to draw me near,
And His the Blood that can for all atone,
And set me faultless there before the Throne.

Nought can I bring, dear LORD, for all I owe
Yet let my full heart what it can bestow;
Like Mary's gift let my devotion prove,
Forgiven greatly, how I greatly love.

TOZER.

1859

1 ST. JOHN ii.　1, 2. If any man sin, we have an advocate with the FATHER, JESUS CHRIST the righteous. And He is the propitiation for our sins.

T. ADAMS.

1860

ST. JOHN xvi.　7. If I go not away, the Comforter will not come unto you; but if I depart, I will send Him unto you.

xiv.　16. And I will pray the Father, that He may abide with you for ever.

SONG OF SOLOMON iv.　16. Awake, O north wind; and come, thou south; blow upon my garden, that the spices thereof may flow out.

PSALM civ.　30. When Thou lettest Thy breath go forth they shall be made : and Thou shalt renew the face of the earth.

cxliii.　10. Let Thy loving Spirit lead me forth into the land of righteousness.

T. ADAMS.

1861

Nearer, my GOD, to Thee,
    Nearer to Thee;
E'en though it be a cross
    That raiseth me,
Still all my song shall be,
Nearer, my GOD, to Thee,
    Nearer to Thee.

Though, like the wanderer,
    The sun gone down,
Darkness comes over me,
    My rest a stone,
Yet in my dreams I'd be
Nearer, my GOD, to Thee,
    Nearer to Thee.

There let my way appear
    Steps unto heaven,
All that Thou sendest me
    In mercy given,
Angels to beckon me
Nearer, my GOD, to Thee,
    Nearer to Thee.

(*From " The Cross of Christ,"* No. 17.)   T. ADAMS.

1862

GENESIS i. 12. The earth brought forth grass, and herb yielding seed after his kind, and the tree yielding fruit, whose seed was in itself, after his kind: and GOD saw that it was good.

ISAIAH lxi. 11. For as the earth bringeth forth her bud, and as the garden causeth the things that are sown in it to spring forth, so the LORD GOD will cause righteousness and praise to spring forth before the nations.

xl. 26. Lift up your eyes on high, and behold Who hath created these things: He is strong in power.

lxv. 18. Be glad and rejoice for ever in that which I create.

(*From " The Rainbow of Peace,"* No. 3.)   T. ADAMS.

1863

PSALM xxxi. 19. (*Bible Version.*) Oh, how great is Thy goodness which Thou hast laid up for them that fear Thee, which Thou hast wrought for them that trust in Thee.

JEREMIAH xxxi. 12. Therefore they shall come and sing in the height of Zion, and shall flow together to the goodness of the LORD.

(*From " The Rainbow of Peace,"* No. 7.)   T. ADAMS.

1864

Abide with me; fast falls the eventide;
The darkness deepens; LORD, with me abide;
When other helpers fail, and comforts flee,
Help of the helpless, O abide with me.

Swift to its close ebbs out life's little day;
Earth's joys grow dim, its glories pass away;
Change and decay in all around I see;
O Thou Who changest not, abide with me.

I need Thy presence every passing hour;
What but Thy grace can foil the tempter's power?
Who like Thyself my guide and stay can be?
Through cloud and sunshine, LORD, abide with me.

I fear no foe with Thee at hand to bless;
Ills have no weight, and tears no bitterness;
Where is death's sting?   Where, grave, thy victory?
I triumph still, if Thou abide with me.

Hold Thou Thy Cross before my closing eyes;
Shine through the gloom, and point me to the skies;
Heaven's morning breaks, and earth's vain shadows flee;
In life, in death, O LORD, abide with me.

DUNSTAN.

1865

Sun of my soul, Thou SAVIOUR dear,
It is not night if Thou be near:
O may no earth-born cloud arise
To hide Thee from Thy servant's eyes.

When the soft dews of kindly sleep
My wearied eyelids gently steep,
Be my last thought how sweet to rest
For ever on my SAVIOUR'S breast.

If some poor wandering child of Thine
Have spurned to-day the voice divine,
Now, LORD, the gracious work begin;
Let him no more lie down in sin.

Watch by the sick; enrich the poor
With blessings from Thy boundless store;
Be every mourner's sleep to-night,
Like infant's slumbers, pure and light.

Come near and bless us when we wake,
Ere through the world our way we take;
Till in the ocean of Thy love
We lose ourselves in heaven above.

DUNSTAN.

1866

PSALM cxiii. 2. Blessed be the Name of the LORD: from this time forth for evermore.

5. Who is like unto the LORD our GOD, that hath His dwelling so high: and yet humbleth Himself to behold the things that are in heaven and the earth?

civ. 13. He watereth the hills from above: the earth is filled with the fruit of Thy works.

14. He bringeth forth grass for the cattle: and green herb for the service of men.

c. 1. O be joyful in the LORD, and come before His presence with a song.

Let us with a gladsome mind
    Praise the LORD, for He is kind;
For His mercies still endure,
    Ever faithful, ever sure. Amen.

MAUNDER.

1867

CHRIST is risen! CHRIST is risen!
He hath burst His bonds in twain,
CHRIST is risen! CHRIST is risen!
Alleluia! swell the strain!
    For our gain He suffered loss
      By Divine decree;
    He hath died upon the Cross,
      But our GOD is He.
CHRIST is risen! CHRIST is risen!
He hath burst His bonds in twain;
CHRIST is risen! CHRIST is risen!
Alleluia! swell the strain!

See the chains of death are broken;
  Earth below and heaven above
Joy in each amazing token
  Of His rising, LORD of love;
    He for evermore shall reign
      By the Father's side,
    Till He comes to earth again,
      Comes to claim His bride.
CHRIST is risen! CHRIST is risen!
He hath burst His bonds in twain;
CHRIST is risen! CHRIST is risen!
Alleluia! swell the strain!

Glorious angels downward thronging
  Hail the LORD of all the skies;
Heaven, with joy and holy longing
  For the Word Incarnate, cries,
    "CHRIST is risen! Earth, rejoice!
    Gleam, ye starry train!
  All creation find a voice;
    He o'er all shall reign."
CHRIST is risen! CHRIST is risen!
  He hath burst His bonds in twain;
CHRIST is risen! CHRIST is risen,
  O'er the universe to reign. Amen.

            MAUNDER.

1868

Christians, awake, salute the happy morn.

St. Luke ii. 8. There were shepherds abiding in the field, keeping watch over their flock by night.

9. And lo, the angel of the Lord came upon them, and the glory of the Lord shone round about them: and they were sore afraid.

10. And the angel said unto them, Fear not: for, behold, I bring you good tidings of great joy, which shall be to all people.

11. For unto you is born this day, in the city of David, a Saviour, Which is Christ the Lord.

Zechariah ix. 9. Rejoice greatly.

Isaiah ix. 6. [*Hallelujah !] For unto us a Child is born, unto us a Son is given: and the government shall be upon His shoulder: and His Name shall be called Wonderful, Counsellor, The mighty God, The Everlasting Father, The Prince of Peace.

> Oh! may we keep and ponder in our mind
> God's wondrous love in saving lost mankind;
> Then may we hope, the angelic hosts among,
> To sing, redeemed, a glad triumphal song.
> He That was born upon this joyful day
> Around us all His glory shall display;
> Saved by His love, incessant we shall sing
> Eternal praise to heaven's Almighty King. Amen.
>
> Maunder.

1869 W. H. Monk,* Isaiah ix., 6. Hallelujah!

1870

Psalm cxlvii. 12. Praise the Lord, O Jerusalem: praise thy God, O Sion.

13. For He hath made fast the bars of thy gates: and hath blessed thy children within thee.

cxlv. 8. The Lord is gracious, and full of compassion: slow to anger, and of great mercy.

9. The Lord is good to all: and His tender mercies are over all His works.

10. All Thy works praise Thee, O LORD; and Thy saints give thanks unto Thee.

lxv. 14. The valleys stand so thick with corn that they laugh and sing.

cxlvii. 12. Praise the LORD, O Jerusalem: praise thy GOD, O Sion. Praise the LORD. Amen.

MAUNDER.

1871

Sing to the LORD of harvest,
  Sing songs of love and praise;
With joyful hearts and voices
  Your hallelujahs raise:
By Him the rolling seasons
  In faithful order move,
Sing to the LORD of harvest
  A song of happy love.

By Him the clouds drop fatness,
  The deserts bloom and spring,
The hills leap up in gladness,
  The valleys laugh and sing:
He filleth with His fulness
  All things with large increase;
He crowns the year with goodness,
  With plenty and with peace.

Heap on His sacred altar
  The gifts His goodness gave,
The golden sheaves of harvest,
  The souls He died to save:
Your hearts lay down before Him,
  When at His feet ye fall.
And with your lives adore Him
  Who gave His life for all. Amen.

MAUNDER.

1872

ISAIAH xii. 5. Sing unto the LORD, for He hath done great things. Sing unto the LORD.

PSALM cxxvi. 3. For He hath done great things for us; whereof we are glad.

cxlvii. 5. Great is the LORD, and great is His power: yea, and His wisdom is infinite.

xcvi. 5. As for the gods of the heathen, they are but idols ; but it is the LORD that made the heavens.

ISAIAH xii. 5. Sing unto the LORD, for He hath done great things, whereof we are glad.

PSALM cxxvi. 5. They that sow in tears shall reap in joy.

6. He that goeth forth and weepeth, bearing precious seed, shall doubtless come again with rejoicing.

ISAIAH xi. 9. The earth shall be full of the knowledge of the LORD, as the waters cover the sea.

PSALM xcvi. 10. Tell it out among the heathen that the LORD is King.

REVELATION xi. 15. And He shall reign for ever and ever.

xix. 16. King of Kings, and LORD of Lords. Hallelujah.

MAUNDER.

1873

ISAIAH xii. 5. Sing unto the LORD, for He hath done great things. Sing unto the LORD.

PSALM cxxvi. 3. For He hath done great things for us ; whereof we are glad.

5. They that sow in tears shall reap in joy.

6. He that goeth forth and weepeth, bearing precious seed, shall doubtless come again with rejoicing.

cxlvii. 5. Great is the LORD, and great is His power: yea, and His wisdom is infinite.

xcvi. 5. As for the gods of the heathen, they are but idols ; but it is the LORD that made the heavens.

ISAIAH xii. 5. Sing unto the LORD, for He hath done great things, whereof we are glad. Amen.

MAUNDER.

1874

Acts xiii. 32. We declare unto you glad tidings, how that the promise which was made unto the fathers,

33. God hath fulfilled the same unto us, in that He hath raised up Jesus again.

Job xix. 25. I know that my Redeemer liveth, and that He shall stand at the latter day upon the earth :

26. And though worms destroy this body, yet in my flesh shall I see God :

Exodus xv. 21. Sing unto the Lord, for He hath triumphed gloriously.

MAUNDER.

1875

Genesis viii. 22. While the earth remaineth, seed-time and harvest, and cold and heat, and summer and winter, and day and night shall not cease.

Psalm civ. 24. O Lord, how manifold are Thy works : in wisdom hast Thou made them all.

cxlv. 16. Thou openest Thine hand : and fillest all things living with plenteousness.

lxv. 9, 11. Thou visitest the earth and blessest it : Thou crownest the year with Thy goodness.

civ. 24. O Lord, how manifold are Thy works : in wisdom hast Thou made them all.

lxv. 13. The pastures are clothed with flocks ; the valleys are covered with corn ; they shout for joy, they also sing.

civ. 24. O Lord, how manifold are Thy works : in wisdom hast Thou made them all.

cl. 6. Let every thing that hath breath praise the Lord.

MAUNDER.

1876

Psalm lvii. 9. Awake up, my glory, awake, lute and harp : I myself will awake right early.

10. I will give thanks to Thee, O Lord, among the people : and I will sing unto Thee among the nations

lxxxvi.   5. For Thou, LORD, art good and gracious : and of great mercy unto all them that call upon Thee.

cxviii.   29. O give thanks unto the LORD, for He is gracious : and His mercy endureth for ever.

HAYNES.

1877

Lo, GOD, our GOD, has come !
   To us a Child is born,
To us a Son is given.
   Bless, bless the blessed morn.
Oh ! happy, lowly, lofty birth,
Now GOD, our GOD, has come to earth.

Rejoice, our GOD has come '
   In love and lowliness,
The Son of GOD has come
   The sons of men to bless.
GOD with us now descends to dwell,
GOD in our flesh, Immanuel.

Praise ye the Lamb that once was slain,
Praise ye the King that comes to reign,
Praise ye the Word made Flesh !
   True GOD, true Man is He !
Praise ye the CHRIST of GOD !
   To Him all glory be !   Amen.

HAYNES.

1878

ST. MARK xiv.   38. Watch ye and pray, lest ye enter into temptation. The spirit is truly ready, but the flesh is weak.

VICARS.

1879

PSALM xxxvii. 27. Flee from evil, and do the thing that is good : and dwell for evermore.

30, 41. The righteous shall inherit the land, and dwell therein for ever, because they put their trust in Him.

30, 32. The righteous shall inherit the land, their goings shall not slide : the LORD upholdeth them with His right hand.

26. The righteous is ever merciful : his seed is blessed.

32. The law of GOD is in his heart : his goings shall not slide ;

30. The righteous shall dwell therein for ever.

29. The wicked shall be punished : as for the seed of the ungodly it shall be rooted out.

27. Flee from evil, and do the thing that is good : and dwell for evermore.

W. J. CLARKE.

1880

COLLECT

For the Tenth Sunday after Trinity.

Let Thy merciful ears, O LORD, be open to the prayers of Thy humble servants ; and that they may obtain their petitions make them to ask such things as shall please Thee ; through JESUS CHRIST our LORD. Amen.

BELL.

1881

ISAIAH i. 18. Come now, and let us reason togetner, saith the LORD : though your sins be as scarlet, they shall be as white as snow ; though they be red like crimson, they shall be as wool.

19. If ye be willing and obedient, ye shall eat the good of the land.

20. But if ye refuse and rebel, ye shall be devoured with the sword : for the mouth of the LORD hath spoken it. Amen.

BRIANT.

1882

Dawns the day, the natal day,
Light of light foretelling,
Ancient shadows melt away,
He with men is dwelling.
  Name transcending,
  Reign unending,
War by peace repelling.

He is King, the glorious King,
Robed in flesh unstained,
Manhood pure and conquering,
Strength by weakness gained,
  GOD possessing
  Endless blessing,
Three in One contained.

Blest is JESUS, by Whose Name
GOD and SAVIOUR are the same;
GOD is He and none beside,
Who this day hath glorified.
GOD hath made this Christmastide.
       Alleluia! Alleluia!

GOD by Whom the world was made,
And on sure foundation laid;
GOD, Who reigned alone on high,
LORD from all eternity.
GOD has come to earth, the Child
Of a maiden undefiled.

Hail! Holy Babe, in Mary's bosom sleeping!
Sleep, sweetest child, Thy friends their watch are
  keeping,
Kneeling around the manger poor and lowly,
Shepherds and angels with Thy mother holy.

Care not, fair Babe, for all that shall befall Thee;
Sleep on and dream of nought that shall appal Thee;
Too soon shalt sigh, GOD's sigh for man outspoken,
Sigh, when the Heart refused by men is broken.

O wondrous thing ! O mystery unsounded !—
God, Who art here in flesh enclos'd and bounded,
Pardon our weakness, help our poor endeavour,
Peace and good-will preserve in us for ever.

Shout, O Zion, and rejoice,
Thou shalt hear the Bridegroom's voice ;
Tears and waiting—all are past ;
King and Spouse is here at last.
    Come then forth to meet Him.

Holy Jesu, may we raise
Willing voices in Thy praise ;
Holy Mary, mother fair,
May we thy pure gladness share,
    Met to-day to greet Him.

Legge.

1883

Isaiah xlix. 13. Sing, O heavens ; and be joyful, O earth ; and break forth into singing, O mountains : for the Lord hath comforted His people, and will have mercy upon His afflicted.

14. But Zion said, The Lord hath forsaken me, and the Lord hath forgotten me.

lv. 7. Return unto the Lord, and He will have mercy upon you ; and to your God, for He will abundantly pardon.

xxx. 18. Therefore will the Lord wait, that He may be gracious unto you, and therefore will He be exalted, that He may have mercy upon you : for the Lord is a God of judgment : blessed are they that wait for His salvation.

xlix. 13. Sing, O heavens ; and be joyful, O earth ; and break forth into singing, O mountains : for the Lord hath comforted His people, and will have mercy upon His afflicted. Sing, O heavens ; and be joyful, O earth ; break forth into singing, O mountains.

Welton.

1884

Jesu, Who from Thy Father's throne,
To this low vale of tears cam'st down,
    In our poor nature drest !
O may the charms of that sweet love,
Draw up our souls to Thee above,
    And fix them there at rest.

St. Luke i. 30. And the angel said unto her, Fear not, Mary : for thou hast found favour with God.

31. And, behold, thou shalt bring forth a son, and shalt call His Name Jesus.

32. He shall be great, and shall be called the Son of the Highest : and the Lord God shall give unto Him the throne of His father David :

Jesu, Who took'st that heavenly Name,
Thy blessed purpose to proclaim,
    Of saving lost mankind !
O, may we bow our heart and knee,
Bright King of Names, in praising Thee,
    And Thy hid sweetness find.

Jesu, draw up our souls to Thee above.

Woods.

1885

Psalm lxxviii. 24. The Lord opened the doors of heaven.

25. He rained down manna also upon them for to eat : and gave them food from heaven.

26. So man did eat angels' food.

cvi. 1. O give thanks unto the Lord, for He is gracious : and His mercy endureth for ever.

Woods.

1886

Numbers xxiv. 17. (*Revised Version.*) There shall come forth a Star out of Jacob, and a Sceptre shall rise out of Israel.

19. Out of Jacob shall One have dominion.

Genesis xlix. 10. And unto Him shall the obedience of the peoples be.

ISAIAH lxiii. 1. Who is this that cometh from Edom, with dyed garments from Bozrah? this that is glorious in His apparel, marching in the greatness of His strength?

xxv. 9. Lo, this is our GOD; we have waited for Him, and He will save us: this is the LORD; we have waited for Him we will be glad and rejoice in His salvation. Amen.

MANSFIELD.

1887

The day is past and over;
  All thanks, O LORD, to Thee;
I pray Thee that offenceless
  The hours of dark may be:
O JESU, keep me in Thy sight,
And save me through the coming night.

The toils of day are over;
  I raise the hymn to Thee,
And ask that free from peril
  The hours of fear may be:
O JESU, keep me in Thy sight,
And guard me through the coming night.

Be Thou my soul's preserver,
  O GOD! for Thou dost know
How many are the perils
  Through which I have to go:
Lover of men, O hear my call,
And guard and save me from them all.

MARKS.

1888

PSALM lxvii. 1. (*Bible Version.*) GOD be merciful unto us, and bless us; and cause His face to shine upon us;

2. That Thy way may be known upon earth, Thy saving health among all nations.

3. Let the people praise Thee, O GOD; let all the people praise Thee.

4. O let the nations be glad and sing for joy; for Thou shalt judge the people righteously, and govern the nations upon earth.

5. Let the people praise Thee, O GOD; let all the people praise Thee.

6. Then shall the earth yield her increase; and GOD, even our own GOD, shall bless us.

7. GOD shall bless us; and all the ends of the earth shall fear Him.

(From " Seed-time and Harvest," No. 2.) WEST.

1889

DEUTERONOMY xxviii. 8. The LORD shall command the blessing upon thee in thy storehouses; He shall bless thee in the land which the LORD thy GOD giveth thee.

PSALM lxxxv. 12. Yea, the LORD shall give that which is good; and our land shall yield her increase.

JOEL ii. 21. Fear not, O land; be glad and rejoice: for the LORD will do great things.

22. Be not afraid, ye beasts of the field; for the pastures of the wilderness do spring, for the tree beareth her fruit, the fig tree and the vine do yield her strength.

24, 26. The floors shall be full of wheat, and ye shall eat in plenty, and be satisfied, and praise the Name of the LORD your GOD, that hath dealt so wondrously with you.

(From " Seed-time and Harvest," No. 5.) WEST

1890

PSALM lxvi. 1. *(Prayer Book Version.)* O be joyful in GOD, all ye lands: sing praises unto the honour of His Name; make His praise to be glorious.

2. Say unto GOD, O how wonderful art Thou in Thy works.

3. For all the world shall worship Thee: sing of Thee and praise Thy Name.

4. O come hither, and behold the works of GOD: how wonderful He is in His doing toward the children of men.

PSALM civ. 24. O LORD, how manifold are Thy works: in wisdom hast Thou made them all; the earth is full of Thy riches.

lxvi. 1-3. O be joyful . . . sing of Thee and praise Thy Name.

Praise GOD, from Whom all blessing flow ;
Praise Him, all creatures here below ;
Praise Him above, angelic host ;
Praise Father, Son, and Holy Ghost.   Amen.

(From " Seed-time and Harvest," No. 13.)   WEST.

1891

JEREMIAH v.   24. Let us now fear the LORD our GOD, that giveth rain, both the former and the latter, in his season : He reserveth unto us the appointed weeks of the harvest.

PSALM xxxi.   21. O how plentiful is Thy goodness which Thou hast laid up for them that fear Thee, and that Thou hast prepared for them that put their trust in Thee, even before the sons of men !

JEREMIAH v.   24. Let us now fear the LORD.

PSALM cxi.   5. He hath given meat unto them that fear Him : He shall ever be mindful of His covenant.

Therefore unto Him we raise
Hymns of glory, songs of praise ;
To the FATHER, and the SON,
And the Spirit, Three in One,
Honour, might, and glory be
Now, and through eternity.   Amen.

WEST.

1892

PSALM cxlv.   21. My mouth shall speak the praise of the LORD, and let all flesh give thanks unto His Holy Name for ever and ever.

15. The eyes of all wait upon Thee, O LORD; and Thou givest them their meat in due season.

16. Thou openest Thine hand, and fillest all things living with plenteousness.

21. My mouth shall speak the praise of the LORD, and let all flesh give thanks unto His Holy Name for ever and ever.   Hallelujah.   Amen.

WEST.

1893

PSALM cxv. 1. Not unto us, O LORD, not unto us, but unto Thy Name give the praise : for Thy loving mercy, and for Thy truth's sake.

2. Wherefore shall the heathen say : Where is now their GOD ?

3. As for our GOD, He is in heaven : He hath done whatsoever pleased Him.

4. Their idols are silver and gold : even the work of men's hands.

5. They have mouths, and speak not : eyes have they, and see not.

6. They have ears, and hear not : noses have they, and smell not.

7. They have hands, and handle not ; feet have they, and walk not : neither speak they through their throat.

8. They that make them are like unto them : and so are all such as put their trust in them.

9. But thou house of Israel, trust thou in the LORD : He is their succour and defence.

10. Ye house of Aaron, put your trust in the LORD : He is their helper and defender.

11. Ye that fear the LORD, put your trust in the LORD : He is their helper and defender.

17. The dead praise not Thee, O LORD : neither all they that go down into silence.

18. But we will praise the LORD from this time forth for evermore. Praise the LORD.

WEST.

1894

1 CORINTHIANS xv. 20. Now is CHRIST risen from the dead, and become the first-fruits of them that slept.

21. For since by man came death, by man came also the resurrection of the dead.

22. For as in Adam all die, even so in CHRIST shall all be made alive.

57. Thanks be to GOD, Which giveth us the victory through our LORD JESUS CHRIST.

55. O death, where is thy sting? O grave, where is thy victory ?

56. The sting of death is sin, and the strength of sin is the law.

57. But thanks be to GOD, Which giveth us the victory through our LORD JESUS CHRIST. Hallelujah ! Amen.

WEST.

1895 T. ADAMS, vv. 20, 21. Alleluia.

1896

O come, Redeemer of mankind, appear,
　Thee with full hearts the Virgin-born we greet ;
Let every age with rapt amazement hear
　That wondrous birth which for our GOD is meet.

How doth Thy lowly manger radiant shine !
　On the sweet breath of night new splendour grows ;
So may our spirits glow with faith Divine,
　Where no dark cloud of sin shall interpose.

All praise and glory to the Father be,
　All praise and glory to His only Son,
All praise and glory, Holy Ghost, to Thee,
　Both now, and while eternal ages run.　Amen.

WEST.

1897

THE COLLECT FOR THE ANNUNCIATION OF THE BLESSED VIRGIN MARY.

We beseech Thee, O LORD, pour Thy grace into our hearts ; that, as we have known the incarnation of Thy Son JESUS CHRIST by the message of an angel, so by His cross and passion we may be brought unto the glory of His resurrection ; through the same JESUS CHRIST our LORD. Amen.

WEST.

1898

With all Thy hosts, O LORD, we sing,
And thanks and praise to Thee we bring ;
For Thou, O long-expected Guest,
Hast come at length to make us blest.

ISAIAH xxv. 9. Lo, this is our GOD ; we have waited for Him, and He will save us : This is the LORD ; we have waited for Him, we will be glad and rejoice in His salvation.

PSALM lxxxv. 9. For His salvation is nigh them that fear Him : that glory may dwell in our land.

10. Mercy and truth are met together : righteousness and peace have kissed each other.

11. Truth shall flourish out of the earth : and righteousness hath looked down from heaven.

ISAIAH xxv. 9. This is the LORD ; we have waited for Him, we will be glad and rejoice in His salvation.

ST. LUKE i. 68. Blessed be the LORD GOD of Israel : for He hath visited and redeemed His people. Amen.

WEST.

1899

My GOD, I love Thee ; not because
    I hope for heaven thereby,
Nor yet because who love Thee not
    Are lost eternally.

Thou, O my JESUS, Thou didst me
    Upon the Cross embrace ;
For me didst bear the nails, and spear,
    And manifold disgrace,

And griefs and torments numberless,
    And sweat of agony ;
Yea, death itself ; and all for me
    Who was Thine enemy.

Then why, O Blessèd JESU CHRIST,
    Should I not love Thee well ?
Not for the sake of winning heaven,
    Nor of escaping hell ;

Not from the hope of gaining aught,
    Not seeking a reward ;
But as Thyself hast lovèd me,
    O ever-loving LORD.

So would I love Thee, dearest LORD,
    And in Thy praise will sing ;
Solely because Thou art my GOD,
    And my most loving King. Amen.

G J. BENNETT.

1900

On the morn of Easter day,
From the tomb wherein He lay,
  CHRIST our Hope rose gloriously;
Trampling down th'infernal king,
Hell and Satan vanquishing,
  He return'd victoriously.

When the risen LORD was seen,
Blessed Mary Magdalene
  Was the herald whom He chose:
On the glorious errand sent,
To His brethren straight she went,
  Bearing joy to end their woes.

O thrice blessed eyes, that first,
When the chains of death were burst,
Sin destroyed and Satan quell'd,
CHRIST, the King of all, beheld!

This was she who was of old
Lost in sin so manifold,
But, at JESU's feet, obtain'd
Grace to pardon all that stain'd.

Lips deploring, heart adoring,
Are the proving of her loving
  JESU more than all the rest;
Whom she worshipp'd, fully knowing
She receiv'd from His bestowing
  Pardon for her troubled breast.

Marys twain, with news of gladness,
Freed the Church of GOD from sadness;
One was the Virgin Mother, one
The Saint whom sin had once undone.

One the gate, whereby salvation
Enter'd in for every nation;
And one the herald, sent to tell
That CHRIST had ris'n, and vanquish'd h-ll.

                              G. J. Brennan.

1901

A few more years shall roll,
A few more seasons come ;
And we shall be with those that rest
Asleep within the tomb :
Then, O my LORD, prepare
My soul for that great day ;
O wash me in Thy precious Blood,
And take my sins away.

A few more storms shall beat
On this wild rocky shore ;
And we shall be where tempests cease,
And surges swell no more :
Then, O my LORD, prepare
My soul for that calm day ;
O wash me in Thy precious Blood,
And take my sins away.

A few more struggles here,
A few more partings o'er,
A few more toils, a few more tears,
And we shall weep no more :
Then, O my LORD, prepare
My soul for that bright day ;
O wash me in Thy precious Blood,
And take my sins away.

'Tis but a little while,
And He shall come again,
Who died that we might live, Who lives
That we with Him may reign :
Then, O my LORD, prepare
My soul for that glad day ;
O wash me in Thy precious Blood,
And take my sins away. Amen. BLAIR.

1902

PSALM xcvi. 7. Ascribe unto the LORD, O ye kindreds
of the people ; ascribe unto the LORD worship and power.
8. Ascribe unto the LORD the honour due unto His
Name : bring presents, and come into His courts.
9. O worship the LORD in the beauty of holiness ; let
the whole earth stand in awe of Him. BLAIR.

1903

§ 1.

St. Luke xii. 37. Blessed are they whom the Lord when He cometh shall find watching. They shall go into Life Eternal, they shall be His people.

Revelation xxi. 3. And God Himself shall be with them, and shall be their God.

(From "Blessed are they who watch," No. 1.)

§ 2.

1 Thessalonians iv. 13. Sorrow not for those that sleep, even as others which have no hope.

14. If we believe that Jesus died and rose again, even so them also which sleep in Jesus will God bring with Him.

St. John v. 25. Behold the hour cometh when the dead shall hear the voice of the Son of God, and they that hear shall live.

1 Thessalonians iv. 16. For the Lord Himself shall descend from Heaven with a shout, with the voice of the archangel, and the trump of God.

Isaiah xxvi. 19. Awake and sing, ye that sleep in the dust. Thy dead men shall live, together with my dead body shall they arise; and the earth shall cast out the dead.

(From "Blessed are they who watch," Nos. 2, 3.)

§ 3.

1 St. John ii. 17. The world passeth away, and the lust thereof; but he that doeth the will of the Lord abideth for ever.

Revelation xxi. 6. I will give unto him that is athirst of the fountain of the water of life freely.

7. He that overcometh shall inherit all things; I will be his God, and he shall be My son.

(From "Blessed are they who watch," Nos. 4, 5.)

§ 4.

REVELATION xii. 10. Now is come salvation and strength, and the kingdom of our GOD, and the power of His CHRIST.

ISAIAH xxv. 9. Lo! This is our GOD, we have waited for Him, He will save us.

(*From " Blessed are they who watch,"* No. 6.)

BLAIR.

1904

PSALM lxxi. 14. I will go forth in the strength of the LORD GOD : and will make mention of Thy righteousness only.

7. O let my mouth be filled with Thy praise : that I may sing of Thy glory and honour all the day long.

BLAIR.

1905

> Before the heavens were spread abroad,
>   From everlasting was the Word ;
> With GOD He was, the Word was GOD,
>   And must divinely be adored.

JOB xxxviii. 7. The morning stars sang together, and all the sons of GOD shouted for joy.

ST. JOHN i. 14. And we beheld His glory, as of the only begotten of the Father, full of grace and truth.

> This is He Whom seers in old time
>   Chanted of with one accord ;
> Whom the voices of the Prophets
>   Promised in their faithful word ;
> Now He shines, the long expected ;
>   Let creation praise its LORD,
>   Evermore and evermore.

> CHRIST, to Thee, with GOD the Father,
>   And, O Holy Ghost, to Thee,
> Hymn, and chant, and high thanksgiving,
>   And unwearied praises be,
> Honour, glory, and dominion,
>   And eternal victory,
>   Evermore and evermore. Amen.

PARKER.

1906

PSALM xcvi. 7. (*Bible Version.*) Give unto the LORD, O ye kindreds of the people, give unto the LORD glory and strength.

6. Honour and majesty are before Him : strength and beauty are in His sanctuary.

xlviii. 8. We wait for Thy loving-kindness, O LORD, in the midst of Thy temple.

xciii. 6. Holiness becometh Thine house for ever.

xcvi. 7. Give unto the LORD, O ye kindreds of the people, give unto the LORD glory and strength.

> Here vouchsafe to all Thy servants
>   What they ask of Thee to gain,
> What they gain from Thee for ever
>   With the blessed to retain.

> Here vouchsafe to all Thy servants
>   What they ask of Thee to gain,
> And to Paradise translated,
>   There in rest with Thee to reign.

> Glory to our GOD, and honour ;
>   Highest He above all heights :
> Father, Son, and Holy Spirit,
>   One in praise, and One in might,
> Might and praise enduring ever,
>   In the changeless worlds of light.   Amen.

PARKER.

1907

PSALM lxxxix. 26. I will set his dominion in the sea : and his right hand in the floods.

27. And he shall call Me, Thou art my Father: my GOD, and my strong salvation.

28. And I will make him My first-born : higher than the kings of the earth.

cxxxii. 14. The LORD hath chosen Sion to be an habitation for Himself.

16. I will bless her victuals with increase : and will satisfy her poor with bread.

17. I will deck her priests with health : and her saints shall rejoice and sing.

lxxxix. 50. Praised be the LORD for evermore. Amen and Amen.

PARKER.

1908

1. Ye holy angels bright,
   Who wait at GOD's right hand,
   Or through the realms of light
   Fly at your LORD's command,
   Assist our song,
   Or else the theme
   Too high doth seem
   For mortal tongue.

2. Ye blessèd souls at rest,
   Who ran this earthly race,
   And now, from sin released,
   Behold the Saviour's Face,
   His praises sound,
   As in His light
   With sweet delight
   Ye do abound.

3. Ye saints, who toil below,
   Adore your heavenly King,
   And onward as ye go
   Some joyful anthem sing;
   Take what He gives
   And praise Him still,
   Through good and ill,
   Who ever lives !

4. My soul, bear thou thy part,
   Triumph in GOD above,
   And with a well-tuned heart
   Sing thou the songs of love !
   Let all thy days
   Till life shall end,
   Whate'er He send.
   Be filled with praise.

RICHARDS.

1909

Cleanse me, LORD, that I may kneel
At Thine altar, pure and white,
They that once Thy mercies feel,
Gaze no more on earth's delights.

Worldly joys like shadows fade
When the heavenly light appears,
But the covenants Thou hast made
Endless, know nor days nor years.

In Thy Word, LORD, is my trust,
To Thy mercies fast I fly,
Though I am but clay and dust,
Yet Thy grace can lift me high.　　WRIGLEY.

1910

ST. LUKE x.　25. Master, what shall I do to inherit
eternal life ?

27. Thou shalt love the LORD thy GOD with all thy
heart, with all thy soul, with all thy strength, and with
all thy mind ; and thy neighbour as thyself.

28. This do, and thou shalt live.　　BOWES.

1911

ST. JOHN iii.　14. As Moses lifted up the serpent in
the wilderness, even so must the Son of man be lifted up :

15. That whosoever believeth in Him should not perish,
but have eternal life.

16. For* GOD so loved the world, that He gave His only
begotten Son, that whosoever believeth in Him should
not perish, but have everlasting life.

17. For GOD sent not His Son into the world to
condemn the world ; but that the world through Him
might be saved.

ST. MATTHEW xxiv.　13. He that shall endure unto
the end shall be saved.

[ROMANS v.　8. But GOD commendeth His love toward
us ; in that, while we were yet sinners, CHRIST died for us.

1. Therefore, being justified by faith, we have peace with
GOD, through our LORD JESUS CHRIST.]　　GOSTELOW.

1912 J. V. ROBERTS. ST. JOHN, iii. 16, 17; ROMANS. v. 8, 1.

1913

Isaiah xli. 18. I will open rivers in high places, and fountains in the midst of the valleys: I will make the wilderness pools of water, and the dry land streams of water.

Joel ii. 21. Fear not, O land ; be glad and rejoice: for the Lord will do great things.

22. For the pastures of the wilderness do spring, and the fig tree beareth her fruit.

23. Be glad, ye children of Zion: rejoice in the Name of the Lord your God.

24. And the floors shall be full of wheat, and ye shall praise the Name of the Lord your God.

21, 23. Fear not, O land, be glad and rejoice ; for the Lord will do great things. Then rejoice in the Name of the Lord. Pettman.

1914

St. Luke ii. 8. There were shepherds abiding in the field, keeping watch over their flocks by night.

9. And lo, the angel of the Lord came upon them, and the glory of the Lord shone round about them: and they were sore afraid.

10. And the angel said unto them, Fear not: for, behold, I bring you good tidings of great joy, which shall be to you and all people.

11. For unto you is born this day, in the city of David, a Saviour, Which is Christ the Lord.

[St. Luke i. 32. He shall be great, and shall be called the Son of the Highest: and the Lord God shall give unto Him the throne of His father David.

33. And He shall reign over the house of Jacob for ever; and of His kingdom there shall be no end.]

> Your King is born in Bethlehem,
> The Son of God in low estate,
>   Come, and adore Him, Christ the Lord.
>
> Bright beams above the guiding star,
> Its heavenly radiance spreads afar,
> Emmanuel, we come to worship Thee,
>   Our Lord and King.

O'er this dark world of sin and woe,
Its beams still shine with heavenly glow,
Redeemed and free our song shall be
From all the ransomed world
       For evermore.   Amen.

                                    PETTMAN.

1915 T. ADAMS, St. Luke i. 32, 33.   Alleluia! Amen.
1916 TOURS, St. Luke ii. 8–11 ; i. 33.   Amen.

1917

ISAIAH lii. 9. Break forth into joy.   Hallelujah!

ST. LUKE ii.   10. Behold, I bring you good tidings of great joy, which shall be to you and all people.

11. For unto you is born this day, in the city of David, a SAVIOUR, Which is CHRIST the LORD.

ISAIAH lii. 9. Break forth into joy.   Hallelujah!

IX.   6. For unto us a Child is born, in the city of David, Which is CHRIST the LORD.   Hallelujah!

                                    STEANE.

1918

PSALM cxlv.   3. Great is the LORD, and marvellous, and worthy to be praised: there is no end of His greatness.

4. One generation shall praise Thy works unto another, and declare Thy power.

15. The eyes of all wait upon Thee, O LORD : and Thou givest them their meat in due season.

16. Thou openest Thine hand, and fillest all things living with plenteousness.

21. My mouth shall speak the praise of the LORD.

3. Great is the LORD, and marvellous, and worthy to be praised : there is no end of His greatness.

21. And let all flesh give thanks unto His holy Name for ever and ever.   Amen.

                                    STEANE.

1919

JOY IN HARVEST.

Almighty Father, God of Love!
  The seasons roll at Thy command,
Oceans below and stars above
  Proclaim the wonders of Thy hand.

Winter returns with snow and cold,
  Spring yields the green and blossom'd thorn,
Summer displays her realms of gold,
  And Autumn stores the fruits and corn.

Over the earth's extensive space
Thy bounteous gifts are richly spread.

May all who reap, who glean, and store,
  United praises sing to Thee;
Much Thou hast given, Thou wilt give more,
  If fervent our devotions be.

ISAIAH ix. 3. They joy before Thee, according to the joy in harvest, and as men rejoice when they divide the spoil.

    God of harvest, God of power,
      God of justice, mercy, grace,
    Guardian of the passing hour,
      Thou shedd'st Thy blessing on our race.

    Crops of plenty to the scythe,
      To the spade and sickle yield,
    They who till the soil now thrive;
      Golden produce crown the field.

    Grateful hearts and thankful minds
      Make the hills and valleys ring;
    Creatures all of varying kinds,
      Should praise God for everything.

PSALM cl. 6., Let everything that hath breath praise the LORD.

STEANE.

1920

PSALM lxii. 1. My soul truly waiteth still upon GOD : for of Him cometh my salvation

6. He truly is my strength and my salvation : He is my defence so that I shall not fall.

8. O put your trust in Him alway, ye people : pour out your hearts before Him, for GOD is our hope.

STEANE.

1921

PSALM cxxxvi. 1. O give thanks unto the LORD, for He is gracious : and His mercy endureth for ever.

cv. 8. He hath been always mindful of His covenant and promise, that He made to a thousand generations.

cvii. 9. For He satisfieth the empty soul, and filleth the hungry soul with goodness.

civ. 13. He watereth the hills from above : the earth is filled with the fruit of Thy works.

14. He bringeth forth grass for the cattle : and green herb for the service of men.

cxxxvi. 1. O give thanks unto the LORD, for He is gracious : and His mercy endureth for ever.

To Thee, O LORD, our hearts we raise
In hymns of adoration,
To Thee bring sacrifice of praise
With shouts of exultation ;
Bright robes of gold the fields adorn,
The hills with joy are ringing,
The valleys stand so thick with corn
That even they are singing. Amen.

STEANE.

1922

ST. JOHN xx. 1. The first day of the week came Mary Magdalene, when it was yet dark, unto the sepulchre, and seeth the stone taken away from the sepulchre.

2. She runneth to Simon Peter, and to the other disciple, whom JESUS loved, and saith unto them, They have taken away the LORD, and we know not where they have laid Him.

1 CORINTHIANS xv. 20. [*Hallelujah !] CHRIST is risen from the dead, and become the first-fruits of them that slept.

21. For since by man came death, by man came also the resurrection of the dead.

22. For as in Adam all die, even so in CHRIST shall all be made alive.

[57. Thanks be to GOD, Which giveth us the victory, through our LORD JESUS CHRIST. Thanks be to GOD.]

20. Alleluia ! CHRIST is risen from the dead.

> Alleluia now we cry
> To our King Immortal,
> Who triumphant burst the bars
> Of the tomb's dark portal;
> Alleluia, with the Son,
> GOD the Father praising;
> Alleluia yet again
> To the Spirit raising.
> Alleluia ! Amen.
>
> STEANE.

1923 STEANE,* 1 Cor. xv., 20—22, 57. Hallelujah! Amen.

1924

ROMANS xiii. 12. The night is far spent, the day is at hand.

11. Now it is high time to awake out of sleep.

12. Let us cast off the works of darkness, and let us put on the armour of light.

PHILIPPIANS iv. 6. Let your requests be made known to GOD.

7. And the peace of GOD, which passeth all understanding, shall keep your hearts and minds through JESU CHRIST.

> O come, Redeemer, come and free
> Thine own from guilt and misery ;
> The gates of heaven again unfold,
> Which Adam's sin had closed of old.
>
> All praise, Eternal Son, to Thee,
> Whose Advent sets Thy people free,
> Whom with the Father we adore
> And Holy Ghost for evermore.

Hosanna in the highest. Amen. STEANE.

1925

GENESIS viii. 22. While the earth remaineth, seed-time and harvest, and cold and heat, and summer and winter, and day and night shall not cease.

LEVITICUS xxvi. 4. I will give you rain in due season, and the land shall yield her increase.

PSALM lxv. 9. Thou visitest the earth and blessest it : Thou makest it very plenteous.

10. The river of GOD is full of water : Thou preparest their corn, for so Thou providest for the earth.

14. The valleys stand so thick with corn, they even laugh and sing.

xxxii. 12. Be glad, O ye righteous, and rejoice in the LORD.

xxxiii. 4. For the word of the LORD is true, and all His works are faithful.

STEANE

1926

ST. LUKE xxiv. 5. Why seek ye the living among the dead ?

6. He is not here, but is risen ; remember how He spake unto you when He was yet in Galilee,

7. Saying, The Son of man must be delivered into the hands of sinful men, and be crucified, and the third day rise again. (6.) He is risen.

I CORINTHIANS xv. 20. Alleluia ! CHRIST is risen from the dead.

> Alleluia ! Alleluia ! Alleluia !
> The strife is o'er, the battle done ;
> Now is the Victor's triumph won ;
> O let the song of praise be sung.
> > Alleluia !

> Death's mightiest powers have done their worst,
> And JESUS hath His foes dispersed ;
> Let shouts of praise and joy outburst.
> > Alleluia. Amen.

STEANE.

1927

ROMANS xiv. 9. CHRIST both died, and rose, and re-vived, that He might be LORD both of the dead and living.

2 CORINTHIANS v. 15. He died for all, that they which live should not henceforth live unto themselves, but unto Him Which died for them, and rose again.

iv. 14. He which raised up the LORD JESUS shall raise up us also by JESUS, and shall present us with you.

Now to GOD the Father, GOD the Son, and GOD the Holy Ghost, be ascribed all power and dominion, both now and for evermore. Amen.

E. W. NAYLOR.

1928

BARUCH iv. 36. O Jerusalem, look about thee toward the east, and behold the joy that cometh unto thee from GOD.

37. Lo, thy sons come, whom thou sentest away, they come gathered together from the east to the west by the word of the Holy One, rejoicing in the glory of GOD.

PHILIPPIANS iv. 5. The LORD is at hand.

E. W. NAYLOR.

1929

PSALM xxvi. 6. I will wash my hands in innocency, O LORD, and so will I go to Thine Altar ;

7. That I may shew the voice of thanksgiving, and tell of all Thy wondrous works. Amen.

CULLEY.

1930

PSALM xli. 1. LORD, I call upon Thee, haste Thee unto me : and consider my voice when I cry unto Thee.

2. Let my prayer be set forth in Thy sight as the incense : and let the lifting up of my hands be an evening sacrifice.

cxlv. 17. The LORD is righteous in all His ways : and holy in all His works.

18. The LORD is nigh unto all them that call upon Him : yea, all such as call upon Him faithfully.

19. He will fulfil the desire of them that fear Him : He also will hear their cry and will help them.

CULLEY.

1931

SAVIOUR, abide with us!
  The day is now far gone:
We would obtain a blessing thus,
  By coming to Thy throne.

We have not reached that land,
  That happy land as yet,
Where holy angels round Thee stand,
  Whose sun can never set.

Our sun is sinking now,
  Our day is almost o'er ;
O Sun of Righteousness, do Thou
  Shine on us evermore !

HANFORTH.

1932

1 ST. PETER iii. 8. Be ye all of one mind, having compassion one of another, love as brethren, be pitiful, be courteous :

9. Not rendering evil for evil, or railing for railing : but contrariwise blessing ; knowing that ye are thereunto called, that ye should inherit a blessing.

10. For he that will love life, and see good days, let him refrain his tongue from evil, and his lips that they speak no guile :

11. Let him eschew evil, and do good ; let him seek peace, and ensue it.

12. For the eyes of the LORD are over the righteous, and His ears are open unto their prayers : but the face of the LORD is against them that do evil. Amen.

GODFREY.

1933

PSALM iv. 9. I will lay me down in peace, and take my rest : for it is Thou, LORD, only that makest me dwell in safety.

cxxi. 2. My help cometh even from the LORD : Who hath made heaven and earth.

3. He will not suffer thy foot to be moved : and He that keepeth thee will not sleep.

7. The LORD shall preserve thee from all evil : yea, it is even He that shall keep thy soul.

A. C. EDWARDS.

1934

PSALM xliii. 4. I will go unto the altar of GOD, even the GOD of my joy and gladness.

cxvi. 15. I will offer unto Thee the sacrifice of thanksgiving, and call upon the Name of the LORD.

COLOSSIANS iii. 1. If ye then be risen with CHRIST, seek those things which are above, where CHRIST sitteth on the right hand of GOD.

2. Set your affection on things above, not on things on the earth.

1 CORINTHIANS xv. 55. O death, where is thy sting? O grave, thy victory?

57. Thanks be to GOD, Which giveth us the victory through our LORD JESUS CHRIST. Amen.

C. HARRIS.

1935

PSALM lxviii. 3. Let the righteous be glad; let them rejoice before GOD : yea, let them exceedingly rejoice.

cxlviii. 13. Let them praise the Name of the LORD : for His Name alone is excellent; His glory is above the earth and heaven.

DEUTERONOMY xxxiii. 12. The beloved of the LORD shall dwell in safety by Him; and the LORD shall cover him all the day long.

PSALM lv. 22. He shall never suffer the righteous to be moved.

lxviii. 3. Then let the righteous be glad; let them rejoice before GOD : yea, let them exceedingly rejoice.

cxlviii. 13. Let them praise the Name of the LORD : for His Name alone is excellent; His glory is above the earth and heaven. Hallelujah!

R. F. LLOYD.

1936

ISAIAH lii. 9. Break forth into joy; sing together, ye waste places of Jerusalem, for the LORD hath comforted His people, and hath redeemed Jerusalem.

ST. LUKE ii. 11. Unto you is born this day in the city of David a Saviour, Which is CHRIST the LORD

O come, all ye faithful,
Joyful and triumphant :
O come ye, O come ye to Bethlehem ;
Come and behold Him
Born, the King of angels ;
O come, let us adore Him, CHRIST the LORD.

Amen.

COLERIDGE-TAYLOR.

1937

PSALM lxxi. 1. In Thee, O LORD, have I put my trust, let me never be put to confusion : but rid me, and deliver me in Thy righteousness. Incline Thine ear unto me : make haste to deliver me.

xxxi. 6. Into Thy hands I commend my spirit : for Thou hast redeemed me, Thou GOD of truth. Amen

COLERIDGE-TAYLOR.

1938

PSALM xxiv. 7. Lift up your heads, O ye gates ; and be ye lift up, ye everlasting doors : and the King of glory shall come in.

8. Who is this King of glory? It is the LORD strong and mighty, even the LORD mighty in battle. Amen.

COLERIDGE-TAYLOR.

1939

PSALM cxviii. 14. The LORD is my strength and my song : and is become my salvation.

17. I shall not die but live : and declare the works of GOD.

O LORD of all, with us abide
In this our joyful Easter-tide ;
From every weapon death can wield
Thine own redeemed for ever shield.

All praise be Thine, O risen LORD,
From death to endless life restored :
All praise to GOD the FATHER be
And HOLY GHOST eternally. Amen.

COLERIDGE-TAYLOR.

1940

EPHESIANS v. 1. Be ye therefore followers of GOD, as dear children ;

2. And walk in love, as CHRIST also hath loved us, and hath given Himself for us an offering and a sacrifice to GOD.

A. S. BAKER.

1941

ST. MATTHEW v. 4. Blessed are they that mourn : for they shall be comforted.

REVELATION vii. 16, 17. They shall hunger no more, neither thirst any more : for GOD shall wipe away all tears from their eyes. BATSON.

1942

PSALM cxxvi. 6. They that sow in tears shall reap in joy.

7. He that now goeth on his way weeping, and beareth forth good seed : shall doubtless come again with joy, and bring his sheaves with him. BATSON.

1943

PSALM cxlv. 10. All Thy works shall praise Thee, O LORD : and Thy saints give thanks unto Thee.

11. They shew the glory of Thy Kingdom, and talk of Thy power ;

12. That Thy power, Thy glory, and mightiness of Thy kingdom may be known unto men.

10. All Thy works shall praise Thee, O LORD : Thy saints give thanks unto Thee.

civ. 24. O LORD, how manifold are Thy works : in wisdom hast Thou made them all ; the earth is full of Thy riches.

13. He watereth the hills from above : the earth is filled with the fruit of Thy works.

14. He bringeth forth the grass for the cattle, and green herb for the service of man.

24. O LORD, how manifold are Thy works : in wisdom hast Thou made them all, the earth is full of Thy riches.

cxlv. 10. All Thy works shall praise Thee, O LORD : Thy saints give thanks unto Thee.

11. They shew the glory of Thy kingdom, and talk of Thy power.

To Thee, O LORD, our hearts we raise
In hymns of adoration,
To Thee bring sacrifice of praise
With shouts of exultation;
Bright robes of gold the fields adorn,
The hills with joy are ringing,
The valleys stand so thick with corn
That even they are singing.
Alleluia. Amen.

ELY.

1944

PSALM xciii. 1. The LORD is King, and hath put on His glorious apparel : the LORD hath put on His glorious apparel, and girded Himself with strength.

2. He hath made the round world so sure, that it cannot be moved.

xcii. 5. O LORD, how glorious are Thy works : Thy thoughts are very deep : Thou art from everlasting.

6. An unwise man doth not well consider this : and a fool doth not understand it.

xciii. 4. The floods are risen, O LORD, the floods have lift up their voice.

5. The waves of the sea are mighty, and rage horribly.

xcv. 5. The sea is His, and He made it : and His hands prepared the dry land.

6, 3. O come, let us worship, and fall down; for the LORD is a great GOD : and a great King above all gods.

6. O come, let us worship, and kneel before the LORD our Maker.

xciii. 4. The floods are risen, O LORD : the floods lift up their waves.

5. The waves of the sea are mighty, and rage horribly : but yet the LORD, Who dwelleth on high, is mightier. Amen.

H. J. KING.

1945

PSALM ciii. 1. Bless the LORD, O my soul : and all that is within me, bless His holy Name.

2. Bless the LORD, O my soul, and forget not all His benefits.

8. The LORD is merciful and gracious, slow to anger, and plenteous in mercy.

9. He will not alway chide, nor keep His anger for ever.

20. Bless the LORD, ye His angels, that excel in strength, that do His commandments, hearkening unto the voice of His word.

21. Bless the LORD, all ye His hosts ; ye ministers of His, that do His pleasure.

22. Bless the LORD, all His works in all places of His dominion : bless the LORD.

19. The LORD hath prepared His throne in the heavens; and His kingdom ruleth over all.

22. Bless the LORD, all His works in all places of His dominion : bless the LORD, O my soul.

KINGSTON.

1946

PSALM xviii. 1. I will love Thee, O LORD, my strength.

2. The LORD is my rock, my fortress, my deliverer; my GOD, my strength, in Whom I will trust; the horn of my salvation, and my high tower.

3. I will call upon the LORD, Who is worthy to be praised.

lvii. 7. My heart is prepared, O GOD : I will sing and give praise.

8. Awake up, my glory; awake, lute and harp.

10. For the greatness of Thy mercy reacheth unto the heavens, and Thy truth unto the clouds.

7, 9. My heart is prepared, O GOD : I will sing and give praise unto Thee among the nations.

11. Be Thou exalted, O GOD, above the heavens : and let Thy glory be above all the earth.

xviii. 49. Therefore will I give thanks unto Thee, O LORD, among the gentiles, and sing praises unto Thy Name. Amen.

KINGSTON.

1947

O Saving Victim, opening wide
The gate of heaven to man below :
Our foes press on from every side,
Thine aid supply, Thy strength bestow.

All praise and thanks to Thee ascend
For evermore, Blest One in Three ;
O grant us life that shall not end
In our true native land with Thee.

KÖNIG.

1948

PSALM ciii. 1. Praise the LORD, O my soul: and all that is within me praise His holy Name.

8. The LORD is full of compassion and mercy: long-suffering, and of great goodness.

13. Yea, like as a father pitieth his own children: even so is the LORD merciful unto them that fear Him.

1. Praise the LORD, O my soul: and all that is within me praise His holy Name. Amen.

ROYLE.

1949

PSALM cxxxvii. 1. (*Bible Version.*) By the rivers of Babylon, there we sat down, yea, we wept, when we remembered Zion.

2. We hanged our harps upon the willows in the midst thereof.

3. For there they that carried us away captive required of us a song; and they that wasted us required of us mirth, saying, Sing us one of the songs of Zion.

4. How shall we sing the LORD's song in a strange land?

5. If 'I forget thee, O Jerusalem, let my right hand forget her cunning.

6. If I do not remember thee, let my tongue cleave to the roof of my mouth; if I prefer not Jerusalem above my chief joy.

SAMSON.

1950

ISAIAH liv. 10. For the mountains shall depart, and the hills be removed; but My kindness shall not depart from thee; neither shall the covenant of My peace be removed, saith the LORD that hath mercy on thee.

SAMSON.

1951

PSALM lxxx. 1. (*Bible Version.*) Give ear, O Shepherd of Israel, that leadest Joseph like a flock; shine forth, that dwellest between the cherubims, shine forth, O Shepherd of Israel.

3. Turn us again, O GOD, and cause Thy face to shine; and we shall be saved.

1. Give ear, O Shepherd of Israel, that leadest Joseph like a flock.

4. How long wilt Thou be angry against the prayer of Thy people?

5. Thou feedest them with the bread of tears; and givest them tears to drink in great measure.

3. Turn us again, O God, and we shall be saved.

1. Give ear, O Shepherd of Israel, that leadest Joseph like a flock; shine forth, that dwellest between the cherubims, shine forth, O Shepherd of Israel.

3. Turn us again, and we shall be saved. Amen.

WHITING.

1952

PSALM cxxxix. 1. (*Bible Version.*) LORD, Thou hast searched me, and known me.

2. Thou knowest my downsitting and mine uprising, Thou understandest my thought afar off.

3. Thou compassest my path and my lying down, and art acquainted with all my ways.

4. For there is not a word in my tongue, but, lo, O LORD, Thou knowest it altogether.

7. Whither shall I go from Thy Spirit? or whither shall I flee from Thy presence?

8. If I ascend up into heaven, Thou art there; if I make my bed in hell, Thou art there.

9. If I take the wings of the morning, and dwell in the uttermost parts of the sea;

10. Even there shall Thy hand lead me, and Thy right hand shall hold me.

23. Search me, and know my heart: try me, and know my thoughts:

24. And see if there be in me any wicked way, and lead me in the way everlasting. Amen.

WHITING.

INDEX OF PASSAGES OF SCRIPTURE, &c.

METRICAL VERSIONS OF THE PSALMS.

					No.						No.
Psalm	iii	...	..	..	1439	Psalm	lv.	...			764
"	viii.	...	...	...	482	"	lxxxiv.	...	...	842,	1581
"	ix.	..	...	...	484	"	lxxxvi.	...	.		83
"	xi	...	...	..	484	"	xciii.		..	..	1417
"	xii.	.	.	..	484	"	c.	..	..	3,	1017
"	xiii.	...	481,	484,	774	"	cxvii.	...	..	517,	1558
"	xviii.	...	..	...	655	"	cxxi.	...	.	...	550
"	xix.	.	.	...	667	"	cxxxiv.	...	...	...	8
"	xxxiii.	.	...	.	1253	"	cxxxv.	...	.	.	517
"	xlii.	..	...	..	338	"	cxxxvii.	...	..	...	1042
"	xliii.	.	..	.	1252	"	cxlv.	...	...	..	560
"	xlvii	.	..	..	1592	"	cxlviii.	...	.	..	517

COLLECTS, PRAYERS, &c.

	No		No
1st Sunday in Advent	886	3rd Collect at Evening Prayer ..	1411
2nd " " ...	887	Miscellaneous Prayers, &c.	1, 11, 12, 15, 40, 49, 70, 73, 214, 635, 640, 704, 706, 756, 775, 796, 849, 866, 961, 970, 1149, 1360, 1507
Epiphany	732		
1st Sunday after the Epiphany	828		
2nd " " "	1654		
3rd " " "	53	The Lord's Prayer ...	843, 1631
Sunday called Quinquagesima .	710	O God, Whose nature ..	902
4th Sunday in Lent	871	From the Litany	817, 1006, 1191, 1542, 1806
Annunciation	1897		
1st Sunday after Easter .. .	799	From the Communion Service:—	
Ascension Day	1184	1st Collect	965
Sunday after Ascension Day ...	827	Kyrie	1584
1st Sunday after Trinity	800	Credo	1586
3rd " "	936	Sanctus 831, 1076, 1373, 1587, 1720	
5th " " 646,	1771	Gloria in excelsis ...	555, 1585
6th " . ..	697	Sursum Corda...	1628
7th " " ..	562	Proper Preface for Easter Day	78
9th " " .	1104	Prevent us, O Lord . ..	1519
10th " " ...	1880		
13th " " ..	937		
15th " " ..	471	Agnus Dei	1589
17th " " ..	678	Benedictus	1588
20th " " ..	958	From the Office for the Visitation of the Sick	255
21st " " ..	731		
23rd " .	1224	From the Burial Service	269, 1541
St Michael and all Angels .	1223	From the Commination Service	202
2nd Collect at Morning Prayer ..	863		

MISCELLANEOUS WORDS, HYMNS, &c.

THE TE DEUM   ...   673, 674, 705, 1285

SEVEN ANTIPHONS   ...   1712

FROM VARIOUS SOURCES.

INDEX OF FIRST LINES.